MW01009506

Industry and Firm Studies

Industry and Firm Studies

4th EDITION

Edited by **Victor J. Tremblay** and **Carol Horton Tremblay**

M.E.Sharpe
Armonk, New York
London, England

Copyright © 2007 by M.E. Sharpe, Inc.

All rights reserved. No part of this book may be reproduced in any form
without written permission from the publisher, M.E. Sharpe, Inc.,
80 Business Park Drive, Armonk, New York 10504.

Library of Congress Cataloging-in-Publication Data

Industry and firm studies / Victor J. Tremblay, Carol Horton Tremblay, editors. — 4th ed.
   p. cm.
  Includes bibliographical references and index.
  ISBN 978-0-7656-1723-1 (cloth : alk. paper); ISBN 978-0-7656-1724-8 (pbk.: alk. paper)
  1. Industrial management—Case studies. 2. Industrial organization—Case studies.
  3. Management games—Case studies. I. Tremblay, Victor J. II. Tremblay, Carol Horton.

HD31.I55 2007
338.5—dc22

2006020317

Printed in the United States of America

The paper used in this publication meets the minimum requirements of
American National Standard for Information Sciences
Permanence of Paper for Printed Library Materials,
ANSI Z 39.48-1984.

BM (c) 10   9   8   7   6   5   4   3   2   1
BM (p) 10   9   8   7   6   5   4   3   2   1

To Bud and Pat

Jason, Sarah, and Mark

Jeff, Tracy, Allison, and Christopher

Paul, Nancy, Nicholas, and Marcus

Gayle, Paul, Cheree, and Jennifer

Contents

I. Industry Studies

II. Firm Studies

Tables and Figures

Tables

Figures

Preface

The study of a particular industry has been a cornerstone of applied research in the field of industrial organization. Traditional industry studies provide students and scholars with information about the structure, conduct, and performance of a particular industry and show how economic and policy analysis can be applied. Such studies can also serve as a platform for future analysis of an industry. One drawback with these studies is that they frequently fail to account for individual firm effects and recent contributions of game theory.

Developments in game theory have revolutionized the fields of industrial organization, marketing science, and management strategy. Game-theoretic models of oligopolistic industries explain how history, market institutions, and firm idiosyncrasies affect firm behavior and industry performance. In order to better understand markets and benefit from the insights of game theory, a number of scholars advocate the study of leading firms as well as individual industries.[1] It is for this reason that this new edition includes both firm and industry case studies.

The chapters in *Industry and Firm Studies* address a wide variety of issues concerning industry structure, policy toward business, and the strategic innovations and blunders of individual firms. The collection may serve as a rich resource for undergraduate- and master's-level courses in industrial organization, applied game theory, and management strategy. The assumed prerequisite is a solid understanding of microeconomic principles. Chapters that use more advanced material provide references for the interested reader.

Part I of the book contains a selection of industries, based on our assessment of reader demand and relevance to current events and policy issues. Larry L. Duetsch, former editor of *Industry Studies,* provided valuable advice on the choice of industries, and we are grateful for his advice in this and other matters. Each chapter provides historical background, summarizes key economic features, and emphasizes one or more important economic or policy issues as they relate to the industry. The chapter on commercial banking discusses the influences of new legislation and innovations in electronic technologies on merger activity and competition. In the brewing chapter, we show how a hostile economic environment shaped firm behavior and how the actions of the leading brewers have been consistent with many game theoretic models. The chapter on soft drinks illustrates how to decompose the effect of collusion and product differentiation on market power. Estimates of market power clarify why a merger between any of the leading soft drink producers would be a violation of the Clayton Act.

Several chapters focus on important public policy issues. The chapters on distilled spirits and cigarettes highlight the economic consequences of government regulations designed to mitigate the externalities associated with cigarette and alcohol consumption. Airline service is the oldest deregulated industry in the United States, and the chapter on airlines explains how the industry has responded to the regulatory reforms of the 1970s and 1980s. The chapter on health insurance describes the evolution of the health insurance market in response to regulatory changes and rising health care costs in the United States. The sports entertainment industry in North America has been exempt from antitrust laws, and the chapter on sports discusses the political motivations for the exemption and its effect on market power. The chapter on motion pictures provides a case study of an industry in which vertical integration, exclusive dealing, and price discrimination are prominent and litigation against the industry's vertically integrated structure established an important antitrust precedent.

Part II contains chapters on individual firms. We believe that students of industrial organization, applied game theory, and business can learn a great deal from studying the actions of firms, particularly those that have made important innovations, experienced supernormal success, or failed unexpectedly. The chapter on General Motors (GM) provides an excellent example, as GM no longer holds the position of dominance in the U.S. automobile industry. The chapter on the Schlitz Brewing Company investigates a leading firm that experienced a sudden and dramatic decline from the shrewd actions of its competitors as well as its own strategic blunders. The chapter on Microsoft demonstrates that the same actions that brought the company early success became antitrust violations once Microsoft reached a dominant position. Finally, the chapter on TiVo illustrates that innovations in product design need not lead to market dominance.

Each chapter is written by an expert in the field, and we are grateful for their fine work on this project. We also received helpful comments on individual chapters and editorial assistance from a number of colleagues and research assistants. We are especially grateful to Yan Du, Natsuko Iwasaki, Yasushi Kudo, Maya Sherpa, and Lisa Duke. Of course, any remaining errors are our own.

Note

1. For a discussion of this approach, see Richard Erickson and Ariel Pakes, "Markov-Perfect Industry Dynamics: A Framework for Empirical Analysis," *Review of Economic Studies* 62, 1 (January 1995); Pankaj Ghemawat, *Games Businesses Play: Cases and Models* (Cambridge, MA: MIT Press, 1997); Stephen Martin, *Advanced Industrial Economics* (Malden, MA: Blackwell Publishers, 2002); R. Preston McAfee, *Competitive Solutions: A Strategist's Toolkit* (Princeton, NJ: Princeton University Press, 2002); and Victor J. Tremblay and Carol Horton Tremblay, *The U.S. Brewing Industry: Data and Economic Analysis* (Cambridge, MA: MIT Press, 2005).

I

Industry Studies

1

Airline Service

The Evolution of Competition Since Deregulation

Steven A. Morrison

After forty years of tight regulation by the federal government, the airline industry was deregulated in 1978. Such a dramatic change in an industry's economic environment is bound to have significant effects, and the airline industry is no exception. Airlines provide an interesting example of how an industry evolves when freed from government regulation. After nearly three decades of deregulation, this evolution is still not complete, although the form to which the industry is evolving is becoming clear.

This evolution has not been without controversy. Each zig and zag of the industry renews the debate about the wisdom of deregulation and the future of the industry. The industry has this high profile because many people are fascinated with aviation. Others devote attention to airlines because airline deregulation was the first of many regulatory reforms (e.g., railroads, trucking, telecommunications, banking) in the late 1970s and 1980s. As the oldest deregulated industry, airlines give analysts insight into other industries. Although the airline industry is a complex one, it is amenable to study because of the wealth of data—a legacy of regulation—the government continues to collect.

This study chronicles and explains the evolution of the domestic passenger airline industry since it was deregulated in 1978.[1] The next two sec-

tions provide a brief history of the government's involvement in the industry and the deregulation movement. The succeeding section describes the technology of the industry and introduces some terminology that will be useful. After a discussion of the demand for air transportation, there is a discussion of what airline deregulation was supposed to accomplish and what it has accomplished. Finally, current trouble spots and policy options are identified.

History of the Industry

The aviation age began in 1903 at Kitty Hawk, North Carolina, when Wilbur and Orville Wright performed the first power-driven, heavier-than-air, controlled flight. It was just eleven years later, in 1914, that scheduled commercial passenger service began. For $5.00 the St. Petersburg–Tampa Airboat Line carried passengers eighteen miles between Tampa and St. Petersburg, Florida. Significant growth in the industry would wait until after World War I, and then it was mail rather than passenger transportation that developed.

The first regular airmail service began in 1918, operated by the Post Office. By 1927, the Post Office had contracted out all airmail service to private carriers. Private carriage was feasible because the federal government undertook the expense of constructing the air infrastructure (e.g., lighted civil airways and beacons for navigation).

Carriers were paid for carrying mail on the basis of its weight and the distance traveled (pound-miles). At one point, after several changes in postage rates and in payments to carriers, carriers received more for carrying mail than the cost of the postage. This posed financial problems for the Post Office and was exacerbated by the incentives carriers had to mail heavy packages to themselves. In 1930, partly in response to such problems, Congress passed legislation to base compensation on capacity and distance (space-miles) instead of pound-miles. Although this ended the problems with the pound-mile system, the space-mile system gave carriers an incentive to use larger aircraft and to use the extra space to carry passengers. Because passenger transportation was not financially feasible without a mail contract, the Postmaster General effectively controlled entry into the industry. Thus subsidized passenger service began, with the Postmaster General as the regulator of commercial air transport.

Aviation continued to develop during the early 1930s, despite the Depression, because of significant technical advances in aircraft design and manufacturing. Reacting to new problems, in 1934 Congress passed an act that divided control of air transportation among three agencies. This also proved unworkable because carriers submitted ridiculously low bids to one agency (zero in at least one case) to win a mail contract, knowing that another agency had the power to raise rates that were too low. Finally, in 1938 Congress passed the Civil Aeronautics Act, which remained basically unchanged until deregulation in 1978. The Act, patterned after the Interstate Commerce Act of 1887 and the Motor Carrier Act of 1935, subjected the industry to public utility-type rate-of-return regulation. To implement the regulations, the Act created what was to become the Civil Aeronautics Board (CAB). This legislation,

enacted during the Great Depression, reflected the widespread distrust of market forces that prevailed then and the belief that government regulation could improve the market outcome.

The Civil Aeronautics Act required carriers to have a certificate of public convenience and necessity issued by the Board. The sixteen carriers operating when the Act was passed received "grandfather" rights and were granted certificates for the routes they served. Other applicants had to show that they were "fit, willing, and able" to perform the proposed service and that the service was "required by the public convenience and necessity."

The Act allowed the entry of new carriers, but the CAB never granted a major (trunk) route award to a new entrant. However, the Board did allow entry into other categories: "local service" carriers providing feeder service for the trunks (1943); air taxi and commuter airlines operating small aircraft, usually with fewer than twenty seats (1952); and supplemental charter carriers (1962). Nonetheless, from the beginning of CAB regulation in 1938 until one year before deregulation in 1978, the Board did not permit entry on any route that already had two or more carriers.[2]

Initially, the CAB set airfares equal to prevailing first-class rail fares. Ultimately the Board set fares as a function of distance so the industry would earn a 12 percent return on its rate base, assuming a 55 percent load factor (percentage of seats filled). The fare formula included a fixed terminal charge and a fixed amount per mile for each of several mileage segments. Because the Board felt that cross-subsidization of short-haul routes by long-haul routes would foster the development of aviation, the formula was designed so fares for long routes were greater than costs and fares for short routes were less than cost. The Board then allowed carriers to file for the fares called for by the formula.

Because fares were based on industry-wide costs, they differed substantially from costs in many markets, even for the same distance. Although airlines effectively were prohibited from engaging in price competition, they were allowed to compete with service quality, especially equipment and flight frequency, which were explicitly not under the Board's control. Carriers added equipment and flights in the lucrative long-haul markets and reduced flights (to the extent allowed) in unprofitable short-haul markets.

There was also an interesting link between the Board's entry policy and its fare policy. Because of the fare formula, an airline's profits depended to a large extent on its route configuration. The Board was aware of this and awarded new routes to balance the advantages and disadvantages that its prior route awards and pricing rule had created.[3]

Besides regulating entry, the Board also regulated exit. To exit a route, a carrier had to obtain CAB approval. Because the Board's restrictive entry policy gave value to a carrier's right to serve a route, firms did not exit the industry through bankruptcy. Instead, they "exited" through mergers, which provided a convenient way for a healthy carrier to acquire route authority.

The Deregulation Movement

Economists began criticizing CAB regulation as early as the 1950s. Gradually, more and more analysts accepted the position that the airline industry did not have characteristics that made economic regulation necessary. The critics argued that airline regulation had led to higher fares than would prevail in an unregulated market, yet the industry was not earning excess profits.

Since the Civil Aeronautics Act regulated "interstate air transportation," airlines operating only within one state were not subject to federal regulation. This aspect of the law set up an interesting "controlled" experiment of sorts: by comparing unregulated intrastate fares with fares on similar interstate routes, a measure of the effects of regulation could be obtained. One particularly influential study pointed out that in 1965 the fare charged by the intrastate carrier Pacific Southwest Airlines (PSA) between San Francisco and Los Angeles (338 miles) was $11.43, while the fare charged by CAB-certificated carriers between Boston and Washington, D.C., (400 miles) was $24.65.[4]

Going beyond the compelling case for deregulation provided by academic studies, a series of events during the 1970s set the stage for deregulation. First, the introduction of wide-body jets in 1970 coincided with a recession and led to excess capacity in the industry. The CAB responded by imposing a moratorium on new route awards and by allowing carriers to agree to capacity limitations on major routes. Both actions were widely criticized.[5] Next, in 1973 fuel prices soared in the wake of the Arab oil embargo. Regulatory reform was seen as a means of fighting inflation and eliminating government red tape.[6] Furthermore, a change in public attitude toward competition and regulation occurred during the decades since the CAB was created. By the 1970s, people viewed government regulation with the same suspicion with which competition had been viewed during the 1930s.[7]

In 1975, the Ford administration sought deregulation of the airlines. Shortly thereafter, during 1976 and 1977, the CAB began to loosen regulatory control by interpreting the existing statute more liberally, a trend that increased dramatically when economist Alfred Kahn was appointed chairman of the CAB in 1977. The resulting liberalizations, such as the Board approval of American Airlines' proposed "Supersaver" fares in 1977, gave legislators an inkling of how a deregulated marketplace would function. Although Congress was won over, airlines themselves—and airline labor groups—remained largely unconvinced of the wisdom of deregulation: Most airlines and unions opposed deregulation.

Finally, in 1978, Congress passed and President

Carter signed the Airline Deregulation Act. The overriding objective of the Act was reliance on competition. Entry regulations were phased out; since 1982 carriers have been free to enter any route they desire, as long as they are fit, willing, and able. Exit regulations were eliminated; carriers can now exit at will. Fare regulation was also phased out. In 1983 the CAB's authority over fares was eliminated. Carriers can charge whatever fares they desire. Finally, in 1985 the CAB ceased to exist; its remaining functions (e.g., international aviation, consumer protection) were transferred to the Department of Transportation.[8]

Technology and Terminology

Do large airlines have a cost advantage over small airlines? If so, small airlines would be unable to compete and the industry would come to be dominated by a few large firms. At the heart of the issue of cost advantages is the production technology of the airline industry. Because there are many ways to measure an airline's size, we must first address the issue of measuring airline output and then consider ways of measuring airline size.

At its most basic level, the unit of output of a passenger airline is transportation of passengers between cities. We could describe the output of an airline by listing the number of passengers it carries from New York to Los Angeles, the number of passengers it carries from Chicago to Denver, and so on. When viewed in this way, air transportation is a multiproduct industry. However, dealing with these multiple products at the disaggregate level would quickly become unwieldy—in 2000 the U.S. domestic airline industry produced more than 425 million (directional) passenger trips between approximately 660 airports, involving approximately 100,000 unique (directional) city pairs.

To summarize the list of outputs of an airline, several more-tractable aggregate measures have

been developed. The simplest of these is a count of passengers. In particular, this measure is usually called revenue passengers enplaned (RPE) because it counts paying passengers each time they board a plane. Although it has some uses, it has two drawbacks. First, because it does not take trip distance into account, a short trip and a long trip both count as one enplanement. Second, if one passenger makes a trip without changing planes (a direct flight) while another passenger travels from the same origin to the same destination but changes planes (a connecting flight), the connecting passenger's trip would be counted as two enplanements, whereas the direct passenger's trip only counts as one enplanement. Thus, this measure of output is sensitive to the way in which the output was actually produced.

A measure of output that overcomes the first problem and could, in principle, overcome the second is revenue passenger miles (RPM). A revenue passenger mile is one paying passenger transported one mile. If an airline carried 100 passengers 500 miles, it would have produced 50,000 revenue passenger miles. Thus, this measure varies with distance flown. When passengers on connecting flights fly a greater distance than would be required by a nonstop flight, this measure also captures the way in which the output was actually produced. In principle (although seldom in practice), each trip could be counted as the minimum number of revenue passenger miles necessary to complete the trip.

There are analogous measures of an airline's capacity. One measure is aircraft departures. Like the RPE measure of output, it fails to take into account the distance flown or the size of the aircraft. Aircraft miles take into account the miles flown, but do not take aircraft size into account. The most frequently used measure of airline capacity is available seat miles (ASM). This is the number of seats available for sale times the distance the aircraft is flown. If an airline flies a 150-seat plane 1,000 miles, it has a capacity of 150,000 available seat miles.

Figure 1.1 **Aircraft Operating Cost per Available Seat Mile**

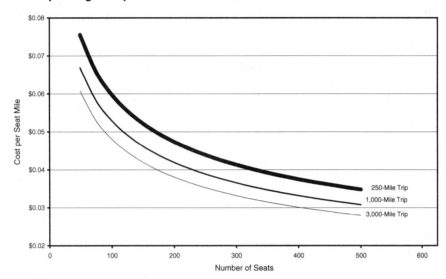

Source: Author's calculations using 1996 aircraft operating cost data from U.S. Department of Transportation, Form 41.

Demand for air transportation varies from route to route, with further variation from day to day and hour to hour on a given route. In addition to the predictable component of demand, there is a random component. Because aircraft come in discrete sizes and cannot be stretched or shrunk to accommodate changes in demand, aircraft usually fly with some empty seats. A measure of how much of an airline's capacity is actually sold is the load factor—the ratio of RPM to ASM. Thus, if an airline flies 10,000 available seat miles and has 7,000 revenue passenger miles, its load factor is 0.70 or 70 percent.

With our measures of output now in hand, we can start to address the question of whether large airlines have lower costs per revenue passenger mile than small airlines. Answering this question seems straightforward. Compare the cost per revenue passenger mile of large carriers with that of small carriers. For example, in 2004 the largest U.S. airline, American Airlines, produced about 130 billion RPM at a cost of $0.146 per RPM.

Aloha Airlines, the twenty-first largest carrier, produced about 2 billion RPM at a cost of $0.197 per RPM. This certainly seems like evidence of increasing returns to scale. However, cost comparisons are not that simple.

To understand the economics of producing air transportation, start with the unrealistic assumption that there are no economies of aircraft size. In other words, assume that an aircraft with 100 seats is 100 times more costly to fly a given distance than an aircraft with one seat. If it were, the cost per available seat mile would be independent of aircraft size, and efficient air transportation would allow each passenger to be transported in one-person aircraft directly from any origin to any destination at any time. If only airlines could operate that way! The reason they do not is there are economies of aircraft size—larger aircraft are cheaper to operate per available seat mile than smaller aircraft.[9] (If they were not, there would be no reason to have large aircraft.) These economies are illustrated in Figure 1.1, which shows aircraft operating cost per seat mile as a function of the number of seats and distance. Herein lies a basic tradeoff in any transportation activity: the tradeoff between low operating costs and convenient service. Passengers prefer frequent service. But providing frequent service means using small aircraft, which have a higher cost per available seat mile.[10] Because of this, airlines do not "schedule" one-person aircraft to leave whenever each passenger wants to leave, and instead schedule larger aircraft to leave at various times throughout the day. This results in less convenient service to passengers, but it is less costly to produce.[11]

As more passengers travel on a route, it becomes possible to use larger aircraft (and have more frequent service), thus lowering the cost per available seat mile. This is what transportation economists call economies of density, where density is measured by the number of passengers traveling on a route between two cities. Because of economies of aircraft size, air transportation has economies of density.[12]

But there is another aspect to the convenience/operating cost tradeoff. Consider a city with many "thin" routes, that is, routes with very few passengers per day. Suppose these routes could each receive once-a-day service with small aircraft or once-every-other-day service with a larger aircraft. In either case, service would be expensive and inconvenient. But there is a third alternative. Why not combine all passengers from the thin routes onto several large planes and take them to a centrally located airport? Once there, they change planes (with other travelers going to or from other such points) and fly to their final destination accompanied by passengers from many origins bound for the same destination. This is the basis for the hub-and-spoke route system. By combining passengers with many origins or destinations on the same plane, travelers receive the benefit of larger aircraft and the benefit of more frequent departures

than they could have with point-to-point service. The downside is the increased travel time and the inconvenience of changing planes. If the number of travelers going from one city to another is large enough, the time and inconvenience costs outweigh the benefits of more frequent service and larger aircraft. Thus, dense routes receive point-to-point service, while less dense routes are combined and use the hub-and-spoke system.

Now we can answer the question of whether large airlines have lower unit costs than small airlines. By "large," we mean an airline that serves many cities. In particular, how do the costs of one airline producing a given number of passenger-miles on its route system compare with the costs of another airline that produces twice as many passenger-miles to twice as many cities?[13] Research indicates that the larger airline will have costs twice that of the smaller airline, so that unit costs are identical. Thus, the production of passenger transportation is characterized by constant returns to scale. Large airlines do not have cost advantages over small airlines. Observed variations in cost between large and small airlines are primarily due to differences in route density and route length.[14] On the production side, at least, there is no reason to believe that large airlines have an advantage.

Demand for Air Transportation

Big airlines do not have a cost advantage over their smaller rivals, but do passengers prefer to fly on larger airlines, giving such airlines demand-side advantages? To investigate this possibility we must explore the nature of passenger demand for air travel.

The demand for air transportation is very peaked. Demand for travel differs from month to month, day to day, and hour to hour. In addition to the peaking, there are random fluctuations in demand that are impossible to predict. For example, demand for this Friday's flight will differ from last Friday's. Compounding the airlines' problems, not everyone with a reservation actually shows up.[15]

Also, there are many different types of travelers. The simplest breakdown of travelers distinguishes pleasure travelers from business travelers. As a generalization, pleasure travelers buy their own tickets and prefer a low fare to convenient service. Business travelers' tickets are purchased by their employers. They tend to be willing to pay a high fare to get convenient service on short notice. In 2001, 50.5 percent of trips by air in the United States were for pleasure, the remaining 49.5 percent comprising business, personal business, commuting, and other.[16]

Economists measure the sensitivity of demand to changes in price and income (or other factors) using the concept of elasticity of demand. In particular, demand elasticity is the ratio of the percentage change in quantity demanded to the percentage change in price or income. No one knows precisely what these elasticities are, but it is generally agreed that demand for air travel is very responsive to changes in income. In particular, the income elasticity of demand is probably around 1.5. This means that if passengers' income rises by 3 percent, with all other factors (price, etc.) constant, demand for air travel will increase by 4.5 percent. When the economy is growing, airlines do very well. However, this is a two-edged sword. During a recession, for example, if income falls by 2 percent, demand for air travel will fall by 3 percent. Because of the high-income elasticity of demand, the airline industry is cyclical—so much so that it grows—and shrinks—faster than the economy as a whole.[17]

The response of demand to changes in price depends on trip purpose. Business travelers have a less elastic demand than pleasure travelers. Once again, precise estimates elude us, but as an approximation, pleasure travelers have a demand elasticity around 1.9, while business travelers have an elasticity of about 0.8.[18]

But do travelers have a preference for large airlines? The answer appears to be yes for at least three reasons.[19] First is information costs. Travelers tend to call or check the Web site of the largest airline that serves their city because they know it is more likely to serve their destination and to have convenient departure times. (Alternatively, the largest carrier is likely to have more affiliated travel agents.) Second, passengers prefer the large integrated route systems of large carriers. This makes it possible to fly to many points worldwide on the same airline, with less chance of a lost bag or a missed connection. Finally, frequent flier programs also enhance the desirability of a large carrier. So even though there is no cost reason that large carriers should dominate the airline industry, passenger preference for large carriers does place small carriers at some disadvantage.

Deregulation: What Was Supposed to Happen

The deregulation movement was based largely on the performance of the California and Texas intrastate airlines. These airlines were the model for what kind of industry the deregulated air transportation industry was supposed to become. Since there were thought to be no advantages to large-scale production, it was expected there would be entry of new airlines, offering low-fare service. These low fares would be possible because these carriers would have low labor costs. In addition, although these new entrants would fly conventional jet aircraft, they would fit them with more seats (i.e., less legroom) and would operate at high load factors (i.e., percentage of seats filled). Barriers to entry into the industry and into particular city-pair markets were thought to be small, so entry—or the threat of entry—would keep airlines from earning excess profits.[20]

Figure 1.2 **Percentage of Domestic Scheduled Passenger Miles Flown by Largest Four and Eight Airlines**

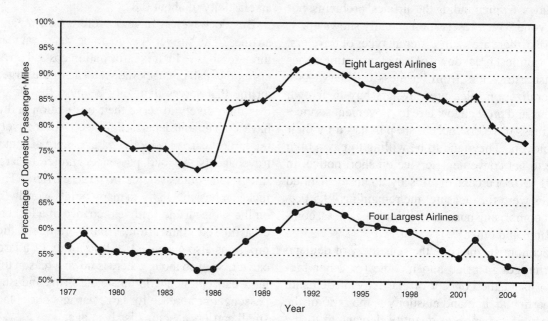

Source: Author's calculations using data from U.S. Department of Transportation, Form 41.

Deregulation: What Actually Happened

Before describing the changes deregulation has brought to the airline industry, we must address two methodological points. First, when did airline deregulation begin? The simple answer—although too simple—is October 28, 1978, when President Carter signed the Airline Deregulation Act. But, as mentioned earlier, the CAB began loosening the constraints of regulation as early as 1976. So comparisons that use 1978 as the starting point probably understate the effect of airline deregulation.

The second point is subtler. Most evaluations of airline deregulation—including this one—simply compare the industry's performance "before" with its performance "after" and ascribe the difference to deregulation. In other words, such "factual" comparisons simply compare what *is* with what *was*. Such an approach assumes that the only changes

in the industry were those induced by deregulation. For example, if fares rise (or fall) because fuel prices rise (or fall), one must ask whether this has anything to do with deregulation. The way around this problem is a counterfactual analysis, in which what *is* is compared with what *might have been*. For example, to see what effect deregulation had on fares, one could compare actual deregulated fares with (an estimate of) what regulated air fares would have been if regulation continued. This is counterfactual because regulated fares never existed in the deregulated environment.

There is no question that factual comparisons can be illuminating. The comparisons provided in this chapter are factual. But you must always ask yourself if something other than deregulation could have contributed to the observed changes.[21] The next six sections chronicle the changes in key areas that have occurred in the wake of airline deregulation.

Table 1.1

Important Airline Mergers, Acquisitions, and Failures

Carriers	Resulting carrier	Year
North Central–Southern	Republic	1979
Republic–Hughes Airwest	Republic	1980
Northwest–Republic	Northwest	1986
Pan American–National	Pan American	1980
Pan American	Ceased operating	1991
Braniff	Ceased operating	1982
Texas International–Continental	Continental	1982
People Express–Frontier	People Express	1985
Texas Air–People Express	Texas Air (holding company)	1986
Texas Air–Eastern	Texas Air (holding company)	1986
Eastern Airlines	Ceased operating	1991
Southwest–Muse	Southwest	1985
Southwest–Morris	Southwest	1993
TWA–Ozark	TWA	1986
Delta–Western	Delta	1986
American–AirCal	American	1987
American–Reno	American	1998
American–TWA	American	2001
USAir–PSA	USAir	1987
USAir–Piedmont	USAir	1987
USAir–Trump Shuttle	USAir	1992
America West–US Airways	US Airways	2005
Midway	Ceased operating	1991
United–Air Wisconsin	United	1992

Source: Author's compilation from various sources.

Industry Concentration

Figure 1.2 plots the domestic airline industry's four- and eight-firm concentration ratios, frequently used measures of industry concentration.[22] In 1977 the eight largest airlines accounted for about 82 percent of total domestic revenue passenger miles and the four largest accounted for 57 percent. By 2004 the eight-firm ratio had fallen somewhat to 77 percent while the four-firm ratio declined as well to 52 percent. In the intervening years, until early 1986, the industry became less concentrated. But from mid-1986 until mid-1988 the industry became much more concentrated because of the mergers that took place during that period. Industry concentration peaked in 1992 and began a more-or-less steady decline since then.

Table 1.1 shows the important airline mergers, acquisitions, and failures that have taken place since airline deregulation. Although it took less than a year after deregulation for the first two carriers to merge, the great merger wave occurred between June 1985 and October 1987, when fourteen mergers were consummated.

Although a standard measure of concentration in many industries, the use of concentration ratios based on revenue passenger miles gives a distorted impression of the degree of competition in the airline industry. The output of airlines is not really revenue

Figure 1.3   **Domestic Competition at the Route Level**

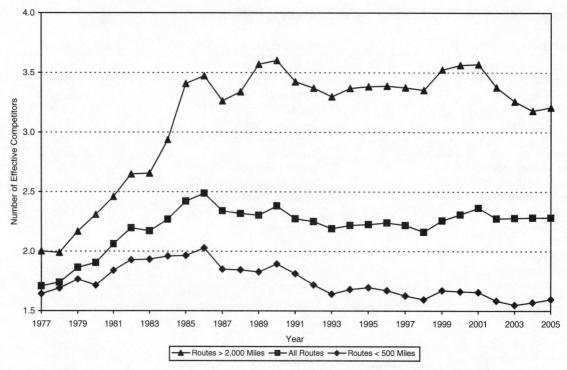

Source: Author's calculations using data from U.S. Department of Transportation, Data Bank 1A.

passenger miles that are just a simple way of aggregating the output of the industry into a single number. (Recall that the airline industry is a multiple-product industry producing and selling thousands of different products—travel between city pairs.) Thus, instead of looking at what has happened to competition in the "national market" for revenue passenger miles, we should look at what has happened to competition at the route level. It is at the route level, after all, that airlines actually compete with one another. Revenue passenger miles produced between Cincinnati and Seattle do not "compete" with revenue passenger miles between Pittsburgh and New Orleans. Measures of the extent of competition at the route level tell a different story than the other more aggregate measures. In Figure 1.3 we see that in 1977, the year

before formal deregulation, the average domestic airline route had about 1.7 "effective competitors."[23] This measure of competition rose steadily through 1986 when, due to mergers, the number of effective competitors per route declined and since 1987 has been relatively stable in the range of 2.2 to 2.4. Based on this route-level measure, airline competition is significantly stronger than it was before deregulation. However, the figure also shows that all routes have not experienced the same gains. Long-haul routes (greater than 2,000 miles) have seen competition increase by 61 percent, while competition on short-haul routes (less than 500 miles) is virtually unchanged from its level in 1977.

Another, perhaps more intuitive, way to look at the extent of route-level competition is to see what has

MORRISON: AIRLINE SERVICE

Figure 1.4 **Revenue Passenger Mile Share of Low-Fare Carriers and RPM Share of Routes with Low-Fare Competition**

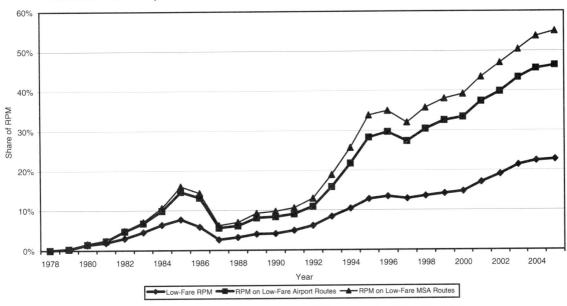

Source: Author's calculations using data from U.S. Department of Transportation, Data Bank 1A.

happened to the percentage of passengers who travel on "competitive" carriers (i.e., those with a route market share less than 20 percent) and those who fly on "monopoly" carriers (i.e., those with a route market share greater than 90 percent). The percentage of passengers captive to monopoly carriers has been cut by nearly half—from 29 percent in 1977 to 16 percent in 2005. During that time, the percentage of passengers flying on competitive carriers more than doubled, from 8 percent to 17 percent.

In addition to the number of competitors on a route, the identity of those competitors is also important. Deregulation allowed entry by existing airlines into new routes, but it also allowed the entry of new, usually low-cost, low-fare airlines into the industry. The extent of competition provided by these new low-fare entrants is shown in Figure 1.4. Competition by new low-fare entrants began rising immediately after deregulation until it reached a peak in 1985. The importance of new low-fare

entrants declined from 1986 through 1987 due to the acquisition of People Express by Texas Air Corporation in 1986 and the significant expansion of the pre-deregulation "legacy" airlines. However, since 1988, the share of domestic passenger miles flown by new entrants has continued to increase and in 2005 reached 23 percent, its all-time high. But this measure understates the influence of low-fare carriers because other carriers that compete against low-fare carriers must match (or at least lower) their fares to compete. Low-fare carriers serve airport-to-airport routes that account for 46 percent of domestic passenger miles. And if a route is considered as connecting two metropolitan areas (some with multiple airports) rather than just two airports, the percentage of domestic traffic on low-fare routes rises to 55 percent.

In addition, the effect of a carrier, especially a low-fare carrier, extends beyond the routes it actually serves. A carrier may also influence fares

Table 1.2

Southwest Airlines' Impact on Fares in 1998

Category	Percentage of domestic passenger miles affected	Fare savings ($ billions)
Actual competition		
Routes served	21.0	6.55
Nearby routes	23.7	3.03
Potential competition		
Serves both endpoint airports	6.5	0.95
Serves one endpoint airport, one nearby airport	2.7	0.18
Serves two nearby airports	0.1	−0.01
Serves one endpoint airport	30.7	1.76
Serves one nearby airport	9.4	0.42
Total	94.2	12.88

Source: Steven A. Morrison, "Actual, Adjacent, and Potential Competition: Estimating the Full Effect of Southwest Airlines," *Journal of Transport Economics and Policy,* 35 (May 2001), pp. 239–56.
Note: Totals may not add due to rounding.

on nearby routes it serves that passengers view as reasonable substitutes for travel on the route in question. For example, Southwest Airlines serves the route from Providence, Rhode Island, to Baltimore–Washington airport in Maryland. These airports are sufficiently close to Boston and Washington Reagan National, respectively, that fares on Southwest also influence fares on that route. In addition, a carrier can provide potential competition on a route it does not serve if carriers that serve the route charge lower fares than they otherwise would to give other carriers less incentive to actually enter the route. Table 1.2 shows that these effects can be substantial, at least in the case of Southwest Airlines, the nation's premier low-fare airline. In 1998, Southwest was the seventh-largest domestic passenger airline with a 7 percent share of domestic scheduled revenue passenger miles. Despite its relatively small size, through its effects on the routes that it serves, on nearby routes, and on routes it is poised to serve, it influenced airfares on routes accounting for 94 percent of the domestic market. As shown in the table, in 1998 the fare

savings attributed to competition from Southwest Airlines were over $12 billion.

Despite the increased competition in general at the route level and the increased role of low-fare carriers, concerns have arisen in the past that in certain markets the dominance of a few firms makes it easier for them to collude and raise fares. However, a study of pricing on thirty-three routes where United Airlines and American Airlines dominated the market (together carrying 75 percent or more of each route's passengers) found strong evidence against collusive pricing behavior.[24]

Another measure of post-deregulation concentration that has been the focus of a lot of attention is the concentration at hub airports where one or sometimes two carriers account for a large share of airport activity. Figure 1.5 shows what has happened to airport concentration over time, as measured by all enplanements and originating enplanements.[25] In 2005, the average airport in the United States was more concentrated based on total enplanements (which include connecting passengers) and somewhat less concentrated based

Figure 1.5 **Airport Concentration**

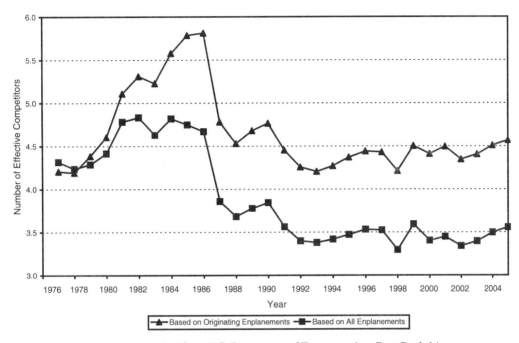

Source: Author's calculations using data from U.S. Department of Transportation, Data Bank 1A.

on originating enplanements (which only include those travelers who are beginning their outbound or return trips) than it was in 1977.

Fares

Although there are other aspects of the industry that are also important—service quality, for example—fares occupy center stage in any discussion of the airline industry and deregulation's effect on it.

A simple way to look at the effect of deregulation on airfares is to see how they have changed relative to the overall price level. In particular, we can calculate real airfares by adjusting actual airfares by the changes in the Consumer Price Index (CPI). This is shown in Figure 1.6, which plots real airline yield from 1970 through 2004. (Yield is revenue per revenue passenger mile and is the standard measure of average airfares.) Real airfares have fallen under

deregulation, regardless of when you consider deregulation to have started. As of 2004, airfares were 55 percent lower than their level in 1976. But can this decrease be attributed to deregulation? As the figure shows, yields had a downward trend even before the beginning of the deregulation movement. Here a counterfactual comparison would help. Results of such a counterfactual for 1998 show that fares were 28 percent lower than they would have been had regulation continued.[26] For 1998, the annual fare savings to travelers attributed to deregulation amounted to $24 billion (1998 dollars).[27]

As interesting as aggregate yield figures are, they may mask changes in how deregulation has affected different routes. Figure 1.7 shows real fare changes (net of taxes) for 18,586 (origin-destination) routes for which fare data were available for both 1978:4 and 2005:4. As can be seen in the figure, there are considerable differences in fare changes among the

Figure 1.6   **Domestic Airline Yield Adjusted for Inflation** (2004 dollars)

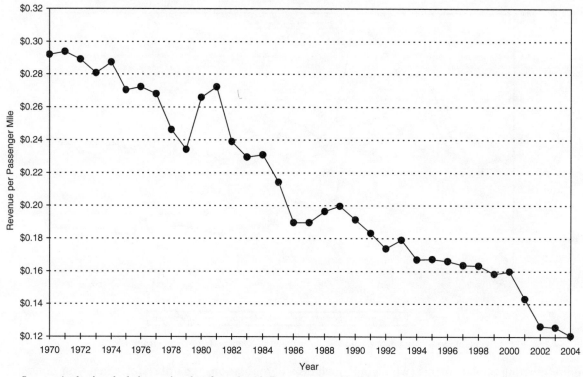

Source: Author's calculations using data from the Air Transport Association.

routes, with about 83 percent of the routes (accounting for about 94 percent of passengers and about 98 percent of passenger miles) experiencing lower average real fares, and about 17 percent facing the same or higher average real fares. The (logarithmic) trend line shows that there is a pronounced relationship of fare changes with distance; on average, short-haul routes have experienced real fare increases while real fares have fallen on long-haul routes. This finding is not at all surprising because the CAB had intentionally set long-haul fares above cost and short-haul fares below cost.

Another feature of fares under deregulation that is lost when looking at yields is the change in the distribution of fares charged on any given route. Even occasional air travelers are aware of the array of fares available, ranging from expensive unrestricted coach fares to deeply discounted fares with a host of restrictions. Airlines also vary fares and the number of discount seats available by time of day. When demand is high, fares are high; when demand is low, fares are lower. Table 1.3 illustrates how varied fares can be on a single flight. The extent of this variation over time is shown in Figure 1.8, which plots a measure of fare dispersion over time for all airlines as well as for a representative low-fare airline (Southwest) and a representative "legacy" airline (American).[28] As is readily apparent in the figure, fares have become more dispersed since deregulation. In 1978, fares on each route showed relatively little variability and stayed that way for the next few years. Fare dispersion increased beginning in 1985 and peaked in 1991. After declining for the first half of the 1990s, dispersion increased,

Figure 1.7 **Real Fare Change as a Function of Distance, 1978:4–2005:4**

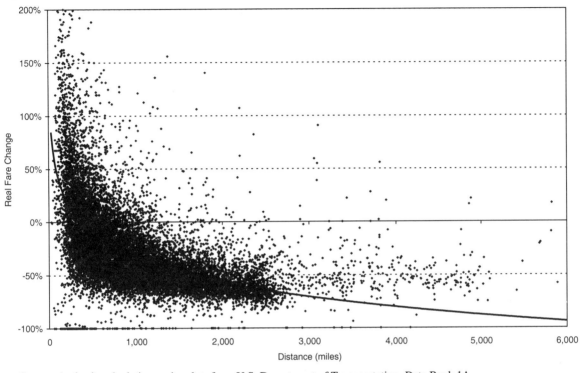

Source: Author's calculations using data from U.S. Department of Transportation, Data Bank 1A.

then fell, in 2002 and 2003 and leveled off in 2004 and 2005. It is important to point out, however, that not all this dispersion is due to price discrimination. Some of the dispersion reflects cost-based price differences, for example, peak versus off-peak fares. Also, business travelers, who pay high fares, have an easier time booking a seat at the last minute than pleasure travelers because airlines carry a larger "inventory" of seats for business travelers (relative to their expected demand) than they do for pleasure travelers. The cost of these "extra" seats is reflected in the fares business travelers pay.

Service Quality

Fares have declined, but what has happened to service quality? One aspect of service quality is how easy it is for a traveler to get a seat on the flight of his or her choice. This is (inversely) related to the load factor, the percentage of seats filled. A low load factor means that, on average, travelers will have a relatively easy time getting a seat on their preferred flight. As load factors increase, travelers face an increasing probability that the flight of their choice will be sold out, necessitating taking a flight with a less preferred departure time. As shown in Figure 1.9, load factors have increased under deregulation. In 2004 the load factor was nearly 76 percent, its highest level since World War II and its immediate aftermath.

Although average load factors have increased, this has not been uniform across routes. In particular, Figure 1.10 shows the average load factor as a function of distance for 1977 and 2004.

Table 1.3

Airline Yield Management

Type of ticket	Number of passengers	Average fare ($)
First class (14 seats, all booked)		
Full first class	5	909
Discount first class	3	529
Paid/free upgrades	5	248
Frequent flier awards	1	0
Coach (115 seats, all booked)		
Full coach	38	530
7-day advance purchase fare	7	64
14-day advance purchase fare	24	101
21-day advance purchase fare	5	186
Frequent flier awards	6	0
Special discount fares (e.g., contract)	35	362

Source: U.S. General Accounting Office, *Aviation Competition: Restricting Airline Ticketing Rules Unlikely to Help Consumers,* GAO-01–831, July 2001.

Note: These data are from an actual flight. The average fare is the average one-way fare for each class of ticket based on the local fare for travelers flying between the origin and destination of this flight and is prorated for the 15 travelers making connections. Because of differences in the fraction of travelers making a connection, the average 7-day advance purchase fare is lower on this particular flight than the average 21-day advance purchase fare. If only local fares were used, the 21-day fare would be lower than the 7-day fare.

Load factors have increased for all distances, but the increase for longer routes is greater than the increase for shorter routes. The relatively greater increase for long routes was expected and took place because, under regulation, long-haul fares were set above cost, which led to low load factors as carriers competed with flight frequency.

Network Structure

Another change that is receiving a lot of attention is the increased reliance on hub-and-spoke route structures under deregulation. One often hears passengers complaining about having to take connecting flights rather than direct flights. One study found that in 1983 passengers were willing to pay nearly $75 to avoid one hour spent at a connecting airport.[29] Although the percentage of passengers who take connecting flights has only increased

from about 29 percent in 1977 to about 31 percent in 2005, a dramatic change has occurred in the nature of those connections. In 1977, about half of all connections were interline connections, where passengers change airlines as well as planes. By 2005, interline connections all but disappeared and were replaced by online connections, where passengers change planes but not airlines. In 2005, about one-half of 1 percent of travelers made interline connections. One study has estimated that travelers find online connections sufficiently more attractive than interline connections that they are willing to pay $38 (2005 dollars) more for online service.[30] But most important of all, the hub-and-spoke route structure gives passengers—from spokes and from the hub—more frequent service than would be possible with single-plane service. Because passengers bound for many destinations are flown in the same plane, more frequent service is possible

Figure 1.8   **Fare Dispersion in the U.S. Domestic Airline Industry**

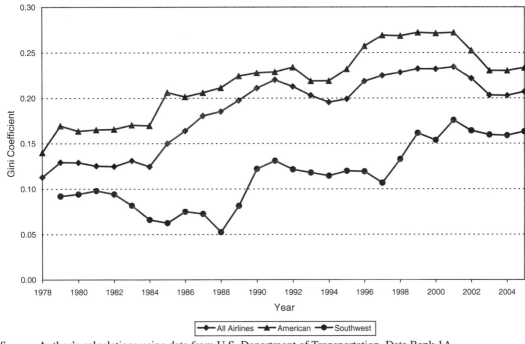

Source: Author's calculations using data from U.S. Department of Transportation, Data Bank 1A.

than with single-plane service. In fact, one study of deregulation found that about two-thirds of the benefits to passengers from deregulation were from increased frequency of service made possible by the hub-and-spoke route structure.[31]

Profits

Figure 1.11 shows the operating profit margin for U.S. scheduled airlines. Operating profit margin expresses operating profits (operating revenue minus operating cost, which excludes interest and taxes) as a percentage of operating revenue. As the figure makes clear, the industry is a cyclical one. During the recession of the early 1980s, industry operating profits were negative. They recovered in 1983 and 1984 and then hovered in the 3–5 percent range. In the early 1990s, due primarily to a recession, the industry sustained three years of

losses. The industry returned to profitability from 1993 to 2000 only to experience significant losses beginning in 2001. However, these industry averages hide wide variations in profitability among firms. In 2004, operating profit margins for major carriers ranged from a negative 39 percent for American Trans Air (ATA) to a positive 9 percent for JetBlue.

But what explains the recent losses?[32] From 2001 to 2004 the U.S. airline industry flew nearly 3 billion passengers. Unfortunately, it lost an average of $13 on each one, generating more than $32 billion in losses. To be sure, the airline industry has always exhibited cyclicity because travelers' demand is sensitive to the performance of the macroeconomy, yet airlines must predict this demand accurately because of the lead time required to acquire aircraft. When airlines overpredict demand, which can happen for any number of reasons, they

Figure 1.9 **Percentage of Seats Filled with Revenue Passengers**

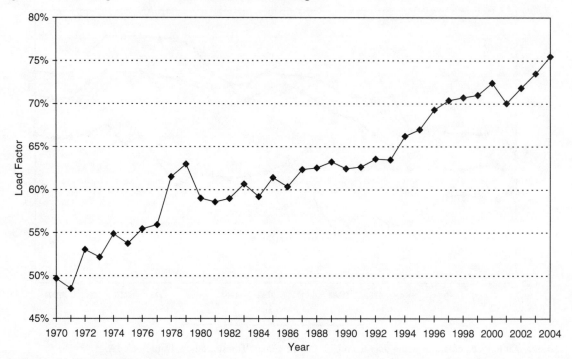

Source: Air Transport Association.

suffer losses. The huge losses since 2000 have resulted because the long-standing challenge of aligning capacity with demand over the business cycle has been exacerbated by the confluence of several events that have significantly reduced the industry's revenues and raised its costs.

An airline's profits depend on its revenue and its costs. Revenue depends on what a carrier is able to charge for its flights and the number of passengers it carries. Costs depend on, among other factors, the price of fuel and the wages and salaries of employees. What has happened to these components of profit during the past several years?

Number of Passengers

Traffic (revenue passenger miles) in 2004 exceeded its previous peak in 2000. Negative traffic growth

is a relatively rare occurrence in the airline industry—the last downturn is only the fifth occurrence of a negative year over year traffic growth since record keeping began in 1930. However, what is unprecedented about this drop in traffic is that it took four years for traffic to rebound.

This downturn in traffic began in February 2001, one month before the recession that began in March 2001 (and ended in November 2001). The downturn was exacerbated by the aftermath of the September 11, 2001, terrorist attacks. Traffic growth has subsequently returned, but why? One reason is that gross domestic product (GDP) is growing. Since its trough in 2001:3, real GDP has been growing by more than 3 percent per year. Another reason is more travelers are feeling that flying is safe enough for them to travel by air. Still another important reason is that the airlines

Figure 1.10   **Relationship of Load Factor to Distance, 1977 and 2004**

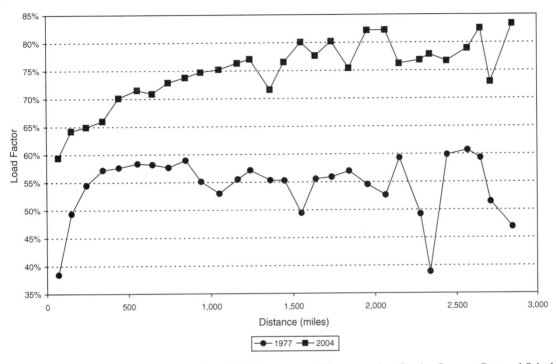

Source: Author's calculations using data from U.S. Department of Transportation, Service Segment Data and Schedule T-100, Data Bank 28DS, Domestic Segment Data.

responded to the initial drop in traffic by reducing fares to induce people to fly.

Fares

As shown in Figure 1.6, fares fell by 25 percent from 2000 to 2004 after adjusting for inflation. This substantial decline in fares has occurred only one other time in the United States, namely after capacity restrictions were eased following the end of World War II.

Because of the dramatic decline in airfares, the rebound in traffic masks underlying changes in passengers' demand for air travel. A "back-of-the-envelope" calculation suggests, under reasonable assumptions about the sensitivity of travel to fare changes, that in 2004 prevailing fares generated

17 percent less traffic than those fares would have generated in 2000.

But what has caused the change in passengers' underlying willingness to pay for air travel? Plausible reasons are that the airline "product" has changed. Increased security leads to earlier arrival at airports and longer trip times; fuller planes—over 75 percent full on average, the highest since right after World War II—make traveling more unpleasant. And alternatives to air travel, teleconferencing and rail travel—at least in the Northeast corridor—have become more attractive options. In addition to these considerations, the traveling public, especially the (formerly) lucrative business travelers, are less willing to pay fares many times higher than their fellow leisure travelers pay.

Figure 1.11 **Operating Profit Margin (All Services), U.S. Scheduled Airlines**

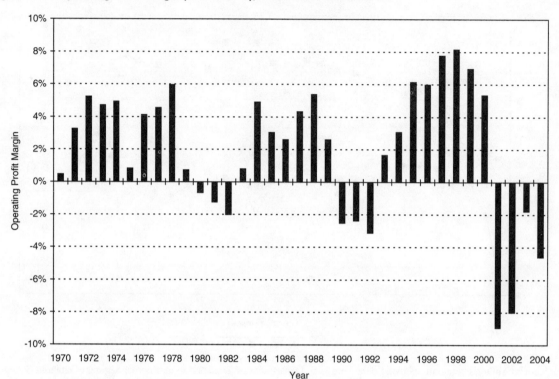

Source: Air Transport Association.

Fuel

In addition to unanticipated reductions in travel demand, the industry is vulnerable to unanticipated increases in costs. Jet fuel, a necessary input into the production of air transportation, accounts for between 10 and 30 percent of airlines' costs, and its price can fluctuate widely from year to year.

Fuel price increases can be a significant drain on airline profits. Relative to the (nominal) price of jet fuel that prevailed in 2000—the last "good" financial year for the airline industry (and one in which the price of fuel was relatively high by previous historical standards)—in 2003 and 2004 the industry lost more than $8 billion due to the higher price of jet fuel.

Labor

Labor represents the biggest single category of airline costs, currently about 28 percent. Legacy airlines, by definition, are those that existed during the period when airlines were regulated (through 1978). In that environment, there was so-called "rent sharing," as unionized workers sought, and received, a share of the "rents" (profits) that the regulated firms earned. Low-cost carriers emerged with the advent of deregulation in 1978 and adopted a more entrepreneurial/cooperative style of labor relations that resulted in lower pay and/or higher worker productivity than legacy carriers were able to achieve with their workforce. The expansion of low-cost carriers has put increasing

Figure 1.12 **Air Travel Safety**

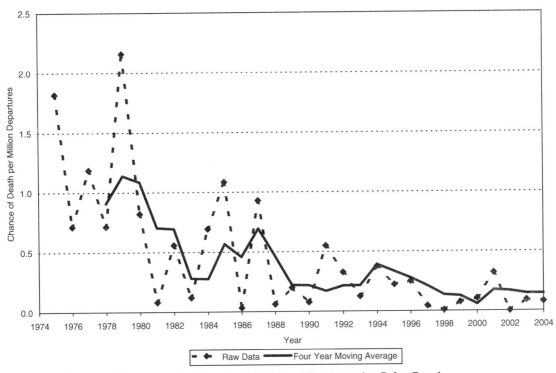

Source: Author's calculations using data from the U.S. National Transportation Safety Board.

pressure on legacy carriers to lower their labor and other costs. Since 2000, food and beverage costs per revenue passenger mile have fallen by 35 percent and travel agent commissions (per available seat mile) have fallen by 69 percent. But since labor is the largest category of airline costs, it too has been the target of cost cutting (and enhanced productivity) by legacy carriers, through negotiation as well as in bankruptcy, as they seek to reduce their costs to compete with low-cost carriers.

Given the demand and cost shocks, the U.S. airline industry finds itself with more capacity than can be profitably supported at the fares that passengers are willing to pay. And in this environment it is difficult, if not impossible, to sustain fare increases to cover increased costs, such as for fuel, causing several legacy carriers to seek bankruptcy protection.

Competitive Environment

As noted, the low-cost carriers have put increased pressure on legacy airlines to reduce their fares and their costs. This pressure has become intense, as low-cost carriers have increased their share of the nation's airline traffic (see Figure 1.4).

Safety

Airline safety invariably comes up in any discussion of airline deregulation. But safety was not deregulated. Safety standards continue to be enforced by the Federal Aviation Administration (FAA). However, some people believe that increased competition in a deregulated marketplace will cause airlines to be less safe by skimping on maintenance or by hiring less-experienced pilots. Others counter that without the protection from competition afforded by regulation, a carrier that was unsafe—or even perceived to be unsafe—would not survive in a regime of free entry by other carriers. Both views make sense. Ultimately, it is an empirical question. What has happened to the safety record of airlines since deregulation? Figure 1.12 shows the probability of an airline passenger dying in an airline accident from 1975 to 2005. The safety record of airlines continues to improve in the deregulated era.[33]

Possible Trouble Spots and Policy Solutions

Any change in an industry's environment as great as that caused by deregulation is bound to have unanticipated consequences. The trouble spots listed below (in no particular order) are not meant to be exhaustive, but they do cover the major areas of concern.

Airport Gates

Before the 1930s, airports were often privately owned, but this ended with the Depression of the 1930s. Today all air carrier airports in the United States are publicly owned, usually by local government agencies. Although deregulation radically changed the airlines' environment, the system of providing airport services remains largely unchanged. Airports still enter into long-term exclusive-use leases of airport gates with airlines, just as they did during regulation. The General Accounting Office (GAO, now called the Government Accountability Office) reports that 88 percent of the gates at sixty-six large and medium-sized airports are leased, and 85 percent of these are leased under exclusive-use terms, where the gate is effectively the property of

the airline to use (or not use) as it sees fit.[34] These contracts, and the difficulty of adding new capacity at airports, may make it difficult for new carriers to enter airports. Post-deregulation airlines reported to the GAO that they had difficulty getting access to gates at Charlotte, Cincinnati, Detroit, Minneapolis, Newark, and Pittsburgh, where the share of gates under exclusive-use leases ranges from 84 percent (Newark) to 100 percent (Minneapolis).[35] The GAO found that the larger a carrier's share of leased gates at an airport, the higher its fares were. In particular, a doubling of a carrier's share of gates is associated with a 3.5 percent increase in that carrier's fares from that airport.[36] Another study found lack of availability of gates due to exclusive and preferential use lease provisions cost travelers $3.8 billion annually in higher fares.[37] Public policy should be directed toward making sure that airport resources are not kept artificially scarce by lease provisions. A few analysts believe that the best way to accomplish this is to sell airports to private operators who would run them to make a profit.

Dominated Hub Airports

Many hub airports have come to be dominated by one or two airlines. A concern is that airlines will use their dominance at such airports to raise fares. Indeed, the U.S. General Accounting Office found that fares in 1988–89 at fifteen dominated hub airports (where one carrier had 60 percent or more of passenger enplanements or two carriers combined had 85 percent or more of passenger enplanements) were 27 percent higher than at a control group of thirty-eight unconcentrated airports.[38] A subsequent study found that, using the same definition of concentrated hub airport, in 1998 there were twelve concentrated hub airports and fares were 23 percent higher than fares at a control group of airports.[39] However, that study also found that when the control group of airports did not include airports served by

Figure 1.13 **Changes in Components of Actual Flight Time Since 1977**

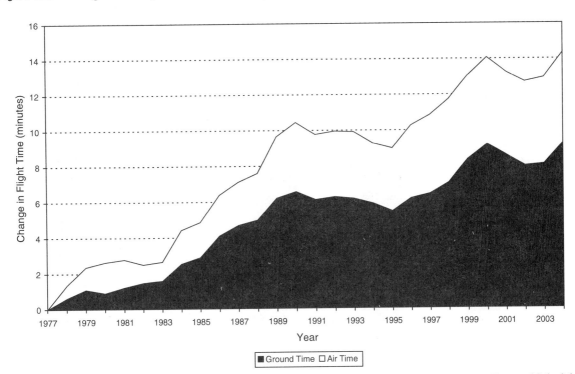

Source: Author's calculations using data from the U.S. Department of Transportation, Service Segment Data and Schedule T-100, Data Bank 28DS, Domestic Segment Data.

Southwest Airlines, the hub premium vanished. Thus, what is called a hub premium appears to be a premium that airlines charge in any market where they do not have competition from Southwest Airlines or other low-fare carriers. Clearly, the key to lower fares at hubs and at other airports as well is increased competition by low-fare carriers, which could be fostered, as noted above, by changes in the terms of gate leases.

Perimeter Rules

Three airports have limitations on the length of flights or the origin/destination of flights that may use the airports. Such restrictions are referred to as perimeter rules. At New York's LaGuardia Airport, the rule prohibits non-stop flights longer than 1,500 miles in order to shift long-haul traffic to Kennedy Airport. At Washington's Reagan National Airport the limit is 1,250 miles and is designed to shift long-haul traffic to Dulles International Airport. Enacted in 1980 to protect the then-new Dallas–Ft. Worth Airport, federal law (the Wright Amendment) prohibits airlines using aircraft with more than fifty-six seats from flying from Dallas Love Field to states other than Texas, Louisiana, Arkansas, Oklahoma, New Mexico, Mississippi, Kansas, Alabama, and Missouri. These restrictions have been estimated to cost travelers nearly $1 billion per year in higher fares.[40]

Figure 1.14 **Percentage Difference in 2004 Between International Fares** (U.S.-Foreign) **and U.S. Domestic Fares** (adjusted for distance)

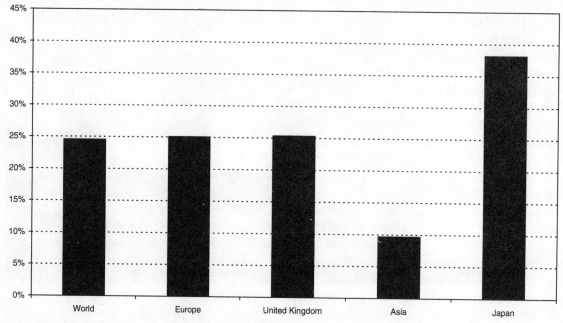

Source: Author's calculations using data from U.S. Department of Transportation, Data Bank 1A.

Congestion

Figure 1.13 shows how aircraft flight times (actual, not scheduled) have increased since 1977, reflecting the increased congestion attendant to the increase in aviation activity. In 2004, the average airline trip took about fourteen minutes longer than the same trip did in 1977. For years, economists have advocated airport takeoff and landing charges that take congestion costs into account. In particular, such fees would equal the cost that an aircraft imposes on other aircraft (including the value of passengers' travel time) that are delayed. Such fees would be quite high at congested airports during peak periods and would be low—perhaps zero—during off-peak periods or at uncongested airports.[41]

International Aviation

Although domestic air travel was deregulated in 1978, international air travel remains governed by bilateral treaties between the United States and the other countries involved.[42] The terms of some of these treaties have been renegotiated in recent years to make them more liberal, but many of these agreements are quite restrictive and are reminiscent of domestic airline regulation. Indeed, the effect of the less competitive environment internationally is shown in Figure 1.14, which shows the difference between U.S. domestic fares and U.S. foreign fares (adjusted for distance). In 2004, international fares were 25 percent higher than domestic fares. Increased use of liberal bilaterals should bring international fares in line with domestic fares.

Conclusions

The deregulated airline industry continues to evolve, apparently toward a system with a handful of large U.S. airlines serving domestic and international routes, with several smaller specialty carriers that serve particular market niches. Recently, due to competitive pressures, the full-service legacy airlines have been forced to reduce their costs and service to better compete with the growing low-cost carrier segment. The airline industry, like many others, is becoming increasingly global, and a similar evolution of other countries' carriers is also taking place.

Although most analysts still agree that there are no advantages of large scale in producing available seat miles, it has become apparent there are significant economies of scale in marketing air transportation, that is, in producing and distributing information.

Although airline markets have not evolved in ways that analysts had predicted, the majority opinion is still that deregulated airline markets, with their imperfections, are better than regulated airline markets with their flaws. The studies of regulated and deregulated markets that have been done in the wake of industry deregulations of the late 1970s and early 1980s have led to a greater awareness that both regulated and deregulated markets fall short of ideal performance. Comparisons of perfect regulation with actual deregulation are as empty as comparisons of perfect deregulation with imperfect regulation. The vast majority of analysts believe that returning the industry to traditional rate and entry regulation would be a mistake. But a belief that some kinds of government regulation are harmful does not indict all forms of government oversight. The role for government in airline markets is to reduce or eliminate those constraints and bottlenecks that limit the ability of carriers to compete against one another.

Notes

1. Domestic and international freight transportation have also been affected, but that is not dealt with here. International passenger transportation is discussed briefly in the policy options section.

2. Elizabeth E. Bailey, "Deregulation and Regulatory Reform of U.S. Air Transportation Policy," in *Regulated Industries and Public Enterprise: European and United States Perspectives,* Bridger M. Mitchell and Paul R. Kleindorfer, eds. (Lexington, MA: Lexington Books, 1980).

3. Stephen Breyer, *Regulation and Its Reform* (Cambridge, MA: Harvard University Press, 1982).

4. Michael E. Levine, "Is Regulation Necessary? California Air Transportation and National Regulatory Policy," *Yale Law Journal,* 74 (July 1965), pp. 1416–47.

5. Melvin A. Brenner, James O. Leet, and Elihu Schott, *Airline Deregulation* (Westport, CT: Eno Foundation for Transportation, 1985).

6. Bailey, "Deregulation and Regulatory Reform."

7. John C. Panzar, "Regulation, Deregulation, and Economic Efficiency: The Case of the CAB," *American Economic Review,* 70 (May 1980), pp. 311–15.

8. The Department of Transportation was also responsible for merger review until 1989, when that authority was turned over to the Antitrust Division of the Department of Justice.

9. There are two reasons for this. First, some factors of production are fixed regardless of aircraft size—for example, the number of pilots and the number of radios and fuel gauges. The second reason is based on aerodynamics. The drag on an aircraft (the force resisting forward motion) is roughly proportional to the surface area of the aircraft. If surface area doubles, drag and fuel cost double, but the capacity (volume) of the aircraft more than doubles. Thus, a larger aircraft has a lower cost per unit of capacity than a smaller aircraft.

10. In 1996, travelers on routes involving "non-hub" communities (those enplaning less than 0.05 percent of the nation's total) would have had 62 percent fewer departures if they had the same aircraft size and load factor as large-hub communities (those enplaning 1 percent or more of the nation's total). See Steven A. Morrison and Clifford Winston, "The Fare Skies: Air Transportation and Middle America," *Brookings Review,* 15 (Fall 1997), pp. 42–45.

11. Those travelers who place a very high value on convenience can charter a plane, which is very convenient—and very expensive.

12. For example, it has been found that if the number of passengers an airline carries increases by 1 percent (holding the number of cities served constant), total cost increases by less than 1 percent (0.80 percent). See Douglas W. Caves, Laurits R. Christensen, and Michael W. Tretheway, "Economies of Density Versus Economies of Scale: Why Trunk and Local

Service Airline Costs Differ," *Bell Journal of Economics,* 15 (Winter 1984), pp. 471–89.

13. Because passengers and cities both double, route density remains constant. Thus, this definition of the concept of scale does not confuse density economies with scale economies.

14. See Caves et al., "Economies." In the foregoing American-Aloha example, the average passenger on American traveled 1,421 miles compared with 556 miles for Aloha.

15. On average, about 20 percent of travelers with reservations do not show up for their flight. As a result, airlines sell more tickets than there are seats available because they know that not everyone with a reservation will show up. Of course, sometimes more people show up than there are seats available, in which case airlines ask for volunteers to give up their seats for some remuneration.

16. These figures were calculated by the author from data in the 2001 National Household Travel Survey, preliminary long-distance trip file, U.S. Department of Transportation.

17. As a consequence, airline stocks are relatively volatile and are characterized by a high "beta," a measure of a stock's volatility relative to the stock market as a whole. Airline betas for eight of the largest U.S. passenger airlines that are publicly traded average 2.67, ranging from 1.32 (Southwest) to 4.9 (American). A beta of 1 indicates that a stock is as volatile as the stock market as a whole. (Data from Salomon Smith Barney.)

18. A survey of estimates of the price elasticity of demand for air transportation reports that the most likely range is 1.10 to 2.70 for vacation trips and 0.40 to 01.20 for non-vacation trips. See Tae H. Oum, W.G. Waters II, and Jong Say Young, "A Survey of Recent Estimates of Price Elasticities of Demand for Transport," World Bank, Working Papers, Transportation Division, WPS 359, January 1990.

19. See Michael W. Tretheway, "The Characteristics of Modern Post-Deregulation Air Transport," Faculty of Commerce, University of British Columbia, 1991.

20. The idea that the threat of entry will keep firms from earning excess profits is known as the contestable markets hypothesis. See William J. Baumol, John C. Panzar, and Robert D. Willig, *Contestable Markets and the Theory of Industry Structure,* rev. ed. (San Diego: Harcourt Brace Jovanovich, 1988).

21. Although the results below do not constitute a counterfactual because other factors (e.g., technological change) may be at work, the conclusions drawn are strongly suggestive and qualitatively consistent with the few rigorous counterfactuals that have been performed for the airline industry using less recent data.

22. The "n" firm concentration ratio is the percentage of the market accounted for by the largest "n" firms. In this case, the market is defined in terms of domestic scheduled revenue passenger miles.

23. The number of "effective competitors" is the inverse of the Herfindahl-Hirshman Index (HHI). The HHI, rather than simply counting the number of carriers in a market, adjusts for unequal market shares by summing the square of each airline's market share. When market shares are expressed as fractions rather than percentages, the HHI approaches zero in the competitive case with a large number of small firms, and equals one in the monopoly case. If two airlines each had a 50 percent market share on a route, the HHI would equal one-half. Inverting this gives two (effective competitors). Similarly, if there were three unequal-sized competitors, with the largest serving two-thirds of the market and the other two each serving one-sixth of the market, the HHI would be one-half, which also translates into two effective competitors. Thus, "effective competitors" has a more intuitive interpretation than the HHI.

24. James A. Brander and Anming Zhang, "Market Conduct in the Airline Industry: An Empirical Investigation," *Rand Journal of Economics,* 21 (Winter 1990), pp. 567–83.

25. There are many measures of airport activity. Two frequently used measures are aircraft departures and revenue passengers enplaned. These measures are good measures of the extent of use of overall airport resources. However, at hub airports the share that a carrier has of enplanements or departures is not a measure of how captive originating travelers are to that carrier. A carrier that hubs at an airport will always have a greater share of total enplanements than it does of originating enplanements.

26. Of course, one has no way of knowing for sure what regulated fares would be. However, a good guess can be made with an updated version of the fare formula that the CAB used during the last few years of regulation. See Steven A. Morrison and Clifford Winston, "The Remaining Role for Government Policy in the Deregulated Airline Industry," in *Deregulation of Network Industries: What's Next?,* Sam Peltzman and Clifford Winston, eds. (Washington, DC: AEI-Brookings Joint Center for Regulatory Studies, 2000).

27. It should be noted that this figure does not take into account that the lower fares that most travelers enjoy today come at the expense of restrictions (e.g., minimum stay of a Saturday night) that are much more prevalent than during regulation.

28. The measure used is the Gini coefficient. This measure has an intuitive interpretation in that twice the Gini coefficient is equal to the expected difference in fares from two randomly selected tickets on a route expressed as a fraction of the average fare on that route. For example, if the Gini coefficient on a route is 0.25 and the average fare is $100, the expected difference in price between two randomly selected tickets would be $50.

29. Steven A. Morrison and Clifford Winston, "Enhancing the Performance of the Deregulated Air Transportation System," *Brookings Papers on Economic Activity: Microeconomics 1989,* pp. 61–112.

30. Dennis W. Carlton, William M. Landes, and Richard A. Posner, "Benefits and Costs of Airline Mergers: A Case Study," *Bell Journal of Economics,* 11 (Spring 1980), pp. 65–83. They estimated that the value of single-carrier service ranged from $14.10 to $17.75 in 1980 dollars. The figure in the text is the average of these figures expressed in 2005 dollars.

31. Steven A. Morrison and Clifford Winston, *The Economic Effects of Airline Deregulation* (Washington, DC: Brookings Institution, 1986).

32. The remainder of this section draws heavily from Steven A. Morrison and Clifford Winston, "What's Wrong with the Airline Industry? Diagnosis and Possible Cures," testimony before the Aviation Subcommittee, Committee on Transportation and Infrastructure, U.S. House of Representatives, September 28, 2005.

33. It cannot be ruled out that the accident record would have improved even more if airlines were still regulated. This question could, in principle, be answered using a counterfactual model of airline safety. However, developing such a model would be extremely difficult. Nonetheless, it is true that air travel is safer than it used to be.

34. See U.S. General Accounting Office, *Airline Competition: Industry Operating and Marketing Practices Limit Market Entry,* GAO/RECD-90-147, Washington, DC, August 1990.

35. See U.S. General Accounting Office, *Airline Deregulation: Barriers to Entry Continue to Limit Competition in Several Key Domestic Markets, GAO/RCED-97-4,* October 1996.

36. See "Effect of Airline Entry Barriers on Fares," statement of Kenneth M. Mead, U.S. General Accounting Office, GAO/T-RECD-60–62, April 5, 1990.

37. See Morrison and Winston, *The Remaining Role.*

38. U.S. General Accounting Office, *Airline Competition: Higher Fares and Reduced Competition at Concentrated Airports,* GAO/RCED-90–102, July 1990.

39. See Morrison and Winston, *The Remaining Role.*

40. Steven A. Morrison and Clifford Winston, "Foul Regulatory Weather Grounds Airline Competition," *Wall Street Journal,* December 3, 1997.

41. A recent contribution points out that increasing delays at airports are not necessarily bad but may reflect the tighter scheduling needed to provide travelers with convenient connecting flights at hub airports. See Christopher Mayer and Todd Sinai, "Network Effects, Congestion Externalities, and Air Traffic Delays: Or Why Not All Delays Are Evil," *American Economic Review,* 93 (September 2003), pp. 1194–215. Another contribution observes that appropriate congestion charges would only charge carriers for delay they impose on other users of the airport, not for delay one carrier imposes on itself by delaying its own flights. At a dominated hub airport this distinction can be important. See Jan K. Brueckner, "Airport Congestion When Carriers Have Market Power," *American Economic Review,* 92 (December 2002), pp. 1357–75.

42. See U.S. General Accounting Office, "International Aviation: DOT's Efforts to Increase U.S. Airlines' Access to International Markets," Statement of John H. Anderson, GAO/RCED-96–32, March 14, 1996.

Selected Readings

Levine, Michael E. "Airline Competition in Deregulated Markets: Theory, Firm Strategy, and Public Policy," *Yale Journal on Regulation,* 4 (1987), pp. 393–494. The author, having served as an airline executive, airline regulator, and academic, presents his views on the way deregulated markets function and how government policy may improve on it.

Morrison, Steven A., and Clifford Winston. *The Economic Effects of Airline Deregulation* (Washington, DC: Brookings Institution, 1986). This study compared regulated airline markets in 1977 with a counterfactual model of the fares and service quality deregulated airlines would have offered in that year.

———. *The Evolution of the Airline Industry* (Washington, DC: Brookings Institution, 1995). This study traces the evolution of the airline industry from before regulation to the present. It presents an empirical profile of the industry and examines the role of government policy in the airline industry.

Transportation Research Board. *Entry and Competition in the U.S. Airline Industry: Issues and Opportunities,* Special Report 255. (Washington, DC: National Research Council, 1999). This report, mandated by Congress, examines the functioning of the deregulated airline marketplace and addresses whether increased federal oversight or regulation is warranted.

U.S. Government Accountability Office, *Legacy Airlines Must Further Reduce Costs to Restore Profitability,* GAO-04–836, August 2004.

2

Banking

An Industry in Transition

Robert M. Adams

The size and scope of the commercial banking industry, together with the unique role it plays in the U.S. economy, make it a particularly important industry to consider in any analysis of competition. The industry has over $8.0 trillion in financial assets (compared to $5.0 trillion in the insurance industry) and 2.1 million employees (more than any other manufacturing industry and more than the motor vehicle, steel, and petroleum industries combined). Banks provide essential deposit services; perform many payment functions; and lend funds to individuals, businesses, and governments.

This chapter focuses on competition in retail commercial banking, which encompasses the provision of basic financial services to households and small businesses by depository institutions chartered to operate as commercial banks. This subset of depository institutions does not include thrift institutions, such as savings banks, savings and loan associations, or credit unions. This chapter does not address the "corporate" (or "wholesale") banking market, which includes the set of services typically demanded by large corporations or other banks. The distinction between retail and wholesale is essential for both policy and analytical purposes. The retail banking industry is especially interesting because it underwent major changes resulting from the removal of legal barriers to entry, an unprecedented merger movement, and the

adoption of electronic technology in the provision of some services during the last decade.[1]

The various changes in retail banking raise questions about competition, barriers to entry, and public policy that are of interest to students of industrial organization and policymakers. This chapter seeks to use empirical evidence and some of the basic concepts of industrial organization to examine implications for competition analysis and public policy in the industry.

Motivation for Banking as a Laboratory for Study

Banking in the United States has traditionally been a regulated industry.[2] Consequently, teachers of industrial organization tend to place it in a special class with other regulated industries that are regarded as not very useful for studying general questions and hypotheses about competition, firm behavior, and performance. It is assumed that regulation inhibits or distorts the normal functioning of the marketplace so that any pricing behavior or firm interrelationships found to exist are not applicable to other industries in general, but are unique to the regulated industry under review. This is a mistaken view of the banking industry.

While banks are subject to various regulations, particularly involving portfolio risk, they have a

Table 2.1

Entry and Exit in Commercial Banking, 1990–2003

Year	Number of new state and national charters	Number of failures	Number of mergers	Number of branches	
				Opened	Closed
1990	165	168	366	2,719	878
1994	49	13	475	2,710	1,147
1995	101	6	475	2,521	1,486
1996	145	5	446	2,487	870
1997	188	1	422	3,122	1,636
1998	194	3	493	2,384	1,485
1999	232	6	333	2,040	1,158
2000	192	6	255	1,881	1,421
2001	129	3	231	1,510	1,072
2002	91	6	203	1,879	1,137
2003	NA	NA	184	1,465	649

Source: Failure data are from the *Annual Report* of the Federal Deposit Insurance Corporation and statistical releases. Mergers and acquisitions data are from Steven J. Pilloff, "Bank Merger Activity in the United States, 1994–2003," *Staff Study* 176 (Federal Reserve Board, May 2004). New bank and branch openings and closings are from the *Annual Report,* Federal Reserve Board, relevant years. For the years 1990–95, new bank and branch data include industrial banks.

wide range of discretion in their behavior and in the extent to which they compete for business. Most notably, banks' prices and profit rates are not subject to review, approval, or other constraints as is the case for public utilities. Consequently, banks may adopt whatever prices local supply-and-demand conditions will allow them to charge (or require them to pay), whether for checking accounts, savings deposits, student loans, safe deposit boxes, or any other bank service.

Entry and exit in banking, while not absolutely free from regulatory review, are also clearly indicative of an environment where broad opportunity for discretionary behavior exists. For example, each year from 1994 to 2003 there were an average 352 bank mergers, 147 new banks chartered, 2,200 new branch offices opened, and 1,306 branch offices closed (Table 2.1). Thus, it is apparent that entry and exit provide important vehicles for competition and strategic behavior within the retail banking

industry. While the tempo of these changes has leveled off in recent years, the effects on competition are still unknown.

Nonprice or quality competition is another important avenue for discretionary behavior by banks. While the basic services provided by retail banks (i.e., insured savings deposits, checking accounts, and loans) may be viewed as relatively homogeneous, nonprice competition among banks is common and important to consumer choice. For example, to differentiate itself from its competitors, a retail bank may choose to offer better service by providing more tellers, extended evening and weekend hours, drive-through windows, banking-by-telephone, twenty-four-hour deposit and cash-withdrawal facilities through automated teller machines (ATMs), and a wide range of products such as safety deposit boxes, Christmas club accounts, extended branch or ATM networks, Internet banking, and other "improvements" in quality.

It is evident that retail banks have a wide range of opportunity for discretionary strategic behavior in pricing, entry and exit, and product/service quality competition. Despite certain elements of regulation in banking, market forces are the primary determinants of prices, output, and quality. Hence, retail banking provides a reasonable alternative to the manufacturing or retail sectors for investigating hypotheses derived from economic theories about the functioning of markets in a free-market system.

Moreover, in several practical respects the retail banking industry provides an attractive laboratory for research on industrial organization. First, detailed, high-quality balance sheet and income statement data are available for all 7,000-plus banks in the industry. Second, the data are essentially comparable across all banking firms. Third, the data are available quarterly or annually and are largely comparable over time. Fourth, unlike firms in the manufacturing sector generally, and even within specific manufacturing industries, retail banks produce fairly homogeneous outputs. Finally, retail banking is essentially a local-market industry, so many different geographic markets exist containing multiple firms in the same industry for which good data are available. This permits cross-sectional studies of the banking industry that do not hold factors constant across highly diverse industries as do studies of manufacturing.

In sum, despite its regulated status, the retail banking industry provides an excellent laboratory for research because of the wide latitude for discretionary firm behavior and the operation of market forces; the unusual detail, quality, and availability of data; and the basic nature of these firms and their scope of operations. Not surprisingly, industrial organization research that has been done on the retail banking industry finds relationships and yields results that are similar to those found for the manufacturing sector.

The Industry and Its Characteristics

An understanding of the key characteristics of the banking industry is needed before we can examine the competition factors and public policy issues involved in retail banking. A common first step used in any analysis of competition is to define the industry, its appropriate product market, and its geographic market. In other words, we must have a basic understanding of which firms are competing, what they are producing, and where they are competing.

From an industrial organization standpoint, these questions are answered by analyzing consumer preferences and substitution patterns across firms, products, or geographic areas. For example, if many consumers are willing to change their banking relationships from local banks to more distant banks, in reaction to minor changes in their prices (e.g., local banks pay a slightly lower interest rate on deposits), then it is probable that the geographic market is relatively large. We should note that, in the event of any change in prices, some customers might switch. We need to know *how many* will switch and whether the likelihood of switching would deter a bank from changing its prices (i.e., would it make the change unprofitable?). The Department of Justice has solidified this notion of market definition in its Merger Guidelines.[3]

Retail Banks Versus Other Intermediaries

Banks are financial intermediaries that play a key role in the saving and investment process of the economy. Such institutions take in money from many individuals in the form of deposits or insurance premiums. They pool these funds and lend them to, or invest them in, companies as well as consumers who would generally find it to be very difficult and inefficient, if not impossible, to raise funds directly from other individuals. Moreover, banks provide the institutional mechanism used by the Federal Reserve to increase or decrease the money supply when it attempts to influence interest rates and, thereby, influence economic activity. A change in the money supply can be accomplished through banks because banks are required to hold in reserve only a fraction (say, 20 percent) of the money that is deposited with them, while the remainder (80 percent) can be loaned out. Thus, when the Federal Reserve conducts open-market operations by purchasing (selling) government securities, the money received by the sellers (paid by the buyers) of securities is deposited in (withdrawn from) banks, effectively increasing (decreasing) the reserves of the banking system. The money supply can increase (decrease) by a multiple of the original sale amount (say $1,000) because the bank (Bank 1) in which the $1,000 is deposited need only hold 20 percent ($200) in reserve. Bank 1 can make a loan equal to 80 percent of the original deposit ($800). That loan will be spent and deposited by the second seller into Bank 2. Bank 2 can make a second loan of 80 percent ($640) of its new deposit. That second loan will be spent and Seller #3 will deposit the amount ($640) in Bank 3 and so on.

This view of banks as financial intermediaries and the mechanism for the transmission of monetary policy, while accurate, puts banking into a somewhat abstract macroeconomic perspective. Such a perspective is not very useful for analyzing the competitive behavior and performance of firms in the banking industry. In fact, this perspective does not even provide us with a good picture of what it is that banks do to make a profit. So, what do banks do? Very simply, they provide a number of basic financial services that most households and small businesses use, namely federally insured checking accounts, federally insured savings accounts, and various kinds of loans (e.g., for a car, a home, or school tuition). The firms that compete for the

consumer's dollar by providing these and some other financial services constitute the retail banking industry. Some nonbank firms (e.g., automobile finance companies and mortgage banks) also offer some of these services, but none offers the full range of services (especially federally insured deposits) that are offered by commercial banks.

A recently popular view is that traditional commercial banks do not form a distinct industry, but are simply part of a broader "financial services" industry. That view, however, is too broad because of the wide array of activities and types of firms it includes, such as insurance companies, investment banks, depository institutions (like banks), finance companies, and brokerage firms. While a single financial conglomerate could undoubtedly provide all of the financial services produced by these different types of firms, these services (1) are used for different purposes, (2) are often purchased by distinct sets of customers, (3) require different expertise to produce, and (4) can be produced efficiently by separate firms. To lump them together as one broad industry would perhaps be comparable to treating all firms in the manufacturing sector that produce internal combustion engines as one industry. Such an industry would include firms that produce automobiles, trucks, chain saws, boat motors, lawn mowers, bulldozers, tanks, airplanes, rockets, and so forth. To treat such a diverse group of manufacturing or financial activities as one industry would make a meaningful industry analysis almost impossible. Indeed, as will be shown later, even within the overall commercial banking industry firms have become sufficiently different that a meaningful analysis requires us to distinguish between the wholesale and retail banking industries.

Moreover, thrifts and credit unions have traditionally been differentiated from retail banks because either they do not offer the full palette of services offered by commercial banks as is typically the case with both thrifts and credit unions, or they provide their financial services to a limited group of people (i.e., membership is limited to a specific class of customers), as is the case with credit unions. The popular press's notion of the banking industry usually includes thrifts as competitors, although at least one recent study finds that banks and thrifts are poor substitutes for one another.[4]

We will treat retail banking as a distinct industry within the financial services sector, while recognizing that varying degrees of competition for specific services are provided by nonbank firms. As a definition of the industry: retail banking encompasses a set of relatively homogeneous firms producing a fairly standard set of financial services used regularly by consumers and small-to-medium-sized businesses.

The "Cluster" of Banking Services

Banks offer a wide variety of services to customers. Individual banks differentiate their set of services from those of other banks not only by offering different interest rates, but also by varying fees, minimum balances, overdraft protection, and so forth (note that branch location is also a form of differentiation). To determine which products (or groups of products) are in the same market, an economist would consider consumer preferences and switching patterns. In 1963, the U.S. Supreme Court decided on the "cluster of products and services" as a definition of the product market for banking.[5] In other words, banks offer a core set of services to individuals and businesses that other types of financial institutions cannot provide. Many banking regulators including the Federal Reserve use the banking cluster for public policy decisions. The Department of Justice, however, rejects the cluster approach and instead uses an approach that separates household consumers from small business customers, because household preferences differ from small-business owner preferences. While the product market as defined by the banking cluster has not found universal empirical support, it does have the benefit that it simplifies an analysis of the industry.[6] This chapter uses the banking cluster as a definition of the product market.

Retail Banking Versus Wholesale/Global Banking

Having gained some idea of the product market for retail banking, we should compare retail banking and wholesale/global banking to further distinguish retail banking as a separate industry. This is more than just a pedagogical exercise, because all commercial banks (both retail and global) traditionally have been lumped together in the same industry. To do so today, however, can lead to poor analysis and poor public policy.

Firms that provide global banking services must have the financial resources and offer the specialized financial services needed by large national and international (foreign or domestic) corporations. These firms may also provide retail banking services, but retail banking customers differ dramatically from global banking customers with regard to the financial services that they need.

Another indication that these are indeed separate industries is that global banking service providers face competition from a greater variety of sources than do providers of retail banking services, because large corporate customers have special financing and information requirements. For example, providers of global banking services face competition from the commercial paper market and investment banks, but providers of retail banking services do not.

The geographic market for many wholesale bank customers is at least national in scope and often global. In contrast, the geographic market for the retail banking industry is still largely local in nature, approximated by Metropolitan Statistical Areas (MSAs) or non-MSA counties, and there is no indication that the preference of bank customers for local services is likely to change anytime soon, because it is presumably caused by the higher information and transaction costs of dealing with distant firms. Recent news articles indicate that local branch networks are still an important aspect of bank competition.[7] Bankers are keenly aware of this preference and treat retail banking as a very local activity requiring a local presence. The notion of a local geographic market for retail banking services is supported by the fact that the number of banking offices in the United States increased from 57,417 to 78,727 between 1985 and 2004, even as the number of banks and banking organizations declined dramatically. The local market nature of community banking may also, to some degree, reflect higher information costs facing nonlocal financial firms.

Simply lumping together firms that provide such distinct products and services to such distinct customers would not define a particularly homogeneous industry and would make analysis difficult. Poor public policy would result because what might be good policy for the wholesale banking industry might be poor policy for the retail banking industry and vice versa. However, in the case that a provider of global banking services does provide retail banking services through a local branch network, that provider is included as a competitor in the market, but we only consider the retail banking part of their operations.

The Local Geographic Market

A key feature of any industry is the geographic scope of the market(s). If firms compete in a national market, it means that they compete more or less directly with all other firms in their industry throughout the country. In contrast, if firms compete in a local market, they compete directly with only those firms in the same geographic area, and price and output changes by firms in other areas will not significantly influence their behavior. Determining whether a particular industry is composed of a single national market or many local markets is crucial for meaningful analysis of an industry, but is often a source of confusion. The problem is that when some of the firms in an inherently local market industry, such as bagel baking, operate across the nation (e.g., Lender's), that industry is often presumed to operate in a national market. That presumption is not correct.

Formally, geographic markets are defined by consumer preferences (i.e., price elasticities). Because price elasticities in banking are very difficult to estimate, we rely on other indirect evidence to define the geographic market. We consider the geographic market to be local rather than national in scope if: (1) customers generally purchase the service or product locally rather than from a distant area, or (2) firms are able to operate at an efficient scale by producing only what can be sold within a local market (like a doughnut producer) rather than having to sell their output nationally (like automobile manufacturers) in order to achieve an efficient scale of production. Using these criteria, we can conclude that retail banking is basically a local market industry. Hence, the most important structural data for analyzing competition will be based on local geographic markets.

Empirical Evidence on the Local Banking Market

Empirical evidence indicates that local market areas are generally the appropriate focus for analysis of the competitive effects of bank mergers. In particular, surveys of both households and small businesses continue to support the relevance of local geographic areas. The Survey of Consumer

Finances (2001) shows that about 95 percent of households that used any financial institution identified a local institution as their primary institution. Sixty-five percent of primary institutions were local commercial banks; savings and loan associations and credit unions accounted for an additional 26 percent of households served by a local primary financial institution.[8] The distance traveled to the financial institutions by households was remarkably small. For example, 50 percent of households obtained checking accounts, savings accounts, money market deposit accounts (MMDAs), and certificate of deposits (CDs) within three miles of their home or workplace. Seventy-five percent obtained these same services within fifteen miles of their home or workplace. The majority of households also typically obtained credit of various kinds within a short distance (three to twenty miles) of home or work.[9] The costs of obtaining price and service information, switching among financial service providers, and traveling significant distances for financial services are likely to be substantial for some households. In addition to information and transactions costs, the need for quick local access to funds for contingencies seems likely to be a particularly important factor in the behavior of some households.[10]

The Survey of Small Business Finances (1998) reveals that local institutions are also the primary suppliers of financial services to small business.[11] The data show that 97 percent of small businesses used a local institution as their primary financial institution, with 88 percent using a local commercial bank and another 9 percent using thrifts. Small businesses relied on institutions located very close to their place of business. Fifty percent of small businesses obtained twelve of the thirteen financial services studied (except leasing) within fifteen miles, and for five of the thirteen services, the distance was four miles or less.

Survey data for households and small businesses indicate that the *demand* for financial services has a strong local orientation. Bank branching behavior is also consistent with the view that local market areas are relevant for analyzing the competitive effects of bank mergers. In particular, the number of banking offices steadily increased from about 57,000 in 1985 to over 78,000 in 2004, even as the number of banking organizations and banks declined sharply from over 11,000 and 14,000, respectively, to about 6,300 and 7,500 (Table 2.2). In fact, the expansion in banking offices has exceeded population growth. Population per banking office fell from 4,311 in 1980 to 3,719 in 2004. These data, combined with the fact that many mergers expand the geographic branch networks of banks, are a strong indication that banks continue to believe that a physical local presence is required in order to supply retail banking services effectively. Whether these changes reflect a response to the demands of retail customers or banks' efforts to reduce their own information and transactions costs in the provision of some retail services is not clear, but the importance of a local presence is. Moreover, the continuing success and viability of smaller, basically local banks is a market indicator of the local nature of banking markets.[12] Finally, several studies have shown that measures of local market concentration are significantly correlated with local market prices.

Structure of the U.S. Banking Industry

Recent changes in the structure of the U.S. banking industry look different depending on whether they are viewed from a nationwide perspective or a local one. While the number of commercial banks nationwide has declined and the deposits held by the ten (and even top fifty) largest banking firms have increased, local market structure has not changed appreciably.

Table 2.2

Changing U.S. Banking Structure, 1985–2004

Year	Number of banks	Number of banking organizations	Number of banking offices	Local market deposit concentration: Average Herfindahl-Hirschman index		National deposit concentration: Percent of deposits held by largest banking firms			
				Metropolitan areas (MSAs)	Non-MSAs	Top 100	Top 50	Top 25	Top 10
1985	14,268	11,021	57,417	1990	4357	52.6	37.1	29.1	17.0
1990	12,194	9,221	63,392	2010	4291	61.4	48.9	34.9	20.0
1995	9,855	7,571	68,073	1963	4171	66.9	55.8	43.0	25.6
1996	9,446	7,313	68,694	1991	4145	68.6	59.0	46.8	29.8
1997	9,064	7,122	70,698	1973	4119	69.1	59.6	47.0	29.9
1998	8,697	6,839	71,231	1975	4088	70.9	62.6	51.2	36.7
1999	8,506	6,742	72,562	1935	4064	70.6	62.3	51.6	36.5
2000	8,239	6,676	73,553	1921	4019	71.3	62.7	51.4	36.1
2001	8,004	6,570	74,587	1889	3978	72.0	64.4	54.9	40.6
2002	7,817	6,491	75,293	1860	3951	72.2	64.5	54.5	40.3
2003	7,697	6,415	76,600	1846	3946	72.3	66.9	58.5	45.0
2004	7,554	6,334	78,727	1820	3934	73.7	67.1	58.3	44.3

Source: Summary of deposits data from the FDIC and Federal Reserve Board.

The total number of commercial banks operating in the United States has declined by about 23 percent, from 9,855 in 1995 to 7,554 in 2004. In this same time period, the percentage of deposits held by the ten largest banking firms increased from 25.6 percent to 44.3 percent. However, average concentration in local markets has been remarkably stable over the past twenty years. The average Herfindahl-Hirschman index (HHI) for MSA markets fell from 1,990 in 1985 to 1,820 in 2004.[13] In rural markets, the average concentration fell from 4,357 in 1985 to 3,934 in 2004.[14] Moreover, the number of banking markets that are already somewhat to very highly concentrated fell some in MSA markets and has not changed significantly in rural markets. According to the Department of Justice Merger Guidelines (1997), a market is highly concentrated when its HHI exceeds 1,800. From 1996 to 2004, the number of MSA markets with an HHI greater than 1,800 fell from 171 (53 percent of MSA markets) to 123 (39 percent of MSA markets).[15] In rural markets (defined as counties), the number of such markets having an HHI exceeding 1,800 fell from 2,116 (93 percent of rural markets) in 1996 to 2,046 (90 percent of rural markets) in 2004.[16]

The number of banking organizations provides another perspective on the structure of local markets. For example, the average number of commercial banks in rural counties increased slightly from about four institutions in 1996 to about five institutions in 2004. In MSA markets, the average number of institutions increased from about nineteen in 1996 to twenty-two institutions in 2004. Moreover, the number of rural counties with four or fewer banking organizations decreased slightly from 1,273 (or 56 percent) to 1,203 (or 53 percent).[17] The percentage of MSA markets with ten or fewer commercial banks fell from 28 percent to 23 percent.

There are several reasons that the nationwide and local views of structure in the U.S. banking industry seem to give contradictory trends. First, with relaxation of branching laws, banks can more easily expand by merger into markets in which they did not previously operate. Such mergers would tend to increase national market concentration and have little or no effect on local market concentration; the number of firms in the local market would not change with such mergers as well. Second, antitrust regulators do not allow mergers to dramatically increase local market concentration.[18] Finally, there tends to be a reduction in market share (known as deposit runoff) for the merged institutions after consummation.[19]

Recent Changes: Mergers, Multimarket Banking, Barriers to Entry, and Electronic Technology

Major changes in retail banking with implications for competition are examined below. These changes have had a major effect on the structure of the industry during the past decade.

Mergers

Legislation by individual states during the 1980s and 1990s, along with important federal legislation allowing full nationwide banking, have led to ongoing unprecedented merger activity and massive structural changes in the banking industry.[20] From 1994 to 2003, over 3,517 banks were acquired, involving about $3.1 trillion in acquired assets, and several mergers occurred that were larger, in real terms, than any previous U.S. bank mergers. Given the importance of market concentration as a measure of competition and the relevance of local markets for retail banking, it would appear that,

to date, the unprecedented merger movement in banking has not adversely affected the competitive structure of local retail banking markets. Effective enforcement of antitrust laws has kept the structure of local retail banking markets stable.

The extraordinary amount of merger activity in banking since 1980 is mainly a response to the removal of legal barriers to geographic expansion, both within and across states, that began in earnest in the mid-1980s and culminated with the passage of legislation allowing full nationwide banking in 1994.[21] The largest mergers may be, in part, a response to the globalization of large-scale wholesale banking and the expansion of branch networks across the country.

Mergers provide a vehicle for banks to expand into a now-permissible nationwide banking environment. It is not surprising to see that the percentage of multimarket banks grew from 18 percent in 1990 to 36 percent in 2003. The percentage of multistate banks grew from 0.5 percent in 1990 (a few banks were allowed to operate in multiple states before the legislative change in branching) to 5 percent in 2003. While interstate banking has become more prevalent in the nationwide banking environment, the majority of banks operate within a single state. Apart from a few highly publicized mega-mergers, the majority of mergers occurred between banks seeking to increase their local networks within a single state. In fact, a significant number of multistate mergers were simple reorganizations of bank holding companies.[22]

There are, of course, various motives for mergers, some of which appear to reflect managers' best interests while others reflect stockholders' best interests. These motives include increasing profits, empire building, developing the capacity to implement new technology, increasing size to avoid being acquired, increasing size to become an attractive acquisition target, positioning for entry into one's area by other banks, employing what is currently perceived to be the smart business strategy (like the "financial supermarket" vogue of the early-to-mid-1980s), reducing costs, increasing market share to gain control over prices, obtaining more core deposits, and diversifying loan originations.

Whatever the motives for individual mergers, and despite the fact that mergers may not generally result in improved performance,[23] economists would generally applaud the removal of barriers to entry for facilitating a more efficient allocation of resources, and, of course, many bankers are pleased with the opportunity to expand their operations. However, it is essential that the antitrust laws that govern bank mergers be seriously enforced. Otherwise, any social benefits from deregulation may be offset by social costs from increased market power.

Multimarket Banking

While the removal of legal restrictions on interstate banking has a variety of possible implications for competition and barriers to entry in retail banking, it is important to analyze the evidence for these phenomena rather than assume that the possible effects have materialized.

It has been suggested that increased geographic expansion and multimarket operation by banks may cause the geographic market for retail competition to expand beyond the local level. The importance of any such tendency, however, can easily be exaggerated because some of the basic forces creating local markets are not fundamentally altered simply by the expansion of firms into additional local markets.

The relevance of competition within a local market context, even when multimarket firms are common, is not unique to banking. An analogy to grocery retailing may be useful. From the demand side, virtually everyone shops for groceries locally because of transactions costs. The fact that there are numerous large grocery chains (e.g., Kroger, American Stores, Safeway, A&P, and Winn-Dixie) operating in many local markets throughout the country or in broad regions does not make the relevant geographic market for analyzing competition in grocery retailing a national or regional market. That there may be a substantial number of multi-market grocery retailers in Chicago, for example, is of little use to the consumer in downstate rural farming communities such as White Hall, where at most one or two such firms might operate. Furthermore, firm entry and exit into grocery retailing in any location is neither costless nor instantaneous. So distant retailers likely have, at most, a limited influence on pricing and the service quality of grocery retailers in a small town.[24]

Another specific example of national chains that compete in local markets is the market of office-supply superstores. The three major competitors with national networks, Staples, Office Depot, and OfficeMax, price their products according to the competition in local markets. Evidence from the Federal Trade Commission, presented in its review of the proposed merger between Staples and Office Depot, showed dramatic differences in advertised prices between markets where all three competitors were located and those where only a single firm was present.[25]

Thus, the fact that firms increase the number of local markets in which they operate should not by itself alter the basic supply-and-demand conditions of the industry. Consequently, it seems unlikely that simply because a bank expands into more local market areas, it will be less responsive to local supply conditions (e.g., the number of competitors, cost of labor, and cost of deposits) and local demand conditions (e.g., consumer preferences for services and growth in demand). The profit-maximizing bank would be expected to price its services to reflect the local supply-and-demand conditions. For example, it would not seem to be profit-maximizing behavior for a bank to charge the same prices in small rural towns that it charges in markets such as San Francisco, Chicago, or New York.

However, in some cases, it may not be profitable to vary prices across local markets. In fact, the evidence indicates that some multimarket banks do not vary deposit rates across local markets, but rather only across states.[26] Does this mean the geographic market is now represented by state and not by MSA or rural county? If consumer preferences have not changed and people still rely on local branches, then the geographic market is still local in scope. Multimarket banks could be pricing deposits uniformly within a state because the costs of researching each individual market in order to tailor prices to local market conditions outweigh the gain in profits from doing so.

Furthermore, large multimarket banks may establish list prices for various services for all of their offices. These prices would serve to provide guidance to local offices, maintain some centralized control over prices for various services, and implement strategies that may emphasize certain services or customers over others (e.g., increase mortgage loans and decrease business loans, or increase core deposits and reduce purchased money).[27] However, the profit-maximization objective suggests that banks, like other retailers, would not adhere rigidly to list prices, but would give local offices the latitude to account for local market conditions in setting prices. Indeed, this matter has received considerable attention recently in connection with "overages"; i.e., the practice of encouraging mortgage loan officers to set interest rates above the bank's base (or list) price by compensating them with some percentage of the difference. Such overages not only provide incentive compensation, but are also a way to account for local supply-and-demand conditions. This pricing strategy for mortgages is particularly

notable because mortgages are often cited as an example of a bank service for which the relevant market is no longer local. Mortgage *originations,* however, continue to be influenced significantly by local market conditions, despite the evolution of nationwide mortgage lending firms and a large market in mortgage-backed securities.[28]

It is worth remembering that multimarket banking is nothing new. It has been around for many years, first within individual states, both by way of branch banking and multibank holding companies, and since the early 1980s among groups of states under regional interstate banking compacts between states. There is no particular reason to suppose that simply broadening such multimarket activity to a national scale would alter what has heretofore functioned as a local market industry where competition takes place at the local level in response to local supply-and-demand conditions.

One recent study analyzed interest rates for several deposit products across MSA markets in the United States. This study found that, while multimarket banks tend to pay the same interest rate across markets, there is significant heterogeneity in interest rates among single-market institutions. This observation reinforces the notion that geographic markets are still local.[29] Other studies found that the presence of a multimarket bank in a specific market causes single-market banks to pay lower deposit rates and charge higher fees than they would in their absence. It seems that multimarket banking has a deleterious effect on competition.[30]

One factor that may create more homogeneity in (or among) local markets is the reduction of legal barriers to entry associated with interstate banking. Especially as multimarket branching proceeds, banks may need to adjust their pricing behavior to account for increased potential for entry. Nevertheless, differences in competitive conditions among local markets will almost surely persist for the foreseeable future, in view of the costs of entry and exit, varying market attractiveness across local markets, and the fact that much of the so-called entry from geographic expansion is by way of merger so that the number of firms and market shares in a local market are not affected.

Clearly legal barriers to entry have declined in retail banking with the passage of federal legislation allowing interstate banking. However, it is possible that substantial economic barriers to entry in retail banking exist despite the substantial elimination of *legal* barriers. It is important to note that legal barriers to entry still exist in banking, making entry into local banking markets by nonbanks, in particular, costly. This chapter does not address the legal barriers to entry, but rather discusses the potential economic barriers to entry in retail banking.

Barriers to Entry

It is clear that the 1990s legislation allowing interstate banking has reduced legal barriers to entry into local retail banking markets. However, both economic theory and empirical evidence indicate that market-based barriers to entry continue to be significant in retail banking. Thus, the assumption that barriers to entry have generally disappeared because interstate banking is now allowed would lead to a misguided competition policy toward bank mergers, and the possible public benefit from bank mergers in the aggregate may be offset by adverse effects on competition.

The conditions of entry are very important for analyzing competition, and the concept has a venerable history in classical microeconomic theory, beginning with Adam Smith, and also in empirical research.[31] In classical microeconomics, freedom of entry and exit is one of the conditions that must hold in order for a market to be perfectly competitive.[32] If no entry barriers exist, a market is

either already competitive or "contestable"; that is, regardless of the structure of a market, monopoly pricing cannot take place because monopoly profits will immediately be "contested" away by new entrants.[33] The authors of the concept of contestability state that "Perfectly contestable markets can be viewed as a benchmark for the study of industry structure—a benchmark based on an idealized limiting case."[34] The other theoretical extreme is when entry is blockaded and no new entry is possible.

The definition and sources of barriers to entry have been controversial topics among economists and antitrust lawyers. The discussion on barriers to entry has resulted in numerous definitions of what constitutes a barrier to entry. These definitions vary on two basic focal points: an entry barrier is anything that allows incumbent firms to earn above-normal profits, or an entry barrier is a cost advantage of incumbent firms.[35] While the former allows for demand-based barriers to entry such as branding, the existence of consumer switching costs, and network effects, the latter focuses exclusively on supply-based cost advantages of incumbents such as scale economies and sunk costs. This chapter uses the more inclusive definition because several of the barriers to entry in retail banking are demand-based.

A number of the basic characteristics of retail banking appear to be sources of market imperfections that could directly or indirectly create barriers to entry. These include: (1) information and transactions costs for buyers and sellers, (2) a local market size that allows for only a small number of efficiently sized sellers, and (3) the existence of sunk costs and frictions associated with entry and exit. At least five barriers to entry may be attributed to market characteristics.

Switching costs exist when customers incur costs (e.g., information and transactions costs) from changing suppliers. Switching costs contribute to barring entry by making it difficult and costly for new entrants to attract customers away from incumbent firms. The adverse effects of imperfect information on the functioning of markets and its contribution to market power has long been a topic of study by economists.[36] In retail banking, the relatively wide range of fees and interest rates, especially in relation to the small size of many transactions, suggests that the search costs of obtaining information that would enable customers to compare banks may be significant relative to the benefits.[37] Furthermore, the great importance of physically convenient (nearby) bank office locations to households and small businesses suggests that transactions costs are very important to retail customers.[38] Finally, a significant contributor to switching costs in retail banking may be that bank customers are typically tied to a specific bank through one or more *ongoing* relationships, especially checking accounts, various forms of savings accounts, and automatic direct deposit and billing arrangements. Consequently, in order to switch current service purchases to a new bank, a customer must, among other things, go to the time and trouble of closing out relationships with the current bank.[39] In contrast, for the purchase of many products such as sporting goods, appliances, clothes, groceries, and electronic equipment, the consumer can switch to a new provider without having to disentangle an ongoing relationship. Each purchase provides an opportunity to switch.

Economies of scale relative to market size apply especially to smaller markets in which a new entrant must achieve a large percentage of the market's output in order to operate at a reasonably efficient scale. A potential entrant is likely to recognize that any attempt to acquire a large share of a market will significantly affect all incumbent firms, which will compete aggressively in reaction to such a threat. The possibility of such a response to new entry may well cause potential entrants to avoid entering smaller markets. In fact, evidence indicates that there is far less entry in small banking markets than in large markets, suggesting that economies of scale relative to market size may be of importance in retail banking.[40] Furthermore, there are many small banking markets in the United States; nearly one-half of the U.S. population lives in rural counties and small MSAs.

Strategic barriers to new entry result from a conscious strategy by established firms to deter entry.[41] An example of such behavior outside of banking is the brand proliferation by major breakfast cereal makers to use up limited shelf space in grocery stores.[42] A significant opportunity for entry deterrence may be emerging in retail banking as major banks establish exclusive contracts to place mini-branches in the major grocery or other retail chains in a given market. For example, in the 1990s, Mellon Bank Corp and NationsBank (acquired by Bank of America) began major moves into supermarket branches.[43] NationsBank signed a multi-year agreement with a grocery chain in Charlotte, North Carolina, to install twenty in-store banking centers and negotiated similar major contracts in several other states.[44] Other banks have signed exclusive agreements. This practice will make it more difficult for a new bank to enter and achieve a sufficiently low-cost structure and an effective competitive market presence. The potential importance of grocery stores as an entry vehicle was noted by a bank analyst for Dain Bosworth, Inc., in connection with Minneapolis-based TCF's expansion into Colorado. He observed, "I've always thought the grocery store was a cheap way to enter a new market and build a customer base. It makes it easier to make an acquisition later."[45] Such exclusive contracts for mini-branches would seem to have the potential to be an effective vehicle to restrict new entry, or at least to make it more costly.

Another possible entry-deterring strategy in retail banking might be site preemption, whereby new offices are opened by incumbents somewhat ahead of demand requirements in a market. Thus, established firms with intimate knowledge of the upcoming growth areas in a local market could open up new offices in such areas even before the demand for additional banking services becomes apparent to outside firms. By the time the demand does become apparent, the best, most convenient sites would be occupied by incumbent firms, and entry would be less attractive to potential entrants. Such behavior would be facilitated to the extent that, as seems plausible, incumbent firms have more information than potential entrants regarding demand conditions and likely future developments in the market. One study empirically tested the notion of strategic branching and found evidence consistent with the practice of "overbranching" by incumbents to deter entry of larger banks into the market.[46]

More generally, retail banking appears to be characterized by conditions that are conducive to employing a strategy of entry deterrence. These conditions include asymmetric information between incumbents and potential entrants, prices that can be changed quickly by incumbents in response to new entry, and the possibility of preemptive investments involving sunk costs or yielding product differentiation (as in new offices). Thus, it appears that the opportunity for strategic entry-deterrence behavior exists in retail banking.

Asymmetric information[47] can create barriers to new entry because potential entrants, knowing less about cost-and-demand conditions in the market than incumbent firms, may consider entry into the market to be risky.[48] Furthermore, incumbents may take advantage of the information asymmetry to set prices that mislead potential entrants by causing them to believe that either demand or the marginal cost of the incumbent firm is lower than is actually the case. The potential entrant would be led to underestimate expected profits after entry. The possibility of such strategic behavior increases the risk of entering a market. However, although asymmetric information between incumbents and potential entrants occurs in retail banking, its practical importance as a barrier to entry has not been determined.

First-mover advantages exist when there are distinct advantages to being one of the first, or at least one of the established, firms in a market. Such advantages may make new entry more difficult and costly.[49] In retail banking, first-mover advantages may stem from the existence of customer switching costs (which are of some significance in retail banking), name recognition and an established reputation in the community, and customer (especially small businesses) reluctance to stop dealing with an established bank that has proven to be a dependable source of credit and other services. First-mover advantages appear to be sufficient to impede some entry, but the extent of their impact has not been determined.

The Empirical Evidence

We have summarized above various basic attributes of retail banking that may impede entry into local banking markets, but we must look to empirical research to determine whether such barriers are actually effective. A number of empirical studies suggest that local banking markets are affected in varying degrees by such barriers.[50] The existence of barriers to entry may be inferred from evidence of less-than-competitive behavior, behavior that presents opportunities for an incumbent to earn supra-normal profits. Such a situation cannot exist for very long unless entry is impeded.

1. Research in retail banking generally finds a significant relationship between profits or prices and measures of structure such as concentration and the number of competi-

tors. That is, research indicates that when concentration measures, such as the HHI, are higher, loan rates and profits tend to be higher, while deposit rates tend to be lower. This finding suggests that barriers to entry prevent supra-normal prices and profits from being quickly competed away.[51]

2. Several studies find substantial inefficiency in the industry not associated with size per se, but presumably related to managerial skill (so-called x-inefficiency). Such research finds substantial cost disparity among firms within various size classes of banks. The existence of widespread cost inefficiencies suggests that existing competition is insufficient to force banks to operate efficiently, and hence that entry barriers exist that inhibit new entry.[52]

3. Some studies have found that high local-market deposit growth over a period of three to four years is associated with relatively high profits, suggesting that competition from incumbent firms is not sufficient to drive high growth-related profits to normal levels fairly quickly and also suggesting that barriers to entry are inhibiting new entry in response to the high growth and profits.[53]

4. Studies have also found that the adjustment of some rates paid by banks to retail depositors is asymmetric. Deposit rates tend to adjust in response to downward changes in general market rates more quickly than to upward changes—an asymmetry that benefits the banks, not their customers. More importantly, this asymmetry is more pronounced in more highly concentrated markets.[54] Because of a lack of competition, banks in more concentrated markets do not raise deposit rates quickly in a rising interest rate environment. Such evidence also suggests that entry barriers inhibit new entry that would otherwise have forced banks to adjust deposit rates in a competitive fashion in response to changes in general market rates.

5. One study has analyzed switching costs, i.e., the costs to customers from changing suppliers, and found evidence that they exist.[55] In markets with higher switching costs, deposit rates are relatively low.[56] The inverse correlation between low deposit rates and high switching costs suggests that such costs weaken competitive forces among firms already in the market and raise barriers to entry of new firms. Although switching costs are not directly associated with concentration, their existence imposes a barrier to the entry of new firms.

In summary, legal barriers to entry into local banking markets have declined substantially since 1980. It appears, however, that there continue to be various underlying economic barriers to entry into retail banking, including imperfect information and switching costs. Furthermore, a large and varied body of empirical research suggests that barriers to entry in retail banking markets exist. At a minimum, it is safe to say that local retail banking markets are not "contestable." Once a market assumes a clearly noncompetitive structure, it seems unlikely that firms will behave in a competitive fashion, or that the market will soon become competitively structured. Under the circumstances, the decline in *legal* barriers to entry should not be taken as a sign that all barriers to entry in retail banking have vanished. They clearly have not. Bank merger policy should take their existence into account as the industry continues its major consolidation.

Moreover, as shown earlier, the opportunity for operating over a wider geographic area that is offered by interstate banking does not alter the basic local market nature of retail banking. Thus, greater multimarket banking does not mean that local markets are irrelevant and bank mergers affecting local market structure will have no effect on competition. Therefore, while interstate banking may indeed have important implications for retail banking structure and competition, these implications require analysis and should not be casually assumed.

Electronic Technology

Electronic banking technology has in recent years been hailed as the wave of the future. Indeed, virtually all back-office and bank-to-bank operations are now performed electronically. Such technology could have profound effects on retail banking and on the competitive effects of bank mergers. If it becomes unnecessary for banks to enter local areas with a physical presence in order to attract customers and provide them with the full range of bank services, local markets will no longer be the relevant areas for analyzing competition. Customers will not be significantly constrained by information and transactions costs in selecting and conducting business with distant banks. Distant suppliers, however, may continue to have higher information costs than local suppliers, at least for some services. For example, a local bank may be better able to monitor the success of a local small business.

The increased activity of out-of-market banks in small business loan and consumer loan business has often been cited as an example of how banks use new technology to overcome the need for proximity. Improvements in technology and methodology have helped banks improve credit-scoring methods to offer loan products to firms and individuals who are not near a branch. It has been argued that the geographic market is

becoming less local because more banks are able to offer loan products to more distant customers. While it is true that banks are able to make these loans, this evidence does not hold for the cluster of services. One subset of these loans tends to be secured (e.g., a mortgage or car loan) and, hence, less risky. These types of loans are often originated by a local vendor (a mortgage broker or car dealer), but they are held by a more distant lender. Another significant portion of these loans are credit cards with low credit limits issued by large banks. Credit card services are not tied to bank branches and, hence, are not part of the cluster of services. Most often, customers obtain credit cards through mail offerings.

The dramatic growth of ATMs and the emergence of "point of sale" (POS) debit transactions are also cited as an indication of the emergence of electronic retail banking. The number of ATMs grew from around 800 in 1972 to about 18,500 in 1980, 61,000 in 1985, and 383,000 in 2004. Similarly, the volume of ATM transactions grew from 900 million in 1980 to 13.6 billion in 2001, and leveled off at 11 billion transactions in 2004 (Table 2.3). Debit cards are a payment option like cash, credit cards, and checks that allow customers access to their money directly at the merchant or "point of sale." POS debit transactions have grown dramatically in the past decade. POS debit grew from 775 million transactions in 1995 to over 6.3 billion transactions in 2004. ATM and POS debit activity, however, must be viewed in perspective. ATMs are used primarily as cash dispensers and basically constitute a convenience offered by many banks to their customers. POS debit services are simply used as a means of payment. Neither of these services is a substitute for a branch, and neither constitutes retail electronic banking. The limitations of ATMs and debit cards are suggested by simple facts. Even as the number of ATMs exploded between 1980 and 2004, and the number

Table 2.3

Number of ATMs, ATM Transactions, and POS Volume, 1980–2004

Year	ATMs	Number of ATM transactions (billions)	Number of POS transactions (millions)
1980	18,500	0.9	NA
1985	61,117	3.6	NA
1990	80,156	5.8	NA
1995	122,706	9.7	775
1996	139,134	10.7	1,096
1997	165,000	11.0	1,600
1998	187,000	11.2	2,000
1999	227,000	10.9	2,428
2000	273,000	12.8	3,107
2001	324,000	13.6	3,648
2002	352,000	10.6	4,500
2003	371,000	10.8	5,006
2004	383,000	11.0	6,274

Source: ATM & Debit News.

of POS debit terminals at merchants exploded as well, the number of brick-and-mortar banking offices continued to increase (from about 57,000 to about 78,000). At the same time, some banks aggressively established "banking centers" in grocery stores, where overhead is low and customer shopping traffic is very high and very regular. This trend, which began in the 1990s, toward establishing a physical presence in grocery stores is another clear indication that full electronic banking is not yet a substitute for a physical presence. Finally, a few studies have analyzed the role of ATM networks on bank choice; they show that local ATM networks are important to consumer choice.[57]

Personal computers (PCs) may have more potential than ATMs to serve as the retail platform to replace branches. Currently, online banking software can offer a fairly standard range of services, including account histories, bill payment, stop payment, loan applications, and various other financial transactions. Pure online banks (i.e., banks without any branch presence) were established in the late 1990s in an attempt to take advantage of the PC as a retail platform. Thus far, pure online banks have not become a viable alternative to traditional banks. In midyear 2000, less than two dozen pure online banks existed, capturing only 5 percent of the U.S. online banking market, and less than 1 percent of all Internet banking customers consider a pure online bank to be their primary bank. Growth in online banking comes primarily from the introduction of online Internet banking services by traditional banks, which view online banking as another way to bring greater convenience to their customers by increasing the number of contact points (branches, ATMs, and now the Internet).[58]

While online banking provides increased convenience for consumers and reduces costs for some banking-type services, online banking is not a general substitute for a bank branch. Moreover, there is anecdotal evidence that some electronic services actually increase switching costs. Electronic services such as direct deposit of paychecks and direct debit of regular payments such as mortgages, utilities, and so forth are costly to change. If an individual changes banks, then each formal arrangement for electronic banking services must be changed as well. As long as most banking customers still choose banks with local branches, retail banking markets will continue to be local.

There continues to be uncertainty about the security of online retail electronic banking. In a 2004 survey of banks on deposit account fraud, identity theft and Internet fraud were the top- and third-ranked threats against deposit accounts.[59] Almost 40 percent of survey participants listed identity fraud as a major threat and about 15 percent listed the Internet as a threat. In fact, these concerns have moved up in rankings over the past four years.[60] These results indicate that, while online bank usage is increasing, consumers remain concerned about online security. This seems to be especially true for pure online banks.

There appear to be good reasons to have doubts about the immediacy of full-fledged electronic retail banking. Many things will need to come together in order for this to take place. The convenient, simple, full-service electronic device will need to be in most homes and small businesses; basic changes in customer behavior will be needed to get customers to be comfortable with banking electronically and to feel secure about having all of their funds moved around as electronic impulses; equipment in homes, banks, and stores will need to be ubiquitous and compatible; and prices of the electronic services will need to be attractive.[61] These changes may well be under way. A recent survey suggests that individuals tend to use the Internet more often to search for information on financial services.

Overall, despite the availability of applicable technology and the great potential for electronic retail banking, electronic banking has a long way to go before it becomes a significant factor in analyzing the competitive effects of bank mergers. In spite of its seeming inevitability, fully electronic retail banking may not be here for a very long time. Economic research and public policy on bank mergers must recognize these market realities in analyzing the competitive effects of bank mergers without getting carried away in the enthusiasm and hyperbole associated with this exciting technology.

Summary

The retail banking industry is clearly undergoing a major transition, as is suggested by the dramatic decrease in the number of banks and the very large increase in nationwide banking concentration. The transition is being driven by the removal of restrictions on interstate banking, an unprecedented merger movement, the installation of thousands of ATMs and POS terminals, and initial experiments with as yet limited forms of electronic "home" banking.

In the future, electronic banking may have a fundamental effect on the analysis of competition in retail banking by making a national market (rather than local markets) the appropriate focus for analysis. However, a variety of evidence indicates that electronic banking has not yet had much effect in this respect. At this time, ATMs, PCs, and telephone banking have provided great convenience for some bank customers, but they have not proven to be good substitutes for local offices or to have significantly reduced the local orientation of the great majority of retail bank customers.

The merger movement is having the most immediate and substantial effect on retail banking in the short run. To some extent, bank mergers may be motivated by the uncertainty caused by the factors associated with the industry's transition. However, the removal of legal barriers to geographic expansion is probably the primary motivation for the merger movement as the industry adjusts to nationwide banking from a legally created fragmented market characterized by fifty separate state banking structures. Whatever the reason, mergers are having a profound effect on the structure of the industry and have the potential to affect competition in retail banking for better or worse.

If public policy toward bank mergers assumes that deregulation of geographic restrictions on entry has eliminated all barriers to entry into local markets and will thus ensure that local markets will remain competitive, regardless of the effect of mergers on local market structure, then competition will be adversely affected. Such a presumption would reflect a failure to recognize that market-based barriers to entry may be significant in retail banking, as suggested by economic theory and empirical evidence. If, on the other hand, the existence of barriers to entry and the potential for mergers to affect local structures and weaken competition are recognized, it should be possible to maintain competition in local banking markets even as the transition of the industry continues. This would allow customers to enjoy the benefits of competition along with other possible benefits of interstate banking such as increased efficiency, greater competition, and an increase in the diversity of banks represented in local markets.

Notes

The views expressed herein are the author's and do not necessarily reflect the views of the Federal Reserve Board. This chapter borrows from three articles: Steven J. Pilloff, "Bank Merger Activity in the United States, 1994–2003," *Board of Governors of the Federal Reserve System Staff Study* 176 (2004); Robin A. Prager, "Bank Merger Activity: The Antitrust Perspective," *Proceedings of the 40th Annual Conference on Bank Structure and Competition* (2004); and Stephen A. Rhoades, "Have Barriers to Entry in Retail Commercial Banking Disappeared?" *Antitrust Bulletin* (Winter 1997). Excerpts reprinted with permission of Federal Legal Publications, Inc.

1. See, for example, a special issue of the *Review of Industrial Organization* entitled "Industrial Organization Topics in Banking" (February 1997).

2. For a complete discussion of the regulatory background in retail banking, see *Federal Deposit Insurance Corporation Banking Review* 11, 1 (1998).

3. U.S. Department of Justice, "Horizontal Merger Guidelines" (April 1997).

4. Robert M. Adams, Kenneth P. Brevoort, and Elizabeth K. Kiser, "Who Competes with Whom? The Case of Depository Institutions," *Journal of Industrial Economics* (forthcoming).

5. *U.S. v. Philadelphia National Bank, et al.*, 374 U.S. 321 (1963).

6. See Alan S. Blinder, "Antitrust and Banking," *Antitrust Bulletin* (Summer 1996). The Department of Justice (DOJ) does not use the "cluster" of banking products in its analysis of merger transactions. However, in most cases, the Federal Reserve and DOJ agree about the competitive effects of merger transactions.

7. See Matthais M. Bekier, Dorlisa K. Flur, and Seelan J. Singham, "A Future for Bricks and Mortar," *McKinsey Quarterly* 3 (2000), and Gerald D. Verdi, "Traditional Banks Should Integrate Web Banking with the Branch Network," *American Banker* (June 16, 2000), p. 116.

8. An institution is defined as local if the institution office used most often is within thirty miles of the home or workplace of the people using the institution. The Survey of Consumer Finances, sponsored by the Federal Reserve Board, is a major national survey of consumers' finances. The survey is managed by Arthur Kennickell, who, along with Gerhard Fries, kindly provided these data. Institution types in the survey include depository institutions (commercial banks, savings and loan associations, savings banks, and credit unions), finance companies, brokerage firms, and "other" financial institutions.

9. Survey of Consumer Finances (2001). These data include checking, savings, leasing, lines of credit, four categories of loans, transactions services, cash management, trust, brokerage, and credit-related services.

10. Despite the introduction of electronic services, local branch networks are still an important factor of bank competition. See Matthais M. Bekier, Dorlisa K. Flur, and Seelan J. Singham, "A Future for Bricks and Mortar," *McKinsey Quarterly* 3 (2000), and Gerald D. Verdi, "Traditional Banks Should Integrate Web Banking with the Branch Network," *American Banker* (June 16, 2000), p. 116.

11. The Survey of Small Business Finances (1998), cosponsored by the Federal Reserve Board and Small Business Administration, is a major national survey of small business finances. Small businesses are defined as those with fewer

than 500 employees. A financial institution is defined as local if it is within thirty miles of the firm. See Marianne P. Bitler, Alicia M. Robb, and John D. Wolken, "Financial Services Used by Small Businesses: Evidence from the 1998 Survey of Small Business Finances," *Federal Reserve Bulletin* (April 2001). John Wolken, who manages the survey, kindly provided these data.

12. The success of small banks is evident from Robert DeYoung, William C. Hunter, and Gregory F. Udell, "The Past, Present, and Probable Future for Community Banks," *Journal of Financial Services Research* 25 (2004), pp. 85–133, and Tim Critchfield, Tyler Davis, Lee Davison, Heather Gratton, George Hanc, and Katherine Samolyk, "Community Banks: Their Recent Past, Current Performance, and Future Prospects," *Federal Deposit Insurance Corporation Future of Banking Study* (2004), 3.1.

13. MSAs and non-MSA counties are widely used as rough initial approximations for local banking markets. The Federal Reserve generally includes thrift deposits at 50 percent when calculating HHIs to assess the competitive effects of proposed bank mergers. These figures are based on banks only. The average HHI with thrift institution deposits included at 50 percent increased from 1,373 in 1985 to 1,609 in 2004.

14. With 50 percent thrift inclusion, the average HHI decreased slightly from 3,766 in 1985 to 3,723 in 2004.

15. With thrifts deposits included at 50 percent, the number of markets with an HHI above 1,800 fell from 115 (36 percent of MSA markets) in 1996 to 81 (25 percent of MSA markets) in 2004.

16. With thrift deposits included at 50 percent, the number of markets with an HHI above 1,800 fell slightly from 2,013 (89 percent of rural markets) in 1996 and 1,972 (87 percent of rural markets) in 2004.

17. Based on 2004 FDIC Summary of Deposits data.

18. Very few bank mergers are actually denied. The sale of local branches (or divestitures) is often required for transactions that would dramatically increase the concentration in local markets.

19. See Steven J. Pilloff, "What's Happened at Divested Bank Offices? An Analysis of Antitrust Divestitures in Bank Mergers in the United States," *Multinational Finance Journal* (forthcoming). The amount of runoff tends to be greater at the divested branches in a merger. The exact reasons for runoff are unknown, though one could hypothesize that the changes in branch brand and bank characteristics are major factors.

20. Steven J. Pilloff, "Bank Merger Activity in the United States, 1994–2003," *Board of Governors of the Federal Reserve System Staff Study* 176 (2004), and Stephen A. Rhoades, "Bank Mergers and Banking Structure in the United States, 1980–98," *Staff Study* 174 (Federal Reserve Board, August 2000).

21. Congress passed the Interstate Banking and Branching Efficiency Act, also known as the Riegle-Neal Act, in September 1994. That law permits nationwide banking through bank holding companies as of September 29, 1995, and nationwide branching as of June 1, 1997.

22. Multibank holding companies are companies created to bypass the interstate branching laws. These companies allowed a single entity to own several banks in different states. With nationwide branching now possible, bank holding companies can consolidate their bank subsidiaries into a single institution.

23. The performance effects of mergers in general are discussed in Nanette Byrnes, Paul C. Judge, Kevin Kelly, and David Greising, "The Case Against Mergers," *Business Week* (October 30, 1995), pp. 122–38, and in banking, Stephen A. Rhoades, "A Summary of Merger Performance Studies in Banking, 1980–93, and an Assessment of the 'Operating Performance' and 'Event Study' Methodologies," *Staff Study* 167 (Federal Reserve Board, July 1994).

24. It has been found that there is substantial variation in grocery prices across local markets and that variation is directly associated with the concentration of grocery supermarkets. See, for example, Ronald W. Cotterill, "Market Power in the Retail Food Industry: Evidence from Vermont," *Review of Economics and Statistics* (August 1986), pp. 379–86.

25. See *Federal Trade Commission v. Staples, Inc. and Office Depot, Inc.*, Civ. No. 97–701.

26. See Lawrence J. Radecki, "The Expanding Geographic Reach of Retail Banking Markets," *Federal Reserve Bank of New York Economic Policy Review* 4, 2 (June 1998), pp. 15–34, and Erik A. Heitfield, "What Do Interest Rate Data Say About the Geography of Retail Banking Markets?" *Antitrust Bulletin* (Summer 1999).

27. See, for example, a customer-segmentation strategy used by NationsBank in Carey G. Gillam, "Less Profitable Customers May Just Have to Wait," *American Banker* (April 24, 1997), p. 1.

28. Bank Rate Monitor's Web site (www.bankrate.com) provides mortgage rate quotes by local regions.

29. Erik A. Heitfield, "What Do Interest Rate Data Say About the Geography of Retail Banking Markets?" *Antitrust Bulletin* (Summer 1999).

30. Timothy H. Hannan and Robin A. Prager, "The Competitive Implications of Multimarket Bank Branching," *Journal of Banking and Finance* (August 2004), and Timothy H. Hannan, "Retail Deposit Fees and Multimarket Banking," *Journal of Banking and Finance* (forthcoming).

31. See Adam Smith, *Wealth of Nations*, Edwin Cannan, ed. (Chicago: University of Chicago Press, 1976), ch. 7; Edward H. Chamberlin, *The Theory of Monopolistic Competition*, 1st ed., 1933 (Cambridge, MA: Harvard University Press, 8th ed., 1965), pp. 200–1; and William J. Baumol, John C. Panzar, and Robert D. Willig, *Contestable Markets and the Theory of Industry Structure* (San Diego: Harcourt Brace and Jovanovich, 1982). For some early empirical work, see

Joe S. Bain, *Barriers to New Competition* (Cambridge, MA: Harvard University Press, 1956). For a more recent treatment of barriers to entry, see Richard J. Gilbert, "Mobility Barriers and the Value of Incumbency," in *Handbook of Industrial Organization,* vol. 1, Richard Schmalensee and Robert Willig, eds. (New York: North-Holland, 1989), ch. 8.

32. The other conditions required for perfect competition to exist include: (1) the existence of a large number of firms such that no one firm can influence price; (2) a homogeneous product (no product differentiation) so that buyers are indifferent about which firm they make purchases from; and (3) perfect knowledge by consumers and producers, which forces competitive prices to exist.

33. The concept of contestable markets is based on very strong assumptions, including that entry and exit are instantaneous and frictionless, there are no sunk costs resulting from entry and exit, and a new firm can enter and become fully established before incumbent firms can initiate a price response.

34. W.J. Baumol, J.C. Panzar, and R.D. Willig, "On the Theory of Perfectly Contestable Markets," *New Developments in the Analysis of Market Structure,* Joseph E. Stiglitz and G. Frank Mathewson, eds. (Cambridge, MA: MIT Press, 1986), p. 339.

35. For a complete discussion of barriers to entry, see R. Preston McAfee, Hugo M. Mialon, and Michael A. Williams, "What Is a Barrier to Entry?" *American Economic Review* (May 2004), pp. 561–70, and Richard Schmalensee, "Sunk Costs and Antitrust Barriers to Entry," *American Economic Review* (May 2004), pp. 471–75.

36. See, for example, Tibor Scitovsky, "Ignorance as a Source of Oligopoly Power," *American Economic Review,* Papers and Proceedings (May 1950), pp. 48–53, and Joseph E. Stiglitz, "Imperfect Information in the Product Market," *Handbook of Industrial Organization,* vol. 1, Richard Schmalensee and Robert Willig, eds. (New York: North-Holland, 1989), ch. 13.

37. The number of fees and charges associated with basic banking services such as negotiable order of withdrawal (NOW) accounts, no interest checking, and savings accounts is impressive. See Timothy Hannan, *Annual Report to Congress on Retail Fees and Services of Financial Institutions* (Federal Reserve Board, 1996).

38. Data on the distance between retail bank customers and their financial service suppliers were collected in the 1993 and 1998 National Survey of Small Business Finances and the 1998 Survey of Consumer Finances, sponsored by the Federal Reserve Board. For a summary of findings on the distance of consumers from their financial service providers, see Myron L. Kwast, Martha Starr-McCluer, and John D. Wolken, "Market Definition and the Analysis of Antitrust in Banking," *Antitrust Bulletin* (Winter 1997), and Dean F. Amel and Martha Starr-McCluer, "Market Definition in Banking: Recent Evidence," *Antitrust Bulletin* (Spring 2002).

39. Several banks are trying to reduce switching costs by offering to change all service relationships for the customer. Other banks offer so called "switch kits," which help the customers change their services on their own.

40. Dean F. Amel and J. Nellie Liang, "Determinants of Entry and Profits in Local Banking Markets," *Review of Industrial Organization* (February 1997), pp. 59–78.

41. The issue of strategic entry deterrence has received a lot of attention. See, for example, Richard J. Gilbert, "Pre-emptive Competition," *New Developments in the Analysis of Market Structure,* Joseph E. Stiglitz and G. Frank Mathewson, eds. (Cambridge, MA: MIT Press, 1986), ch. 3, and Jean Tirole, *The Theory of Industrial Organization* (Cambridge, MA: MIT Press, 1988), pp. 338–52.

42. An analysis of this behavior may be found in Richard Schmalensee, "Entry Deterrence in the Ready-to-Eat Breakfast Cereal Industry," *Bell Journal of Economics* (Autumn 1978), pp. 305–27.

43. See Brett Chase, "Mellon Deal Hints More's In-Store for Northeast," *American Banker* (September 13, 1996), p. 4, and "NationsBank, Grocer Plans Banking Centers," *American Banker* (November 8, 1996), p. 4.

44. See "NationsBank, Grocer Plans Banking Centers," *American Banker* (November 8, 1996), p. 4, and Olaf de Senerpont Domis, "Wells Fargo to Expand Supermarket Strategy in the Midwest," *American Banker* (September 3, 1999).

45. Brett Chase, "TCF Financial Using Grocery Store Chain to Expand into Colorado," *American Banker* (November 19, 1996), p. 4.

46. Andrew Cohen and Michael J. Mazzeo, "Competition, Product Differentiation, and Quality Provision: An Empirical Equilibrium Analysis of Bank Branching Decisions," Federal Reserve Board Finance and Economics Discussion Series Working Paper (2004).

47. In the literature on the theory of the banking firm, asymmetric information between investors (depositors) and intermediaries (banks) is a key reason for the existence of the intermediaries, which can capitalize on the information they have for evaluating and investing in assets. A parallel argument could be used to explain, at least partially, the existence of local banking offices and their advantages over distant providers. See, for example, Anthony M. Santomero, "Modeling the Banking Firm: A Survey," *Journal of Money, Credit, and Banking,* Part 2 (November 1984), pp. 576–602. A more recent discussion directed specifically at information advantages of local banks is in Leonard I. Nakamura, "Small Borrowers and the Survival of the Small Bank: Is Mouse Bank Mighty or Mickey?" *Business Review* (Federal Reserve Bank of Philadelphia) (November/December 1994), pp. 3–15.

48. The implications of asymmetric information were recognized by Adam Smith, *Wealth,* ch. 7, and have received considerable attention, especially since Paul Milgrom and

John Roberts, "Limit Pricing and Entry Under Incomplete Information: An Equilibrium Analysis," *Econometrica* (March 1982), pp. 443–59. See Tirole, *Industrial Organization,* p. 306, and David Encaoua, Paul Geroski, and Alex Jacquemin, "Strategic Competition and the Persistence of Dominant Firms: A Survey," *New Developments in the Analysis of Market Structure,* Joseph E. Stiglitz and G. Frank Mathewson, eds. (Cambridge, MA: MIT Press, 1986), p. 59.

49. The opportunities for first movers to engage in strategic nonprice behavior to deter entry are discussed in Encaoua, Geroski, and Jacquemin, ibid., ch. 2.

50. Research also suggests that legal barriers did significantly affect local market competition in the past. See, for example, Dean F. Amel and J. Nellie Liang, "The Relationship Between Entry into Banking Markets and Changes in Legal Restrictions on Entry," *Antitrust Bulletin* (Fall 1992), pp. 631–49.

51. For a review of price-concentration studies in banking, see Leonard W. Weiss, "A Review of Concentration-Price Studies in Banking," *Concentration and Price,* Leonard W. Weiss, ed. (Cambridge, MA: MIT Press, 1989), pp. 219–65. See also Timothy Hannan, "The Functional Relationship Between Prices and Market Concentration: The Case of the Banking Industry," *Empirical Studies in Industrial Organization,* D.B. Audretsch and J.J. Siegfried, eds. (Netherlands: Kluwer Academic Publishers, 1992), pp. 35–59; Stephen A. Rhoades, "Market Share Inequality, the HHI and Other Measures of the Firm-Composition of a Market," *Review of Industrial Organization* (December 1995), pp. 657–74; Allen N. Berger and Timothy H. Hannan, "Using Efficiency Measures to Distinguish Among Alternative Explanations of the Structure–Performance Relationship in Banking," *Managerial Finance* 23 (May 1997); and Steven J. Pilloff, "Multimarket Contact and Competition: Evidence from the Banking Industry," *Review of Industrial Organization* (March 1999).

52. See, for example, Allen N. Berger and David B. Humphrey, "The Dominance of Inefficiencies over Scale and Product Mix Economies in Banking," *Journal of Monetary Economics* 28 (1991), pp. 117–48, and Simon H. Kwan and Robert A. Eisenbeis, "An Analysis of Inefficiencies in Banking: A Stochastic Cost Frontier Approach," *Economic Review* 2 (Federal Reserve Bank of San Francisco, 1996), pp. 16–26.

53. See, for example, Stephen A. Rhoades, "Market Share Inequality," pp. 657–74.

54. See David Neumark and Steven A. Sharpe, "Market Structure and the Nature of Price Rigidity: Evidence for the Market for Consumer Deposits," *Quarterly Journal of Economics* (May 1992), pp. 657–80; Timothy H. Hannan and Allen N. Berger, "The Rigidity of Prices: Evidence from the Banking Industry," *American Economic Review* (September 1991), pp. 938–45; and William E. Jackson, III, "Market Structure and the Speed of Price Adjustments: Evidence of

Non-Monotonicity," *Review of Industrial Organization* (February 1997), pp. 37–57.

55. Steven A. Sharpe, "The Effect of Consumer Switching Costs on Prices: A Theory and Its Application to the Bank Deposit Market," *Review of Industrial Organization* (February 1997), pp. 79–94.

56. Switching costs are proxied by the mobility and turnover of the population in a market. It is notable that because non-MSA markets tend to experience relatively little population mobility and turnover, switching costs are likely to be generally more important in non-MSA than in metropolitan markets.

57. Timothy H. Hannan, Elizabeth K. Kiser, Robin A. Prager, and James J. McAndrews, "To Surcharge or Not to Surcharge: An Empirical Investigation of ATM Pricing," *Review of Economics and Statistics* 85, 4 (2003), pp. 990–1002, and Joy Ishii, "Interconnection Pricing and Compatibility in Network Industries: ATM Networks in the Banking Industry," 2005.

58. See Robert DeYoung, "The Financial Performance of Pure Play Internet Banks," *Economic Perspectives* (First Quarter 2001), and Karen Furst, William Lang, and Daniel E. Nolle, "Internet Banking: Developments and Prospects," *Economic and Policy Analysis Working Paper* (September 2000).

59. *American Bankers Association Deposit Account Fraud Survey Report* (2004).

60. In the 2000 *ABA Deposit Account Fraud Survey Report,* identity theft and Internet fraud were the fourth and fifth most important threats.

61. For a discussion of the challenges that these uncertainties create for bankers, the continuing critical role of branches as a retail platform for the banking industry, and a possible strategy to employ as we move (perhaps very slowly) toward a world of retail electronic banking, see Stephen A. Rhoades, "Bank Mergers and Industrywide Structure, 1980–94," *Staff Study* 169 (Federal Reserve Board, January 1996).

Selected Readings

Antitrust Bulletin (Fall 1992). This special issue on banking examines various antitrust policy issues in banking. It also presents research on industrial organization topics, including the effects of mergers on efficiency and the relationship between entry and legal barriers to entry.

Antitrust Bulletin (Summer 1996). This special issue on banking examines antitrust policy toward banking, competition issues surrounding ATM networks, and the views of key policymakers on antitrust policy concerning banking.

Antitrust Bulletin (Summer 1999). This special issue includes several articles on the definition of banking markets and the calculation of market shares. Other articles discuss the bank merger movement, ATM network mergers, and some general antitrust topics such as entry and exit and predation.

Review of Industrial Organization (February 1997). This special issue on banking provides a good illustration of the traditional industrial organization topics on which research is conducted in the context of the banking industry. Among the topics analyzed are the determinants of entry, the effect of switching costs on prices, and the relationship between market structure and performance.

Rose, Peter S. *The Changing Structure of American Banking.* New York: Columbia University Press, 1987. This book provides a very useful historical perspective on industry structure and institutional developments in commercial banking. It also provides a fairly extensive overview of research on a fairly wide range of topics related to banking competition and structure.

3

Brewing

Games Firms Play

Victor J. Tremblay and Carol Horton Tremblay

Since recorded history, people have combined water, cereal grain, and yeast to make beer. Ancient brews were dark in color and fairly sweet until bittering agents such as hops were added to preserve freshness over a thousand years ago. Today, grains, hops, and water are cooked together in large vats. Spent grains are removed and yeast is added to the remaining liquid, called wort, which starts the fermentation process. This converts the sugars in the wort into alcohol and carbon dioxide. The final product is then aged, filtered, pasteurized, and packaged into cans, bottles, or kegs.

Beer draws much of its flavor from malt, the most commonly used grain in the brewing process. Malt is roasted barley that can range from pale in color when lightly roasted to almost black when roasted at high temperatures. Beer becomes darker and heartier when brewed with darker malt and with top fermenting yeast. Top fermented styles of beers include ales, porters, and stouts. Porter and stout are not only darker but generally have higher alcohol content than ale. Lager is made with bottom fermenting yeast and is lighter in color and milder in flavor than ales, porters, and stouts. Many lagers are made lighter by using paler malt and replacing some of the malt with adjuncts, usually corn or rice. Brewers can also increase bitterness by using more hops and can increase alcohol content by adding sugar to the wort and extending fermentation time.

Today, U.S. consumers have access to a wide variety of styles and brands of beer. The largest domestic firms, called the macro brewers, produce a pale lager beer. These include the Anheuser-Busch, Miller, Coors, and Pabst brewing companies. Traditional domestic lager is brewed with some corn or rice and is marketed at three price points: popular, premium, and super-premium. The leading super-premium brand, Michelob by Anheuser-Busch, was an all-malt beverage until 1961 when rice was added to lighten its flavor.[1] To keep costs and prices low, popular-priced beer is typically brewed with 60 to 65 percent corn or rice, compared to 25 to 30 percent for premium beer.[2] A typical 12-ounce can of premium lager, such as Budweiser, has about 145 calories and is about 4.6 percent alcohol by volume. "Light" beer, such as Coors Light, is an extremely pale lager, with about 30 percent fewer calories and 10 percent less alcohol than premium lager.[3] Other lager styles that are marketed by the leading U.S. brewers include malt liquor, dry beer, and ice beer. Brands in these categories frequently have 10 to 20 percent more alcohol than premium lager.

Darker beers and ales are produced by foreign brewers and by many small domestic brewers, originally called microbreweries. Most of these foreign and small domestic firms brew all-malt beer, ale, porter, and stout, products that do not compete directly with the lighter lagers brewed by the macro brewers. On average, these darker beers have about 180 calories per 12-ounce serving and are about 5.4 percent alcohol by volume. Because some domestic microbreweries have become quite large, they are now called domestic specialty brewers. Beer brewed by the domestic specialty brewers is generally known as craft-style beer to distinguish it from imports.

With these beer styles and brewers in mind, we turn to the strategies used by the major players as they compete in the U.S. brewing industry. We begin by providing a discussion of the industry and the contentious economic environment that has shaped the strategic actions of brewers.[4] We find that many of these actions are consistent with the strategies found in game-theoretic models. For example, brewers were forced into a preemption race in television advertising during the 1950s and 1960s and into a war-of-attrition game in the 1970s, which continues even today. Common games and strategies found in the U.S. brewing industry include the prisoners' dilemma, mixed strategies, trigger strategies, brand proliferation, devolution strategies, and Hail Mary strategies.[5]

Games Brewers Play

The actions chosen by firms depend on the business environment, government regulations, and strategic considerations. Consumer preferences and technology shape environmental conditions, which are reflected in a firm's demand and cost functions. Although most environmental conditions are exogenous, a firm can make strategic investments in order to manipulate its business environment. For example, a successful advertising campaign may increase product demand, and investments in research and development may lower future production costs. In imperfectly competitive industries like brewing, a firm's profits will be affected by the actions of its rivals as well as its own actions. Thus, a successful firm will develop a strategy that takes into account the expected response of its rivals to any action taken by the firm. This is the purview of game theory. We compare game-theoretic predictions about the cooperative and noncooperative actions of firms to the behavior of firms in the U.S. brewing industry.

In the last half century, two major changes in market conditions influenced strategic activity in the U.S. brewing industry. First, the advent of television after World War II gave an advantage to firms that marketed their products nationally. Pressure to attain national status grew in the 1950s and 1960s as television became more popular. U.S. households with a television set increased from 9 percent in 1950 to 95 percent by 1970. An important advantage of national television advertising is that it reaches a given audience at lower cost than local television advertising. For example, in 1980 the price of advertising during sporting events was about 43 percent lower for national compared to local television ads.[6] This competitive advantage caused the major brewers to race to gain national status in order to use television advertising to foster a premium image for their flagship brands. Ulrich Doraszelski and Sarit Markovich term this a preemption race in advertising.[7] As a result, this strategic investment in advertising made the national brewers tougher competitors, or "top dogs" in the taxonomy of Drew Fudenberg and Jean Tirole, causing the exit of their smaller regional competitors.[8]

Second, changes in technology provide a cost advantage to large-scale brewers. One example is canning and bottling lines in the packaging industry. A high-speed canning line could fill and seal 750 cans per minute in 1966 and 2,000 cans per minute by 1987. To operate just one full-time canning line efficiently, a firm would need to produce about 0.82 million barrels per year in 1966

Figure 3.1   **Average Cost of Production for Various Brewers, 2004**

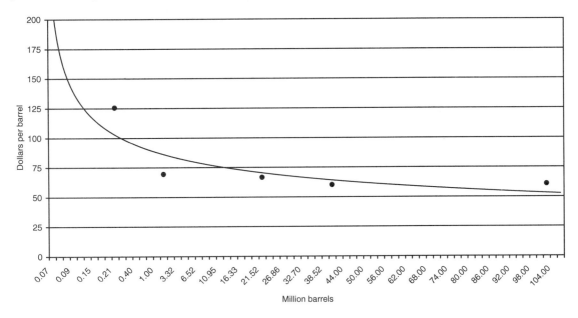

Source: Beer Industry Update: A Review of Recent Developments, 2005.

and about 2.18 million barrels by 1987. These and other innovations caused the industry leaders to build larger breweries and greatly expand their total brewing capacity. Evidence from industry experts, cost function estimation, and survivor tests suggest that minimum efficient scale (MES) at the firm level rose from 1 million barrels in 1960 to about 8 million barrels in 1970, 16 million barrels in 1980, and 23 million barrels in 2001.[9] The raw data on the cost of goods sold per barrel, plotted in Figure 3.1, suggest that MES may have exceeded 23 million barrels by 2004.[10]

The rapid growth in MES put a great deal of pressure on smaller brewers to grow in size. Because market demand increased more slowly than MES, not all existing firms could grow sufficiently to reach MES. This can be seen in Figure 3.2, which compares the actual number of brewers with the number of brewers that would exist if each firm produced at MES. From 1960 through 2000,

there were too many firms for them all to produce at MES. Thus, many firms were inefficiently small and could grow only by gaining market share from competing brewers. This forced brewers into a war of attrition, a game in which there are too many firms than can efficiently produce and profitably survive in an industry.[11] The war produced tough competition and low profits in brewing. For example, the average profit-to-sales ratio was 2.72 percent in U.S. brewing from 1960 to 1994, compared to 4.82 percent in U.S. manufacturing for the same period.

The preemption race in advertising and the war of attrition sparked vigorous competition as firms struggled to survive. In the mid-1970s, product differentiation and brand proliferation became important strategies for firm success. In what follows, we first consider product differentiation and the emergence of new products and brands in the brewing industry. This sets the stage for

Figure 3.2 **Actual and Efficient Number of Macro Brewers**

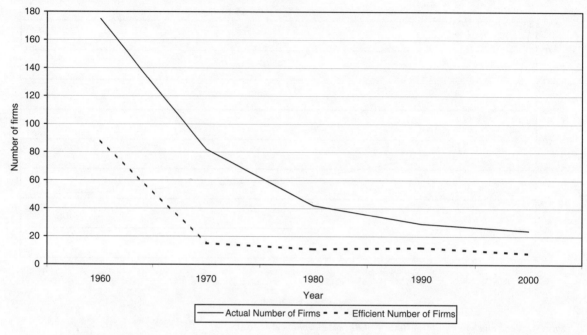

Source: The Office of R.S. Weinberg, St. Louis, and Victor J. Tremblay and Carol Horton Tremblay, *The U.S. Brewing Industry: Data and Economic Analysis* (Cambridge, MA: MIT Press, 2005).

subsequent discussion by identifying products and brands that are tied to pricing, advertising, and other strategies.

Product Differentiation and Brand Proliferation

An early decision when entering a market is the choice of brands and product characteristics. The major brewers choose to market a portfolio of different styles and brands of beer. In 2005, for example, Anheuser-Busch marketed thirty brands of domestic malt beverages, Coors offered sixteen, Miller offered thirty-five, and Pabst offered over thirty. Of the leading specialty brewers, the Boston Beer Company offered twenty-one and the Sierra Nevada Brewing Company offered thirteen different brands of beer.

Consumer demand for variety drives product differentiation and brand proliferation. Strategic considerations might also stimulate proliferation. For example, firms may flood the market with a wide variety of brands of different styles in order to leave few, if any, profitable product niches for potential entrants to exploit. The economics literature categorizes product differentiation as vertical and horizontal. Differentiation is horizontal when consumers disagree over the preference ordering of the horizontal characteristic. In brewing, this would include bitterness, as some consumers prefer bitter beer and others a milder beer. Products differ vertically if consumers agree on the preference ordering of the characteristic. Product quality is one example, as all consumers prefer a high-quality to a low-quality good, *ceteris paribus*. Unlike spirits and wine, beer quality depreciates over time, so product freshness is an important vertical characteristic in brewing.

Before the mid-1970s, almost all of the beer consumed in the United States was traditional lager beer. Because the horizontal characteristics of one brand were so similar to those of another brand, firms tried to differentiate their brands along the quality dimension. The national brewers' "premium" brands typically sold for a higher price than regional brewers' "popular-priced" brands. Premium brands are more expensive to produce, but the cost difference is small compared to the price difference. In the early 1970s, for example, the cost of producing a 12-ounce container of premium Budweiser was half a cent more than the cost of producing popular-priced Busch, two brands produced by Anheuser-Busch. Yet the price premium for Budweiser was fifteen cents. Immediately after World War II, most of the cost difference between the premium brands of national brewers and the popular-priced brands of regional brewers was due to differences in transportation costs, as the national brewers shipped their beer around the country from a single brewing facility in either Milwaukee (Miller, Pabst, and Schlitz) or St. Louis (Anheuser-Busch). Transportation costs for these "shipping brewers" began to fall in the 1950s, however, with the construction of a faster interstate highway system and as they built new brewing facilities in multiple locations. Today Anheuser-Busch, for example, has relatively low transportation costs due to its network of eleven breweries located around the country. In spite of the decline in shipping costs, the price of premium beer over popular-priced beer has actually risen over time. To illustrate, the price difference between premium and popular-priced beer was about 25 percent in 1953 compared to 38 percent in 2004. Perhaps a higher price increases the image of the national brands or signals a higher level of quality.

The national brewers claim that their national brands are of superior quality. Premium beer is brewed with a large percentage of malted barley, which is more expensive than corn and rice. The belief that all-malt beer is superior in quality may have been inspired by Germany's beer purity law of 1516, the *Reinheitsgebot* (meaning, literally, "commandment for purity"). This law required that all German beer be made from three ingredients: *gerste, hopfen,* and *wasser* (barley malt, hops, and water). The role of yeast was unknown at that time. Beer made from a larger percentage of barley malt has a heartier flavor, but there is no evidence that this is a vertical characteristic, as some consumers prefer lighter lagers that are made with more corn or rice. For example, men on average prefer all-malt beer, while women on average prefer a lighter lager.[12] The viewpoint that the use of barley malt, rice, or corn creates horizontal rather than vertical differentiation is consistent with the recent opinion of the Court of Justice of the European Communities. In 1987, the Court ruled that the German purity law was illegal, as its modern use did not ensure beer quality but was, in fact, a barrier to free trade.

Veblen effects and perceived differences in quality may be more likely explanations for the high price consumers are willing to pay for premium beer. A Veblen effect occurs when a consumer purchases a good to impress others.[13] This is normally associated with high-status brands that sell for high prices. As the average consumer in the United States grew wealthier, demand for high-quality and high-status goods increased. Veblen effects may explain the higher prices paid for premium beer because blind taste tests reveal that most consumers cannot distinguish one brand of traditional domestic lager from another.[14] The demand for high-status goods was initially met by premium beer and later by super-premium, import, and domestic craft-style beer. By offering both

Figure 3.3   **U.S. Macro, Craft, and Import Sales, 1950–2004**

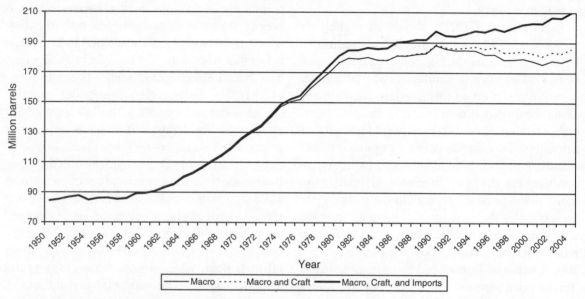

Source: The Office of R.S. Weinberg, St. Louis.

popular-priced and high-status brands, brewers are able to price-discriminate between consumers who prefer high-status brands and consumers who are more price conscious. Status and quality can be conveyed and enhanced by advertising, and some consumers may believe that more intensive advertising spending signals higher quality. The topic of advertising as a strategic variable will be discussed in a later section.

As traditional domestic lager became lighter and more homogeneous through the 1970s, some consumers became dissatisfied with the lack of variety. This was a time when import demand began to grow and the microbrewery movement emerged (Figure 3.3). Import and domestic craft-style beer are generally bitterer, due to higher hop content, and have a maltier flavor, due to a higher malt content. They are also higher in alcohol, calories, and carbohydrates. These differences can be seen in Table 3.1 for the major brands of import, domestic specialty, and traditional lager brands.

At the same time, the macro brewers began to develop new styles of beer and introduce new brands. Miller was the first major brewer to brand-proliferate, a strategy that was common to the tobacco industry and began at Miller when the company was acquired by the Philip Morris Tobacco Company in 1970. Through the mid-1970s, Miller introduced Miller Ale, Miller Malt Liquor, Lowenbrau, and Miller Lite. Of these, only Miller Lite was a hit. Although Miller did not invent light beer, Miller Lite was the first successful light brand. Previous light brands were promoted as diet beers, and part of the success of Miller Lite is attributed to the company's decision to market it as a light rather than a diet beer. The success of Lite induced other brewers to brand-proliferate. In 1970, today's largest four macro brewers (Anheuser Busch, Coors, Miller, and Pabst) produced an average of three brands, consisting of malt liquor and of traditional lager at different price points. This number had risen to thirty by 2005.

Table 3.1

Alcohol, Calorie, and Carbohydrate Content for a Twelve-Ounce Container of the Leading Brands of Beer

Style	Brand (brewer)	Alcohol by volume	Calories	Carbohydrates (grams)
Regular domestic lager				
	Budweiser (A-B)	5.0	143	10.6
	Busch (A-B)	4.6	133	10.2
	Coors Original	5.0	142	10.6
	Michelob (A-B)	5.0	155	13.3
	Miller Genuine Draft	4.7	143	13.1
	Miller High Life	4.7	143	13.1
	Old Milwaukee (Pabst)	4.6	145	12.5
	Pabst Blue Ribbon	5.0	153	12.0
Light and low carb				
	Aspen Edge (Coors)	4.1	94	2.6
	Bud Light (A-B)	4.2	110	6.6
	Budweiser Select (A-B)	4.3	110	6.6
	Coors Light	4.2	102	5.0
	Michelob Light (A-B)	3.3	134	6.7
	Michelob Ultra (A-B)	4.2	95	2.6
	Miller Lite	4.2	96	3.2
Malt liquor (ML) and ice beer				
	Bud Ice (A-B)	5.5	148	8.9
	Colt 45 ML (Pabst)	6.1	174	11.1
	Icehouse (Miller)	5.5	149	9.8
	King Cobra ML (A-B)	5.9	166	11.7
	Magnum ML (Miller)	5.6	157	11.2
	Old English 800 ML (Miller)	7.5	202	13.4
Domestic specialty				
	Anchor Steam	4.9	153	16.0
	Samuel Adams Lager (Boston)	4.7	160	18.0
	Samuel Adams Stout (Boston)	4.6	195	23.9
	Sierra Nevada Pale Ale	5.6	200	12.3
	Black Butte Porter (Deschutes)	5.2	180	n.a.
Imports (country of origin)				
	Corona Light (Mexico)	4.5	105	5.0
	Guinness Extra Stout (Ireland)	6.0	194	17.6
	Heineken (Netherlands)	5.4	166	9.8

Sources: Modern Brewery Age Weekly, May 16, 2005, and company Web pages.
Note: Busch and Old Milwaukee are popular-price brands. Pabst was a premium brand until the early 1960s, and Miller High Life was a premium until the early 1990s. Pabst and High Life are popular-priced brands today.

Product- and brand-proliferation were especially intense during the era of the beer wars, 1971–89. By filling up the product space with new products and brands, the macro brewers made it increasingly more difficult for the weaker regional brewers to find a successful market niche. In fact, Miller Lite was developed to combat the successful Coors Banquet. In the early 1970s, Coors was a strong regional brewer, and Coors Banquet was the number one brand west of the Rocky Mountains. Banquet was

Figure 3.4   **Market Share of the Leading Beer Segments, 1970–2004**

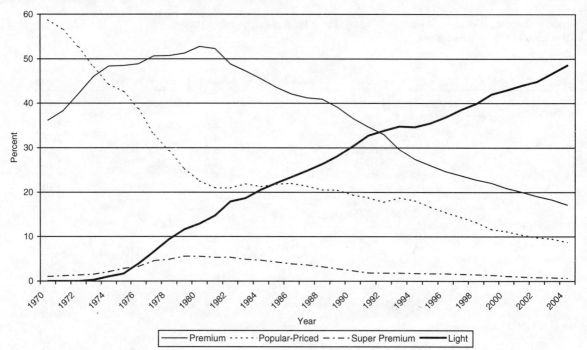

Source: Beer Industry Update: A Review of Recent Developments, 1997–2005.

lower in calories and alcohol than other leading premium brands and was marketed as "America's Fine Light Beer." The introduction of Miller Lite squeezed Banquet between regular premium beer and Miller Lite in terms of calories and alcohol content. As a result, Banquet experienced a steep sales decline beginning in 1977. Coors's survival is attributable to the company's successful introduction of Coors Light in 1978 and to its subsequent introduction of several heartier beers in the premium and super-premium categories: Herman Joseph's in 1982, Killian's Irish Red in 1982, and Coors Extra Gold in 1985.

Of the new product styles introduced by the macro brewers, light beer has proven to be the most successful.[15] As documented in Figure 3.4, light beer has gained considerable market share at the expense of other segments, particularly the

popular-priced brands produced predominantly by the regional brewers. From 1973 to 2004, the domestic market share of light beer rose from 0.3 to 48.6 percent, while the share of popular-priced beer declined from 48.1 to 8.7 percent.

By producing all-malt lagers, porters, and stouts, import suppliers and domestic specialty brewers have successfully minimized direct competition with the domestic macro brewers. The brewing facilities of the largest macro brewers are not designed to produce small quantities of craft-style beer, the one segment where the leading macro brewers do not have an important presence. This limits competition between the macro brewers and the import and domestic specialty suppliers. It also explains why most small regional brewers produce craft-style beer today. These include the Yuengling & Sons, Latrobe, and High Falls (Genesee) brew-

Figure 3.5   **Market Share of Specialty, Import, and Malt Alternatives**

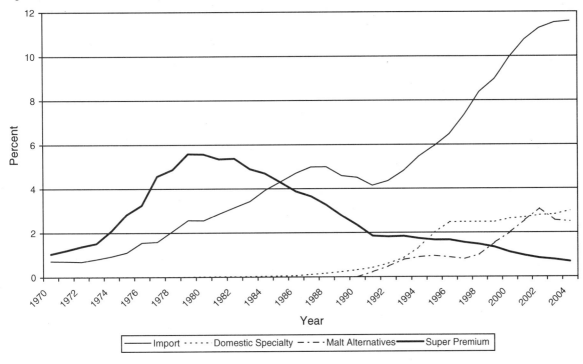

Source: Beer Industry Update: A Review of Recent Developments, 1977–2005.

ing companies. The relative success of the specialty and import sectors can be seen in Figure 3.5. The figure suggests that consumers now prefer craft and import beer over super-premium beer.

Of late, beer companies have faced stiff competition for the alcoholic beverage consumer from wine and spirits suppliers. In response, the macro brewers have introduced a number of flavored malt beverages. These are called malt alternatives, which consist of a lager beer that is filtered to remove any malt flavor and is usually sweetened with a fruit flavor. Their sales trends are depicted in Figure 3.5. The strategic response of the brewing industry to the growing success of the wine and distilled spirits industries will be addressed in a later section.

Pricing Strategies

Prices vary considerably from one style of beer to another. Imports sell at a relatively high price (Table 3.2), due in part to high shipping costs. In 2004, the average imported beer was about 25 percent more expensive than similar styles of beer produced by the domestic specialty brewers. Whether brewed as a regular or light beer, domestic premium brands are priced at 38 percent more than popular-priced brands. Of all malt beverage styles, malt alternatives command the highest price and are about 74 percent more costly than regular premium beer. Their higher price reflects higher production costs because malt alternatives require greater filtering and added flavorings. A high price

Table 3.2

Price Trends by Segment of Malt Beverages

Segment	Average price per case		
	2002	2003	2004
Imports	23.51	23.67	24.53
Domestic specialty	18.43	19.06	19.63
Regular			
Premium	15.51	15.84	16.20
Popular priced	11.22	11.43	11.71
Light			
Premium	15.52	15.82	16.16
Popular priced	11.31	11.55	11.79
Malt alternatives	26.89	27.61	28.13

Source: Beer Industry Update: A Review of Recent Developments (2005).

Note: The price is the average supermarket price, measured in dollars per case of 24 12-ounce containers.

may also enhance a premium image, as quality appears to be important to potential consumers who are interested in wine coolers and sophisticated mixed drinks.

Prior to the mid-1970s, however, most macro brewers focused their marketing efforts on a single flagship brand of regular domestic beer, such as Budweiser by Anheuser-Busch, Coors Banquet, Miller High Life, and Pabst Blue Ribbon. Although there were slight differences among brands, blind taste test results reveal that most consumers could not distinguish one brand of macro brew from another. In a market where firms produce perfectly homogeneous goods and compete by simultaneously choosing prices, the static Bertrand-Nash equilibrium predicts that price competition will be fierce. This is called the Bertrand paradox because the Bertrand model predicts that pricing will be perfectly competitive, even in an oligopoly market, when brands are perfectly homogeneous. It also illustrates one of the most famous outcomes of game theory, the prisoners' dilemma. In a game characterized by a prisoners' dilemma, it is always best for an individual player to deviate from co-

operation.[16] In an oligopoly market, all firms are better off by jointly setting the monopoly or cartel price, but each firm has an incentive to undercut its competitors when acting independently. One way to avoid competitive pricing is for firms to differentiate their products. In brewing, extensive product differentiation did not occur until the mid-1970s. Thus, one would expect pricing to have been competitive before that time.

Concentration and Price Competition

In a Cournot-Nash or in a repeated game, the number of competitors may also affect the degree of price competition. This is an issue of concern in brewing, as the number of independent macro brewers has continued to decline. After beer production ceased with Prohibition (1920–32), the number of independent brewing companies, what we term macro brewers, reached 733 in 1935 and declined to 22 firms by 2004 (Figure 3.6). This element of market structure is called industry concentration, which characterizes the number and size distribution of firms. One way to describe industry concentration is with a concentration curve, which plots the cumulative market shares attributable to the largest one, two, three, . . . n firms in the industry. An upward shift in the concentration curve implies greater industry concentration, which will occur as the number of firms in the industry declines or as the largest firms gain market share, *ceteris paribus*. Concentration curves for domestic beer production of the largest forty firms in brewing are plotted in Figure 3.7 for 1970 and 2004. They show that concentration grew considerably. This can also be seen by using common indices of industry concentration: the four-firm concentration ratio (CR_4) and the Herfindahl-Hirschman index (HHI).[17] These indices are plotted in Figure 3.8 and reveal the steady increase in brewing industry concentration during the period. For example,

Figure 3.6   **Number of U.S. Macro Brewers, 1934–2004**

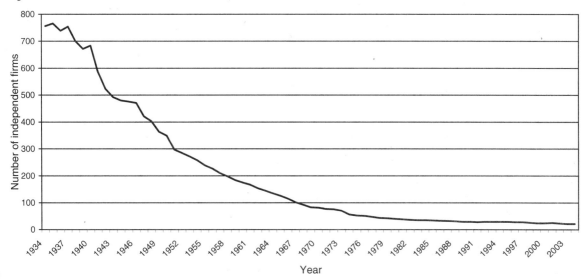

Source: The Office of R.S. Weinberg, St. Louis.

the market share of domestic beer production for the largest four firms was 44.2 percent in 1970 and reached 94.0 percent by 2004.[18] According to the standards established by the Department of Justice, the brewing industry would have been classified as moderately concentrated by 1972 and highly concentrated since 1981.[19] The high level of concentration and the growing degree of product differentiation suggest that price competition may have begun to diminish in brewing by the early 1980s.

A common measure of the degree of price competition or market power is the Lerner index. This is defined as $(p\text{-}mc)/p$, where p is the market price and mc is marginal cost. When a market is perfectly competitive, price equals marginal cost and the Lerner index equals 0. With less competition, price rises above marginal cost and the index becomes positive. Thus, a higher value of the Lerner index implies less price competition. Because marginal cost is generally unobservable, average cost is frequently used to approximate marginal cost. With

this substitution, the index is called a price-cost margin. Although the price-cost margin provides a poor estimate of market power unless there are constant returns to scale, it does provide an accurate picture of how profitability changes over time, assuming that accounting methods remain the same and the market is never far from long-run equilibrium.

Competition and Profits During Three Eras: 1950–70, 1971–95, and 1996–2004

The price-cost margin, plotted in Figure 3.9, indicates that profitability in the brewing industry declined in the 1950s, remained low in the 1970s and 1980s, and has risen substantially since 1995. In spite of greater product differentiation and industry concentration, price competition remained high until the mid-1990s. To better understand the forces that have influenced profits over time, we focus our study on three periods or regimes. The first, 1950–70, corresponds to a time when

Figure 3.7   **Concentration Curves for the U.S. Brewing Industry, 1970 and 2004**

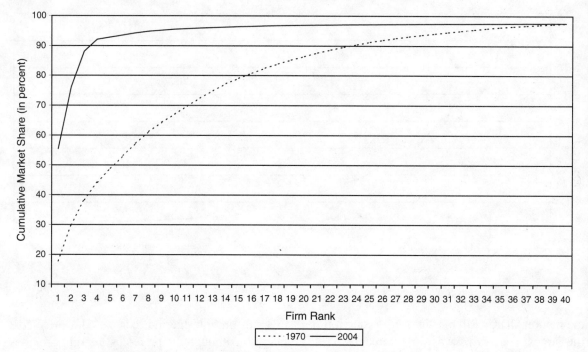

Source: The Office of R.S. Weinberg, St. Louis.

the major brewers produced nearly homogeneous goods and fought a preemption race in television advertising. The preemption race fostered tougher price competition and lower price-cost margins as leading brewers invested more heavily in television advertising. Markets were regional rather than national in scope during this time, however, and some regions of the country may have been insulated from intense competition, especially early on in this regime.

The second period, 1971–95, identifies the so-called beer wars. By the beginning of this period, the market became national in scope and the leading brewers built large new brewing facilities around the country to lower shipping costs and take advantage of growing MES. From 1970 to 1979, capacity expansion of the three largest brewers at the time (Anheuser-Busch, Miller, and

Schlitz) far outstripped growth in market demand. Total beer consumption increased by about 36 percent, while Anheuser-Busch increased its brewing capacity by almost 100 percent, Miller by almost 500 percent, and Schlitz by more than 80 percent. In addition, Philip Morris purchased Miller in 1970, a merger that caused Miller to mimic tobacco companies and undertake a brand-proliferation strategy during the 1970s. Another important event was Coors's expansion into new regional markets in an effort to become a national brewer during the 1980s. Coors sold beer in twenty-one states in 1980 and served every state by 1991. The substantial increase in MES forced firms into a war of attrition, a war that was intensified by the merger between Miller and Philip Morris and by the expansion of Coors. Thus, price and other forms of competition were fierce during this

Figure 3.8   **Concentration in the U.S. Brewing Industry, 1947–2004**

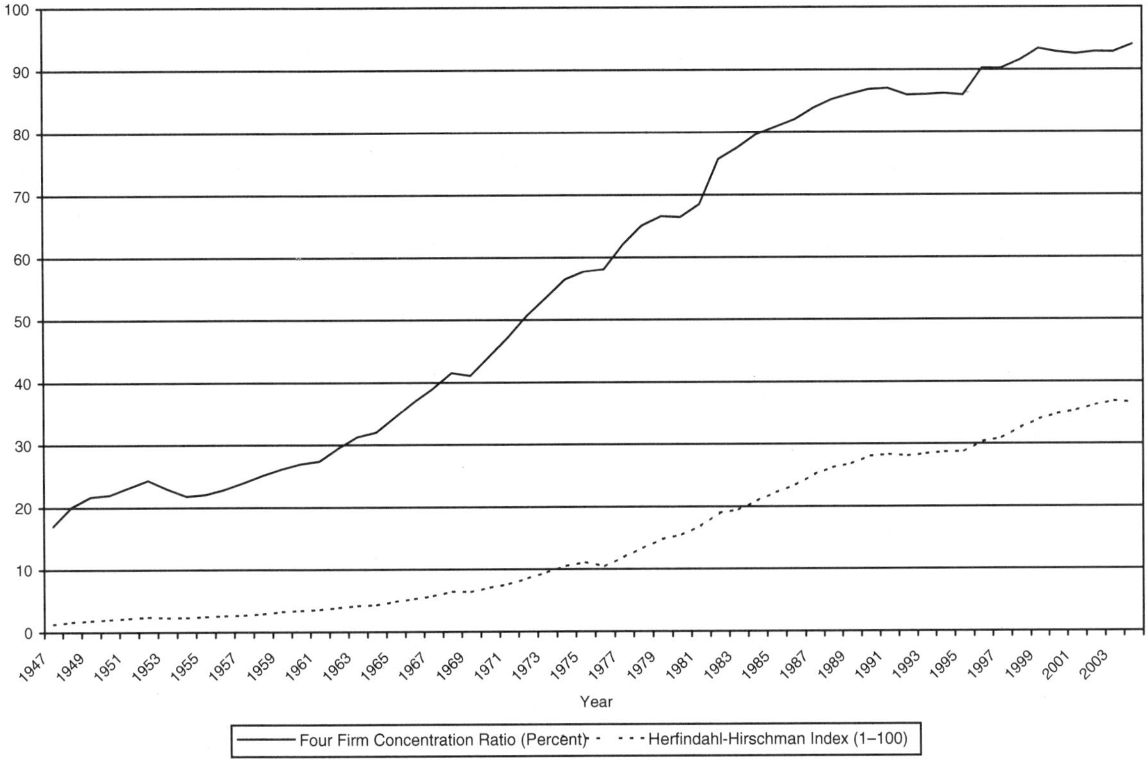

Source: The Office of R.S. Weinberg, St. Louis.

regime, which explains the record low price-cost margins.

The third period, 1996–2004, represents a time when competition appears to have subsided. By 1996, all of the remaining regional companies had exited, were on the verge of failure, or had contracted to serve a local niche market. The dominant three brewers, Anheuser-Busch, Coors, and Miller, took over almost all of the domestic beer production. Their market share of domestic beer production grew from 81.9 percent in 1995 to 94.0 percent in 2004.[20] The historically high price-cost margins suggest that industry concentration may have been sufficiently high to suspend intense competition in brewing during this period.

Trigger Strategies

One strategy that has been used in brewing to encourage cooperation is the trigger strategy. To illustrate how this works, consider a market in which each firm sets its price at a noncompetitive level (e.g., at the cartel price) if all rivals had set their prices at a noncompetitive level in the previous period. If a competitor chooses a more competitive price, this will trigger a harsh punishment in the form of a substantial price cut in the next period (normally to the Nash equilibrium price). By punishing noncooperative behavior, a trigger strategy will support cooperation as long as the punishment phase is sufficiently long, the

Figure 3.9   **Price-Cost Margins in Brewing (Before Taxes), 1950–2004**

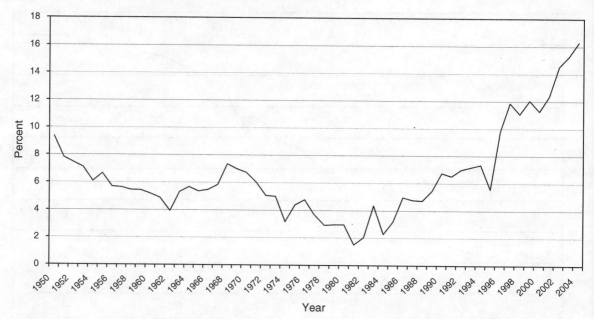

Source: Brewers Almanac (various issues) and U.S. Treasury Department, Internal Revenue Service, Source Book.

discount of future profits is not too great, and the number of firms is sufficiently small. If effective, firms will cooperate and a punishment phase will never be observed. A punishment phase can occur, however, if firms miscalculate the present value of future profits, perhaps because the length of the punishment phase is unknown.

There is evidence that Anheuser-Busch has used such a strategy to support higher beer prices. The first known example occurred in the mid-1950s after a union agreement led to higher wages for brewery workers. Anheuser-Busch responded to this cost increase by raising the price of Budweiser, a price increase that was not followed by many of its rival brewers. Evidence from the St. Louis area indicates that Anheuser-Busch retaliated by lowering the price of Budweiser by as much as 20 percent. After cutting price for over a year, Anheuser-Busch raised the price of Budweiser once again. This time, rivals followed with a price

increase of their own. There is no question that Anheuser-Busch was attempting to use a punishment phase to facilitate coordination. According to court testimony, the president of Anheuser-Busch is quoted as saying that he ordered the price cuts to "punish them [rival firms] for refusing to increase prices. . . ."[21] The punishment phase occurred in 1954, a year when price-cost margins took a noticeable dip (see Figure 3.9).

Similar events are documented in 1988 and 1995, when Miller and Coors discounted the prices of their flagship brands in order to gain market share from the remaining large regional brewers, the Heileman and Stroh brewing companies. Anheuser-Busch responded to these episodes with warning statements that Coors and Miller would "pay dearly if they continued the price slashing. . . ."[22] Threats of a price war were effective, as less competitive pricing ensued (see Figure 3.9).

Aggressive advertising campaigns can also trigger a punishment phase in pricing. In late 2004, Miller began a series of attack ads against Bud Light, the best-selling brand of light beer. The ads stated that Miller Lite has "more taste and half the carbs of Bud Light." Initially, Anheuser-Busch responded with its own attack ads, but ultimately resorted to a price cut of its Bud Light brand in the summer of 2005. Price cuts on other Anheuser-Busch brands soon followed. This form of punishment may have worked, as Miller executives complained that such price cuts are not in the interest of the industry and encouraged all brewers to use advertising to promote a positive beer image. Anheuser-Busch subsequently announced that it would raise prices in 2006.[23]

Mixed Strategies

The final pricing strategy common to the macro brewers is the use of a mixed strategy to market their flagship brands. This occurs when a brand is discounted unexpectedly with the intent of attracting the attention of price-conscious shoppers. To use a mixed strategy, a firm must identify a regular price, a discount price, and a probability of setting a discount price. When certain regularity conditions hold, a Nash equilibrium in mixed strategies will occur when it is optimal for one or more firms to discount their products in any particular time interval with some positive probability.[24] Unpredictability is important for a mixed-pricing strategy to be effective, since anticipated price cuts could be matched by rivals and consumers could postpone purchases until the next sale period.

Anheuser-Busch pioneered the mixed-price strategy in brewing by offering temporary discounts for Budweiser. The strategy has become common practice among the leading macro brewers.[25] Brewers must apply discounting judiciously, however, since a high price may be used by some consumers as a signal of high quality. In the past, brewers that overused discounting found that the reputation of their flagship brands became tarnished. Excessive discounting of Pabst Blue Ribbon in the 1960s and of Miller High Life in the 1990s caused sales to eventually drop and these brands to slide into the popular-priced category.

Advertising

Advertising can be an important strategic variable because it influences consumer demand and raises sunk costs. High sunk costs deter entry and generally result in high levels of industry concentration.[26] According to Joe Bain, advertising is "significant" and "substantial" when the intensity of advertising, measured by the ratio of advertising expenditures divided by sales revenues, exceeds 5 percent.[27] The brewing industry meets this criterion, as the advertising-to-sales ratio was 8.7 percent in 2004. This is similar to the advertising-to-sales ratios of other beverages and exceeds those of the cigarette, automobile, and pharmaceutical industries.

Advertising may inform consumers of product characteristics, increase brand loyalty by persuasive means, or create product images that become tied to the product.[28] The characteristics of beer, especially traditional domestic lager, are well-known to consumers, so there is little role for informative advertising. During the 1960s, a period of intense advertising competition, Raymond Bauer and Stephen Greyser found that consumers classified only 4 percent of beer advertising as informative.[29] The one exception occurs when a new brand is introduced. In order to inform consumers of its existence, the advertising-to-sales ratio is usually over five times the industry average in the first year that the new brand is introduced.

One reason that brewers spend so much money on advertising, even for established brands, is that beer advertising is "combative." Empirical studies confirm that advertising influences firm demand

Figure 3.10 **Advertising per Barrel in the U.S. Brewing Industry, 1950–2004**

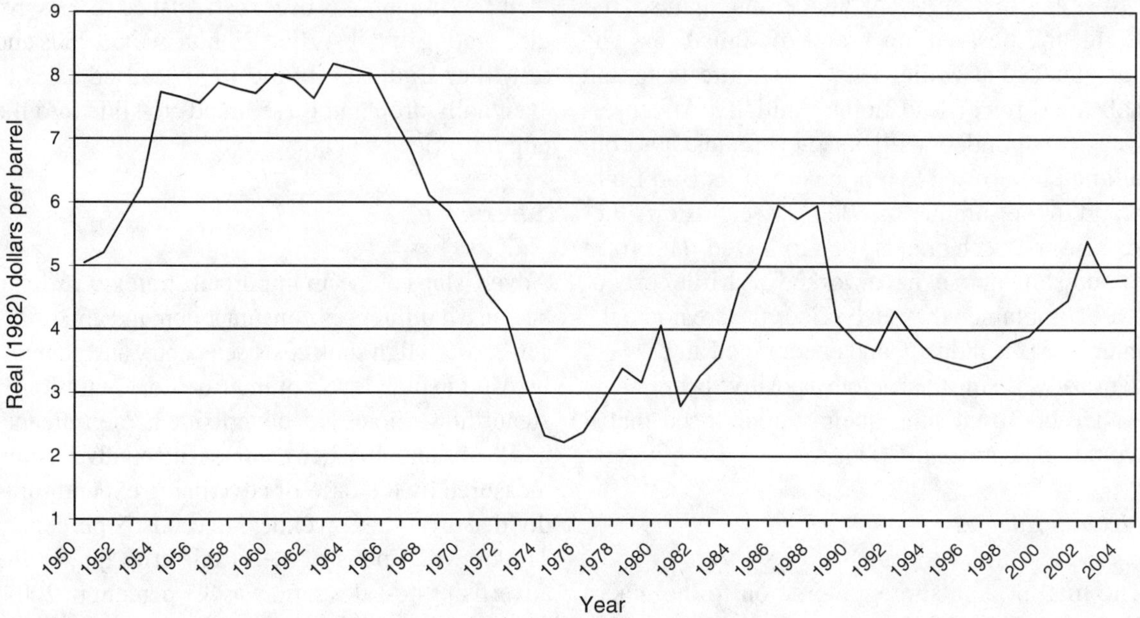

Source: Brewers Almanac (various issues) and *Beer Industry Update: A Review of the Evidence*, 1977–2005.

but has little or no effect on total beer demand. This form of advertising is said to be combative because one brewer's advertising can increase demand for its product only by stealing customers from rival brewers. In this setting, firms face a prisoners' dilemma in advertising. This occurs because one firm's advertising imposes a negative externality on its competitors. When each firm behaves independently to maximize its own profit, the Nash equilibrium level of advertising will exceed the level that maximizes industry profits.[30] Much like the price wars in a Bertrand type game in prices, advertising wars will occur. This may explain why beer advertising among the macro brewers tends to be persuasive and image enhancing, as these forms of advertising are designed to cultivate brand loyalty, thereby impeding the business-stealing effect of rival advertising. As discussed previously, some wealthy consumers may also be willing to

pay a higher price for heavily advertised premium brands if advertising creates brand names and images that are associated with prestige and high quality. When effective, this form of advertising creates subjective product differentiation, which may reduce price competition.

Figure 3.10 plots real advertising spending per barrel (measured in 1982 dollars), for the brewing industry, 1950–2004.[31] Advertising spending per barrel does not follow a simple pattern and can be better understood by investigating different events that affected advertising competition in brewing. As discussed above, television advertising became an important marketing outlet for the large national brewers during the 1950s and 1960s, resulting in heated competition in television advertising spending. From the early 1950s through the mid-1960s, real advertising spending exceeded $7.00 per barrel, which is well above the industry average of

Figure 3.11 **Advertising per Barrel for the Leading Brewers, 1969–2004**

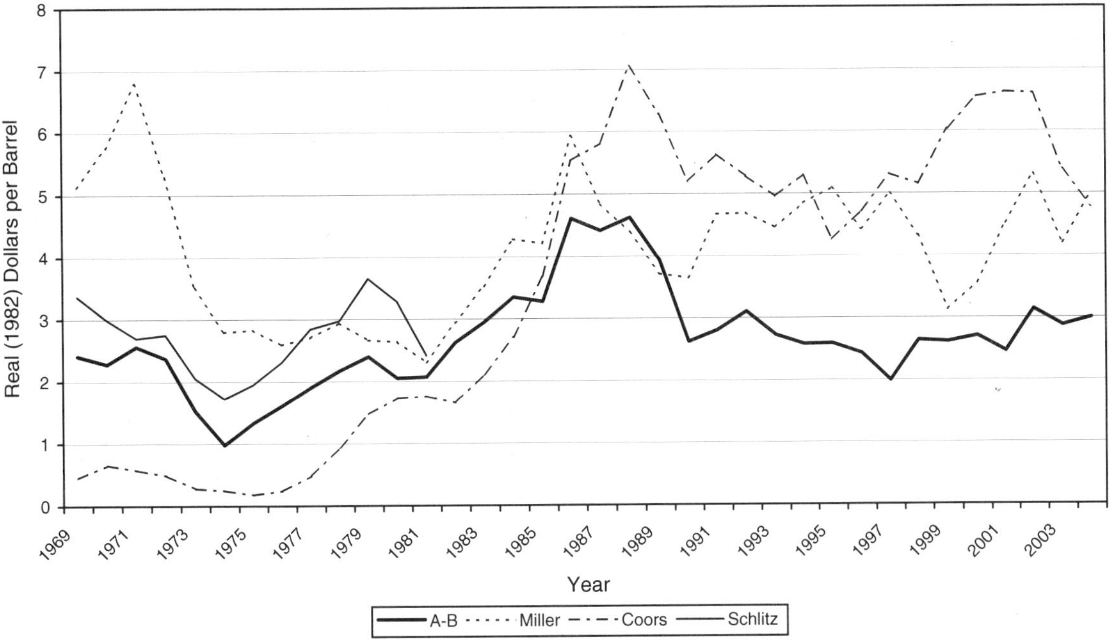

Source: Beer Industry Updates: A Review of Recent Developments, 1977–2005.

$5.13 for 1950–2004. The high level of advertising spending and low price-cost margins during the 1950s and 1960s are also consistent with a prisoners' dilemma in advertising. The winners in this stage of the advertising race were Anheuser-Busch, Schlitz, and Pabst, companies that marketed their beer nationally and substantially gained market share from competing brewers.

The next important event that affected competition in brewing began in 1970 when Philip Morris bought Miller. The first move by Philip Morris was to increase Miller's advertising spending. By 1971, Miller spent $6.80 a barrel on advertising, over two and a half times the amount spent by the other leading brewers (Anheuser-Busch, Schlitz, and Coors). Next, Miller introduced new brands and made substantial investments in new brewing facilities. In response to increases in MES, Miller

increased its brewing capacity by almost five times from 1970 to 1979. These investments caused Miller's sales to rise and its advertising spending per barrel to fall (Figure 3.11). The other leading brewers responded in kind, and it appears that cuts in advertising spending were used to help finance investments in brewing facilities. In addition, total beer sales rose steeply during the 1970s (see Figure 3.3), which also pushed down advertising spending per barrel.

The third event of importance regarding advertising competition was Coors's efforts to become a national brewer. Coors entered twenty-eight new states from 1980 to 1988, which required considerable advertising spending and investment in new distribution networks. Coors's advertising spending per barrel rose from $0.94 to $7.06 from 1978 to 1988. This started an advertising war among the leading brewers, as the market demand for macro beer grew very little and advertising became more combative (see Figure 3.11). During this time, advertising spending rose from $2.17 to $4.62 per barrel for Anheuser-Busch and $2.94 to $4.38 per barrel for Miller. The advertising war subsided once Coors reached national status in 1991, and advertising spending at the industry level has remained at or below the long-run industry average of $5.13 a barrel since that time.

Exit and Devolution Strategies

Changing market conditions and resulting strategic battles caused the number of traditional macro brewers to decline from 421 in 1947 to 22 firms by 2004. To be successful on a large scale, a brewer needed to have survived the preemptive race in advertising during the 1950s and 1960s, built efficient new brewing facilities during the 1970s, introduced a successful brand of light beer in the 1970s, and maintained a premium image for core brands. At this point in the game, the winners are Anheuser-Busch, Coors, and Miller. Another survival route for the traditional brewer was to retreat to a local niche market by producing craft-style beer. This strategy reduces competition with the national brewers and enables them to compete in the faster growing domestic specialty sector of the market.

Two firms fared well through the preemption race in advertising, but both later undermined their own success with serious strategic blunders. The first was Pabst, the industry leader in 1949 and the third largest brewer through most of the 1960s. Pabst's major mistake was to discount its Blue Ribbon brand, which repositioned it from a premium to a popular-priced brand in the early 1960s. This proved successful at first, since popular-priced beer dominated industry sales with a market share of over 75 percent in 1961. Unfortunately for Pabst,

sales in the popular-priced category began to decline by the late 1960s. For example, the market share of popular-priced beer fell to 59 percent by 1970 and 23 percent by 1980. Today, this segment accounts for less than 10 percent of sales. In hindsight, the repositioning of Blue Ribbon was a mistake, and at present the future of Pabst appears to be in doubt. Pabst has a declining market share, and all of the company's beer is brewed under contract with Miller. The other example of a successful firm that stumbled is the Schlitz Brewing Company, the last brewer to hold the number one spot before Anheuser-Busch took it over in 1957. Schlitz remained the number two brewer until the late 1970s, when its sales began a steep decline. Cost-cutting measures that lowered the perceived quality of Schlitz beer, poorly timed and unsuccessful introductions of new brands, and a failed marketing campaign are partially to blame for the problems at Schlitz. In chapter 12 of this volume, Avi Goldfarb makes an effective case that the marketing battles between Anheuser-Busch and Miller in the mid-1970s, precipitated by Philip Morris's acquisition of Miller, also contributed to the demise of Schlitz.

Brewers facing a slippery slope toward failure took several different routes before exiting the market. Those with relatively weak financial positions and little chance of reaching MES chose to exit the industry rather quickly. In most cases, these firms were purchased by another domestic macro brewer.[32] With so many firms on the chopping block, several firms chose to grow in size by purchasing failing brewers. Through the 1970s, the Department of Justice and the Federal Courts made it almost impossible for the leading brewers to grow by merger. Thus, only smaller, less efficient firms were able to purchase a failing brewer. As a result, most of the growth of the leading brewers came from building new brewing facilities.

The dominant strategy that evolved under these

conditions for the mid-sized firms was the harvest or devolution strategy. When under financial stress, a firm would make deep cuts to overhead costs, frequently eliminating all spending on advertising and maintenance of plant and equipment. By drastically cutting costs, exit was delayed until the company's physical capital and product goodwill sufficiently depreciated. These cuts allowed the firm to cut price and stay in business for many years. Because strict enforcement of the anti-merger laws made it impossible for the leading brewers to grow by merger, mid-sized brewers such as Heileman and Stroh were able to purchase failing breweries at relatively low cost. From 1961 through 1987, Heileman made seventeen horizontal acquisitions. When an acquisition included successful brands but inefficient brewing facilities, the acquired facilities would be closed and the new brands would be brewed at one of Heileman's existing, more efficient plants. When weak brands but more efficient facilities were purchased, the acquired brands would be discontinued and the new plant would replace one of Heileman's existing, less efficient plants. This strategy proved successful for Heileman until the supply of failing brewers dried up in the 1980s. With no new brands or facilities to replace depreciated ones, Heileman declared bankruptcy in 1991 and was sold to Stroh in 1996. Stroh went out of business in 1999, putting an end to the devolution strategy in brewing. All other small regional breweries have either gone out of business or retreated to local niche markets.

Hail Mary Strategies

It is common for a firm on the brink of business failure to pursue an unconventional strategy in its struggle to survive. Even though chances are low, such a strategy could save the firm from bankruptcy. The strategy poses little downside risk, as the firm will fail anyway unless a dramatic turn-around takes place. Pursuit of an unconventional strategy in the face of failure is called a Hail Mary strategy, named after the long passes thrown by a trailing football team at the end of the game in a desperate attempt to complete a winning touchdown pass. Odds are against the play's succeeding. Nevertheless, a long pass is thrown, knowing that the miracle pass completion would reverse the team's fortunes. Another important feature of this theory as it applies to business is that successful firms will monitor the unconventional strategies of other firms and mimic them if they prove to be successful.[33]

Such behavior is common practice in brewing. In the words of industry expert Robert S. Weinberg, "There seems to be an inverse relationship between having the means to take risks, and the willingness to take them."[34] The most common type of Hail Mary strategy found in brewing is the introduction of a new or unconventional brand or product. There are several notable examples of unconventional brands. The first is Old Frothenslosh, a brand of the Pittsburgh Brewing Company that was introduced in the 1960s and reintroduced in the 1970s. The Old Frothingslosh labels contained Day-Glo colors. The brand was marketed by a 300-pound woman named Fatima Yechburg, and promoted as the "pale stale ale" and the "only brew you can find in the dark." Second, during Jimmy Carter's presidency the Falls City Brewing Company worked with the president's brother, Billy Carter, to develop and market Billy Beer in the late 1970s. Finally, the Eastern Brewing Company developed a brand called Nude Beer. Each container had a silver scratch-off patch that, when rubbed off, revealed a picture of a nude woman. These brands met with limited success and were discontinued once their novelty faded. None of the leading brewers have resorted to such gimmicks.

One could also view the first introduction of light beer as a Hail Mary strategy. Light was initially introduced by three struggling regional brewers in the 1960s: Piel in 1961, Rheingold in 1967, and Meister Brau in 1968. Although light beer is the dominant beer category today, these pioneering brands were unsuccessful and did not save their failing parent companies. Part of the problem is that they were marketed as diet beers, a term that may not have appealed to beer drinkers. Light beer became a hit with the introduction of Miller Lite, a brand that was first marketed nationally in February 1975. Recall that Miller pursued a brand-proliferation strategy after being purchased by Philip Morris in 1970. Lite's success is attributable to the advertising support it received from Philip Morris, as well as Miller's decision to avoid the diet beer connotation. Instead, Lite was marketed as a beer that is "great tasting" and "less filling." The success of Miller Lite became quickly apparent, and all of the leading brewers followed by introducing their own versions of light beer by 1978.

The behavior of Schlitz provides an excellent case study, as the company resorted to the use of unconventional strategies once its financial fortunes began to wane. Until the mid-1970s, Schlitz was a leading brewer and its actions were conservative and predictable. This changed when Schlitz began to fail in 1977, as the company tried several unconventional strategies until it was acquired by Stroh in 1981. In the 1970s, the advertising campaigns of the most successful brewers were humorous and emphasized quality. To turn the company around, however, Schlitz tried an aggressive new advertising theme in 1977. The ad featured a formidable boxer who drank Schlitz. When asked to switch to another brand, the boxer glared into the camera in a threatening manner and asked, "You want to take away my gusto?" The ads were quickly taken off the air as they were viewed as menacing, and they were later called the "drink Schlitz or I'll kill you" campaign.[35] In the final stages of decline, Schlitz resorted to blind taste-test commercials that aired live during the professional football playoffs and Super Bowl XV (1980–81). In these commercials, 100 Budweiser or Miller beer drinkers were asked to compare and evaluate the taste of their favorite beer with Schlitz. In spite of the fact that many preferred Schlitz, the campaign was unsuccessful. This was the first attempt by a major brewer to pursue blind taste-test commercials on a large scale; subsequent attempts at blind taste-test commercials by other declining brewers have also proven unsuccessful.[36]

More recently, brewers under financial stress have resorted to the so-called "beer-n-babes" advertising campaigns.[37] In fact, one could argue that the use of sexually provocative ads is an indicator that a brewer is under financial stress. To illustrate, Stroh was in financial trouble during the early 1990s, experiencing a 44 percent decline in market share from 1989 to 1995. In 1991 the company used a "Swedish Bikini Team" (five women wearing blond wigs and bikinis) to market its Old Milwaukee brand. Even though their jobs were at stake, a group of female employees filed a lawsuit against Stroh, claiming that the ads encouraged sexual harassment. Stroh responded by dropping the ads. This legacy continues as Pabst, another declining firm and the current owner of Old Milwaukee, revived the Swedish Bikini Team to market Old Milwaukee in 2005.[38] Miller has also resorted to such tactics. In an effort to turn around a gradual but steady decline in market share since 1999, Miller introduced its so-called catfight ads in 2002–3. In these ads, two beautiful women, arguing over whether or not Miller Lite's best quality is that it "tastes great" or is "less filling," end up ripping off each other's clothes in a brawl in a water fountain. Rance Crain, editor-in-chief of *Advertising Age,* described these ads as "blatant sexism and exploitation of the female body."[39]

Domestic specialty brewers have also used sex to promote beer. After experiencing a decline in sales, the Boston Beer Company aired a "sex for Sam" radio advertisement in 2002, offering a free trip to a Boston concert to couples who engaged in sex in a public place. Company president James Koch later apologized for the ads. The ads and publicity associated with them may have been successful, however, as Boston's sales rose in 2002 for the first time in six years. Another specialty brewer chose its name to make this connection explicit, The Great Sex Brewing Company of Redding, California, and has used such marketing slogans as "Let's Have Some Great Sex" and "It's Great Sex Time."

Internationalization of the Brewing Industry

In the last several years, leading brewers around the world have expanded their geographic scope with a series of international mergers. In 2002, Miller was purchased by South African Brewers of the United Kingdom, and the new company is known internationally as SABMiller. In 2005, SABMiller bought a controlling interest in Bavaria SA, South America's second largest brewer. Coors acquired Carling Breweries of the United Kingdom in 2002, and Coors and the Molson Brewing Company of Canada merged in 2005 to form the Molson-Coors Brewing Company. The industry leaders, Anheuser-Busch and SABMiller, are vying for a presence in China, the world's largest beer-drinking nation. State-owned breweries in China have sought foreign help with privatization, and Anheuser-Busch has purchased the Harbin Brewing Group of China. SABMiller has purchased three breweries in Shanghai and has recently expanded the brewing capacity of a Chinese partner, China Resource Breweries Limited.

Several forces motivate a firm to internationalize. First, sufficiently low transportation costs and trade restrictions are required. The extent of scale economies can also be important. When MES is large relative to the size of a national market, one way for a firm to reach MES is to expand into foreign markets. With sufficiently low transportation costs and trade barriers, unit costs may fall as the firm expands globally. The automobile industry fits this description and provides one explanation for the wave of international mergers in the industry during the last decade. There are substantial scale economies associated with the production of many automobile components, enabling a firm to attain lower unit-production costs as it serves a larger share of the world market. For example, Ford was able to lower its unit cost of production after acquiring Swedish-based Volvo in 1999. By designing and producing a common frame for its mid-sized Ford and Volvo cars, total production of mid-sized frames increased and unit costs fell.

In other markets like soft drinks, products are marketed internationally, not because of scale economies in production but because of scale economies in the creation of a premium image. For an international brand like Coca-Cola that uses a unifying marketing theme, brand equity that is created in one country stays with consumers who travel or move to another country. A unifying, worldwide theme would be more effective for marketing campaigns that focus on a vertical characteristic, like a premium image for a high-quality good, than for a horizontal characteristic. Marketing a horizontal characteristic, like a mango- versus lemon-flavored soft drink, may be region-specific and therefore of limited effectiveness globally. A marketing campaign that emphasizes a product's high quality will appeal to all consumers around the world, as everyone prefers a high-quality to a low-quality good, *ceteris paribus*.

Marketing, more than production efficiencies, appears to be driving internationalization of the brewing industry. Like soft drinks, the premium brands receive most of the marketing effort of the leading international brewers. For example,

74

Figure 3.12 **Market Share of Alcoholic Servings for Beer, Wine, and Spirits in the United States, 1970–2004**

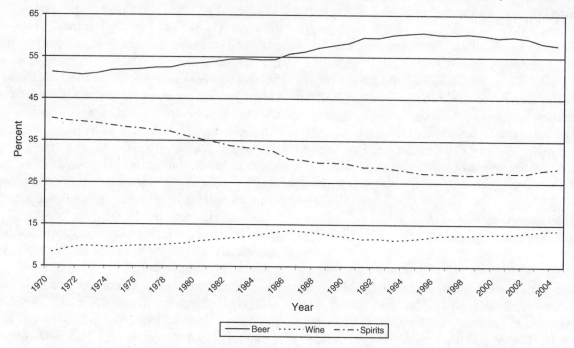

Source: Alcohol Epidemiologic Data System, T.M. Nephew et al. Alcohol Epidemiologic Data Reference Manual, U.S. Apparent Consumption of Alcoholic Beverages Based on State Sales, Taxation, or Receipt Data. Washington, D.C., NIAAA.

Anheuser-Busch markets Budweiser internationally, promoting product quality and its "King of Beers" theme. Foreign brands with a reputation for excellence, such as Guinness Stout and Heineken, are also receiving greater marketing support around the world. Although marketed internationally, these brands are frequently brewed locally. In Japan, for example, Budweiser and Heineken are brewed under contract by the Kirin Brewing Company, and Guinness is brewed under contract by the Sapporo Brewing Company.

Strategic Interactions Among Beer, Wine, and Spirits Producers

The latest challenge facing the beer industry is competition from the wine and spirits industries.

Beer's share of the market for alcoholic beverages rose from the early 1970s through the mid-1990s, primarily at the expense of the distilled spirits industry (Figure 3.12). Beer's share has slipped of late, from 60.6 percent in 1998 to 57.9 percent in 2004, and several analysts claim "beer is dead."[40] Wine consumption rose moderately in the mid-1980s, riding the temporary wine cooler craze. A more sustained increase in wine demand began in 1995 after a medical study at the University of Wisconsin found that moderate consumption of red wine reduces the risk of heart disease. Subsequent research has shown that part of the benefit comes from ethanol but that red wine provides added benefits due to its high concentration of antioxidants.

One explanation for these trends is the change in demographics. An important determinant of

Figure 3.13   **Per-Capita Beer Consumption in Gallons and Percentage of U.S. Population (18–44), 1950–2004**

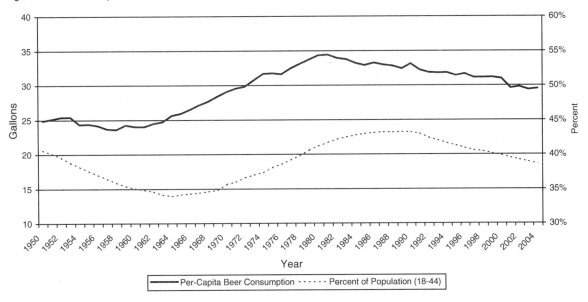

Source: The Office of R.S. Weinberg, St. Louis, and *Statistical Abstract of the United States.*

per-capita beer demand is the size of the primary beer-drinking population, which is eighteen to forty-four years of age. Figure 3.13 reveals a close relationship between these two variables. Demand studies suggest that older consumers prefer spirits and wine to beer. Thus, beer demand is likely to stagnate or fall with the aging U.S. population.

Changes in marketing policies may also be a factor. Unlike beer and wine producers, distilled spirits producers had agreed to a voluntary ban on all broadcast advertising since Prohibition. Motivated by declining demand and an interest in competing on a level playing field with beer and wine, Seagram Americas violated the industry's voluntary ban in June 1996. Other spirits producers followed, and the Distilled Spirits Council of the United States voted to rescind the voluntary broadcast advertising ban on November 7, 1996. Although opposition from consumer and public

health organizations has limited the growth of broadcast advertising of distilled spirits, spirits producers have increased their advertising spending relative to beer and wine since the ban was lifted. In 1996, spirits producers spent $118 million on advertising, beer producers spent $713 million, and wine producers spent $83 million. From 1996 to 2004, advertising spending for spirits increased by 97 percent, while beer spending increased by 65 percent and wine spending increased by 38 percent. The increased marketing efforts of distilled spirits producers may have played a role in their growing share of the alcohol market since 1999.

According to James Arndofer, another factor working against the beer industry is the fact that many wealthy consumers and young adults who normally prefer beer are trading up to fashionable mixed drinks and high-priced wine and spirits brands.[41] For example, sales of wines priced at over

$11 a bottle rose by 19 percent in early 2005.[42] Because prestige and perceived quality are frequently linked to price, beer is at a distinct disadvantage. When bottled and properly stored, wine quality can improve and spirits quality does not diminish with age. Thus, the price of a high-quality bottle of wine or spirits rises over time as the supply of a particular vintage falls with consumption. For example, a prominent Web merchant lists a five-liter bottle of red Bordeaux at over $4,000 and a 750-millimeter bottle of single-malt scotch at over $2,500. Beer is different, however, because beer quality deteriorates immediately after packaging. Most two-year-old containers of beer are undrinkable, and it is very rare to find even an imported brand of beer selling for more than $20 for a 6-pack of 12-ounce bottles.

The leading domestic specialty brewer, Boston, has responded by introducing a series of "extreme beers" to compete for upscale spirits and wine drinkers. These include Samuel Adams Millennium, which was brewed just once in 1999, and Samuel Adams Utopia, first introduced in 2001. These extreme beer brands are unique in that they are noncarbonated and high in calories and alcohol. For example, Utopia is fermented with champagne yeast, has about 642 calories per 12-ounce serving, and is 25 percent alcohol by volume.[43] Millennium sold for $200 per 32-ounce bottle, and Utopia is marketed in a 24-ounce decanter that sells for $100.[44] An inability to store beer for long periods limits the growth potential of extreme beers, however.

To appeal to young adults, the macro brewers have introduced a variety of malt alternatives. These brews target young adults who prefer sweeter mixed drinks and soda pop to traditional beer. For example, the Zima brand by Coors comes in lemon-lime, orange, black cherry, and green apple flavors. Tequiza, by Anheuser-Busch, is a light lager beer that is flavored with lime and blue agave, a plant used to make tequila. Anheuser-Busch's new B^E (pronounced B-to-the-E) brand is a malt alternative that is similar to an energy or sports drink. It is slightly sweet and brewed with caffeine, ginseng, and guarana (a Brazilian stimulant). Malt alternatives contain more alcohol, calories, and carbohydrates than regular domestic beer. For example, a 12-ounce container of Zima Hard Orange is 5.9 percent alcohol by volume and contains 231 calories and 30 grams of carbohydrates. B^E is sold in 10-ounce cans and contains 6.6 percent alcohol, 203 calories, 22.5 grams of carbohydrates, and 54 milligrams of caffeine.[45]

Sales of malt alternatives grew from 1 to over 3 percent of the malt beverage market from 1998 to 2002. This motivated distilled spirits producers to create their own malt alternative brands, such as Smirnoff Ice. Distilled spirits versions derive their alcohol from brewing rather than distilling because malt beverages are taxed at a much lower rate than distilled spirits.[46] The share of malt alternatives began to slip after 2002, and has fallen to 2.5 percent in 2004. Thus, it is unclear whether malt alternatives will have much of a lasting effect on the drinking habits of the young adults who prefer mixed drinks. Given their sweetness, it is also unlikely that regular beer drinkers will do more than sample a malt alternative beverage.

Although demographic trends are working against the brewing industry, it remains to be seen if the young adult trend toward mixed drinks will prove lasting and if the strategic responses of U.S. beer companies will be effective.

Conclusion

Two key events motivated strategic behavior among firms in the U.S. brewing industry. The invention of television and its impressive gain in popularity during the 1950s and 1960s created a new and powerful marketing tool for the national brewers. Second, technological change in the 1970s increased scale economies, giving large-scale brewers a cost advantage over smaller regional firms. Market demand was insufficient to support more than a few firms of sufficient size to exploit national advertising and attain minimum efficient scale. Fierce competition ensued.

In this setting, U.S. brewers chose a variety of strategies, many of which can be found in game theory literature. The leading national brewers invested heavily in advertising, especially during the 1950s and 1960s, and later built super-sized brewing facilities in order to reach scale efficiency. During the beer wars of the 1970s and 1980s, the leading brewers also chose a brand proliferation strategy to usurp market share from their smaller regional competitors. The evidence also shows that Anheuser-Busch used a trigger strategy to support higher beer prices, although not always with success. Finally, the leading domestic brewers have begun to internationalize as the market becomes global.

Competitive pressure and the actions of the leading brewers created unfavorable market conditions for smaller regional brewers. As a result, they took a variety of different strategic paths. In the last fifty years, Coors is the only regional brewer to successfully gain national status. This was accomplished by increasing advertising spending and investing in distribution systems in new states. Other surviving regional brewers have retreated to local niche markets by brewing brands of craft-style beer that do not compete directly with the brands of the national brewers. Of the 421 macro brewers in 1947, 399 exited the market by 2004. Some exited rather quickly, but others pursued one of two strategies. Several regional brewers postponed their demise by using a devolution strategy: slashing costs and milking all of the remaining brand equity and productive capacity out of their plant and equipment. Others chose a Hail Mary strategy: a risky action or gimmick that has a low expected return but, if successful, could save the company from almost certain demise.

In most cases, the strategic actions of successful and failing firms have been rational and in keeping with the principles of game theory. There is some evidence, however, that a handful of firms made strategic blunders due to a lack of foresight or inadequate understanding of strategic principles. In such cases, an understanding of game theory may have enabled management to identify strategies that better fit the changing conditions in the brewing industry.

Notes

We wish to thank Bob Weinberg of the Office of R.S. Weinberg, St. Louis, for graciously providing data on firm output and the number of independent macro and specialty brewers. We also wish to thank Yan Du, John Hall, Natsuko Iwasaki, Yasushi Kudo, Maya Sherpa, and Andrew Stivers for providing helpful comments on an earlier version of the chapter.

1. James D. Robertson, *The Connoisseur's Guide to Beer* (Ottawa, IL: Jameson Books, 1984).

2. Ted Goldammer, *The Brewers' Handbook* (Clifton, VA: KVP Publishers, 1999).

3. "Can You Judge a Beer by Its Label?" *Consumer Reports,* (June 1996), pp. 10–17.

4. The interested reader can find a more complete discussion of the data and the economics of the brewing industry in our previous work: Victor J. Tremblay and Carol Horton Tremblay, *The U.S. Brewing Industry: Data and Economic Analysis* (Cambridge, MA: MIT Press, 2005).

5. For a review of the game theoretic concepts found in this chapter, see Robert Gibbons, *Game Theory for Applied Economists* (Princeton, NJ: Princeton University Press, 1992); Luis M.B. Cabral, *Introduction to Industrial Organization* (Cambridge, MA: MIT Press, 2000); Dennis W. Carlton and Jeffery M. Perloff, *Modern Industrial Organization* (Boston: Addison Wesley, 2005); Lynne Pepall, Daniel J. Richards, and George Norman, *Industrial Organization: Contemporary Theory and Practice* (Cincinnati, OH: South-Western, 2004); Oz Shy, *Industrial Organization: Theory and Applications* (Cambridge, MA: MIT Press, 1995); Don E. Waldman and Elizabeth J. Jensen, *Industrial Organization: Theory and Practice* (Boston: Addison Wesley, 2000). For further discussion of games involving a war of attrition, a preemptive race, devolution strategies, and Hail Mary strategies, see Jeremy L. Bulow and Paul D. Klemperer, "The Generalized War of Attrition," *American Economic Review* 89, 1 (March 1999), pp. 175–89; Ulrich Doraszelski and Sarit Markovich, "Goodwill and Awareness Advertising: Implications for Industry Dynamics," working paper, Department of Economics, Harvard University, 2005; Pankaj Ghemawat and Barry Nalebuff, "The Devolution of Declining Industries," *Quarterly Journal of Economics* 105,

1 (February 1990), pp. 167–86; Debra J. Aron and Edward P. Lazear, "The Introduction of New Products," *American Economic Review* 80, 2 (May 1990), pp. 421–26.

6. Douglas F. Greer, "Beer: Causes of Structural Change," in *Industry Studies,* ed. Larry L. Duetsch, p. 34 (Armonk, NY: M.E. Sharpe, 2002).

7. Doraszelski and Markovich, "Goodwill and Awareness Advertising: Implications for Industry Dynamics."

8. Drew Fudenberg and Jean Tirole, "The Fat-Cat Effect, the Puppy-Dog Ploy, and the Lean and Hungry Look," *American Economic Review* 74, 2 (May 1984), pp. 361–68.

9. MES is defined as the minimum level of production needed to reach constant returns to scale. Evidence on the size of MES in brewing can be found in Tremblay and Tremblay, *The U.S. Brewing Industry: Data and Economic Analysis,* and Victor J. Tremblay, Carol Horton Tremblay, and Natsuko Iwasaki, "The Dynamics of Industry Concentration for U.S. Micro and Macro Brewers," *Review of Industrial Organization* 26, 3 (May 2005), pp. 307–24.

10. The sample includes five brewers for which financial data are available. These include two specialty brewers, Redhook Brewing Company (with a unit cost of $125.56) and the Boston Beer Company ($69.43), and three macro brewers, Coors ($66.59), Miller ($60.18), and Anheuser-Busch ($60.83).

11. Bulow and Klemperer, "The Generalized War of Attrition."

12. Originally, an important reason for the German purity law was to shift beer ingredients from wheat to barley. Wheat was needed for bread production and vital to the nutrition of the German people during the late Middle Ages.

13. Thorstein Veblen, *The Theory of the Leisure Class* (New York: Macmillan, 1899).

14. See Tremblay and Tremblay, *The U.S. Brewing Industry: Data and Economic Analysis* (chapter 7, 2005) for a review of the extensive literature on consumer blind taste tests of different brands of beer.

15. The other new styles developed by the macro brewers include low-alcohol beer, with half the alcohol of regular beer (offered from 1983–91), dry beer (1988–98), and ice beer (1993–). Ice beer is the only type still brewed today, but its market share has declined since 1999.

16. For a review of the prisoners' dilemma and static oligopoly games of Bertrand (price) and Cournot (output), see Robert Gibbons, *Game Theory for Applied Economists* (Princeton, NJ: Princeton University Press, 1992); Jean Tirole, *The Theory of Industrial Organization* (Cambridge, MA: MIT Press, 1988); Luís M.B. Cabral, *Introduction to Industrial Organization* (Cambridge, MA: MIT Press, 2000); Don E. Waldman and Elizabeth J. Jensen, *Industrial Organization: Theory and Practice,* 2nd ed. (Boston: Addison Wesley, 2001); Lynne Pepall, Daniel J. Richards, and George Norman, *Industrial Organization: Contemporary Theory and Practice* (St. Paul, MN: South-Western College, 1999); and Dennis W. Carlton and Jeffrey M. Perloff, *Modern Industrial Organization,* 3rd ed. (Reading, MA: Addison-Wesley, 2000).

17. CR_4 is defined as the market share of the largest four firms in the industry, and HHI is defined as the sum of the squared values of each firm's market share. When market share is measured in percentages, CR_4 ranges from 0 to 100 and HHI ranges from 0 to 10,000. To make comparisons easier, we divide HHI by 100 so that it ranges from 0 to 100. These indices are discussed in most industrial organization textbooks, including Luís M.B. Cabral, *Introduction to Industrial Organization,* Dennis W. Carlton and Jeffrey M. Perloff, *Modern Industrial Organization,* Lynne Pepall, Daniel J. Richards, and George Norman, *Industrial Organization: Contemporary Theory and Practice,* and Don E. Waldman and Elizabeth J. Jensen, *Industrial Organization: Theory and Practice.*

18. These concentration measures are only accurate if the market is properly defined. National figures are used here because the market became national by the late 1960s. Imports are ignored because this allows us to better understand the distribution of the domestic producers and because the import brands are not perfect substitutes for the traditional lager produced by the macro brewers.

19. The Merger Guidelines of the Department of Justice classify an industry as moderately concentrated when HHI ranges from 10,000 to 18,000 and as highly concentrated when HHI exceeds 18,000.

20. Although Pabst is an independent brewer, all of Pabst's beer has been brewed under contract by Miller since 2003.

21. Roland H. Koller, "The Myth of Predatory Pricing: An Empirical Study," *Antitrust Law and Economics Review* 4, 4 (Summer 1971), pp. 105–23.

22. "A Warning Shot from King of Beers," *Business Week,* (December 18, 1989), p. 124.

23. For further discussion of these events, see *Modern Brewery Age Weekly,* "Miller Begins New Wave of Attack Ads" (October 25, 2004), pp. 1–2; "Anheuser Strikes Back, with Humor this Time" (November 29, 2004), p. 1; " Regulators Reject A-B Complaints About Miller" (April 18, 2005), pp. 1–4; "Miller Says it Will Continue Aggressive Marketing Plan" (June 20, 2005), pp. 1, 5–6; "Beer Wholesalers See Looming 'Price War' in Citigroup Survey" (August 1, 2005), pp. 1, 5; "Transcript of Analysts Panel from NBWA" (October 17, 2005), p. 1; "U.S. Brewers Look for Image Enhancement" (November 17, 2005), pp. 1, 3; "Anheuser Tells Analysts that Sales are Improving" (December 6, 2005), pp. 1, 3.

24. For a detailed description of a mixed-strategy Nash equilibrium, see Robert Gibbons, *Game Theory for Applied Economists.*

25. "While the Big Brewers Quaff, the Little Ones Thirst," *Fortune,* (November 1972), p. 103.

26. John Sutton, *Sunk Costs and Market Structure: Price Competition, Advertising, and the Evolution of Concentration* (Cambridge, MA: MIT Press, 1991).

27. Joe S. Bain, *Industrial Organization* (New York: Wiley, 1959).

28. For an excellent review of the economics of advertising, see Kyle Bagwell, *The Economic Analysis of Advertising,* monograph, Department of Economics, Columbia University, 2005. For a discussion of the social costs of advertising in brewing, see Tremblay and Tremblay, *The U.S. Brewing Industry: Data and Economic Analysis,* and Jon P. Nelson, "Beer Advertising and Marketing Update: Structure, Conduct, and Social Costs," *Review of Industrial Organization* 26, 3 (May 2005), pp. 269–306.

29. Raymond A. Bauer and Stephen A. Greyser, *Advertising in America: The Consumer View* (Cambridge, MA: Harvard University Press, 1968).

30. In contrast, if a firm's advertising attracts customers to its own and its rivals' brands, then the firm will ignore this positive externality and advertise less than is jointly maximizing. See Tremblay and Tremblay, *The U.S. Brewing Industry: Data and Economic Analysis,* and Andrew Stivers and Victor J. Tremblay, "Advertising, Searching Costs, and Welfare," *Information Economics and Policy* 17, 3 (July 2005), pp. 317–33, for further discussion of this point.

31. Due to data limitations, for the remainder of the chapter we use this measure of advertising intensity instead of the advertising-to-sales ratio.

32. In our previous work, we document 215 horizontal mergers and acquisitions among the macro beer companies from 1950 to 2002: Tremblay and Tremblay, *The U.S. Brewing Industry: Data and Economic Analysis.*

33. Aron and Lazear, "The Introduction of New Products."

34. "The Year in Review: 1993," *Modern Brewery Age* (March 21, 1994), pp. 8–39.

35. "Getting Schlitz Back on Track," *Fortune* (April 24, 1978), pp. 47–49.

36. Tremblay and Tremblay, *The U.S. Brewing Industry: Data and Economic Analysis.*

37. Lauren Clark, "Beer & Babes Go Back a Long Way," *All About Beer Magazine* (September 2002), pp. 28–77.

38. "Swedish Bikini Team Lives!" *Modern Brewery Age Weekly* (February 7, 2005), p. 1.

39. "Can Miller Beer Survive the Mess It's In?" *Advertising Age* (July 7, 2003).

40. James B. Arndofer, "The Death of Beer," *Advertising Age* (May 2, 2005).

41. Arndofer, "The Death of Beer."

42. "Wine Industry Reports that Sales of More Expensive Wines are Booming," *Modern Brewery Age Weekly* (June 6, 2005), p. 6.

43. "Koch Reviews Utopias," *Modern Brewery Age Weekly* (July 18, 2005), p. 4.

44. Although more affordable than extreme beers, Anheuser-Busch introduced Michelob Celebrate during the holiday season of 2005, which has 10 percent alcohol by volume and sells for about $15 for a 24-ounce bottle.

45. By comparison, a 7-ounce cup of coffee contains 80–135 milligrams of caffeine, and tea contains about 40 milligrams. A 12-ounce container of Coke contains 34 milligrams of caffeine, and Pepsi contains 38 milligrams of caffeine.

46. On average, the federal tax rate on an ounce of ethanol is $0.10 for beer and $0.21 for spirits.

Selected Readings

The following books and book chapters provide a more complete discussion of the economics of the U.S. brewing industry.

Elzinga, Kenneth G. "Beer," in *The Structure of American Industry,* eds. Walter Adams and James W. Brock. Upper Saddle River, NJ: Prentice-Hall, 2004.

Greer, Douglas F. "Beer: Causes of Structural Change," in *Industry Studies,* ed. Larry L. Duetsch. Armonk, NY: M.E. Sharpe, 2002.

Scherer, F.M. "Beer," in *Industry Structure, Strategy, and Public Policy,* ed. F.M. Scherer. New York: Harper Collins, 1996.

Tremblay, Victor J., and Carol Horton Tremblay. *The U.S. Brewing Industry: Data and Economic Analysis,* Cambridge, MA: MIT Press, 2005.

The following books and articles review the game-theoretic strategies discussed in this chapter.

Bulow, Jeremy L., and Paul D. Klemperer. "The Generalized War of Attrition," *American Economic Review* 89, 1 (March 1999), pp. 175–89.

Cabral, Luis M.B. *Introduction to Industrial Organization.* Cambridge, MA: MIT Press, 2000.

Carlton, Dennis W., and Jeffery M. Perloff. *Modern Industrial Organization.* Boston: Addison Wesley, 2005.

Doraszelski, Ulrich, and Sarit Markovich. "Goodwill and Awareness Advertising: Implications for Industry Dynamics." Working paper, Department of Economics, Harvard University, 2005.

Ghemawat, Pankaj, and Barry Nalebuff. "The Devolution of Declining Industries," *Quarterly Journal of Economics* 105, 1 (February 1990), pp. 167–86.

Gibbons, Robert. *Game Theory for Applied Economists.* Princeton, NJ: Princeton University Press, 1992.

Pepall, Lynne, Daniel J. Richards, and George Norman. *Industrial Organization: Contemporary Theory and Practice.* Cincinnati, OH: South-Western, 2004.

Shy, Oz. *Industrial Organization: Theory and Applications.* Cambridge, MA: MIT Press, 1995.

Tirole, Jean. *The Theory of Industrial Organization.* Cambridge, MA: MIT Press, 1988.

Waldman, Don E., and Elizabeth J. Jensen. *Industrial Organization: Theory and Practice.* Boston: Addison Wesley, 2000.

4

Cigarettes

Old Firms Facing New Challenges

Frank J. Chaloupka

The cigarette industry in the United States has many features that have long fascinated industrial organization economists. From the early rise and subsequent breakup of the tobacco trust through the decades of dominance by a small number of firms, the industry has been best described as a product-differentiated oligopoly with a few firms accounting for nearly all output. At its peak, nearly half of all adults consumed its products. Some aspects of the industry have changed considerably since the mid-twentieth century, largely the result of the growing evidence on the health consequences of smoking and the policy interventions, litigation, and changing social norms that followed. Smoking rates are half what they were a few decades ago, unprecedented entry has taken place in recent years, and the industry's operating environment is increasingly hostile. The industry, however, appears to be weathering the storm and remains one of the most profitable in the country. This chapter reviews the evolution of the cigarette industry, and discusses its structure, conduct, and performance.

A Brief History

The Rise and Fall of the Tobacco Trust

Prior to the mid-nineteenth century, nearly all of the demand for tobacco products centered on chewing tobacco, pipe tobacco, snuff, and cigars. It is thought that cigarettes first appeared in Seville sometime in the late seventeenth century, with beggars gathering the remains of cigars, wrapping them in paper, and smoking them.[1] Cigarettes slowly spread through Europe and other countries (including the United States) and, given their relatively low price, became a popular alternative to cigars. Robert Gloag is credited with opening the first British cigarette factory in 1856, followed soon after by a tobacco merchant from London named Philip Morris.[2] Similar factories began to appear in the United States soon after. Manufacturing at the time was a very labor-intensive process relying on hand rolling of cigarettes; estimates indicate that the most proficient hand-rollers could produce up to 300 cigarettes per hour.[3] Hand-rollers were often imported from other countries, including Russia and Poland, and there was significant supervision to ensure high-quality products. Somewhat surprisingly, despite the importance of tobacco growing to the U.S. economy, much of the tobacco initially used in producing these cigarettes was imported Turkish tobacco; competing domestic varieties of tobacco were similarly heavy, dark leaves that produced strong-tasting cigarettes with limited appeal. Consequently, cigarettes remained expensive compared to most tobacco products and accounted for a small share of overall tobacco product consumption. Eventually, some producers began to mix the more expensive Turkish tobacco with relatively inexpensive, domestically grown tobacco, but demand remained low.

Some features that would come to characterize the cigarette market of the twentieth century began to emerge in the industry's early days. One such feature is the brand advertising that many producers engaged in, the related packaging of these brands, and the brand loyalty that was stimulated. This early branding/packaging conjured up images of sophistication, élan, and mystery with names like Vanity Fair, High Life, and Orientals, and accompanying colorful imagery on the packs. A second major change was the shift from the use of mostly imported tobacco leaf to domestically grown leaf. This happened first with the use of the "bright" leaf, a lighter variety of tobacco grown, cured, and aged in a distinctive way (which legend suggests was discovered by accident) that results in a yellow leaf. This was followed by the emergence of "white burley," another lighter variety of tobacco leaf. The availability of these milder cigarettes led to a significant increase in cigarette demand during and after the Civil War era. This growth did not escape the notice of federal authorities, who imposed the first federal cigarette excise tax on cigarettes—$0.008 per pack of 20—in 1864. The tax would be raised several times during the war, peaking at 10 cents per pack in 1867.

Most important, however, was the invention of the first mechanized cigarette-rolling machine by James A. Bonsack. This was a time when production in a variety of industries was being mechanized. Bonsack's machine, patented in 1881, was developed in response to then-leading cigarette producer Allen & Ginter's offer of a cash prize of $75,000 for the first viable cigarette-rolling machine.[4] In contrast to the 3,000 cigarettes *per day* that a skilled hand-roller could produce, the Bonsack rolling machine could produce as many as 12,000 cigarettes *per hour*—a fortyfold increase. In addition, the Bonsack machine and the standardized output it produced eliminated the need for highly skilled labor and intensive supervision, greatly reducing the labor costs associated with cigarette manufacturing.

Bonsack leased his machine to manufacturers at a price that cut direct manufacturing costs in half. Interestingly, Allen & Ginter, whose contest stimulated Bonsack's invention, were slow to adopt the new machine, given that they had built their reputation on the quality of their hand-rolled cigarettes and given some bugs in the machines that limited their utility.[5] Instead, W. Duke, Sons & Co., a loose-tobacco producer run by James Buchanan "Buck" Duke, was the first U.S. company to take advantage of this new technology. Duke took a chance on the Bonsack machine, leasing two of them (at a reduced cost given the problems other manufacturers had experienced with the machines). After months of tinkering with them, Duke and his mechanics worked out the bugs and had the machines operating smoothly. Duke's success with the machines led him to negotiate a unique deal with Bonsack under which he would buy as many of the machines as Bonsack would provide, but would pay at least 25 percent less than any of his competitors would pay in their future leases.[6]

Duke capitalized on the significant cost advantage he had over his competitors and cut prices for the Duke brands in half. Despite the significant price cut, he was able to earn substantial profits that were reinvested in expanding manufacturing capacity and in aggressive pricing, marketing, and distribution practices. By 1889, W. Duke, Sons & Co. was the leading U.S. cigarette manufacturer, with 40 percent market share, and was spending the then-astounding amount of $800,000 to promote its brands. Marketing efforts included using picture cards featuring prominent businessmen and the attractive "Sporting Girls," more sophisticated packaging, and a variety of promotional events, as well as inducements to distributors and retailers to promote their brands (often at the expense of their efforts to promote other companies' brands)—variations of which continue to be important marketing techniques in today's cigarette market.[7]

Duke's rivals found it hard to compete, given the cost disadvantage they faced and given Duke's aggressive marketing and distribution practices. In 1890, Duke was able to persuade his four leading competitors to join forces with him in creating the American Tobacco Company. When formed, the new "tobacco trust" controlled approximately 90 percent of the U.S. cigarette market. This mirrored the development of similar trusts in many other markets (e.g., Standard Oil, U.S. Steel, and Eastman Kodak).

Over the next two decades, the tobacco trust acted aggressively to maintain its position. American Tobacco obtained exclusive rights to the Bonsack cigarette-rolling machine and purchased patents on other machines, allowing it to maintain its cost advantage over potential competitors. It engaged in a variety of often unfair business practices targeting its competitors, including efforts to organize strikes among their workers, entering into exclusive distribution deals with distributors, and bidding up the prices for tobacco leaf in the markets where its competitors operated. Perhaps most significant was its use of "fighting brands" in markets where it faced competition; these brands were often sold below the trust's production and distribution cost at a price that could not be matched by competitors. Many of the independents were driven out of business by the trust, while others were absorbed by it. During this period, it acquired approximately 250 of its competitors; many were shut down after acquisition, while others continued as members or subsidiaries of the trust. At the same time, American Tobacco vigorously exported its products to foreign markets and, in response to high tariffs in

many countries, invested directly in a number of countries, establishing its own production facilities and/or acquiring local producers.

The significant reduction in cigarette prices resulting from the mass production of cigarettes, a sharp drop in the federal cigarette tax following the Civil War (to a low of 1 cent per pack from 1883 to 1897), the increasing availability of cigarettes and the aggressive marketing of them, among other factors, contributed to a sharp rise in cigarette consumption during the last few decades of the nineteenth century and the early years of the twentieth (Figure 4.1).

Despite its success, American Tobacco faced several challenges around the turn of the century. Tobacco farmers unhappy about the trust's exertion of its monopsony power entered into alliances not to sell their produce to the trust and attacked their colleagues who did; in some areas, government forces were eventually called in to quell the violence.[8] As cigarette smoking became more popular (including among women and children), the anti-smoking campaign that emerged in the mid-nineteenth century gained momentum. Opponents attacked smoking as unhealthy and immoral (the same arguments, often from the same individuals and organizations, that were being used to support prohibition of alcohol in many states). These early anti-smoking advocates were successful in getting several state governments to adopt legislation outlawing the sale of cigarettes within their borders, while some of these and others banned smoking in public places.

The most significant challenge, however, came from the federal government under the Sherman Act, adopted in 1890. In 1907, the U.S. Department of Justice brought suit against American Tobacco Company, its subsidiaries, and various others for antitrust violations. In 1911, two weeks after issuing a similar decision against Standard Oil, the U.S. Supreme Court found American

Figure 4.1 **Cigarette Consumption, 1865–1910**

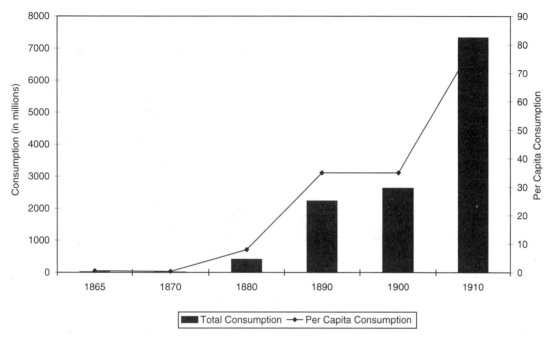

Source: Orzechowski and Walker, *The Tax Burden on Tobacco*, 2006.

Tobacco guilty of monopolizing the cigarette and related tobacco product markets. The Court cited American Tobacco's acquisition of rivals (often with the intent of closing them), exclusive arrangements with distributors, predatory pricing, and other unfair business practices as evidence of its intent to monopolize the market. As a result of the Court-imposed remedies, sixteen firms emerged from the breakup of the tobacco trust. These included four major cigarette companies: a new American Tobacco Company (ATC), R.J. Reynolds Tobacco Company (RJR), Liggett & Myers Tobacco Company (L&M), and P. Lorillard Company (Lorillard).[9] In addition, American Tobacco Company was divested of its foreign holdings, most notably Imperial Tobacco Ltd., which eventually monopolized the market in Great Britain, and British American Tobacco

Company (BAT), which focused on manufacturing in the British colonies and elsewhere.

The Boom Years

The breakup of the tobacco trust, multiple increases in federal cigarette excise taxes (from 2.5 cents per pack in 1988 to 8 cents per pack in 1951), the adoption of cigarette excise taxes in most states (beginning with Iowa in 1921), two world wars, the Great Depression, some early links between cigarette smoking and negative health outcomes, and another antitrust conviction could not slow the rapid growth of the U.S. cigarette industry over the next several decades (Figure 4.2). Per capita consumption rose nearly 500 percent from 1910 to 1920 and another 400 percent over the following three decades. Some of the early growth, particu-

Figure 4.2 **Cigarette Consumption, 1910–1960**

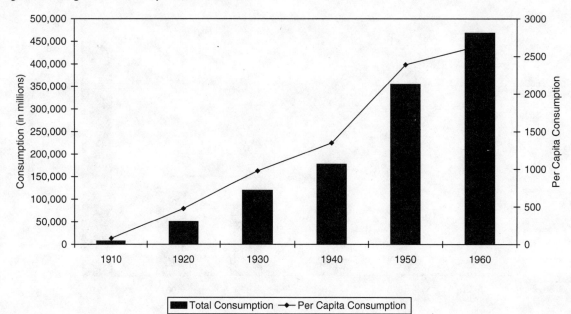

Source: Orzechowski and Walker, *The Tax Burden on Tobacco*, 2006.

larly among men, has been attributed to the distribution of free cigarettes to soldiers during World War I, many of whom returned addicted. Early state bans on smoking were repealed. Perhaps most important in this growth, however, were the development and marketing of new, milder brands that appealed to many more consumers.

Shortly after the breakup of American Tobacco, three firms—ATC, L&M, and Lorillard—controlled over 90 percent of the U.S. market. RJR (which prior to the breakup had not produced cigarettes) was a minor player in the market. However, this soon changed with RJR's introduction of its Camel brand. The growth of Camel, and RJR as a result, is a nice illustration of the combined importance of the product, pricing, and other marketing strategies that track the rise and fall of other brands/companies over time. With respect to product, Camel was a blend of relatively mild flue-cured bright tobacco, a flavored, sweetened burley tobacco (unique to

Camel at the time), and a small amount of Turkish tobacco (hence the imagery used on the pack and in advertising); eventually, some Maryland tobacco was added to the mix given its slower burn. This combination came to be known as the American blend of tobacco.[10] The exotic mix was noted on the pack and became a feature of RJR's advertising campaign. The new brand was initially introduced at a relatively low price, and RJR further lowered price through the distribution of coupons; after the brand gained a foothold in the market, however, RJR raised prices above those of many other brands and explicitly advertised Camels as a premium brand selling at a premium price. Finally, because of its lack of established brands, RJR was able to focus nearly all of its considerable advertising effort on promoting Camel. The combination was highly successful, making RJR the clear market leader, with a 40 percent market share, by the end of World War I.

Other companies quickly followed RJR's lead in developing new mixes of tobacco for use in their brands, as well as in concentrating much of their marketing effort on a single brand. ATC focused on its Lucky Strike brand, while L&M concentrated on its Chesterfield brand. While both lost considerable market share to RJR, they were relatively successful compared to Lorillard, which had stayed out of the fray and lost more than 90 percent of its share in the decade following the breakup of the trust. The marketing campaigns of the time generated some memorable slogans that were used for many years, including RJR's "I'd Walk a Mile for a Camel," ATC's "Reach for a Lucky Instead of a Sweet," and L&M's "They Satisfy."

While aggressively advertising their products and competing to distribute them widely through wholesalers and retailers, the post–World War I period was marked by a relative lack of price competition. Instead, the pricing strategies that would come to characterize the industry for many years began to appear, with one firm (typically RJR at the time) increasing its prices and other firms quickly matching the price change. This changed with the onset of the Great Depression, falling incomes, and the first real decline in cigarette demand in the early 1930s. Despite these factors and falling tobacco-leaf prices, the major companies raised their prices in 1931 to a level that resulted in retail prices of 14–15 cents per pack. This created an opportunity for new firms to enter the market or for existing firms to significantly expand their shares by competing on price. Many did so with what came to be known as their 10-cent brands, which notwithstanding their limited advertising and promotion quickly gained almost a quarter of the market by 1932.

The big three of the time (RJR, ATC, and L&M) responded to the success of the 10-cent brands by cutting their wholesale prices, by 12 percent in January 1933 and by an additional 10 percent the following month, with ATC leading the way. In addition, they put pressure on distributors and retailers to reduce their margins so that the retail prices of their premium brands would fall to 10 cents. The price competition from the big three drove many of the new firms from the market. However, two of them—Philip Morris (PM) and Brown & Williamson (B&W, BAT's U.S. subsidiary)—gained a toehold that would allow them to eventually become significant players in the U.S. cigarette market. In due course, the price war ended with an RJR price increase in 1934 that was matched by the others, albeit at a lower level than the pre-price war prices. RJR was the primary loser in the price war, seeing its market share fall by nearly half by 1940, in part because it cut its advertising budget to compensate for the lower prices. ATC emerged from the war as the new industry leader, with nearly 30 percent of the market.

The big three's response to the 10-cent brands drew the attention of the U.S. Department of Justice, which eventually led to their 1941 conviction for violating the Sherman Act, a decision eventually upheld by the Supreme Court in 1946. Much of this decision was based on their pricing strategies, including the apparently predatory pricing they engaged in during the 1933–34 price war. Other circumstantial evidence of collusion was also presented, most notably their apparently monopsonistic behavior at tobacco auctions where companies would not bid unless all were present, bids that resulted in all companies paying the same prices for tobacco leaf, and the lack of bids by some companies on tobacco grades of particular interest to other companies.[11] Given the lack of evidence that there were any explicit arrangements among firms, the Court determined that the parallel behavior of the firms was sufficient to establish a conspiracy. Several commentators have noted that the Court's decision in this case was not supported by economic reasoning, given the lack of evidence that firms were jointly restricting output to raise prices and profits and the lack of evidence that their tobacco-leaf purchasing strategies depressed leaf prices and production costs. In contrast to the earlier antitrust conviction that led to the breakup of the tobacco trust, the Court did not impose any structural penalties; instead, firms were fined up to $250,000 (a minor penalty given their profits at the time) and some minor constraints were imposed.

In the end, the Court's decision had little to no impact on the U.S. cigarette industry. For the next fifty years, the combined market share of the top six firms (ATC, B&W, L&M, Lorillard, PM, and RJR) exceeded 99 percent, although there have been significant changes in the shares of individual firms, as described below. Demand continued to grow in the 1940s, with overall cigarette consumption about doubling between 1940 and 1950, and smoking prevalence among adults rising to well over 40 percent.

Stagnation and Decline

The rapid growth of the U.S. cigarette industry during the first half of the twentieth century was halted as research evidence linking smoking to lung cancer began to appear in the 1950s. The health concerns associated with tobacco use date back to the early 1600s, as evidenced by King James I of England's statement in his *Counterblaste to Tobacco* that smoking "is a custome lothsome to the eye, hatefull to the nose, harmefull to the braine, dangerous to the lungs, and in the blacke stinking fume thereof, nearest resembling the horrible Stigian smoke of the pit that is bottomelesse." Similar concerns were raised over the years and contributed to the growth of the early anti-smoking movement described above. This early movement, however, was based largely on anecdotal evidence on the health consequences of cigarette smoking

rather than scientific evidence. The first scientific studies began to appear in the 1920s and 1930s. A good example of this early research was a 1938 publication by a Johns Hopkins University biologist, Raymond Pearl, which noted that 67 percent of his sample of nonsmokers lived past the age of sixty years, compared to only 46 percent of smokers.

As the health evidence began to emerge in the 1920s and 1930s, the industry responded with implicit and explicit health claims in its advertising. Some ads referred to the featured brand as being less irritable than others (e.g., an RJR ad for Camels featuring Lou Gehrig stating "'They Don't Get Your Wind' Athletes Say"), while others touted the weight-control benefits of cigarettes (e.g., the infamous "Reach for a Lucky Instead of a Sweet"). Over time, the claims would become more explicit (e.g., the Camel ad introduced in 1946 stating that "More Doctors Smoke Camels than Any Other Cigarette").

These ads, coupled with the product design and other marketing strategies discussed above, contributed to the success of the leading brands. By 1950, the three leading brands (Camel, Lucky Strike, Chesterfield), and Philip Morris's Commander brand) accounted for over 80 percent of the market.

More rigorous epidemiological studies on the health effects of smoking appeared in the 1940s and early 1950s, many of which concluded that cigarette smoking causes lung cancer. The scientific evidence was translated for and disseminated to the general public through a series of magazine and newspaper articles, beginning with a 1952 report in the *Christian Herald* that was reprinted in *Reader's Digest* in December of that year. The publication of the article, "Cancer by the Carton," proved to be a watershed event for the industry. Subsequent and increasingly stronger articles in *Time, Consumer Reports,* and other publications added fuel to the fire. For the first time, consumer concerns about the health consequences of smoking led to a sharp decline in cigarette consumption, with per capita consumption falling by over 8 percent between 1953 and 1955.

The companies responded to the emerging scientific evidence with a combination of strategies similar to those that had helped fuel the industry's early growth, along with some new tactics that would continue to be used in the coming decades. In a December 1953 meeting at the Plaza Hotel in New York City, executives from five of the big six cigarette companies (all but L&M), other tobacco company executives, and representatives from the public relations firm of Hill and Knowlton gathered to discuss their response to the growing evidence on the health consequences of smoking. This was the first meeting of company executives since the late 1930s and appears to be the origin of a concerted effort to address the "health problem."[12] One outcome of the meeting was the creation of the Tobacco Industry Research Committee (TIRC), later renamed the Council for Tobacco Research (CTR). TIRC was funded by the major tobacco companies (with the exception of L&M) to support research on the health impact of tobacco use, a public relations effort to suggest that the industry was concerned about the health consequences of smoking.

A second outcome was the publication of "A Frank Statement to Cigarette Smokers" in hundreds of newspapers across the country in January 1954 (Figure 4.3). The "Frank Statement" was an ad announcing the creation of TIRC, and laying out the joint position that the industry would take on the relationship between smoking and health over the next several decades. While some nuances of the position changed over time, the central tenets were that the scientific evidence that smoking caused disease was inconclusive, that the industry did not believe that smoking harms health, that more research was needed to prove a causal relationship, and that the industry was committed to supporting this research (through the TIRC) and to working with others to resolve the questions about smoking and health. The "Frank Statement" was signed by the leaders of the top cigarette companies (with the exception of L&M), various tobacco growers and warehousers' associations, and others.

Behind the scenes, industry scientists were working aggressively to develop new products that would directly address the health concerns, and that would change the fortunes of major companies. The first major innovation was the development and mass marketing of filter-tipped cigarettes. While filter tips had been around for decades, they had not gained much ground in the market; in 1950, filter-tipped cigarettes accounted for less than 1 percent of all sales. Alterations in the design of the filter and the health concerns created by the emerging scientific evidence, however, changed this percentage. Among the key changes in design was the development of the cellulose acetate filter, variations of which are still used today; this filter was first marketed by B&W on its Viceroy brand. Other filter designs were employed (e.g., the charcoal filter). Perhaps most notorious was the asbestos-based Micronite filter used by Lorillard in its Kent brand (eventually replaced with a cellulose filter). By the mid-1950s, all major companies were aggressively marketing filter-tipped brands, often advertising these brands as healthier than other cigarettes (e.g., B&W's ads for its Viceroy brand stating that "Filtered cigarette smoke is better for your health"). Philip Morris introduced a filter-tipped version of Marlboro in the mid-1950s and began a campaign (the "Marlboro Man") to reposition the brand that had initially been marketed to women. RJR introduced its Winston brand in 1954, soon to become the leading filter-tipped brand. By 1956, filter-tipped cigarettes accounted for over one-quarter of U.S. cigarette consumption.

Figure 4.3

A Frank Statement
to Cigarette Smokers

RECENT REPORTS on experiments with mice have given wide publicity to a theory that cigarette smoking is in some way linked with lung cancer in human beings.

Although conducted by doctors of professional standing, these experiments are not regarded as conclusive in the field of cancer research. However, we do not believe that any serious medical research, even though its results are inconclusive should be disregarded or lightly dismissed.

At the same time, we feel it is in the public interest to call attention to the fact that eminent doctors and research scientists have publicly questioned the claimed significance of these experiments.

Distinguished authorities point out:

1. That medical research of recent years indicates many possible causes of lung cancer.

2. That there is no agreement among the authorities regarding what the cause is.

3. That there is no proof that cigarette smoking is one of the causes.

4. That statistics purporting to link cigarette smoking with the disease could apply with equal force to any one of many other aspects of modern life. Indeed the validity of the statistics themselves is questioned by numerous scientists.

We accept an interest in people's health as a basic responsibility, paramount to every other consideration in our business.

We believe the products we make are not injurious to health.

We always have and always will cooperate closely with those whose task it is to safeguard the public health.

For more than 300 years tobacco has given solace, relaxation, and enjoyment to mankind. At one time or another during these years critics have held it responsible for practically every disease of the human body. One by one these charges have been abandoned for lack of evidence.

Regardless of the record of the past, the fact that cigarette smoking today should even be suspected as a cause of a serious disease is a matter of deep concern to us.

Many people have asked us what we are doing to meet the public's concern aroused by the recent reports. Here is the answer:

1. We are pledging aid and assistance to the research effort into all phases of tobacco use and health. This joint financial aid will of course be in addition to what is already being contributed by individual companies.

2. For this purpose we are establishing a joint industry group consisting initially of the undersigned. This group will be known as TOBACCO INDUSTRY RESEARCH COMMITTEE.

3. In charge of the research activities of the Committee will be a scientist of unimpeachable integrity and national repute. In addition there will be an Advisory Board of scientists disinterested in the cigarette industry. A group of distinguished men from medicine, science, and education will be invited to serve on this Board. These scientists will advise the Committee on its research activities.

This statement is being issued because we believe the people are entitled to know where we stand on this matter and what we intend to do about it.

TOBACCO INDUSTRY RESEARCH COMMITTEE

5400 EMPIRE STATE BUILDING, NEW YORK 1, N. Y.

SPONSORS:

THE AMERICAN TOBACCO COMPANY, INC.
Paul M. Hahn, President

BENSON & HEDGES
Joseph F. Cullman, Jr., President

BRIGHT BELT WAREHOUSE ASSOCIATION
F. S. Royster, President

BROWN & WILLIAMSON TOBACCO CORPORATION
Timothy V. Hartnett, President

BURLEY AUCTION WAREHOUSE ASSOCIATION
Albert Clay, President

BURLEY TOBACCO GROWERS COOPERATIVE ASSOCIATION
John W. Jones, President

LARUS & BROTHER COMPANY, INC.
W. T. Reed, Jr., President

P. LORILLARD COMPANY
Herbert A. Kent, Chairman

MARYLAND TOBACCO GROWERS ASSOCIATION
Samuel C. Linton, General Manager

PHILIP MORRIS & CO., LTD., INC.
O. Parker McComas, President

R. J. REYNOLDS TOBACCO COMPANY
E. A. Darr, President

STEPHANO BROTHERS, INC.
C. S. Stephano, D'Sc., Director of Research

TOBACCO ASSOCIATES, INC.
(An organization of flue-cured tobacco growers)
J. B. Hutson, President

UNITED STATES TOBACCO COMPANY
J. W. Peterson, President

The increasingly explicit health claims in cigarette advertising drew attention from the Federal Trade Commission (FTC), the agency charged with ensuring that advertising is not false, deceptive, or misleading. The first group of FTC cigarette advertising investigations culminated in a cease-and-desist order based on the FTC's decision that the comparative health claims being made in various brand advertising could not be substantiated; this order included a ban on comparisons of tar and nicotine content. Importantly, the FTC rules applied to specific brands, not new brands (or new versions of existing brands), and most notably the filter-tipped brands. This loophole was closed a few years later with the FTC's 1955 cigarette advertising guidelines that prohibited health claims in cigarette advertising and that applied to all brands; in addition, the guidelines prohibited advertising of tar and nicotine content not supported by "competent scientific proof." At the same time, however, *Consumer Reports* was annually publishing listings of the tar and nicotine content of leading cigarette brands. Given this "scientific proof," companies began to aggressively advertise the tar and nicotine content of their filtered brands in the mid- to late 1950s, a period that has come to be known as the "Tar Derby." Some estimates suggest that the "Tar Derby" lowered measured tar content of cigarettes by as much as 40 percent in the late 1950s. The FTC again stepped in and, in 1959, negotiated a voluntary agreement with the cigarette industry that prohibited statements about tar and nicotine content in cigarette advertising, ending the "Tar Derby." Some commentators suggest that this agreement had the unintended effect of reducing incentives to produce less harmful cigarettes (to the extent that such cigarettes might exist).

The other major product innovation of the 1950s was the development and marketing of menthol cigarettes. The first mentholated brand—"Spud"—was patented in 1925 by Lloyd "Spud" Hughes.[13] The first to capture a modest share of the market was B&W's Kool brand, introduced in 1933; however, for the next twenty years, menthol brands were more of a novelty, never gaining a significant share of the market. Not surprisingly, given their flavor and given the health claims contained in the advertising of the time, advertising for the mentholated brands highlighted their mild, soothing taste. Other companies developed and marketed similar mentholated brands (e.g., Lorillard's Newport brand). As with filter-tipped cigarettes, the health concerns of the 1950s spurred the growth of these brands, most notably the Salem brand introduced by RJR in 1956. Kool and Salem would be the leading menthol brands for many years, accounting for as much as 10 percent of the market by the end of the 1950s.

The development and marketing of filter-tipped cigarettes, including some menthol brands, along with their aggressive marketing and the slow reactions by the FTC, helped to counter the emerging evidence on the health consequences of cigarette smoking. By 1963, cigarette sales had rebounded, rising almost 17 percent from their 1955 low; smoking prevalence among adults was well over 40 percent. Filter-tipped cigarettes accounted for nearly 60 percent of the market, and almost one in six cigarettes consumed was mentholated. Interestingly, the shift to filtered cigarettes almost certainly reduced production costs and had a positive impact on industry profitability, given that the length of the cigarette including the filter was the same as that of nonfiltered cigarettes and given the use of less expensive, lower grades of tobacco in these cigarettes, the stronger taste of which was diluted by the filter.[14]

Stronger scientific evidence on the health consequences of smoking continued to emerge throughout the 1950s and early 1960s, prompting President Kennedy to form an advisory committee to review this evidence in 1962. This committee, led by Surgeon General Luther Terry, included representatives from federal agencies, private health associations, and the tobacco industry. After more than a year reviewing over 11,000 studies, the committee released its report on January 11, 1964. This first Surgeon General's report concluded that cigarette smoking caused lung cancer and was a contributing factor for emphysema, chronic bronchitis, and cancers of the mouth, throat, respiratory tract, and larynx, and that smokers had higher death rates from cardiovascular disease and liver cirrhosis (but that these last associations were not proven to be causal).

The 1964 Surgeon General's report prompted im-

Figure 4.4   **Cigarette Consumption, 1960–2005**

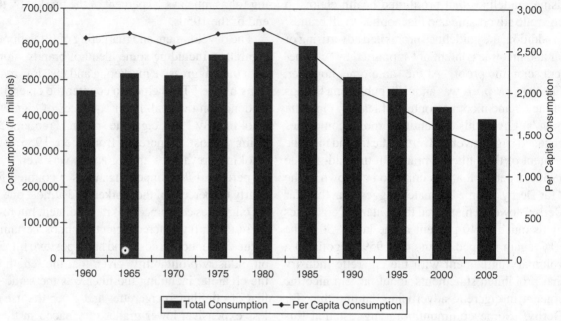

Source: Orzechowski and Walker, *The Tax Burden on Tobacco*, 2006.

mediate and sustained public policy efforts to reduce cigarette smoking unlike those targeting any other legal consumer product. At the federal level, these would include: continued dissemination of information on the growing list of health consequences resulting from cigarette smoking and other tobacco use through Surgeon General's reports and other channels, mandatory warning labels on cigarette packaging and, eventually, advertising that have been strengthened over time; a ban on cigarette advertising on television and radio; broadcast of anti-smoking advertising on television under the Federal Communication Commission's Fairness Doctrine; and some restrictions on smoking. State and local governments were similarly active, adopting policies that: raised cigarette excise taxes; restricted or banned smoking in a number of public places and in private worksites; required schools to educate youth about the health consequences of smoking; limited

youth access to cigarettes; and more. Together, these efforts eventually reversed the rise in smoking and produced a sharp decline over the last two decades of the twentieth century (Figure 4.4).

Cigarette demand in the United States continued to grow, albeit slowly and unevenly, in the two decades after the release of the first Surgeon General's report and in the face of policy interventions aimed at reducing tobacco use, before falling more or less steadily after 1983. The persistence of demand in the face of the increasing information about the health consequences of cigarette smoking reflected the success of the industry's strategies during this period. As with filtered and menthol cigarettes in the 1950s, changes in product design and the aggressive marketing of products perceived to be healthier were major factors. One such innovation was "light" or "mild" cigarettes that delivered significantly less tar (based on machine-measured readings) than existing brands. ATC, for example, introduced its Carlton brand in 1964 one week before the release of the Surgeon General's report. Lorillard soon followed with its True brand, and RJR introduced its Doral brand in the late 1960s. These and other companies developed light versions of existing brands (e.g., Philip Morris's Marlboro Lights brand that was introduced in 1972). As with the filter-tipped cigarettes of the 1950s, the new light cigarettes were almost certainly less costly to produce than other cigarettes given the use of reconstituted tobacco sheet (formed from a combination of tobacco stem and dust that were previously unused waste products).

Confusion about the health impact of light cigarettes contributed to their success; many in the public health community, for example, viewed light cigarettes as less harmful than other cigarettes. Reversing its earlier position by 1970, the FTC now required cigarette advertising to include tar and nicotine information. While some evidence indicated that the compensatory behavior of smokers minimized the benefits, if any, of smoking "light" cigarettes, it was decades before this was widely known; even today, many smokers continue to believe that light cigarettes are safer than others.[15] As with filtered cigarettes in the 1950s, the market share of "light" cigarettes (those with 15 mg or less of tar) grew quickly, rising from 0.2 percent of the market in 1965 to more than half the market by 1981.[16]

A second design innovation was the use of various additives, most notably ammonia, in producing cigarettes; these additives enhanced the delivery of nicotine while at the same time reducing measured tar and nicotine levels. PM was a leader in this area, introducing ammonia into its Marlboro brand as early as 1965; other firms were slow to follow. This design change, coupled with the hugely successful Marlboro Man advertising campaign, are key factors in the emergence of PM as the industry leader in the 1970s.

Eventually, the combination of increasing information on the health consequences of cigarette smoking (as well as on the consequences for nonsmokers of exposure to tobacco smoke), a sustained tobacco control movement, a progressively more comprehensive and stronger set of federal, state, and local policy interventions aimed at reducing smoking, and increasingly strong antismoking norms began to have an impact. Per capita cigarette consumption in the United States began declining more or less continuously in the mid-1970s.

At least in part in response to the increasing pressures on the industry coupled with stagnant and eventually declining domestic demand, as well as in response to the general trend across industries, cigarette companies began to diversify their operations in the 1960s. Over time, the six major companies acquired a variety of nontobacco businesses, including food and alcoholic beverages; by the early 1970s, every major domestic cigarette company had diversified. In addition, given the growing demand for cigarettes in foreign markets (particularly in developing countries where there were few, if any, active tobacco control efforts), several companies initiated or significantly expanded their international business.

The diversification and globalization strategies of some companies were highly successful, while those of others were not, and have helped to shape the industry as it is known today. Firms whose strategies were less successful eventually returned to a focus on their domestic tobacco operations, while others became major multinational conglomerates. The scope of their current activities varies significantly. PM has become the largest cigarette company, and its Marlboro brand is the best-selling cigarette in the world; its parent company, Altria, is also the parent company for Kraft Foods, among others. Lorillard is one subsidiary of Loews Corporation, a highly diversified, primarily U.S.-

focused company. RJR, after significant diversification in the past, has refocused on cigarettes and other tobacco products for the United States and international markets; after its merger with B&W, it is now part of Reynolds American Inc., which is also the parent company of Santa Fe Natural Tobacco Co. Inc. and Lane Limited, a specialty tobacco producer. L&M, now known as Liggett Group LLC, is one part of Vector Group Limited, a largely domestic, cigarette-focused company that also includes Vector Tobacco and Liggett Vector Brands among its subsidiaries.

The Litigation Era

Cigarette companies have been the targets of three waves of litigation over the past fifty years.[17] Following the early evidence on the health consequences of cigarette smoking, and largely unique to the United States, hundreds of smokers brought product liability lawsuits against cigarette companies. These early cases were generally based on one of two (or sometimes both) legal theories: negligence and implied warranty. Negligence was based on the idea that cigarette companies were aware of the health consequences caused by their products and that they did not take steps to inform consumers about the risks from using them. Implied warranty is a broader legal theory that suggests that the seller is providing some guarantee, even if it is not expressly stated, about the quality of the product being sold, when used as intended. Companies spent significant resources fighting these lawsuits; as a result, few of these early cases went to trial, and none resulted in a judgment against a cigarette company. Some analysts suggest that the lack of success of these early lawsuits was in part the result of government policy, specifically the mandated warning labels on cigarette packs and advertising and the prohibition on health claims in cigarette advertising.

The second wave of litigation began in the 1980s and was modeled after the success of lawsuits brought against asbestos companies. As with the early lawsuits, cigarette companies spent considerable resources fighting the new cases. Plaintiffs in these cases were a bit more successful in countering this, often pooling their own resources and taking advantage of newly available tobacco-related litigation information clearinghouses. The legal theory behind many of these cases was based on strict liability, which holds the producer liable for the consequences that arise from defects in their products, even if they were not negligent. While continuing to deny that there were any risks from cigarettes, companies successfully argued that smoking was a free choice and that any health consequences that resulted were the result of the smoker's "contributory" negligence, the "blame the smoker" defense. As in the first wave of cases, the mandated health warnings were used as evidence that smokers chose to smoke despite being warned about the consequences of doing so. One of these cases, *Cipollone v. Liggett Group Inc.*, resulted in a jury verdict in favor of the plaintiff, but this decision was reversed on appeal. However, internal documents discovered in this and other second-wave cases planted the seeds for a new wave of litigation.

Particularly important in sparking the third wave of litigation was the growing recognition of the addictive properties of nicotine and the emerging evidence that cigarette companies had manipulated the nicotine contained in their cigarettes. This led to a congressional investigation that included a defining moment in the history of the industry—the 1994 hearing at which the heads of all leading U.S. cigarette and other tobacco companies testified that they did not believe that nicotine was addictive, testimony that would soon be proven to be false by a flood of internal documents released through new litigation. The internal company documents would demonstrate, among other things, that the companies knew about the health consequences caused by smoking from their internal research, despite their public statements to the contrary; that they understood that nicotine was a powerful, addictive drug; that they manipulated the nicotine delivered by cigarettes through the use of additives and other design features; and much more. The new cases, given the strong evidence contained in the documents, went forward using a variety of legal theories, including those that had been used unsuccessfully in the past., including negligence, express and implied warranty, strict liability, fraud, and conspiracy.

Many of the third-wave cases were initiated, beginning in 1994, by large health-care providers (e.g., Blue Cross and Blue Shield) and by state attorneys general (because of Medicaid) on the grounds that they incurred significant costs from treating the diseases caused by the greater levels of cigarette smoking that resulted from the companies' practices. Some included antitrust arguments based on claims that the companies acted collusively to keep less harmful products from being developed and marketed. In addition to these cases brought by large organizations, numerous individual smoker cases proceeded, along with a new group of class action lawsuits on behalf of large groups of individuals (smokers and nonsmokers) harmed by smoking. These new cases were much more successful than those of the first two waves and led to numerous judgments against the cigarette companies; the compensatory and punitive damages awarded were often substantial (and at times reduced in the appeals process).

Realizing that the tide had begun to turn against them, cigarette companies began settling many of these cases, particularly the cases brought by states seeking reimbursement for the Medicaid costs of treating smoking-attributable diseases. In July 1997, the first of these cases was settled; under the settlement, Mississippi (one of the first states to file suit) would receive a minimum of $3.3 billion over twenty-five years, with annual payments of at least $135 million in perpetuity; the agreement also included a clause that would apply the terms of future state settlements to Mississippi, if those were better than the terms of the initial settlement (as proved to be the case). Florida settled just over a month later, for $11 billion over twenty-five years, and at least $440 million per year afterward; this agreement included an additional $200 million to fund a two-year youth smoking prevention campaign. A few months later (in January 1998), Texas settled for $14.5 billion over twenty-five years and a minimum of $580 million per year thereafter. Finally, after a lengthy trial and in the middle of closing arguments, Minnesota (which had joined forces with Blue Cross and Blue Shield of Minnesota) settled in May 1998. The state would receive $6.1 billion over twenty-five years and BCBS would receive an additional $469 million, along with subsequent payments in perpetuity. The Minnesota settlement contained a number of other provisions, including bans on a variety of marketing activities in Minnesota (including some that extend beyond Minnesota), the disbanding of the industry's Council for Tobacco Research and Tobacco Institute, and the creation of a depository for internal industry documents revealed through litigation that would be maintained at industry expense for ten years.

While these cases were being tried and settled, cigarette companies were working actively behind the scenes on a "global settlement" agreement that would have ended all pending state lawsuits against the industry, as well as those brought by other governmental agencies and all class action lawsuits. Some of the provisions of this settlement would have been clear violations of federal antitrust law; as a result, any agreement required congressional approval. Multiple proposals were introduced in

Congress, many of which would have gone well beyond the terms of the original global proposal. The McCain bill had the greatest momentum and included provisions that, among other things, would have: required industry payments of $516 billion over twenty-five years (almost $150 billion more than proposed in the global settlement), and additional payments in perpetuity; increased the federal cigarette excise tax by $1.10 per pack; allowed FDA regulation of tobacco; and significantly constrained cigarette company marketing activities. As a result, the industry withdrew its original global settlement proposal; a scaled-back agreement that settled the state and other government lawsuits was reached. This Master Settlement Agreement (MSA) with forty-six states, the District of Columbia, the Commonwealth of Puerto Rico, Guam, the U.S. Virgin Islands, American Samoa, and the Northern Marianas has had a substantial impact on the cigarette industry.

The main provisions of the November 1998 MSA included: $206 billion in payments to states over twenty-five years and additional payments in perpetuity; creation of a foundation (what became the American Legacy Foundation) that would research efforts to prevent youth smoking, along with initial funding of nearly $1.5 billion for a mass-media program to educate consumers about the health risks from smoking (with an additional $300 million per year after five years under certain circumstances); constraints on cigarette company marketing activities, including a ban on transit and outdoor advertising, limits on sponsorship, and bans on the use of cartoon characters in advertising or on packaging; a ban on product placement in entertainment; bans on the distribution and sale of branded merchandise; a ban on the distribution of free samples (except where minors were prohibited); and other limits on cigarette company marketing and lobbying activities. The terms of the MSA required that annual payments to states be adjusted based on several factors including inflation and changes in cigarette sales. Other clauses in the MSA reduced industry payments under specific circumstances; most notable are the clause that ended the annual $300 million payment for the national education program when participating manufacturers' combined market share fell below 99.05 percent (something that happened almost immediately), and a clause that would disproportionately reduce payments to the states if it was determined that the MSA was a "significant factor" in the participating companies' loss of market share.

Given that the annual settlement payments are tied to current cigarette sales, they effectively act like a tax on cigarettes. Consequently, the MSA had an immediate impact on cigarette prices; on the day that the agreement was reached, the participating cigarette companies raised prices by 45 cents per pack, passing virtually all of the costs of the agreement along to smokers. This is in sharp contrast to what would have happened had a different payment structure been established (one based on past sales, for example, that would have been more like a fixed or sunk cost). To at least some observers' surprise, cigarette company marketing expenditures also rose sharply after the MSA, despite the constraints on marketing contained in the agreement. The net effect of the higher prices and increased marketing effort (much of which focused on price promotions, as described below) was a significant reduction in cigarette smoking; one recent study estimates that the MSA reduced per capita consumption by over 8 percent in the years immediately following the agreement.[18] Perhaps even more surprisingly, the market value of cigarette companies and their profits increased in the years following the MSA.[19] This is likely the result of the opportunity the agreement created for a coordinated price increase as well as the resolution of the risk of more costly judgments against the industry in the state lawsuits. However, as described below, the terms of the MSA and the large price increases it induced led to an opportunity for new entry that has sharply reduced the combined market share of the major cigarette companies, as described below. The long-term impact of the MSA on the industry remains to be seen.

The "success" of the states' lawsuits led the federal government to initiate its own litigation against major cigarette companies, filing suit in September 1998. The federal lawsuit sought to recoup the health-care costs the government had incurred in treating diseases caused by smoking and alleged that the major companies had engaged in a decades-long conspiracy to deceive the public about the health consequences of smoking, beginning with the 1953 meeting at the Plaza Hotel and the subsequent release of the "Frank Statement." The alleged conspiracy included their consistent denials of the health risks from smoking as well as the addictive nature of smoking, their manipulation of the nicotine contained in cigarettes, and their marketing practices, including those targeting children and those for light and low-tar cigarettes.[20] The health-care cost component of the case was thrown out early in the proceedings; the conspiracy portion of the case proceeded under the federal Racketeer Influenced and Corrupt Organizations (RICO) statutes. The case eventually went to trial in the District of Columbia's Federal District Court in September 2004. The bench trial ended in June 2005; the Department of Justice's closing arguments were quite controversial given the differences between the government's proposed remedies and those that had been proposed by some of its expert witnesses, with some observers suggesting political interference in the case. In response to this controversy, the District Court judge allowed major public health groups to become parties to the case; these "intervenors" proposed significantly stronger remedies than those proposed by the government in its closing arguments. As of this writing, no decision had been issued in this case.

Structure

Industry Concentration

For much of the twentieth century, the cigarette industry was one of the most concentrated industries in the United States. In the early 1900s, the industry was dominated by the ATC's "Tobacco Trust," accounting for well over 90 percent of the market. Following the breakup of the trust, a handful of firms have dominated the market. As illustrated in Figure 4.5, the four-firm concentration ratio has exceeded 80 percent since the breakup of the trust. In 1995, following Brown & Williamson's acquisition of American Tobacco, the four-firm concentration ration was 98.1 percent and the top five firms controlled over 99.9 percent of the U.S. cigarette market. Since that time, however, concentration has generally been declining as a number of small firms entered the market following the 1998 MSA. By 2003, the four-firm concentration ratio had fallen to 84.0 percent, its lowest level since 1969. The merger of RJR and B&W, approved by the FTC in 2004, has had a modest impact on industry concentration, given the declining market shares of the two companies in the years prior to the merger.

In terms of manufacturing establishments, total U.S. cigarette production in 2002 came from fifteen manufacturing establishments owned by thirteen companies, most of which were located in Virginia and North Carolina. Of these, only nine had one hundred or more employees and another three had between twenty and ninety-nine employees.[21]

Individual Firm Market Shares

The high overall industry concentration throughout the twentieth century masks the substantial changes

Figure 4.5   **Four-Firm Concentration Ratio, 1947–2003**

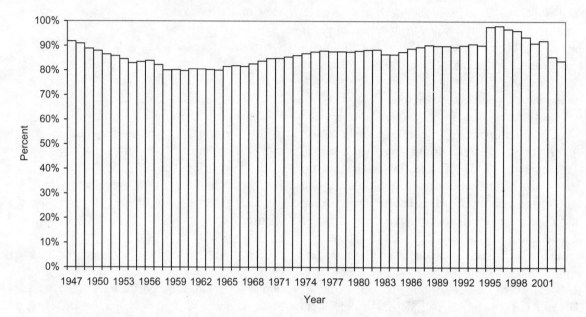

Source: R. Goldstein, "Cigarette Production, 1949–1999," report prepared for the Roswell Park Cancer Institute, Buffalo, NY (2003); Price Waterhouse Coopers reports on Master Settlement Agreement payments, various years.

in the fortunes of individual firms. Figure 4.6 illustrates the changes over time in the market shares of individual firms. The two largest firms following the breakup of the trust have all but disappeared from the market: ATC, with its acquisition by B&W in 1995 (and B&W's subsequent merger with RJR in 2004), and L&M, with just over a 2 percent market share in recent years. Of the original "big three," only Lorillard remains. Other companies have seen their shares rise and fall over time, most notably RJR, which dominated the market for much of the mid-twentieth century before losing over 40 percent of its share over the past few decades. In contrast, Philip Morris was a relatively small player in the market through the first half of the century before growing rapidly starting in the mid-1960s, accounting for nearly half of the U.S. cigarette market over the past decade.

Product Differentiation and Brand Market Shares

Much of the ebb and flow of firm market shares is tied to the fate of particular brands, as shown in Figure 4.7. In most years, the majority of cigarette consumption is accounted for by a small number of cigarette brands. RJR's early success can be attributed to the rapid acceptance of its Camel brand, while its later success relates to the growth of its Winston and Salem brands. Philip Morris's dominance over the past few decades can be attributed to the growth of its Marlboro brand starting in the 1960s; in 2003, about four of every ten cigarettes consumed was a Marlboro. As described elsewhere in this chapter, the rise and fall of various brands can be tied to innovations in product design and the success or failure of marketing campaigns.

Figure 4.6 **Cigarette Company Market Shares, 1913–2003**

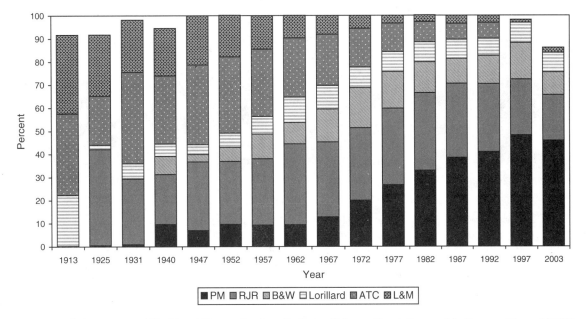

Source: U.S. Department of Health and Human Services, *Reducing Tobacco Use: A Report of the Surgeon General* (2000); Federal Trade Commission, *Competition and the Financial Impact of the Proposed Tobacco Industry Settlement* (1997); Price Waterhouse Coopers reports on Master Settlement Agreement payments, various years.

While design innovations account for the growth of various brands and/or firms over time, these spread quickly throughout the industry so that cigarettes remain a relatively homogeneous product. Notwithstanding this, companies spend considerable resources trying to differentiate their brands. One indicator of this is the number of cigarette brands subjected to the FTC's tar and nicotine testing process. In March 1972, the FTC reported test results for 130 varieties of cigarettes sold domestically; by 2002, results were reported for 1,298 varieties.[22] These include multiple variations of a given brand that together are known as a brand family. In 2002, for example, there were thirty-six varieties contained in the Marlboro family, with variations based on length (85 mm vs. 100 mm), flavor (menthol vs. nonmenthol), and strength (full flavor, milds, medium, light, and

ultra light). Other variations exist for other brands, including some nonfilter brands. Some evidence indicates that the proliferation of cigarette brands has been effective in increasing demand.[23] Over the past few years, a variety of flavored brands have appeared, including: pineapple-coconut (Kauai Kolada), citrus (Twista Lime), toffee (Winter Warm Toffee), and mint-flavored Camels (Winter MochaMint); Midnight Berry, Mocha Taboo, and Mintrigue versions of Kool; and several others.[24] The recent introduction of these flavored cigarettes has been highly controversial given their potential appeal to youth.

Internal industry documents provide fascinating discussions on the efforts of the companies to differentiate their products through advertising, marketing a variety of cigarettes to different market segments. For example, internal PM documents

Figure 4.7 **Brand Shares, Selected Years**

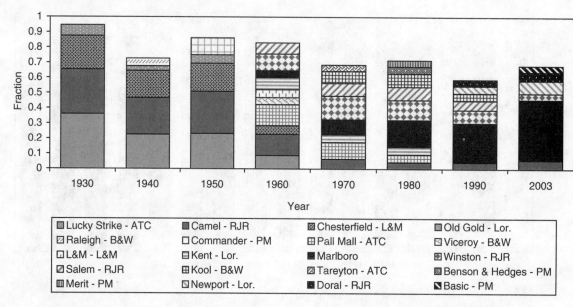

Source: R. Goldstein, "Cigarette Production, 1949-1999," report prepared for the Roswell Park Cancer Institute, Buffalo, NY (2003); Tobacco Reporter, *2004 Maxwell Tobacco Fact Book* (2004); Gene Borio, Tobacco Timeline, www.tobacco.org (accessed May 5, 2006).

Note: Brands with market shares of 4 percent or above in a given year are shown for that year; some brands shown in one year are sold in other years, but do not reach 4 percent share in those years; shares represent share for a brand "family."

describe how the slim and super slim varieties of its Virginia Slims brand, sold in pastel-colored packs, have a greater appeal to women.[25] A recent review of these documents provides a nice discussion of the different psychosocial, economic, demographic, and other population segments identified by the companies; labels for these segments are quite descriptive, including: "the rugged man," "unsettled dreamers," "insecure and pessimistic," "frustrated blue collar," "lively taste-oriented female," "social strivers," and many more.[26] Brands and marketing campaigns were developed by the companies to reach these different market segments. The explosion in the number of brands over the past few decades reflects, at least in part, the increasing sophistication of the companies' market segmentation efforts.

Barriers to Entry

The historically high concentration in the cigarette industry resulted from significant barriers to entry. Since the breakup of the tobacco trust in 1911, there have been only two periods when significant entry occurred. Both involved periods when cigarette prices were high, creating an opportunity for new firms to enter or fringe firms to expand their operations. The first, as described above, was in the early 1930s when the dominant firms of the time—ATC, RJR, and L&M—raised industry prices such that retail prices were 14 to 15 cents per pack for most leading brands, despite falling tobacco-leaf prices and the onset of the Great Depression. New entrants and small existing firms took advantage of this opportunity with the introduction of their 10-cent brands and quickly grew to nearly one-quarter of the market before the big three responded by cutting prices to the same level. While most of the new firms were not able to survive, two of them—Philip Morris and Brown & Williamson—eventually became major players in the U.S. markets.

From the mid-1930s through the mid-1990s, no significant entry occurred. Several factors contribute to this, including strong brand loyalty sustained, in large part, by sizable advertising and promotion expenditures, limited distribution channels, and the falling demand for cigarettes. Cigarettes enjoy extremely high rates of brand loyalty among smokers, perhaps more so than any other consumer product. While smokers may occasionally smoke a different brand, most of the cigarettes that most smokers consume will be their usual brand. Estimates suggest that few smokers change brands in any given year. Much of this brand switching is among brands in the same brand family (e.g., from Marlboro to Marlboro Light) or to another brand produced by the same company (e.g., from Camel to Winston). Very little switching involves changing from one brand of a particular company to a different company's brand.

This brand loyalty is reinforced by the sizable advertising and promotional expenditures of cigarette companies (discussed below). Economies of scale in marketing are substantial, in contrast to relatively modest economies of scale in cigarette manufacturing.[27] Government policies restricting cigarette marketing have almost certainly made it more difficult for new firms to enter by taking away relatively cost-effective ways of introducing new brands. Research indicates, for example, that the federal ban on television and radio cigarette advertising reduced competition within the industry and increased the market power of existing firms.[28] State and local restrictions on advertising, the restrictions contained in the MSA, and voluntary industry restrictions are likely to have a similar impact. Other marketing efforts have directly rewarded smokers' brand loyalty by providing valuable merchandise as a "reward" for smoking particular brands (e.g., the loyalty programs like Marlboro Miles and Camel Cash programs).

Similarly, other marketing expenditures have rewarded the loyalty of distributors and retailers, making it difficult for new brands to access traditional distribution channels (e.g., Philip Morris's Retail Leaders and Wholesale Leaders programs). Cigarettes are distributed by thousands of wholesalers in over a million retail outlets. Major cigarette companies have numerous sales reps involved in all aspects of wholesale and retail distribution, from setting up point-of-sale displays to providing incentives and promotions to wholesalers and retailers. A new firm trying to introduce a new brand nationally would need to invest a considerable amount to compete effectively with the distribution efforts of major companies. Interestingly, the wholesaler/retailer loyalty programs and their impact on access to shelf space and the positioning of cigarette brands have been the subject of much disagreement among major cigarette companies, with various companies initiating lawsuits against others claiming that these programs are anticompetitive. To date, these lawsuits have been unsuccessful.

In addition, the generally declining demand for cigarettes in the United States over the past two-plus decades reduces the incentives for new entry, even in the face of high profitability within the industry. This is particularly true given the extensive and expensive litigation risks that could face a new firm.

Despite these factors, a second wave of entry has taken place over the past decade, at least in part spurred by the large price increases that followed the MSA and the state legislation implementing the agreement. Industry cigarette prices were increased several times prior to the MSA, as companies settled lawsuits with individual states, beginning with Mississippi in July 1997 and followed by Florida, Texas, and Minnesota; these individual state settlements account for much, if not all, of the more than 25-cent-per-pack increase in the wholesale price of cigarettes between March 1997 and August 1998. The November 1998 agreement settling the lawsuits with the other forty-six states, the District of Columbia, and other jurisdictions was accompanied by a same-day 45-cent-per-pack increase in the wholesale prices of the leading companies.

The four leading cigarette companies at the time—PM, RJR, B&W, and Lorillard—were the initial signatories to the MSA; they are collectively referred to as the Original Participating Manufacturers (OPMs). The OPMs were subject to a variety of payments, including initial payments (through 2003), annual and strategic contribution payments (in perpetuity), and other payments (of varying duration, for the establishment of a national foundation, to cover states' attorneys' fees and other activities). Their November 1998 price increases were designed to cover these costs.

Over time, other companies have agreed to the terms of the MSA; for example, the then-fifth-largest firm (L&M) and two of the larger fringe firms (Commonwealth and Santa Fe, both with well below 1 percent market share at the time) joined immediately, while several others signed on within the first ninety days. These firms received some advantages from joining early, in that they are not required to make payments on their grandfathered market share (the larger of 125 percent of 1997 market share or 1998 market share). Other firms joined the MSA in subsequent years; they do not receive the same preferential treatment that the early signatories received. Collectively, these companies are referred to as the Subsequent Participating Manufacturers (SPMs). As of early

2006, there are over forty SPMs in operation. The SPMs are subject to some (e.g., the annual and strategic contribution payments) but not all of the payments required of the OPMs; this gives them a small advantage over the OPMs in terms of their MSA-related costs, with the early signatories receiving additional advantages given that their grandfathered market share is not included in calculating their share of MSA payments. A few of the SPMs have seen significant growth from 1997 to 2003, most notably Commonwealth Brands (whose market share rose nearly 400 percent to almost 2.8 percent) and L&M (whose market share nearly doubled to over 2.2 percent).

In addition, there are a number of small cigarette companies that have chosen not to participate in the MSA; these firms are known as the Non-Participating Manufacturers (NPMs). In order to keep the NPMs from gaining a significant cost advantage over the OPMs and SPMs, the MSA included several provisions targeting these firms. However, loopholes in the MSA and noncompliance by the NPMs allowed the NPMs to price well below the participating manufacturers; this, combined with other factors, allowed the NPMs to gain significant market share in the post-MSA period. By 2003, these firms accounted for over 8 percent of the market, almost 2,000 percent growth collectively since 1997 (Figure 4.8).

The key provision of the MSA targeting the NPMs is found in Exhibit T of the agreement. This exhibit calls for settling states to adopt legislation requiring the NPMs to pay an amount equivalent to what they would have paid had they joined the MSA, with these payments held in escrow for twenty-five years against future health-care cost claims made against the NPMs.[29] States failing to adopt this model statute would face significant reductions in the payments they received under the MSA. Not surprisingly, all settling states quickly adopted the model statute (also referred

Figure 4.8   **Market Share by MSA-Participant Status, 1997–2003**

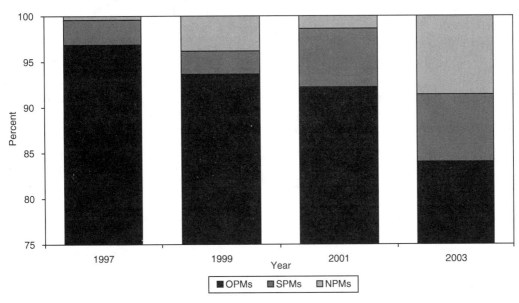

Source: Price Waterhouse Coopers reports on Master Settlement Agreement payments, various years. Note that the vertical axis begins at 75 percent for illustrative purposes.

to as the qualifying statute).[30] The model statute had a number of problems that some NPMs were quick to exploit, not the least of which was allowing them as much as almost sixteen months to make their escrow payments (payments were due by April 15 of the following year). This allowed some of the more unscrupulous NPMs to enter a state's cigarette market, sell for a period of time at a price well below what they could sell at if making the required escrow payment, and then leave the market (at times reemerging under a different name), or otherwise avoid making the escrow payments. Many NPMs are located overseas and use nontraditional distribution channels, making it more difficult for state authorities to identify them and to enforce the escrow statutes.[31] Given the process, a noncompliant NPM might operate for as long as two years in a state without making its escrow payments before a complaint was filed and an injunction issued prohibiting it from selling

in that state. Some of the early NPM growth was almost certainly fueled by this noncompliance.

States quickly realized the problems with implementing the model statute, stimulating a new wave of "complementary legislation" targeting the NPMs. The resulting statutes generally prohibited the application of state excise tax stamps on cigarette brands that are not included in the state's list of approved products; for a brand to be included on this list, its manufacturer must certify that it is either a participating manufacturer or, for the NPMs, that it is in compliance with the model statute.[32] The first of these statutes was adopted in 2001; by 2004, all but a few of the settling states had some form of complementary legislation in place. In addition, many states adopted provisions requiring quarterly escrow payments from NPMs. These policies have facilitated state enforcement efforts and raised NPM compliance with the model statute.[33]

While states were tightening their escrow provisions, compliant NPMs were exploiting another loophole in the MSA, the so-called cap release or allocable share release provision contained in Exhibit T that was a part of the model statute adopted in all settling states. The cap release required a state to return the difference between an NPM's escrow payments to the state and the payments the state would have received from that company had it been a participating manufacturer. The difference between the two becomes significant for an NPM that is operating in a single state or a small number of states because its escrow payments are based on all sales within each state, while the payments it would make as an SPM are based loosely on its share of national sales. For example, suppose that an NPM sells its cigarettes in only one state and that that state's share of MSA payments is 2 percent. Assuming that the escrow payment per cigarette is the same as the per cigarette cost had the firm been an SPM, that NPM would be entitled to a rebate of 98 percent of the escrow payments it made to that state.[34] This enabled compliant NPMs that operated in a limited geographic region to gain a significant cost advantage over participating manufacturers, an advantage that almost certainly contributed to the increased market shares of some NPMs. As this became apparent, states responded with yet another wave of legislation aimed at closing this loophole—the allocable share repeal statutes amending the model statute to eliminate the escrow rebate; the first of these was enacted in 2003, with most settling states adopting such legislation by 2004.

In addition to the cost advantages compliant and noncompliant NPMs were able to achieve, at least one other factor likely contributed to the growth of the NPMs (and to that of the SPMs): the increased availability of new distribution channels, notably the opportunity to sell cigarettes on the Internet and the growth in the number of discount tobacco product stores. The number of tobacco stores rose by almost 60 percent from 1997 to 2002, while the number of electronic and mail order tobacco product vendors rose by 160 percent in this period.[35] Anecdotal evidence suggests that both types of outlets offer a greater variety of brands, particularly the discount and deep discount brands that account for much of the SPMs' and NPMs' sales.

Whether or not the growth of these recent entrants will be sustained remains to be seen. The recent state efforts to eliminate any cost advantages compliant NPMs might obtain under the MSA, coupled with enforcement efforts targeting noncompliant NPMs, are likely to slow, if not reverse, the upward trend in the market share of NPMs. The finding in favor of participating manufacturers in the recent MSA "significant factor" proceeding may result in reductions in OPM and SPM payments to the states, reducing any disadvantages to them from participating in the MSA.[36] As with the entry of the firms producing the 10-cent brands in the 1930s, it seems likely that the more recent wave of entry induced by the MSA will lead to at least a few successful firms that may have a lasting impact on the future of the industry.

Conduct

Pricing

With few exceptions, cigarette prices have historically been relatively stable and well above their competitive level. These prices, however, have not been set at the level that would occur if the firms were setting prices jointly to maximize profits, given that nearly all empirical treatments of cigarette demand produce elasticity estimates in the inelastic range (most short-run estimates fall in the range from -0.25 to -0.50, with long-run estimates about double the short-run estimates).[37] If firms were jointly maximizing profits, increases in prices would produce disproportionate increases in profits given the inelasticity of demand. Some evidence of pricing above competitive levels comes from research on the impact of state and federal cigarette excise tax increases on prices. In general, these studies find that cigarette tax increases result in increases in cigarette prices that are at least as large as the increase in the tax, suggesting that producers are not sharing the burden of the tax increase, as would be the case in a competitive industry.[38]

For much of its history, cigarette industry pricing strategies have been characterized by price leadership, with the dominant firm of the time initiating most price changes, which are matched almost immediately by identical changes in other firms' prices. This pricing strategy evolved in the years after the breakup of the tobacco trust. As described above, RJR quickly became the dominant firm in the market following the introduction of its Camel brand. Efforts by other firms to raise prices during this period were not matched by comparable price increases by RJR, and the increases were soon abandoned. In contrast, RJR quickly responded to price reductions by other firms with larger reductions in its own prices. The big three of the time quickly learned that competing on price was not in their best interests, with other firms accepting RJR's pricing strategies throughout the 1920s and into the early 1930s. The rise of the 10-cent brands in 1931 and the ensuing price war led by ATC's price cuts (which were matched by RJR and L&M) was the one exception to this. In the shakeout that followed the price war, RJR again assumed its price leadership role.

As the industry evolved, the leadership position changed, with ATC taking on this role for much of the 1940s. The emergence of filter-tipped cigarettes in the 1950s resulted in a division of this role, with ATC continuing to lead in the nonfiltered segment of the market and RJR assuming the lead in the new filter-tipped segment. Eventually, as Philip Morris and its Marlboro brand grew, PM assumed the lead. The evolution of industry pricing strategies and PM's leadership role in the 1970s and after is nicely described in a 1976 PM internal document on "Pricing Policy":

> The cigarette industry is characterized by economists as a "kinky oligopoly." This charming term implies that the general price level is determined by a small number of firms (price leaders); that no economic advantage can be obtained by any one firm pricing below the general price level; and that major disadvantages accrue to a firm that attempts a price above the general level. In short, the general price level results from some sparring among the potential price leaders, after which the rest of the industry accepts the resulting price structure.[39]

The report goes on to note that RJR and ATC had played the leadership role for many years and that price increases during this time were relatively modest, but that things had changed by the 1970s, with PM playing the leadership role: "We no longer follow the market; whether we initiate a price increase or not, our decision is a key factor in establishing a new industry price level, and we must examine any price move in the light of our own judgment of the appropriate level."

This report provides a fascinating look at how PM and the rest of the industry priced cigarettes in the late 1970s. It clearly described the tradeoffs between price competition and other marketing efforts (discussed below), noting that the lack of price competition in the industry provided revenues that could be invested in other marketing efforts to maintain or increase market share. Similarly, it recognized that prices were below the level that would maximize joint profits. In the end, after discussing a variety of pricing strategies, the report concluded that a "full inflation price relief" strategy—one that increased prices so as to keep pace with the relatively high inflation of the time—was the

Figure 4.9   **Inflation-Adjusted Cigarette Prices and Key Components, 1970–2005**

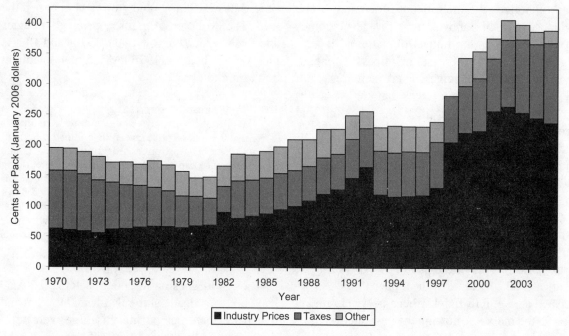

Source: Orzechowski and Walker, *The Tax Burden on Tobacco* (2006); Tobacco Reporter, *2004 Maxwell Tobacco Fact Book* (2004); U.S. Department of Agriculture, *Tobacco Outlook* (2006). Data are as of November 1 each year.

appropriate strategy. In the end, as illustrated by Figure 4.9, inflation-adjusted industry prices rose somewhat during the late 1970s and early 1980s, while inflation-adjusted retail prices fell somewhat as a result of the stability of nominal state and federal cigarette excise taxes.

Pricing strategies changed in the 1980s, at least in part reflecting the industry's response to federal and state cigarette excise tax increases. Some analysts contend that the January 1983 8-cent-per-pack increase in the federal cigarette excise tax (the first increase since 1951) served as a coordinating mechanism for an oligopolistic industry price increase, observing that retail prices rose by about 16 cents per pack, after accounting for changes in costs. Again, internal industry documents are informative in describing how the industry handled

the tax increase. Writing several years later, PM analyst Myron Johnston states:

> We increased prices five times between February of 1982 and January of 1983. In less than a year, the price went from $20.20 to $26.90 per thousand ($2.70 more than the tax), and this fact was not lost on consumers, who could legitimately blame the manufacturers for the price increases. While price increases of this magnitude might have been tolerated during the rapid escalation in the overall inflation rate between 1977 and 1981, the increase in the price of cigarettes in 1982–83 was made even more dramatic by the fact that the overall rate of inflation was slowing considerably.[40]

The industry price increases of the late 1970s and early 1980s, coupled with the first real increases in state and federal cigarette excise taxes in many years, created an opportunity for gains from a new approach. L&M, the smallest of the big six, with a market share of about 2 percent in the early 1980s, initiated the first real price competition the industry had seen in decades with the introduction of a line of discount "generic" cigarettes priced well below other brands. L&M's generic cigarettes captured about 4 percent of the market by 1984. Other firms were quick to respond with the introduction of their own discount brands, repositioning of existing brands as discount brands (e.g., RJR's Doral brand), and related efforts (e.g., the introduction of packs of twenty-five cigarettes at the same price as packs of twenty, such as PM's Players 25).

Over the next few years, a three-tier pricing structure emerged, with the lowest-priced deep-discount brands (e.g., L&M's generic cigarettes and B&W's GPC brand), mid-priced discount brands (e.g., PM's Basic brand), and the highest-priced premium brands (e.g., Marlboro, Camel, and Newport). Over time, the price gap between premium brands and other brands increased; by 1992, discount cigarettes were priced about 40 cents per pack below premium brands, despite minimal differences in production costs. Given the relatively elastic demand within price tiers and the high degree of substitutability across at least adjacent price tiers,[41] the discount brands gained significant market share, accounting for nearly 40 percent of the market by early 1993.

While PM established itself as a key player in the industry in the 1930s through its 10-cent brands, it was not as successful in this wave of price competition; for the first time in over two decades, Marlboro's market share was falling. In a bold move, on April 2, 1993—now known as Marlboro Friday—Philip Morris reasserted its leadership position by cutting Marlboro prices by 40 cents per pack. This was initially accomplished through a series of promotional efforts and was made permanent in August 1993 with a comparable wholesale price reduction. PM's Marlboro Friday

price reductions were matched almost immediately by reductions in other firms' premium brand prices. The impact was substantial; PM stopped the erosion in its market share and reversed the slide in Marlboro's share, with both resuming their upward trend throughout the 1990s. Over the next few years, the discount and deep discount share of the market fell by about one-third.

As described above, the MSA and other settlement-induced price increases of the late 1990s created a new opportunity for low-priced brands to gain a toehold in the cigarette market. Some commentators have suggested that industry prices have increased well beyond what would have been necessary to cover settlement costs and other cost increases, a suggestion supported by the growth in real industry prices illustrated in Figure 4.9 in the years immediately following the initial MSA-related price increase in late 1998.

Economic theories of addiction provide one explanation for this greater than necessary price increase.[42] Specifically, when demand for the industry's product is rising and firms have market power, they may price below the level that would maximize short-term profits in order to "hook" new consumers who are not yet addicted and are likely to be more price sensitive (consistent with the empirical evidence for cigarette demand that indicates that smoking among youth and young adults is two to three times more sensitive to price than is smoking among adults). This strategy implies a steady stream of new consumers that keeps demand above what it would be if prices were set to maximize short-run profits, thus raising long-run profitability. In contrast, firms with market power in an industry producing an addictive product and expecting future reductions in demand (in response, for example, to policy efforts aimed at reducing the use of its product) have incentives to increase prices more rapidly given their declining future prospects. This dynamic profit maximization strategy may help explain the relatively large increases in prices around the 1983 federal cigarette excise tax increase, as well as those that occurred in the wake of the MSA.

However, this strategy increases the potential for price competition from new entrants. Coupled with the loopholes in the agreement and the lack of compliance with MSA-related legislation among at least some nonparticipating manufacturers described above, a new era of price competition began. The response of the major cigarette companies has been modest to date: Most firms' wholesale prices have not been increased since 2002 (resulting in the absorption of the 2003 federal cigarette excise tax increase by these firms); they have increased their price-related marketing efforts significantly (described below); and, perhaps most importantly, they have pushed states to strengthen policies targeting the NPMs and to more aggressively enforce these policies. As a result, the new entrants and some existing fringe firms gained significant market share at the expense of some of the major firms (particularly RJR and B&W). The long-run impact of this entry and resulting price competition remains to be seen.

Advertising and Promotion

Cigarettes have long been one of the most heavily marketed products in the United States. In 2003, the top cigarette companies spent a combined $15.15 billion on advertising and promotion.[43] This is an incredible amount given the high degree of brand loyalty among consumers, the lack of real innovation in product design, and the long-term declines in smoking prevalence and cigarette consumption.

As described above, the rise of cigarette companies is directly linked to the success of key brands; marketing efforts have played a major role in this success. The early Camel, Lucky Strike, and Chesterfield advertising campaigns contributed to the dominance of these brands from the 1920s and into the 1950s. Leo Burnett's iconic Marlboro Man played a major role in the transformation of PM's Marlboro brand from a brand targeted to women to the most widely smoked brand in the world. More recently, RJR's Joe Camel campaign spurred resurgence in the popularity of its Camel brand.

Cigarette marketing has received much attention from policymakers, despite the mixed evidence on its impact on smoking. As described above, the FTC investigated a number of health claims in cigarette advertising in the 1940s and 1950s, eventually establishing guidelines for industry advertising in 1955; the agency has continued to monitor advertising for related claims ever since. In the late 1960s, one antismoking advertisement for every three prosmoking commercials was televised under the FCC's Fairness Doctrine. These came to an end when all broadcast cigarette advertising was banned under the Public Health Cigarette Smoking Act, effective January 2, 1971. Industry marketing expenditures fell in the years immediately following the ban, but by 1975 exceeded their 1970 level by more than one-third. More recently, as part of the MSA, other forms of cigarette advertising and promotion have been either banned or restricted. These constraints include: a ban on most outdoor and transit advertising; restrictions on sponsorship; a ban on product placement in movies, television shows, and other media; a ban on the distribution of free samples (except in adult-only facilities); a ban on branded merchandise; and a ban on the use of cartoon characters in cigarette advertising, promotions, or packaging. In contrast to the initial fall in expenditures following the broadcast ban, cigarette company advertising and promotional expenditures have increased at an increasing rate since the MSA.

Figure 4.10 illustrates this, showing inflation-adjusted, per-pack cigarette advertising and

Figure 4.10   **Inflation-Adjusted Cigarette Marketing Expenditures per Pack, 1975–2003**

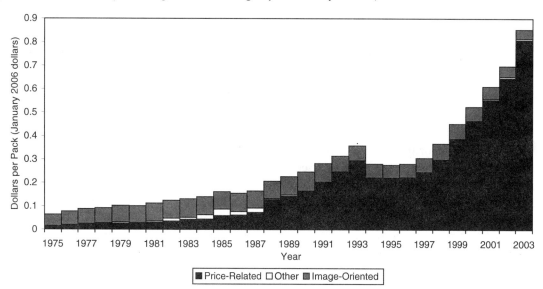

Source: Federal Trade Commission, *Cigarette Report for 2003* (2005). "Price-Related" expenditures include those on retail valued added promotions, promotional allowances, coupons, sampling, and specialty item distribution; "Image-Oriented" expenditures include those on billboard, transit, magazine, newspaper, direct mail, point-of-sale, sponsorship, and Internet advertising. Some of these sub-categories are included in "Other" expenditures, given that the FTC did not report some categories separately until later years.

promotion expenditures for major cigarette companies from 1975 through 2003, based on data reported annually by the FTC. Marketing expenditures illustrated in Figure 4.10 are aggregated into two categories: image-oriented advertising expenditures and price-related promotional expenditures. The image-oriented category includes expenditures on billboard, transit, magazine, newspaper, point-of-sale, direct mail, sponsorship, and Internet advertising. The price-related promotion category includes expenditures on retail value added promotions, promotional allowances, coupons, sampling, and specialty item distribution. Retail value added promotions include those that involve "free" cigarettes (e.g. buy-one-get-one-free promotions) and those that provide a gift (e.g., a lighter, baseball cap, or other item of value) with the purchase of cigarettes.

Promotional allowances include payments to wholesalers and retailers for product placement, as well as volume rebates and various incentive payments that result in lower retail prices. Expenditures on specialty item distribution reflect the expenditures on programs that provide merchandise as rewards for brand loyalty (e.g., the Marlboro Miles program). Some of the expenditures included in the price-related category do not directly affect retail cigarette prices (e.g., some promotional allowances are for placement), but are grouped in this way given the categories reported by the FTC over time; in the most recent FTC reports, promotional allowances have been disaggregated into those for price discounts and those for other activities (largely placement), with price discounts accounting for the vast majority of these expenditures. In earlier years, some of the price-related expenditures are included in the "other" category, given that these were not separately reported by FTC (e.g., coupons and retail value-added promotions prior to 1988).

Two key conclusions emerge from Figure 4.10. First, real cigarette company advertising and promotional expenditures per pack have risen sharply over time, with per-pack expenditures in 2003 about triple their level in 1995 and more than twelve times larger than in 1975. The only significant decline in real expenditures occurred in the mid-1990s and reflects the change in marketing strategies associated with Marlboro Friday specifically—the shift from using price promotions to reduce price to a direct reduction in industry prices. Second, there has been a marked shift over time in the relative importance of the two broad marketing categories. Price-related promotional expenditures accounted for less than one-quarter of marketing expenditures in the early 1980s, but account for the overwhelming majority of expenditures—95 percent—by 2003. The shift in emphasis from more traditional image-oriented advertising to price-related promotions began in the mid-1980s, shortly after the publication of the first empirical studies on the greater price elasticity of youth and young adult smoking. Internal industry documents clearly show that these early studies received much attention from company marketing officials and others, that the findings of these studies were consistent with internal research, and that these findings spurred interest in price-related marketing efforts.[44] Many of the price-related marketing expenditures are for activities that resemble price discrimination, given that they are offered selectively on different brands, in different types of outlets, and in different markets. Some evidence suggests that these marketing expenditures have become increasingly concentrated in a small number of brands, most notably the brands most smoked by young smokers.[45]

Product Design

New product development is closely tied to the success of various cigarette companies and brands over time. As described above, the use of the American blend of various types of tobacco in its Camel cigarettes was perhaps the most important factor in the early rise of RJR. While other companies quickly developed comparable products, the advantage RJR gained from being first, combined with its aggressive marketing of the brand and the ensuing loyalty of Camel smokers, accounts for the company's leadership position in the industry from the years following the breakup of the tobacco trust through the mid-1950s.

Similarly, the spread of information on the health consequences of cigarette smoking spurred new product innovations in the 1940s and 1950s, most notably the development of filter-tipped cigarettes. Firms that were quick to introduce and market filter-tipped brands benefited almost immediately. Lorillard, for example, whose market share had been stagnant, around 5 percent for many years, saw a more than doubling of its share in the years following its introduction of Kent in 1953; the brand alone captured over 8 percent of the market within a few years. The same phenomenon applied a decade later as companies brought a variety of low-tar brands to market following the release of the first Surgeon General's report in 1964. During this period, there was an inherent tension within the industry, given that the development and marketing of "safer" cigarettes implicitly acknowledged the health consequences of cigarette smoking, something that the industry denied until recently. As described above, there was much confusion over the health impact of filter-tipped and low-tar cigarettes, with some public health authorities encouraging their use as less harmful alternatives to other cigarettes. In recent years, however, it has become clear that there are no significant health benefits that result from smoking low-tar cigarettes; nevertheless, many smokers continue to perceive these brands as less harmful than others.

In terms of its impact on the industry, perhaps the most important innovation in product design of the past fifty years was PM's reformulation of Marlboro in the mid-1960s. Internal industry documents revealed through litigation describe cigarette company research that demonstrated the importance of nicotine as the active ingredient in cigarettes as well as of the addictive properties of nicotine. These documents also provide examples of efforts to change the chemistry of cigarette smoke through the use of various additives, so as to improve taste while reducing measured tar and nicotine content.[46] Ammonia was ultimately identified as one such additive that would increase the free nicotine contained in smoke (facilitating more rapid absorption of nicotine in the lungs and producing a more immediate impact on the smoker) while reducing the acidity of cigarette smoke, effectively increasing the "kick" provided by nicotine while at the same time reducing measured tar and nicotine levels. Philip Morris was the first to use ammoniated tobacco in its brands—most notably Marlboro—with internal RJR documents indicating ammonia use beginning in the mid-1960s and increasing significantly over the following decade. One RJR document compared tar and nicotine levels for Marlboro and Winston, showing that levels fell by about two-thirds for the two brands over time, but that the free nicotine produced by Marlboro remained constant over time, while that for Winston fell by about two-thirds.[47] Other internal documents credit PM's use of ammoniated tobacco in its Marlboro brand for the rapid rise in Marlboro and PM's market share in the 1960s and 1970s.

Other companies eventually discovered the chemistry that contributed to Marlboro's success and began using ammonia in their cigarettes as well (e.g., RJR began using ammoniated tobacco in its Camel brand in the mid-1970s and in its Winston brand a few years later). Other design changes were adopted with the same goal of increasing the nicotine contained in cigarette smoke, including B&W's efforts to genetically engineer tobacco leaf with greater nicotine content and the addition of ventilation holes to filters that reduced the acidity of cigarette smoke. While these design changes contributed to the growth of some brands, none achieved the same success that PM had with Marlboro. Coupled with the highly effective Marlboro Man advertising campaign, Philip Morris became the leading U.S. cigarette company and Marlboro became the country's (and the world's) leading cigarette brand.

Efforts to develop "safer" cigarettes continued in the 1970s and beyond. One of the more notable efforts of the 1970s was L&M's "XA Project," which used additives to neutralize some of the carcinogens produced by cigarette smoking (polycyclic aromatic hydrocarbons [PAHs]). Using some of the same testing procedures (specifically skin-painting tests on mice) that had been used to demonstrate the cancer-causing properties of tar, L&M scientists demonstrated significantly reduced risks from "XA Project" cigarettes. However, given ongoing industry litigation challenging the validity of these tests and given the potential liability that would result from marketing a "safe" cigarette (essentially acknowledging that all other cigarettes were unsafe), other companies successfully pressured L&M to abandon the project.

One innovation that made it a bit further was Premier. In the 1980s, RJR invested hundreds of millions of dollars in developing Premier, a "smokeless" product that looked like a cigarette but functioned quite differently. Using a unique technology, Premier heated rather than burned tobacco, potentially reducing the carcinogens inhaled through cigarette smoke. RJR test-marketed Premier in 1988; consumers found the product difficult to use (packaging included detailed instructions on how to ignite the heating element) and bad tasting and smelling. At the same time, given the product's design, public health officials argued that it was not a cigarette, but rather a different type of nicotine delivery device that should be subject to regulation as a drug by the Food and Drug Administration (FDA). Given the regulatory challenges and its rejection by consumers, RJR dropped Premier in 1989. Despite the lack of commercial success, companies continued to invest in efforts to develop "safer" cigarettes.

Perhaps the most contentious recent innovation in product design is the development and marketing of "potentially reduced exposure products" (PREPs).[48] These include cigarette-like products that heat rather than burn tobacco (e.g., RJR's Eclipse and PM's Accord). RJR incorporated the lessons learned from its failure with Premier in developing Eclipse a few years later. Changes in the product design produce a smokelike vapor that results in more of a cigarette taste, while significantly changing the composition of the "smoke" so as to significantly reduce tar levels. PM's Accord uses a different technology, employing a battery-powered heating element to produce a similar effect. RJR is marketing Eclipse as a more socially acceptable, potentially safer product:

> Compared to other cigarettes, Eclipse reduces secondhand smoke by 80 percent, produces no ashes and leaves no lingering odor or visible staining on glass or fabrics. Based on extensive scientific studies, R.J. Reynolds has also concluded that Eclipse may present less risk of certain, but not all, smoking-related diseases when compared to other cigarettes. Eclipse demonstrates R.J. Reynolds' commitment to developing products that have the potential to reduce the risks associated with smoking.[49]

Other PREPs are modified tobacco products that purportedly reduce the carcinogens in cigarettes through various techniques. Notable brands include: Star Scientific's Advance, which uses a unique curing process to reduce carcinogens known as tobacco-specific nitrosamines (TSNAs); Vector's Quest, which uses genetically modified tobacco that contains less nicotine; and Vector's Omni, which includes additives that are supposed to reduce TSNAs and PAHs (apparently adopting a variation of the approach L&M had used in its XA Project). In addition, noncigarette tobacco products (smokeless tobacco products like U.S. Smokeless Tobacco's Revel and tobacco lozenges like Star Tobacco's Ariva) are being marketed as safe alternatives to cigarettes; of note among these products is RJR's test marketing of a smokeless product called Camel Snus in the summer of 2006.

The claims that these products are less harmful than other cigarettes have yet to be supported by independent, scientific research. Nevertheless, many are being marketed as healthier than other cigarettes. To date, none have gained significant market share.

Performance

Profitability

Cigarette manufacturing has long been one of the most profitable industries in the United States, a fact that remains true today, despite the significant litigation costs incurred by industry firms. Figure 4.11 shows the revenues, operating income, and profit margins from the domestic operations of major cigarette companies.[50] The average profit margin for the industry was approximately 17 percent in 2005, well above that in most other industries. In recent years, profit margins have typically been correlated with a firm's share of the premium cigarette market; hence PM and

Figure 4.11   **Revenues, Income, and Profits of Largest U.S. Cigarette Companies, 2005**

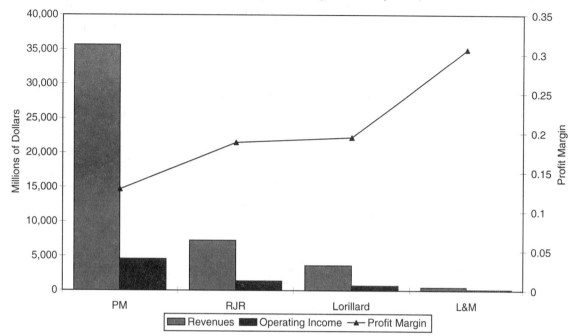

Source: Company 10-K filings, 2006: PM (Altria), RJR (Reynolds American), Lorillard (Loews Corporation), and L&M (Vector Holdings). No filing could be found for Commonwealth Brands, the fourth largest cigarette manufacturer in 2005.

Lorillard's relatively high margins.[51] As noted above, recent research suggests that the profitability of cigarette companies improved following the resolution of state lawsuits brought by states against the industry.

Public Health

No discussion of the performance of the cigarette industry is complete without a discussion of the health impact of cigarette smoking. Cigarette smoking is the leading cause of preventable death in the United States, with recent estimates indicating that smoking caused an average of 438,000 premature deaths per year from 1997 through 2001.[52] This is approximately one in five of all deaths in the United States each year, and each death results in an average loss of fourteen years

of potential life. The most recent U.S. Surgeon General's report concludes that:

- Smoking harms nearly every organ of the body, causing many diseases and reducing the health of smokers in general.
- Quitting smoking has immediate as well as long-term benefits, reducing risk for diseases caused by smoking and improving health in general.
- Smoking cigarettes with lower machine-measured yields of tar and nicotine provides no clear benefit to health.

The list of diseases caused by smoking has been expanded to include abdominal aortic aneurysm, acute myeloid leukemia, cataract, cervical cancer, kidney cancer, pancreatic cancer, pneumonia, periodontitis, and stomach cancer. These are in addition to diseases previously known to be caused by smoking, including bladder, esophageal, laryngeal, lung, oral, and throat cancers, chronic lung diseases, coronary heart and cardiovascular diseases, as well as reproductive effects and sudden infant death syndrome.[53]

In addition to the direct health consequences of smoking, there are additional health consequences from nonsmokers' exposure to environmental tobacco smoke (ETS). These include deaths from lung cancer and coronary heart disease, as well as increased risk of a variety of respiratory diseases (including asthma, bronchitis, and pneumonia) in infants and children.[54] Similarly, smoking during pregnancy raises the likelihood of low-birth weight birth, premature birth, stillbirth, infant death, and other pregnancy complications, as well as raising the risk of sudden infant death.[55]

Clearly, cigarettes are unlike any other legal consumer product in terms of the health consequences resulting from their use. As described above, however, cigarette companies spent decades denying the health risks of smoking.

Public Policy

The emergence of scientific evidence on the health consequences of cigarette smoking in the mid-twentieth century stimulated an unprecedented, sustained, and somewhat successful antismoking campaign in the United States. Federal, state, and local governments have been quite active in this campaign, using a variety of policy interventions to encourage adult smokers to quit and to discourage young people from taking up smoking. Much of this effort, particularly in recent years, has focused on preventing youth initiation, given the growing evidence that the vast majority of adult smokers began smoking before age twenty.

Government intervention in cigarette markets is motivated by three significant market failures that generate inefficient outcomes.[56] First, there is an information failure in that many consumers do not fully understand the health consequences of smoking; to the extent that consumers have general information about the health effects of smoking (e.g., that smoking causes lung cancer), there is evidence indicating that they have distorted perceptions of the risks of smoking compared to other health risks and/or do not fully internalize these risks. The extent of this imperfect information in the United States is the subject of much debate[57]; perhaps the best example of this is the continued belief among many that light and low-tar cigarettes are less harmful than other cigarettes, as described above. Second, there is an additional information failure related to the addictive nature of cigarette smoking. Most smokers, when initiating smoking, significantly underestimate the risk of becoming addicted to nicotine, only coming to fully appreciate the strength of the addiction years later when, as most adult smokers eventually do, they attempt to quit. Survey data from the United States and other countries clearly indicate that the vast majority of adult smokers regret ever starting smoking and, given the chance to do it over, would not begin.[58] These two information failures are particularly significant given that most smoking initiation occurs among young people who have the least appreciation for the long-term health consequences of smoking and limited, at best, understanding of addiction. Among tenth-grade students, for example, nearly one-third do not perceive "great risk" from smoking one or more packs of cigarettes daily.[59] Similarly, most high school seniors who smoked but did not believe they would still be smoking five years later are still smoking when resurveyed.[60] Finally, there are clear externalities from cigarette smoking. As described above, there are significant health consequences for nonsmokers resulting from exposure to ETS. The evidence on whether or not there are net financial externalities as well (e.g., from publicly funded treatment of diseases caused by smoking) is mixed.

Many policy interventions directly target these market failures.[61] Support for research on the health consequences of cigarette smoking, the dissemination of findings from this research through the Surgeon General's reports and other channels, mandatory health warning labels on cigarette packaging and advertising, school-based educational programs, and mass-media antismoking campaigns that provide information on the consequences of smoking directly address the imperfect information about the health consequences of smoking. Similarly, these activities, coupled with publicly supported smoking cessation efforts (e.g., state "quit-lines" that provide cessation counseling and subsidization of pharmacotherapies for smoking cessation), help address the addiction-related information failures and their consequences for at least some smokers who want to quit. Bans on various forms of cigarette advertising and promotion, as well as the FTC's regulation of the content of remaining advertising, are steps toward limiting the dissemination of potentially misleading information and reducing young people's exposure to the positive imagery contained in cigarette advertising at a time when they may be most receptive to it.

Similarly, restrictions on smoking in a variety of public places and in private workplaces directly address some of the externalities resulting from nonsmokers' exposure to environmental tobacco smoke. These restrictions have been expanded and strengthened in recent years, with many states and localities banning smoking in virtually all indoor public places (including workplaces). The litigation brought by states seeking compensation for publicly funded health-care costs for treating smoking-related diseases focused on some of the financial externalities caused by smoking. Still other policies targeting youth, such as prohibitions

on the retail sales of tobacco products to minors and restrictions on youth purchase, use, or possession of these products, directly address some of the concerns arising from the relatively larger impact of information failures on young people. Finally, increases in cigarette excise taxes have become a widely used and powerful policy tool for reducing cigarette smoking, particularly among the younger and/or less educated populations that are most responsive to price and that may respond less to other interventions. While tobacco control policies and other efforts have been considerably strengthened over time, this progress has been slowed by the continued opposition to most of these efforts from the cigarette and other tobacco product manufacturers.

By some measures, the antismoking campaign of the past half century has been highly successful. Adult smoking prevalence in 2004 was about half its level in the year following the release of the first Surgeon General's report.[62] After rising for much of the mid-1990s, youth smoking prevalence has fallen steadily since the MSA; high school senior smoking prevalence is at its lowest level in the thirty years for which data have been regularly collected.[63] Per-capita cigarette consumption in 2005 was less than half of its 1976 peak.[64] As a result, lung cancer death rates are declining, as are some of the other health consequences of smoking.

While there has been much progress in reducing smoking, approximately 44.5 million adults continued to smoke in 2004, and estimates indicate that 3,900 adolescents ages twelve through seventeen initiate smoking every day, while 1,500 of them initiate daily smoking.[65] Prevalence is higher in some population subgroups, particularly those that are less educated and/or have low incomes, and there are substantial geographic differences in smoking rates (in large part related to the historical significance of tobacco growing and manufacturing across regions and in the resulting policy environment). The majority of adult smokers express an interest in quitting and many try to quit smoking each year, but few are successful. Exposure to ETS remains high, with about 60 percent of nonsmokers presenting biological evidence of ETS exposure and an estimated 22 percent of minors exposed to ETS at home.[66] Given these patterns, many millions of people currently alive will die prematurely from diseases caused by smoking. Moreover, comprehensive efforts to reduce smoking appear to be on the wane. Perhaps most disappointing to the public health community has been the failure of most states to use MSA payments they receive to support tobacco control programs. While these programs received unprecedented funding in the years following the MSA, the funds dedicated to these programs fell well short of CDC-recommended levels in nearly all states, with funding levels in many states falling in recent years.[67]

Conclusions

A New Millennium, a New Industry?

The U.S. cigarette industry is clearly in transition as it enters the twenty-first century. After decades of obfuscation, cigarette companies now publicly state that cigarette smoking causes a number of health consequences and that nicotine is addictive (although there are substantial differences across companies in the extent and explicitness of these public statements).[68] The major tobacco companies have developed their own youth smoking prevention programs, some of which have included large-scale antismoking advertising targeting children and their parents.[69] Spurred by the successes of the 1990s, litigation against the industry has continued and expanded. Cigarette demand is declining rapidly, in part in response to continually stronger state and local tobacco control policies, comprehensive tobacco control

programs, and generally increasing antismoking sentiment. Numerous new firms have entered the market, reducing the combined market share of the major companies to levels not seen for many decades. Firms are developing and marketing new products, some of which are purported to be less harmful than existing cigarettes. Proposals to grant the FDA authority to regulate cigarettes and other tobacco products are being debated, with cigarette companies divided in their support for FDA regulation.[70] How these and other developments will impact the future of the U.S. cigarette industry is unclear. One thing is certain, however: The U.S. cigarette industry of the twenty-first century will be as intriguing and controversial as it has been throughout its history.

Notes

I thank Tyler LaPlante for the outstanding research assistance he provided in developing this chapter. I have served as an expert witness and consultant in litigation and other proceedings involving cigarette companies, most recently in *U.S. v. Philip Morris, et al.*

1. Historical accounts differ on when cigarettes first appeared, with most suggesting the late seventeenth or early eighteenth century. See, for example, Susan Wagner, *Cigarette Country: Tobacco in American History and Politics* (New York: Praeger, 1971, pp. 32–33, and Wikipedia's entry for "Cigarette," http://en.wikipedia.org/wiki/Cigarette (accessed May 12, 2006).
2. S. Wagner, *Cigarette Country*, p. 33.
3. S. Wagner, *Cigarette Country*, p. 37.
4. Richard Kluger, *Ashes to Ashes* (New York: Alfred A. Knopf, 1996), p. 19.
5. Howard Cox, *The Global Cigarette: Origins and Evolution of British American Tobacco, 1880–1945* (Oxford: Oxford University Press, 2000), p. 30; R. Kluger, *Ashes to Ashes*, p. 20.
6. R. Kluger, *Ashes to Ashes*, p. 22.
7. R. Kluger, *Ashes to Ashes*, pp. 23–26; S. Wagner, *Cigarette Country*, pp. 37–38.
8. S. Wagner, *Cigarette Country*, p. 40.
9. These abbreviations will be used throughout the chapter for consistency; over time, the names of some of the companies changed (e.g., Liggett & Myers became the Liggett Group, while American Tobacco Company became American Brands).

10. S. Wagner, *Cigarette Country,* p. 50.

11. F.M. Scherer and David Ross, *Industrial Market Structure and Economic Performance* (Boston: Houghton Mifflin, 1990), pp. 340–41.

12. This meeting represents a critical event in the ongoing U.S. Department of Justice (DOJ) case against the major cigarette companies. The DOJ describes the meeting as the start of a decades-long conspiracy to hide or distort the scientific evidence on the health consequences of smoking.

13. Charyn D. Sutton and Robert G. Robinson, "The Marketing of Menthol Cigarettes in the United States: Populations, Messages, and Channels," *Nicotine & Tobacco Research* 6, Supplement 1 (February 2004), pp. S83–S91.

14. Gideon Doron, *The Smoking Paradox: Public Regulation in the Cigarette Industry* (Cambridge, MA: Abt Books, 1979).

15. The compensatory behavior includes deeper inhalation and blockage of air vents on filters; the limits of the FTC machine readings for tar and nicotine, compensation, and related issues are discussed in depth in National Cancer Institute Monograph 13, *Risks Associated with Smoking Cigarettes with Low Tar Machine-Measured Yields of Tar and Nicotine* (Bethesda, MD: National Institutes of Health, National Cancer Institute, 2001). A collection of papers describing smokers' perceptions of the risks from these products is contained in the *Nicotine & Tobacco Research* supplement on "Tobacco Risk Perceptions and Behavior: Implications for Tobacco Control" 6, Supplement 3 (December 2004).

16. Federal Trade Commission, *Report to Congress Pursuant to the Public Health Cigarette Smoking Act* (Washington DC: Federal Trade Commission, various years).

17. Much of this discussion is based on the review of tobacco litigation contained in U.S. Department of Health and Human Services, *Reducing Tobacco Use: A Report of the Surgeon General* (Atlanta, GA: U.S. Department of Health and Human Services, 2000).

18. Theodore H. Keeler, Teh-Wei Hu, Michael Ong, and Hai-Yen Sung, "The U.S. National Tobacco Settlement: The Effects of Advertising and Price Changes on Cigarette Consumption," *Applied Economics* 36 (2004), pp. 1623–39.

19. Frank A. Sloan, Carrie A. Matthews, and Justin G. Trogdon, "Impacts of the Master Settlement Agreement on the Tobacco Industry," *Tobacco Control* 13 (2004), pp. 356–61; Stuart J. Fowler and William F. Ford, "Has a Quarter-Trillion-Dollar Settlement Helped the Tobacco Industry?" *Journal of Economics and Finance* 28 (Fall 2004), pp. 430–44.

20. For more details, see the Department of Justice's amended complaint available online at: www.usdoj.gov/civil/cases/tobacc02/DOJ%20Web%20-%20Amended%20Complaint.pdf.

21. U.S. Census Bureau, 2002 Economic Census, Cigarette Manufacturing, Detailed Statistics.

22. Correspondence from Joan E. Fina, attorney at the FTC, regarding FOIA02004–000200 Cigarette Tar, Nicotine & Carbon Monoxide Numbers for 1999–2002 (2003), online at: www.ftc.gov/foia/cigarette2004–00020.pdf.

23. Henry Saffer, "Tobacco Advertising and Promotion," in Prabhat Jha and Frank J. Chaloupka, eds., *Tobacco Control in Developing Countries,* pp. 215–36 (Oxford: Oxford University Press, 2000).

24. Campaign for Tobacco-Free Kids, "Big Tobacco Still Targeting Kids," online at: www.tobaccofreekids.org/reports/targeting.

25. Melanie Wakefield, Christopher Morley, Judith K. Horan, and K. Michael Cummings, "The Cigarette Pack as Image: New Evidence from Tobacco Industry Documents," *Tobacco Control* 11, Supplement 1 (2002), pp. i73–i80.

26. Benjamin Lê Cook, Geoffrey Ferris Wayne, Lois Keithly, and Gregory Connolly, "One Size Does Not Fit All: How the Tobacco Industry Has Altered Cigarette Design to Target Consumer Groups with Specific Psychological and Psychosocial Needs," *Addiction* 98 (2003), pp. 1547–61.

27. Scherer and Ross, *Industrial Market Structure and Economic Performance,* p. 140.

28. Stephen J. Farr, Carol Horton Tremblay, and Victor J. Tremblay, "The Welfare Effect of Advertising Restrictions in the U.S. Cigarette Industry," *Review of Industrial Organization* 18 (2001), pp. 147–60; Carol Horton Tremblay and Victor J. Tremblay, "Re-Interpreting the Effect of an Advertising Ban on Cigarette Smoking," *International Journal of Advertising* 18 (1999), pp. 41–49; E. Woodrow Eckard, Jr., "Competition and the Cigarette TV Advertising Ban," *Economic Inquiry* 29 (1991), pp. 119–33; Mark L. Mitchell and J. Harold Mulherin, "Finessing the Political System: The Cigarette Advertising Ban," *Southern Economic Journal* 54 (1988), pp. 855–62.

29. Exhibit T provides the rationale for the escrow payments:

> It would be contrary to the policy of the State if tobacco product manufacturers who determine not to enter into such a settlement could use a resulting cost advantage to derive large, short-term profits in the years before liability may arise without ensuring that the state will have an eventual source of recovery from them if they are proved to have acted culpably. It is thus in the interest of the State to require that such manufacturers establish a reserve fund to guarantee a source of compensation and to prevent such manufacturers from deriving large, short-term profits and then becoming judgment-proof before liability may arise (Master Settlement Agreement, Section I, paragraph f).

> Full text of MSA available online at: www.naag.org/backpages/naag/tobacco/msa/msa-pdf/.

30. National Association of Attorneys General (NAAG), *Model Complementary Legislation: Introduction and Analysis* (Washington DC: National Association of Attorneys

General, 2003); available online at: www.naag.org/up-load/1043252723_CompLegSummaryandAnalysis.pdf.

31. Ibid.

32. Ibid.

33. Ibid.

34. The details are somewhat more complicated, but the net effect is about the same.

35. U.S. Census Bureau, 1997 and 2002 Economic Census, Retail Trade statistics.

36. An independent arbitrator—Nobel laureate economist Daniel McFadden—recently determined that the MSA had been a "significant factor" in the participating manufacturers' combined market share loss in 2003 (relative to the 1997 pre-MSA baseline), triggering a potential reduction in the MSA payments these companies make to states. Whether or not payments will ultimately be reduced is unclear and depends, at least in part, on whether or not states can demonstrate that they have "diligently enforced the provisions of the MSA targeting the NPMs."

37. U.S. Department of Health and Human Services (US-DHHS), *Reducing Tobacco Use: A Report of the Surgeon General* (Atlanta, GA: U.S. Department of Health and Human Services, 2000).

38. See USDHHS (2000) for a review of relevant studies.

39. Philip Morris, "Pricing Policy," September 28, 1976; Bates Number 2023769635–2023769655.

40. Myron Johnston, Philip Morris, "Handling an Excise Tax Increase," September 3, 1987; Bates Number 2022216179–2022216180.

41. John A. Tauras, Richard M. Peck, and Frank J. Chaloupka, "The Role of Retail Prices and Promotions in Determining Cigarette Brand Market Shares," *Review of Industrial Organization* 28 (2006), pp. 253–84.

42. Gary S. Becker, Michael Grossman, and Kevin M. Murphy, "An Empirical Analysis of Cigarette Addiction," *American Economic Review* 84 (1994), pp. 396–418; Mark H. Showalter, *Essays in Applied Econometrics: Essay III: Monopoly Behavior with Intertemporal Demand,* PhD dissertation, Massachusetts Institute of Technology, 1991.

43. Federal Trade Commission, *Cigarette Report for 2003* (2005); these reflect expenditures of parent companies for PM, RJR, B&W, Lorillard, L&M, Commonwealth, Santa Fe, and Vector brands.

44. Frank J. Chaloupka, K. Michael Cummings, Christopher P. Morley, and Judith K. Horan, "Tax, Price and Cigarette Smoking: Evidence from the Tobacco Documents and Implications for Tobacco Company Marketing Strategies," *Tobacco Control* 11, Supplement 1 (2002), pp. i62–i72; Frank J. Chaloupka, written testimony in *US v. Philip Morris et al.,* available online at: www.usdoj.gov/civil/cases/tobacc02/Chaloupka%20Direct%20-%20final.pdf.

45. See the testimony of industry marketing executives, other industry representatives, and various expert witnesses

in the federal tobacco litigation (*US v. Philip Morris et al.*), as well as at least some company Web sites, for a discussion of the increased focus of marketing efforts on a limited number of brands. Written testimony of government witnesses is available online at: www.usdoj.gov/civil/cases/tobacc02/, and that of industry witnesses is available at: www.altria.com/media/03_06_03_04_05_04_dojwitnessfilings.asp.

46. In 1994, major cigarette companies provided the U.S. Department of Health and Human Services with a list of 599 additives used in producing their cigarettes.

47. "Ammonia Key to Marlboro's Success," Associated Press, December 11, 1999.

48. Much of the discussion that follows draws heavily on Dorothy Hatsukami and Stephen Hecht, *Hope or Hazard? What Research Tells Us About "Potentially Reduced-Exposure Products"* (Minneapolis: University of Minnesota Transdisciplinary Tobacco Use Research Center, 2005).

49. Online at: www.rjrt.com/company/brandsPortfolio.aspx (accessed May 18, 2006).

50. Profit margin is defined as operating income divided by revenues.

51. L&M's margin in 2005 was higher than in other recent years, due to a one-time revenue gain from sale of some of its assets.

52. Centers for Disease Control and Prevention (CDC), "Annual Smoking-Attributable Mortality, Years of Life Lost, and Productivity Losses–United States, 1997–2001," *Morbidity and Mortality Weekly Report* 54 (2005), pp. 625–28.

53. USDHHS, *The Health Consequences of Smoking: A Report of the Surgeon General* (Atlanta, GA: Author, 2004).

54. National Cancer Institute, *Health Effects of Exposure to Environmental Tobacco Smoke* (Bethesda, MD: National Institutes of Health, National Cancer Institute, 1999).

55. USDHHS, *The Health Consequences of Smoking: A Report of the Surgeon General.*

56. More detailed discussions of these market failures can be found in Prabhat Jha, Philip Musgrove, Frank J. Chaloupka, and Ayda Yurekli, "The Economic Rationale for Intervention in the Tobacco Market," in Prabhat Jha and Frank J. Chaloupka, eds., *Tobacco Control in Developing Countries* (Oxford: Oxford University Press, 2000), and Prabhat Jha and Frank J. Chaloupka, *Curbing the Epidemic: Governments and the Economics of Tobacco Control* (Washington, DC: World Bank, 1999).

57. See, for example, the testimony of several industry and government expert witnesses in the *US v. Philip Morris et al.* litigation cited above.

58. Geoffrey T. Fong, David Hammond, Fritz L. Laux, Mark P. Zanna, K. Michael Cummings, Ron Borland, and Hana Ross, "The Near-Universal Experience of Regret Among Smokers in Four Countries: Findings from the International Tobacco Control Policy Evaluation Survey," *Nicotine &*

Tobacco Research 6 Supplement 3 (December 2004), pp. S341–S351.

59. University of Michigan News Service, "Decline in Youth Smoking Appears to be Nearing Its End," online at: www.monitoringthefuture.org/pressreleases/05cigpr_complete.pdf.

60. Lloyd D. Johnston, Patrick M. O'Malley, Jerald G. Bachman, and John E. Schulenberg, *Monitoring the Future: National Survey Results on Drug Use, 1975–2004, Vol. II: College Students and Adults Ages 19–45* (Bethesda, MD: National Institute on Drug Abuse, 2005).

61. For more detailed reviews on the use and impact of interventions aimed at reducing cigarette smoking in the United States and elsewhere, see: Frank J. Chaloupka and Kenneth E. Warner, "The Economics of Smoking," in Anthony J. Culyer and Joseph P. Newhouse, ed., *Handbook of Health Economics,* pp. 1539–627 (New York: Elsevier Science B.V., 2000); USDHHS, *Reducing Tobacco Use: A Report of the Surgeon General;* and Prabhat Jha and Frank J. Chaloupka, eds., *Tobacco Control in Developing Countries.*

62. Prevalence data reported by CDC online at: www.cdc.gov/tobacco/research_data/adults_prev/prevali.htm.

63. University of Michigan News Service, "Decline in Youth Smoking Appears to Be Nearing Its End," online at: www.monitoringthefuture.org/pressreleases/05cigpr_complete.pdf.

64. Orzechowski and Walker, *The Tax Burden on Tobacco* (Arlington: Orzechowski and Walker, 2006).

65. CDC, "Cigarette Smoking Among Adults—United States, 2004," *Morbidity and Mortality Weekly Report* 54 (2005), pp. 1121–24; CDC "Fact Sheet: Youth and Tobacco Use: Current Estimates" (2005), online at: www.cdc.gov/tobacco/research_data/youth/Youth_Factsheet.htm.

66. CDC "Fact Sheet: Secondhand Smoke" (2004), online at: www.cdc.gov/tobacco/factsheets/secondhand_smoke_factsheet.htm.

67. American Heart Association, American Cancer Society, Campaign for Tobacco-Free Kids, and American Lung Association, *A Broken Promise to Our Children: The 1998 State Tobacco Settlement Agreement Seven Years Later* (2005), online at: www.tobaccofreekids.org/reports/settlements/2006/fullreport.pdf.

68. For example, on its Web site, RJR states:

R.J. Reynolds Tobacco Company (R.J. Reynolds) believes that smoking, in combination with other factors, causes disease in some individuals. The U.S. Surgeon General and other public health and medical officials, including the U.S. Centers for Disease Control and Prevention (CDC), have concluded that smoking causes many chronic diseases including heart disease and lung cancer. (See the 2004 Surgeon General's Report [SGR], "The Health Consequences of Smoking.") There is universal awareness of those conclusions and individuals should rely on them when making decisions regarding smoking (www.rjrt.com/smoking/summaryCover.aspx, accessed May 20, 2006).

With respect to addiction, the RJR Web site states:

Smoking is addictive as that term is commonly used today. Many smokers find it difficult to quit and some find it extremely difficult. However, we disagree with characterizing smoking as being addictive in the same sense as heroin, cocaine or similar illegal substances. Any smoker with a sincere desire and determination to stop smoking can—and should—quit. The best way to reduce the risks of smoking, of course, is to quit (www.rjrt.com/smoking/summaryCover.aspx, accessed May 20, 2006).

PM goes a bit further on its Web site with respect to the health consequences of smoking:

Philip Morris USA agrees with the overwhelming medical and scientific consensus that cigarette smoking causes lung cancer, heart disease, emphysema and other serious diseases in smokers. Smokers are far more likely to develop serious diseases, like lung cancer, than non-smokers. There is no safe cigarette. (www.philipmorrisusa.com/en/health_issues/defaultasp, accessed May 20, 2006).

And with respect to addiction:

"Philip Morris USA agrees with the overwhelming medical and scientific consensus that cigarette smoking is addictive. It can be very difficult to quit smoking, but this should not deter smokers who want to quit from trying to do so" (www.philipmorrisusa.com/en/health_issues/default.asp, accessed May 20, 2006).

69. There is little evidence, however, that these efforts have been effective in preventing youth smoking initiation. Instead, some research indicates that they have been counterproductive and may contribute to increases in the likelihood that youth smoke (e.g., Melanie Wakefield, Yvonne Terry-McElrath, Sherry Emery, Henry Saffer, Frank J. Chaloupka, Glen Szczypka, Brian Flay, Patrick O'Malley, and Lloyd Johnston, "Impact of Televised Tobacco Industry Smoking Prevention Advertising on Youth Smoking—Related Beliefs, Intentions, and Behavior," *American Journal of Public Health* 96 (December 2006), pp. 2154–60.

70. PM has been the most vocal supporter of FDA regulation. Some analysts view this support skeptically, suggesting that the primary reason for PM's support is that this regulation would help protect its position as the market leader by making it more difficult for other firms to develop and market new, less harmful products.

Selected Readings

Chaloupka, Frank J., and Kenneth E. Warner. "The Economics of Smoking." In Anthony J. Cuyler and Joseph P. Newhouse, eds., *The Handbook of Health Economics*. New York: Elsevier Science B.V., 2000.

Jha, Prabhat, and Frank J. Chaloupka, eds. *Tobacco Control in Developing Countries*. Oxford: Oxford University Press, 2000.

Kluger, Richard. *Ashes to Ashes: America's Hundred Year Cigarette War, the Public Health, and the Unabashed Triumph of Philip Morris*. New York: Alfred A. Knopf, 1996.

Tenant, Richard. *The American Cigarette Industry*. New Haven: Yale University Press, 1950.

Wagner, Susan. *Cigarette Country: Tobacco in American History and Politics*. New York: Praeger, 1971.

5

Distilled Spirits

Spirited Competition or Regulated Monopoly?

Jon P. Nelson

In December of 1932, a joint resolution was passed in Congress calling on the states to act on the Twenty-first Amendment repealing the Prohibition Amendment. By December 1933, thirty-six states had ratified the amendment, thus ending fourteen years of alcohol prohibition, lawlessness, and corruption.[1] The "Noble Experiment" was over, and President Franklin D. Roosevelt hailed the "return of individual freedom," expressing confidence that the American people would restrain from "excessive use of intoxicating liquors."[2] Repeal of Prohibition gave the states the right to ban or restrict the distribution and sale of alcohol beverages within their borders, including regulation of hours and days of operation, container sizes, local advertising, price changes, and so forth. The predictable result was a patchwork of laws that represents a natural laboratory for economic research. Three states voted to remain dry and to continue lucrative opportunities for moonshiners and bootleggers. Although dry in name only, Kansas finally ended statewide prohibition in 1948, Oklahoma in 1959, and Mississippi in 1966.[3] Twenty-seven states resumed the sale of alcohol beverages through licensed private retail outlets (the "open license" states). License states with local options also allow local governments to choose between "wet" or "dry" status, typically through municipal or countywide referendums. The other eighteen states decided to operate wholesale and retail monopolies for off-premise liquor and wine sales, and are collectively known as the "monopoly control" states.[4] Some of these states are license states for wine, but Pennsylvania and Utah also monopolize retail sale of table wine. At the federal level, regulatory authority rests with the Treasury Department's Alcohol and Tobacco Tax and Trade Bureau (TTB). Some of TTB's alcohol authority is shared with the Federal Trade Commission (FTC) and the Food and Drug Administration (FDA). In summary, the liquor industry is a highly regulated sector of the economy, which raises issues of regulatory objectives, methods, and effects.

Although Prohibition applied to all alcohol beverages, hard liquor was singled out as the source of the worst abuses of "tied-house" saloons, wherein retailers were partially owned by suppliers. As a result, laws and regulations that govern the distribution and sale of distilled spirits are more stringent than similar laws for beer and wine. This difference extends to federal and state alcohol taxes. One consequence of differential regulation and taxation is consumer substitution among beverages due to price or accessibility differences.[5] Another consequence is that changes in the production and distribution of liquor attract greater public attention and scrutiny. For example, in June of 1996, the now defunct distiller Joseph

E. Seagram aired television advertisements for Crown Royal Canadian Whiskey on an NBC-TV affiliate in Corpus Christi, Texas, thereby breaking the industry's long-standing voluntary ban of broadcast advertising (on radio since 1936 and TV since 1948).[6] Reactions to the ads included a full-page protest in the *New York Times* and a "Just Say No" bill introduced in Congress by Democratic representative Joseph Kennedy of Massachusetts. President Bill Clinton asked the industry to go back to the ban, calling Seagram's TV ads "simply irresponsible." He also requested an investigation by the Federal Communications Commission (FCC). Although a full-scale FCC inquiry never materialized, the chain of events during 1996–2002 is illustrative of the compromises that characterize regulatory processes. First, the industry never advertised extensively on network TV, and instead has placed ads on cable TV programs. Second, in late 2001, NBC-TV announced its intention to allow alcohol ads after 9 P.M. on programs such as *Saturday Night Live*, and the controversy shifted focus onto the network. NBC eventually reinstated its voluntary ban to realign itself with the other three major networks. Third, absent explicit directions from Congress, the FCC's authority was questioned by many observers, who pointed out that the FTC had primary jurisdiction over matters relating to deceptive or unfair advertising in all media, including broadcasting. As a new equilibrium emerged and other public issues came to the forefront, the broadcast advertising controversy largely fizzled away as a topic for intense public scrutiny. In the end, neither spirited competition nor significantly tighter regulation emerged as a clear-cut policy.

The U.S. distilled spirits industry is characterized by a three-tier structure that eliminates vertical integration among key sectors: Licensed producers/suppliers sell to licensed wholesale distributors, and the wholesalers sell to licensed retailers. As mandated by federal and state laws, each tier must operate independently from the other two tiers. Some states add a fourth tier and require that on-premise retailers purchase supplies from licensed off-premise retailers. In about a third of the states, price-posting laws require that price changes be published thirty to ninety days before they become effective. Decreased demand, regulation, and other legal pressures forced major consolidations in the production and wholesale sectors during the 1990s, and the industry is now moderately concentrated. The largest U.S. producers also are integrated or partnered into a global industry that is dominated by a few large worldwide producers. Some products, such as Scotch whiskey and tequila, are produced exclusively in other countries and imported in bottled and bulk forms by licensed agents. Between 1977 and 1997, the number of U.S. liquor producers in the *Census of Manufacturers* declined from 64 to 44 and the number of distilleries fell from 104 to 60. The *1997 Census of Wholesale Trade* lists 1,531 establishments classified as "wine and distilled alcoholic beverage wholesalers," compared to 1,610 in 1987 and 1,813 in 1977. However, the trade association for the sector, the Wine and Spirits Wholesalers of America, claims that its 500 members account for 90 percent of sales at the wholesale level. Many wholesalers operate in narrow geographic markets, but local markets in the 1960s that had a dozen or more wholesale-tier competitors now have only two to four full-service competitors.[7] These structural changes in liquor production and distribution create concerns about the future competitiveness of the industry.

This study examines the structure of the distilled spirits industry and its leading firms, selected aspects of industry regulation, and the controversies that surround advertising of distilled spirits. The next two sections summarize the industry's market structure, including product and brand identification, concentration, product differentiation, identity and strategies of the leading distillers, recent mergers, and entry conditions. The following section presents the so-called economic theory of regulation as a framework to examine past, present, and future alcohol regulations. Following descriptions of the major federal regulatory agencies, the theory is applied to several episodes in the liquor industry. Lastly, the study examines empirically two aspects of distilled spirits advertising: first, the causal relationship (if any) between liquor sales and advertising; and, second, the possible targeting by liquor advertisers of adolescent magazine readers. The data used for the empirical investigations are contained herein, and the reader is encouraged to replicate or extend the econometric analyses.

Market Structure and Leading Brands

Product Identification

Production of distilled spirits consists of two essential stages: (1) fermentation, whereby the sugars in an organic substance such as grain mash, fruit juices, sugarcane, or potatoes are converted to alcohol; and (2) distillation, whereby the fermented beverage is boiled and condensed to make the final product. Both pot stills and continuous column stills are employed at the distillation stage. Liquor production is not labor-intensive: U.S. distilled spirits producers (NAICS 312140) had 5,600 employees in 2002, including 3,700 production workers. One-third are employed in the state of Kentucky. In addition to the principal raw materials, other key inputs are glass and plastic containers, cooperage or barrels used in aging, and paperboard boxes and containers. Distilled spirits are divided into three major categories: brown spirits including American whiskey and bourbon and Canadian, Irish, and Scotch whiskeys; white spirits including vodka, gin, rum, and tequila; and

specialties including brandies, schnapps, cordials, liqueurs, and pre-prepared cocktails. A relatively recent development is the mass marketing of low-alcohol flavored alcohol beverages and pre-prepared cocktails. In 2004, this category captured 4 percent of sales compared to only 2 percent in 1984. Within each beverage category, it is common to divide brands according to positioning by price: super-premium, premium, and popular or value-priced brands. Total sales of all types of spirits by volume in 2004 were 393.8 million gallons or 165.65 million 9-liter cases.[8] Imports account for about 40 percent of supplier sales by volume. Supplier sales revenues were $16.4 billion and wholesaler sales were $23.0 billion, whereas retail sales were estimated at $49.4 billion. On-premise retail sales were $28.3 billion, and $21.1 billion was spent for off-premise consumption. The typical retail markup is 25 to 30 percent of the wholesale price for off-premise sales, but on-premise markups at bars and restaurants can exceed 500 percent. The biggest sales period is from Thanksgiving to New Year's Eve, accounting for 30 to 35 percent of yearly sales of distilled spirits.

Market Concentration

In 2004, there were twenty liquor suppliers in the United States with sales exceeding 1 million cases or $100 million of revenue. These twenty suppliers account for 90 percent of the industry's sales volume and 87 percent of sales revenue. The top six producers/suppliers in the United States are: Diageo NA, 22.5 percent of volume; Constellation Brands, 9.5 percent; Bacardi USA, 9.2 percent; Jim Beam Brands, 8.6 percent, Allied Domecq/Pernod Ricard USA, 7.7 percent; and Brown-Forman Beverages, 6.5 percent. The industry's four-firm concentration ratio is 49.8 percent, while the twenty-firm Herfindahl-Hirschman Index or HHI is 924. Using the Merger Guidelines issued by the

FTC and the Department of Justice (DOJ), the HHI value is slightly below the critical value of 1,000 that marks the line between an unconcentrated and a moderately concentrated industry. However, in two recent merger cases, the FTC used narrower product market definitions based on price-positioning to assess competitive impacts of mergers between leading producers of spirits. These lawsuits and the FTC's market definitions are discussed below. Further, the geographic market area for suppliers is global, and many of the top U.S. suppliers are subsidiaries of multinational corporations. Since 2000, imports can enter the United States on a duty-free basis, except for imported rums. However, tariffs and regulations often limit U.S. exports to other countries, especially developing countries and countries with nontariff barriers. For example, China has an estimated 35,000 distilleries and is the world's largest producer and consumer of distilled spirits.[9] While recent trade negotiations yielded significantly lower tariffs, U.S. liquor exports to China are minimal. A particular trade problem is the nontariff practices of government monopolies, such as Canada's provincial liquor control boards, which limit the number of imported products that retailers can carry and restrict the stocking of new imported products. These practices serve to insulate the home market from the full forces of global competition.

Consumption and Price Trends

Table 5.1 shows that, in 2004, apparent consumption of distilled spirits was 393.8 million gallons or about 1.89 gallons per capita for the adult population ages twenty-one years and older. This is 14 percent less than record sales of 449.5 million gallons in 1981. The record year for per capita adult use was 1971, when consumption reached 3.06 gallons. Between 1971 and 2004, liquor consumption per capita declined by 38 percent. Some of the de-

crease is due to consumer purchases of other beverages (beer, wine, soft drinks, and bottled water) and increased consumption of higher-priced premium spirits, especially by wealthy or status-conscious individuals. Nevertheless, it is a simple fact that U.S. adults are imbibing less when it comes to distilled spirits. A possible economic reason is an increase in the relative price. However, as shown in Table 5.1, the relative or real price of distilled spirits declined substantially between 1953 and 1983, and after that date it either remained constant or decreased slightly. In part, the price decline reflects that federal and state excise taxes on liquor failed to keep pace with general inflation in the economy. This trend is often singled out as a justification to increase taxes as a way to address social problems attributed to alcohol, including underage consumption.[10] Further, the price index for distilled spirits has risen less than that for beer, leading to a decline in the price of spirits relative to beer. Another demand variable, real disposable income, doubled between 1953 and 1983, but income gains after that date have been generally smaller. After 1983, real income on a per capita basis rose by 60 percent, and stood at $17,673 in 2004 compared to $11,130 in 1983. Due to a high-income elasticity of demand, any real income gains should increase the demand for distilled spirits. One expectation was that aging (and wealthier) baby boomers would consume less beer, and this might spark a renewed interest in distilled spirits, well-established brands, and traditional cocktails. This shift has been modest, and many of the industry's new products feature unusual flavor combinations and colors that are designed to appeal to consumers in the twenty-one to twenty-nine age bracket. Unique low-alcohol brands such as Heaven Hill's Hpnotiq liqueur, a blue-hued combination of vodka, fruit juice, and cognac, might not be recognized by earlier generations of drinkers.

Retail prices for alcohol beverages reflect excise

Table 5.1

Distilled Spirits Sales, Consumption, and Prices, 1950–2004

Year	Sales (mil. gal.)	Per capita (gal.)	Spirits price (82/84=100)	Beer price (82/84=100)	Consumer price index	Real price spirits	Real income ($ per capita)
1950	190.0	1.95	NA	NA	24.1	NA	5,528
1951	193.8	1.97	NA	NA	26.0	NA	5,587
1952	183.7	1.85	NA	NA	26.5	NA	5,693
1953	194.7	1.94	58.9	38.9	26.7	220.5	5,858
1954	189.5	1.87	59.2	40.4	26.9	219.9	5,852
1955	199.6	1.95	59.5	40.1	26.8	221.9	6,037
1956	215.2	2.08	60.1	40.7	27.2	220.9	6,120
1957	212.1	2.03	62.1	41.5	28.1	221.0	6,167
1958	215.5	2.05	62.3	41.4	28.9	215.6	6,128
1959	225.5	2.12	63.1	41.7	29.1	216.9	6,218
1960	234.7	2.17	64.0	42.3	29.6	216.3	6,266
1961	241.5	2.21	64.4	42.4	29.9	215.5	6,367
1962	253.7	2.30	64.6	42.6	30.2	214.1	6,563
1963	259.0	2.32	65.4	43.0	30.6	213.6	6,718
1964	275.9	2.44	65.7	43.4	31.0	211.8	7,100
1965	294.2	2.58	65.9	43.8	31.5	209.1	7,415
1966	308.9	2.68	66.3	44.4	32.4	204.5	7,691
1967	324.8	2.79	67.0	45.2	33.4	200.5	7,900
1968	345.5	2.91	68.0	46.5	34.8	195.4	8,150
1969	363.2	3.01	68.7	47.7	36.7	187.2	8,288
1970	371.5	3.05	70.4	49.2	38.8	181.5	8,494
1971	382.3	3.06	71.3	51.0	40.5	176.2	8,705
1972	393.4	3.00	72.8	51.5	41.8	174.1	8,948
1973	404.4	3.01	73.2	52.3	44.4	164.8	9,450
1974	417.2	3.03	74.3	57.3	49.3	150.7	9,407
1975	423.4	3.02	76.5	63.4	53.8	142.2	9,433
1976	425.9	2.98	77.7	65.0	56.9	136.6	9,687
1977	432.6	2.98	78.8	66.0	60.6	130.0	9,939
1978	445.3	3.01	82.0	69.6	65.2	125.8	10,294
1979	448.2	2.99	85.1	76.9	72.6	117.2	10,484
1980	449.4	2.90	89.8	84.8	82.4	109.0	10,643
1981	449.5	2.85	94.9	90.9	90.9	104.4	10,769
1982	437.7	2.74	98.2	95.2	96.5	101.8	10,837
1983	431.1	2.65	100.4	100.7	99.6	100.8	11,130
1984	426.1	2.59	101.4	104.2	103.9	97.6	11,872
1985	416.3	2.49	105.3	106.7	107.6	97.9	12,193
1986	394.2	2.37	113.3	108.7	109.6	103.4	12,490
1987	388.2	2.30	114.4	110.9	113.6	100.7	12,685
1988	378.1	2.21	116.1	114.4	118.3	98.1	13,176
1989	371.5	2.15	119.9	118.2	124.0	96.7	13,493
1990	374.5	2.17	125.7	123.6	130.7	96.2	13,690
1991	346.3	1.97	139.2	138.4	136.2	102.2	13,596
1992	354.7	1.97	141.5	143.5	140.3	100.9	13,959
1993	342.7	1.88	143.2	143.2	144.5	99.1	13,922
1994	334.5	1.84	144.3	143.4	148.2	97.4	14,126
1995	326.7	1.78	145.7	143.9	152.4	95.6	14,361
1996	326.5	1.75	147.5	147.4	156.9	94.0	14,652
1997	329.9	1.76	150.8	148.2	160.5	94.0	14,992
1998	334.2	1.77	152.7	148.5	163.0	93.7	15,653
1999	343.1	1.80	156.2	151.9	166.6	93.8	15,968
2000	353.8	1.79	162.3	156.8	172.2	94.3	16,608
2001	357.4	1.78	168.0	160.7	177.1	94.9	16,705
2002	364.5	1.79	171.4	164.7	179.9	95.3	17,012
2003	378.4	1.84	173.1	168.5	184.0	94.1	17,244
2004	393.8	1.89	175.3	174.6	188.9	92.8	17,673

Source: Adams Liquor Handbook 2005 (Norwalk, CT: Adams Business Media, 2005) for sales and adult per capita consumption; U.S. Bureau of Labor Statistics Web site for consumer price indexes, www.bls.gov/cpi/home.htm; and *Economic Report of the President* for real disposable personal income per capita, www.gpoaccess.gov/eop/tables05.htm.

Notes: Spirits price index is estimated for 1950–77 based on the price index for whiskey. Real income per capita is expressed in constant 1982/84 dollars using the implicit price deflator for GDP.

Table 5.2

Federal and State Alcohol Taxes, 2004

Tax and units	Spirits ($)	Beer ($)	Wine ($)
Federal tax rates:			
$ per proof gallon[a]	13.50	6.17	4.86
$ per wine gallon[b]	10.80	0.58	1.07
$ per 31-gallon barrel	—	18.00	—
$ per 750 ml. bottle (25.4 oz)	2.14	—	0.21
$ per six-pack (72 oz.)	—	0.33	—
State tax per proof gallon:			
California	4.12	2.13	0.91
Florida	8.12	5.11	10.22
Hawaii	7.48	9.89	6.27
Illinois	5.62	1.97	3.32
Kentucky	2.40	0.85	2.27
Missouri	2.50	0.64	1.36
New York	8.05	1.17	0.86
Texas	3.00	2.11	0.91
Wisconsin	4.06	0.64	1.14
License state median	4.69	2.00	3.13

Sources: Adams Liquor Handbook 2005; Distilled Spirits Council of the United States (DISCUS), *State Data Book* (Washington, DC: DISCUS, 2005); Federation of State Tax Administrators, *State Comparisons, January 1, 2005,* http://www.taxadmin.org/fta/rate/tax_stru.html.

[a]A proof gallon is one gallon at 100 proof or 50 percent alcohol by volume.

[b]A wine gallon of spirits is assumed to be 40 percent alcohol by volume or 80 proof; beer is 9.4 proof; and wine is 22 proof.

taxes levied by federal and state governments. Once referred to as sumptuary taxes, these taxes are now called sin taxes. Despite the label, it does not follow that excise taxes are set to regulate the external costs of alcohol consumption. Until recently, taxes on alcohol were often used as a revenue-increasing measure during and following wartime conflicts. In 1789, a young U.S. government imposed a tax on imported spirits to offset a portion of the Revolutionary War debt assumed from the states. In 1791, the tax was extended to domestic production of distilled spirits. Discriminatory enforcement led to a short-lived armed insurrection by frontier settlers in southwestern Pennsylvania, known as the Whiskey Rebellion of 1794.[11] Additional tax increases in 1864 and 1865 resulted in so much illegal distilling activity that Congress eventually rolled back the tax to the former level. Alcohol taxes also were levied on a "temporary" basis to help pay for World War II and the Korean Conflict. Between 1951 and 1984, the federal tax on distilled spirits was fixed at $10.50 per proof gallon. In real terms, the inflation-adjusted tax fell from $10.50 in 1951 to only $2.63 in 1984, a decline of 75 percent. The Tax Reform Bill of 1984 increased the tax to $12.50 per proof gallon, effective October 1, 1985. The Omnibus Budget Reconciliation Act of 1990 further increased the tax to $13.50 per proof gallon, effective January 1, 1991. Table 5.2 displays the distribution in 2004 for federal excise taxes by beverage, selected state taxes, and the median tax rate for the license states. Because federal and state alcohol taxes are not uniform across beverages, differential tax rates are a source of continuing

Figure 5.1 **Percentage Change in Per Capita Ethanol Consumption, 1977–2003** (gal. per capita ages 14 and older)

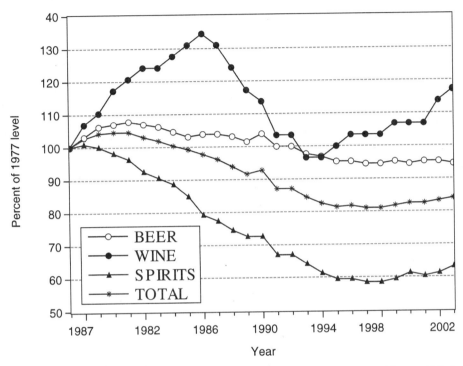

Source: National Institute on Alcohol Abuse and Alcoholism, Surveillance Report #73 (Washington, DC: Author, 2005).

controversy. The table demonstrates that both federal and state taxes per proof gallon are higher for distilled spirits compared to beer and wine. Some policy discussions point to this disparity as a reason to equalize taxes based on alcohol content.[12] The variation in state rates also is a topic of economic interest, such as the difference in taxes on table wine in California and Florida. Economic theories of regulation discussed below provide insight into these differences in state tax rates.

In part, the decline in spirits consumption reflects a long-term shift in American drinking practices toward lighter beers and table wines, and away from hard liquor. In order to compare trends for different alcohol beverages, it is necessary to express consumption in units of pure alcohol (ethanol). The

National Institute on Alcohol Abuse and Alcoholism estimates the average ethanol content of each beverage and converts sales into gallons of pure alcohol, and expresses these gallons on a per capita basis for persons ages fourteen and older.[13] Figure 5.1 shows the percent changes for each beverage since 1977. In 1969, the per capita ethanol amounts for beer and spirits were nearly identical: 1.12 gallons for beer and 1.13 gallons for spirits. The value for wine was 0.26 gallons per capita. In 1990, the values were 1.34 gallons for beer, 0.33 gallons for wine, and 0.77 gallons for spirits. The per capita values for 2003, which is the latest year available, were 1.22 gallons for beer, 0.34 gallons for wine, and 0.67 gallons for spirits. In percentage terms, the current distribution of ethanol consumption is

55 percent for beer, 15 percent for wine, and 30 percent for spirits. Thus, a portion of the market losses in the distilled spirits industry is due to consumer substitution toward beer and wine, but all forms of alcohol use have declined since the peak level of 2.76 gallons per capita attained in 1980–81.

Product Differentiation

Some industries produce an almost infinite variety of products (e.g., breakfast cereals), but for others, such as personal computer operating systems, product variety or differentiation is quite limited. Product variety arises due to producer strategies in combination with consumer preferences for location, service, physical characteristics, brand names, subjective image differentiation, and advertising. Consumers cannot be faulted for desiring variety, but tradeoffs exist where better quality or service increases the price of a brand or advertising creates barriers to entry and mobility.[14] Hence, public policy might rationally seek to either increase or decrease the degree of product differentiation. An antitrust remedy that encourages entry is an example of a policy that promotes variety, while an advertising ban can reduce variety and make entry more difficult. Consider an industry where entry is easy and product characteristics can be tailored to differences in consumer tastes. New firms enter as long as they can expect to make a profit. Each entrant introduces a brand that appeals to some (but not all) consumers, so entry also determines the extent of product variety in the marketplace. Each firm faces a downward-sloping demand function due to sunk costs of entry associated with new brands, incomplete information on the part of consumers, and switching costs. If entry is relatively easy, the real price of each brand eventually falls until additional entry is no longer profitable. An equilibrium in terms of the number of brands (firms) is determined by the equality of each brand's price and its average cost of production, which applies to all brands (firms) in the market. In equilibrium, the matching between consumer tastes and variety will be imperfect because the number of brands is smaller than the number of consumers. The incomplete matching of consumer tastes and varieties results in product differentiation and a downward-sloping demand function for a given brand. As a consequence, consumers are faced with choices along a price–attribute locus, which records the tradeoff between price and variety. The implicit price of a product attribute is referred to as a compensating differential or hedonic price. Empirical estimation of implicit prices is an econometric exercise with a long tradition in economics, which aids the construction of constant quality price indexes.[15]

Products can be differentiated vertically or horizontally. Vertical differentiation occurs if all consumers prefer the brand with a larger amount of a given characteristic (e.g., age of a whiskey). Horizontal differentiation occurs if consumers disagree about the desirability of an attribute (Scotch vs. bourbon). Richard Caves and Peter Williamson discuss four broad characteristics that form the basis for either vertical or horizontal product differentiation.[16] First, some products or services can be tailored to individual consumer preferences or produced on a made-to-order basis. Many service industries fit this category, such as the professional services provided by an attorney or physician. Second, differentiation is enhanced if product characteristics can be bundled or packaged in different ways, such as the models and options that exist for automobiles or the numerous brands of distilled spirits. This type of differentiation is aided by research and development, market analysis of consumer preferences, trial and error, and advertising. Third, in some cases, consumers desire post-sale service such as repairs to automobiles, which can or must be custom tailored to the consumer. Fourth, consumers always are constrained by information costs and switching costs in choosing the best brand, and information sources differ according to their perceived accuracy.

There are two additional aspects of product differentiation that are important.[17] First, there are sunk costs associated with the development, production, and marketing of each brand, which can create an entry barrier. Market power is created or enhanced if incumbent firms can successfully exploit this entry barrier. Second, consumers will (rationally) make choices along the price–attribute locus based on incomplete information and also will take account of switching costs among brands, which are largely sunk costs. Advertising and other marketing activities by incumbents can successfully exploit consumers' ignorance of product attributes and the price–attribute locus. The entry/mobility barrier created by advertising's sunk costs can be substantial in some markets, especially if past advertising does not depreciate quickly.[18]

Leading Brands by Category

In contrast to the beer industry in which a few brands are dominant, there are numerous brands of distilled spirits that enjoy some degree of market success. Some brands, such as Bacardi rum, are industry leaders, but even brands that sell in much smaller quantities have well-recognized brand names within their beverage category or market segment. Examples include Beefeater and Gilbey's in the gin category, Finlandia and Three Olives vodka, and Cutty Sark and Glenlivet Scotch whiskey. In some cases, brand-name recognition is due to past success or price positioning, but the spirits industry has not suffered from the uniformity of consumer preferences that characterizes mass marketing of many consumer products. Distilled spirits brands can be classified according to major

category (brown, white, specialties) and beverage category, and within each category according to retail price (super-premium, premium, value). Table 5.3 shows the share of distilled spirits consumed by category during four selected years: 1980, 1990, 2000, and 2004. The table illustrates the long-term shift by U.S. consumers away from whiskeys and toward white spirits, especially vodka and rum. The decline in whiskey consumption extends to domestic whiskey and imports, with the smallest losses incurred in the Canadian category. The top five beverage categories by volume in 2004 were vodka (26.7 percent of sales volume), rum (12.6 percent), cordials and liqueurs (12.1 percent), American whiskey (11.6 percent), and Canadian whiskey (9.4 percent). Table 5.4 displays information on sales and advertising of the top twenty-five brands of spirits in the year 2004. It is apparent in the table that some leading brands advertise relatively little. The top 4 brands account for 15 percent of industry sales; the top 10 brands, 27 percent; the top 25 brands, 44 percent; the top 50 brands, 61 percent; the top 100 brands, 75 percent; and the top 150 brands, 83 percent.

In contrast, the top four brands of beer now control about 50 percent of the market and the top ten brands have two-thirds of the market. This difference reflects several economic forces operating in the two industries. First, spirits are produced in a large number of categories, while brewers have focused on Pilsner-style lager beers in premium regular and light versions. The diversity of categories and consumer preferences results in a greater array of liquor products and brands. Second, economies of scale in production are more important in beer, reflecting the greater length of production runs and differences in bottling and canning technologies. Some of the larger distilleries are substantial, such as Pernod Ricard's distillery in Cincinnati, Ohio, which has an annual capacity of 8 million cases. This capacity represents about 5 percent of the

Table 5.3

Percentage Share of Distilled Spirits Consumption by Category, 1980–2004

Category	1980	1990	2000	2004	Change 80–04
Straights and bonds	14.0	10.4	8.9	8.4	−5.6
Blends	8.9	6.0	3.9	3.2	−5.7
Total American whiskey	22.9	16.4	12.8	11.6	−11.3
Canadian	12.8	12.7	10.4	9.4	−3.4
Scotch	12.7	8.4	6.2	5.5	−7.2
Irish	0.3	0.2	0.2	0.3	−0.0
Total imported whiskey	25.8	21.2	16.8	15.2	−10.6
Total whiskey	48.7	37.7	29.6	26.8	−21.9
Gin	9.4	8.5	7.5	6.6	−2.8
Vodka	18.8	22.2	24.4	26.7	+7.9
Rum	6.8	8.5	11.4	12.6	+5.8
Tequila	1.7	2.8	4.9	5.0	+3.3
Total whites	36.7	42.0	48.2	50.9	+14.2
Brandy and cognac	4.0	4.7	6.0	6.1	+2.1
Cordials and liqueurs	8.2	11.1	11.7	12.1	+3.9
Prepared cocktails	2.3	4.5	4.5	4.0	+1.7
Total specialties	14.5	20.3	22.2	22.2	+7.7
Total non-whiskey	51.3	62.3	70.4	73.2	+21.9

Source: Adams Liquor Handbook 2005 and earlier editions.

Notes: American whiskeys are classified according to the type of grains in the mash, proof, and length and manner of aging. Straight whiskeys (bourbon, Tennessee, rye) are unblended and contain no neutral spirits. Bourbon is a straight whiskey that must contain a minimum of 51 percent corn, be distilled at less than 160 proof, and be aged for at least two years. Tennessee whiskey has these same characteristics, but must be filtered through a bed of sugar maple charcoal. Bonded whiskey is 100-proof bourbon that is aged for at least four years in a government-supervised warehouse. Blended whiskeys are made from varying proportions of different straight whiskeys and neutral spirits.

total U.S. spirits market, including imports, or 8 percent of the domestic segment of the market. However, in both industries, production economies of scale apply only to the mass-produced segment of the market. Third, shipping and storage costs are different for beer and spirits. The higher price of distilled spirits on a volume basis supports transportation over greater distances, so imports account for 38 to 40 percent of the spirits market compared to 10 to 11 percent of the beer market.[19] At the retail level, premium-priced domestic beer sells for about $5–$7 per six-pack or $8.90–$12.45 per gallon. Spirits prices vary by beverage and price

category, but premium Scotch is priced at $20–$25 per 750-ml. bottle or $100–$125 per gallon.

Advertising by Leading Brands

A fourth economic factor is more difficult to evaluate, but important and controversial. Beer is heavily advertised on TV, but liquor is not. Distilled spirits advertisers have historically been faced with restrictions that did not allow them to promote their products and brands on radio and television. As a result, spirits marketers have relied on print advertising media, including magazines, newspapers,

Table 5.4

Top Twenty-five Distilled Spirits Brands, 2004 (ranked by sales of 9-liter cases)

Rank and brand	Category	Supplier	9-L cases (000)	Advertising ($000)	Intensity ($ per Case)
1. Bacardi	Rum	Bacardi USA	8,450	21,280	2.52
2. Smirnoff	Vodka	Diageo	7,498	7,167	0.96
3. Captain Morgan	Rum	Diageo	4,758	16,990	3.57
4. Absolut	Vodka	Absolut Spirits	4,640	35,602	7.67
5. Jack Daniel's	Straight	Brown-Forman	4,235	20,980	4.95
6. Crown Royal	Canadian	Diageo	3,429	16,533	4.82
7. Jose Cuervo	Tequila	Diageo	3,408	14,451	4.24
8. Jim Beam	Straight	Jim Beam Brands	3,200	10,663	3.33
9. DeKuyper	Cordial	Jim Beam Brands	2,810	164	0.06
10. Seagram's Gin	Gin	Pernod Ricard USA	2,774	2,159	0.78
11. E & J	Brandy	E & J Gallo Winery	2,485	41	0.02
12. Seagram's 7	Blended	Diageo	2,460	504	0.20
13. Canadian Mist	Canadian	Brown-Forman	2,105	1,446	0.69
14. Hennessy	Cognac	Moet Hennessy USA	2,002	6,333	3.16
15. Stolichnaya	Vodka	Allied Domecq USA	1,935	6,318	3.27
16. Black Velvet	Canadian	Constellation Brands	1,902	834	0.44
17. McCormick	Vodka	McCormick Distilling	1,869	—	—
18. Skyy	Vodka	Skyy Spirits USA	1,880	10,545	5.61
19. Popov	Vodka	Diageo	1,850	—	—
20. Jagermeister	Liqueur	Sidney Frank Imports	1,800	435	0.24
21. Grey Goose	Vodka	Bacardi USA	1,760	23,035	13.09
22. Barton	Vodka	Constellation Brands	1,595	87	0.05
23. Gordon's	Vodka	Diageo	1,500	—	—
24. Tanqueray	Gin	Diageo	1,440	1,880	1.31
25. Dewar's	Scotch	Bacardi USA	1,400	3,122	2.23

Source: Adams Liquor Handbook 2005.
Note: Total twenty-five brands account for 44 percent of industry sales and 46 percent of advertising outlays.

and billboards. Thus, it is possible that TV advertising of beer has encouraged homogeneous consumer preferences and contributed in other ways to the long-term shift toward beer consumption. Tests of this hypothesis, however, fail to support it.[20] In 2003, beer producers spent $1,083 million on advertising, including $883 million on broadcast advertising (81.5 percent). Spirits producers spent $391.7 million, including $327.6 million on print advertising (83.6 percent). The content and placement of spirits and beer ads are monitored by the TTB, state alcohol regulatory agencies, and self-appointed watchdog groups, such as the Center for Science in the Public Interest and the Center on Alcohol Marketing and Youth. Each industry also has a system of advertising self-regulation, which includes a code of conduct. Following a 1999 report to Congress by the FTC, the spirits and beer industries overhauled their codes to require a minimum of 70 percent adult audience for all broadcast and print media—the previous standard was 50 percent—and both industries instituted a system of third-party review of controversial ads. In September 2003, the FTC issued a report that endorsed self-regulation. While these changes have placated some congressional critics, controversial

Table 5.5

Advertising and Prices by Category and Leading Brands, 2004

Category and leading brands	Case sales (000)	Advertising ($000)	Intensity ($ per case)	Typical price ($ per 750 ml)
American whiskey	19,239	48,350	2.51	—
Jack Daniel's[a]	4,235	20,980	4.95	19.49
Jim Beam[a]	3,200	10,663	3.33	13.49
Seagram's 7[a]	2,460	504	0.20	10.49
Evan Williams[a]	930	5,078	5.46	10.49
Canadian whiskey	15,543	20,470	1.32	—
Crown Royal	3,429	16,533	4.95	22.99
Canadian Mist[a]	2,105	1,446	0.69	8.49
Black Velvet[a]	1,902	834	0.44	8.99
Canadian Club	1,380	228	0.17	12.99
Seagram's V.O.	1,293	471	0.36	13.99
Scotch whiskey	9,114	42,104	4.62	—
Dewar's	1,400	3,122	2.23	24.99
Clan MacGregor[a]	720	—	—	8.99
Johnnie Walker Black	715	8,342	11.67	32.99
Johnnie Walker Red	685	166	0.24	24.99
Chivas Regal	483	7,877	16.31	29.99
Glenlivet	217	6,508	29.99	33.99
Glenfiddich	145	7,165	49.41	33.99
Vodka	44,262	139,092	3.14	—
Smirnoff[a]	7,498	7,167	0.96	11.99
Absolut	4,640	35,602	7.67	19.49
Stolichnaya	1,935	6,318	3.27	19.49
Skyy[a]	1,880	10,545	5.61	15.99
Grey Goose	1,760	23,035	13.09	26.99
Rum	20,800	58,892	2.83	—
Bacardi[a]	8,450	21,280	2.52	12.49
Captain Morgan[a]	4,758	16,990	3.57	14.99
Malibu (42 proof)	1,300	2,914	2.24	13.99
Castillo[a]	1,200	—	—	8.99
Gin	10,972	19,580	1.78	—
Seagram's Gin[a]	2,774	2,159	0.78	10.99
Tanqueray	1,440	1,880	1.31	21.99
Gordon's Gin[a]	885	—	—	10.99
Bombay Sapphire	705	9,645	13.68	23.99
Beefeater	620	2,348	3.79	19.49
Gilbey's Gin[a]	550	—	—	9.49

Sources: Adams Liquor Handbook 2005 for sales and advertising; *Pennsylvania Wine & Spirits Quarterly, Holiday 2005* for prices as of December 2005.

[a] Brands bottled in the United States.

issues remain, such as beer advertising in connection with college sports broadcasts, sponsorship of automobile racing teams, alleged targeting of underage magazine readers, and direct shipping of alcohol products, especially wine.[21]

Table 5.5 shows advertising outlays in 2004 by leading brands in six spirits categories: American whiskey, Canadian whiskey, Scotch whiskey, vodka, rum, and gin. Also shown are typical prices charged in 2005, which are used to determine a brand's position within the category. For example, the Scotch category includes three super-premiums (Glenlivet, Glenfiddich, Johnnie Walker Black), three premiums (Dewar's, Johnnie Walker Red, Chivas Regal), and one value brand (Clan Mac-Gregor). The latter brand is imported in bulk and bottled in the United States. The table illustrates the wide variation that exists in advertising expenditures and advertising intensity per case. Some value brands advertise very little, if at all, while many super-premiums are characterized by high advertising intensities that serve to differentiate the brand from its competitors. However, if a brand's major competitors also advertise heavily, these expenditures might simply result in a stalemate for market shares and reduced profits. In game theory, this outcome is known as the "prisoners' dilemma," and it suggests that spirits producers might rationally seek some government-enforced limits on their advertising expenditures or methods. The industry's adoption of the FTC's new advertising code is consistent with this prediction.

Brand advertising in the distilled spirits industry also has been attacked for possible spillover effects on market demand and related social problems such as underage drinking and drunk driving. In the economics literature, the spillover effect is represented by an advertising-sales response function, which depicts the relationship between industry advertising outlays and industry sales. Some investigators hypothesize that the response function is S-shaped, with a region of increasing marginal returns to outlays, followed by a region of decreasing marginal returns.[22] Evidence that supports the relationship at the industry level is lacking generally, although studies that examine advertising bans provide possible clues about its existence or nonexistence.[23] However, the spillover hypothesis only makes economic sense for successful advertising campaigns when sales of a leading brand increase substantially, and might therefore generate a spillover effect that stimulates primary market demand.

Case Study: Advertising Spillovers and Absolut Vodka

As a case study of the spillover hypothesis, consider the importance of advertising by the second-leading vodka brand, Absolut Vodka. In 1980, vodka consumption in the United States was 0.56 gallons per adult and total spirits consumption was about 2.90 gallons per adult. By 2004, these two amounts had declined to 0.50 gallons and 1.89 gallons, respectively. Although the vodka category declined in absolute terms, vodka's share of the spirits market rose from 19 percent of sales in 1980 to 26 percent in 2004, making it the largest single category. However, the spillover hypothesis addresses total or per capita consumption, and not market shares. In 1980, a new brand of vodka entered the crowded U.S. market for spirits. A premium-priced brand, Absolut Vodka is produced by Vin & Sprit AB, the Swedish government's alcohol monopoly (no alcohol advertising of any kind is allowed in Sweden). The brand's U.S. advertising campaign is known for its creative print ads, which feature the distinctive Absolut bottle and a two-word message that plays on its name, such as "Absolut Perfection" and "Absolut Joy." The campaign evolved over time to feature artists, cities and locations, objects, holidays, designer-name clothes, and other novel or upscale images. By 1989, Absolut was the third-best brand by sales among vodkas and the twelfth-leading spirits brand overall. By 2004, Absolut was the second-best seller among vodkas (behind Smirnoff) and the fourth-leading brand overall. Absolut's sales rose from about 2.25 million cases in 1989 to 4.64 million in 2004, an increase of more than 100 percent. Total sales of vodka remained stable at about 35 million cases per year between 1989 and 1999, and increased marginally to 44 million cases in 2004. Nevertheless, vodka sales per capita declined by 35 percent between 1980 and 2004. Absolut Vodka, and vodka brands generally, are heavily promoted, but this has not translated into either increased vodka sales or greater consumption of distilled spirits. In 1984, Absolut spent about $9.65 per case on advertising, compared to $1.52 per case for category leader Smirnoff. In 1989, Absolut spent $10.6 million on advertising, principally in magazines, making it the third-leading brand by total advertising expenditure (behind Dewar's Scotch and Smirnoff Vodka). Total spending on spirits was $272.8 million ($1.75 per case). In 1999, Absolut spent $32.4 million ($8 per case), making it the leading brand ranked by total advertising expenditure. In 2004, total spending on spirits was about $439 million ($2.65 per case), while Absolut's expenditure was $35.6 million ($7.67 per case). As indicated, vodka sales per capita and consumption of spirits have declined over time. In this example, successful advertising by Absolut translated into increased brand sales, but any primary or market-wide spillovers must be very small in magnitude. Absolut's remarkable success at the brand level did not breed success at the category or industry level, indicating that an industry-wide advertising response function does not exist. Further evidence on advertising-related issues is provided below.

Leading Firms and Recent Mergers

The Six Majors

In 2004, the top six firms ranked by U.S. sales volume were: (1) Diageo NA; (2) Constellation Brands; (3) Bacardi USA; (4) Jim Beam/Fortune Brands; (5) Allied Domecq/Pernod Ricard USA; and (6) Brown-Forman Beverages. Each of these firms has a portfolio of brands and, except for Constellation, spends in excess of $15 million annually on advertising. It is noteworthy that the brand names are well-known to the U.S. public, but the names of the firms behind these brands are not highly recognizable. It is interesting to focus on the differences among the firms and how each firm's business plan or strategy is tailored to its brand portfolio.[24]

Diageo North America

The industry's leader had 2004 sales revenue of $3,866 million based on case sales of 37.3 million, and a market share of 22.5 percent. Diageo spent $90.4 million on advertising ($2.42 per case). Diageo has concentrated on the premium and super-premium segments, although its business strategy indicates that it will focus on "complete category participation." Its brand portfolio includes six of the top twenty brands, including Smirnoff (vodka), Captain Morgan (rum), Crown Royal (Canadian), Seagram's 7 Crown (blended whiskey), and Popov (vodka). It also has strong positions with other leading brands, including Jose Cuervo (tequila), Tanqueray (gin), Bailey's (liqueur), and Johnnie Walker Black/Red (Scotch). These ten brands account for 75 percent of Diageo's sales volume. As a separate company, Diageo Plc was created in 1997 by the merger of Guinness Plc and Grand Metropolitan Plc. In late 2000, at a combined cost of $8.15 billion, Diageo and Pernod Ricard acquired the rights to Seagram Ltd.'s global operations, following the acquisition of the latter company by Vivendi Universal. Diageo Plc also participates in the beer and wine sectors (Guinness, Harp, Beaulieu, Sterling, and others) but recently increased its focus on distilled spirits through the sale of other holdings, including Pillsbury and Burger King.

Constellation Brands

Formerly Canandaigua Brands, Constellation is a broadly diversified worldwide producer and distributor of imported beer (Corona and others), wine (Robert Mondavi, Estancia, Almaden, and others), and distilled spirits. It is the world's largest producer of wine. It had liquor sales in 2004 of 15.73 million cases, revenues of $806 million, and a market share of 9.5 percent. Although it is the number two firm by volume, it is only number six by sales revenue. Constellation's advertising expenditures in 2004 were only $1.663 million ($0.11 per case), which was twentieth largest in the industry. About half of Constellation's sales are due to its position in six brands: Black Velvet (Canadian), Barton Vodka, Paul Masson Brandy, Skol (vodka), Fleischmann's Royal (vodka), and Canadian LTD. Constellation's Mr. Boston brands are value leaders in several categories. The firm's market position is partly due to a focus on the vodka category and its marketing of a large number of brands. Constellation's Fact Sheet indicates that it presently markets more than ninety brands of distilled spirits, including ten different vodkas, eight gins, and eleven Canadian whiskeys. In July of 2005, Constellation Brands was added to the S&P 500 Index.

Bacardi USA

This firm is the import/marketing subsidiary of Bacardi Ltd., a privately held producer of spirits, wines, and flavored alcohol beverages. Although Bacardi's assets in Cuba were seized in 1959, it currently has production facilities in nine countries, including Canada, Mexico, and Puerto Rico. In 2004, Bacardi USA had sales revenue of $1,597 million, case sales of 15.225 million, and a market share of 9.2 percent. Its advertising expenditures in 2004 were $62.517 million ($4.11 per case), which was second largest behind only Diageo. Bacardi USA's success is based largely on its signature brand, Bacardi Rum, which accounts for 55 percent of company sales. Its other lead-ing brands include Grey Goose (vodka), Dewar's (Scotch), Castillo (rum), Bombay Sapphire (gin), and Bacardi Party (prepared cocktails). The top six brands account for more than 90 percent of sales volume. In recent years, Bacardi's position in the rum category has been eroded by upstarts Captain Morgan and Malibu, which focused their marketing on younger adult drinkers. Bacardi's share of the rum category was 59 percent in 1991, 48 percent in 1998, and 41 percent in 2004. Since 1998, Bacardi has responded with an advertising campaign built around the theme "Bacardi by Night," which is one of the industry's most costly campaigns. Traditionally, Bacardi Rum has ranked among the top two or three most heavily advertised brands. In 2004, it had advertising outlays of $21.3 million, which placed it third behind Absolut ($35.6 million) and Grey Goose ($23.0 million), and just ahead of Jack Daniel's ($21.0 million). These four brands—two of which are marketed by Bacardi—account for about 23 percent of industry advertising compared to only 12 percent of industry sales.

Jim Beam Brands

The parent company of Jim Beam Brands is Fortune Brands, a $7 billion producer of home products (Moen faucets, Master Lock, Therma Tru doors, and others), golf products (Titleist, Cobra, Footjoy, and others), wines (Clos du Bois, Geyser Peak, and others), and distilled spirits. In 2004, Jim Beam Brands had case sales of 14.175 million, revenues of $988 million, and a market share of 8.6 percent. Beam's expenditures on advertising were $15.910 million ($1.12 per case). The company's leading brands are Jim Beam (straight whiskey), DeKuyper (cordial), Windsor Supreme (Canadian), Kamchatka (vodka), Kessler (blended whiskey), and Wolfschmidt (vodka). These six brands account for 65 percent of company sales volume. Many of these are value brands, although the company also produces a number of premium whiskeys (Old Grand-Dad, Knob Creek, and others) and is the U.S. distributor of Absolut Vodka. In July of 2005, Fortune Brands and Pernod Ricard completed the acquisition of Allied Domecq Plc. Fortune spent $5 billion to obtain the rights to more than twenty spirits and wine brands, including Sauza (tequila), Courvoisier (cognac), Canadian Club, Teacher's (Scotch), and Maker's Mark (straight whiskey). According to Fortune's press release, the acquisition doubles its sales volume and revenues and makes it the fourth-largest spirits company in the world.

Allied Domecq/Pernod Ricard USA

Allied Domecq was a subsidiary of Allied Domecq Plc, a London-based company. In July of 2005, the company was purchased by Pernod Ricard, a French wine and spirits company, and Fortune Brands. According to information released by Pernod Ricard, the acquisition makes it the world's second-largest producer of wine and spirits, and the number one producer outside the United States. Because a number of Domecq brands were sold to Fortune, separate data are reported for Domecq and Ricard. In 2004, Domecq USA had sales of 12.8 million cases and revenues that totaled $1,379 million. Ricard USA had case sales of 5.95 million and revenues of $674 million. Advertising expenditures in 2004 were Domecq, $29.243 million ($2.28 per case), and Ricard, $31.526 million ($5.29 per case). Ricard's advertising outlays reflect its marketing of several premium brands, including Chivas Regal (Scotch), Glenlivet (Scotch), and Wild Turkey (straight whiskey). The combined brands of Domecq and Ricard also include Seagram's Gin, Stolichnaya (vodka), Malibu (rum), Kahlua (liqueur), Hiram Walker (cordials), Beefeater (gin), Seagram's Vodka, and Ballentine's (Scotch). The acquisition gives Pernod Ricard a diverse product line, with substantial volume in most beverage categories and considerable strength in premium Scotch, premium vodka, and liqueurs.

Brown-Forman Beverages

A U.S.-based distiller founded in 1870, Brown-Forman has its corporate headquarters in Louisville, Kentucky. In addition to distilled spirits, the firm produces wine (Fetzer, Sonoma-Cutrer, Korbel, Bolla, and others) and consumer durables (Hartmann luggage). In 2004, Brown-Forman had liquor case sales of 10.83 million, revenue of $1,113 million, and a market share of 6.5 percent. Brown's advertising expenditures were $41.54 million ($3.84 per case). About half of the expenditures were for a single premium-priced brand, Jack Daniel's Tennessee Whiskey. Brown-Forman's brand portfolio includes six leading brands: Jack Daniel's (straight whiskey), Canadian Mist, Southern Comfort (cordial), Jack Daniel's Country Cocktails (prepared cocktails), Early Times (straight whiskey), and Finlandia (vodka). These six brands account for 90 percent of company sales volume, with Jack Daniel's share being 39 percent. In contrast to the other leading firms, Brown-Forman has maintained its focus on the traditional "brown" market segment.

Table 5.6 summarizes market-share data for the six leaders and two groups of smaller producers. It is apparent that there is more than one successful business strategy in the spirits industry. Two of the leading firms, Bacardi USA and Brown-Forman, rely heavily on the success of a single premium brand, and promote these brands heavily. Two other firms, Constellation and Jim Beam, have focused on the value-segment of the market, and have much lower advertising outlays per case. The remaining two firms, Diageo and Domecq/Ricard, offer broad product lines, with considerable strength in premium-priced categories. No other firm has

Table 5.6

Industry Sales and Advertising by Groups of Firms, 2004

Group	Case sales (000)	Revenue ($ 000)	Percent of industry	Advertising outlays ($ 000)	Percent of industry	Intensity ($ per case)
Top six firms	112,013	10,423	63.4	272,791	62.1	2.44
Next three firms	15,916	1,865	11.3	75,714	17.2	4.76
Next ten firms	21,333	2,032	12.4	65,764	15.0	3.10
All others	16,388	2,117	12.9	25,023	5.7	1.53
Total industry	165,650	16,437	100.0	439,292	100.0	2.65

Source: Adams Liquor Handbook 2005.
Note: Top six firms includes data for Pernod Ricard USA.

been able to match Diageo's brand portfolio, where its top six brands account for 13 percent of total sales of spirits. It is noteworthy that the advertising intensity for the top six firms is below that of the next three smaller firms (Absolut, Moet Hennessy, Heaven Hill) and the next ten smaller firms. In part, this reflects promotional economies of scale and attempts by smaller firms to capture market shares through advertising. Recent examples of elevated advertising outlays for smaller brands include Evan Williams (straight whiskey), Ketel One (vodka), Cointreau (liqueur), Remy Red (liqueur), Macallan (Scotch), Skyy (vodka), Three Olives (vodka), Glenfiddich (Scotch), and Frangelico (liqueur). Sales of these brands are dwarfed by the industry leaders, but in a differentiated market this has not prevented competition based on price positioning and advertising outlays.

Recent Mergers and Entry/ Mobility Barriers

The distilled spirits industry has a complex market structure, with at least ten beverage categories, three price segments within each category, and numerous brands. The extent of consumer substitution among beverage categories or between price segments is not very well understood, which complicates the identification of economic markets. The guiding principle in identifying a market is that the definition should include all products that play a significant role in the determination of prices. According to the DOJ/FTC Merger Guidelines, a market for antitrust analysis is defined as follows:

> A product or group of products and a geographic area in which it is produced or sold such that a hypothetical profit-maximizing firm, not subject to price regulation, that was the only present and future seller of those products in that area likely would impose at least a "small but significant and nontransitory" increase in price, assuming the terms of sale of all other products are being held constant.[25]

In order to understand the substance of this statement, consider the following question: Would a merger between Firm A and Firm B result in a significant price increase of, say, 5 percent or more, either because the merged firms have significant market power or because they can more easily collude with other firms? A market for antitrust analysis is found by adding products (or geographic regions) as long as the answer to this question is affirmative. Notice that the guidelines usually result in narrow market definitions, which means that the analysis of entry barriers is crucial.

In April of 1998, the FTC issued a complaint in the proposed merger between Guinness Plc and Grand Metropolitan Plc, and the successor corporation, Diageo Plc.[26] As noted in the complaint, respondent Guinness was engaged in the sale and distribution of distilled spirits in the United States, including its premium Scotch brands, Dewar's White Label and Johnnie Walker Red, and premium gin brands, Tanqueray and Tanqueray Malacca. Respondent Grand Met also produced premium Scotch, including J&B Rare, J&B Select, and The Famous Grouse. Grand Met's premium gin brands sold in the United States were Bombay Original and Bombay Sapphire. According to the FTC's complaint, premium gin and premium Scotch brands are limited to brands bottled in England and Scotland, respectively. The complaint alleged that the likely effect of the merger was to substantially lessen competition in these two markets by eliminating direct competition between Guinness and Grand Met; by increasing the likelihood of unilateral exercise of market power; and by increasing the likelihood of collusion on prices. However, aside from basic data on brand shares and market concentration, the complaint lacked an analysis of other economic aspects of the market, such as the extent of entry barriers or ease of collusion in a differentiated market. Further, FTC Commissioner Mary Azcuenaga went so far as to characterize the market definitions as "wacky." The terseness of the complaint is typical under the premerger provisions of the Hart-Scott-Rodino Act of 1976, which emphasizes early (and quick) approval or disapproval of mergers. Following the complaint, the full Commission found reason to deny the merger unless the merging firms divested themselves of three brands: Dewar's Scotch, Bombay Original gin, and Bombay Sapphire gin. In order to close the merger deal, the three contested brands were sold to Bacardi USA, which at the time did not compete in the premium Scotch and gin categories.

In a second case filed in December of 2001, the FTC contested the proposed sale of Seagram brands by Vivendi Universal to Diageo Plc.[27] In this merger, Diageo had tried to anticipate antitrust concerns by engaging Pernod Ricard as a third party in the merger. The business acquired by Diageo would be limited to Seagram's Captain Morgan rum assets, while Pernod Ricard would acquire all other brands, including Seagram's Gin, Chivas Regal Scotch, Glenlivet Scotch, and Martell Cognac. The FTC staff again defined several narrow market segments for competitive analysis of the merger, including premium rum, popular gin, premium Scotch, super-premium Scotch, and premium cognac. The basis for the complaint paralleled that used in the 1998 merger of Guinness and Grand Met. As a condition for approval of the merger, the Commission required that Diageo divest its Malibu rum assets and that it be prevented from obtaining "commercially sensitive information" relating to the brands acquired by Pernod Ricard. In order to close the merger deal, Diageo sold its Malibu rum assets to Allied Domecq, thereby obtaining approval of the other aspects of the merger.

In these and similar merger cases involving differentiated products, narrow market definitions make economic sense if consumer substitution among price segments is limited and entry/mobility barriers in the market segments are high. Previous court decisions indicate that the federal courts have accepted antitrust markets defined according to price segments, but with enough reservations to leave the issue in doubt.[28] Earlier FTC decisions that examined price segmentation include two mergers in the wine industry: the 1973 acquisition of Franzia Brothers Winery by Coca-Cola Bottling Company of New York; and the 1969 acquisition of United Vintners by Heublein Inc. These decisions also are of interest for the attention paid to entry barriers and advertising in an alcohol beverage industry. In the Coca-Cola/Franzia case, Administrative Law Judge (ALJ) Lewis Parker identified four market segments (table, dessert, sparkling, and "pop" wines) and three price segments (premium, mid-premium, and popular priced).[29] The FTC's complaint alleged that the acquisition would eliminate competition between Franzia, a producer of popular-priced California table, dessert, and sparkling wines, and Coke's Mogen David division, a producer of sweetened kosher "berry" wines. Complaint counsel alleged that "wine is wine," but defendants' witnesses testified that Mogen David represented a distinctly different product that had "no real competition in the markets it dominates" (93 FTC 165). The ALJ substantially agreed with these witnesses, and concluded that an "all wine market is a theoretical construction which does not take into account the realities of the market in which the merged companies operate" (93 FTC 189). Hence, the merger was a product extension merger, rather than a horizontal merger, and the FTC staff had not proven that the merger would lessen competition in narrower market segments. Upon appeal, the full Commission disagreed in part, arguing that there was a continuum of products in the wine market arrayed by price and sweetness and that Mogen David's position in this array did not exclude it from the continuum altogether (93 FTC 204). Due to consumers' willingness to trade up among wine brands, the Commission also rejected defendants' notion that wines compete within narrow price ranges. Thus, this decision is inconsistent with the FTC's market definitions in the recent liquor industry mergers. After examining the post-acquisition evidence, the Commission concluded that the Coca-Cola/Franzia merger posed little threat to market competition. The decision also drew a careful distinction between ease of entry on a minimal basis in a price segment and entry at a level at which the entrant is able to provide meaningful competition in the bulk of the market. The decision reasoned, "it is entry of the latter sort with which we must be principally concerned in evaluating the state of competition in an industry" (93 FTC 210). As a precedent, this decision establishes that in markets with differentiated products, competition can occur along a continuum of prices and beverage categories.

In a second wine industry merger case, the FTC challenged Heublein's acquisition of United Vintners.[30] At the time of the acquisition, Heublein was an importer of table and dessert wines (Lancer's Rose, Harvey's Sherries & Ports), and recently had acquired several small California wineries. United was the nation's second-largest seller of wines, including all types of table, dessert, and sparkling wines (Italian Swiss Colony, Inglenook). The complaint defined the relevant market as "all wine," and argued that major barriers to entry existed for any firm attempting "significant entry into the wine business" (96 FTC 396). In a lengthy opinion, ALJ Alvin Berman found that table, dessert, and sparkling wines were "well-defined submarkets, which in themselves constitute product markets for antitrust purposes" (96 FTC 385), and rejected defendants' contention that "standard" and "premium" wines must be treated as separate markets. He concluded, "a broad spectrum of prices is apparent among wines, all of which are clearly substitutable in end use" (96 FTC 480). He also found significant barriers to entry in the wine industry, including (1) capital requirements and long payout periods; (2) difficulties of obtaining effective wholesale distributors; (3) limits on obtaining effective retail shelf space; (4) advertising and brand recognition; (5) state laws and regulations; and (6) entrenchment of two dominant firms, Gallo Winery and United Vintners. Upon appeal, the full Commission dismissed the complaint. Citing the Coca Cola/Franzia decision, the Commission defined the relevant market as "all wines." The Commission noted that the wine market was not highly concentrated and, within this broadly defined market, United had a market share of 17.9 percent and Heublein's share was only 0.79 percent. The Commission determined that "Heublein was but one among an unusually large number of potential entrants and expanders" (96 FTC 584), and many of these firms, including Heublein, were major firms selling liquor that had small holdings ("toeholds") in the wine market. Thus, the removal of one potential competitor was of little competitive significance. Finally, with respect to advertising, the Commission found that "where such product differences exist, an advantage in advertising costs is less likely to be of competitive importance [and] it is also more likely to be competitively useful, encouraging product variations by informing consumers of a wide range of different products" (96 FTC 596). In summary, the FTC's earlier decisions in two wine mergers are inconsistent with its recent opinions in two liquor merger cases.

The Regulatory Environment

The Economic Theory of Regulation

What economic factors explain the regulation of industries, products, and businesses? What explains the standards or rules of regulation applied to different markets and industries? Until the late 1960s, economics lacked a positive theory of regulation. When economists discussed regulation, they usually viewed it as inherently serving the noble "public interest" or at least attempting to do so. This view was challenged by accumulating evidence indicating numerous technical and allocative inefficiencies associated with regulation. However, simply labeling this as "politics as usual" ignores the fact that there are purposeful political agents supplying the regulations. Furthermore, the economic agents affected by regulation clearly have it in their self-interest to be concerned about the enactment of regulation and its form. These private interests comprise the demand side of the market for legislation and rules.

The revolution in economic thinking came in 1971 with the publication of an article by George Stigler, titled "The Theory of Economic Regulation."[31] Stigler's article contained two insights that have motivated research on the origins and uses of regulation. First, he observed that "the state has one basic resource which in pure principle is not shared with even the mightiest of its citizens: the power to coerce."[32] He hypothesized that this power provides "the possibilities for the utilization of the state by an industry to increase its profitability,"[33] such as direct subsidies, price fixing, control over entry, and control over inter-industry competition. Second, he observed, "political boons are not obtained by the industry in a pure profit-maximizing form."[34] This means that regulation is not a free good for the industry, since it involves an essential transfer of wealth that will be opposed by other interest groups. The prediction is that regulation and regulatory agencies will not serve a single economic interest to the exclusion of others; rather political agents must trade off among competing interests through compromises on rules, cross-subsidization, and even deregulation. These political compromises erect constraints on the pure pursuit of profits by the regulated industry such as redistribution of market power among individual firms, procedural delays and costs, and admission of powerful outsiders to the internal workings of the firms and industry.[35] Further, demanders of regulation who are more effective in delivering votes and other resources will obtain larger and more permanent transfers of wealth, so Stigler's theory also is a model of the optimal size of effective political coalitions. In summary, an idealistic public-interest view of regulation is cast aside in favor of a model in which regulations and rules are the outcome of rational self-interested political and economic behavior.[36]

Stigler's theory is well-tailored to situations involving a regulatory agency that has authority over a single industry (e.g., the defunct Civil Aeronautics Board and the airlines), or what came to be termed "economic regulation." The theoretical prediction is that the agency will tend to be "captured" by the industry for the simple reason that member firms have a large per capita stake in the outcome and are better able to organize as an effective political coalition.[37] In this setting, the costs of regulation tend to be dispersed widely over the broad population of consumers and taxpayers. Stigler's theory would seem to fit less well in the area of "social regulation" such as controls designed to improve health, safety, and the environment. Because social regulations affect many industries, the costs tend to be allocated to concentrated groups, whereas the benefits of regulation are widely dispersed. However, the theory has yielded insights here as well. First, expanded application of social regulation is in the interest of the firms that are already in compliance. Second, larger firms often are at an advantage due to fixed costs of compliance, so smaller firms can be driven from the market through a process of raising rivals' costs.[38] Third, standards are sometimes differentiated between competing industries or between incumbent producers and new producers. By obtaining discriminatory regulations or setting different standards for new producers, competition and entry can be controlled. Fourth, within the industry, trade-offs are possible between groups of consumers and input suppliers, such that economic surplus or "rent" is redistributed. For example, products supplied to some customer groups might be exempt from environmental regulation or differentially priced, resulting in cross-subsidization of one customer group by others. The advantage to the regulated firms is that the subsidized customers become an ally in dealings with the regulatory agency. Finally, "rent seeking" is not a costless process, and the theoretical prediction is that competition for rents increases economic costs to the level of the available rent. Hence, the deadweight loss under regulation can exceed the losses that would be associated with simple monopoly.[39]

Bootleggers and Baptists

It is said that politics makes for strange bedfellows. Building on this old adage, Bruce Yandle pointed out that politicians in a democracy must find ways to dress their actions in public-interest clothing.[40] Regulators find it easier to enact rules that are supported by a public-welfare group (e.g., Baptists), even though the rules might primarily transfer wealth to some rent-seeking private interest group (bootleggers). Of course, the exact identity of the two groups will vary with circumstances. The underlying parable is that Baptists favor strict regulation of the legal sale of alcohol, including a ban of Sunday sales. Bootleggers want to limit competition from legal sources, so they have an effective ally that can clothe the regulations in the public interest. Regulators also gain because Sunday bans are easy to enforce. Any costs of the regulation are borne largely by legal operators of liquor stores (who might be Baptists), but their actions are more observable than those of the bootleggers. Hence, opposition is constrained by the moral smoke screen of the public interest. While regulation of alcohol sales is endorsed by Baptists on moral grounds, a ban of Sunday sales is symbolic because it does not directly prevent consumption and indirectly it encourages the sale of illegal alcohol. As Yandle points out, "it is the details of regulation that usually win the endorsement of bootleggers, not just the broader principle that matters most to Baptists."[41] It also might be in the interest of the rent-seeking bootleggers to subsidize the activities of the public-spirited Baptists, which makes it more difficult to empirically identify rent-seeking activity from public-interest behavior.[42] With this as background, three case studies are discussed that illustrate the workings of alcohol regulation and application of the economic model.

Federal Regulatory Agencies

Alcohol and Tobacco Tax and Trade Bureau

Following the repeal of Prohibition and the collapse of the National Recovery Act, Congress passed the Federal Alcohol Administration (FAA) Act of 1935. This act established a Federal Alcohol Administration within the Department of the Treasury.[43] The FAA Act grants authority for both categories of regulation—economic and social—but historically it has been interpreted as authorizing economic regulation.[44] The administration underwent several changes in name and function, and effective July 1, 1972, it was named the Bureau of Alcohol, Tobacco and Firearms (ATF). Federal regulation and taxation of the alcohol and tobacco industries remained a part of ATF until January of 2003. Under the Homeland Security Act, these functions were transferred to a new Treasury unit, the TTB. While control of intrastate sale of alcohol is delegated to the states, TTB is the primary federal agency that regulates manufacture and sale of alcohol products intended for interstate commerce. TTB licenses alcohol importers, manufacturers, and wholesalers, and regulates the size of containers, labeling of containers, and alcohol advertising. TTB also is responsible for collecting federal taxes on alcohol beverages and suppressing illegal production. At the federal level, TTB shares authority over alcohol purity and advertising with the FDA and FTC, respectively, but these agencies usually defer to TTB on these matters. The TTB's authority extends to the following functions and duties:

(1) collecting federal excise taxes and classifying alcohol products for excise tax purposes; (2) investigating applications and issuing permits for the operation of distilleries, wineries, and breweries; (3) regulating the production, packaging, bottling, labeling, and storage of alcohol products; (4) ensuring that labeling and advertising of alcohol beverages provide adequate information to the consumer concerning the identity and quality of the product; (5) preventing misleading labeling or advertising; (6) regulating alcohol marketing and promotional practices by producers and wholesalers; and (7) enforcing the provisions of the Alcohol Beverage Labeling Act, which mandates a warning statement that appears on all alcohol beverage products. In order to carry out these functions, TTB has three operating divisions: (1) Trade Investigations Division, which oversees product integrity, importer rules, compliance with trade practice rules, and review of new entrants; (2) Tax Audit Division, which deals with audits of tax returns and other tax-related claims; and (3) Advertising, Labeling, and Formulation Division, which focuses on the prevention of consumer deception in advertising, marketing, and labeling, and enforces the Alcohol Beverage Labeling Act (ABLA). In addition, TTB's Special Service Division includes the Beverage Alcohol Laboratory, which oversees the integrity and purity of alcohol products.

Case Study: TTB's Regulation of Alcohol Health Claims

Unlike most manufactured foods and beverages, alcohol beverages do not list ingredients on the label. In 1940, the FDA agreed to defer to Treasury in matters of alcohol labeling, and Treasury decided not to require ingredient labeling. Although alcohol producers are required to use FDA-approved ingredients and additives, this decision is a source of continuing controversy.[45] In 1972, ATF and FDA were petitioned by a watchdog group, the Center for Science in the Public Interest (CSPI), to require ingredient listings for alcohol beverages. After ATF withdrew its proposed regulations as unnecessary, costly, and potentially misleading, the FDA in 1975 announced that it would undertake regulatory action to enforce ingredient labeling (40 *Federal Register* 54455). However, it was prevented from doing so by a federal court.[46] Although a few additives are now listed, CSPI and other organizations have continued to press for a uniform "Alcohol Facts" label, but TTB's response has been largely limited to a 2004 White Paper on "Serving Facts Information on Alcohol Beverages."[47] Any producer that desired to compete through ingredient labeling would find it difficult to do so, but it might have the Baptist-leaning CSPI on its side. This episode sets the stage for a more recent example of alcohol labeling and advertising involving regulation of health claims and health-related claims.

In the mid-1980s, scientific-research reports began to appear indicating that there might be a health benefit associated with alcohol consumption, especially moderate daily consumption of red wine, or what was called the "French Paradox" in a report on *60 Minutes* that aired on TV in 1991. Briefly, the research linked moderate drinking to lower rates of heart disease, especially among older individuals and women. ATF had a strict policy of not approving any substantive health claims for alcohol, but in 1993 it announced its intentions to engage in rule making on guidelines with respect to health claims in the labeling and advertising of alcohol beverages. In the meantime, it would continue to consider the issue on a case-by-case basis. In 1995–96, several wine producers sought approval of "directional" labels that encouraged individuals to seek advice from a physician on the health benefits and risks of moderate wine consumption or to consult the Government's *Dietary Guidelines for Americans*, which in 1995 recognized that moderate drinking reduces the risk of coronary heart disease. In February 1999, after extensive review, ATF approved two directional health claims for wine labels. When numerous public health groups and individuals objected, ATF proposed to amend the regulations on health claims to require proper qualification, sufficient detail and specificity, and identification of categories of individuals for whom any positive benefits would be outweighed by negative health effects (64 *Federal Register* 57413). Few industry members expressed an interest in labels that were so detailed and qualified.[48] Within the framework of the theory of regulation, the comments received on the rule making provide insight into common positions adopted by some industry members and public health groups (68 *Federal Register* 10076). The trade associations for the spirits and beer industries opposed health and health-related labels as a violation of the ABLA and also opposed any change in TTB's advertising regulations. The spirits industry commented, "America's distillers do not recommend that consumers drink beverage alcohol for health reasons" (68 *Federal Register* 10081). These comments, of course, were echoed by numerous health-related groups, including the Food and Drug Administration, American Medical Association, American Cancer Association, Mothers Against Drunk Driving, and the Southern Baptist Convention (68 *Federal Register* 10085). In March of 2003, TTB issued final regulations that allowed substantive health statements in labels that were nonmisleading and "sufficiently detailed" with respect to health risks and, in the case of directional labels, accompanied by a disclaimer. TTB conceded "the regulations make it difficult to make a substantive health claim . . . because of the level of qualification and explanation" (68 *Federal Register* 10100). After ten years of agency consideration, there was little or no change in the status quo.[49] Such stability is characteristic of a regulatory environment, which often discourages risk-taking and product innovations.

Federal Trade Commission

The FTC is an independent regulatory agency, which was created in 1914 with the substantive mandate to prevent unfair methods of competition.[50] Although this broad mandate was understood to mean antitrust injuries to competitors, and not false or misleading advertising, the FTC immediately concerned itself with false advertising complaints. A Supreme Court decision in 1931 (283 U.S. 643) brought a halt to many advertising cases, requiring the FTC to demonstrate a harmful effect on a competitor even if the ad had deceived consumers. In 1938, Congress enacted the Wheeler-Lea Act, which expanded the FTC's mandate to include a prohibition against unfair or deceptive acts or practices. This allowed the FTC to protect consumers as well as competition (or competitors). However, the words *unfair* and *deceptive* lacked operational definitions, and the FTC struggled for many years with these terms as a practical guide to consumer protection. Under procedures established in 1983, the FTC "will find deception if there is a representation, omission or practice that is likely to mislead the consumer acting reasonably in the circumstances, to the consumer's detriment" (103 FTC 110). Thus, *deception analysis* does not ask about countervailing or offsetting benefits. It assumes either false or misleading statements that have no benefits or that the injury could be avoided at low cost by limiting the ads or practices. Hence, the deception test creates a shortcut by assuming that when a material falsehood exists, the practice could not pass a cost-benefit test.[51] In antitrust analysis, the comparable test is known as a per se rule. In contrast, the current treatment of unfairness grew out of actions taken by the FTC in the 1970s, when its expanded authority was used to legislate

against many advertising and marketing practices such as ads on children's TV programs.[52] After a series of stinging rebukes by Congress, the FTC in 1984 altered the unfairness definition to mean an act or practice is unfair: (1) if it causes or is likely to cause substantial consumer injury; (2) if the injury is not reasonably avoided by consumers; and (3) if the injury is not offset by countervailing benefits to consumers or competition (104 FTC 949). This establishes a cost-benefit test of unfairness or rule of reason. When Congress reauthorized the FTC in 1994, it codified the three-part consumer injury test for unfairness. Congress also rejected the use of "public policy considerations" as the primary basis for unfairness actions, which appears to make it more difficult for the FTC to clothe itself in the public interest. However, a recent episode involving advertising of alcohol beverages suggests that the FTC's Bureau of Consumer Protection continues to operate under older notions of unfairness.

Case Study: FTC's 1999 and 2003 Alcohol Advertising Reports

In 1999, and again in 2003, the joint Congressional Committees on Appropriations directed the FTC to investigate the effectiveness of the alcohol industry's voluntary guidelines for advertising and marketing to underage audiences.[53] The FTC's 1999 Report pointed out that alcohol use by teenagers and youth had declined substantially since the peak levels of the late 1970s, but it nevertheless expressed the view that underage alcohol use presented a constant challenge to the industry, government agencies, and consumer organizations.[54] The report failed to address reasons for the decline in underage alcohol use. The report also stated "while many factors may influence an underage person's drinking decisions, including among other things parents, peers and the media, there is reason to believe that advertising also plays a role."[55] However, the report did not present a comprehensive review of the relevant literature or weigh the importance of advertising relative to the other factors as required by the 1984 version of the unfairness test. Further, the report argued that industry self-regulation of advertising was "an appropriate mechanism because many forms of government intervention raise First Amendment concerns."[56] Among other things, this thorny statement ignores the possible effects of industry self-regulation on competition, especially advertising carried out by smaller firms and emerging brands. In its 1999 Report, the FTC recommended several "best practice" changes in the industry's "code of conduct," including: (1) a 70 percent adult audience standard for placement of advertisements in all media; (2) changes in advertising content and placement to avoid targeting of underage youth; and (3) creation of third-party external review boards with responsibility to address complaints from the public or other industry members. However, the recommendations were unaccompanied by a cost-benefit analysis indicating the likely effects (if any) of the changes on underage drinking or the consequences for industry competition of third-party review.[57] In 2003, despite a high level of compliance with the existing 50 percent adult standard, the beer and spirits industries altered their codes and adopted the FTC's recommended 70 percent standard. Further, both industries instituted external review panels to assess complaints about content and placement of advertisements, and one unidentified firm went so far as to use an outside panel to act as a sounding board during the creative stage.[58] This blurs the line between private and public enterprise. Given the difficulties likely to be encountered in meeting the tougher 70 percent standard, it can be expected that public health watchdog groups will press for legislation making mandatory an external review of all advertisements, even though the TTB is authorized to do this.

Moreover, alcohol producers have always taken the position that advertising affects only brand shares, so the change to the new standard means that public health advocates can easily question the industry's belief in its own position, i.e., if advertising affects only brand shares, why did the industry make the change to the 70 percent standard? (The author has personally witnessed this happen.) The answer, of course, rests in the shifting balance of powers that is characteristic of a regulated industry as well as the incentives faced by a regulatory agency that might be trying to generate support from Congressional Appropriations Committees.[59]

Case Study: Location and Pricing of Monopoly Control States

Following the repeal of Prohibition, eighteen states adopted statewide control of wholesale or retail sales of alcohol. The control state system is not an American invention, as similar systems already existed in Canada and the Scandinavian countries. Officials associated with the control states are able to dress up monopoly in public interest clothes, but this ignores the fact that all states also derive revenue from the taxation of alcohol. Given that a government is going to collect a certain amount of tax revenue, both taxpayers and tax collectors have an incentive to minimize the economic costs of collection (e.g., paperwork, evasion, enforcement costs). Collection costs are higher if there are low-tax or untaxed substitutes available to consumers. Unlike the license states, the control states rely on internal taxation of alcohol by using a complex system of markups of producer prices and ad valorem or per gallon taxes. Except for Iowa and Utah, the control states can be divided into two groups according to location: the northern control states, located on or near the Canadian border, Idaho, Maine, Michigan, Montana, New Hampshire, Ohio, Oregon, Pennsylvania, Vermont, Washington, and

Wyoming, and the southern control states, located in or near the Appalachian mountains, Alabama, Mississippi, North Carolina, Virginia, and West Virginia. As pointed out by Daniel Benjamin and Terry Anderson, the principal sources of low-cost bootleg liquor during Prohibition were Canada and the Appalachian region.[60] Hence, the higher costs of tax enforcement in northern border states and southern Appalachian states meant that a system of state monopolies would be a better method for maximizing the government's net revenue from alcohol sales, even if there are somewhat higher costs of operating the government's monopoly compared to privately licensed alcohol wholesalers and retailers. An economic model of organization emphasizes the trade-offs between unrestricted private enterprise, restricted private enterprise, and government monopoly. The nonrandom location of control states suggests that temperance may be less important than suggested by monopoly spokespersons or advocates. This outcome is supported by the small differences in alcohol consumption in control states compared to the license states.[61]

Having chosen the monopoly organizational form, a state alcohol agency also must decide rules of operation and a price structure. Behind these rules and prices are possibilities for rent-sharing and cross-subsidization of consumers. Control states generally have operated fewer retail stores per capita, have fewer hours of operation per day or week, engage in less advertising and in-store assistance, carry fewer brands, and so forth.[62] These visible symbols of alcohol temperance appeal to Baptist-leaning individuals. These rules affect the transaction costs of alcohol purchases, which are reflected in a higher full cost of consumption. However, it follows from the model of regulation that control states might charge lower pecuniary prices, both to ward off the sale of low-taxed alcohol and to retain the political support of alcohol producers and users. The available historical evidence indicates that prices for many brands sold by control states were below those charged by license states.[63] Lastly, the price structure can be used to create political support by charging relatively low prices on inexpensive popular-priced brands compared to premium brands. Again, the historical evidence is consistent with the prediction from the economic model.[64] This example illustrates the interdependence of interests under regulation, including temperance groups and those interested in other factors, such as tax revenue.

Alcohol Advertising: Two Empirical Examples

Politically powerful interest groups, such as the American Medical Association, have argued that alcohol advertising should be banned or restricted due to its effects on public health and drinking by underage individuals, including a complete ban on all TV advertising of alcohol.[65] This view has been recited by many groups and individuals, but usually without complete reference to the empirical literature on the topic. Several exhaustive reviews of the empirical literature on alcohol advertising have failed to establish an effect of advertising or advertising bans on alcohol consumption, including underage use.[66] This section addresses two empirical issues associated with liquor advertising: first, the causal relationship (if any) between advertising and consumption of distilled spirits, and second, the alleged targeting by liquor advertisers of adolescent magazine readers.

A Causality Test for Liquor Sales and Advertising

Table 5.7 displays data on sales and advertising of distilled spirits during the period 1964–2004. It is apparent that spirits advertising peaked in the late 1970s, and declined substantially after that time.

The exact magnitude of the decline depends on the measure chosen, but real advertising per gallon peaked in 1979 and then declined by 66 percent to a low of $0.36 per gallon in 1996. It is of interest that real total advertising and sales of spirits are highly correlated, but it is well-known that correlation does not prove causation. For example, the simple correlation between real total advertising and per capita sales is 0.949. And for real advertising per gallon and per capita sales, the simple correlation is 0.913. A high correlation might demonstrate that advertising leads to (or "causes") higher sales, but the opposite also could be true. That is, it could be that once a brand or market segment meets with consumer preferences, this enables a higher level of advertising outlays as producers attempt to lock in their gains at the brand level. Similarly, it could be the case that sales and advertising are simultaneously determined, especially if the data frequency is annual. Further, the data series themselves are positively autocorrelated, and failure to account for autocorrelation of a variable can lead to spurious statistical relationships.[67] The correlation of sales with its own lagged (past) value is 0.990 and the correlation of real total advertising with its own lagged value is 0.974. Both of these values exceed the simple correlations reported above. Given these data, this section presents a Granger causality test of the relationship between real advertising and consumption of distilled spirits. The discussion uses basic econometrics, and the reader is advised that a more technical treatment of the issue is available using higher-frequency data.[68]

The basic idea of Granger causality is simple. Consider two variables such as advertising (X) and consumption of distilled spirits (Y). First, there should be a reasonable or rational relationship between the two variables that would support a causal relationship. Second, if X causes Y, then changes in X should precede changes in Y. The test asks how much of Y can be explained by its lagged values

and, having accounted for autocorrelation, then to see if adding lagged values of X can improve the prediction of Y. If it does, there is information in the values of X that aids the explanation of Y, and X is said to Granger-cause Y. Note that Granger causality does not necessarily indicate "cause and effect" in the usual sense because there might be other variables that cause both X and Y or it may be that X and Y are simultaneously determined. A failure of Y to Granger-cause X helps rule out these other possibilities, and the test is run for both possible causal flows, i.e., does X cause Y, and vice versa? For aggregate consumption and advertising in the economy, an early test for causal flow was conducted by Richard Schmalensee, who looked at various leads and lags between real per capita aggregate consumption in the economy and real per capita aggregate advertising.[69] Schmalensee observed that the advertising in the next quarter was more highly correlated with current consumption than was current advertising or lagged advertising. Additional statistical tests led him to conclude, "We must accept the null hypothesis that advertising affects neither aggregate total consumption nor aggregate consumption spending on goods."[70] A more definitive test of the aggregate relationship is found in a famous 1980 study by Richard Ashley, Clive Granger, and Richard Schmalensee, which concluded that aggregate advertising in the economy does not cause aggregate consumption, but consumption might be causing advertising.[71]

In order to conduct a test of Granger causality for distilled spirits, the sales and advertising data in Table 5.7 were transformed by taking their logarithms, and first-differencing the logged variables, e.g., $dln(Y_t) = ln(Y_t) - ln(Y_{t-1})$, where ln indicates the natural log operator and d indicates the differencing operator. The resulting variables are annual growth rates. Taking logs helps reduce heteroscedasticity, while differencing removes trends in the variables and helps ensure that the transformed data series

Table 5.7

Distilled Spirits Advertising and Consumption, 1964–2004

Year	Nominal ads (mil. $)	Cost index (82/84=100)	Real total ads (mil. $ 82/84)	Ads per gal. ($ per gal.)	Ads per cap. ($ per cap.)	Spirits (gal. per cap.)
1964	112.8	38.0	296.8	1.08	2.63	2.44
1965	127.1	40.0	317.8	1.08	2.79	2.58
1966	135.3	41.0	330.0	1.07	2.86	2.68
1967	145.3	42.0	346.0	1.07	2.97	2.79
1968	157.2	43.0	365.6	1.06	3.08	2.91
1969	163.8	45.0	364.0	1.00	3.02	3.01
1970	164.1	46.0	356.7	0.96	2.93	3.05
1971	164.8	48.0	343.3	0.90	2.75	3.06
1972	180.6	46.0	392.6	1.00	2.99	3.00
1973	180.2	46.0	391.7	0.97	2.92	3.01
1974	200.2	48.0	417.1	1.00	3.03	3.03
1975	196.6	51.0	385.5	0.91	2.75	3.02
1976	217.1	54.0	402.0	0.94	2.81	2.98
1977	218.3	58.0	376.4	0.87	2.59	2.98
1978	277.3	64.0	433.3	0.97	2.93	3.01
1979	335.3	70.0	479.0	1.07	3.20	2.99
1980	348.3	77.0	452.3	1.01	2.92	2.90
1981	377.1	85.0	443.6	0.99	2.81	2.85
1982	385.9	92.0	419.5	0.96	2.63	2.74
1983	361.5	100.0	361.5	0.84	2.22	2.65
1984	346.2	108.0	320.6	0.75	1.95	2.59
1985	302.9	116.0	261.1	0.63	1.56	2.49
1986	259.9	122.0	213.0	0.54	1.28	2.37
1987	253.1	126.0	200.9	0.52	1.19	2.30
1988	240.5	134.0	179.5	0.47	1.05	2.21
1989	277.2	141.0	196.6	0.53	1.14	2.15
1990	284.6	148.8	191.3	0.51	1.11	2.17
1991	272.2	158.4	171.8	0.50	0.98	1.97
1992	230.1	163.2	141.0	0.40	0.78	1.97
1993	212.7	168.9	125.9	0.37	0.69	1.88
1994	207.7	174.8	118.8	0.36	0.65	1.84
1995	234.0	180.4	129.7	0.40	0.71	1.78
1996	225.7	190.3	118.6	0.36	0.64	1.75
1997	267.1	197.6	135.2	0.41	0.72	1.76
1998	291.3	209.8	138.8	0.42	0.74	1.77
1999	321.6	218.2	147.4	0.43	0.77	1.80
2000	377.1	224.7	167.8	0.47	0.85	1.79
2001	415.5	229.2	181.3	0.51	0.90	1.78
2002	406.6	239.7	169.6	0.47	0.83	1.79
2003	391.7	249.3	157.1	0.42	0.76	1.84
2004	439.3	258.3	170.1	0.43	0.82	1.89

Sources: Nominal ads from *Impact* for 1975–2004 and *Adams/Jobson Liquor Handbook* for 1964–1974; media unit cost index for magazines from Universal McCann; spirits per adult from *Adams Liquor Handbook 2005.*

Table 5.8

Granger Causality Regression Results, 1965–2004

Variable	dln (spirits per capita)	dln (spirits per capita)	dln (spirits per capita)	dln (real total ads)	dln (ads per capita)
Constant	−0.0033 (0.887)	−0.0033 (0.850)	−0.0029 (0.741)	−0.0020 (0.133)	−0.0145 (0.930)
dln (spirits per capita): L1	0.2023 (1.400)	0.1811 (1.144)	0.1836 (1.160)	1.3263 (2.110)*	1.4215 (2.276)*
dln (spirits per capita): L2	0.4993 (3.614)*	0.4727 (3.031)*	0.4766 (3.045)*	−0.1034 (0.167)	−0.2030 (0.329)
dln (real total ads): L1	—	0.0283 (0.631)	—	0.1494 (0.840)	—
dln (real total ads): L2	—	−0.0042 (0.093)	—	0.1148 (0.639)	—
dln (ads per capita): L1	—	—	0.0260 (0.045)	—	0.1488 (0.830)
dln (ads per capita): L2	—	—	−0.0048 (0.105)	—	0.0758 (0.420)
Adjusted-R^2	0.3990	0.3702	0.3689	0.1803	0.1688
D-W statistic	2.1488	2.1414	2.1466	1.9381	1.9533
B-G statistic (p-value)	1.1440 (0.564)	1.5490 (0.461)	1.6186 (0.445)	1.0283 (0.598)	0.7049 (0.703)
F-statistic (p-value)	—	0.1994 (0.820)	0.1647 (0.849)	2.3139 (0.115)	2.6325 (0.087)

Notes: All variables are expressed as logged first-differences (growth rates), where L1 and L2 indicate the first- and second-lags of the growth variables. Number of observations is 38. T-statistics are in parentheses; asterisks indicate statistically significant coefficients at the 5 percent level or better. The critical value at the 10 percent significance level for the F-test statistic is 2.488 (d.f. = 2, 33). Restricted regressions for the advertising variables are omitted from the table. D-W is the Durbin-Watson statistic for first-order serial correlation (Durbin h could not be calculated). B-G is the Breusch-Godfrey Lagrange-multiplier test statistic for general serial correlation (none found).

are stationary. The econometric test is conducted by, first, regressing the growth rate of spirits consumption on lagged values of itself, which is a restricted regression. The number of lagged terms is determined by the highest value of the adjusted-R^2 statistic. Second, lagged values of advertising growth rates are added to the regression, and an F-test is used to examine the joint significance of the advertising coefficients. Third, the regressions and F-test are repeated with advertising growth as the dependent variable and lagged values of spirits growth in the unrestricted regression. The null hypotheses are that real advertising does not Granger-cause spirits consumption in the first unrestricted regression, and consumption does not Granger-cause spirits advertising in the second unrestricted regression. If a calculated F-statistic exceeds its critical value, the null hypothesis is rejected. In order to conclude that advertising growth (X) causes sales growth (Y), the null hypothesis that X does not cause Y should be rejected and the

null hypothesis that Y does not cause X should not be rejected. The tests below obtain the opposite outcome for liquor; that is, sales growth causes advertising, but advertising growth does not cause sales. This repeats the findings in Ashley, Granger, and Schmalensee for aggregate advertising and consumption.

Table 5.8 shows the Granger regressions for growth of spirits consumption per capita, real total advertising, and real advertising per capita. The sample period is 1965–2004. Two lags of each growth variable are used in the restricted and unrestricted regressions. Regression (1) is the restricted regression for growth of spirits consumption. Regressions (2) and (3) are the unrestricted regressions, which include lagged values for growth of real total advertising and real advertising per capita, respectively. The values for the F-statistics indicate that the null hypothesis for advertising is not rejected, which means that advertising does not Granger-cause spirits consumption. Regressions

(4) and (5) show the unrestricted regressions for the advertising variables. For real total advertising growth, the calculated F-statistic is slightly below the critical value of 2.488, and for real advertising per capita, it is slightly above the critical value. Furthermore, the first lag of spirits growth is statistically significant in both regressions. While this is not overwhelming evidence, it indicates that spirits consumption causes advertising, and not vice versa. The results suggest that banning advertising would not reduce consumption of distilled spirits, which is consistent with the results obtained in empirical studies of advertising bans.

Do Liquor Advertisers Target Adolescent Magazine Readers?

In 2003, the alcohol beverage industry spent more than $1.6 billion on advertising in measured media outlets, including $394 million on ads placed in magazines. Magazine advertising expenditures for distilled spirits were $274 million or 70 percent of the industry's amount. Industry critics allege that some of these activities intentionally target adolescent audiences and thereby contribute importantly to social problems associated with underage alcohol consumption. Compared to broadcast media, advertising in magazines might be prone to demographic targeting of selected audiences due to content differences, portability, and ability to connect with the reader's lifestyle and preferences. Do spirits advertisements target adolescent magazine readers? The evidence on the affirmative side is based largely on a series of descriptive reports commissioned by a watchdog organization, the Center on Alcohol Marketing and Youth (CAMY).[72] CAMY's studies measure the youth audience as a percentage of the total audience for different alcohol brands and media outlets, which are aggregated to obtain measures of advertising exposure per capita for youth and adults. For magazines, the exposure measure takes account of an advertisement's frequency and reach (audience composition), but fails to account for audience size. Because underage youth constitute about 15 percent of the total U.S. population, CAMY characterizes any audience containing more than 15 percent adolescents as "youth-oriented." This designation is used regardless of other aspects of placement decisions, such as the number of adults in the audience or the number of adult readers per copy. Further, CAMY's studies are descriptive and based on the simplistic notion that intentional targeting occurs whenever the 15 percent threshold is exceeded. Magazines such as *Popular Mechanics* and *Sports Illustrated*, with 17 percent and 25 percent youth readership, respectively, are characterized as "youth-oriented," despite other features of the audience and magazine. In order to improve on these descriptive reports, the present study estimates a model of the demand for media space across magazines, conditional on reader demographics, magazine characteristics, and the price of a standardized advertisement.

Advertisers' demand for media space and time is derived from consumers' demand for low-cost information about the existence and attributes of products and brands, including information that is persuasive in nature. Assume the advertiser has solved the problem of media mix and must next decide on the choice of space in available magazines. Magazines can be described in terms of various characteristics of the readers (age, gender, race, income); characteristics of the magazine (subject matter, paid circulation, audience size, single-copy sales, number of issues); and the magazine's price for a standardized advertisement, e.g., the cost of a one-page four-color (P4C) advertisement. Specifying the demand function as a count data model leads to the following formulation of the expected number of occurrences (counts) of alcohol ads, N_i, placed in the i-th magazine during a given time period:

$$E(N_i) = exp\left(X_i'\beta + Z_i'\theta + \alpha P_i + \delta \ln(issues_i)\right) \qquad (1)$$

where exp stands for the exponential function, X is a vector of reader demographics, Z is a vector of magazine characteristics, P is the price of a P4C advertisement, and β, θ, and α represent the coefficients. Holding incidence rates constant, weekly magazines have more annual alcohol advertisements than monthly magazines. Equation (1) treats the number of annual issues of each magazine as the "exposure" variable, which implies that the elasticity coefficient should be close to unity. The price variable is identified by the existence of different real prices for a standardized advertisement due to differences across magazines that reflect unobserved costs of supply that apply to all advertisers, including alcohol advertisers. Hence, the price term in equation (1) is exogenous. Audience size is measured by readers per copy, and is a measure of the marginal benefits of advertising that should be important for placement decisions. For count data, the Poisson model offers a number of advantages, but distribution plots suggested that the negative binomial model might be more appropriate.[73]

Table 5.9 presents the data used in the empirical analysis. The analysis uses the cumulative count of spirits ads in each of thirty-five magazines for the five-year period 1997–2001. This empirical approach ignores year-to-year fluctuations in placements, which are not of particular interest, and also reduces the number of zeros in the ad counts. More important, it is often argued that advertising has lagged effects on adolescent behaviors, and examination of cumulative placements for a given time period captures this broader concern. Data on ads per magazine are from reports by Competitive Media Reporting and are drawn from a study by Craig Garfield, Paul Chung, and Paul Rathouz.[74] The key explanatory variables in the study are readership demographics, which are obtained from

Mediamark Research, Inc. (MRI). For adults, the MRI readership data are based on face-to-face interviews and self-reported readership by 13,000 persons. For youth, a mail survey is used. For each magazine sampled, MRI takes the readership estimates and extrapolates them to the nation. In the present study, youth readers are defined as the age group twelve to nineteen years, and constitute about 14 percent of the U.S. population that is twelve years and older. The null hypothesis is that increased youth readership does not result in an increase in the number of alcohol ad placements. The demographic data also include the median adult reader age, median adult reader income, and percentage of adult male readers. Magazine characteristics include the price of a standardized advertisement, percentage of single-copy sales, adult readers per copy, and annual number of issues. The regression model also includes a binary dummy variable for three African American magazines (*Ebony*, *Jet*, and *Vibe*).

The count data are highly skewed, suggesting that the standard Poisson regression model may be inappropriate due to overdispersion of the data. Overdispersion can arise if there is a high fraction of zeros (nonoccurrences) or because the counts reflect dependence in the placement of ads. Further, the Poisson model imposes the strong condition that the probability of successive events is constant. Two additional count data models were estimated: negative binomial model and zero-inflated Poisson model. The latter model combines a binary (0, 1) variable with a standard count variable. Table 5.10 presents the empirical results for the three regression models. The coefficients indicate the proportional increase in the expected number of placements for a unit increase in an explanatory variable. More generally, positive coefficients indicate that advertisers tend to favor or "target" magazines with the reader characteristic in question, while negative coefficients indicate

Table 5.9

Spirits Ads and Readership for Thirty-five Magazines (cumulative ads 1997–2001)

Magazine (issues)	Reader demographics					Magazine data		
	No. of spirits ads	Youth readers (%)	Adult median age	Adult income ($ 000)	Adult males (%)	Ad cost ($)	Percent news-stand	Readers per copy
Allure (12)	50	38.0	38.1	44.7	12.9	71.08	31.8	4.29
Better Homes & Garden (12)	7	6.6	44.8	50.1	22.0	30.41	5.1	4.35
Car & Driver (12)	51	20.8	33.6	56.0	88.2	85.06	11.2	6.42
Cosmopolitan (12)	410	14.7	31.6	45.8	15.9	44.79	70.2	6.10
Ebony (12)	199	19.2	38.4	34.1	38.6	28.60	14.2	6.09
Elle (12)	226	19.6	30.0	47.9	14.6	71.58	32.0	4.90
Entertainment Weekly (48)	785	23.7	32.0	46.9	43.2	57.18	7.3	5.22
Essence (12)	126	20.2	37.6	34.9	26.9	41.71	24.6	6.56
Family Circle (17)	0	5.6	46.0	44.4	10.1	35.17	36.9	4.38
Field & Stream (12)	170	12.2	39.3	44.1	80.6	50.78	1.8	6.03
Glamour (12)	121	21.1	30.7	48.3	7.9	46.46	51.8	5.15
Good Housekeeping (12)	0	5.6	46.2	45.9	13.0	40.69	25.8	5.45
In Style (12)	383	28.6	32.2	62.1	12.5	48.68	60.5	3.65
Jet (52)	193	19.6	38.3	34.3	45.1	57.93	12.8	9.14
Life (13)	15	17.1	40.9	47.1	49.0	42.98	23.0	9.65
Marie Claire (12)	154	32.3	27.6	47.2	4.8	67.10	59.8	3.00
Motor Trend (12)	11	21.8	34.6	52.3	90.2	84.09	12.5	5.36
National Geographic (12)	43	17.0	44.2	53.1	54.1	25.83	3.4	4.38
Newsweek (52)	417	14.1	43.4	61.1	54.6	51.92	6.1	5.94
People Weekly (52)	400	12.8	39.7	52.5	34.1	42.46	40.6	9.97
Popular Mechanics (12)	67	19.8	39.3	49.1	86.4	62.55	15.7	6.57
Popular Science (12)	38	27.0	40.0	56.5	83.3	41.27	9.9	3.99
Reader's Digest (12)	0	10.3	48.0	42.3	40.9	32.35	5.7	3.26
Road & Track (12)	49	24.6	36.3	60.9	90.7	92.29	18.6	6.71
Rolling Stone (24)	903	35.2	27.7	48.6	62.9	68.67	15.1	6.49
Soap Opera Digest (52)	1	16.0	35.8	35.2	7.9	30.16	34.1	5.88
Spin (12)	299	45.2	24.4	51.3	65.2	68.44	19.5	5.92
Sport (12)	24	43.6	34.8	46.0	77.4	49.56	5.3	3.58
Sporting News (52)	207	28.6	38.2	53.6	86.7	55.05	5.1	5.32
Sports Illustrated (53)	1470	21.3	36.5	51.3	78.0	57.14	2.7	6.79
Time (52)	143	11.2	43.2	55.4	52.1	44.00	5.6	5.30
TV Guide (52)	11	17.8	40.2	41.5	43.9	29.04	16.9	2.77
Vibe (12)	360	45.6	26.3	37.3	51.2	68.39	27.9	7.53
Vogue (12)	171	22.7	33.2	47.6	12.9	65.66	45.3	8.47
Woman's Day (17)	0	6.5	44.7	45.8	7.0	37.18	40.8	4.95

Sources: Cumulative number of spirits ads for 1997–2001 from Garfield et al. "Alcohol Advertising in Magazine and Adolescent Readership," *JAMA* (May 14, 2003); percent youth readers from *MRI Magazine* (Teen) for 1999; adult age, adult income, adult males, and adult readers per copy from *MRI Magazine Report* for 1999; cost per thousand readers for a P4C ad from *SRDS Magazine Advertising Source* for 1999; and annual number of issues from MRI Circulation Report, www.mriplus.com.

the opposite effect. Regardless of the model, the results fail to demonstrate that spirits advertisers are targeting adolescent readers. The coefficient for youth readers is negative, rather than positive.

Additional statistical tests indicated the negative binomial model is the preferred model for advertising count data. The remaining discussion focuses on these results. The coefficient for median age

Table 5.10

Count Data Regression Results for Spirits Ads in Magazines

Variable	Poisson model		Zero-inflated Poisson model		Negative Binomial model	
Constant	14.07	(0.328)*	13.91	(0.329)*	15.74	(3.599)*
Percent youth readers (ages 12–19)	−0.122	(0.004)*	−0.119	(0.004)*	−0.107	(0.030)*
Adult reader median age (years)	−0.440	(0.009)*	−0.432	(0.009)*	−0.506	(0.077)*
Adult reader median income ($ 000)	0.147	(0.004)	0.144	(0.004)*	0.180	(0.038)*
Percent adult male readers (male share of total adults)	0.020	(0.001)*	0.019	(0.001)*	0.018	(0.010)**
Black mags binary (1 = Ebony, Jet, Vibe)	2.629	(0.084)*	2.562	(0.085)*	2.774	(0.754)*
Price of P4C ad (cost per thousand readers)	−0.052	(0.002)*	−0.051	(0.002)*	−0.057	(0.018)*
Percent single-copy sales (percent newsstand sales)	−0.012	(0.002)*	−0.012	(0.001)*	−0.023	(0.016)
Adult readers per copy (pass-along rate)	0.096	(0.011)*	0.097	(0.011)*	0.248	(0.115)*
Log of annual no. of issues (log of issues)	1.164	(0.030)*	1.150	(0.030)*	0.684	(0.289)*
Log likelihood value	−1.272		−1.257		−190.0	
Alpha dispersion parameter (s.e.)	—		—		0.745	(0.187)*

Notes: Dependent variable is a count of cumulative number of spirits ads for each magazine, including zero counts, for the period 1997–2001. Number of observations is 35. Robust standard errors are in parentheses; one and two asterisks indicate statistically significant coefficients at the 5 and 10 percent levels, respectively. Estimates obtained using Stata 8.2.

of adult readers is significantly negative, which implies that spirits advertisers favor younger adult audiences. Adult median income and percentage of adult male readers are both significantly positive. Hence, the demographic results indicate that spirits advertisers favor magazines with more men and young adult readers, but not adolescents. The binary variable for African American magazines is significantly positive. The other empirical results pertain to the cost of a standardized advertisement and features of the magazine. The price of a P4C ad is significantly negative, which shows the importance of treating advertising placements as an economic decision rather than just a marketing ploy. The measure of audience size—adult readers per copy—is significantly positive. The variable for single-copy sales is not significant in the negative binomial model. The exposure variable—annual number of issues—is always significantly positive. Overall, the results provide no evidence that the spirits industry is using magazine ad placements to "target" underage youth. The methods used here improve on an earlier study by Garfield, Chung,

and Rathouz, which failed to control for audience size and the price of an advertisement. This is especially important for distilled spirits, the alcohol beverage that relies most heavily on magazine advertising.

Summary

This chapter has examined the structure and regulation of a declining industry. Sales of distilled spirits in the United States are almost 40 percent below the record level attained in 1971. Reasons for the decline are not well understood, but it cannot be due to lack of advertising or, in recent years, a lack of new brands and products. The major firms in the industry have adapted through merger and positioning of their brand portfolios. The industry remains competitive, but further declines in sales and number of firms might threaten this condition. The spirits industry also is highly regulated and, in contrast to most other industries, its marketing and retailing activities are subject to close supervision by federal and state agencies. Distillers have a First

Amendment right to communicate with their customers, but regulatory agencies are often petitioned by watchdog groups and others, who present a one-sided view of the powers of advertising to stimulate or create product demand. This chapter presented empirical evidence on the advertising-spillover hypothesis, and found it lacking in support. Advertising by successful brands has not stimulated market demand at the category level or beyond. If anything, causality flows from sales growth to advertising, rather than vice versa. Further, an analysis of liquor advertising in magazines failed to support the notion of youth targeting. It is well to remember that, in a free society, the appropriate response to speech that offends is more speech, and not censorship by watchdog interest groups. Anything less is to give in to monopoly.

Notes

1. Analyses of the adoption of prohibition and its repeal are found in B. Goff and G. Anderson, "The Political Economy of Prohibition in the United States, 1919–1933," *Social Science Quarterly* 75 (June 1994), pp. 270–83; M. Munger and T. Schaller, "The Prohibition-Repeal Amendments: A Natural Experiment in Interest Group Influence," *Public Choice* 90 (March 1997), pp. 139–63; J.A. Miron, "An Economic Analysis of Alcohol Prohibition," *Journal of Drug Issues* 28 (Summer 1998), pp. 741–62; and K.S. Strumpf and F. Oberholzer-Gee, "Local Liquor Control from 1934 to 1970," in J.C. Heckelman, J.C. Moorhouse, and R.M. Whaples, eds., *Public Choice Interpretations of American Economic History*, pp. 425–45 (Boston: Kluwer Academic, 2000). See also D.E. Kyvig, *Repealing National Prohibition*, 2nd ed. (Kent, OH: Kent State University Press, 2000).

2. "Nation Celebrates Repeal; Roosevelt Wars on Illicit Trade and Return of Saloon," *Washington Post*, December 6, 1933, p. 1.

3. H.D. Holder and C.J. Cherpitel, "The End of U.S. Prohibition: A Case Study of Mississippi," *Contemporary Drug Problems* 23 (Summer 1996), pp. 301–30. Mississippi was officially dry from 1908 to 1966, but bootlegged liquor was sold openly through licensed outlets and a state tax was used to extract revenues on "tangible personal property." According to Holder and Cherpitel, the end of state prohibition in Mississippi merely substituted legal for illegal consumption, with no change in real consumption levels.

4. Ranked by fiscal year 2004 sales (in millions), the eighteen control states are: Pennsylvania ($1,388); Michigan ($800); Washington ($609); Ohio ($553); Virginia ($491); North Carolina ($486); New Hampshire ($373); Alabama ($290); Oregon ($289); Mississippi ($194); Utah ($168); Iowa ($135); Maine ($89); Idaho ($86); Montana ($71); West Virginia ($60); Wyoming ($56); and Vermont ($47). Some states control only wholesales, and this is reflected in the ranking. The amounts for Pennsylvania and Utah reflect retail sales of table wine.

5. For evidence, see J.P. Nelson, "Advertising Bans, Monopoly, and Alcohol Demand: Testing for Substitution Effects using State Panel Data," *Review of Industrial Organization* 22 (February 2003), pp. 1–25; and B. Trolldal and W. Ponicki, "Alcohol Price Elasticities in Control and License States in the United States, 1982–99," *Addiction* 100 (August 2005), pp. 1158–65.

6. See R.M. O'Neil, *Alcohol Advertising on the Air: Beyond the Reach of Government?* (Washington, DC: Media Institute, 1997); and M. Grimm, "A Spirited Debate," *American Demographics* 24 (April 2002), pp. 48–50. The industry's voluntary ban began after a threat in 1934 by the Federal Radio Commission to conduct hearings on the renewal applications of radio stations that carried liquor advertisements. As an independent agency, the FCC was known during the 1970s for its regulatory zeal under the so-called Fairness Doctrine, which resulted in free counter-ads by antismoking groups during 1967–70 and eventually led to the 1971 ban of cigarette ads on TV and radio. After numerous inquires and considerations, the FCC finally announced in 1987 that the Fairness Doctrine had a chilling effect on speech generally, and could no longer be sustained as an effective public policy; see S.J. Simmons, *The Fairness Doctrine and the Media* (Berkeley, CA: University of California Press, 1978); and T.W. Hazlett, "The Fairness Doctrine and the First Amendment," *The Public Interest* 96 (Summer 1989), pp. 103–16.

7. U.S. International Trade Commission, Office of Industries, *Industry & Trade Summary: Distilled Spirits* (Washington, DC: Author, 2000), p. 10. Other sources of basic information are: Adams Beverage Group, *Adams Liquor Handbook 2005* (Norwalk, CT: Adams Business Media, 2005); Euromonitor International, *Spirits in the USA* (London: Author, 2005); and U.S. Department of Agriculture, Foreign Agricultural Service, *U.S. Market Profile for Distilled Spirits* (Washington, DC: Author, 2005).

8. Sales and revenue data are from *Adams Liquor Handbook 2005*. Distilled spirits sales by volume are commonly expressed either in wine gallons (128 fluid ounces) or 9-liter cases of twelve 750-ml. bottles (2.378 gallons). Proof is 2x the percentage of alcohol by volume (80 proof = 40APV). A proof gallon is equal to 128 fluid ounces containing 50 percent ethyl alcohol (ethanol) by volume (100 proof). Imports of distilled spirits are commonly expressed in proof gallons,

whereas industry statistics use wine gallons or 9-liter cases. The conversion from proof gallons to wine gallons varies, but one proof gallon equals about 0.80 wine gallons.

9. World Advertising Research Center, *World Drink Trends 2005* (Henley-on-Thames, UK: Author, 2005), p. 141.

10. Excise taxes as a revenue-raising or corrective device are discussed in public finance textbooks such as J. Gruber, *Public Finance and Public Policy* (New York: Worth, 2006); see also Congressional Budget Office, *Federal Taxation of Tobacco, Alcoholic Beverages, and Motor Fuels* (Washington, DC: Author, 1990).

11. See S.R. Boyd, ed., *The Whiskey Rebellion* (Westport, CT: Greenwood Press, 1985); and T.P. Slaughter, *The Whiskey Rebellion: Frontier Epilogue to the American Revolution* (London: Oxford University Press, 1986).

12. National Research Council, Institute of Medicine, *Reducing Underage Drinking: A Collective Responsibility* (Washington, DC: National Academies Press, 2004), pp. 240–44; see also "Higher 'Sin' Taxes: A Low Blow to the Poor," in G.S. Becker and G.N. Becker, *The Economics of Life*, pp. 147–48 (New York: McGraw-Hill, 1997); and "Effects of Changes in Alcohol Prices and Taxes," in National Institute on Alcohol Abuse and Alcoholism, *10th Special Report to the U.S. Congress on Alcohol and Health*, pp. 341–54 (Washington, DC: Author, 2000).

13. National Institute on Alcohol Abuse and Alcoholism, *Apparent Per Capita Alcohol Consumption: National, State, and Regional Trends, 1977–2003*, Surveillance Report #73 (Washington, DC: Author, 2005).

14. In most industries, there are well-defined groups of firms within the industry, referred to as strategic groups. If two groups of firms have the same risk-adjusted profitability, the market is efficient (although not necessarily competitive). If the average returns differ, there are barriers to mobility or expansion within the industry. Thus, mobility barriers are the technical and strategic costs of expansion faced by an incumbent firm if it tries to enter a different market segment; see R. Caves and M. Porter, "From Entry Barriers to Mobility Barriers: Conjectural Decisions and Contrived Deterrence to New Competition," *Quarterly Journal of Economics* 91 (May 1977), pp. 241–61; M.E. Porter, "The Structure Within Industries and Companies' Performance," *Review of Economics and Statistics* 61 (May 1979), pp. 214–27; M.E. Porter, *Competitive Strategy: Techniques for Analyzing Industries and Competitors*, rev. ed. (New York: Free Press, 1998); and S. Oster, *Modern Competitive Analysis*, 3rd ed. (New York: Oxford University Press, 1999).

15. The classic statement of the hedonic price model is S. Rosen, "Hedonic Prices and Implicit Markets: Product Differentiation in Pure Competition," *Journal of Political Economy* 82 (January/February 1974), pp. 34–55.

16. R.E. Caves and R.J. Williamson, "What Is Product Differentiation, Really?" *Journal of Industrial Economics* 34 (December 1985), pp. 113–32. Empirically, Caves and Williamson analyzed the basis for product differentiation in thirty-six Australian industries for the period 1968–78. Using factor analysis, they found that gross markups above cost and domestic market shares were positively related to import prices; positively related to differentiation based on advertising; and positively related to differentiation based on complexity of product attributes. They stressed that both the complexity of product attributes and the costliness of information are responsible for differing degrees of product differentiation among industries.

17. See J. Sutton, *Sunk Costs and Market Structure: Price Competition, Advertising, and Evolution of Concentration* (Cambridge, MA: MIT Press, 1992). Sutton's theory yields the prediction that in advertising-intensive industries, such as distilled spirits, "some small set of firms must at some point emerge as high advertisers, whose combined market share exceeds some lower bound, however large the market becomes" (p. 174). See also K. Bagwell, "The Economics of Advertising," in M. Armstrong and R. Porter, eds., *Handbook of Industrial Organization*, 3rd ed. (Amsterdam: North-Holland, forthcoming).

18. It is generally accepted that advertising depreciates over a matter of months, rather than years; see D.G. Clarke, "Econometric Measurement of the Duration of Advertising Effect on Sales," *Journal of Marketing Research* 13 (November 1976), pp. 345–57; and E.M. Landes and A.M. Rosenfield, "The Durability of Advertising Revisited," *Journal of Industrial Economics* 42 (September 1994), pp. 263–76.

19. If shipping costs are constant per unit (e.g., per gallon), then transportation costs reduce the price of "high quality" imported spirits relative to lower-priced imported brands and, other things equal, this will raise the demand for premium imported brands. This proposition is known as the Alchian-Allen substitution theorem (or the "shipping the good apples out" conjecture). For a recent empirical test, see D.L. Hummels and A. Skiba, "Shipping the Good Apples Out: An Empirical Confirmation of the Alchian-Allen Conjecture," *Journal of Political Economy* 112 (December 2004), pp. 1384–402.

20. J.P. Nelson, "Broadcast Advertising and U.S. Demand for Alcoholic Beverages," *Southern Economic Journal* 65 (April 1999), pp. 774–90.

21. All fifty states regulate to some degree the interstate shipment of alcohol directly to their residents, but wine is most affected by direct shipment laws. Because several states exempted in-state wineries or have other discriminatory provisions, at least eight lawsuits were filed in federal courts that challenged the constitutionality of these laws. In May of 2005, the Supreme Court consolidated two cases, and held that states that discriminate against out-of-state shippers violate the Constitution's Commerce Clause and that such discrimination is not permitted by the Twenty-first

Amendment; see *Granholm v. Heald* (544 U.S. 460). The political economy of direct shipment laws is analyzed by G.A. Riekhof and M.E. Sykuta, "Politics, Economics, and the Regulation of Direct Interstate Shipping in the Wine Industry," *American Journal of Agricultural Economics* 87 (May 2005), pp. 439–52.

22. A test of the spillover hypothesis for distilled spirits is found in M.P. Gius, "Using Panel Data to Determine the Effect of Advertising on Brand-Level Distilled Spirits Sales," *Journal of Studies on Alcohol* 57 (January 1996), pp. 73–76. On the advertising-response function, see J.L. Simon and J. Arndt, "The Shape of the Advertising Response Function," *Journal of Advertising Research* 20 (August 1980), pp. 11–28; and G. Assmus, J.U. Farley, and D.R. Lehmann, "How Advertising Affects Sales: Meta-Analysis of Econometric Results," *Journal of Marketing Research* 21 (February 1984), pp. 65–74.

23. The evidence on advertising bans is addressed in J.P. Nelson and D.J. Young, "Do Advertising Bans Work? An International Comparison," *International Journal of Advertising* 20, 3 (2001), pp. 273–96; J.P. Nelson, "Cigarette Demand, Structural Change, and Advertising Bans: International Evidence, 1970–1995," *Contributions to Economic Analysis & Policy* 2 (August 2003), pp. 1–27; J.P. Nelson, "Alcohol Advertising Bans, Consumption, and Control Policies in Seventeen OECD Countries, 1975–2000," unpublished paper (2006); and J.P. Nelson, "Advertising Bans in the United States," in R. Whaples, ed., *EH.Net Encyclopedia,* (May 2004), online at: www.eh.net/encyclopedia/contents/Nelson.AdBans.php.

24. Sources for this section include the individual company Web sites and the publications listed above in note 7.

25. Federal Trade Commission, *1992 Horizontal Merger Guidelines, with April 8, 1997 Revisions to Section 4 on Efficiencies* (Washington, DC: Author, 1997), p. 4, available on the FTC Web site.

26. Federal Trade Commission, "In the Matter of Guinness PLC, Grand Metropolitan PLC, and Diageo PLC," File No. 971 0081, Docket No. C-3801 (1997–1998), available on the FTC Web site. An econometric test of market segmentation for distilled spirits is found in M.P. Gius, "The Extent of the Market in the Liquor Industry: An Empirical Test of Localized Brand Rivalry, 1970–1988," *Review of Industrial Organization* 8, 5 (1993), pp. 599–608. Gius finds that the market is segmented, but not to the extent suggested by the FTC complaint. Empirically, he divides products into "browns" and "whites," and within brown spirits into "premium" and "non-premium" brands.

27. Federal Trade Commission, "In the Matter of Diageo PLC and Vivendi Universal S.A.," File No. 011 0002, Docket No. C-4032 (2001–2002), available on the FTC Web site.

28. See *U.S. v. The Gillette Company*, 828 F. Supp. 78 (1993), holding that there was a relevant market for premium fountain pens, but neither technological nor legal barriers to entry limited competition in the market segment.

29. *In the Matter of Coca-Cola Bottling Company of New York, Inc.*, 93 FTC 110 (1979).

30. *In the Matter of Heublein, Inc., et al.*, 96 FTC 385 (1980).

31. G.J. Stigler, "The Theory of Economic Regulation," *Bell Journal of Economics and Management Science* 2 (Spring 1971), pp. 3–21.

32. Ibid., p. 4.

33. Ibid., p. 4.

34. Ibid., p. 6.

35. Ibid., p. 7.

36. In addition to Stigler's article, important contributions were made by R.A. Posner, "Taxation by Regulation," *Bell Journal of Economics and Management Science* 2 (Spring 1971), pp. 22–50; S. Peltzman, "Toward a General Theory of Regulation," *Journal of Law and Economics* 19 (August 1976), pp. 211–40; and G.S. Becker, "A Theory of Competition Among Pressure Groups for Political Influence," *Quarterly Journal of Economics* 98 (August 1983), pp. 371–400. See also T.R. Beard, D.L. Kasserman, and J.W. Mayo, "A Graphical Exposition of the Economic Theory of Regulation," *Economic Inquiry* 41 (October 2003), pp. 592–606.

37. In 1982, without consulting the alcohol industry, the Reagan Administration proposed elimination of the Federal Bureau of Alcohol, Tobacco and Firearms, and transfer of some its duties to other federal agencies. The industry quickly rejected this opportunity, citing, among other things, the fear of dealing with fifty sets of state regulations; see "Deregulation Plan Has an Industry 'Dumbfounded,'" *New York Times,* August 27, 1982, p. A-10.

38. S.C. Salop, D.T. Scheffman, and W. Schwartz, "A Bidding Analysis of Special Interest Regulation: Raising Rivals' Costs in a Rent Seeking Society," in B. Yandle and R. Rogowsky, eds., *The Political Economy of Regulation: Private Interests in the Regulatory Process*, pp. 102–27 (Washington, DC: FTC, 1984); and T.G. Krattenmaker and S.C. Salop, "Anticompetitive Exclusion: Raising Rivals' Costs to Achieve Power Over Price," *Yale Law Journal* 96 (December 1986), pp. 209–93.

39. For a survey of the rent-seeking literature, see W.C. Mitchell and M.C. Munger, "Economic Models of Interest Groups: An Introductory Survey," *American Journal of Political Science* 35 (May 1991), pp. 512–46. See also F.S. McChesney, *Money for Nothing: Politicians, Rent Extraction, and Political Extortion* (Cambridge, MA: Harvard University Press, 1997).

40. B. Yandle, "Bootleggers and Baptists: The Education of a Regulatory Economist," *Regulation* 7 (May/June 1983), pp. 12–16; B. Yandle, "Bootleggers and Baptists in the Market for Regulation," in J.F. Shogren, ed., *The Political Economy of Government Regulation*, pp. 29–53 (Boston: Kluwer, 1989);

and B. Yandle, "Bootleggers and Baptists in Retrospect," *Regulation* 22 (Fall 1999), pp. 5–7.

41. Yandle, "Bootleggers and Baptists in Retrospect," p. 5.

42. J.F. Shogren, "The Optimal Subsidization of Baptists by Bootleggers," *Public Choice* 67 (November 1990), pp. 181–89.

43. Information in this section is drawn mainly from the TTB Web site. There are very few studies of the ATF or TTB that focus on regulation of alcohol. An exception is R.G. LaForge, *Misplaced Priorities: A History of Federal Alcohol Regulation and Public Health Policy*, unpublished Ph.D. dissertation, Johns Hopkins University, 1987. LaForge's comprehensive study examines the development of federal alcohol policy from 1933 to 1986, including controversies related to alcohol health warnings, ingredient labeling, and advertising.

44. LaForge, p. 21.

45. Under the FAA Act, standards of identity for spirits and wine are published in the *Code of Federal Regulation*, but these only list basic ingredients and not additives and optional ingredients (beer is exempt). All labels are subject to an approval process referred to as a certificate of label approval (COLA), which authorizes the certificate holder to bottle and remove or import alcohol beverages that bear labels identical to the approval label. There is no formal mechanism for FAA certification of advertising copy, which means that review is often instituted following complaints from competitors or watchdog groups. In November of 2004, TTB announced that it would take a more proactive approach with respect to monitoring advertising.

46. *Brown-Forman Distillers Corp., et al., v. Mathews, et al.*, 435 F. Supp. 5 (1976). The opinion in this case contains an excellent history of labeling regulation since the repeal of Prohibition.

47. In 1973, CSPI petitioned for a warning label on the effects of inebriation. ATF responded in 1978 by issuing a notice of proposed rule making on warning labels that would address alcohol use by pregnant women (43 *Federal Register* 2186). Ultimately, these concerns resulted in congressional passage of the Alcohol Beverage Labeling Act of 1988 (P.L. 100-690), which required a health-warning label that is administered by TTB. Since November of 1989, all labels on alcohol products have contained the message, "GOVERNMENT WARNING: (1) According to the Surgeon General, women should not drink alcoholic beverages during pregnancy because of the risk of birth defects. (2) Consumption of alcoholic beverages impairs your ability to drive a car or operate machinery, and may cause health problems."

48. Constitutional issues surrounding the health-claims example are summarized in E. Bierbauer, "Liquid Honesty: The First Amendment Right to Market the Health Benefits of Moderate Alcohol Consumption," *New York University Law*

Review 74 (October 1999), pp. 1057–98; and B. Lieberman, "The Power of Positive Drinking: Are Alcoholic Beverage Health Claims Constitutionally Protected?" *Food and Drug Journal* 58, 3 (2003), pp. 511–20.

49. See B.M. Owen and R. Braeutigam, *The Regulation Game: Strategic Use of Administrative Process* (Cambridge, MA: Ballinger, 1978). They argue that a major consequence of regulation is to "slow down or delay the operation of market forces" (p. 18) and that under administrative procedures, economic agents acquire a "legal right to the status quo" (p. 30), which can be used strategically to limit competition from outsiders.

50. This section reflects ongoing research by the author on FTC regulation of alcohol and tobacco advertising; see Nelson, "Advertising Bans in the United States." There are numerous reviews of the FTC's authority, but many focus on antitrust and not consumer protection. See S. Stone, *Economic Regulation and the Public Interest: The Federal Trade Commission in Theory and Practice* (Ithaca, NY: Cornell University Press, 1977); K.W. Clarkson and T.J. Muris, eds., *The Federal Trade Commission Since 1970: Economic Regulation and Bureaucratic Behavior* (Cambridge, UK: Cambridge University Press, 1981); B.R. Hasin, *Consumers, Commissions, and Congress: Law, Theory, and the Federal Trade Commission* (New Brunswick, NJ: Transaction Books, 1987); J.C. Miller, *The Economist as Reformer: Revamping the FTC, 1981–1985* (Washington, DC: American Enterprise Institute, 1989); B. Boyer, "The Federal Trade Commission and Consumer Protection Policy: A Postmortem Examination," in K. Hawkins and J.M. Thomas, eds., *Making Regulatory Policy*, pp. 93-132 (Pittsburgh: University of Pittsburgh Press, 1989); and M.E. Budnitz, "The FTC's Consumer Protection Program During the Miller Years: Lessons for Administrative Agency Structure and Operation," *Catholic University Law Review* 46 (Winter 1997), pp. 371–451.

51. See H. Beales, R. Craswell, and S.C. Salop, "The Efficient Regulation of Consumer Information," *Journal of Law and Economics* 24 (December 1981), pp. 491–539; G.T. Ford and J.E. Calfee, "Recent Developments in FTC Policy on Deception," *Journal of Marketing* 50 (July 1986), pp. 82–103; E.T. Sullivan and B.A. Marks, "The FTC's Deceptive Advertising Policy: A Legal and Economic Analysis," *Oregon Law Review* 64, 4 (1986), pp. 593–635; J.I. Richards, *Deceptive Advertising: Behavioral Analysis of a Legal Concept* (Hillsdale, NJ: Erlbaum, 1990); and P.H. Rubin, "The Economics of Regulating Deception," *Cato Journal* 10 (Winter 1991), pp. 667–90.

52. The unfairness standard was first articulated by letter on December 17, 1980, and later adopted in a 1984 decision; see *FTC Unfairness Policy Statement*, appended to *International Harvester Co.* (104 FTC 949). See also R. Pitofsky, "Beyond Nader: Consumer Protection and the Regulation of Advertising," *Harvard Law Review* 90 (Febru-

ary 1977), pp. 661–701; E.R. Jordan and P.H. Rubin, "An Economic Analysis of the Law of False Advertising," *Journal of Legal Studies* 8 (June 1979), pp. 527–53; R.D. Petty, "FTC's Advertising Regulation: Survivor or Casualty of the Reagan Revolution," *American Business Law Journal* 30 (May 1992), pp. 1–34; and J.H. Beales, "The Federal Trade Commission's Use of Unfairness Authority: Its Rise, Fall, and Resurrection," *Journal of Public Policy & Marketing* 22 (Fall 2003), pp. 192–200.

53. Federal Trade Commission, *Self-Regulation in the Alcohol Industry: A Review of Industry Efforts to Avoid Promoting Alcohol to Underage Consumers* (Washington, DC: Author, 1999); and Federal Trade Commission, *Alcohol Marketing and Advertising: A Report to Congress* (Washington, DC: Author, 2003). Both reports are available on the FTC Web site.

54. According to reports released by the University of Michigan's Monitoring the Future (MTF) survey, thirty-day prevalence of alcohol use by twelfth graders reached an all-time high of 72.1 percent in 1978, declined to 50 percent in 2000, and stood at 47 percent in 2005. Thirty-day prevalence rates in 2005 for eighth and tenth graders were 17.1 percent and 33.2 percent, respectively, which are the lowest levels attained since the reporting began for younger age groups in 1991; see the MTF Web site for these data.

55. Federal Trade Commission (1999), p. 4.

56. Ibid., p. 3. While commercial speech is afforded protection under the First Amendment, the protection granted is less than that given noncommercial speech. Under the Supreme Court's *Central Hudson* doctrine, 447 U.S. 557 (1980), a governmental restriction of commercial speech must satisfy four criteria (or prongs) to survive First Amendment scrutiny: (1) the speech must concern lawful activity and must not be false or misleading; (2) the asserted government interest in restricting speech must be substantial; (3) the restriction must directly and materially advance the government's interest; and (4) the restriction must be no more extensive than necessary to serve the government's interest. The Supreme Court applied the doctrine in *44 Liquormart, Inc. v. Rhode Island*, 517 U.S. 484 (1996) and struck down a state ban of alcohol price advertising. For additional discussion of this case, see Nelson, "Advertising Bans in the United States."

57. During the first two years under the new Code, the Distilled Spirits Institute (DISCUS) received thirty-one complaints about liquor ad placement and contents, and twenty-three of the complaints were filed by other industry members; see the DISCUS Web site. The Code's self-policing aspect is reminiscent of Trade Practice Conferences instituted by the FTC during and following the Great Depression. These joint agreements among competitors were questioned for potentially collusive effects; see Anon., "Trade Rules and Trade Conferences: The FTC and Business Attack Deceptive Practices, Unfair Competition, and Antitrust Violations," *Yale Law Journal* 62 (May 1953), pp. 912–53.

58. Federal Trade Commission (2003), p. 11.

59. See also P. Pennock, "The Evolution of U.S. Temperance Movements Since Repeal: A Comparison of Two Campaigns to Control Alcoholic Beverage Marketing, 1950s and 1980s," *Social History of Alcohol and Drugs* 20, 1 (2005), pp. 14–65.

60. D.K. Benjamin and T.L. Anderson, "Taxation, Enforcement Costs, and the Incentive to Privatize," in *The Privatization Process: A Worldwide Perspective*, pp. 39–55 (Lanham, MD: Rowman & Littlefield, 1996). See also B.L. Benson, D.W. Rasmussen, and P.R. Zimmerman, "Implicit Taxes Collected by State Liquor Monopolies," *Public Choice* 115 (June 2003), pp. 313–31.

61. See Nelson, "Advertising Bans, Monopoly, and Alcohol Demand: Testing for Substitution Effects Using State Panel Data," p. 7.

62. For more on the economics of state monopolies, see J.K. Smith, "An Analysis of State Regulation Governing Liquor Store Licenses," *Journal of Law and Economics* 25 (October 1982), pp. 301–19; A. Zardkoohi and A. Sheer, "Public Versus Private Liquor Retailing: An Investigation into the Behavior of the State Governments," *Southern Economic Journal* 50 (April 1984), pp. 1058–76; S. Swidler, "Consumption and Price Effects of State-Run Liquor Monopolies," *Managerial and Decision Economics* 7 (March 1986), pp. 49–55; J.P. Nelson, "State Monopolies and Alcoholic Beverage Consumption," *Journal of Regulatory Economics* 2 (March 1990), pp. 83–98; D.S. West, "Double Marginalization and Privatization in Liquor Retailing," *Review of Industrial Organization* 16 (June 2000), pp. 399–415; and D.G. Whitman, *Strange Brew: Alcohol and Government Monopoly* (Oakland, CA: Independent Institute, 2003).

63. Benjamin and Anderson, p. 45.

64. S. Peltzman, "Pricing in Public and Private Enterprises," *Journal of Law and Economics* 14 (April 1971), pp. 109–47.

65. See AMA Board of Trustees, "Alcohol: Advertising, Counteradvertising, and Depiction in the Public Media," *Journal of the American Medical Association* 256 (September 19, 1986), pp. 1485–88; and American Medical Association, *H-30.990: Alcoholic Beverages Advertising Ban* (Chicago: Author, 2005).

66. National Institute of Alcohol Abuse and Alcoholism, "Alcohol Advertising: What Are the Effects?" in *10th Special Report to the U.S. Congress on Alcohol and Health*, pp. 412–26 (Washington, DC: Author, 2000); J.P. Nelson, "Alcohol Advertising and Advertising Bans: A Survey of Research Methods, Results, and Policy Implications," in M.R. Baye and J.P. Nelson, eds., *Advances in Applied Micro-Economics: Advertising and Differentiated Products*, pp. 239–95 (Amsterdam, Netherlands: Elsevier Science, 2001); and

National Research Council, Institute of Medicine, *Reducing Underage Drinking: A Collective Responsibility* (Washington, DC: National Academies Press, 2003).

67. E.R. Berndt, *The Practice of Econometrics: Classic and Contemporary* (Reading, MA: Addison-Wesley, 1991), p. 381.

68. See N.E. Coulson, J.R. Moran, and J.P. Nelson, "The Long-Run Demand for Alcohol and the Advertising Debate: A Cointegration Analysis," in M.R. Baye and J.P. Nelson, eds., *Advances in Applied Micro-Economics: Advertising and Differentiated Products*, pp. 31–54 (Amsterdam, Netherlands: Elsevier Science, 2001).

69. R. Schmalensee, *The Economics of Advertising* (Amsterdam, Netherlands: North-Holland, 1972), pp. 48–95.

70. Ibid., p. 58.

71. R. Ashley, C.W.J. Granger, and R. Schmalensee, "Advertising and Aggregate Consumption: An Analysis of Causality," *Econometrica* 48 (July 1980), pp. 1149–68. Aggregate advertising is pro-cyclical in the economy, rather than counter-cyclical as might be claimed by advocates of the spillover hypothesis; see the series of articles on advertising during the 2001 recession appearing in the *Wall Street Journal*: "Ad Slump May Be Worse Than Thought," August 14, 2001, p. B-2; "Decline in Ad Revenue Worsens," November 28, 2001, p. B-14; "Bargain Prices Lure Some to Increase Ads," December 12, 2001, p. B-4; and "TV Ad Spending Likely to Stay Flat," April 25, 2002, p. B-11.

72. Center on Alcohol Marketing and Youth, *Overexposed: Youth a Target of Alcohol Advertising in Magazines* (Washington, DC: Author, 2002); and Center on Alcohol Marketing and Youth, *Youth Overexposed: Alcohol Advertising in Magazines, 2001 to 2003* (Washington, DC: Author, 2005).

73. For discussion of count data models, see A.C. Cameron and P.K. Trivedi, *Regression Analysis of Count Data* (Cambridge, UK: Cambridge University Press, 1998); and R. Winkelmann, *Econometric Analysis of Count Data*, 4th ed. (Berlin: Springer, 2003).

74. C.F. Garfield, P.J. Chung, and P.J. Rathouz, "Alcohol Advertising in Magazines and Adolescent Readership," *Journal of the American Medical Association* 289 (May 14, 2003), pp. 2424–29. See also J.P. Nelson, "Advertising, Alcohol, and Youth," *Regulation* 28 (Summer 2005), pp. 40–47; and J.P. Nelson, "Alcohol Advertising in Magazines: Do Beer, Wine, and Spirits Ads Target Youth?" *Contemporary Economic Policy* 24 (July 2006), pp. 357–69.

Selected Readings

Baye, M.R., and J.P. Nelson, eds. *Advances in Applied Microeconomics: Advertising and Differentiated Products* (Amsterdam, Netherlands: Elsevier Science, 2001).

Calfee, J.E. *Fear of Persuasion: A New Perspective on Advertising and Regulation* (Washington, DC: AEI Press, 1997).

Cook, P.J., and M.J. Moore, "Alcohol," in A.J. Culyer and J.P. Newhouse, eds., *The Handbook of Health Economics*, Vol. 1B, pp. 1629–73 (Amsterdam, Netherlands: Elsevier, 2000).

Cook, P.J., and M.J. Moore, "Environment and Persistence in Youthful Drinking," in J. Gruber, ed., *Risky Behavior Among Youths: An Economic Analysis*, pp. 375–437 (Chicago: University of Chicago Press, 2001).

McChesney, F.S. *Money for Nothing: Politicians, Rent Extraction, and Political Extortion.* Cambridge, MA: Harvard University Press, 1997.

Nelson, J.P. "Advertising Bans in the United States," in R. Whaples, ed., *EH.Net Encyclopedia* (May 2004), online at: www.eh.net/encyclopedia/contents/Nelson.AdBans.php.

Sutton, J. *Sunk Costs and Market Structure: Price Competition, Advertising, and the Evolution of Competition.* Cambridge, MA: MIT Press, 1991.

Selected Web Sites

Alcohol and Tobacco Tax and Trade Bureau, U.S. Department of the Treasury: www.ttb.gov.

Distilled Spirits Council of the United States: www.discus.org.

Monitoring the Future, University of Michigan: www.monitoringthefuture.org.

National Alcohol Beverage Control Association: www.nabca.org.

National Institute of Alcohol Abuse and Alcoholism, U.S. National Institutes of Health: www.niaaa.nih.gov.

U.S. Federal Trade Commission: www.ftc.gov.

Wine & Spirits Wholesalers of America, Inc.: www.wswa.org.

6

Health Insurance

Designing Products to Reduce Costs

Lee R. Mobley and H.E. Frech III

Introduction

A health insurer contracts to pay all or a portion of bills for medical services deemed "necessary" in return for a fixed premium. Consumers demand this service because it reduces risk. The cost of this service is the difference between the premium and the expected benefits, which is known as the loading charge. The degree of competition affects the size of the loading charge and the amount of innovation insurers will undertake to reduce the administrative costs that underlie it.

But efficiency in the provision of health insurance involves more than just minimizing administrative costs. Insurance also profoundly affects the rate of use and price of health services. When much of the cost of medical services is covered by insurance, more services will be used and patients will devote less effort to seeking providers with lower prices. These harmful effects of insurance on the provision and pricing of medical care services have led insurers to design policies to lessen its impact. These policies have included increasing the use of deductibles and coinsurance and, more recently, administrative utilization controls. The degree of competition in the health insurance market influences how much insurers use such policies. Thus, the degree of competition affects not only the resources that go into administering insurance

but, much more importantly, it affects the resources that go into medical services.

Up until about the early eighties, insurers largely ignored their adverse impact on medical costs. Since then, the health insurance market has become more competitive and, partly as a result, cost-containment efforts have increased markedly. In section two of this chapter, we discuss the health insurance market in the early days, up to about 1980. In sections three and four, we stress changes since 1980 that have made insurance markets more competitive. We conclude with some thoughts on what the market will be like in the future.

The Early Days, Up to About 1980: Traditional Insurance Firms

U.S. health insurance is provided by both public and private firms. The public providers are Medicare (federal health insurance for the elderly) and Medicaid (federal and state insurance for the poor and disabled). In the recent past, most U.S. private health insurance was sold by two major types of firms, commercial insurers and nonprofit organizations. First were the commercial health insurers, both profit seeking and mutual, who made up about half of the private insurance market in 1975. The other half of the market was covered by the mostly nonprofit Blue Cross and Blue Shield insurances.

Figure 6.1 **Persons Covered by Blue Cross/Blue Shield (BCBS) and All Other Commercial Insurers, Expressed as a Proportion of the Total Number of Persons with Private Insurance Protection, 1970–2003**

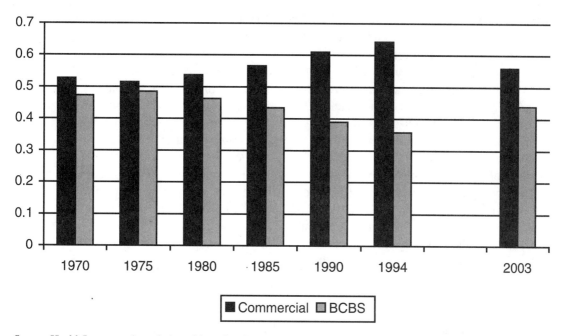

Source: Health Insurance Association of America, *Source Book of Health Insurance Data*, 1996, p. 41, and James Robinson, "Consolidation and the Transformation of Competition in Health Insurance," *Health Affairs* 23, 6 (2004), pp. 11–24.

The commercial half of the market was populated by hundreds of firms, none of which had a market share of more than 1 or 2 percent. Entry was easy, and firms entered (and exited) at a high rate. Concentration ratios among the commercial firms were comparatively low. Over 85 percent of individuals insured for hospital expenses were covered under group policies, implying that the market was dominated by informed buyers. Indeed, it is best to think of the commercial insurers as competitively providing a schedule of prices for various types of insurance. The consumer (or more commonly her/his union or employer representative) chose from this competitively determined schedule. Thus, the commercial part of the market seemed to be reasonably competitive. However, we discuss below how competitive conditions varied

considerably across geographic regions, depending upon the degree of local dominance by the Blue Cross and Blue Shield plans.

In 1975, the other half of the industry was comprised of the Blue Cross and Blue Shield plans (Figure 6.1). The Blue Cross plans were organized by hospitals to provide hospital insurance, and the Blue Shield plans were organized by physicians to provide physician services insurance. The Blues were organized (and largely still are) as legally nonprofit public service firms. These firms were controlled by boards of directors with heavy representation of hospital and physician interests. Typically, the Blues were organized under special enabling acts so that additional entry was not allowed. Thus, Blue Cross/Blue Shield plans had considerable market power by about 1975. This contrasted sharply with the situation of commercial insurers, where entry was relatively easy and common.

There were two sources of market power for the Blues. First, they were regulated and taxed more favorably than their competitors. Second, for both historical and continuing reasons, the Blues could often obtain discounts from doctors and hospitals that were greater than their competitors'.[1] One might expect these regulatory and discount advantages to lead to a complete monopoly for the Blue plans, but this is not what one observes. The Blues' share of the national private health insurance market was quite stable from about 1940 to about 1975, hovering near 50 percent. It slowly declined to about 36 percent by 1994 (Figure 6.1). In the nineties, some of the Blues' plans reincorporated as for-profit firms, and both the for-profit and nonprofit firms developed new managed care insurance products to compete with other managed care insurers. By 2003, the Blues had regained some market share and held 44 percent of the national private group insurance market.

There are several explanations for the fact that the Blues have not come to monopolize insurance markets. It is more convenient for employers to deal with one insurance firm for all of their insurance needs. This gives commercial insurers, who sell many types of insurance, an advantage. Also, the regulatory advantages conferred on the Blue plans were used to "purchase" two items of value to those controlling and influencing the plans. The first was administrative slack/inefficiency. (Examples include more executive staff, attractive and spacious offices, salaries higher than necessary to attract staff, and so on.) This weakening of the incentives to minimize costs is a general problem in regulation.[2] The second item "purchased" was more complete insurance. The mechanism by which more complete insurance was induced is a special kind of discriminatory price—an all-

or-nothing price. Consumers were confronted with an attractive price because of the regulatory advantages, but only very complete insurance was offered. However, one could not choose from the entire possible menu of insurance plans when dealing with the Blues. Large deductibles (say $1,000 to $5,000) were especially rare. While the Blues' all-or-nothing pricing did induce some consumers to purchase overly complete insurance, others chose to purchase a policy with larger cost-sharing from commercial insurers. Commercial insurers survived largely because (1) their Blue competitors were inefficient, and (2) the Blues left a portion of the market to them by refusing to sell insurance with large consumer copayments.

The Impact of Blue Cross/Blue Shield Market Power on Medical Care Costs

The effect of the high market power of Blue Cross and Blue Shield is more serious than one might think because of the linkage of the policies of the Blue plans to the cost of health care. The Blues have leverage in affecting medical care costs. The traditional Blue plans preferred more complete insurance with less consumer cost-sharing (such as deductibles and coinsurance). There are two reasons for this. First, more complete insurance raises the demand for medical care. The medical providers who controlled or influenced the Blue plans obtained higher revenues as a result. Most of the Blues could not simply use their market power in a profit-maximizing manner and return the funds to the medical providers in the form of dividends or overpayments for services. Their nonprofit status ruled out such transfers. So, increasing the demand for medical care was virtually the only major way in which the firms could benefit the providers. A second reason for the preference of the Blue plans for complete insurance was ideology—the belief that there should be no "financial barriers" to medical care.

The Blues' practice of promoting policies with minimal cost-sharing led to a lower level of cost-sharing in the overall market. Many consumers were led to purchase plans that included less cost-sharing than the plans they would have purchased otherwise because the Blues offered an attractive premium for plans with full coverage. But because such practices led to less cost-sharing in the aggregate, health-care costs have been driven higher than they would have been otherwise.[3]

Moral Hazard: Insurance Raises Use

Economists have criticized the use of overly complete insurance because of its subsidy effect. When the patient pays only a small fraction of the cost of medical care, there is an inducement to utilize more care and pay a higher price for it. Consumers wind up demanding medical care that has less value to them than it costs to produce. This is called the moral hazard effect of insurance. It is a problem for all types of insurance, but a worse problem for health insurance.

Most insurance offers an objectively fixed dollar payment contingent on a loss. Often the dollar payment is equal to the value of the loss. For example, automobile collision insurance pays the value of the loss as determined by claims adjusters and estimates from body shops. Health insurance is different because there is no objective way to determine the magnitude of the loss incurred by the patient. Instead, the insurance pays all or part of the cost of the health care. The insurance payment reduces the effective price of the health care to the consumer. Thus, the consumer slides down the demand curve, demanding more at the lower effective price. This subsidy causes consumers to buy more health care, including some health care that is worth far less to them than it costs to produce. Given the moral hazard problem, there is an optimal extent of insurance coverage (less

than 100 percent coverage) that balances the moral hazard welfare loss of more insurance against the risk reduction benefits of more insurance. In a completely free, competitive, and undistorted market, consumers would purchase such optimal insurance.[4]

The problem for the health-care economy is that there are two major distortions pushing consumers in the direction of excessively complete health insurance. The first is the tax treatment of health insurance. Employer payments for health insurance are deductible as costs of doing business. At the same time, these payments are not taxable as income to employees. Thus, there is a tax subsidy toward purchasing more health insurance equal to the sum of the federal and state marginal income tax rates. This is a large subsidy indeed, varying from 28 to about 50 percent.[5] The second distortion is the market power of the Blue Cross/Blue Shield plans, which attempt to promote even more complete health insurance.

Phelps states that the health sector could be about 10 to 20 percent smaller without the tax subsidy for health insurance, which is equivalent to about 1 to 2 percent of the gross national product.[6] Feldstein has studied the problem of the U.S. consumer who has excessively complete health insurance and estimates a welfare loss in the billions of dollars from the use of overly complete health insurance.[7] Since the Blue plans induce purchase of more complete insurance, consumer welfare losses of overinsurance are exacerbated.

Consumer Choice and Search: Insurance Raises Prices

Health insurance reduces the incentives for consumers to search for and choose low-priced physicians and hospitals. Because of the insurance coverage, most of the savings from searching out and choosing the low-price provider accrue to the insurer, not to the consumer. This effect is at its worst for 100 percent coverage. All the benefits from the choice of a low-price seller benefit the insurer entirely, not the consumer who must perform the search and make the choice. These consumers will rationally select the most preferred doctors and hospitals, regardless of cost. Further, they cannot be wooed away by price competition. Indeed, there can be no price competition at all for consumers with such insurance.

This effect of insurance is still strong for the popular 20 percent coinsurance plan. Here, for each $100 saved by seeking out a low-price provider, the insurer keeps $80 of the savings, while the consumer obtains only $20. Even though coinsurance improves incentives when compared to full coverage, the incentives are still weak.

Only one type of traditional health insurance preserves correct incentives for consumer search and choice of low-price providers. This is the type sometimes called indemnity insurance (though the term is used loosely and inconsistently). Here, the benefit is a fixed dollar amount per unit of service. As long as the benefit amount is set below most providers' prices, the consumer keeps the entire gain if he or she finds a less expensive provider. If the consumer finds and chooses a doctor who charges $100 less for a procedure, he or she keeps the entire difference. Consumers with no insurance also have this ideal incentive for search and choice.

Consider the impact of health insurance on the degree of price competition among doctors and hospitals. When customers have more complete coverage, the provider has less incentive to reduce price. The price-cutter will pick up a few new customers who will switch, but only a few. On the other hand, if the provider raises prices above competitive levels, he or she will lose only a few customers. Thus, traditional health insurance reduces the incentives for providers to compete on price. This is a major reason that health care is so costly.

Modern Trends, Since About 1980: New Forms of Insurance

In the mid-1970s, traditional insurance (commercial insurances and the Blues) covered almost all people who were privately insured. In the eighties, new forms of insurance emerged, designed to manage care and costs more effectively. These include health maintenance organizations (HMOs) and preferred provider organizations (PPOs). HMOs combine the insurer with the doctors and hospitals to eliminate the moral hazard incentive to overuse medical care that is inherent in traditional third-party insurance.[8] PPOs are contracts among insurers, providers, and consumers. The providers agree to serve PPO consumers on preferential terms, offering a lower price per unit of service and agreeing to cooperate with utilization review restrictions mandated by the insurer. In turn, consumers are given financial incentives (such as reduced coinsurance and additional covered services) to favor PPO providers. For the PPO to be financially successful, a significant number of patients must change their source of medical care to preferred providers.

In 1984, HMOs and PPOs had less than 1 percent of the private group health insurance market. By 1993, the HMO and PPO plans provided serious competition to the traditional insurances, serving almost 50 percent of the market.

By 1993 a new breed of health insurance product, the Point of Service (POS) plan, became a popular addition to HMOs and PPOs. A POS plan is a health product usually offered by an HMO that has indemnity-like options that work like this: The HMO's primary care doctors in the POS plan usually make referrals to other providers in the plan, but members can refer themselves outside the plan and still get some coverage. If the doctor makes a referral out of the HMO's provider network, the plan pays all or most of the bill. If the member refers him- or herself to a provider outside the

Figure 6.2 **Managed Care Plans (HMO, PPO, and POS) as a Percentage of the Private Group Insurance Business, 1984–2005**

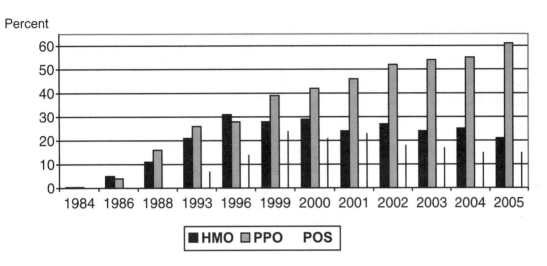

Source: Health Insurance Association of America, *Source Book of Health Insurance Data*, 1992, p. 22, for data 1984–1988; Kaiser Family Foundation and Health Research and Educational Trust, *Employer Health Benefits Annual Survey*, 2005, Section 5: "Market Shares of Health Plans" (accessed online December 2005): www.kff.org/insurance/7315/sections/ehbs05-sec5-1.cfm, for data 1993–2005.

network and the service is covered by the plan, they have to pay coinsurance. The POS product is similar to a PPO. Over the nineties, POS plans thrived. Figure 6.2 shows that the private group insurance market has changed dramatically in recent years. PPOs and POS plans have transformed the nature of fee-for-service health insurance, and HMOs, which were quite popular in the 1990s, have seen their market shares taken by the more flexible PPO and POS plans. The PPO, POS, and HMO plans greatly altered the incentives and the type of competition observed in the market. By 2005, traditional insurance covered only about 3 percent of the private group insurance market, while PPOs dominated the managed care plan types with a 61 percent market share (Figure 6.2).

Another change that accompanied the growth of POS products is that most large employers are now self-insured. When an employer self-insures,

it typically hires either an insurer or a firm specializing in claims processing (i.e., a third-party administrator, or TPA) to process claims. So the term *self-insurance* is a misnomer. The employee is still insured by someone else, not by him- or herself. But the risk is borne by the employer or union group rather than an insurance company.

Although many employers use commercial insurers (HMOs, PPOs, and Blue Cross/Blue Shield plans) as administrators of their self-insured plans, these insurers must compete with professional third-party administrators (TPAs) for employer business. Professional TPAs are firms that specialize in managing the full spectrum of fringe benefits offered by the firm, which may include a broad variety of benefits such as life insurance, health club memberships, or tuition reimbursement. Offering a range of benefits in a cafeteria-style package that employees can tailor to fit their own needs helps retain em-

Figure 6.3   Growth Rate in Private Group Health Insurance Premiums

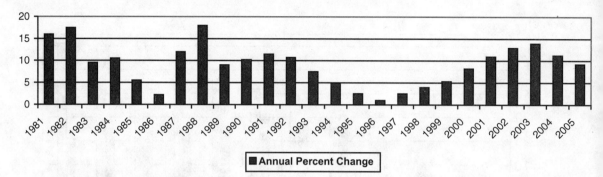

Source: Health Insurance Association of America, *Source Book of Health Insurance Data*, 1992, p. 29; Prospective Payment Assessment Commission, *Medicare and the American Health Care System: Report to Congress*, June 1996, p. 19; and the Kaiser Family Foundation (KFF) and Health Research Educational Trust (HRET) Employer Health Benefits 2005 Annual Survey, accessed online December 2005: www.kff.org/insurance/7315/sections/ehbs05-1-1.cfm.

ployees, but can be administratively challenging to manage. Employers have taken a much more active interest in the benefit structures they offer and administration of their plans. More importantly, self-insurance is a means of avoiding costly state regulations on private insurance coverage.

Because most of the non-elderly population is insured through employment-based group policies, the rising costs of medical care have been felt by employers as insurance premiums have increased. Between 1970 and 1980, the amount of insurance premiums paid by U.S. employers for group insurance policies rose 352 percent. During the mid-eighties, premium increases averaged 6 to 8 percent annually, but by 1990 they again reached double-digit levels, dipped in the mid-nineties, then increased again in the late nineties, peaking in 2003 and then declining again (Figure 6.3).[9]

In order to slow premium growth, employers have shifted employees from traditional insurance plans into managed care plans, with premiums 9 to 12 percent lower. Most employers continue to offer traditional insurance as a choice among insurance plans for employees, but many are drop-

ping this option. Also, employers are increasing consumer cost-sharing to control the moral hazard that causes premiums to rise over time. To do this, employers have increased the share of the premium paid by employees, and raised coinsurance and deductibles.[10] These recent changes in insurance have made insurance markets more competitive and were somewhat successful in slowing the growth rate in group health insurance premiums in the nineties. The upswing in the late nineties occurred about the same time that HMOs became less popular (relative to the more lenient PPO and POS plans). Because PPO and POS plans offer more choice and looser cost controls, the increase in average premiums as they gained market share in the late nineties is not surprising (Figures 6.2 and 6.3). As discussed below, legislation, such as insurance mandates, may have also contributed to rising premiums in the latter nineties.

Managed Care

Increased cost-sharing is a simple and reliable way to reduce health benefit costs, but it has not

Figure 6.4 **National Health Expenditures as a Percentage of GDP**

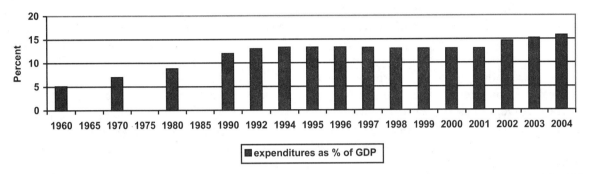

Source: Health Care Financing Administration Web site, 6/2001: www.HCFA.gov/stats, and *An Overview of the U.S. Healthcare System: Two Decades of Change, 1980–2000* (Baltimore: Center for Medicare & Medicaid, Office of the Actuary, National Health Statistics Group, 2000).

been the only method of cost containment used by third-party payers. Insurers and employers are increasingly using administrative mechanisms to review the appropriateness of use of services. One technique that is now common is pre-admission certification, a procedure that determines, before hospitalization, whether a hospital stay is appropriate. Many plans also require a pre-hospitalization interview between the patient and admitting physician for elective (nonemergency) procedures, and review individual cases during a hospital stay to limit time in the hospital. Some plans require second opinions before approving plans for surgery. Some insurers have given administrators discretion on a case-by-case basis to expand coverage to new services for a specific case if there is a likelihood of reducing overall treatment costs for a patient. Monitoring quality of care and case management activities have become increasingly important to insurers in response to competitive pressures from the marketplace and administrative oversight by government and industry payers.

These cost-containment and increased cost-sharing activities, also known as managed care, were effective in containing rising health-care costs

in the nineties. The growth of spending on health care as a percentage of gross domestic product (GDP) rose steadily from 5.1 percent in 1960 to about 12.2 percent in 1990, causing considerable alarm and generating the impetus to better manage health-care spending. In the nineties, national health expenditures per GDP leveled off at about 13.2 percent, and industry observers attribute the stability over the nineties to the spread of managed care practices (Figure 6.4). (A quick glance back at Figure 6.2 shows that managed care insurances really became a significant force in the nineties.)

National savings from managed-care practices derive from several sources: (1) lower managed-care premiums, (2) lower premiums for other insurers competing with managed-care plans, and (3) slowing in the adoption of cost-increasing medical technology. These savings are so large that the estimated cost of eliminating managed care would be about $329 billion from 2002 to 2005, which translates into about $3,600 per household. This is about 8 percent of private health insurance costs. In addition, about 6.4 million people would lose medical insurance coverage, through premium increases, if managed care were eliminated.[11]

Figure 6.4 shows that, in the new millennium, expenditures as a percentage of GDP appear to rise again, after their decade of stability in the nineties. There are many possible underlying causes, including increasing hospital prices, increasing use of hospital outpatient services, and increasing use of prescription drugs.[12] The spread of new medical technologies has been named as a cost driver.[13] Adverse health behaviors such as the trend toward greater numbers of morbidly obese and diabetic adults contribute to the rise in expenditures because health costs are much higher for these populations.[14] Also, people with expensive chronic diseases have become more likely to obtain treatment in recent times.[15] However, the aging of the population may not be an important cost driver for the under-sixty-five population because differences in spending by age are not large enough and the U.S. population is not aging quickly enough.[16] The interplay of these various factors on the rising expenditures per capita is complicated, and will no doubt be an area of ongoing active research.[17]

One possible market-based explanation for the rise in expenditures since the nineties is that HMOs, which were quite effective in curtailing unnecessary costs, have become less popular as the PPO and POS forms of insurance have increased market share. As discussed below, these forms of insurance are not as strict in utilization controls and allow consumers more freedom and choice, which raises costs. One explanation for rising premiums can be easily ruled out. Rising premiums are not due to higher insurer profit rates. Indeed, industry profits have varied over the underwriting cycle, between –6 percent and +5 percent for some insurers.[18] Also, new state regulations of insurance have continued to be passed by legislators so that by 2002 there were seventy state-level mandates on the books.[19] As we will see below, these sorts of regulation may impede efficient plan design and result in higher premiums and expenditures.

Health Maintenance Organizations (HMOs)

HMOs combine the insurer with a group of selected doctors that constituents can use to receive full coverage of the plan's health benefits. Profits for HMOs are higher if fewer services are provided since revenue comes from premium payments made in advance. When premium payments are less than costs, the HMO bears the risk (unless the HMO's providers are reimbursed on a per-person insured [capitated] basis, in which case the providers bear the risk). Thus, the HMO's own incentives to use "efficient" providers that supply fewer services opposes the HMO subscriber's incentive to demand many services because the out-of-pocket price is zero or near zero. Health maintenance organizations restrain utilization by nonprice rationing. The necessity of competing for new members prevents HMOs from providing too few services. Empirical evidence from as early as 1987 shows that employers whose employees chose HMOs as their health insurance paid substantially lower premiums, and that there was a lower profit margin on HMO insurance. This means that HMOs were a significant competitive force in health insurance markets by the latter eighties.[20]

Pressure from HMOs led to competitive responses from traditional insurers. First, insurers became more innovative in the design of traditional policies by developing PPOs and POS plans, and introducing managed care into traditional insurance policies. These responses worked to reduce the quantity- and price-increasing effects of health insurance. Second, some of the larger traditional insurers went into the HMO business. Insurers bring to the HMO business access to capital, underwriting and claims processing experience, and extensive marketing organizations. Insurer entries to the managed-care market accelerated the growth of HMOs and PPOs, magnifying the competitive impact of this development.

The growth of HMOs was rapid (Figure 6.2). They increased their market share from about 0.45 percent in 1983 to about 21 percent in 1993, and by 2000, HMOs served about 30 percent of the private group market. An even more astonishing growth trend is noted for PPOs, with market shares even higher than HMOs from 1988 on. The growth in managed-care plan options increased the competitiveness of the health insurance market in several ways. These new market entrants were particularly valuable for competition because many of them came from backgrounds other than traditional health insurance and because they introduced different products into the market. Because of their ability to channel patients to providers with whom they contracted, even plans with small market shares were able to negotiate substantial discounts.

Preferred Provider Organizations (PPOs)

Preferred provider organizations differ from HMOs in that services from providers outside of the preferred panel are still covered (though with more cost-sharing) and providers are not usually at-risk for the volume of services used by patients (as they might be in a capitated HMO). The ability to receive some payment for care received from non-plan providers is a significant attraction of the PPO plan.

Preferred provider organizations reduce the tendency of insurance to raise prices of medical services. They not only provide an acceptable way for consumers to be given incentives to choose a low-priced, low-cost provider, but facilitate the consumer's search process by providing a directory of preferred providers. Through utilization review, PPOs also often reduce the impact of insurance on the use of services.

The development of PPOs has proceeded rapidly from their inception in the early 1970s. By 1988,

PPOs insured about 16 percent of those with group insurance. By 1993, this had grown to about 26 percent, and by 2000, to about 42 percent, a higher share than was held by HMOs (Figure 6.2). PPOs continued to dominate the private group market and by 2005 attained over 60 percent share, with HMOs falling to 21 percent share and POS plans garnering about 15 percent share, leaving only about 3 percent share for the traditional insurances. This rapid development made the market for health insurance more competitive. The entrance of PPOs has allowed new entrants, such as TPAs, to build market share.

Diversification of managed care into both HMO and PPO plan types also enabled the spread of managed care into regions of the United States that were historically opposed to HMOs, such as the Southeast (Figure 6.5). In 1994, sixteen states had less than 30 percent combined market share for HMOs and PPOs, and only one (Minnesota) had combined PPO and HMO market shares greater than 50 percent. By 2002, thirty-two states had combined PPO and HMO market shares greater than 50 percent, and only one state (South Carolina) had combined HMO and PPO market shares less than 33 percent.

State Regulations, Self-Insurance, and Third-Party Administrators

While the insurance industry has become more competitive, and many new products have been developed to meet employers' demand for increased consumer cost-sharing and slower premium growth, consumer groups have retaliated against managed care. Most states have passed laws that regulate the health insurance industry, mandating coverage and conditions for competition within the state.[21] These regulations hinder the ability of markets to produce the full range of insurance products that are demanded.

168

INDUSTRY STUDIES

Figure 6.5   **HMO and PPO Penetration in 1994 and in 2002**

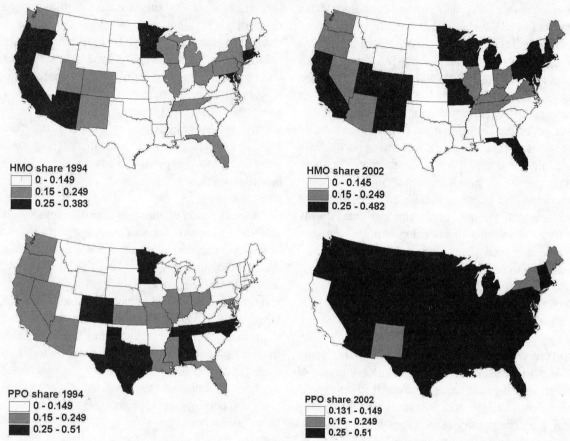

HMO share 1994
0 - 0.149
0.15 - 0.249
0.25 - 0.383

HMO share 2002
0 - 0.145
0.15 - 0.249
0.25 - 0.482

PPO share 1994
0 - 0.149
0.15 - 0.249
0.25 - 0.51

PPO share 2002
0.131 - 0.149
0.15 - 0.249
0.25 - 0.51

Source: InterStudy, "The InterStudy Competitive Edge: HMO Report," St. Paul, Minnesota, various years.

Large employers that are self-insured are exempt from state insurance regulation under the Federal Employee Retirement Income Security Act (ERISA) of 1974. Thus, large firms may avoid the market regulations by covering employees with group insurance plans designed specifically for their employee pool. Self-insurance is attractive because of improved cash management (employers pay claims directly rather than paying a premium in advance), exemption from state insurance regulation (both premium taxes and restrictions on benefit structures), and increased control over the design of the health benefit plan as a component of the complete benefit package.

Being able to avoid the state regulations by custom-designing insurance for employees gives self-insured firms a cost advantage over firms that purchase regulated insurance. This advantage has induced many more firms to self-insure than would otherwise be the case. In 1980 less than 25 percent of all group coverage was through self-insured plans, rising by 1990 to about 58 percent.[22] More recently, the trend seems to have reversed: In 1996 about 57 percent of all group coverage was through self-insured plans, and by 2001 this had declined to about 50 percent.[23] This decline is most likely due to the change in self-insurance product mix, as self-insured employers switched from mostly indemnity plans in the early nineties to HMO and POS plans by 2001. Indemnity plans may be easier to offer as self-insurance because the employer simply assumes the financial risk, then buys stop-loss (catastrophic) insurance to cover any catastrophic expenses. Managed-care plans are more difficult to use by self-insured firms because they must find a network of providers and also arrange for other managed-care services such as quality assurance and disease management.

Increased use of self-insurance increases the competitiveness of the insurance market in several ways. First, as employers gain more control over their plans, cost-containment initiatives are likely to be incorporated more rapidly. The ability to pursue a benefit structure with cost-sharing is facilitated since the Blue Cross/Blue Shield advantage based on exemption from premium taxes is eliminated. Second, self-insurance has opened the insurance market to an additional type of competitor, the TPA. The entry of a new type of competitor is providing an additional spur to competition and innovation with group insurance.

Tax and Regulatory Advantages of Blue Cross/Blue Shield

The tax advantages of the Blues have been eroding. Governments questioned whether public policy goals were being accomplished with the forgone tax revenue. In 1986 the federal government sharply curtailed the exemption of the Blues from federal income tax. State governments have increasingly monitored the public service activities that the plans perform and have insisted on minimum levels of activity if tax advantages are to be retained. A few Blue plans have concluded that the costs of public service

activities they are expected to undertake exceed the resources available from tax advantages and have reincorporated as mutual or for-profit insurers.

By 2003, the nonprofit and for-profit Blues plans *combined* had the largest market share among private insurers in every state except Nevada and California. The Blues plans are formally owned by forty different local companies, some covering multiple states and others covering only one state or part of a state, while the three largest *national* health insurance firms (United Health Group, Aetna, and CIGNA) cover people in the vast majority of the states. Although the Blues have separate, smaller local companies in the different states, by 2003 they dominated the national plans in almost every state, and held more than 50 percent of the private insurance market in twenty states.[24]

There has been a trend toward Blue Cross/Blue Shield plans competing with each other. Under antitrust attack from state attorneys general, collusion among the Blue Cross/Blue Shield plans is weakening. For example, using the antitrust laws, the state of Maryland sued the Maryland and District of Columbia Blue plans to end their explicit agreement dividing the state of Maryland.[25] In Ohio, several plans compete statewide as a result of an antitrust settlement with the state attorney general.

Why Insurance Has Become More Competitive

The previous section discussed a number of developments that have changed the degree and nature of competition in the health-insurance market. This section attempts to identify the forces that are behind these developments.

Changing Attitudes of Employers

During the last few years, top corporate management has taken a more active interest in containing the costs of employee health-benefit programs. A study in 1981 showed that corporate purchasers of health care had little interest in cost containment.[26] There is substantial evidence now of increased leadership in cost containment at the top levels of corporate management and an upgrading of the position of employee benefits manager. Why did the change occur at this time?

Perhaps the central reason is the growth in the proportion of compensation costs going toward health benefits, which increased from 1.6 percent of wages and salaries in 1965 to 5.3 percent in 1985. By 1998, employers spent an average of $4,100 per employee on health care, which was about 36 percent of all non-wage employee benefits, totaling about $291 billion.[27] When more dollars are involved, sharp increases in premiums are more likely to capture the attention of top management. While health benefit costs had been growing relative to other compensation for some time, the sharply rising proportion in the 1980s made health-care cost containment a more important source of cost savings. The curtailment of health insurance benefits for those who had them and tightening of control by employers over utilization and coverage in the nineties resulted in cost containment but also led to a popular backlash against managed care, which culminated in legislation introduced in February 2001 (HSR 526, the Bipartisan Patient Protection Act of 2001, also known as the "patient bill of rights"). One provision in the bill is expanded liability, which would enable larger lawsuits by patients against their health insurers and employers. Industry insiders fear that the expanded liability would further reduce employer-provided health insurance.[28]

As health-care costs and premiums rise, employers reduce coverage and the ranks of the uninsured swell. With the rise of managed care in the nineties, health-care costs stabilized and appeared to be contained. But with the backlash against managed care at the end of the nineties, health-care costs (and premiums) began to rise again. The number of uninsured Americans increases and declines with this insurance cycle and events in the public insurance market.

The number of non-elderly uninsured increased by 4.2 million between 1994 and 1998. Although there was an increase in employer-sponsored coverage, this was more than offset by a decline in Medicaid and state-sponsored insurance. The number of uninsured then declined between 1998 and 2000 by 2.1 million because there were increases in the number of people with public coverage, along with continuing growth in the number of people with employer-sponsored insurance. Between 2000 and 2003, the uninsured increased again by 5.1 million because of the decline in employer-sponsored insurance due to the economic slowdown and rising health-care costs. This decline was only partially offset by increases in Medicaid and state-sponsored insurance, thus the number of uninsured increased. There has been speculation that the rise in the uninsured in recent years may be due to immigrants to the United States who lack health insurance. This can hardly be the whole story because, among the 5.1 million new uninsured in this decade, there were four times more native citizens than nonnatives.[29]

Medicare and Medicaid Policies

Budgetary concerns led to important policy developments in the Medicare and Medicaid programs, which in turn led to changes in the market for private health insurance. From the perspective of private insurers, the most critical development in Medicare policy has been the prospective payment system (PPS), which changed the way that providers were paid. Prior to PPS, providers were reimbursed based on reported costs, which gave no incentives to control costs. The PPS reimburses providers a fixed amount for each unit of service

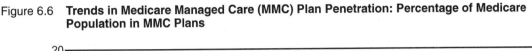

Figure 6.6   **Trends in Medicare Managed Care (MMC) Plan Penetration: Percentage of Medicare Population in MMC Plans**

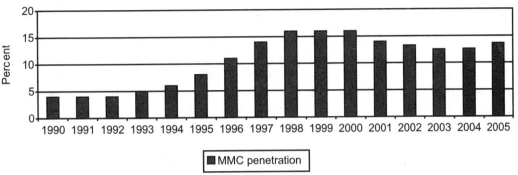

Source for data 1990–2002: Trends-and-Indicators-in-the-Changing-Health-Care-Marketplace-2002-Chartbook, May 2006, Kaiser Family Foundation: www.kff.org/insurance/upload/Trends-and-Indicators-in-the-Changing-Health-Care-Marketplace-2002-Chartbook.pdf.
   Source for data 2003–2005: from *13 Month Trend Report,* updated November 2, 2005, obtained from CMS Web site: http://new.cms.hhs.gov/HealthPlansGenInfo/44_ReportsFilesData_01_TrendReports.asp.

provided, with the reimbursement rates determined before service is performed (prospectively). The most critical development in Medicaid has been the tightening of eligibility requirements. In addition, both programs have expanded enrollments in managed-care options: Managed care plans served about 54.4 percent of Medicaid and about 17.16 percent of Medicare enrollees in 2000.[30] Medicaid participation in managed care continued to grow and reached more than 60 percent of enrollees by 2004. Changes in payments to plans implemented with the Balanced Budget Act (BBA) of 1997 resulted in many Medicare-managed plans pulling out of rural markets and reducing their offerings in urban markets, involuntarily disenrolling many constituents. This resulted in a drop in the proportion of elderly in Medicare managed-care plans. Consequently, the Centers for Medicare and Medicaid have focused on improving reimbursements and risk-sharing arrangements to stimulate reentry and expansion by Medicare managed-care plans.[31] The Medicare Modernization Act of 2003 included many sweeping changes designed to

stimulate enrollment in Medicare managed care, including the passage of the Part D prescription drug benefit offered by all Medicare Advantage (managed-care) plans since January 2006. As an alternative to obtaining drug benefits bundled with Medicare managed-care plan benefits, the elderly can choose stand-alone Part D drug insurance plans to use with other forms of health insurance. Having these two options and at least two of each plan type in every part of the country is expected to introduce considerable competition into the insurance market for elderly coverage.

These changes have increased interest in managed care among the elderly, and enrollments began increasing soon after the 2003 legislation was passed. Figure 6.6 shows the trends in enrollments in Medicare managed-care plans over the period 1990–2005. These penetration rates rise steadily until a little after the BBA was implemented, then fall sharply, then begin rising again in the mid-2000s.

Both the prospective payments system and tightened Medicaid eligibility have made private purchasers (employers and insurers) more sensitive to the issue of cost shifting—that is, the practice of hospitals charging different prices to different payers. Medicare's prospective payment system (PPS) has private payers worried that Medicare could reduce its payments below cost, so that the shortfall would be shifted to them (cost-shifting) through increased markups of charges over costs. Actually, the opposite occurred during the first few years of PPS because profits on Medicare service increased. But the pressure of the federal deficit reduced the generous Medicare reimbursement that was present under early PPS, and hospital margins on PPS fell to very low levels by 2002.[32] Medicaid eligibility reductions have led to similar risks for private purchasers. Many people who are no longer eligible for Medicaid due to tighter real-income standards for welfare eligibility are still admitted to hospitals, and some of them are not insured. Charitable contributions have shrunk to practically nothing in recent years, 1.6 percent of hospital revenues in 1999, down to 1.1 percent in 2003.[33] Thus, hospitals can recoup the costs of caring for these uninsured patients only by charging other patients more (if they have sufficient market power).

Private purchasers have taken two courses in response to the specter of increased cost shifting. First, some have organized politically to support state government actions to reduce payment differentials. These actions have included traditional state rate-setting efforts, policies regulating payment differences, and policies that directly address uncompensated care (services provided to uninsured patients who do not pay their bills). The latter category includes selective Medicaid eligibility extensions and the development of mechanisms to make payments to hospitals that provide significant amounts of uncompensated care. Such payments are often funded through taxes on hospital revenues from all private patients.

Second, private purchasers have obtained discounts from full charges for both hospital and physician services. The key to obtaining favorable prices is the ability to channel patients to providers that agree to a discounted price, hence the development of PPOs and HMOs. Medicare managed-care plans behave like private HMOs and PPOs, negotiating fees with physicians and hospitals. As more and more Medicare patients enroll in managed care, the proportion who are subject to prospective payments falls, as negotiated payments take their place. This further increases the financial pressure from treating uninsured patients in hospitals, as hospitals are left with fewer and fewer "profitable" patients to shift these costs onto.

Professional Standards Review Organizations

The professional standards review organization (PSRO) program was mandated by Congress in the late 1960s but has been phased out by now. It mandated a system of claims review designed to reduce medical care and especially hospital care use. These agencies might be seen as public sector precursors to the current managed-care revolution taking place in the private insurance market. Perhaps because the local PSRO organizations were controlled by the local physicians and hospitals, research studies found them to be ineffective.[34]

Nonetheless, the PSROs may have contributed to the development of more effective utilization review in both the private and public sectors. The program gained practical experience and stimulated the interest of policymakers in developing better techniques. What was learned from the PSRO program was not lost since many of the organizations continued as private peer-review organizations and since the staffs of those that disbanded often found employment with insurers and other private-sector organizations offering utilization review services.

The PSRO experience also conditioned providers to utilization review activities.

Antitrust Enforcement in Health Care

For years, the growth of innovative health insurance schemes (such as HMOs) was delayed by boycott threats from physician groups. However, the development of antitrust law and the attention of antitrust law enforcement agencies have reduced the barriers to new forms of financing.

Prior to 1963, national hospital accreditation standards conferred great economic power on local medical societies. To be accredited, hospitals were required to exclude from their medical staff physicians who were not members of their local medical societies. By ejecting HMO physicians from medical society membership, local medical societies were able to block or hinder the development of these organizations.[35] In 1963, a court decision eliminated the requirement of local medical society membership as a prerequisite to hospital access.[36] We believe that this uncelebrated court decision is the key to understanding the decline of the ability of organized medicine to hinder physician and hospital competition. Further, it also led to the weakening of the American Medical Association's influence on national health policy.

Groups of physicians have also boycotted insurers who used new cost-control measures. For example, in objection to utilization controls, the Michigan State Medical Society boycotted the local Blue Shield plan. The eventual result was a cease and desist order from the Federal Trade Commission (FTC) in 1983.[37]

More recently, physicians have mobilized to seek exemption from tough antitrust laws that prohibit their collusion against managed-care plans. Federal legislation of this type was introduced in 1999 (HR 1304, the Quality Health-Care Coalition Act of 1999). Industry experts estimate that the cost of these physician antitrust waivers would be an increase in private insurance premiums of about 13 percent, which is substantial. This in turn would further reduce the enrollment in private insurance, increasing the ranks of the uninsured.[38]

A recent example of antitrust enforcement involved a new PPO in the small cities of Modesto and Turlock in Stanislaus County, California. The county medical society formed its own PPO and quickly signed on most of the local physicians. The Medical Society's PPO prohibited its member doctors from signing up with any other organizations, thus effectively denying competing PPOs and HMOs entry into the Modesto and Turlock markets. Only when threatened with an antitrust suit by the U.S. Department of Justice did the Stanislaus County Medical Society disband its PPO.[39] In Fort Worth, the North Texas Specialty Physicians organization effectively colluded to raise fees paid by health plans. They were successfully sued by the FTC.[40]

Third-Party Administrators

Since employers do not usually have specialized knowledge of the health-care market and of health insurance, they have sought outside help in managing their self-insured plans. Originally, this function was undertaken by TPAs such as Dual-Plus or AdMar in Los Angeles, Affordable Health Care Concepts in Sacramento, and Martin E. Segal Co. in Denver. These firms smoothed the transition to self-insurance and doubtless saved both money and managerial headaches. But more important for the evolution of a more competitive and efficient marketplace, these small independent firms, most of which began as either benefit or actuarial consulting firms, invented the modern PPO and provided the necessary expertise for its early growth.

One might have expected the established insurance firms to be the innovators. Instead, these small new TPAs and consultants provided the necessary entrepreneurship that transformed the entire industry. As Havinghurst observed, the health insurance industry has been all too willing to strive for consensus and avoid innovation.[41] The entry of the new TPAs has changed that. Under the pressure of this new competition, commercial insurers and Blue Cross/Blue Shield plans have begun to offer TPA services and organize PPOs.

The process recalls Schumpeter's theory that most competition is likely to come from new products or ideas rather than from producing old products at a slightly lower cost. Through "creative destruction," once-dominant firms are displaced by newer firms offering new products.[42] On the other hand, Schumpeter expected large firms operating in concentrated, oligopolistic markets to be especially innovative. Among health insurers, then, one would expect the Blue Cross/Blue Shield plans to be the most innovative, followed by the commercial carriers. That's not at all what has occurred. The innovations have come from small TPAs and consulting firms.

More Physicians

The national physician/population ratio is rising rapidly. The number of graduates of U.S. medical schools doubled from 1965 to 1981, and the number of foreign-trained physicians has also grown.[43] This raised the number of physicians per 1,000 population from 1.68 in 1970 to more than 2.0 by 1980. The ratio rose steadily during the eighties, reaching an all-time high in 1989 of 2.61. There was a sharp dip in 1990, to 2.16, and then continued growth to 2.6 by 1996.[44] A neglected benefit of this growth has been easier development of innovative health insurance schemes and a general growth of price competition. However, physician supply has grown unevenly, and regions with sparse populations have fewer physicians and less competitive physician, hospital, and health insurance markets.

New physicians are especially likely to cut prices to increase their patient loads, either directly or by joining a PPO. Since new physicians have fewer regular patients, price reductions are more likely to increase their revenues. In addition, they have not yet formed a network of friendships and working relationships with other doctors and thus are less susceptible to subtle professional pressure to avoid competing too sharply. The net result is more competition and lower physician incomes.

Managed care has also had an impact on the mix of physicians by encouraging growth in the family and general practice areas and reducing the demand for specialists. The average physician earned almost 4 percent less in 1994 than in 1993, the first drop in earnings since 1982 (when current income statistics were first collected). But the averages conceal considerable variation in the 1985–1994 income changes by physician specialty. Physicians at the upper end of the income distribution (specialists) saw a larger than average drop in income, while those at the bottom (general care and family practice physicians) saw healthy increases in income. The narrowing of the income gap between primary care physicians and specialists can largely be attributed to growth in managed-care plans. In 1986, only 43 percent of physicians provided some services to managed-care plans. In 1995, more than 83 percent of all patient care physicians had at least one managed-care contract.[45]

Competition in the Future

The health-care financing system is still in transition. The current system will continue to respond to powerful forces for change. Of course, predicting the future is difficult, and predicting the direction of the health-care system is no exception. Because of this transitional state, there is considerable variation across regions in the types of health plans and health care available. For example, there is considerable variation in the geographic penetration of HMOs and PPOs (Figure 6.5). This is partly responsible for the geographic variation in medical treatments that is observed across regions. This variation in treatments for the same diseases across regions means that some patients are getting too much care, while others may not be getting enough. Either situation can place the patient at risk and increase costs.[46]

Two factors make prediction about health-care markets particularly uncertain. One is that the system is at the early stage of a cycle of innovation. Some of the current innovations may be discarded, and some of those that will ultimately succeed may not have appeared yet, or at least may not have been widely noticed yet. The second factor concerns the reaction of the public sector. To date, public officials have generally applauded the degree of innovation in the private financing of health care. However, the popular view could quickly change.

One early indication of public opinion regarding recent developments was a provision in the Omnibus Budget Reconciliation Act of 1986 that limits the degree to which hospitals and HMOs can offer incentives to physicians to cut utilization. More recently, in September 1996, the federal government enacted direct federal controls on the content of health-insurance benefits packages. These federal mandates represent a major change in federal policy toward health insurance. Even more recent proposed regulation—aimed at expanding liability for insurance companies and employers, and another piece aimed at loosening antitrust constraints facing physician groups—is a continuing risk to health plans and to competition. One extensive survey of the literature compiles the cost savings from managed-care practices, and

estimates the tremendous cost of eliminating it.[47] It is hoped that sound policy will prevail over the politics of special interests.

Why Mandates Are Bad Economic Policy

Two federal mandates force insurers to cover mental health benefits with the same policy limits (coinsurance, deductibles, etc.) as other health care services, and force insurers to pay for at least forty-eight hours of inpatient care for mothers and newborns. These federal mandates supersede the ERISA exemption from state law through self-insurance that large employers have used to avoid similar state regulations. Thus the federal stance has shifted from one that protected employer groups from state health insurance mandates to one that subjects them to federal insurance mandates.

There is wide agreement among health economists that insurance mandates reflect the lobbying of legislators by special interest groups (e.g., the American College of Obstetricians and Gynecologists and the National Mental Health Association) to obtain off-budget regulatory transfers. Transfers of income go to the providers of the regulated services and do not show up in state or federal government budgets. The mandates thus allow legislators to reward special interest groups without generating any obvious costs. The costs show up later in the form of higher insurance premiums, less consumer choice among alternatives, and increasing numbers of uninsured individuals, among other things.

These federal regulations are harmful in several ways: (1) they limit consumer choice, (2) they limit the utilization control for a service (obstetric care) that is quite price-responsive, and (3) they limit the ability to control utilization and fraud abuse for a service (mental health care) for which "need" is difficult to objectively verify.[48] Thus they inhibit the workings of the market, impeding its ability to supply desired products efficiently.

Between 1970 and 1996, the number of state mandates increased twenty-five-fold. State-mandated benefits raise the cost of insurance and may increase the numbers of uninsured individuals; recent estimates show that one-fifth to one-quarter of uninsured individuals now lack coverage because of mandates.[49] But there has been a small offsetting effect. This happened as mandates led more firms to self-insure than would otherwise be the case, which increased competition in the insurance industry. While mandates have increased growth in PPO and TPA-administered (self-insured) health plans, they have also slowed growth in the HMO sector, which is directly subject to mandated regulations in some states.[50]

Antitrust Enforcement in Health Care

Federal antitrust enforcement in health care is unlikely to change. Even the Reagan administration's relatively permissive antitrust policy did not reduce vigilance toward the health-care industry. The Clinton and Bush administrations have kept the pressure on health care.

There is some recent evidence that managed care has affected the structure of the health-care industry by causing greater integration of hospitals with physician groups to facilitate contracting with managed care plans.[51] In 1994, 27.6 percent of community hospitals were integrated with physician groups, but this grew to 33.2 percent by 1996, then declined to 26.4 percent by 2000.[52] Hospitals affiliated with multihospital chains and larger hospitals were much more likely to have integrated. Because physicians are the key components in the production of health-care services, hospitals that vertically integrate with groups of physicians have more power in bargaining with insurance plans.

Horizontal mergers and consolidations in the health-care industry reached record numbers in the 1980s and escalated to set new records in the 1990s, with no signs of abatement. The HMO industry was engaged in a major wave of mergers in the 1990s, and consolidation in this industry gave them greater clout in bargaining with hospitals. The private group insurance industry in general has become increasingly consolidated, and by 2003 the Blues, United Health Group, Aetna, and CIGNA controlled more than 60 percent of the private group market in thirty-four states and more than 70 percent in twenty-three states. However, the increasing trend among large multistate employers to self-insure moderates the market held by these giants, which must compete for their business with the TPAs.[53]

The trends in HMO mergers and in hospital mergers appear to move in tandem. With continued consolidation in the industry, communities and regulators are becoming increasingly concerned about whether the public interest is being served. With the elimination of excess hospital capacity through merger and consolidation, insurers will find themselves in a weaker bargaining position (as hospital supply becomes less elastic). The integration of the hospital with physician groups enables the hospital to increase its market power. Of course, if excess capacity is eliminated and physicians become integrated with either hospitals or insurance plans, health market dynamics will be completely different than they are today.

Other Factors Affecting Change in the Future

The forces that have caused change are likely to continue. The supply of physicians will continue to increase for the foreseeable future. Although federal government subsidies to medical school expansion are a thing of the past, few would predict public efforts to reduce class sizes.

Employers will continue to look for ways to contain health-care costs. With marginal tax rates substantially lower as a result of the 1981 and 1986 tax reforms, incentives to contain the costs of health benefit programs are now stronger. Further, a cap on the amount of employer contributions to health benefit plans that can be deducted from taxes might be enacted within the next few years. All of the proposed health-care reforms in 1993 included some type of cap. A philosophy of reducing marginal tax rates (or avoiding future increases) through broadening the tax base is now widely accepted in Congress. With such incentives, employers are likely to continue increasing cost-sharing and experimenting with managed care. The control of medical care cost inflation is far from perfect today, due to the separation of the purchaser (the employer) and the consumer (the employee). In the future, the HMO/PPO contract to control consumer use is expected to become much more specific, more effective in containing costs, and more prevalent.[54]

A tightening of Medicare prospective payment rates for hospitals, laboratory tests, and medical durable equipment over the next few years appears inevitable. Hospitals have found Medicare patients to be highly profitable under PPS. Payment rates for durable equipment and laboratory tests are outdated and not aligned with costs of production. This has resulted both from errors in setting initial rates and from faster than expected responses by hospitals, equipment distributors, and laboratories to the new incentives. Reductions in Medicare payments relative to costs will increase the incentives for private payers to negotiate prices with hospitals through HMOs and PPOs. Like airline passengers after deregulation, it could be a rare patient who pays list price.

The force most difficult to predict is the policy response to the increasing proportion of patients that are uninsured. While health insurance cover-age in the public sector remained relatively stable between 1979 and 1997, private insurance declined from about 71.9 percent to about 64.5 percent. Coverage provided by employers has declined, and there has been an increase in employee contribution (cost-sharing). Workers in peripheral jobs are increasingly less likely to have insurance than those in core jobs. Health insurance enrollment has declined in industries composed of small firms and those with large minority workforces.[55] The combination of Medicaid eligibility restriction and changes in the economy has resulted in a larger proportion of the population without health insurance. Access to charity care has probably been reduced by the competitive pressures on providers who are losing the wherewithal to cross-subsidize these patients. As noted earlier, charitable contributions to hospitals are very minor now. Further, they are often targeted toward research, not care for the uninsured.

The policy response to this problem is likely to affect health insurers and their new competitive tools. Some policies to help the uninsured would not harm health insurance competition (e.g., expanding Medicaid to cover more of the uninsured).[56] However, one possible reaction to the uninsured problem would be uniform national health insurance. Most forms of this would eliminate the current competitive, innovative health insurance system and replace it with some kind of highly regulated private or government system (e.g., one of the national health insurance plans proposed in 1993). Such a uniform plan is not necessary to deal with the plight of the population that does not have insurance, but it has some political or ideological appeal. A uniform national health insurance plan would narrow the choices in the current market and would end competition to reduce costs through innovative health insurance. This would be both unnecessary and unfortunate.

Notes

1. H.E. Frech and W. Ginsburg, "Competition Among Health Insurers," in W. Greenberg, ed., *Competition in the Health Care Sector: Past, Present, and Future,* pp. 167–88 (Germantown, MD: Aspen Systems Corp., 1978); H.E. Frech III, "Monopoly in Health Insurance: The Economics of Kartell v. Blue Shield of Massachusetts," in H.E. Frech III, ed., *Health Care in America: The Political Economy of Hospitals and Health Insurance*, pp. 293–322 (San Francisco: Pacific Research Institute for Public Policy, 1988); Killard W. Adamache and Frank A. Sloan, "Competition Between Non-Profit and For-Profit-Health Insurers," *Journal of Health Economics* 2 (1983), pp. 225–43; and Roger Feldman and Warren Greenberg, "The Relation Between the Blue Cross Share and the Blue Cross 'Discount' on Hospital Charges," *Journal of Risk and Insurance* 48 (1981), pp. 235–46.

2. See Paul Milgrom and John Roberts, *Economics, Organization, and Management* (Englewood Cliffs, NJ: Prentice-Hall, 1992), pp. 288–32; and Timothy Brennan, "Is Cost-of-Service Regulation Worth the Cost?" *International Journal of the Economics of Business* 7, 1 (February 1996), pp. 15–42.

3. See Frech and Ginsburg, "Competition Among Health Insurers."

4. H.E. Frech III, "Market Power in Health Insurance," *Journal of Industrial Economics* 27, 1 (September 1980), pp. 55–72. The optimality of competitively supplied insurance with moral hazard holds since there is no governmental or public policy that can reduce the moral hazard. This is called constrained Pareto optimality, where the unavoidable existence of the moral hazard is the constraint.

5. Mark V. Pauly, "Taxation, Health Insurance and Market Failure in the Medical Economy," *Journal of Economic Literature* 24, 2 (June 1986), pp. 629–75.

6. Charles E. Phelps, *Health Economics* (New York: HarperCollins, 1992), p. 303.

7. Martin S. Feldstein, "The Welfare Loss of Excess Health Insurance," *Journal of Political Economy* 81, 2 (March/April 1973), pp. 251–80.

8. H.E. Frech III and Paul B. Ginsburg, *Public Health Insurance in Private Medical Markets: Some Problems of National Health Insurance* (Washington, DC: American Enterprise Institute for Public Policy Research, 1978), chap. 5.

9. This undulating pattern of rising and falling annual growth rates in insurance premiums over time is known as the insurance underwriting cycle, which typically completes a full undulation over the course of about ten years. For an explanation of why this occurs, see "As the Health Insurance Underwriting Cycle Turns: What Next?" by Joy M. Grossman and Paul B. Ginsburg, *Health Affairs* 23, 6 (Nov/Dec 2004), pp. 91–102.

10. Prospective Payment Assessment Commission, *Medicare and the American Health Care System: Report to Congress,* June 1996, p. 19.

11. H.E. Frech III, James Langenfeld, and Michaelyn Corbett, "Managed Health Care Effects: Medical Care Costs and Access to Health Insurance," working paper in economics #12–00, University of California, Santa Barbara, November 2000.

12. B.C. Strunk and P.B. Ginsburg, "Tracking Health Care Costs: Trends Turn Downward in 2003," *Health Affairs,* Web Exclusive (June 9, 2004).

13. T. Bodenheimer, "High and Rising Health Care Costs. Part 2: Technologic Innovation," *Annals of Internal Medicine* 142, 11 (June 2005), pp. 932–37.

14. P. Hogan, T. Dall, and P. Nikolov, "Economic Costs of Diabetes in the US in 2002," *Diabetes Care* 26, 3 (March 2003), pp. 917–32; K.E. Thorpe, C.S. Florence, D.H. Howard, and P. Joski, "The Impact of Obesity on Rising Medical Spending," *Health Affairs* (July–December 2004) Supplement, Web Exclusives: W4–480–6.

15. K.E. Thorpe, C.S. Florence, and P. Joski, "Which Medical Conditions Account for the Rise in Health Care Spending?" *Health Affairs* (July–December 2004) Supplement, Web Exclusives: W4–437–45.

16. B.C. Strunk, and P.B. Ginsburg, "Aging Plays Limited Role in Health Care Cost Trends," *Data Bulletin: Center for Studying Health Systems Change* 23 (September 2002), pp. 1–2. www.hschange.org/CONTENT/473/473.pdf, accessed online February 23, 2006.

17. A. Mehrotra, R.A. Dudley, and H.S. Luft, "What's Behind the Health Expenditure Trends?" *Annual Review of Public Health* 24 (2003), pp. 385–412.

18. Joy M. Grossman and Paul B. Ginsburg, "As the Health Insurance Underwriting Cycle Turns: What Next?" *Health Affairs* 23 (2004), pp. 91–102.

19. James Henderson, J. Steward, B. Taylor, and C. Conover, "State-Level Health Insurance Mandates and Premium Costs," paper presented at the Southeastern Health Economics Study Group, October 2005, Moore School of Business, Columbia, SC.

20. W. David Bradford and Lee R. Mobley, "Employment-Based Health Insurance and the Effectiveness of Intra-Firm Competition Between Insurance Providers," *Southern Economic Journal* 70, 4 (2004), pp. 1012–31.

21. Fred Hellinger, "The Expanding Scope of State Legislation," *Journal of the American Medical Association* (*JAMA*) 276, 13 (October 2, 1996); James Henderson et al., "State-Level Health Insurance Mandates and Premium Costs."

22. Gail Jensen, Kevin Cotter, and Michael Morrisey, "State Insurance Regulation and Employers' Decisions to Self-Insure," *Journal of Risk and Insurance* 62, 2 (1995), p. 185.

23. Jon R. Gabel, Gail A. Jensen, and Samantha Hawkins, "Self-Insurance in Times of Growing and Retreating Managed Care," *Health Affairs* 22, 2 (March/April 2003), pp. 202–10.

24. James Robinson, "Consolidation and the Transformation of Competition in Health Insurance," *Health Affairs* 23, 6 (2004), pp. 11–24.

25. *State of Maryland v. Blue Cross and Blue Shield Assn.*, 620 F. Supp. 907 (1985).

26. Harvey Sapolsky, Drew Altman, Richard Greener, and Judith D. Moore, "Corporate Attitudes Toward Health Care Costs," *Milbank Memorial Fund Quarterly* 59 (1981), pp. 561–75.

27. U.S. Chamber of Commerce, *Employee Benefits 1985* (Washington, DC: U.S. Chamber Research Center, 1986), and online at www.uschamber.com/_labor+day+facts.htm.

28. Statement by Chip Kahn, president, HIAA, in a press release March 21, 2001: "HIAA Encouraged by President Bush's Concern About Unlimited 'Patient Protection' Liability" (www.hiaa.org/news/news-current/press-releases/release6.html); the U.S Chamber of Commerce opposes this bill. Available online at www.uschamber.com/_Political+Advocacy/Issues+Index/Health+Care/Managed+Care/default.htm.

29. Kaiser Commission on Medicaid and the Uninsured, "Are Immigrants Responsible for Most of the Growth of the Uninsured?" Publication Number: 7411 (11-04-2005). Available online December 2005: www.kff.org/uninsured/7411.cfm.

30. HCFA, "Medicare Managed Care Market Penetration Report, All Plans," June 2000, and "Medicaid Enrollment and Medicaid Managed Care Enrollment by State," December 31, 1999, and "National Statistics," December 31, 2005: MCOL (Managed Care Online), www.mcareol.com/factshts/mcolfact.htm.

31. The following reports describe one demonstration project that resulted in the entry of thirty-three new Medicare PPO plans: L. Greenwald, G. Pope, W. Anderson, L. Mobley, N. West, S. Bernard, J. Kautter, and E. Root, *Medicare Preferred Provider Organization (PPO) Case Study and Implementation Report* (January 2004); Centers for Medicare & Medicaid Services: http://new.cms.hhs.gov/Reports/downloads/greenwald_2004_2.pdf. Also see: L. Greenwald, L. Mobley, M. Bruhn, N. West, L. Andrews, P. Salib, G. Pope, and S. Haber, *Medicare Preferred Provider Organization (PPO) Geographic Service Area Report* (May 2003), Centers for Medicare & Medicaid Services: http://new.cms.hhs.gov/Reports/downloads/greenwald_2003_2.pdf.

32. MEDPAC Report to Congress, June 2004. "A Data Book: Healthcare Spending and the Medicare Program," Chart 7–12, p. 88. Accessed online March 2006, www.medpac.gov/publications/congressional_reports/Jun04DataBook_Entire_report_links.pdf.

33. Urban Institute's National Center for Charitable Statistics (NCCS) GuideStar National Nonprofit Organization Research Database, 1999 and 2003: www.urban.org/publications/900054.html, accessed online March 2006.

34. C. Snyder and G. Anderson, "Do Quality Improvement Organizations Improve the Quality of Hospital Care for Medicare Beneficiaries?" *JAMA* 293, 23 (June 15, 2005), pp. 2900–07; K. Sheikh, C. Bullock, S.D. Preston, "Evaluation of Quality Improvement Interventions for Reducing Adverse Outcomes of Carotid Endarterectomy," *Medical Care* 42, 7 (July 2004), pp. 690–99.

35. Clark C. Havinghurst, "Professional Restraints on Innovation in Health Care Financing," *Duke Law Journal* 2 (1978), pp. 303–87.

36. *Griesman v. Newcomb Hospital,* 40 N.J. 384, 192 A.2d 817 (1963).

37. *In re Michigan State Medical Society,* 101 F.T.C. 191 (1983).

38. Monica Noether, "The Cost of Physician Antitrust Waivers," Charles Rivers Associates, March 3, 2000, available in pdf file at www.hiaa.org/pubs/pubs-titles/Research.htm; the U.S Chamber of Commerce opposes this legislation, see press release January 10, 2000: "Doctors Should Not Receive Collective Bargaining Power, Antitrust Exemption Proposal Would Drive Up Costs, Increase Number of Uninsured Americans"; available online at www.uschamber.com/Press+Room/2000+Releases/January+2000/00–6b.htm.

39. Jon Gabel and Dan Ermann, "Preferred Provider Organizations: Performance, Problems, and Promise," *Health Affairs* 4, 1 (Spring 1985), pp. 24–40.

40. FTC, *In the Matter of North Texas Specialty Physicians, a corporation,* Docket No. 9312, FTC Commission Decision, Nov. 29, 2005.

41. Havinghurst, "Professional Restraints."

42. Joseph A. Schumpeter, *The Theory of Economic Development* (Cambridge: MA: Harvard University Press, 1934).

43. Monica Noether, "The Effect of Government Policy Changes on the Supply of Physicians: Expansion of a Competitive Fringe," *Journal of Law and Economics* 29, 2 (October 1986), pp. 231–62.

44. Source: *Statistical Abstract of the U.S.,* various years; the American Medical Association (AMA), "Socioeconomic Characteristics of Medical Practice, 1996," August 1998 (www.HCFA.org).

45. Carol Simon and Patricia Born, "Physician Earnings in a Changing Managed Care Environment," *Health Affairs,* 15, 3 (1996).

46. H.E. Frech, James Langenfeld, and Michaelyn Corbett, "Managed Health Care Effects: Medical Care Costs and Access to Health Insurance," working paper in economics #12–00, University of California, Santa Barbara, November 2000.

47. Ibid.

48. E. Haavi Morreim, "The Futility of Medical Necessity," *Regulation* 24, 2 (Summer 2001), pp. 22–26.

49. Gail Jensen and Michael Morrissey, "Mandated Benefit

Laws and Employer Sponsored Health Insurance," HIAA, January 1999 www.HIAA.org); Michael Morrisey, "Mandates: What Most Proposals Would Do," *American Enterprise* 3, 1 (January 1, 1992), pp. 63–65; H.E. Frech III, "Risks That Rise with Health Mandates," *Washington Times* (October 22, 1996); Fred Hellinger, "The Expanding Scope."

50. Mandates have raised HMO premiums more than premiums of traditional indemnity plans. See James Henderson, J. Steward, B. Taylor, and C. Conover, "State-Level Health Insurance Mandates and Premium Costs," paper presented at the Southeastern Health Economics Study Group, October 2005, Moore School of Business, Columbia, SC.

51. Michael Morrisey, Jeffrey Alexander, Lawton Burns, and Victoria Johnson, "Managed Care and Physician/Hospital Integration," *Health Affairs* 15, 4 (1996); Gail Jensen and Michael Morrisey, "Mandated Benefit Laws and Employer Sponsored Health Insurance," HIAA, January 1999 (www. HIAA.org).

52. Gloria J. Bazzoli, Linda Dynan, Lawton R. Burns, and Clarence Yap, "Two Decades of Organizational Change in Health Care: What Have We Learned?" *Medical Care Research and Review* 61 (September 2004), pp. 247–331.

53. James Robinson, "Consolidation and the Transforma-tion of Competition in Health Insurance," *Health Affairs* 23, 6 (2004), pp. 11–24.

54. Clark Havinghurst, *Health Care Choices: Private Contracts as Instruments of Health Reform* (Washington, DC: AEI Press, 1995).

55. Henry Farber and Helen Levy, "Recent Trends in Employer-Sponsored Health Insurance Coverage: Are Bad Jobs Getting Worse?" working paper #402, Princeton University, July 1998, and Lisa Cubbins, et al., "Economic Change and Health Benefits: Structural Trends in Employer-Based Health Insurance," *Journal of Health and Social Behavior* 42, 1 (March 2001).

56. Press release by Chip Kahn, HIAA president, April 5, 2001, "Senate Amendment a Victory for Millions of Uninsured Americans," stated: "Today's Senate action—together with President Bush's tax package—indicates that there is growing momentum in Washington for helping the nearly 43 million Americans who lack health coverage. It also is important that both measures complement the employment-based health insurance system, which more than 170 million Americans depend upon to pay for their health care." Available online at: www.hiaa.org/news/news-current/press-releases/release1. html.

7

Motion Pictures

Competition, Distribution, and Efficiencies

Stanley I. Ornstein

Introduction

The history of the motion picture industry spans over 100 years. During that period the industry has endured competitive challenges from network television, cable and satellite, massive corporate reorganizations, and years of government and private antitrust attacks. Since the passage of the Sherman Antitrust Act in 1890, few industries have been so drastically altered by government antitrust action as the motion picture industry. But it has survived, gaining prosperity through technological improvements in filmmaking and exhibition, and by capitalizing on new channels for distributing movies. Born from innovations in the photography of moving objects and the projection of images onto a screen, the industry rose from humble beginnings in the 1890s. The first theatrical screening was in New York City in 1896, following a vaudeville act. Movie viewing was widespread by 1910, and reached enormous popularity in the 1920s, 1930s, and 1940s. In the 1930s and 1940s upward of 400–500 feature films were produced per year in the United States, and theater attendance in many years reportedly averaged 85 to 90 million per week, or over 4 billion annually, well above contemporary attendance levels of approximately 1.4 to 1.6 billion.[1]

Following World War II, the vertically inte-grated structure of the top movie distributors, with common ownership of production, distribution, and exhibition, was dissolved by government antitrust actions, and, under court order, many of the industry's well-established marketing and distribution practices, such as "block booking," "blind bidding," and exclusive dealing franchise arrangements were prohibited.[2] Movies then faced the challenge of network television, which some believed would destroy the movie business. With declining theater attendance, thousands of motion picture theaters were closed. However, over the last thirty years the industry has rebounded, capitaliz-ing on the introduction of videocassettes, DVDs, and pay cable television; experiencing huge growth in foreign revenues; and attaining a post-1970 peak in North American theatrical admissions in 2002 of 1.64 billion.

This study offers an overview of the industry's evolution: its organizational structure, marketing and distribution practices, alleged antitrust trans-gressions, responses to forced dissolution, and contemporary economic performance. Industry studies provide an opportunity to broaden our understanding of economic practices. The motion picture industry provides vivid examples of promi-nent economic phenomena, including vertical in-tegration, exclusive dealing, price discrimination, and adaptations to inherently risky investments.

The courts' dissolution of the industry's vertically integrated structure and curtailment of various distribution practices in 1948 provides a natural before-and-after experiment for examining the factors leading to vertical integration and the consequences of abandoning such integration. Price discrimination has been an integral part of the motion picture industry for over seventy-five years. As we will see, the demand for movies lends itself to price discrimination, and practices arose to exploit this opportunity. Finally, the movie business is very risky. The box office outcome of any given movie is highly uncertain. The risk of investing in movies has had a substantial effect on the industry's business practices, structure, and evolution.

Production, Distribution, and Exhibition

The movie industry traditionally operates at three levels: (1) production—the financing, development, and making of motion pictures; (2) distribution —the licensing, distribution, and promotion of movies; and (3) exhibition—the screening of movies. All three stages are obviously highly dependent on one another. Until the 1950s, the top five studios were vertically integrated companies, combining production, distribution, and exhibition. In 1948 the U.S. Supreme Court, in effect, required the top five studios to divest their ownership of movie theaters and halt a variety of distribution practices for violations of the Sherman Antitrust Act, destroying an integral part of their organizational structure and thereby increasing the costs of distributing movies.[3]

Table 7.1 lists the major studio-distributors of films and their relative shares over time of domestic box office revenues (known as "rentals"). Columbia, Twentieth Century Fox, MGM/UA, Paramount, Universal, and Warner Brothers have been major distributors since at least the 1920s and 1930s. As seen from the changing shares, the distributors' fortunes have risen and fallen over time as blockbuster movies have propelled first one and then another distributor to the top in various years. However, as noted, the success of movies is uncertain, with the majority of them losing money. The major hit movies must earn enough to compensate for the many losing investments. Distributors are generally unable to maintain a number one position for more than a few consecutive years, indicating how difficult it is to consistently produce and distribute hit movies. As one example, Sony (Columbia/Tri-Star) reported a $3.2 billion loss on its movie operations in 1994.[4] Sony had a series of poorly performing movies, gaining only 9 percent of theater rentals. However, Sony scored with major successes in 1997, propelling it to a top rental share of 20 percent. The hits disappeared from 1999 to 2001, Sony's share fell back to approximately 9 percent, but it was again on top with a 17 percent share in 2002. Similar large swings are evident in the box office shares of other major studios.

Motion pictures are rented under license to exhibitors, with the box office receipts divided in an agreed proportion between distributor and exhibitor. The distributor receives a percentage of box office receipts, with the percentage declining the longer the movie runs. In one type of first-run movie license, the distributor receives 70 percent of box office receipts for the first week or two, with the percentage declining weekly thereafter. Under another formula for first-run movies, the theater owner receives a negotiated sum to cover overhead expenses, and the box office is split 90/10 for the distributor in the first few weeks, with the distributor's share declining over time. These revenue shares are important because most movies earn the majority of their box office receipts within the first three to four weeks. On average, studio-distributors receive approximately 50 percent of box office receipts, although this can vary widely

Table 7.1

North American Theatrical Rental Shares of Distributors

Year	Time Warner (Warner Bros.)	Disney (Buena Vista)	Dream-works	News Corp (20th Century Fox)	MGM/UA	Miramax	New Line	Sony (Columbia)	Viacom (Paramount)	General Electric (Universal)
2005	16	10	6	16	2	2	5	10	9	11
2004	13	12	10	10	2	4	5	14	7	10
2003	13	17	3	9	4	4	10	13	7	12
2002	12	13	6	10	4	4	10	17	8	10
2001	15	11	5	11	6	8	7	9	11	12
2000	12	15	10	10	1	6	5	9	11	15
1999	14	17	4	11	4	4	4	9	12	13
1998	11	16	7	11	3	6	8	11	16	6
1997	11	14	2	11	3	7	6	20	12	10
1996	16	21		13	5	4	5	11	13	8
1995	16	19		8	6	4	7	13	10	13
1994	16	19		9	3	4	6	9	14	13
1993	19	16		11	2	3	3	11	9	14
1992	20	19		14	1	1	2	13	10	12
1991	14	14		12	2	1	4	9	12	11
1990	13	16		14	3	1	4	13	15	14
1985	18	3		11	9		1	10	10	16
1980	14	4		16	7			14	16	20
1975	9	6		14	11			13	11	25
1970	5	9		19	9			14	12	13

Source: Variety, January 18, 1989, January 13, 1993, and January 6–12, 1997; Standard & Poor's, *Industry Surveys, Movie and Home Entertainment*, April 18, 1996, February 27, 1997, May 10, 2001, and March 24, 2005; National Association of Theater Owners, *2000–2001 Encyclopedia of Exhibition*, and *2005–2006 Encyclopedia of Exhibition*, and ww.boxofficemojo.com.

Notes: Other distributors at various times included Lorimar, Embassy Pictures, Gramercy, and Orion. Dreamworks (excluding Dreamworks animation) was purchased by Viacom's Paramount in 2005. Miramax was acquired by Disney in 1993 and spun off in 2005. New Line was acquired by Warner Brothers in 1996. Sony includes Tri-Star since 1984. A Sony-led consortium acquired MGM in 2004. General Electric acquired Universal in 2003.

Table 7.2

Top North American Theater Chains

Exhibitor	Number of screens			
	1994	1997	2000	2005
Regal Cinemas	722	1,978	4,449	6,264
AMC	1,636	1,930	2,736	3,308
Carmike Cinemas	2,035	2,590	2,821	2,450
Cinemark USA	1,214	1,459	2,227	2,347
Loews Cineplex			2,726	1,427
Cineplex Odeon	1,643	1,550		
Sony Theatres	912	988		
United Artists Theatre Circuit	2,204	2,237	1,858	
National Amusements	848	898	1,076	1,099
General Cinema Theatres	1,221	1,202	1,060	
Hoyts Cinemas	519	817	967	
Act III Theatres	568	703		
Famous Players	441	511	868	
Edwards Theatres		426	743	
Century Theatres		408	722	985
Wallace Theater Company		132	544	458
Silver Cinemas		153	540	
Kerasotes Theatres		404	521	609
Marcus Theatres			487	503

Source: Variety, January 4, 1987, and January 20, 1988; Standard & Poor's, *Industry Surveys, Leisure Time,* April 6, 1995, and Standard & Poor's, *Industry Surveys, Movies and Home* Entertainment, February 27, 1997; National Association of Theater Owners, *1997–1998 Encyclopedia of Exhibition, 2000–2001 Encyclopedia of Exhibition,* and *2005–2006 Encyclopedia of Exhibition;* and *Los Angeles Times,* March 5, 2006, p. C1.

Notes: AMC acquired Loews Cineplex in January 2006, giving AMC 5,672 total screens. Loews Cineplex was formed by the merger of Cineplex Odeon and Sony Theatres in 1998. Regal Cinemas acquired Act III Theatres in 1999, United Artist and Edwards Theatres in 2001, and Hoyts Cinemas in 2003. Viacom, owner of National Amusements, acquired Famous Players of Canada in 1994. Cineplex Odeon acquired Famous Players in 2005. AMC acquired General Cinema in 2002.

over movies and time. Profits from theater concession good sales (popcorn, candy, soft drinks, video games, etc.) go solely to the exhibitor.[5]

Leading exhibitor firms in 2005 are shown in Table 7.2. The top ten exhibitors account for approximately 50 percent of all screens in the United States. Exhibition has experienced large-scale consolidation through mergers and acquisitions since the early 1980s, and through internal expansion by the largest exhibitors. The largest theater chain in 2005, Regal, began in 1989 and grew primarily by acquisition until the mid-1990s, and then grew by a combination of acquisitions and new theater construction. Loews Cineplex resulted from the 1998 merger of Sony's Loews Theaters, with approximately 900 screens, and Cineplex Odeon, with approximately 1,600 screens. AMC and Loews were acquired independently in 2004 and taken private, and in January 2006 they merged, solidifying AMC's second-place position. With the merger, the two largest exhibitor chains own approximately 31 percent of all U.S. screens. Others, such as Cinemark USA and National Amusements, have also grown through acquisitions. As a result of differences across firms in acquisitions and new theater construction programs, the size ranking of exhibitors has shifted dramatically since the 1980s, producing increasing concentration in screen ownership.

The growth in number of screens has outpaced the rise in attendance for years. This was especially true in the 1990s. A construction boom in theaters from 1994 to 1999 added over 10,000 new screens. The leading firms incurred large debt, which resulted in a series of theater firm bankruptcy filings in 1999 and 2000. Firms falling into bankruptcy reorganization included such leading names as Regal, Carmike, Loews Cineplex, United Artists, and General Cinema; major regional firms like Edwards and Silver Cinemas; and smaller chains.[6] Some chains planned over 20 percent reductions in their total screens. With large excess capacity in screens and efforts through bankruptcy reorganization to regain profitability, hundreds of older screens were closed, with little increase in the total number of screens from 1999 through 2004.

These two tables illustrate the dynamic nature of the motion picture industry. Intense competition and the vagaries of individual movie success change the rankings of distributors, generally from year to year. In theater exhibition, changes in ownership due to acquisitions and bankruptcies have fostered greater concentration in ownership and changed the fortunes of individual firms. We will return to contemporary industry developments and performance later in this study. However, we start with industry history, for to understand the industry today, one needs to examine its historic development.

Early History

At the inception of the industry, manufacturers of motion picture cameras and projectors produced the movies, for in order to sell their equipment, they had to supply movies.[7] The movies were short, one-reel episodes of five to twenty minutes in length. They could be drama, Westerns, comedy, or outdoor scenic movies. Movies were sold outright to exhibitors and viewed by individuals in penny arcades or in theaters along with vaudeville acts. Movies soon graduated to modest theaters for showings, known as nickelodeons for their five-cent admission fee, and thousands of nickelodeons opened throughout the country. Exchange firms arose to facilitate movie trading among exhibitors who sought variety in movie viewing for their customers, and as a means to reduce the costs of acquiring movies. Exchange firms evolved into early versions of modern-day distributors, acquiring movies from producers and renting them to exhibitors. By 1911 there were a reported 150 exchanges (distributors) and 11,500 movie theaters in the United States. There were also dozens of motion picture producers. Movie theater chains were forming, and where they dominated local markets through movie booking agencies, some thought they exercised monopsony power, using that power in bargaining with distributors on movie rental rates.[8]

Feature-length films of four- and five-reel length, replacing the short one-reel movies, were widespread by 1913. To attract larger audiences, theaters became more lavish in architecture and size, and in providing patrons with more amenities and comforts. Distributors, in turn, grew more sophisticated in selecting theaters for each movie and in setting rental rates according to theater size and location. At the same time that theaters and distributors were multiplying rapidly, ten manufacturers of patented movie equipment formed the Motion Picture Patents Company in 1908 as a means to eliminate what had been years of intra-industry patent infringement lawsuits, and also in an attempt to exclude competition in the production, distribution, and marketing of movies.[9] The Motion Picture Patents Company's attempts to monopolize the industry failed; however, it pioneered in various aspects of movie distribution. The Motion Picture Patents Company vertically integrated into distribution in 1910 in an attempt to monopolize distribution, forming the General Film Company, which acquired most of its former independent distributors. The General Film Company established for the first time a national distribution system of film rentals, classifications of theaters, time periods or "runs" for first-run, second-run, third-run movies, and so forth, and geographic zones or "clearances," which amount to exclusive exhibition territories for a given movie. Although it was innovative in distribution practices to maximize revenues, the company failed to move into feature film production, hastening its demise. The Motion Picture Patents Company was dissolved in 1918, after being found guilty in 1915 of attempting to monopolize the motion picture industry and after losing major patent lawsuits. Long before its dissolution, however, numerous new entrants had successfully challenged the Motion Picture Patents Company in all phases of the business: the manufacturing of cameras and projectors, and movie production, distribution, and exhibition.

As one example of new entry, Paramount Pictures was formed in 1914 by combining five distribution-exchanges and regional distributors. Paramount secured contracts to distribute movies for three leading production companies. For its distribution services, Paramount retained 35 percent of the box office receipts it received from exhibitors, similar to the fees charged by distributors today. Paramount secured exhibitors for its producers, forming franchise or exclusive dealing relationships with exhibitors who screened Paramount's full line of movies. Paramount also helped finance new production by providing advances to producers against box office receipts and by contracting with exhibitors for future play dates.[10] By 1914, blocks of movies for an entire year were being licensed to distributors and exhibitors (block booking), requiring exhibitors to take lesser movies in order to receive movies scheduled to have appearances by the leading movie stars of the day. In addition to Paramount, other national distributors included Mutual, Universal, and Fox. As noted, the Motion Picture Patents Company's early attempt to monopolize failed primarily due to widespread entry from rival producers, distributors, and exhibitors. But the company pioneered in vertical integration between production and distribution and in the distribution practices—runs and clearances—that provided the basis for price discrimination.

Vertical Integration

From 1915 to the 1930s there was large-scale vertical integration into production, distribution, and exhibition. Movie production studios integrated forward into distribution and exhibition, distributors integrated into production and exhibition, and exhibitor groups integrated backward into distribution and production. In 1916 the Famous Players-Lasky studio bought Paramount, the distribution company, and in 1919 started vertically integrating into theaters, acquiring 300 theaters by mid-1921. In 1917 theater owners organized the First National Exhibitors Circuit to act as a purchasing agent for movies, and vertically integrated into distribution and movie production. By 1920 over 600 theaters were in the group. Eventually its best theaters were acquired by Famous Players-Lasky-Paramount, which became Paramount Pictures. Other theater chains integrating backward into distribution, and production included Fox, which became Twentieth Century Fox in the 1930s, and Loews Theaters, which first acquired Metro in the 1920s. Loews/Metro put together the studios that became Metro-Goldwyn-Mayer (MGM). In the late 1920s, Warner Brothers, which pioneered in the first sound motion pictures, invested heavily in theaters, acquiring 500 theaters by the mid-1930s. A fifth vertically integrated studio, RKO, was formed in 1929 by the Radio Corporation of American (RCA) in order to sell sound equipment to movie producers, and it eventually acquired approximately 200 theaters.

Table 7.3

Theater Ownership by the Top Five Major Distributors, 1945

Firm	Theaters owned	Joint ownership with independent owners	Total
Paramount	1,395	993	2,388
Twentieth Century Fox	636	66	702
Warner Bros.	501	20	521
Loews	135	21	156
RKO	109	187	296
Joint ownership with top five firms	361		361
Total	3,137	1,287	4,424

Source: Michael Conant, *Antitrust in the Motion Picture Industry, Economic and Legal Analysis (*Berkeley and Los Angeles: University of California Press, 1960).

These studios—Paramount, Twentieth Century Fox, Loews (MGM), Warner Brothers, and RKO —controlled the bulk of first-run theaters in large and small cities in the 1930s and 1940s through ownership, leases, or franchise (exclusive dealing) contracts with independent theaters. The five major theater-owning studios cross-licensed each other's movies in cities or areas where they did not own theaters. Theater ownership as of 1945, both individually and jointly, is shown in Table 7.3. The number of theaters owned by the vertically integrated firms represented about 24 percent of the approximately 18,000 U.S. theaters in 1945. The top five distributors accounted for 70 percent of first-run theaters in the ninety-two largest market areas (100,000 population and above), and approximately 60 percent of first-run theaters in cities of 25,000 to 100,000, generating the vast majority of movie revenues. The top eight distributors, which included Columbia, Universal, and United Artists (although these firms did not own theaters), accounted for 95 percent of film rental payments to distributors over the period 1935 to 1944.[11]

Vertical integration was adopted during a period of intense competition as a more efficient means of distributing and marketing movies. Numerous firms challenged the Motion Picture Patents Company during its attempt to monopolize the movie industry. Producers competed for major stars to enhance box office appeal, in the quality of movies produced, and for the best distributors and exhibitors. Exhibitors and distributors competed for box office receipts and for the best movies. Firms sought to reduce costs and enhance demand by integrating into two or all three levels of production, distribution, and exhibition. A variety of factors drove this movement to vertical integration. First, producers integrated into distribution, seeking greater control over the licensing, promotion, and theater placement of their movies. Second, according to some commentators, producers and distributors became concerned about contracting for exhibition outlets, fearing they would be foreclosed from the best outlets once exhibitors integrated backward into production, as in the case of the First National Exhibitors Circuit. By integrating into exhibition, producers had a secure network of outlets in at least some parts of the country. With guaranteed distribution and exhibition, producers could more easily finance movie production. In similar fashion, exhibitors were concerned about gaining an adequate supply of movies when producer–distributors integrated forward into exhibition, fearing they would lose movies to the distributor-owned theaters. By integrating backward into production and distribution, exhibitors sought to gain a secure supply of movies. However, such concerns were questionable. Self-sufficiency in the supply of movies for exhibition is not a tenable competitive position. Exhibitors and distributors want the best movies, regardless of source. No firm with exhibition outlets has ever been able to rely solely on its own movies as a source of supply.

Third, revenues to support the industry came from box office receipts, and exhibitors controlled the box office. Dishonest exhibitors had many avenues to cheat on rental agreements and the distribution of box office receipts. Among the practices used were: understating tickets sold, delaying payment, screening at more than the authorized location, and reproducing movie prints. Such cheating was widespread, requiring large expenditures to monitor exhibitor behavior.[12] Ownership of theaters and exclusive dealing arrangements could drastically reduce these losses. Such integration also ensured the setting of admission prices consistent with the distributor's wish to maximize box office receipts through price discrimination. Fourth, some producer-distributors believed they could operate first-run theaters more economically under ownership than by contracting with numerous independent exhibitors. Licensing movies is costly, requiring individual negotiations with exhibitors, transporting prints, advertising, and the monitoring and collection of box office receipts. Ownership could possibly reduce some of these costs, such as contracting and monitoring box office receipts.

In addition, "adjustments," a type of financial settling-up, are regularly made to contract terms when movies either do poorly or exceptionally well at the box office. Adjustments change the terms of the initial license, such as length of run, percentage shares of box office rentals, and advertising expense sharing between exhibitor and distributor. Rather than have a movie play to a relatively empty theater, negotiations can shorten a run or move the film to a smaller theater. Because distributors and exhibitors must work together on a long-term cooperative basis, it is in the distributors' interest not to impose prohibitive losses on exhibitors. Adjustments to license terms have been part of the distribution process since at least the 1930s. Theater ownership internalizes certain costs, such as licensing and adjustments, and, in principle, can reduce the overall cost of distribution and exhibition.

Price Discrimination

From approximately the World War I era onward, movies were released to theaters in a tightly controlled, temporal pattern.[13] Motion pictures first appeared for a specific number of days in first-run theaters, then were moved to second-run theaters, next to third-run, and so forth. Admission prices varied by run, with the highest price for first-run, next highest in second-run, and so on. Movies were licensed or rented to theaters for a specific run, measured in days. From the 1920s into the 1940s, 75 percent of first-run films had runs of more than twenty-eight days, and some up to 100 days or more.[14] Theaters were granted geographic zone clearances, guaranteeing the theater an exclusive territory for screening; that is, the movie could not be shown by another theater within a prescribed distance. For example, approximately two-thirds of first-run theaters had geographic clearances of ten miles or more. Studio-distributors designated which theaters were first-run, generally reserving that status for their own theaters and those of their top rivals. As indicated, the majority of first-run theaters in major population centers were owned or partially owned by the top five studio-distributors: Paramount, Warner Brothers, Twentieth Century

Fox, MGM, and RKO. Other first-run exhibitors were affiliated with the major distributors though exclusive dealing franchise arrangements. Because the majority of box office revenues came from first-run movies, many exhibitors sought first-run status for their theater. Distributors also engaged in resale price maintenance, setting minimum admission prices for theaters in their rental contracts.

In addition to time and zone clearances, resale price maintenance on admission prices, and block booking, movies in the 1930s were typically rented to exhibitors "blind," with no advance information on the movies' contents. In the 1930s, a year's supply of films for exhibitors was acquired in a block during a two- or three-month buying (rental) season. Exhibitors were required to take blocks of films with no prior knowledge of the film's actors, storyline, and so on from various distributors for the following year's screenings. The films were yet to be staffed and produced. Theaters contracted for various numbers of films depending on their run status, with first-run theaters contracting for fewer films than, say, third-run theaters, because the latter would change films more frequently, sometimes two or three times in a week. Bulk purchasing (rental) through block booking provided exhibitors with films and distributors with assured outlets for their films. It also aided in minimizing movie inventory costs and, given that the movies were rented in advance, it ensured their financing.

The system of controlling exhibition prices by time and zone clearances, and through resale price maintenance, was clearly designed to maximize box office revenue by capturing the maximum area under the demand curve for movies. Prices were set according to individual consumer segments of demand, with differential pricing across each demand segment. Consumers with the highest demand viewed movies in first-run theaters and paid the highest admission price; then came consumers with a somewhat lower demand, viewing movies

in second-run theaters at lower prices; then came consumers for third-run theaters, and so on. This method of differential pricing, matching price to relative consumer demand, produced far greater admission revenues for distributors and exhibitors to share than a uniform price for all consumers would have achieved. Maximization of box office receipts was further aided by resale price maintenance. Because exhibitors gained all concession good profits and split box office receipts with distributors, they had an incentive to sacrifice box office receipts to increase concession sales. Fixing minimum admission prices in licensing contracts protected the distributor's interest in maximizing box office receipts.

Antitrust Charges and the
Paramount Case

Few industries have been subject to more antitrust lawsuits than the motion picture industry. From approximately 1912 to the present, a variety of distributors and exhibitors have been embroiled in either a major government antitrust suit or in suing each other in one of literally hundreds of private suits. Government suits typically alleged some form of collusive activity and monopolization, by either distributors or exhibitors. Private suits, often by exhibitors against distributors or against other exhibitors, generally alleged some form of anticompetitive discrimination in issuing licenses or some practice that foreclosed rivals from competing for movies.

From at least the 1920s onward, independent movie theater owners objected repeatedly to the control of first-run movie theaters by studio-distributors and the rental of movies by block booking and blind bidding. Many independent theater owners sought first-run movie status from distributors, only to be denied the opportunity. Numerous examples exist of first-run status being granted only after a theater sold out or sold a partial interest to one of the top five producers.[15] When advance information about a movie was made available, theater owners also objected to being forced to take undesired movies through block booking in order to receive those they preferred, while the major studios' theaters allegedly escaped such pressure. Independents also objected to contracting for movies without receiving information about the contents or an advance screening. Believing themselves victimized by unfair discriminatory competition, disaffected independent theater owners sought protection from distributors, turning first to the Federal Trade Commission (FTC) and then to the Department of Justice (DOJ). The FTC filed a complaint against the (then) major studios in 1921, charging them with unfair competition through block booking and the control of first-run movie houses.[16] Following a lengthy investigation, the FTC concluded that block booking was an unfair trade practice and issued a cease-and-desist order that was never enforced. Again responding to exhibitors' complaints, the DOJ brought an antitrust case against the eight largest studio-distributors in 1938, charging them with monopolizing the motion picture industry through their control of production, distribution, and exhibition. As a remedy, the DOJ sought the divestiture of theater ownership from production and distribution. After one week at trial, the parties retreated to negotiate, which led to a consent decree in November 1940 whereby the five major producers agreed to temporarily limit block booking to five films at a time and to end blind bidding by having trade screenings for exhibitors. Curiously, despite years of complaints against blind bidding, few exhibitors attended the trade screenings.[17] The government, in turn, agreed not to pursue the forced divestiture of theaters for a three-year period.

The DOJ reopened the case in 1944, again seeking the divestiture of theaters as a remedy for alleged monopolization. In June 1946, a district court found that the top eight distributors had engaged in an illegal restraint of trade.[18] The court prohibited the firms from: (1) fixing admission prices; (2) agreeing to maintain uniform clearances; (3) engaging in excessive or unreasonable clearances, formula deals, or master agreements,[19] (4) pooling arrangements in exhibiting movies,[20] and (5) block booking. The court concluded that competitive bidding on a picture-by-picture, theater-by-theater basis would solve the problem of discrimination against independent exhibitors, but it rejected the government's request for movie theater divestiture.

On appeal to the Supreme Court, the defendants were found to have monopolized the exhibition of first-run movies in major cities through vertical integration and complex licensing contracts and distribution practices.[21] Monopoly was found to exist at the exhibition level, as evidenced by the percentage of first-run theater ownership and domestic movie rentals controlled by the defendants. Theater control through vertical integration and franchising was held to exclude competition in the distribution and exhibition of movies. The Court agreed with the lower court that the solution was theater-by-theater licensing of individual pictures, but it rejected competitive bidding in favor of the divestiture of theaters and the end to franchising, and it directed the lower court to reconsider divestiture as the appropriate remedy. The Supreme Court also held that clearances and runs were not illegal as long as a fixed and uniform system of clearances did not prevail across all distributors. Final court decisions required the top five distributors to divest ownership in their domestic theaters and the new theater circuits to sell some of their theaters. By February 1953, all of the firms but Loews had spun off their theater circuits, and Loews followed, belatedly, in 1959.[22]

The government spent the next twenty-five years

reviewing all proposed acquisitions by the successor theater companies. An estimated 500 petitions for acquisitions were reviewed for their potential anticompetitive consequences. Maurice Silverman, the DOJ lawyer in charge of the reviews, spent the remainder of his career, until he retired in 1975, working on the petitions.[23] In 1968 the successor to Twentieth Century Fox Theaters, National General Theaters, sought to acquire Warner Brothers Studios for $500 million, but Silverman blocked the acquisition. Most acquisitions were of a lesser magnitude, involving the acquisition of a few theaters. In 1974 the government stopped reviewing acquisition petitions, and in 1985 the DOJ effectively terminated the *Paramount* consent decrees because there was little likelihood of a return to the level of vertical integration existing before the *Paramount* decision and theatrical screenings faced increasing competition from home viewing.

Post-*Paramount* Performance

The court-ordered massive restructuring of movie distribution and exhibition provides a basis for testing the government's position that the industry's structure and complex distribution practices were adopted as part of a conspiracy to monopolize motion picture production, distribution, and exhibition by blocking competition from independent exhibitors and producers. It also provides a basis for examining the distributors' use of vertical integration, by ownership or by contract in the form of exclusive dealing. We first look at the charge of monopolization.

Tests of Monopolization

Assuming the eight firms had behaved monopolistically, raising rental shares and admission prices above the competitive level, then after the court-imposed restructuring a return to lower competitive prices should be evident. Admission prices and rental shares should decline and output should rise. An unambiguous test of this proposition is clouded, unfortunately, by the fact that the demand and supply of movies was changing. Movie admission revenue fell from $1.69 billion in 1946 to $1.12 billion in 1957.[24] Paid indoor movie theater admissions fell from 3.35 billion in 1948 to 1.96 billion in 1954 and 1.28 billion in 1958.[25] A number of factors contributed to the decline in movie attendance. A high birthrate following World War II limited leisure time for young families. People moved in large numbers to the suburbs, away from the (then) main concentration of downtown movie theaters, although this was offset in part by the growth of drive-in theaters. Drive-ins grew in number from approximately 300 in 1946 to 4,500 in 1956.[26] Of major importance was the spread of television ownership from 1948 onward and its effect on the demand for motion pictures. In 1949 approximately 12 percent of homes with electricity had a television set. At the end of 1957, 86 percent had a television set.[27] Nevertheless, it is instructive to examine the available evidence on changes in price and output.

Did distributors' rental shares of box office receipts fall, as a return to competition would predict? Distributors calculated that their average revenue share *rose* after the *Paramount* decisions, from 26 percent in 1947 to 35 percent in 1953.[28] Exhibitors estimated a more modest distributor rental share rise, from approximately 33 percent in 1947 to 36 percent in 1955. A third study indicates a distributor share increase from approximately 30 percent in 1948 to 40 percent in 1954.[29] These results are inconsistent with the view that the eight firms were acting as monopolies, extracting economic rents from independent exhibitors, because a return to competition would lower rental shares.

If the courts were correct, a return to competition in exhibition would also be reflected in lower admission prices. Resale price maintenance was prohibited, removing the floor on admission prices, and more theaters competed for first-run movie customers, which should have lowered prices. However, the average admission price, in real terms, rose from $0.46 in 1948 to $0.61 in 1950, a 33 percent rise, and remained near $0.60 in real terms until the 1960s.[30] Lower demand for movies due to television and a return to competition should have reduced admission prices. One possible explanation for the price rise is that, as more low-priced sub-run theaters closed, and more theaters shifted to first-run competition, the overall average price of admission rose. Under monopoly, output is restricted and price is raised. The output of films by the top nine distributors first rose from 249 in 1947 to 320 in 1951, consistent with a prior monopolistic restriction on output, but it then fell to 301 in 1953 and 215 in 1955.[31] More broadly, film production declined from an average of 421 new releases per year in the United States in the 1940s to 338 new releases per year in the 1950s.[32] To the extent that television reduced the demand for movies, the total number of new movies would fall. In addition, the end to block booking, which tied grade B movies to grade A movies, would also tend to reduce total production unless there were offsetting price discounts, because exhibitors would move toward fewer, better-quality films. The evidence on monopolization thus is far from clear, but whatever the possible competitive gains from ending vertical integration and the other offending distribution practices, they were not reflected in lower prices to consumers or a larger revenue share for exhibitors.

The Restructuring of Distribution

The government claimed that the basis for monopolizing production, distribution, and exhibition was provided by the complex system of distributing movies through agreements involving theater ownership, exclusive dealing, block booking, runs and clearances, theater pooling arrangements, and resale price maintenance. Missing from the government's position was any awareness of whether there were, in addition, efficiency gains that would be lost by eliminating this complex structure of distribution. The contested practices began as early as World War I, during an era of intense competition in the industry, suggesting the practices were a response to competitive pressures to reduce costs and enhance the demand for movies. If so, ending the practices, whatever the effects on competition, would raise the costs of distribution.

Before analyzing distribution practices after the *Paramount* case, some background information on movie licensing is needed. Motion picture licenses are granted in one of three ways: competitive bidding, competitive negotiations, and noncompetitive negotiations.[33] In competitive bidding, distributors send formal letters to competing exhibitors requesting bids on a forthcoming movie. Terms may include a nonrefundable rental guarantee, an advance payment against box office receipts, percentage terms for sharing box office receipts, cooperative advertising expense sharing, boundaries for geographic clearances, length of run, and the opening date. For peak demand periods, the summer months and Christmas, bids are often requested six months or more in advance. Competitive bidding by exhibitors on a movie-by-movie basis is costly, both in terms of preparing bids and evaluating bids from a variety of exhibitors in different locations. It also shifts the risks of a movie's failure to the exhibitor because adjustments to license terms after the opening date would defeat the purpose of competitive bidding. If exhibitors knew that license terms would be adjusted, their bids could be grossly overstated because overbidding would have no harmful consequences.

In competitive negotiations, a distributor negotiates with a few exhibitors in an area for the right to license a movie, rather than opening competition to all exhibitors. In noncompetitive negotiations, a distributor negotiates with a single exhibitor in an area. This took place under exclusive dealing contracts with exhibitors and by necessity in one-exhibitor towns. It also took place in earlier periods when exhibitors banded together to form booking agencies in order to gain leverage in negotiating movie rental terms with distributors and to capture the cost advantages of economies of scale.

Unavoidably, distributors and exhibitors must negotiate with one another and work to resolve conflicting interests over hundreds of movies from year to year. Numerous issues can divide the parties. Distributors want secure play dates during peak demand periods when available screens may be scarce. Exhibitors want the best movies, at peak demand as well as other times, and are always concerned over the risk of a box office flop, especially when they must guarantee payment in advance. Both sides seek to maximize their share of box office receipts. They may sustain significant costs when a movie fails, and each has an incentive to shift the costs to the other party. The process of licensing itself can be costly, involving negotiations over the numerous issues indicated above—revenue sharing, advertising expense sharing, length of run, geographic clearances, coverage of theater overhead expenses, and up-front financial guarantees by exhibitors. Any cheating on license terms is costly to distributors.

Organizational arrangements involving ownership and contracting arose to minimize the various costs of distribution and the potential conflicts between distributors and exhibitors. For example, block booking of yet-to-be-produced movies greatly reduced the costs of movie distribution relative to movie-by-movie distribution. With block booking, distributors dealt with about 10,000 contracts per year. Under individual-movie, theater-by-theater

contracting in the 1950s, distributors handled hundreds of thousands of contract negotiations per year.[34] In the 1950s, when exhibitors found the cost of dealing on a movie-by-movie basis much higher than block booking, they returned to booking movies in groups.[35] As stated earlier, block booking also assured distributors of future exhibition and play dates, supporting the financing of future movies.

Vertical integration and exclusive dealing also served to reduce distribution costs. They provided long-term, stable relationships between distributors and exhibitors, where reputation and trust could be established through repetitive dealing. In block booking, for example, exhibitors learned to trust the overall quality of a studio's movie production. By standardizing licensing between a distributor and a network of closely affiliated exhibitors, conflicts could more easily be avoided and the costs of distribution reduced. Conflicts over post-licensing adjustments, when a movie does poorly, are internalized under vertical integration because a single owner bears the costs of low revenues. In regard to cheating on license terms, there is little incentive to cheat on license terms under vertical integration because only theater owners, not employee–managers, can benefit directly from violating license terms. Long-term exclusive dealing relationships or franchising served to reduce exhibitor cheating and overall conflicts with distributors. Cheating on license terms could result in an exhibitor's being terminated, and the loss of these benefits to exhibitors placed a restraint on their incentives to violate license terms. Franchise contracts also covered rental terms over an extended period, at least one movie season, saving the costs of negotiating on a movie-by-movie basis. Exclusive dealing also provided a secure source of future movies. One reflection of an increase in distribution costs is the extent of conflicts between distributors and exhibitors. Evidence showing an increase in the number of conflicts between distributors and exhibitors following the *Paramount* decision supports the view that integration, either by ownership or by exclusive dealing contract, served to reduce the costs of distribution. The record shows that hundreds of private lawsuits were filed in the 1950s between distributors and exhibitors, based on alleged cheating on license terms agreed to by exhibitors and on alleged discrimination across exhibitors on license terms granted by distributors.[36] The Antitrust Division of the DOJ reported in 1953 that they had received about 1,000 complaints from exhibitors and that about one-third of all correspondence received was from exhibitors complaining about distributors on such issues as runs, clearances, and the criteria used for choosing exhibitors.[37] As further evidence of increased conflict between distributors and exhibitors, Congress held hearings to investigate the motion picture industry in both 1953 and 1956 in response to complaints by exhibitors of unfair treatment and that distributors were violating the terms of the *Paramount* consent decrees.[38] This explosion of complaints appears to be: (1) a direct result of eliminating vertical integration and exclusive dealing, which served for many years to reduce disputes between distributors and exhibitors and thus reduced the costs of distribution, and (2) a reflection of exhibitor and distributor attempts to adapt to new rules of movie licensing following *Paramount*. Thus, whatever anticompetitive behavior can be attributed to vertical integration in the motion picture industry, it also contributed to reducing the costs of distributing and exhibiting motion pictures.

If vertical integration and exclusive dealing provided the most efficient means of dealing with the conflicts between distributors and exhibitors and of minimizing the costs of movie distribution, their loss would cause distributors to develop alternatives. Two alternative organizational arrangements arose to replace vertical integration and exclusive

dealing. One was a sub-rosa form of exclusive dealing, known in the industry as "tracking" or a "marriage." In tracking, a distributor deals with the same exhibitor in a city or area on a long-term basis, but no formal exclusive dealing or franchising contract exists. The parties are committed voluntarily to a long-term relationship because it is in their mutual self-interest to reduce the costs of distribution.

A second form of distribution that flourished in the 1950s is known as "film splitting."[39] In split agreements, exhibitors in an area agree to rotate the selection of upcoming movies among themselves, avoiding competitive bidding. Exhibitors decide which exhibitor will negotiate with a distributor for a given movie. Distributors send bid letters to all the exhibitors in an area, but only the designated exhibitor negotiates for the movie. If an agreement cannot be reached, the distributor can negotiate with a second designated exhibitor or turn to an exhibitor outside of the split agreement. Split agreements appear to be a blatant form of exhibitor collusion, intended to avoid competing for movie licenses. However, their use as an anticompetitive tactic remains somewhat of a mystery. Splitting was widely adopted by the industry in the 1950s, and for thirty years it was condoned by the DOJ, which possibly felt it helped protect small exhibitors and thus was in the spirit of the *Paramount* decision. Even more significantly, those most likely harmed by an exhibitor cartel, the distributors who could have stopped split agreements by private antitrust actions, fully accepted and participated with exhibitors in the split agreements. Acceptance of split agreements by distributors from the 1950s onward indicates that the agreements provided economic efficiencies such as savings in distribution costs, benefiting both exhibitors and distributors. Not until 1985 and 1986 did the DOJ take decisive action against exhibitors, filing thirteen lawsuits against split agreements throughout the country.

Tracking and split agreements dominated movie allocations to exhibitors following *Paramount*. The 1946 district court's solution to exhibitor problems, competitive bidding, was largely rejected by both sides following the *Paramount* decision. Loews reported that for an average picture with 15,000 theater bookings in 1955, competitive bidding was used in only 3.2 percent of the licenses.[40] Universal Pictures had a similarly low rate of competitive bidding. In contrast, tracking represented a form of integration and allowed for noncompetitive negotiations. Tracking provided the efficiencies of long-term distribution relationships, achieved through repetitive dealing and subsequent settling-up through adjustments, but without vertical integration through ownership or formal exclusive dealing arrangements. Tracking also avoided the costs of competitive bidding and reduced the incentives for exhibitor cheating because, unlike competitive bidding, it allowed for adjustments. The benefits from split agreements in the 1950s appear to be a more or less ensured exhibitor for a movie, an avoidance of the transaction costs and higher risks of competitive bidding, and a reduced likelihood of lawsuits by exhibitors charging distributors with discrimination in license terms because each exhibitor was given an equal opportunity to receive good movies. Splitting provided a weak form of block booking. Implicit in distributors' participation in split agreements was that some exhibitor would screen their movie, reducing the risks of production. Because distributors could have ended split agreements, the end result must have been that rental shares to distributors under split agreements were no less than alternative approaches to licensing.

Distributors and exhibitors have shifted between tracking, splitting, and competitive bidding as the relative costs and benefits of each licensing method have changed over time. In the 1950s, splitting and tracking dominated distribution. In the 1970s competitive bidding dominated distribution. According to General Cinema and Disney, between one-half and two-thirds of all distribution in the 1970s was by competitive bidding.[41] According to another commentator, in the early 1990s there was little competitive bidding.[42]

The relative costs and benefits of alternative forms of distribution change over time with shifts in the supply and demand for movies, changes in the technology and cost of distributing movies and monitoring exhibitors, and changes in the law on distribution. For example, splitting is probably rare today because it was found to be per se illegal under the Sherman Antitrust Act in the 1980s.[43] Competitive bidding increased in frequency as the supply of movies decreased relative to the number of screens for viewing. The average annual supply of movies was 338 in the 1950s, but only 246 in the 1970s. The number of new releases fell from 282 in 1971 to 167 in 1977, rising to 232 in 1983.[44] From 1971 to 1977 the number of screens increased by 18 percent, from 14,070 to 16,554, while the annual output of new movies over the same period fell by 40 percent. It is not surprising to find that competitive bidding dominated distribution during this period. The number of new movies in the 1990s and 2000s has far exceeded levels in the 1970s, at over 400 movies annually, consistent with less use of competitive bidding.

Current Trends in Industry Performance

Contemporary indicators of industry performance and the demand for first-run movies in theaters are shown in Table 7.4. In the modern era, domestic box office admissions bottomed out in 1971 at a headcount of 820 million and grew slowly since then, reaching a high in 2002 of 1.64 billion and declining to 1.40 billion in 2005. As an indicator of the demand for movies, total admission

Table 7.4

Total Admissions, Screens, Average Admission Price, and Box Office Gross, 1967–2004

Year	Admissions (millions)	Percent change	Total screens	Percent change	Admissions per screen	Percent change	Average ticket price	Percent change	Average ticket price in real dollars	Percent change	Box office gross (millions)	Box office gross percent change	In real dollars	Percent change
1967	926.5		13,000		71,269		1.20		2.93		1,110.0		2,711.0	
1968	978.6	5.62	13,190	1.46	74,193	4.10	1.31	9.17	3.02	3.21	1,282.0	15.50	2,960.3	9.20
1969	911.9	-6.82	13,480	2.20	67,648	-8.82	1.42	8.40	3.12	3.24	1,294.0	0.94	2,845.7	-3.87
1970	920.6	0.95	13,750	2.00	66,953	-1.03	1.55	9.15	3.23	3.34	1,429.2	10.45	2,975.5	4.56
1971	820.3	-10.90	14,070	2.33	58,301	-12.92	1.65	6.45	3.31	2.66	1,349.5	-5.58	2,709.7	-8.94
1972	934.1	13.87	14,370	2.13	65,003	11.50	1.70	3.03	3.33	0.45	1,583.1	17.31	3,099.1	14.37
1973	864.6	-7.44	14,650	1.95	59,017	-9.21	1.76	3.53	3.33	0.06	1,523.5	-3.76	2,882.5	-6.99
1974	1,010.7	16.90	15,384	5.01	65,698	11.32	1.89	7.39	3.22	-3.41	1,908.5	25.27	3,248.0	12.68
1975	1,032.8	2.19	15,969	3.80	64,675	-1.56	2.05	8.47	3.30	2.46	2,115.0	10.82	3,400.1	4.68
1976	957.1	-7.33	15,976	0.04	59,909	-7.37	2.13	3.90	3.25	-1.25	2,036.0	-3.74	3,110.6	-8.51
1977	1,063.2	11.09	16,554	3.62	64,226	7.21	2.23	4.69	3.26	0.03	2,372.0	16.50	3,462.6	11.31
1978	1,128.2	6.11	16,755	1.21	67,335	4.84	2.34	4.93	3.23	-0.77	2,644.0	11.47	3,649.9	5.41
1979	1,120.5	-0.65	17,095	2.03	65,569	-2.62	2.52	7.69	3.23	0.71	2,821.0	6.69	3,641.9	-0.22
1980	1,021.5	-8.87	17,675	3.39	57,793	-11.86	2.69	6.75	3.17	-2.65	2,748.5	-2.57	3,235.8	-11.15
1981	1,067.0	4.45	18,144	2.65	58,807	1.75	2.78	3.35	3.05	-3.58	2,956.6	7.57	3,247.5	0.36
1982	1,175.4	10.16	18,295	0.83	64,247	9.25	2.94	5.76	3.06	0.13	3,452.7	16.78	3,590.5	10.56
1983	1,196.9	1.83	18,884	3.22	63,382	-1.35	3.15	7.14	3.15	3.03	3,766.0	9.07	3,766.0	4.89
1984	1,199.1	0.18	19,589	3.73	61,213	-3.42	3.36	6.67	3.22	2.34	4,030.6	7.03	3,886.9	2.68
1985	1,056.1	-11.93	21,097	7.70	50,059	-18.22	3.55	5.65	3.30	2.46	3,749.4	-6.98	3,488.5	-9.79
1986	1,017.2	-3.68	22,365	6.01	45,482	-9.14	3.71	4.51	3.34	1.08	3,778.0	0.76	3,399.9	-2.54
1987	1,088.5	7.01	22,679	1.40	47,996	5.53	3.91	5.39	3.38	1.35	4,252.9	12.57	3,680.5	8.26
1988	1,084.8	-0.34	23,129	1.98	46,902	-2.28	4.11	5.12	3.40	0.49	4,458.4	4.83	3,688.7	0.22
1989	1,262.8	16.41	22,921	-0.90	55,094	17.46	4.23	2.92	3.40	1.35	5,033.4	12.90	3,961.2	7.39
1990	1,188.6	-5.88	23,814	3.90	49,912	-9.41	3.99	-2.92	3.14	-7.66	5,021.8	-0.23	3,790.6	-4.31
1991	1,140.6	-4.04	24,639	3.46	46,292	-7.25	4.23	6.02	3.19	1.68	4,803.2	-4.35	3,488.2	-7.98
1992	1,173.2	2.86	25,214	2.33	46,530	0.51	4.21	-0.47	3.06	-4.24	4,871.0	1.41	3,441.5	-1.34
1993	1,244.0	6.03	25,626	1.63	48,544	4.33	4.15	-1.43	2.93	-4.10	5,154.2	5.81	3,543.1	2.95
1994	1,291.7	3.83	26,689	4.15	48,398	-0.30	4.14	-0.24	2.85	-2.94	5,396.2	4.70	3,626.0	2.34
1995	1,262.6	-2.25	27,843	4.32	45,347	-6.30	4.18	0.97	2.81	-1.30	5,493.5	1.80	3,573.2	-1.46
1996	1,338.6	6.02	29,731	6.78	45,024	-0.71	4.35	4.07	2.83	0.74	5,911.5	7.61	3,735.1	4.53
1997	1,387.7	3.67	31,865	7.18	43,549	-3.27	4.42	1.61	2.79	-1.30	6,365.9	7.69	3,965.5	6.17
1998	1,480.7	6.70	34,168	7.23	43,336	-0.49	4.59	3.85	2.86	2.38	6,949.0	9.16	4,277.4	7.87
1999	1,465.2	-1.05	37,131	8.67	39,460	-8.94	4.69	2.18	2.89	0.97	7,448.0	7.18	4,548.6	6.34
2000	1,420.8	-3.03	36,280	-2.29	39,162	-0.76	5.08	8.32	3.10	7.47	7,661.0	2.86	4,602.0	1.17
2001	1,487.3	4.68	35,173	-3.05	42,285	7.98	5.39	6.10	3.24	4.36	8,412.5	9.81	4,976.6	8.14
2002	1,639.3	10.22	35,836	1.88	45,745	8.18	5.66	5.01	3.35	3.41	9,519.6	13.16	5,568.1	11.89
2003	1,574.0	-3.98	35,995	0.44	43,728	-4.41	5.81	2.65	3.40	1.49	9,488.5	-0.33	5,488.1	-1.44
2004	1,536.1	-2.41	36,652	1.83	41,910	-4.16	6.03	3.79	3.49	2.63	9,539.2	0.53	5,476.7	-0.21
2005	1,402.7	-8.68	38,852	6.00	36,104	-13.85	6.21	2.99	3.57	2.23	8,991.2	-5.74	5,105.6	-6.78

Source: National Association of Theater Owners, 2000–2001 Encyclopedia of Exhibition and 2005–2006 Encyclopedia of Exhibition; Motion Picture Association of America, U.S. Economic Review: 1992, 1997, and 2000 and US Entertainment Industry: 2005 MPA Market Statistics; Goldman Sachs, Movie Industry Update–1993, April 7, 1993; and U.S. Department of Labor, Bureau of Labor Statistics, Producer Price Index data at www.bls.gov.

Note: Average ticket prices and box office gross for 1967 through 1996 were deflated using the entertainment CPI, 1982–84 = 100. The entertainment CPI covers products beyond movies, including theater, opera, concerts, sporting events, sporting equipment, toys, hobbies, and reading materials. Average ticket prices and box office gross for 1997 through 2004 were deflated using the recreation CPI, 12/1997 = 100. The Bureau of Labor Statistics discontinued the entertainment CPI in 1997. The recreation CPI began in 1993 to take the place of the entertainment CPI.

is incomplete because it measures only theater attendance. Aggregate movie demand includes DVDs, pay television, network and syndicated television, and Internet downloads. Nontheatrical revenues represent approximately 70 percent of total movie sales.

Domestic box office gross was relatively flat in the early 1990s, but it grew subsequently with rising attendance and average ticket prices. Again, a focus on exhibitor performance alone overlooks the much larger demand for movies in nontheatrical channels of distribution.

While admissions grew slowly until 2002, paradoxically, the total number of screens, as indicated earlier, rose at a phenomenal rate in the 1990s. The number of screens grew by 56 percent in the short period of 1990 to 1999. Given the long-term growth in number of screens and slow growth in attendance, admissions per screen have fallen sharply since the 1970s.

New multi- and megaplex theater construction, with eight screens and more per site, has been growing for years. As replacements for the large single-screen and small multiscreen theaters of an earlier era, they offer a number of economic advantages. Movies can be moved to different size theaters within the complex, depending on audience demand. Centralized operations, such as ticket sales and admission, concession good sales, and restrooms, can service a large number of individual theater screens, achieving economies of scale in facilities and staff relative to separate theaters. Furthermore, by offering a variety of movies, exhibitors reduce their risk relative to dependence on a single movie. For patrons, a wide variety of movies are available at a single location, providing convenience and possibly reduced search costs, and blockbuster movies can be shown on two or three screens, further accommodating movie customers.

Although the price of motion picture admission is often complained about, average ticket prices in real terms remained relatively flat from the late 1960s to the early 1980s, when prices began to rise slowly. The basis of the price series in Table 7.4 changed in 1989, so price comparisons pre- and post-1989 are most likely not appropriate. The price series from 1989 onward, however, shows a surprising fall in real ticket prices from 1990 to 1996, but real prices have risen in recent years. In addition, it is important to keep in mind that the quality of exhibition in new theaters, in terms of seating, sound, and movie technology, has improved greatly and the price series is not adjusted for quality changes.

The focus of this study has been on domestic economic and competitive performance because that is of greatest public policy interest. However, the industry is international in scope, with U.S.-produced movies generating foreign revenues for distributors larger than those produced in the United States. In 2005, U.S. distributors earned $9 billion in domestic box office revenues.[45] The main revenue-generating countries outside the United States are Japan, Germany, France, Canada, United Kingdom/Ireland, Spain, and Australia. Foreign market sales in 2005 were $14.25 billion, well above those produced in the United States.

Channels of Distribution

The rise of new technologies in delivering movies has drastically altered distribution channels. Until the introduction of television in the late 1940s, movie receipts came exclusively from box office admissions. Television allowed home viewing of movies. Television networks became a substantial source of movie revenues starting in the 1960s. In the 1980s, VCR ownership spread rapidly, as did cable system and pay movie channel subscriptions.

Table 7.5 shows the dramatic shift in movie-generated revenues in the 1980s from box office

Table 7.5

Distribution of Domestic Theatrical Revenues (in millions of dollars)

Gross and percentage of total

	1983		1984		1985		1986		1987		1988		1989		1990		1991		1992	
Box office rentals	1,700	54	1,800	47	1,635	40	1,650	38	1,830	38	1,920	35	2,165	35	2,260	32	2,160	29	2,100	26
Pay TV	550	17	600	16	635	15	600	14	575	12	630	11	670	11	725	10	750	10	770	9
Home video	400	13	950	25	1,335	32	1,630	37	1,915	40	2,460	45	2,760	44	3,220	46	3,760	50	4,230	52
Television	410	13	410	11	450	11	450	10	425	9	425	8	525	8	600	9	650	9	675	8
Other	100	3	60	2	56	1	62	1	65	1	90	2	105	2	150	2	220	3	370	5
Total	3,160	100%	3,820	100%	4,111	100%	4,392	100%	4,810	100%	5,525	100%	6,225	100%	6,955	100%	7,540	100%	8,145	100%

Source: Goldman Sachs, *Movie Industry Update–1993*, April 1993.

sales to videocassette rentals and sales. Starting with virtually 100 percent of movie revenues in the 1940s, box office receipts fell to a little more than 50 percent of total domestic receipts by the early 1980s. Cable television pay channels were second to box office revenues, followed by videocassettes, which still lacked large-scale VCR penetration in U.S. television households. By 1984 theatrical box office accounted for less than 50 percent of domestic movie revenues for the first time in history. Videocassette revenues grew rapidly with the spread of VCR ownership. In 1980 about 2 percent of U.S. households with televisions had a VCR. This rose to 50 percent in 1987 and 80 percent by 1992.[46] In 1992 videocassettes accounted for over 50 percent of movie receipts for the first time. U.S. consumers spent approximately twice as much to watch movies on videocassettes as they did to view movies in theaters. Present estimates find consumers spending more than twice as much for home movie rental and purchases of DVDs and videocassettes compared to theater admissions.[47] Nevertheless, successful theater exhibition often leads to a movie's success in other distribution channels. Future demand is built on theatrical box office success, favorable reviews, word-of-mouth advertising, and promotion and advertising for theatrical and home viewing release.

Price Discrimination

In the early years, distributors price-discriminated through the timed releases of movies from first-run to second-run to third-run theaters, and so forth. Gone are most second-run theaters and all subsequent-run theaters. Along with temporal price discrimination by run, there has long been daily differential pricing, between early and evening screenings and across classes of customers, such as discount prices for children, students, and seniors. The modern equivalents of price discrimination

are timed releases of movies to first-run theaters and then, in sequence, to hotels and airlines, pay television, home video, network television, and syndicated television. As in the earlier era, prices decline with later releases, reflecting differing segments of the demand for movies. For over seventy-five years, distributors have attempted to capture the maximum revenues from movie rentals and sales by price discrimination according to differing demands for movie viewing. With each new technology that allowed viewing at home—network television, cable pay channels, and videocassettes and DVDs—the channels of distribution have changed, but the same differential pricing strategy to maximize revenues has always prevailed.

Industry Restructuring: Vertical Integration and Conglomerate Organization

Vertical Integration

Four major distributors—Paramount, Warner Brothers, Columbia, and Universal—returned to theater ownership in the mid-1980s. A relaxation of consent decrees under the *Paramount* decision allowed Paramount and Warner Brothers to vertically integrate once again into theaters. Columbia and Universal were not bound by *Paramount* consent decrees because they did not own theaters in the 1940s. In the mid-1980s the then-parent company of Universal, MCA, purchased 50 percent of Cineplex Odeon, including about 500 screens in Canada. Columbia/Tri-Star, later acquired by Sony, purchased the former Loews and USA Cinema theater chains. Sony acquired Cineplex Odeon in 1998, forming Loews Cineplex. Viacom, purchaser of Paramount in 1994, and Time Warner, formed by the merger of Time, Inc., and Warner Communications in 1990, were partners in Cinamerica theaters, with over 300 screens, which they sold to WestStar

Table 7.6

Conglomerate Operations Including Studio-Distributors

Area	Time Warner (Warner Bros.)	Disney	News Corp. (20th Century Fox)	Sony Corp. (Columbia)	Viacom (Paramount)	General Electric (Universal)
New movies	*	*	*	*	*	*
Film library	*	*	*	*	*	*
Theaters	*			*	*	*
TV shows	*	*	*	*	*	*
Broadcast TV station(s)	*	*	*		*	
Broadcast TV network(s)	*	*	*		*	
Basic cable network(s)	*	*	*		*	*
Pay cable network(s)	*	*			*	
Cable or satellite systems	*		*			
Recorded music	*	*		*		*
Theme parks	*	*			*	*
Publishing	*	*	*		*	
Audio players				*		
Video players				*		
Retailing	*	*			*	
Internet access	*					

Source: Standard & Poor's, *Industry Surveys, Movies and Home Entertainment,* February 27, 1997, May 10, 2001, and March 24, 2005.

Cinemas. In 1988 National Amusement theaters affiliated with Viacom. With these acquisitions and continued new theater building programs, these studios accounted for approximately 4,500 screens, or 12 percent of North American screens.

Vertical integration for anticompetitive purposes, the view that dominated the government's thinking up to the 1980s, cannot explain this return by distributors to ownership of theaters. With only 12 percent of all screens, the distributors could not possibly collude to effect monopoly pricing and foreclosure of rivals. Only the expectation of fundamental efficiency advantages can explain this rebirth of vertical integration. These cost advantages include those mentioned earlier: control of box office receipts, adjustments in license terms after a movie opens, promoting movies, and reduced transaction costs between distributor and exhibitor in licensing movies. However, not all distributors believe the gains from domestic theater ownership are large enough relative to the investment cost and risk. Such large sophisticated companies as Disney and Twentieth Century Fox have not integrated into theaters in North America.

Conglomerate Ownership

The major studio-distributors are generally part of massive, highly diversified conglomerate firms, with ownership of a broad class of entertainment and information products. Table 7.6 shows leading movie studio-distributors, their parent companies, and main areas of product ownership and production. Each firm in Table 7.6 produces movies and television shows, and some own television stations, cable systems, cable channels, theme parks, publishing and newspaper operations, music firms, and retail outlets.

Conglomerate firm ownership of movie studio-distributors is not a new phenomenon. Gulf & Western, one of the largest conglomerate firms formed in the 1960s, with such diverse business lines as agriculture, apparel, automotive parts, and financial services, purchased Paramount Pictures in 1967. Also in 1967, Avco, another 1960s major conglomerate, acquired Embassy, a long-time movie producer. Warner Communication was acquired by Time, Inc., in 1990, but Warner was a diversified firm prior to the acquisition, with interests in movies, music, books and magazines, cable television, and video games. Twentieth Century Fox, before being acquired by News Corp., the international newspaper publisher, had ownership interests in movies, television stations, music, publishing, soft drink bottling, and ski resorts.

More recently, Sony, the producer of home electronic equipment, acquired CBS records in 1988 and Columbia, previously owned by Coca-Cola, in 1989. In 1994 Viacom, Inc., owner of cable channels and movie theaters, acquired both Paramount Communications and Blockbuster Video, the retail chain. In June 1995, Seagram, the beverage company, acquired 80 percent of MCA, owner of Universal, from Matsushita, the Japanese conglomerate, and then sold it to Vivendi in 2000. Vivendi, in turn, sold a majority ownership of Universal in 2004 to General Electric, which had previously acquired NBC Television. In February 1996, the Disney Company acquired Capital Cities/ABC, owner of ABC television, newspapers, and 80 percent of ESPN, the cable sports channel. Some of this acquisition activity has been encouraged by the relaxation of rules limiting joint ownership of television stations and newspapers, and allowing television networks to own programming for syndication.

A popular explanation for conglomerate ownership is to reap the gains from a diversified portfolio of assets with relatively uncorrelated income streams, reducing the overall business risk of the firm. As noted, motion picture production has long been regarded as a relatively high-risk business. The popular view was that out of every ten movies, six or seven lost money, one or two broke even, and two or three made money. Combining moviemaking with a countervailing, steadier stream of income offers a means to reduce overall risk. A commonly offered explanation for combining various forms of entertainment products with media firms is that joint ownership facilitates intra-firm promotion and marketing of entertainment products by utilizing a variety of complementary distribution channels. For example, cable and television channels can promote each other's programming; movies can enhance related book and music sales; and movie characters can improve retail sales. Another common explanation for conglomerate ownership is to capitalize on the synergistic capabilities of management skills.

Whether the expected synergistic effects of conglomerate ownership of movies will materialize for present owners is yet to be determined. Some past movie studio owners, such as Coca-Cola, Matsushita, Seagram, and Vivendi, sold out after disappointing performance in the production of movies. As in all competitive endeavors, some mergers and acquisitions prove successful in stimulating demand and lowering costs, and others do not, leading to divestiture. Some firms are more skillful than others in combining firms with different corporate cultures and in gaining from synergistic opportunities. However, many highly diversified firms formed in the conglomerate merger wave of the 1960s, such as Gulf & Western, International Telephone and Telegraph, Litton Industries, and Teledyne, ultimately failed to provide the expected stock market performance predicted by conglomerate ownership and were split up in the 1980s. These and other conglomerate firms divested hundreds of disparate firms in the 1980s, returning to a core set of businesses. Whether a similar fate awaits current firms with motion picture divisions is unclear. Viacom, however, with poor stock performance from 2000 to 2005, announced a split in 2005 into two smaller conglomerate companies, with Paramount Pictures and Viacom's cable networks like MTV and Nickelodeon in one company and CBS television, television and radio stations, publishing, theme parks, and outdoor advertising in a second company.[48] For now, however, conglomerate ownership rules the movie business.

Conclusions

Government can alter the structure and conduct of an industry through regulation and lawsuits, but under open-market competition, fundamental economic principles and forces shape the structure and conduct of an industry.[49] The history of the motion picture industry provides a vivid example of this process. The industry's structure and conduct were drastically altered by the *Paramount* decision, putting an end to the vertical integration of distributors into theaters, formal exclusive dealing arrangements, and numerous other distribution practices. Hundreds of theaters became first-run houses overnight, and hundreds closed in the ensuing years. Yet distributor–theater relationships continued to be ruled by competitive pressures for economic efficiency. Distribution by tracking was used as a means to capture the gains formerly provided by exclusive dealing arrangements. Split agreements were adopted to avoid the costs and risks of competitive bidding. Even after block booking was ruled to be anticompetitive, many theaters chose to book in small blocks in order to lower licensing costs.[50] And when, after many years, distributors were given the freedom to own theaters again, some distributors chose to reintegrate into theater ownership. Because merger for monopoly in exhibition was impossible in the

1980s and 1990s, the efficiency gains to vertical integration guided distributors back to theater ownership. The government's 1948 decree against theater ownership was, in a sense, overridden in the 1980s and 1990s by the efficiencies of vertical integration.

Moreover, despite the best efforts of government in 1948 to protect small theatrical owners by deconcentrating first-run exhibition, exhibition has returned to a relatively concentrated structure. The top five exhibition firms owned or controlled approximately 24 percent of the 18,000 screens in 1945 (see Table 7.3). In 2005, the top five exhibition firms owned 41 percent of the 38,852 screens in North America (see Table 7.2). With the merger of AMC and Loews in 2006, this share rose to 46 percent. Small neighborhood theaters were largely eliminated by home viewing of movies via network television, cable, videocassettes, and DVDs, as well as by the economic efficiencies of multi- and megaplex theaters. Government intervention surely had a profound effect on the structure of exhibition in the 1950s, but, in the long term, economic forces have reshaped exhibition to be even more concentrated in ownership than before the government's intervention.

As in the case of the persistent drive for efficiency in distribution, neither government intervention nor major changes in channels of distribution have altered the industry's ability to price differentially across consumers. Most revenues now come from nontheatrical sources, primarily DVDs, videocassettes, cable, and satellite television. This reverses the historic flow, in which first-run theaters produced the majority of revenues. Nevertheless, differential pricing and the timed release of movies have been utilized for over eighty years to capture the greatest amount of revenues.

During the industry's golden era in the 1930s, few could have foreseen the rise of television in the 1950s and its impact on the industry. In the 1960s few could have foreseen the rise of videocassettes in the 1980s, DVDs in the 1990s, and the great influx of revenues they generated. What technological changes will sweep the industry in the next twenty years—given digitalization of movies, distribution over the Internet, and unknown future innovations—and the impact they will bring is a story yet to be told. But, as in the past, industry structure and conduct will be conditioned by the competitive drive to increase the demand for movies and to gain efficiencies in their distribution.

Notes

1. See Table 7.4 and Harold L. Vogel, *Entertainment Industry Economics* (Cambridge, UK: Cambridge University Press, 1986), Table S2.2.

2. In block booking, large groups of movies, a year's supply, were licensed to exhibitors during the fall booking season. In blind bidding, exhibitors rented movies without advance screening and, in earlier years, without knowledge of the movie's story, writers, and actors. In franchising, the exhibitor agreed to rental fees and typically had exclusive rights to license the distributor's movie for a year or more.

3. *United States v. Paramount Pictures, Inc.,* 344 U.S. 131 (1948); 85 F. Supp. 881 (S.D.N.Y., 1949).

4. *Los Angeles Times,* July 11, 1997, p. D1.

5. Nat D. Fellman, "The Exhibitor," in Jason E. Squire, ed., *The Movie Business Book,* pp. 313–22 (Englewood Cliffs, NJ: Prentice-Hall, 1983).

6. *Los Angeles Times,* June 21, 1997, p. D2.

7. This section draws on the history presented in: Mae D. Huettig, *Economic Control of the Motion Picture Industry* (Philadelphia: University of Pennsylvania Press, 1944); Ralph Cassady, Jr., "Monopoly in Motion Picture Production and Distribution, 1908–1915," *Southern California Law Review* 32 (1959), pp. 325–90; Michael Conant, *Antitrust in the Motion Picture Industry: Economic and Legal Analysis* (Berkeley and Los Angeles: University of California Press, 1960); and Arthur De Vany and Ross D. Eckard, "Motion Picture Antitrust: The Paramount Case Revisited," *Research in Law and Economics* 14 (1991), pp. 51–112.

8. *Federal Trade Commission v. Stanley Booking Corp.,* 1 FTC 212 (1918).

9. Robert Anderson, "The Motion Picture Patent Company: A Reevaluation," in Tino Balio, ed., *The American Film Industry,* pp. 133–52 (Madison: University of Wisconsin Press, 1985).

10. De Vany and Eckard, "Motion Picture Antitrust," pp. 70–71.

11. Conant, *Antitrust in the Motion Picture Industry,* pp. 49–50.

12. One source estimated that 20 to 25 percent of theaters engaged in some form of revenue cheating in 1947; see Conant, *Antitrust in the Motion Picture Industry,* p. 71. Accounts of cheating on receipts were also in the 1980s, see *Daily Variety,* March 7, 1985, p. 5; May 13, 1985, p. 1; and May 21, 1985, p. 1.

13. Conant, *Antitrust in the Motion Picture Industry,* pp. 61–76.

14. Ibid., p. 66.

15. Ibid., pp. 55 and 64.

16. *Federal Trade Commission v. Famous Players-Lasky Corp.,* 11 FTC (1927).

17. Conant, *Antitrust in the Motion Picture Industry,* p. 99.

18. *United States v. Paramount Pictures, Inc.,* 66 F. Supp. 323 (S.D.N.Y., 1946).

19. A formula deal involved a distributor and theater chain setting rental terms on the basis of a percentage of the national theatrical gross for a movie. One advantage of a formula deal was that it reduced the incentive for an exhibitor to cheat on reporting box office receipts. Master agreements based the share of box office receipts on all the theaters in a chain, rather than on a theater-by-theater basis.

20. In pooling arrangements independent exhibitors joined together, much like a cooperative, to gain the advantages of economies of scale. Managed by a member or committee of members, they booked movies and provided such services as bookkeeping and auditing. Pooling arrangements among the top five firms' theaters allegedly entailed the pooling of profits as well, as would take place in a cartel. They were found to be illegal.

21. *United States v. Paramount Pictures, Inc.,* 344 U.S. 131 (1948).

22. The consent decrees applied only to domestic theaters. At the time, Paramount controlled over 400 screens in Canada, and Twentieth Century Fox and Warner Brothers each controlled over 400 theaters abroad, with large holdings in England.

23. Ed Cray, "Hollywood Unchained," *California Lawyer* (February 1986), pp. 33–35, 54.

24. U.S. Department of Commerce, *National Income Supplement to Survey of Current Business,* 1954, pp. 206–08; and U.S. Department of Commerce, *U.S. Income and Output,* 1958, p. 151.

25. U.S. Bureau of the Census, *Census of Business, Selected Services, Summary Statistics,* 1948, 1954, and 1958. This source reports movie admission revenues falling from $1.25 billion in 1948 to $838 million in 1958.

26. *Film Daily Yearbook,* 1959, p. 106. The *Film Daily*

was an industry daily newspaper published between 1915 and 1970. The *Film Daily Yearbook* was published annually by Film Daily, New York, between 1918 and 1969.

27. *Electrical Merchandising,* McGraw-Hill Publishing Co. Inc., January 1951–January 1958, as reported in Conant, *Antitrust in the Motion Picture Industry,* p. 13.

28. *Motion Picture Distribution Trade Practices, 1956: Hearings Before a Subcommittee of the Select Committee on Small Business,* 84th Congress, 2d Session, p. 305.

29. Robert W. Crandall, "The PostWar Performance of the Motion-Picture Industry," *Antitrust Bulletin* 20 (Spring 1975), pp. 49–88.

30. Stanley I. Ornstein, "Motion Picture Distribution, Film Splitting, and Antitrust Policy," *Hastings Communications and Entertainment Law Journal* 17 (Winter 1995), pp. 415–44.

31. *Film Book Daily* yearbooks, 1949 and 1959.

32. Motion Picture Association of America.

33. For discussion of licensing, see *United States v. Capital Services, Inc.,* 586 F. Supp. 134 (E.D. Wis. 1983) and 756 F. 2d 502 (7th Cir. 1985); Fellman, "The Exhibitor," pp. 315–22; and Ralph Cassady, Jr., "Impact of the Paramount Decision on Motion Picture Distribution and Price Making," *Southern California Law Review* 31(1957–58), p. 150.

34. *1956 Hearings,* statement of Charles L. Feldman, vice president, Universal Pictures.

35. Conant, *Antitrust in the Motion Picture Industry,* p. 145, n. 136.

36. Ibid., 178–79; James S. Gordon, "Horizontal and Vertical Restraints of Trade: The Legality of Motion Picture Splits Under the Antitrust Laws," *Yale Law Journal* 75 (1965), pp. 239–60.

37. *Motion Picture Distribution Trade Practices: Hearings Before Select Subcommittee on Monopoly of the Senate Select Committee on Small Business,* 83rd Congress, 1st Session, 1953, p. 14.

38. *1953* and *1956 Hearings.*

39. Ornstein, "Motion Picture Distribution."

40. *1956 Hearings,* pp. 372 and 474.

41. *General Cinema v. Buena Vista Distribution Company,* 532 F. Supp. 1244, 1271 (E.D. Cal. 1982).

42. D. Barry Readon, "The Studio Distributor," in Jason E. Squire, ed., *The Movie Business Book,* 2nd ed., pp. 309–19 (New York: Simon & Schuster, 1992). See also Daniel R. Fellman, "Theatrical Distribution," in Jason E. Squire, ed., *The Movie Business Book,* 3rd. ed., pp. 364–374 (New York: Simon & Schuster, 2004).

43. *United States v. Capital Services,* 756 F. 2d 502 (7th Cir. 1985).

44. Vogel, *Entertainment Industry Economics,* p. 45; Thomas Guback, "Theatrical Film," in Benjamin M. Compaine, ed., *Who Owns the Media? Concentration of Ownership in the Mass Communication Industry,* 2nd ed., pp. 179–249 (White Plains, NY: Knowledge Industry Publications, 1979).

45. Motion Picture Association, Worldwide Market Research, "U.S. Theatrical Market: 2005 Statistics" (March 2006), pp. 4–5.

46. *Arbitron Ratings/Television Updates* Quarterly Reports. VCR home penetration reached 91 percent in 2003, with DVD penetration about half of that figure. Standard & Poor's Industry Studies, *Movies and Home Entertainment* (March 24, 2005), p. 9.

47. One source reports consumers spent $24.1 billion in 2004 on home screenings versus $9.5 billion at the box office. Standard & Poor's, "Industry Surveys, Movies and Home Entertainment" (March 24, 2005), p. 8.

48. *Los Angeles Times,* June 15, 2005, p. C1.

49. Stanley I. Ornstein, "Antitrust Policy and Market Forces as Determinants of Industry Structure: Case Histories in Beer and Distilled Spirits," *Antitrust Bulletin* 26 (Summer 1981), pp. 281–313.

50. In 1950, after block booking supposedly ended, 3,700 theaters booked Paramount Pictures movies in blocks, with a right to cancel 20 percent of those booked. Conant, *Antitrust in the Motion Picture Industry,* p. 145, n. 136.

8

Soft Drinks

The Carbonated Soft Drink Industry in the United States

Ronald W. Cotterill, William Putsis, Adam N. Rabinowitz, and Inga Druckute

Introduction

The carbonated soft drink industry (CSD) in the United States is a mature industry that is dominated by three very large global food and beverage conglomerates. Coca-Cola, Pepsi, and Cadbury Schweppes ("Big Three") accounted for 89 percent of CSD industry volume in the United States in 2004. Globally, Coca-Cola had a 51.4 percent market share, with Pepsi holding a 21.8 percent share, and Cadbury Schweppes accounting for 6 percent in 2003.[1] Indeed, Coca-Cola's "I'd like to teach the world to sing" campaign was the first truly "global" advertisement ever produced, in many ways reflecting Coke's global reach. While the global environment continues to grow in importance and be a crucial area for future growth, we will focus on the U.S. market in this chapter for two main reasons: (1) the U.S. market is reasonably independent, and hence lends itself nicely to separable empirical research, and (2) the market for carbonated soft drinks in the United States is the most developed and tends to lead trends elsewhere.

In the United States, as is typical throughout the world, competition across manufacturers occurs at the brand level, with each manufacturer marketing multiple brands under the same umbrella (e.g., Coca-Cola Classic, Diet Coke, and Coca-Cola C2, all under the Coca-Cola "umbrella"). Thus, the industry can be characterized as a differentiated product oligopoly, with each firm having three primary competitive weapons at its disposal. First, they compete on price primarily through "promotion"—an industry term used to describe periodic sales (often with special in-store displays) and price reductions (both temporary and permanent). Second, firms compete on advertising in the television, radio, magazine and Internet channels to create and sustain consumer loyalty for their brands. Third, they compete by introducing new brands, ranging from simple line extensions such as Coca-Cola with Lime, while others are entirely new product introductions such as Red Bull and Sierra Mist.

The conduct and performance of the CSD industry must be considered within the context of the larger beverage sector of the U.S. economy. Table 8.1 provides detail on the per capita consumption of different beverages for 1992, 1998, and 2004. In 2004, Americans drank an average of 52.3 gallons of CSD, up from 47.3 gallons in 1992. For 2004, that is equivalent to 557 12-ounce cans of soda per year or 1.5 cans of soda per day for the average American. While per capita consumption of all commercially sold beverages increased from 91 gallons in 1992 to 107 gallons in 2004, Americans consumed only 22.7 gallons of milk in 2004,

Table 8.1

Per Capita Consumption of Nonalcoholic Beverages: All Distribution Channels

	1992	1998	2004
Carbonated soft drinks	47.30	53.80	52.30
Low calorie	13.90	13.90	15.80
Regular	33.40	39.90	36.50
Milk	26.65	24.51	22.65
Fruit juices*	7.89	9.39	9.11
Bottled water	9.20	14.40	23.20
Energy and sports drinks	N/A	N/A	N/A
Tea and coffee	N/A	N/A	N/A
All beverages	91.04	102.10	107.26

Source: USDA Economic Research Service Food Availability Database, available online at: www.ers.usda.gov/data/food-consumption/FoodAvailIndex.htm.

Note: Consumption in gallons.

* Fruit juices excludes fruit drinks.

down from 26.7 gallons in 1992 (a trend that, in part, led to the now famous "Got Milk?" advertising campaign). Thus, the average American drank only 8 ounces of milk per day; by contrast, per capita annual consumption of fruit juice increased from 7.9 gallons in 1992 to 9.1 gallons in 2004. Commercially sold bottled water is the growth champion of the beverage sector, increasing from 7.2 gallons per capita (annually) in 1992 to 23.2 gallons per capita (annually) in 2004.

Table 8.2 provides a more detailed look at consumption per household through the primary retailing channel: supermarkets. Annual editions of the Information Resources, Inc., *Marketing Fact Book* provide this information for a grocery product that is scanned at checkout in supermarkets. Supermarket sales of CSD per household increased from 33.2 gallons in 1992 to 40.5 gallons in 2004, while milk sales decreased from 28.3 gallons to 25.9 gallons over the same period.[2] While at first glance it may appear that consumers are switching from milk to soda at the local supermarket, a closer examination indicates that this is not the case. Ultra High Temperature (UHT) pasteurized milk products with a

very long shelf life, including all organic milk, are included in the non–fruit drink category in Table 8.2. Also included there are soy milks. These are new products that were not available in 1992. When one adds the 2.8 gallons per household of UHT regular, UHT organic, and soy milk that consumers purchased in 2004 to the fresh milk purchases, one sees that consumers bought 28.7 gallons of milk and milk substitutes.[3] Thus, consumption of milk products purchased from supermarkets actually did not decline between 1992 and 2004. The decline in milk consumption has occurred away from home at restaurants, schools, and other institutional eating locations (which is one primary reason for the recent drive by nutrition and health advocates to limit soft drink consumption in schools).

Table 8.2 provides information on the dollars spent annually as well as the gallons, and the average price per gallon for each beverage. In 2004, for example, the typical household spent $99.58 on CSD and purchased 40.52 gallons at an average price of $2.46 per gallon. The same typical household spent $80.52 on milk and purchased 25.91 gallons at an average price of $3.11 per gal-

Table 8.2

Ready-to-Drink Beverages per Household: Supermarkets

	1992					1998					2004				
	Volume	Volume share (%)	Dollars	Dollar share (%)	Price per gallon	Volume	Volume share (%)	Dollars	Dollar share (%)	Price per gallon	Volume	Volume share (%)	Dollars	Dollar share (%)	Price per gallon
Carbonated soft drinks	33.20	41.3	74.77	36.6	$2.25	39.70	43.2	91.26	36.4	$2.30	40.52	38.1	99.58	34.0	$2.46
Milk	28.32	35.2	67.69	33.1	$2.39	26.21	28.5	73.40	29.3	$2.80	25.91	24.3	80.52	27.5	$3.11
Fruit juices and fruit drinks	13.09	16.3	51.69	25.3	$3.95	15.62	17.0	65.78	26.3	$4.21	17.45	16.4	71.42	24.4	$4.09
Bottled water*	5.09	6.3	7.49	3.7	$1.47	8.22	8.9	10.69	4.3	$1.30	14.13	13.3	23.58	8.0	$1.67
Non-fruit drinks			N/A			0.20	0.2	$1.39	0.6	$6.99	4.78	4.5	2.04	0.7	$0.43
Energy and sports drinks	0.59	0.7	2.27	1.1	$3.88	0.95	1.0	4.08	1.6	$4.30	2.01	1.9	9.05	3.1	$4.50
Tea and coffee	0.11	0.1	0.49	0.2	$4.32	1.00	1.1	3.80	1.5	$3.82	1.67	1.6	7.07	2.4	$4.22
All beverages	80.41		204.42			91.90		250.40			106.48		293.27		

Source: Information Resources, Inc., *Marketing Fact Book* (Chicago, IL: 1992, 1998, and 2004).

Notes: Volume is a 12-oz. (gallon) equivalent. Drink mixes and frozen drinks are excluded from ready-to-drink beverages.
*Bottled water includes noncarbonated water, carbonated water, club soda, seltzer, sparkling water, and mineral water.

lon. Fruit juices and fruit drinks cost an average of $4.09 per gallon in 2004, while bottled water cost an average of $1.67 per gallon. Energy and sport drinks (Red Bull and Gatorade are by far the largest brands) cost a whopping $4.50 per gallon. Tea and coffee drinks (Snapple and Frappuccino are leading brands) are also money machines, costing the end-use consumer $4.23 per gallon in 2004. Note that CSDs are lower priced than all other beverages except bottled water.

These trends raise several questions about the organization, conduct, and performance of the CSDs industry. From a strategic and antitrust policy viewpoint, does competition from other beverages limit the market power of the big three companies: Coca-Cola, Pepsi, and Cadbury Schweppes? How do new brand introductions and advertising influence the market share and the market power of CSD firms? Do brands have market power, i.e., does a brand manager face a downward sloping brand-level demand curve rather than a perfectly elastic (flat) demand curve? If so, what is the source of that pricing power? Is it unilateral power due to brand differentiation, or is it coordinated power due to some form of tacit collusion among the major players in the market? Should one of the big three be allowed to merge with another? For example, what would happen to prices if Coke and Pepsi merged? Is the shift away from milk due, at least in part, to the marketing strategies of the CSD industry? Is that shift concentrated in the under-18 age group? Has consumption of zero-calorie diet soda increased? Is increased regular CSD consumption related to the documented increase in obesity among children as well as adults in the United States? If so, is government regulation possible? Is it justified? How has the industry responded?

In order to address these questions, at least in part, the next section provides a brief history of the CSD industry, explains the distribution channel

structure of the industry, and identifies segments and leading brands within the CSD industry. It also describes the operations of the big three: Coca-Cola, Pepsi, and Cadbury Schweppes. The third section explains the primary marketing strategies: new brands, advertising, and pricing/trade promotions. The last section analyzes three policy issues. The first policy analysis uses estimated brand-level demand curves for the Cola/Pepper segment to determine the source and degree of market power that specific brands possess. It introduces two new market power indices, the Cotterill Index of total market power and the Chamberlin Quotient measure of the degree of tacit collusion. This section also reintroduces Rothschild's 1942 index of unilateral market power. In the second policy section we use estimated demand elasticities for the CSD industry's top two brands, Coca-Cola Classic and Pepsi, to illustrate how the antitrust agencies would evaluate a merger of the two brands into a single firm. Finally, we review the research on the link between CSD and obesity. Included in this section are opposing research results and the regulatory rationale as well as the industry rebuttal. On the regulatory side, the state of Connecticut recently passed a law that prohibits all CSDs in public schools, and other states have such initiatives in play. In response to the increasing state legislation and threats of lawsuits, the industry announced that it voluntarily will withdraw all non-diet sodas from public, parochial, and private schools in the United States.[4]

The Carbonated Soft Drink Industry: Brief History and the Current Market Structure

The history of the carbonated soft drink market is an interesting one that sheds some light on the industry structure and conduct of today.[5] The first marketed (noncarbonated) soft drinks actually appeared in the seventeenth century (they were made from water and lemon juice sweetened with honey). In Paris, vendors carried tanks of lemonade on their backs and dispensed cups to customers in the streets. Carbonated soft drinks date back to the mineral water found in natural springs—scientists discovered that carbon dioxide was behind the bubbles in natural mineral water. Over time, scientists and entrepreneurs devised various methods for adding carbonation to beverages. In 1767, the first drinkable man-made glass of carbonated water was created by Dr. Joseph Priestly in the United Kingdom. In 1798, the term *soda water* was first coined, and in 1810, the first U.S. patent was issued for the "means of mass manufacture of imitation mineral waters" to Simons and Rundell of Charleston, South Carolina.

However, carbonated beverages did not achieve great popularity in America until the 1830s, when an easily mass-manufactured apparatus for making carbonated water was created and offered for sale to soda fountain owners. By 1920, the U.S. Census had reported that over 5,000 bottlers were in operation. The first ginger ale was created in Ireland in 1851, the first root beer was mass-produced for public sale in 1876, the first cola-flavored beverage was introduced in 1881, and the first "no-cal" beverage was introduced in 1952. By the 1950s, American pharmacies with soda fountains became a popular part of culture and persisted en masse until the late 1960s. Over time, customers soon wanted to take their "health" drinks home with them, and a soft drink bottling industry grew from consumer demand. Today, the interplay between the "Big Three" players on the manufacturing side, the bottlers on the distribution end, the retailers downstream, and the end-use consumers is a complex and ever-evolving maze of horizontal and vertical relationships that requires a deep understanding of the players as well as the dynamic interactions across each.

The "Big Three"

Coca-Cola Company

Coca-Cola was originally invented by Dr. John Pemberton, a pharmacist from Atlanta, and first sold to the public at the soda fountain in Jacob's Pharmacy in Atlanta on May 8, 1886. Sales in the first year were a far cry from what we observe today. Indeed, the first year operated at a loss ($50 in revenue versus $70 in cost). As the popular tale relates, until 1905 the soft drink did indeed contain extracts of cocaine.[6] Pemberton sold the business to another Atlanta pharmacist and businessman, Asa Candler, in 1887 for $2,300. Over the years, in part due to Candler's aggressive marketing, sales grew rapidly to the point that, by the late 1890s, Coca-Cola was one of America's most popular fountain drinks. The process of selling syrup to independent bottling companies licensed to sell the drink began around the turn of the century and persists to the present day.

Today, Coca-Cola products are sold in more than 200 countries as the company has grown to become the largest manufacturer, distributor, and marketer of nonalcoholic beverage concentrates and syrups in the world. They have expanded beyond CSDs into juice and juice-related drinks, sports drinks, water products, teas, coffees, and other beverages.[7] Coca-Cola entered the sports drink market with PowerAde, which had an 18.1 percent market share in 2004, still a distant second to the original sports drink, Gatorade. In the single-serve bottled water market, Coca-Cola first introduced Dasani water in 1999. Dasani has since expanded to a market share of 12.1 percent. In 2005, the Coca-Cola Company reported over $23 billion in net operating revenues with a stock market valuation of over $95 billion.

One of the most important public policy issues surrounding the Coca-Cola Company over the years has been its use of branding to enhance its leading share position in the CSD market, to create entry barriers, and to increase its market power. In 2004, the Coca-Cola Company had a combined 43.1 percent share of the CSD market in the United States. Table 8.3 shows the Coca-Cola Company portfolio of carbonated soft drink brands. In 2004, Coca-Cola Classic accounted for 41.5 percent of the company share, down from 46.31 percent. Over 75 percent of the company's soft drink portfolio is made up of just three brands, Coca-Cola Classic, Diet Coke, and Sprite. Of those three, only Diet Coke has shown growth in volume from 1998 to 2004.

PepsiCo, Inc.

Like many pharmacists at the turn of the twentieth century, Caleb Bradham of New Bern, North Carolina, had a soda fountain in his drugstore. His most popular beverage was something he called "Brad's drink," made of carbonated water, sugar, vanilla, rare oils, pepsin, and cola nuts. "Brad's drink," created in the summer of 1893, was later renamed Pepsi-Cola in 1898 after the pepsin and cola nuts used in the recipe. In 1898, Caleb Bradham bought the trade name Pep Cola for $100 from a competitor from Newark, New Jersey, and the new name was trademarked on June 16, 1903. Unfortunately, Bradham gambled on the fluctuations of sugar prices during World War I, betting that sugar prices would continue to rise, but they fell instead. Pepsi- Cola went bankrupt in 1923. In 1931, Pepsi-Cola was bought by the Loft Candy Company, which struggled to make a success of Pepsi and even offered to sell Pepsi to the Coca-Cola Company (which refused to even offer a bid).

Today, the company is a diversified conglomerate with a complete product line across the food and beverage categories. Its Frito-Lay division is the leading snack and chip company in the world, while its Quaker Foods division is a market leader in cereals, rice, and pasta products. Noncarbonated beverages also do quite well, with Gatorade, acquired with the purchase of Quaker Foods, leading the sports drink market in 2004 with a 72 percent share. Aquafina is Pepsi's bottled water brand, also a market leader in the single-serve bottled water market with a 13.6 percent share in 2004. In June of 2006, Pepsi-Cola North America introduced Starbucks Ice Coffee; Starbucks Strawberries and Crème Frappuccino, a coffee-free blend of strawberries and low-fat milk; and Starbucks DoubleShot Light, an espresso drink. In July, the company introduced Pepsi Jazz, a carbonated, no-calorie soda with flavors such as black cherry French vanilla and strawberries and cream. For 2005, PepsiCo reported over $32 billion in net revenue and a stock market valuation over $98 billion.

Table 8.4 shows the portfolio of carbonated soft drinks brands for PepsiCo. In 2004, PepsiCo, Inc., had a combined 31.7 percent share of the CSD market in the United States. Similar to Coca-Cola, the top three brands with Pepsico (Pepsi-Cola, Mountain Dew, and Diet Pepsi) account for over 75 percent of the company's portfolio, with only Diet Pepsi seeing a positive volume growth from 1998 to 2004. Interestingly, about half of the current PepsiCo portfolio of CSD is made up of brands introduced since 2000. Yet the aggregate market share of these new brands in Table 8.4 is less than 10 percent of the CSD market.

Cadbury Schweppes

In 1783, in Geneva, Switzerland, Jacob Schweppes independently developed a process of adding carbonation into mineral water, and Schweppes was born. A number of years later, in the United Kingdom in 1824, John Cadbury began selling

Table 8.3

Coca-Cola Portfolio of Carbonated Soft Drink Brands

Brand	Date intro-duced*	1998			2004			1998 to 2004	
		Gallons (millions)	Market share (%)	Share of company (%)	Gallons (millions)	Market share (%)	Share of company (%)	Volume growth (%)	Market share change (%)
Coca-Cola Classic	1886, 1985	3,056.25	20.62	46.31	2,749.05	17.90	41.51	−10.05	−2.72
Diet Coke	1982	1,277.70	8.62	19.36	1,497.00	9.75	22.61	17.16	1.13
Sprite	1961	977.70	6.60	14.82	870.75	5.67	13.15	−10.94	−0.93
Caffeine-Free Diet Coke	1983	269.55	1.82	4.08	255.00	1.66	3.85	−5.40	−0.16
Fanta	1960	46.65	0.31	0.71	195.00	1.27	2.94	318.01	0.95
Barq's	1890	154.65	1.04	2.34	155.55	1.01	2.35	0.58	−0.03
Cherry Coke	1985	97.20	0.66	1.47	118.80	0.77	1.79	22.22	0.12
Mr. Pibb	1972	107.55	0.73	1.63	99.15	0.65	1.50	−7.81	−0.08
Diet Sprite	1974	80.10	0.54	1.21	95.40	0.62	1.44	19.10	0.08
Diet Coke with Lime	2004	—	—	—	67.50	0.44	1.02	—	—
Mello Yello	1979	63.60	0.43	0.96	67.20	0.44	1.01	5.66	0.01
Sprite Remix	2003	—	—	—	58.65	0.38	0.89	—	—
Minute Maid Regular & Diet	1985	182.25	1.23	2.76	56.40	0.37	0.85	−69.05	−0.86
Vanilla Coke	2002	—	—	—	53.40	0.35	0.81	—	—
Caffeine-Free Coke Classic	1983, 1988	87.45	0.59	1.33	47.70	0.31	0.72	−45.45	−0.28
Diet Cherry Coke	1986	10.80	0.07	0.16	39.45	0.26	0.60	265.28	0.18
Coke C2	2004	—	—	—	37.50	0.24	0.57	—	—
Fresca	1966	38.85	0.26	0.59	35.40	0.23	0.53	−8.88	−0.03
Diet Vanilla Coke	2002	—	—	—	27.90	0.18	0.42	—	—
Diet Coke with Lemon	2001	—	—	—	15.00	0.10	0.23	—	—
Diet Barq's	N/A	13.50	0.09	0.20	13.20	0.09	0.20	−2.22	−0.01
Tab	1963	7.50	0.05	0.11	5.40	0.04	0.08	−28.00	−0.02
Surge	1997	77.70	0.52	1.18	0.30	0.00	0.00	−99.61	−0.52
Citra	1997	31.50	0.21	0.48	0.15	0.00	0.00	−99.52	−0.21
Coca-Cola II	1990	6.75	0.05	0.10	N/A	N/A	N/A	N/A	N/A
Others	—	12.00	0.08	0.18	19.65	0.13	0.30	63.75	0.05
Total Coca-Cola	—	6,599.25	44.53	100.00	6,622.20	43.12	100.00	0.35	−1.41

Source: Beverage Digest *Fact Book 2005, Statistical Yearbook of Non-Alcoholic Beverages,* 10th ed. (Bedford Hills, NY: 2005).

* Not necessarily introduced by Coca-Cola.

Table 8.4

PepsiCo, Inc. Portfolio of Carbonated Soft Drink Brands

Brand	Date intro- duced*	1998			2004			1998 to 2004	
		Gallons (millions)	Market share (%)	Share of company (%)	Gallons (millions)	Market share (%)	Share of company (%)	Volume growth (%)	Market share change (%)
Pepsi-Cola	1898	2,099.70	14.17	45.15	1,769.25	11.52	36.39	−15.74	−2.65
Mountain Dew	1964	997.65	6.73	21.45	972.00	6.33	19.99	−2.57	−0.40
Diet Pepsi	1964	794.55	5.36	17.09	937.50	6.10	19.28	17.99	0.74
Sierra Mist	2000	—	—	—	208.20	1.36	4.28	—	—
Diet Mountain Dew	1988	124.50	0.84	2.68	195.30	1.27	4.02	56.87	0.43
Caffeine-Free Diet Pepsi	1987	147.30	0.99	3.17	144.60	0.94	2.97	−1.83	−0.05
Mug Root Beer	1950	117.60	0.79	2.53	102.00	0.66	2.10	−13.27	−0.13
Wild Cherry Pepsi	1988	59.55	0.40	1.28	91.80	0.60	1.89	54.16	0.20
Caffeine-Free Pepsi	1987	137.85	0.93	2.96	77.55	0.50	1.59	−43.74	−0.43
Mountain Dew Code Red	2001	—	—	—	68.85	0.45	1.42	—	—
Slice	1984	96.30	0.65	2.07	43.50	0.28	0.89	−54.83	−0.37
Diet Sierra Mist	2001	—	—	—	42.15	0.27	0.87	—	—
Mountain Dew Live Wire	2003	—	—	—	38.85	0.25	0.80	—	—
Diet Pepsi Vanilla	2003	—	—	—	30.30	0.20	0.62	—	—
Pepsi One	1998	50.10	0.34	1.08	28.80	0.19	0.59	−42.51	−42.51
Pepsi Vanilla	2003	—	—	—	23.70	0.15	0.49	—	—
Mountain Dew Pitch Black	2004	—	—	—	16.35	0.11	0.34	—	—
Diet Pepsi Twist	2001	—	—	—	16.05	0.10	0.33	—	—
Pepsi Edge	2004	—	—	—	12.90	0.08	0.27	—	—
Diet Mountain Dew Code Red	2002	—	—	—	12.45	0.08	0.26	—	—
Pepsi Holiday Spice	2004	—	—	—	8.25	0.05	0.17	—	—
Pepsi Twist	2001	—	—	—	6.90	0.04	0.14	—	—
Diet Slice	1984	16.05	0.11	0.35	5.55	0.04	0.11	−65.42	−0.07
Others	—	9.00	0.06	0.19	5.40	0.04	0.11	−40.00	−0.03
Total Pepsico	—	4,650.30	31.38	100.00	4,862.55	31.66	100.00	4.56	0.28

Source: Beverage Digest, *Fact Book 2005, Statistical Yearbook of Non-Alcoholic Beverages,* 10th ed. (Bedford Hills, NY: 2005).

* Not necessarily introduced by PepsiCo.

tea and coffee. These sales were bolstered by his increasing sales of cocoa and chocolate. Cadbury Schweppes was formed in 1969 via a merger of Schweppes (predominantly beverages) and Cadbury (predominantly confectionary/chocolate). Hence, the merger in 1969 was of giants in the carbonated soft drink (CSD) and confectionary (Cadbury) market, reflecting their primary lines of business. Today, Cadbury Schweppes has the largest share of the global confectionary market and a strong regional presence with carbonated soft drinks in North America. Their CSD portfolio was enhanced greatly through numerous acquisitions over the years, including A&W in 1993 and Dr Pepper/7 Up in 1995. Outside of the CSD market, Cadbury Schweppes acquired Snapple beverages in 2000. In 2005, Cadbury Schweppes had over $11 billion in revenue and a stock market valuation over $21 billion.

Table 8.5 illustrates the Cadbury Schweppes portfolio of carbonated soft drinks. In 2004, Cadbury Schweppes had a combined 14.4 percent share of the CSD market in the United States. Unlike Coca-Cola and PepsiCo, only 55 percent of the company share is vested in the top three brands (Dr Pepper, Diet Dr Pepper, and 7 Up). However, the diet trend continues, as Diet Dr Pepper is the only one of the top three to show a positive volume growth from 1998 to 2004.

Other Players

Table 8.6 shows the market share of the top ten carbonated soft drink companies in the United States. In addition to the big three that we have already discussed, there are other fringe players in the CSD market, most notably Cott Corporation, whose current 5.5 percent market share has doubled over the last six years. Cott produces mostly private label sodas for large retail chains, such as the President's Choice line for Wal-Mart Stores,

Inc. Sales of private label soft drinks through Wal-Mart accounted for approximately 40 percent of Cott's 2005 annual sales.[8] Other players include National Beverage (2.4 percent in 2004) and a series of specialty label brands with a combined 1.7 percent market share.

The dominance of the big three becomes quite apparent when one examines Table 8.7, the top ten brands of carbonated soft drinks in 1998 and 2004. In 2004 Coca-Cola owned four of the top ten brands, Coke Classic, Diet Coke, Sprite, and Caffeine-Free Diet Coke. These four brands had a combined 35 percent of the carbonated soft drink market. During this same period, PepsiCo also owned four of the top ten brands, Pepsi-Cola, Mountain Dew, Diet Pepsi, and Sierra Mist, for a combined market share of 25.3 percent. Cadbury Schweppes claimed ownership of the remaining two, Dr Pepper and Diet Dr Pepper, for a combined 7 percent market share. These ten brands account for 67.3 percent of the carbonated soft drink market. Interestingly, the top ten brands account for 6 percent less market share in 2004 as compared to the top ten in 1998. Both Coke Classic and Pepsi-Cola have seen a significant decrease in volume during this period, while Diet Coke and Diet Pepsi have increased volume sales by about 15 percent.

The Vertical Structure of the Industry

The big three manufacturers generally distribute syrup to independent or captive bottlers who, in turn, distribute to point-of-purchase. See, for example, the Pepsi Bottling Group[9] and the Coca-Cola Bottlers' Association.[10] Independent bottlers are often well organized and often powerful in their own right. This has led the big three to acquire control over bottlers in various ways. Coca-Cola, through majority ownership of Coca-Cola Enterprises, owns and controls many large

Table 8.5

Cadbury Schweppes Portfolio of Carbonated Soft Drink Brands

Brand	Date intro-duced*	1998 Gallons (millions)	1998 Market share (%)	1998 Share of company (%)	2004 Gallons (millions)	2004 Market share (%)	2004 Share of company (%)	1998 to 2004 Volume growth (%)	1998 to 2004 Market share change (%)
Dr Pepper	1885	899.10	6.07	42.57	861.15	5.61	38.64	−4.22	−0.46
Diet Dr Pepper	1963	140.40	0.95	6.65	210.15	1.37	9.43	49.68	0.42
7 Up	1929	316.35	2.13	14.98	171.90	1.12	7.71	−45.66	−1.02
Sunkist	1977	91.35	0.62	4.33	157.80	1.03	7.08	72.74	0.41
Canada Dry	1904	127.95	0.86	6.06	120.30	0.78	5.40	−5.98	−0.08
A&W Root Beer	1919	80.85	0.55	3.83	88.80	0.58	3.98	9.83	0.03
Diet 7 Up	1970	89.55	0.60	4.24	69.90	0.46	3.14	−21.94	−0.15
Squirt	1938	82.20	0.55	3.89	68.10	0.44	3.06	−17.15	−0.11
RC Cola	1934	N/A	N/A	N/A	60.00	0.39	2.69	N/A	N/A
Diet Rite	1962	N/A	N/A	N/A	54.90	0.36	2.46	N/A	N/A
Diet A&W	1974	16.95	0.11	0.80	35.70	0.23	1.60	110.62	0.12
Welch's	1974	28.20	0.19	1.34	29.55	0.19	1.33	4.79	0.00
Diet Rite Flavors	1997	N/A	N/A	N/A	29.25	0.19	1.31	N/A	N/A
Sundrop	1953	30.60	0.21	1.45	29.25	0.19	1.31	−4.41	−0.02
Caffeine-Free Diet Dr Pepper	1983	13.35	0.09	0.63	22.05	0.14	0.99	65.17	65.17
Crush	1916	30.15	0.20	1.43	21.00	0.14	0.94	−30.35	−0.07
IBC	1919	23.25	0.16	1.10	19.80	0.13	0.89	−14.84	−0.03
A&W Cream	1986	16.65	0.11	0.79	19.35	0.13	0.87	16.22	0.01
Vernors	1866	23.40	0.16	1.11	18.75	0.12	0.84	−19.87	−0.04
7 Up Plus	2004	—	—	—	12.75	0.08	0.57	—	—
Cherry 7 Up	1987	14.25	0.10	0.67	11.55	0.08	0.52	−18.95	−0.02
Stewart's	1924	N/A	N/A	N/A	10.05	0.07	0.45	N/A	N/A
Diet Cherry 7 Up	1987	6.15	0.04	0.29	7.95	0.05	0.36	29.27	0.01
Dr Pepper Cherry Vanilla	2004	—	—	—	7.95	0.05	0.36	—	—
dnL	2002	—	—	—	6.00	0.04	0.27	—	—
Caffeine-Free Dr Pepper	1983	20.07	0.04	0.01	4.95	0.03	0.22	−15.38	−0.01
RC Diet	1986	N/A	N/A	N/A	4.05	0.03	0.18	N/A	N/A
Cherry RC	1985	N/A	N/A	N/A	1.65	0.01	0.07	N/A	N/A
Red Fusion	2002	—	—	—	1.20	0.01	0.05	—	—
Hires	1876	18.99	0.04	0.01	0.60	0.00	0.03	−88.57	−0.03
Others	—	N/A	N/A	N/A	8.25	0.05	0.37	N/A	N/A
Total Cadbury Schweppes	—	2,111.85	14.25	100.00	2,228.85	14.51	100.00	5.54	0.26

Source: Beverage Digest *Fact Book 2005, Statistical Yearbook of Non-Alcoholic Beverages,* 10th ed. (Bedford Hills, NY: 2005).

* Not necessarily introduced by Cadbury Schweppes.

Table 8.6

Top Ten Carbonated Soft Drink Companies: All Channels

Company	1998 Share (%)	2004 Share (%)	Share change (%)	1998 Gallons (millions)	2004 Gallons (millions)	Percent volume change
Coca-Cola Co.	44.5	43.1	−1.4	6,599.25	6,622.20	0.3
PepsiCo, Inc.	31.4	31.7	0.3	4,650.30	4,862.55	4.6
Cadbury Schweppes	14.4	14.5	0.1	2,135.85	2,228.85	4.4
Cott Corp.	2.7	5.5	2.8	405.00	847.35	109.2
National Beverage	2.0	2.4	0.4	291.00	374.10	28.6
Big Red	0.3	0.4	0.1	50.55	62.25	23.1
Red Bull	N/A	0.3	N/A	N/A	45.00	N/A
Hansen Natural	N/A	0.2	N/A	N/A	30.30	N/A
Monarch Co.	0.5	0.1	−0.4	69.00	14.70	−78.7
Rockstar	*	0.1	—	*	14.55	—
Royal Crown[a]	1.3	—	—	189.15	—	—
Seagram[b]	0.3	—	—	42.00	—	—
Private label/other	2.6	1.7	−0.9	387.90	257.25	−33.7
Industry total	100.0	100.0		14,820.00	15,359.10	3.6

Source: Beverage Digest Special Issue, February 12, 1999; Beverage Digest Press Release, March 4, 2005.
* Rockstar was introduced in 2001.
[a] Royal Crown has since been acquired by Cadbury Schweppes.
[b] Seagram was acquired in parts by Pepsico, Diageo, Pernod Ricard, and Coca-Cola Co.

Table 8.7

Top Ten Carbonated Soft Drink Brands: All Channels

Brand	1998 Share (%)	2004 Share (%)	Share change (%)	1998 Gallons (millions)	2004 Gallons (millions)	Percent volume change
Coca-Cola Classic	20.6	17.9	−2.7	3,056.25	2,749.05	−11.2
Pepsi	14.2	11.5	−2.7	2,099.70	1,769.25	−18.7
Diet Coke	8.6	9.7	1.1	1,277.70	1,497.00	14.6
Mountain Dew	6.7	6.3	−0.4	997.65	972.00	−2.6
Diet Pepsi	5.4	6.1	0.7	794.55	937.50	15.2
Sprite	6.6	5.7	−0.9	977.70	870.75	−12.3
Dr Pepper	6.1	5.6	−0.5	899.10	861.15	−4.4
Caffeine-Free Diet Coke	1.8	1.7	−0.1	269.55	255.00	−5.7
Diet Dr Pepper	0.9	1.4	0.5	140.40	210.15	33.2
Sierra Mist	*	1.4	—	*	208.20	—
7 Up	2.1	1.1	−1.0	316.35	171.90	−84.0
Minute Maid	1.2	0.4	−0.8	182.25	56.40	−223.1
Top 10 Total	73.3	67.3	−6.0	10,870.80	10,330.05	−5.2

Source: Beverage Digest Special Issue, February 12, 1999; Beverage Digest Press Release, March 4, 2005; and Beverage Digest *Fact Book 2005, Statistical Yearbook of Non-Alcoholic Beverages,* 10th ed. (Bedford Hills, NY: 2005).
* Sierra Mist was introduced by PepsiCo in 2000.

bottlers. Cadbury Schweppes currently is in the process of buying independent bottlers in the United States.[11]

Vertical restraints imposed by the syrup manufacturers on the conduct of the independent bottlers and retailers have been a major policy issue. The most common restraint is the imposition of exclusive territories on independent bottlers. Do they enhance logistic efficiency and marketing coordination, or do they extend manufacturer market power in the channel? William Comanor found that territorial restrictions resulted in two anticompetitive effects: (1) intrabrand competition is diminished because bottlers of the same manufacturer are forbidden from competing for sales to the same customer, and (2) interbrand competition is suppressed because the gross margins that are higher in the absence of intrabrand competition can be used to enhance the selling efforts of the manufacturer.[12]

Muris et al. provide an alternative view that focuses on the long-run development of the industry.[13] The syrup manufacturer's granting of exclusive and perpetual territories to the bottler was considered necessary to: (1) induce a bottler to make asset-specific investments, and (2) ensure that the bottlers' efforts and gains would not eventually be expropriated by the syrup manufacturers. The early decades of bottling were not characterized by effective national "pull" advertising options; therefore the bottlers had to invest in high outlays for local "pull" promotions to increase demand. The bottlers, who had already invested heavily in plant and equipment, required assurance that they would be the recipients of the rewards of their investments. Territorial exclusivity protected these bottlers from losing their "rightful returns" to those bottlers that would otherwise ship into the "developed" territories without having to expend effort and resources in developing the label.

Ultimately, vertical relationships are about the pricing arrangements between the manufacturer (e.g., Coca-Cola) and the retailer and the vertical coordination of trade promotions and other point-of-purchase marketing programs. Typically, trade promotions are temporary price reductions with an agreed-upon performance program at retail such as "put the brand on special display and advertise the special price in the weekly local newspaper advertisement circular." Trade promotions are initiated by the product manager at the manufacturer level. If the bottler is independent, it can decide whether to participate and how much to pass through to the retailer. Integrated or captive bottlers are under the full control of the manufacturer. Ultimately, the retailer also has discretion on how much to pass through to consumers. This issue of pass-through has received much attention in recent years.[14]

Vertical issues including independent versus integrated bottling structures and coordination of trade promotions provide for a complicated picture involving manufacturers, bottlers-distributors, and retailers. However, previous research has demonstrated that the dominant consideration is the horizontal interaction among brands (manufacturers) in differentiated food product market channels and in the CSD industry.[15] Cotterill et al. report that the retail prices of brands sold through captive bottlers are not significantly different from those handled by independent bottlers.[16] Accordingly, we focus primarily on the horizontal aspects in this chapter.[17]

CSD Competitive Strategies

Firms compete in the CSD industry in three major ways. First, new product introductions play an important competitive role as firms seek growth in the industry and attempt to satisfy consumer demand. Often, new soft drink brands are following trends or copying competitors' new brand introductions.[18] Second, advertising serves as an

Figure 8.1   **Coca-Cola New Brand Market Shares**

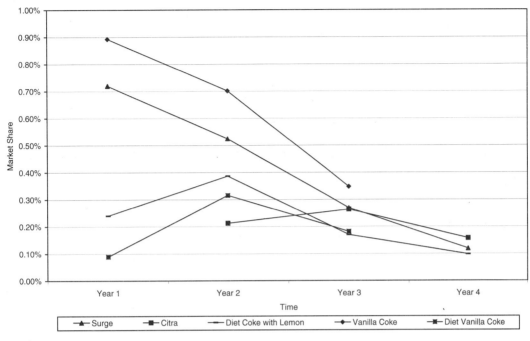

Source: Based on Beverage Digest, *Fact Book 2005, Statistical Yearbook of Non-Alcoholic Beverages*, 10th ed. (Bedford Hills, NY: 2005).

important competitive instrument as new brands attempt to break through to the market as well as keeping established brands fresh and popular. The third competitive strategy in the CSD industry is a combination of pricing and trade promotions. In particular, trade promotions provide manufacturers with an important mechanism to move product and adjust retail pricing in this industry.

CSD Competitive Strategies: New Product Introductions

The search for competitive advantage through the perfect new product is unending. The CSD market has had a number of interesting but not well advised new product introductions over the years. Who could forget (or remember) Cajun Cola, Toca-Cola, Coco-Cola, Yum-Yum Cola, French Wine of

Cola, King-Cola, Coca Ree, Afri Cola, or even the highly promoted New Coke and Crystal Pepsi.[19] These last two were major failures that lost tens of millions of dollars. Simply put, it is often quite difficult to succeed with a new brand in the beverage industries. Nonetheless, new product introductions play a significant role in the strategic interaction among the major players in any differentiated product market. Figures 8.1 through 8.3 examine the market share of some recent introductions in the market by the big three.

One thing to note for all three companies is that share tends to decline quickly after the initial promotional support, and some declines are often precipitous. PepsiCo, in Figure 8.2, has had a few winners, most notably Sierra Mist, over the past few years. Part of the explanation of the success of Sierra Mist lies with the level of promotional

Figure 8.2   **PepsiCo New Brand Market Shares**

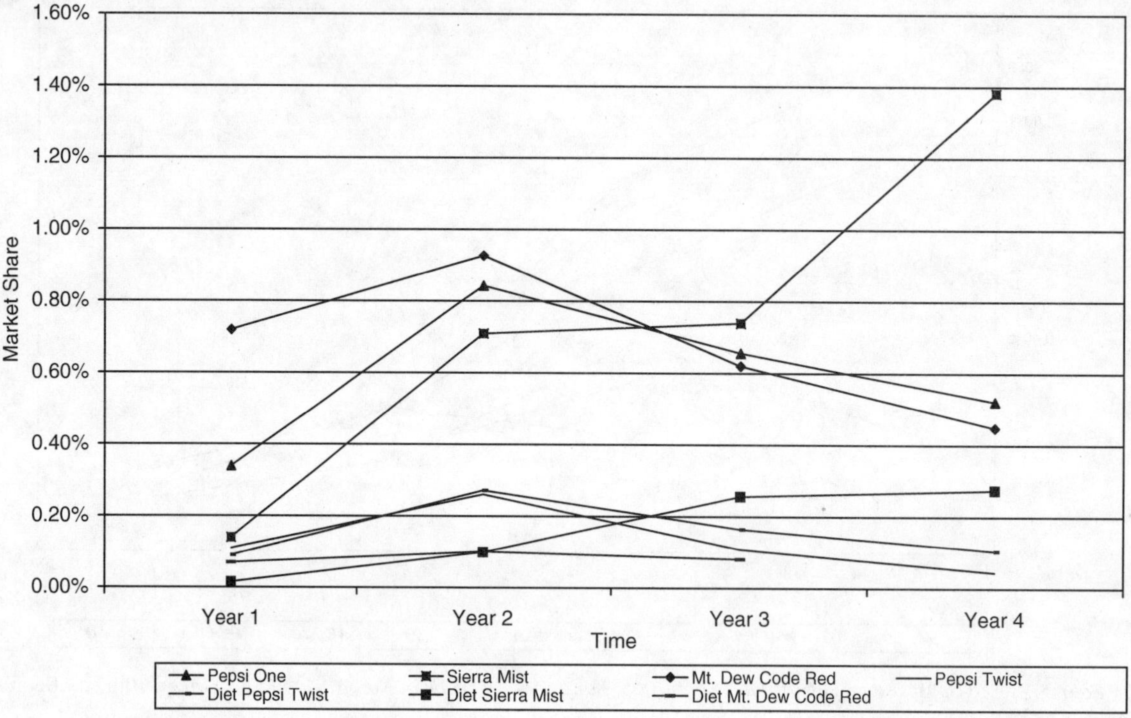

Source: Based on Beverage Digest, *Fact Book 2005, Statistical Yearbook of Non-Alcoholic Beverages*, 10th ed. (Bedford Hills, NY: 2005).

and advertising support. As seen in Table 8.8, in the first four years advertising spending went from just over $6 million to over $18 million in year two, just under $25 million in year three, and over $46 million in year four. However, since advertising support can be determined at least in part as a formulaic percentage of sales, it is not clear if increased sales are a function of increased advertising support or if increased advertising spending is the result of increased sales.

Table 8.8 documents the new brand introduction record for the big three between 1997 and 2004. Unlike the first year of Sierra Mist, it is often the case that a large amount of advertising dollars is spent on new product introductions. This is true for each of the big three. The Coca-Cola Company spent over $22 million in the first year of Vanilla Coke, while PepsiCo spent over $25 million in the first year of Pepsi One, Pepsi Blue, and Pepsi Vanilla. Cadbury Schweppes has invested over $10 million on advertising Red Fusion and most recently 7 Up Plus. It is evident that this trend continued in 2004 when Coca-Cola and Pepsi introduced their new low-calorie, low-sugar, low-carbohydrate soft drinks Coke C2 and Pepsi Edge, with over $30 million in advertising. Pepsi Edge quickly fizzled out, being discontinued by the end of 2005, and Coke C2 has been expected by some experts to follow a similar path.

Given the inherent failure rate of new soft drink product introductions over time, why spend so much time and effort on these new product introductions? There have been numerous explanations

Figure 8.3 **Cadbury Schweppes New Brand Market Shares**

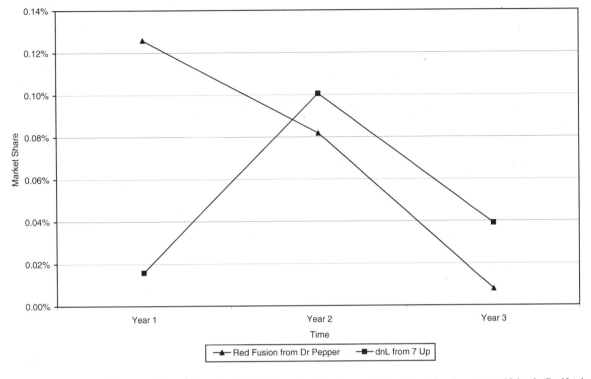

Source: Based on Beverage Digest, *Fact Book 2005, Statistical Yearbook of Non-Alcoholic Beverages*, 10th ed. (Bedford Hills, NY: 2005).

offered over the years, but three are perhaps the most compelling:

- Repetitive brand entry (proliferation) raises entry barriers.[20] It is important to note that in terms of share of voice alone, the big three players have the ability to drown out any spending of smaller rivals in this industry. Thus, ongoing new product brand introduction—with the associated hype and promotional/advertising support—makes it exceedingly difficult for smaller rivals to launch any new products into this space.
- Proliferation increases the ability of the big three to raise price relative to weaker and private label brands.[21] The lack of credible

entry threats and the dominant shelf-space positioning can decrease consumer sensitivity to price within the category.[22]

- Proliferation can increase the overall demand faced by the firm.[23] One explanation for this is that new brands create a "buzz" that has positive parent brand association, although such effects are likely to be context-specific.[24]

CSD Competitive Strategies: Advertising

Similar to new brand introductions, advertising's impact is both multidimensional and contextual. Tables 8.9 and 8.10 depict the levels of advertising spending in this industry.

Table 8.8

Selected New Brand Introductions of The Big Three, 1997–2004

Brand	Company	Year intro-duced	Year 1			Year 2			Year 3			Year 4		
			Gallons (millions)	Market share (%)	Total adver-tising dollars (000)	Gallons (million)	Market share (%)	Total adver-tising dollars (000)	Gallons (million)	Market share (%)	Total adver-tising dollars (000)	Gallons (million)	Market share (%)	Total adver-tising dollars (000)
Surge	Coca-Cola	1997	103.5	0.72	13,611.0	77.7	0.52	17,846.7	40.1	0.27	18,967.4	17.7	0.12	243.8
Citra	Coca-Cola	1997	N/A	N/A	1,119.1	21.0	0.21	6,711.6	26.2	0.26	10,100.4	15.6	0.16	98.4
Pepsi One	PepsiCo	1998	50.3	0.34	25,780.2	125.6	0.84	50,831.9	98.0	0.66	36,603.6	78.3	0.52	25,130.5
Sierra Mist	PepsiCo	2000	20.9	0.14	6,129.9	106.5	0.71	18,155.0	111.9	0.74	24,989.9	210.3	1.38	46,641.3
Mt. Dew Code Red	PepsiCo	2001	108.0	0.72	9,754.5	140.3	0.93	6,421.2	94.4	0.62	10,336.9	68.9	0.45	600.5
Diet Coke with Lemon	Coca-Cola	2001	36.0	0.24	N/A	58.5	0.39	5,768.0	25.8	0.17	679.3	15.0	0.10	N/A
Pepsi Twist[a]	PepsiCo	2001	16.5	0.11	17,922.1	39.5	0.26	29,117.6	16.5	0.11	14,884.3	6.9	0.04	N/A
Diet Pepsi Twist[a]	PepsiCo	2001	13.5	0.09	N/A	41.1	0.27	N/A	25.1	0.16	N/A	16.1	0.10	N/A
Diet Sierra Mist	PepsiCo	2001	2.3	0.01	N/A	15.0	0.10	N/A	39.0	0.26	N/A	42.2	0.27	N/A
Vanilla Coke	Coca-Cola	2002	135.0	0.89	22,678.8	106.7	0.70	13,655.7	53.4	0.35	10,797.1			
Pepsi Blue	PepsiCo	2002	25.5	0.17	27,523.4	7.4	0.05	1,119.5						
Red Fusion from Dr Pepper	Cadbury Schweppes	2002	19.1	0.13	12,428.9	12.5	0.08	266.5	1.2	0.01	0.5			
Diet Vanilla Coke	Coca-Cola	2002	13.5	0.09	229.2	48.0	0.32	N/A	27.9	0.18	N/A			
Diet Mt. Dew Code Red	PepsiCo	2002	10.5	0.07	N/A	15.3	0.10	N/A	12.5	0.08	N/A			
dnL from 7 Up	Cadbury Schweppes	2002	2.4	0.02	N/A	15.3	0.10	3,945.6	6.0	0.04	N/A			
Sprite Remix	Coca-Cola	2003	82.5	0.54	10,500.6	58.7	0.38	25.9						
Mt. Dew Live Wire	PepsiCo	2003	52.5	0.35	10,366.6	38.9	0.25	2,222.2						
Pepsi Vanilla	PepsiCo	2003	33.0	0.22	26,511.8	23.7	0.15	35.0						
Diet Pepsi Vanilla[b]	PepsiCo	2003	24.0	0.16	249.5	30.3	0.20	63.7						
Diet Coke with Lime	Coca-Cola	2004	67.5	0.44	6,619.9									
Coke C2	Coca-Cola	2004	37.5	0.24	35,077.5									
Mt. Dew Pitch Black	PepsiCo	2004	16.4	0.11	N/A									
Pepsi Edge	PepsiCo	2004	12.9	0.08	32,249.5									
7 Up Plus	Cadbury Schweppes	2004	12.8	0.08	10,926.2									
Pepsi Holiday Spice	PepsiCo	2004	8.3	0.05	3,462.5									
Dr Pepper Cherry Vanilla	Cadbury Schweppes	2004	8.0	0.05	363.6									

Source: Beverage Digest Fact Book 2005, Statistical Yearbook of Non-Alcoholic Beverages, 10th ed. (Bedford Hills, NY: 2005); Multi-Media Service, Class/Brand $. (New York: Competitive Media Reporting, Inc., 1997–2002); Multi-Media Service, Class/Brand $. (New York: TNS Media Intelligence, 2003–2004).

Notes: In year 5 the market share for Surge and Citra had dropped to less than 0.1 percent and the market share for Pepsi One dropped below 0.4 percent. Sierra Mist has secured a strong position in the market by year 5 with a share greater than 1.3 percent.

[a] Pepsi and Diet Pepsi Twist advertising dollars are combined; [b] Diet Pepsi Vanilla advertising is combo advertising with Pepsi Vanilla.

Table 8.9 shows national advertising dollars of the leading carbonated soft drink companies during 1992, 1998, and 2004. It is quite apparent that the media of choice for soft drinks is television, where approximately 90 percent of the advertising dollars are spent each year. During 1992 and 1998, the Coca-Cola Company was the advertising leader in the CSD market, spending over $200 million and accounting for over 40 percent of CSD advertising. While its advertising spending in dollar terms has not decreased over this period, its *share* of advertising spending has declined with the significant increase in advertising by PepsiCo. In 2004, PepsiCo spent approximately $287 million, almost double its advertising expenditure in 1992, claiming the top spot in share of advertising expenditure (41.2 percent) for soft drinks. On the other hand, Cadbury Schweppes was a minor advertiser of CSDs until its acquisitions of A&W Brands and, more importantly, Dr Pepper/7 Up Company. In 2004, Cadbury Schweppes accounted for roughly 20 percent of CSD advertising. It is also interesting to see how advertising spending on categories of CSD has evolved over time, more recently focusing on the regular CSD market. Table 8.9 shows how advertising spending on the "regular" CSD market was 64.9 percent in 1992 and 85.6 percent in 2004. Thus, low-calorie "diet" brands account for a much lower proportion of advertising in 2004.

Table 8.10 illustrates the advertising dollars of leading soft drink brand advertisers. All ten of the top individual brands in terms of total advertising spending in the soft drink industry in 2004 were brands owned by the big three, with Coca-Cola Classic and Pepsi spending well over $100 million in advertising. The top four brands (Coca-Cola Classic, Pepsi, Dr Pepper, and Mountain Dew in 2004) accounted for over 50 percent of all advertising spending in the carbonated soft drink market. It

is apparent that well-established brands advertise and keep the brands fresh.

The role of branding, advertising, and "share of voice" (percentage of total category advertising contributed by each brand) is always a key issue in largely undifferentiated product markets, but it has dominated the CSD market for quite some time. In order to understand, at least in part, why this is the case, Figure 8.4 demonstrates the importance of share, in particular as it pertains to share of voice and entry barriers.[25] It is exceedingly difficult for a new brand to enter this market given the high cost of developing and maintaining the brand for low-share brands.

There is a clear relationship between advertising spending per gallon and the annual sales volume. Just to gain a small share of voice, the smaller players in this market must spend a disproportionate share of revenue on advertising. Indeed, the brand-building requirements can be prohibitively expensive, and, even after having spent an inordinate percentage of revenue on advertising in order to build a brand, you still end up "drowning" in a sea of competitors' advertising. Hence, it is not at all difficult to see why new entrants have such a difficult time succeeding in this industry: While Coke Classic is spending a mere $0.04 per gallon on advertising, Sierra Mist needs to spend $0.20 per gallon (a factor of 5!) and is still outspent 3-to-1 by Coke Classic ($41.4 million versus $123.9 million, see Table 8.10). And this does not even include the preexisting brand equity that Coke Classic brings to the table. Thus, advertising and brand, along with selected new product introductions, must be used selectively and strategically by manufacturers.

Much like the impact of new brand introductions, previous research has suggested that advertising's impact is derived from a number of sources:

- Barriers to entry: Bayus and Putsis have suggested that external factors such as advertis-

Table 8.9

National Advertising Dollars of Leading Carbonated Soft Drink Companies

Company	1992					1998					2004				
	Media total	Share of $ spent (%)	Print	TV	Radio	Media total	Share of $ spent (%)	Print	TV	Radio	Media total	Share of $ spent (%)	Print	TV	Radio
Regular carbonated soft drinks															
A&W Brands	8,019.7	1.7	84.4	7,683.3	252.0	Acquired by Cadbury Schweppes in 1993					Acquired by Cadbury Schweppes in 1993				
Cadbury Schweppes	10,566.1	2.2	483.4	8,020.0	2,062.7	87,010.3	15.3	1,002.1	85,961.5	46.7	106,621.9	15.3	4,845.6	101,629.0	147.3
Coca-Cola	139,029.0	29.5	13,271.7	119,507.4	6,249.9	212,760.6	37.4	17,094.7	195,561.9	104.0	234,190.8	33.6	19,025.6	210,491.8	4,673.4
Dr Pepper/7 Up	42,814.0	9.1	782.9	40,822.9	1,208.2	(Acquired by Cadbury Schweppes in 1995)					(Acquired by Cadbury Schweppes in 1995)				
Pepsico Inc	85,705.8	18.2	5,731.2	75,506.4	4,468.2	162,017.8	28.5	12,086.4	147,898.9	2,032.5	254,386.8	36.5	15,293.8	236,077.9	3,015.1
Total regular CSD	305,612.3	64.9	22,553.1	263,026.4	20,032.8	466,785.5	82.0	32,023.1	431,608.5	3,153.9	596,560.2	85.6	39,517.6	548,933.3	8,109.3
Low-calorie carbonated soft drinks															
A&W Brands	3,077.1	0.7	0.0	3,077.1	0.0	Acquired by Cadbury Schweppes in 1993					Acquired by Cadbury Schweppes in 1993				
Cadbury Schweppes	0.6	0.0	0.0	0.6	0.0	30,140.1	5.3	493.3	29,646.8	0.0	31,117.4	4.5	1,033.2	30,084.2	0.0
Coca-Cola	68,777.1	14.6	5,834.8	61,448.0	1,494.3	28,726.5	5.0	8,411.6	20,096.2	218.7	29,422.9	4.2	4,198.0	25,224.9	0.0
Dr Pepper/7 Up	31,520.3	6.7	56.8	31,233.3	230.2	(Acquired by Cadbury Schweppes in 1995)					(Acquired by Cadbury Schweppes in 1995)				
Pepsico Inc	59,368.3	12.6	1,134.8	56,662.5	1,571.0	39,883.2	7.0	1,000.3	38,637.9	245.0	32,897.5	4.7	4,612.4	28,257.6	27.5
Total Low-Calorie CSD	165,234.9	35.1	8,178.1	153,662.9	3,393.9	99,690.3	17.5	10,192.2	89,016.2	481.9	93,437.8	13.4	9,843.6	83,594.2	0.0
Total carbonated soft drinks*															
A&W Brands	11,096.8	2.4	84.4	10,760.4	252.0	Acquired by Cadbury Schweppes in 1993					Acquired by Cadbury Schweppes in 1993				
Cadbury Schweppes	10,566.7	2.2	483.4	8,020.6	2,062.7	117,858.1	20.7	1,730.0	116,081.4	46.7	138,524.6	19.9	6,550.2	131,827.1	147.3
Coca-Cola	207,806.1	44.1	19,106.5	180,955.4	7,744.2	242,814.1	42.6	26,503.6	215,987.8	322.7	265,912.0	38.1	24,300.4	236,890.3	4,721.3
Dr Pepper/7 Up	74,334.3	15.8	839.7	72,056.2	1,438.4	(Acquired by Cadbury Schweppes in 1995)					(Acquired by Cadbury Schweppes in 1995)				
Pepsico Inc.	145,074.1	30.8	6,866.0	132,168.9	6,039.2	202,503.2	35.6	13,262.3	186,963.4	2,277.5	287,429.8	41.2	19,978.9	264,408.3	3,042.6
Grand Total	470,847.2		30,731.2	416,689.3	23,426.7	569,421.1		43,774.6	522,010.7	3,635.8	697,204.0		55,141.8	633,905.0	8,157.2

Source: Multi-Media Service, *Class/Brand $* (New York: Competitive Media Reporting, 1992 and 1998). *Multi-Media Service, Class/Brand $* (New York: TNS Media Intelligence, 2004).

Note: Advertising dollars in thousands (000).

* Total carbonated soft drinks does not sum to regular and low calorie because of additional combo advertising not displayed here.

Table 8.10

National Advertising Dollars of Leading Soft Drink Brand Advertisers

Brand	Company	1992 Media total	1992 Share of $ spent (%)	1992 Print	1992 TV	1992 Radio	1998 Media total	1998 Share of $ spent (%)	1998 Print	1998 TV	1998 Radio	2004 Media total	2004 Share of $ spent (%)	2004 Print	2004 TV	2004 Radio
Coca-Cola Classic	Coca-Cola	90,716.2	19.3	5,891.1	82,182.3	2,642.8	115,490.8	20.3	6,600.3	108,883.4	7.1	123,861.8	17.8	1,207.1	120,112.0	2,542.7
Pepsi	PepsiCo	63,224.6	13.4	2,786.7	57,043.6	3,394.3	82,685.6	14.5	529.2	81,296.5	859.9	103,878.8	14.9	3,557.0	100,165.3	156.5
Dr Pepper	Schweppes* Cadbury	28,794.6	6.1	147.0	28,165.1	482.5	55,247.5	9.7	523.9	54,714.0	9.6	68,584.8	9.8	1,622.6	66,914.7	47.5
Mountain Dew	PepsiCo	10,672.6	2.3	60.6	9,631.5	980.5	39,773.9	7.0	3,069.3	36,704.6	0.0	52,631.7	7.5	1,119.6	50,923.7	588.4
Sprite	Coca-Cola	28,540.8	6.1	242.8	27,564.3	733.7	56,483.4	9.9	3,061.4	53,418.0	4.0	43,908.0	6.3	0.0	42,623.1	1,284.9
Sierra Mist	PepsiCo	First introduced by PepsiCo in 2000										41,381.9	5.9	826.2	39,848.4	707.3
Coca-Cola C2	Coca-Cola	First introduced by Coca-Cola in 2004										35,077.5	5.0	4,699.4	30,378.1	0.0
Diet Pepsi	PepsiCo	43,243.5	9.2	554.9	41,301.2	1,387.4	13,938.7	2.4	792.9	13,008.8	137.0	32,897.5	4.7	4,612.4	28,257.6	27.5
Pepsi Edge	PepsiCo	First introduced by PepsiCo in 2004										32,249.5	4.6	2,801.2	29,448.3	0.0
Diet Dr Pepper	Schweppes* Cadbury	18,757.0	4.0	0.0	18,554.7	202.3	30,139.5	5.3	493.3	29,646.2	0.0	24,903.5	3.6	911.0	23,992.5	0.0
Diet Coke	Coca-Cola	64,094.1	13.6	3,451.9	59,238.5	1,403.7	27,690.8	4.9	7,375.9	20,096.2	218.7	22,803.0	3.3	4,198.0	18,605.0	0.0
7 Up	Schweppes* Cadbury	13,372.9	2.8	491.0	12,183.5	698.4	27,057.9	4.8	202.3	26,821.1	34.5	22,071.9	3.2	21.9	22,050.0	0.0
Diet 7 Up	Schweppes* Cadbury	12,763.3	2.7	56.8	12,678.6	27.9			N/A			770.4	0.1	40.0	730.4	0.0
Pepsi One	PepsiCo	First introduced by PepsiCo in 1998					39,883.2	7.0	1,000.3	38,637.9	245.0			N/A		
Surge Citrus	Coca-Cola	First introduced by PepsiCo in 1997					17,846.7	3.1	31.4	17,785.1	30.2			N/A		

Source: Multi-Media Service, Class/Brand $ (New York: Competitive Media Reporting, 1992 and 1998). Multi-Media Service, Class/Brand $ New York: TNS Media Intelligence, 2004.
Note: Advertising dollars in thousands (000).
* 7 Up and Dr Pepper were owned by Dr Pepper/7 Up Company in 1992.

Figure 8.4   **The Value of Market Share of the Leading Soft Drink Brand Advertisers, 2004**

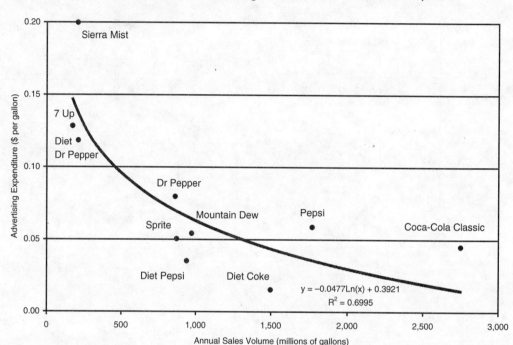

Source: Derived using data from *Multi-Media Service, Class/Brand $.* New York, NY: TNS Media Intelligence, 2004. Beverage Digest, *Fact Book 2005, Statistical Yearbook of Non-Alcoholic Beverages.* 10th ed. Bedford Hills, NY: 2005.
   Note: New brands Coca-Cola C2 and Pepsi Edge with advertising expenditures of $0.94/gallon and $2.50/gallon, respectively, are excluded from this chart.

ing spending by incumbent firms can result in a decreased likelihood of success on new product introductions due to the difficulties inherent in establishing a new and accepted brand name.[26]

- Increased brand loyalty and decreased price sensitivity: Advertising makes consumers less price sensitive as brand loyalties are developed, but possibly only after a threshold level is obtained.[27] This suggests that advertising for low-share brands has little effect below some threshold spending level, providing a distinct advantage for brands with high brand awareness and high dollar spent/share of voice.

- Strategic interaction on like–like instruments: Companies compete both horizontally and vertically in this market, but Steenkamp, Nijs, Hanssens, and Dekimpe have shown that, while the competitive interaction can be aggressive, they demonstrate that the pattern of interaction tends to be on like–like instruments (e.g., promotion changes often prompt promotion response, changes in advertising spending would promote a competitive response in advertising, etc.).[28]

8.1

$$S_{Coke} = 0.443714 - 0.6711\ln(P_{Coke}) + 0.5253\ln(P_{Pepsi}) + 0.0864\ln(P_{RC}) + 0.0594\ln(P_{Dr}) - 0.003Exp_{Cola} + 0.0113Hisp$$

$$(-19.65)^{**} \qquad (18.44)^{**} \qquad (7.400)^{**} \qquad (4.750)^{**} \qquad (-0.428) \qquad (7.502)^{**}$$

To gain a complete picture of competitive interaction in this market requires analysis of brand proliferation and advertising spending on entry, entry barriers, and the exercise of market power.

CSD Competitive Strategies: Pricing and Trade Promotions

The analysis of pricing for any branded food product, including carbonated soft drinks, is more complicated than one might think. To simplify, we assume that soft drink manufacturers, such as Coca-Cola and Pepsi, control the marketing programs of their bottlers and that retailers are passive. This means manufacturers set retail prices for their brands.[29] Using scanner data from U.S. supermarkets in forty-five cities over twenty quarters, Cotterill, Franklin, and Ma estimated demand and price reaction equations for several brands of CSD (additional detail on the data employed in the study can be found there).[30] Here we will use those econometric results to examine pricing for only two brands: Coca-Cola Classic (Coke) and Pepsi, the leading CSD brands.[31] Focusing on two brands allows us to use graphs as well as equations to dissect pricing in a differentiated product oligopoly.

With this two-brand model one can identify actual demand curves, actual reaction curves, and equilibrium prices and quantities. One can also analyze the impact of trade promotions, a very important pricing tactic in food industries, on equilibrium prices and quantities. A typical supermarket has over 30,000 items. Changing the price on a package or the shelf price tag simply does not register with the typical consumer. Therefore, from time to time, branded food manufacturers offer retailers trade promotion programs to communicate price reductions (sales) to consumers. A typical trade promotion has a reduction in retail price. It also has signs on the shelf declaring a reduced price or a coupon dispenser attached to the shelf with cents-off coupons, or an aisle-end display with large "special price" signs. Finally, each supermarket chain's weekly food advertisement circular in the local newspaper may picture the product and announce the "price special." As we will see, CSD firms rely heavily on trade promotions to communicate price reductions and to move product.

Equations 8.1 and 8.2 are the estimated demand curves for the Coke Classic and Pepsi brands. Market share rather than quantity is the dependent variable and the natural logarithm of prices; dollar expenditures in the Cola category and the percentage of the city population that is Hispanic are the explanatory variables.[32]

Note that the signs on the prices are as economic theory predicts. In the Coke demand equation (8.1), for example, the estimated coefficient on $\ln(P_{Coke})$ is negative (−0.6711). A lower Coke price increases Coke market share when all other explanatory variables are constant. The estimated coefficient on $\ln(P_{Pepsi})$ is positive (0.5253): A higher Pepsi price when all other explanatory variables are constant causes consumers to switch to Coke. This indicates that Coke is a substitute for Pepsi, as we would expect. The other brands in the demand model, Royal Crown Cola (P_{RC}) and Dr Pepper (P_{Dr}), are also substitute products.

The numbers in parentheses below the estimated coefficients are t-ratios. They measure the strength of the estimated coefficients, i.e., whether they are

$$S_{Pepsi} = 0.461375 + 0.5253\ln(P_{Coke}) - 0.6112\ln(P_{Pepsi}) + 0.0396\ln(P_{RC}) + 0.0463\ln(P_{Dr}) - 0.0041Exp_{Cola} - 0.0122Hisp$$

$$\qquad (18.44)** \qquad (-20.80)** \qquad (3.677)** \qquad (3.998)** \qquad (-0.668) \qquad (-9.353)**$$

where:

S_j = the dollar market share of brand, j = Coke, Pepsi

P_i = the price of brand, i = Coke, Pepsi, Royal Crown, Dr Pepper

Exp_{Cola} = Dollar Expenditure on Cola/Pepper Brands

$Hisp$ = Percent of the market area population that is Hispanic

statistically different from zero or not. T-ratios with two (one) asterisks are significant at the 1 percent (5 percent) level. The 1 percent level is stronger than 5 percent; however, both indicate that the estimated parameters are statistically different from zero. If all the estimated parameters are zero, a model has no predictive ability; essentially it is useless. In this instance, prices do predict Coke and Pepsi market shares as demand theory counsels. Expenditure is less robust. Its estimated coefficients in both demand equations are not significantly different from zero. The percentage of the Hispanic population has a positive and significant impact on Coke share, and it has a negative and significant impact on Pepsi share. Therefore, markets with a higher Hispanic population have a higher share of Coke.

If one holds all variables constant at their mean values, except the price of the brand and its market share, one obtains the equation of a demand curve.[33] Doing this and taking the anti-logarithms yields the following demand equations for Coke and Pepsi.

$$P_{Coke} = 7.276 \ e^{-1.490} S_{Coke} \qquad 8.3$$

$$P_{Pepsi} = 7.571 \ e^{-1.636} S_{Pepsi} \qquad 8.4$$

Figure 8.5 is a graph of the Coke demand curve. At its average price, $3.71, its market share is 45.2 percent. Figure 8.6 for Pepsi indicates that at its average price, $3.65, its share is 44.6 percent. Note that these brand demand curves have negative slope. Firms that sell homogeneous products in a competitive market face perfectly flat (infinitely elastic) demand curves and have no influence over price. Here in this differentiated product oligopoly both Coke and Pepsi have market power, i.e., the ability to raise the price of a brand without losing all sales to other firms. If Coke and Pepsi have no market power, the brand demand curves in Figures 8.5 and 8.6 would be flat. Pepsi and Coke would be sold only at the "market" price. They would be price takers, not price makers. Note also that these two brands at average prices account for 89.8 percent of the cola/Pepper category. Royal Crown and Dr Pepper are truly fringe players to a dominant duopoly, Coke and Pepsi.

At this stage in the analysis, we do not know the equilibrium of Coke and Pepsi prices and shares—they depend on the game being played and upon the values of exogenous variables such as dollar expenditure in the cola category and the percentage of Hispanic consumers in the demand equation. Cotterill, Franklin, and Ma modeled the game that CSD brand managers play as a Bertrand-Nash model for differentiated goods (BNDG).[34] This model differs from the Bertrand-Nash model for homogeneous goods because in equilibrium, brands can have different prices and prices can be above marginal cost. In BNDG, price is the

Figure 8.5 **The Demand Curve for the Classic Coca-Cola Brand When All Other Variables Are at Their Average Values**

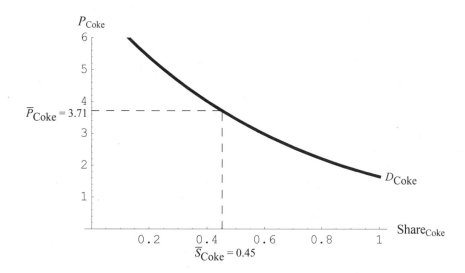

Figure 8.6 **The Demand Curve for the Pepsi Brand When All Other Variables Are at Their Average Values**

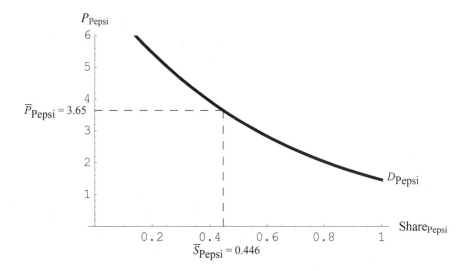

choice variable that each brand manager sets to maximize brand profits given demand curve and cost conditions. Each manager has some conjecture concerning how other brand managers react to his price change. If a manager conjectures that no other brand manager will change price, then her price conjectures are zero and one has the standard Bertrand-Nash differentiated goods model. Otherwise, with non-zero price conjectures, one has a generalized Bertrand-Nash differentiated goods model.

Cotterill, Franklin, and Ma estimate the reaction equations for the more general model.[35] The intersection of the price reaction equations determines equilibrium prices, then one substitutes prices into the demand equation to determine the equilibrium market shares. Since Classic Coke and Pepsi are the dominant brands in the cola/Pepper category, we will focus on Coke and Pepsi pricing strategies to determine their equilibrium prices and shares. This comes close to the "market" equilibrium values that would arise in a more general model that includes the strategic reactions of other brands. Again, using the results from Cotterill, Franklin, and Ma and holding all other explanatory variables, including other prices, at their average values, one can obtain the following price reaction functions for the Classic Coke and Pepsi brands.[36]

$$\ln(P_{Coke}) = 1.14361 + 0.236 \ln(P_{Pepsi})$$

$$- 0.0025(AvWtP \operatorname{Re} d_{Coke}) \qquad 8.5$$

$$- 0.0021(\%VolMer_{Coke})$$

In Equation 8.5, Coke's price is a function of (reaction to) Pepsi's price and two trade promotion variables that the Coke manager controls: the first is the average percentage price reduction on all Coke sold on promotion during the quarter; and the second is the percentage of Coke volume that was sold under some sort of trade promotion

deal during the quarter. Together these capture the depth and time duration of Coke's trade promotion. As we expect, both variables are negatively and significantly related to price in Coke's reaction function (8.5). An increase in trade promotions by Coke management lowers Coke retail prices. A decrease in trade promotions raises Coke price. Note also that Coke tends to follow Pepsi's price moves. The coefficient of $\ln(P_{Pepsi})$ in (8.5) means that a 10 percent increase in Pepsi price leads Coke to increase price 2.36 percent. Coke's price reaction function is positively sloped with regard to Pepsi price. Since the products are substitutes, this is consistent with (confirms) the generalized Bertrand oligopoly model. As we will show below, an increase in Pepsi price shifts the Coke demand curve out, so, other factors held constant, Coke's profit-maximizing price increases.

Equation 8.6 (see middle of next page) is the price reaction function for Pepsi. Again, Pepsi trade promotion variables drive Pepsi price, and Pepsi reacts positively to an increase in Coke price. A 10 percent increase in Coke price leads to a 16.3 percent increase in Pepsi price.

If we fix the trade promotion variables for Coke and Pepsi at their average values, one obtains reaction functions that one can graph in two dimensions: Coke and Pepsi prices. Figure 8.7 is the graph of these reaction functions (R_i, i = Coke, Pepsi) that also are given as Equations 8.7 and 8.8.

$$R_{Coke} : P_{Coke} = 2.73216 P_{Pepsi}^{0.236} \qquad 8.7$$

$$R_{Pepsi} : P_{Pepsi} = 2.9482 P_{Coke}^{0.1626} \qquad 8.8$$

Note that if one holds the trade promotion variables constant, in this example at their average values, the reaction functions are two equations with two unknowns, the prices. Thus one can solve for the profit-maximizing (equilibrium) prices of this generalized Bertrand duopoly pricing game.

Figure 8.7 **Price Reaction Curves for the Classic Coca-Cola and Pepsi Brands When All Other Explanatory Variables Are at Their Average Values**

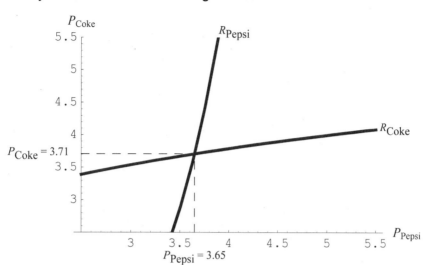

$$\ln(P_{Pepsi}) = 1.255 + 0.1626\ln(P_{Coke}) - 0.0021(AvWtP\operatorname{Re}d_{Pepsi}) - 0.0014(\%VolMer_{Pepsi}) \qquad 8.6$$

where:

$AvWtPRed_i$ = Average Weighted Price Reduction (%) when the brand is on trade promotion, i = Coke, Pepsi

$\%VolMer_i$ = Percent Volume Sold on Trade Promotion (Any Merchandising), i = Coke, Pepsi

In Figure 8.7 the interaction of the reaction curves gives the equilibrium prices. Coke's equilibrium price is $3.71 and Pepsi's is $3.65.

These are, in fact, the average values for Coke and Pepsi. Therefore, the equilibrium market shares are the average market shares for Coke and Pepsi, namely, 45.2 percent and 44.6 percent, respectively, as illustrated in Figures 8.5 and 8.6. The equilibrium will not be at the average values if one or more explanatory variables are set at other than average value.[37]

Next we use this model to gain insight into Coke and Pepsi pricing strategies. Note in Figure 8.7 that the reaction curves are close to being horizontal for Coke and vertical for Pepsi. If they were horizontal (Coke) and vertical (Pepsi), then a shift in either would have no effect on the price of the other. Horizontal and vertical only occur if the cross price coefficients in the demand equations (8.1 and 8.2) are both zero. This is a most unlikely event for any brand in a differentiated product oligopoly because it means that the brand is in a market unto itself, i.e., it is a monopoly. Increases in its price do not cause consumers to switch to another brand; there are no substitutes for the brand. This insight and the estimation results as displayed in Figure 8.7

Figure 8.8   **The Impact of a 20 Percent Reduction in Trade Promotion by Coca-Cola**

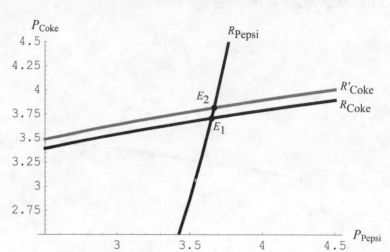

indicate that Coke and Pepsi are substitutes and some competition does exist between them.

Figure 8.8 illustrates how a 20 percent reduction in Coca-Cola Classic's trade promotion variables shifts its reaction curve up. Reducing promotion (sale) events elevates Coke's price to the new equilibrium E_2. Pepsi's price at E_2 is also higher.

Now we analyze how a decrease in Coke trade promotion affects the market shares for Pepsi as well as Coke. Figure 8.9 illustrates the shift in Coke's equilibrium price and share. E_1 is the initial equilibrium. After a 20 percent decrease in the values of the Coke Classic price reduction and percent volume sold on trade promotion variables in Equation 8.7, Coke's new equilibrium in Figure 8.9 is at E_2.

Here is how we move from E_1 to E_2 in Figure 8.9. As reported in Table 8.11, when one solves the two price reaction equations at the new level of Coke promotion, one finds that Coke price increases 11 cents to $3.82, a 2.96 percent increase. Pepsi reacts positively to this price change and increases its price two cents. This higher Pepsi

price shifts Coke's demand curve out in Figure 8.9. Coca-Cola Classic's market share decreases only 1.7 percentage points to 43.5 percent. If Pepsi did not react (i.e., no sympathetic increase in Pepsi's price), then Coke's price increase would decrease its share more, 2.0 percentage points to 43.2 percent, and equilibrium is at E'_2. The fact that Pepsi follows Coke's price lead enhances Coke's pricing power.

Figure 8.10 shows what happens to Pepsi when Coke reduces trade promotions 20 percent. Pepsi's equilibrium shifts from E_1 to E_2. Since Figures 8.9 and 8.10 have the same scale, one can see that the reduction in Coke's trade promotion and Pepsi's rather muted price reaction result in a rather large increase in Pepsi's market share. As Table 8.11 indicates, it increases 1.2 percentage points to 45.8 percent. If Pepsi had not raised price, its share would have increased even more to 46.1 percent and equilibrium at point E'_2 in Figure 8.10. This analysis indicates that Pepsi essentially lets Coke reduce its trade promotion without matching it with a similar price increase. Coke loses (1.2/1.7)

Figure 8.9   **The Effect of the Change in Pepsi's Price on Coca-Cola's Demand**

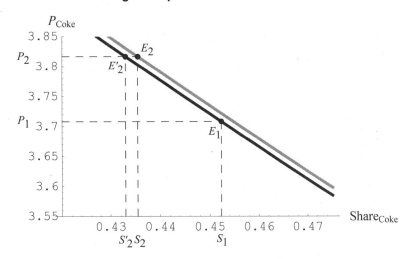

Table 8.11

The Impact of a 20 Percent Reduction in Trade Promotion by Coke

	Initial equilibrium (E_1)	20% reduction in $AvWtPRed_{Coke}$ and % $VolMer_{Coke}$, (E_2)	Absolute Δ	Percentage Δ	(E'_2)	Absolute Δ	Percentage Δ
P^*_{Coke}	3.71	3.82	0.11	2.96	3.82	0.11	2.96
P^*_{Pepsi}	3.65	3.67	0.02	0.55	3.65	0.0	0.0
S^*_{Coke}	45.2%	43.5%	−1.7	−3.76	43.2%	−2.0	−4.42
S^*_{Pepsi}	44.6%	45.8%	1.2	2.69	46.1%	1.5	3.36

Source: Calculations based on Ronald W. Cotterill, Andrew W. Franklin, and Li Yu Ma, "Measuring Market Power Effects in Differentiated Product Industries: An Application to the Soft Drink Industry," Food Marketing Policy Center Research Report, No. 32 (Storrs, CT: University of Connecticut, April 1996). Available online at http://www.fmpc.uconn.edu.

71 percent of its share loss to Pepsi. The rest goes to Royal Crown and Dr Pepper.

Clearly, Pepsi and Coke are each other's main competitors. If Pepsi's reaction coefficient on Coke's price in Equation 8.8 were higher than 0.163, Pepsi's price increase would be greater. In this instance, Coke's demand curve would shift out more in Figure 8.9 and Coke would lose less share with its 11-cent price increase. In Figure 8.10, Pepsi's demand curve would shift out by the same amount, but Pepsi's price would be higher. Hence, it would capture less share on the top curve in Figure 8.10. Such an increase in price is often described as an increase in tacit collusion. It improves the profit of both competitors.

One finds a very similar result if we analyze a 20 percent decrease in trade promotions by Pepsi. Coke's price increases very little and it captures most of Pepsi's share loss. Similarly, it would be instructive to analyze a 20 percent increase in trade

Figure 8.10   **The Effect of the Change in Coke's Price on Pepsi's Demand**

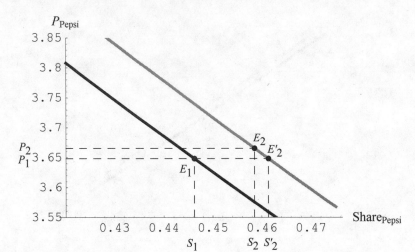

promotions by Coke or Pepsi (you might try this using graphs where the demand curves shift in the opposite direction).

This analysis of competition between Coke and Pepsi is entirely consistent with the commonly observed alternating trade promotion offers by companies: One week one is on sale, and the other is on sale the next.[38] Marginal consumers switch between brands. Neither Coke nor Pepsi cuts price much to deter this shift at the margin.

Policy Analysis in the CSD Industry

Coca-Cola and Pepsi are large global firms with dominant shares of the CSD industry in many countries where they operate, including the United States. Few deny that these companies possess market power. Coca-Cola and Pepsi are "price makers," not "price takers." They create market price and advertising structures that smaller fringe firms regard as part of the market environment when planning their own marketing strategies.

From a policy perspective, two critical and related issues arise from the market pricing power of Coca-Cola and Pepsi: (1) What is the source of each brand's market power? Is it unilateral or coordinated market powers or both? What is the mixture? Unilateral market power emanates from brand loyalty in differentiated product markets or market share dominance in homogenous product markets. Coordinated market power comes from tacit collusion and price followship (what happens if other firms follow).[39] (2) Once one understands the source of their market power and its strength, how do antitrust laws apply to strategic moves by these companies?

In this section, we will address each question in turn. First, we will focus on the sources and levels of power in the Cola sector of the CSD, and then we shift our attention to the Clayton Antitrust Act and as elaborated in U.S. Horizontal Merger Antitrust Guidelines. Finally, another policy topic of interest is the link between CSD consumption and obesity. We will review some relevant research on the issue, and state level initiatives to ban all CSDs, including diet sodas, in public schools and the industry response.

Figure 8.11 **Measurement of Market Pricing Power**

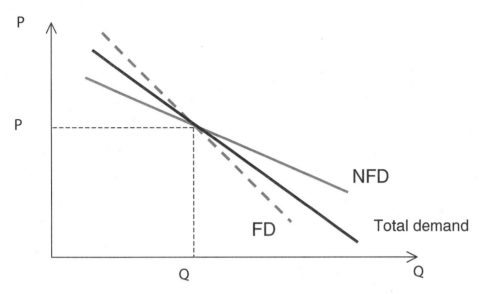

Sources and Levels of Market Power in the Cola Sector of the CSD

Analysis of market power in the United States and elsewhere currently uses a common economic approach that analyzes the possible exercise of coordinated and/or unilateral market power. This, however, has not always been the case; historically, the United States focused primarily on coordinated effects, which are sometimes called tacit collusion. Firms in a tight oligopoly may coordinate pricing via price signaling and/or price followship practices. Would a merger enhance this ability to tacitly collude and elevate prices?

In the European Union, early antitrust enforcement focused on the unilateral power that a dominant firm might possess and whether a horizontal merger would create or enhance a dominant firm's pricing power. In the 1980s, economists generalized the dominant firm model for a homogeneous product such as coal or steel to differentiated products such as CSD or breakfast cereal. A CSD brand, for example, possesses unilateral market power to the extent that other brands are not strong substitutes for it.[40] This is the market power that the demand curves for Coke (Figure 8.5) and Pepsi (Figure 8.6) capture. A brand manager can raise price, even when other firms do not change price, and not lose all sales to other firms.

A brand may also possess coordinated market power if it is part of a portfolio of brands that are jointly priced and if the large firms that have such portfolios signal and follow each other's price moves. In this case, the prices of other brands are not constant. One has an entirely new type of demand curve, one that measures "followship." In contrast to the Marshallian, or partial demand curve, which assumes that all other prices remain constant, this total demand curve incorporates the reactions of other brands to a price change.

To analyze how much unilateral and coordinated market power a brand such as Pepsi has, we turn our attention to Figure 8.11. The brand is initially at equilibrium (P^*, Q^*). If this was a perfectly competitive market (i.e., other available brands are perfect substitutes), then any increase in this brand's price would result in zero sales. Its demand curve in this undifferentiated market is perfectly flat at value P^*. The nonfollowship demand curve illustrates what occurs when the brand is differentiated, but not so strongly differentiated that it has no substitutes, and when no substitute brand reacts and changes its price. In other words, this is the partial equilibrium (Marshallian) demand curve that we estimated and used in the last section.

Now we turn to total demand curves. Each incorporates price reactions by other brands into its demand schedule.[41] Define a total demand curve as follows. A total demand curve gives the schedule of quantities that a brand manager can sell at different prices when the impact via cross-price elasticities of other brands' reactions to the price change is included. Mathematically, for the Coke and Pepsi brand example, one has the following formula for the total elasticity:[42]

$$\eta_i^T = \eta_{ii} + \eta_{ij}R_{ji} \qquad 8.9$$

where:

i = Coke or Pepsi

j = brand of the rival

η_i^T = the ith brands' total elasticity

η_{ii} = the ith brands' partial own price elasticity (holding the other price constant at some value)

η_{ij} = the cross price elasticity for the ith quantity with regard to the jth price

R_{ji} = the price reaction elasticity that gives the percent change in price j for a 1 percent change in price i.

The total demand curve illustrated in Figure 8.11 is less elastic than the Non-Followship Demand (NFD) curve because the price reaction curves generally have positive slopes ($R_{ji} > 0$), and brands in an industry generally are substitutes ($\eta_{ij} > 0$). Since η_{ii}, the partial own price elasticity, is negative, the total own price elasticity is less elastic than the partial. This implies that near (P^*,Q^*) the total demand curve has a steeper negative slope than the NFD (Marshallian) demand curve.

As tacit collusion becomes more powerful, a brand's total demand curve rotates to become even less elastic. If tacit collusion is perfect (i.e., rather than pricing independently, the Coke and Pepsi brand managers tightly follow each other's price moves and jointly maximize profits for the two brands), one obtains the Followship Demand (FD) curve in Figure 8.11. It is the least elastic of the three demand curves. Since the elasticity as defined has negative values, mathematically one has:

$$\eta_{ii} < \eta_i^T < \eta_i^C < -1 \qquad 8.10$$

where:

η_{ii} = unilateral own price elasticity

η_i^T = total own price elasticity

η_i^C = fully collusive own price elasticity

With Figure 8.11 and these three demand curves for a particular brand in hand, we now can measure the brand's total market power, i.e., the power that comes from unilateral and coordinated pricing. Intuitively, one can visualize Figure 8.11 as a fuel gauge in a car. The price axis measures how much fuel is in the tank. If the demand curve needle is perfectly flat at P^*, the tank is empty ... no market power. If the demand curve needle rotates to the NFD level, one has some market power and it is due to unilateral features of the brand, including brand loyalty created by the characteristics of the product and advertising. As the fuel gauge needle rotates to the total demand position, one registers the impact of price followship as well as the unilateral power. The fuel tank is full (market power) when the total demand curve rotates and is identical to the FD curve.

One can measure the level and source of market power with the following indexes. The Cotterill Index (*CI*) defines the degree of total market power that a brand possesses.[43] It is:

$$CI = \frac{\eta_i^C}{\eta_i^T} = \frac{fully\ collusive\ elasticity}{total\ elasticity}$$

$$8.11$$

and $$0 \le CI \le 1$$

A brand's total market power is complete when collusion is perfect and the total demand curve is identical to the FD curve in Figure 8.11. This gives $\eta_1^T = \eta_1^C$ and the *CI* = 1. The market power "tank" is full.

One can decompose the observed degree of total market power that is measured by the Cotterill Index into its two components: unilateral and coordinated market power. The Rothschild Index (*RI*) gives the degree of unilateral market power that a brand possesses.[44] It is:

$$RI = \frac{\eta_i^C}{\eta_{ii}} = \frac{fully\ collusive\ elasticity}{unilateral\ elasticity}$$

$$8.12$$

and $$0 < RI < 1$$

Note that when the unilateral elasticity is negative infinity, the unilateral demand curve is perfectly flat in Figure 8.11 and the brand has no unilateral market power. Then the *RI* = 0. If the brand has no substitutes, then the FD curve is effectively its market demand curve. Moreover, the unilateral demand curve is identical to it and the *RI* = 1. In between these extremes the brand has a modicum of unilateral market power.

If the *CI* = 0, the *RI* = 0. A brand that has no coordinated and unilateral power has no unilateral power. Also the *CI* ≥ *RI*. A brand can have unilateral power but no coordinated power.

A third index, the Chamberlin Quotient (*CQ*), measures the proportion of total market power that is due to tacit collusion.[45] It is

$$CQ = \frac{CI - RI}{CI} = 1 - \frac{\eta_i^T}{\eta_{ii}}$$

$$8.13$$

Cotterill, Franklin, and Ma provide elasticity and market power index estimates for all brands of regular soft drinks.[46] Table 8.12 reproduces their results for the Coca-Cola Classic and Pepsi brands. The Marshallian partial (unilateral) elasticity for Coke is −3.1078. Coke's total elasticity is less elastic and −2.825. Therefore, as demonstrated in the last section, when Coke changes its price, substitute brands tend to follow that price change. This reduces consumers' switching options, so Coke quantity does not go down as much for a given price increase. Note, however, that the fully collusive elasticity for Coke is much less elastic, −2.20. If all substitute brands follow Coke's price move, a 1 percent increase in Coke price only reduces Coke quantity 2.2 percent. If no brands follow, the unilateral loss is 3.0178 percent.

The Cotterill Index indicates that the combination of unilateral and coordinated power exploit 77.89 percent of fully collusive/monopoly pricing power. The Rothschild Index for Coke in Table 8.12 indicates that Coca-Cola Classic has a large amount of unilateral market power. At 0.7291 it means that Coke's unilateral market power is 72.91 percent of fully collusive/monopoly pricing power. The Chamberlin Quotient confirms that most of the existing power is unilateral. Only 6.39 percent of its total power is due to other brands' following Coke's price changes. Tacit collusion exists; however, it is not an important source of market power.

The reported results for Pepsi are even stronger. Its total power index is 83.72 percent. Pepsi's unilateral power, as measured by its Rothschild Index, is 75.47 percent of fully collusive/monopoly pricing power. Only 9.86 percent of Pepsi's pricing

Table 8.12

Brand-Level Elasticities and Indices of Market Power for the Coca-Cola Classic and Pepsi Brands

	Unilateral	Total	Fully collusive	Cotterill index (col3/col2)	Rothschild index (col3/col1)	Chamberlin quotient 1−(col2/col1)
	(1)	(2)	(3)	(4)	(5)	(6)
Coke	−3.0178	−2.825	−2.2004	0.7789	0.7291	0.0639
Pepsi	−2.8858	−2.6013	−2.1778	0.8372	0.7547	0.0986

Source: Ronald W. Cotterill, Andrew W. Franklin, and Li Yu Ma, "Measuring Market Power Effects in Differentiated Product Industries: An Application to the Soft Drink Industry," Food Marketing Policy Center Research Report no. 32, (Storrs: University of Connecticut, April 1996).

power is due to other brands, following its price changes.

These results demonstrate that the top two CSD brands have considerable pricing power due to brand loyalty and their strong consumer franchise. Only a small amount of exercised pricing power is due to coordinated pricing games.[47]

Analysis of the Price Impacts of a Merger Between the Coca-Cola Classic and Pepsi Brands

The possession and exercise of market power is not in itself illegal. This is true, not only for uni-lateral power derived from strong brand loyalty, but also for coordinated market power that arises from tacit collusion. Simply following other firms' price changes is not illegal. However, a merger or acquisition that increases either type of market power, and consequently the price for one or more brands, is unlawful. It violates the Clayton Antitrust Act and similar merger-oriented antitrust policies in other nations, including countries in the European Union.

Here, we will illustrate the economic analysis that is at the core of the evaluation of changes in unilateral market power when two differentiated products merge.[48] Currently Coca-Cola Classic

and Pepsi are managed separately. When Coke raises its price, Pepsi does not follow in lock step. Consumers now have the opportunity to switch to lower-priced Pepsi, the closest substitute to Coke. What if one of the companies acquired the other's brand? For example, assume Coke acquires the Pepsi brand. Then, when they raise the price of Coke Classic, they can also raise the price of Pepsi, effectively trapping consumers that would have switched to Pepsi.

Internalizing the cross price elasticities in this fashion means that the profit-maximizing price for both brands will increase. In this example the merger increases the unilateral market power of the brands and therefore violates the Clayton Antitrust Act. Here is how one arrives at this conclusion. Following Hausman, Leonard, and Zona, the percentage increase in a brand's price due to the merger is:[49]

$$\alpha_j = \frac{100}{\left(\dfrac{e_{jj}}{1+e_{jj}}\right)(1-\theta_j^{M*})} - 100 \qquad 8.14$$

where:

e_{jj} = brand j unilateral own price elasticity.
θ_j^{M*} = brand j markup over marginal cost after the merger.[50]

We have estimates of the unilateral own price elasticities. One obtains estimates of the post-merger markups from the first order condition (FOC) of the joint profit maximization problem.

The post-merger profit maximization problem now includes both brands:

$$MAX_{p_1, p_2} \; \pi = (p_1 - MC_1) \; q_1(p_1, p_2) +$$

$$(p_2 - MC_2) \; q_2(p_1, \; p_2) \qquad 8.15$$

The FOC can be written as follows:

$$S_1 + S_1 \eta_{11} \theta_1^M + S_2 \eta_{21} \theta_2^M = 0 \qquad 8.16$$

$$S_2 + S_1 \eta_{12} \theta_1^M + S_2 \eta_{22} \theta_2^M = 0 \qquad 8.17$$

Given the market shares, S_1 and S_2 and the elasticities, η_{11}, η_{21}, η_{22}, and η_{12}, one has two equations and two unknowns, the markups θ_1^M and θ_2^M.[51] One solves for the markups. For Coca-Cola Classic, at the average share values with the corresponding estimated elasticities, the post-merger markup over marginal cost is 0.424725. For Pepsi it is 0.44284. Using values of the unilateral own price elasticities, one finds that the merger would lead to a 16.2 percent increase in Classic price and a 17.2 percent increase in Pepsi price.

As with any analysis this precise, there are potentially significant caveats. First, we have ignored other dimensions of competition, including advertising and new brand introductions; however, to the extent that they underlie the estimated brand-level demand curve slopes, they are included. Second, we have assumed that the merger generates no cost efficiencies. The marginal costs for both brands remain unaffected by the merger. If there are cost efficiencies, one can expand the analysis to estimate them, and their incorporation will reduce the price increases.[52] Conceivably, they could more

than offset the gain in market power and lead a profit-maximizing firm to cut price on one or both brands after the merger.[53] Another caveat is that price increases of this magnitude may alter the market shares and demand elasticity values that are exogenous (constant) in this price-enhancement computation. One may need a nonlinear specification of the two FOC equations wherein share and elasticities are functions of prices. One then must solve nonlinear equations, a more complicated but feasible task. Finally, this model is static. Dynamic substitution and reaction effects due to changes in price and possibly advertising would require a dynamic model.

Even with these caveats, the analysis of market power and mergers leads to general conclusions concerning the carbonated soft drink industry. Brands possess substantial unilateral market power. Most brands face significant substitutes, but those substitutes do not constrain unilateral price moves much, at least in the static models presented here. There is little tacit collusion. Prices do not move in concert. Mergers of brands that are next-best substitutes such as Coca-Cola Classic and Pepsi, the two leading brands in the CSD industry, will elevate prices. This suggests that the Federal Trade Commission will never allow a merger between any of the three leading CSD firms because such a merger will lead to a substantial increase in market power.

Obesity and Carbonated Soft Drinks

Each twelve-ounce can of sweetened soft drink contains the equivalent of ten teaspoons of sugar.[54] Sixty-five percent of U.S. adults are either overweight or obese.[55] "Annually obesity-related diseases in adults and children account for more than 300,000 deaths and more than $100 billion per year in [health] treatment costs."[56] The evidence is incontrovertible. Obesity is the largest chronic health problem that Americans have today.

Recently, researchers have asked whether there is a link between sugar consumption via soft drinks and obesity, an issue that is particularly heated regarding children. Many have sought to eliminate all soft drinks from schools to combat poor nutrition, obesity, and related long-term health costs.

Doctors, health-care professionals, and nutritionists have documented the link between soft drink consumption and obesity. A study published in the *Journal of the American Medical Association* illustrates the rigorous experimental design that these epidemiological studies use.[57] That study examined the association between consumption of sugar-sweetened beverages and weight change. It analyzed 51,603 women for whom complete dietary information and body weight were tracked in 1991, 1995, and 1999. Schulze et al. reports[58]:

> Those with stable consumption patterns had no difference in weight gain, but weight gain over a 4-year period was highest among women who increased their sugar-sweetened soft drink consumption from 1 or fewer drinks per week to 1 or more drinks per day (multivariate-adjusted means, 4.69 kg for 1991 to 1995 and 4.20 kg for 1995 to 1999) and was smallest among women who decreased their intake (1.34 and 0.15 kg for the two periods, respectively) after adjusting for lifestyle and dietary confounders.[59]

The authors conclude that higher consumption of sugar-sweetened beverages is associated with a greater magnitude of weight gain. This study also concludes that increased sweetened beverage consumption significantly increases the occurrence of type 2 diabetes.[60]

The issue of soft drink consumption and obesity among children is even more explosive. "Results from the 1999–2002 National Health and Nutrition Examination Survey (NHANES) using measured heights and weights indicate that an estimated 16 percent of children and adolescents ages 6–19 years are overweight. This represents a 45 percent

increase from the overweight estimates of 11 percent obtained from NHANES III (1988–94)."[61] Soft drink consumption by adolescents has increased by 300 percent in 20 years.[62] This is direct evidence of the well-known "couch potato" phenomenon. Kids spend several hours daily watching television and playing video games with a soft drink in hand.

Soft drink availability, and promotion, in schools is also an issue. According to an August 2005 survey by the American Beverage Association, 45 percent of all school vending sales are sweetened soda.[63] Soft drink distributors pay schools to place vending machines, resulting in a significant source of income for many cash-strapped school systems. Our review of per capita consumption from all sources and from retail supermarkets in the introduction implicated increased CSD consumption away from home locations, including schools.

Consider the following facts that the American Academy of Pediatrics present in their Policy Statement titled "Soft Drinks in Schools."

- Serving sizes have increased from 6.5 oz in the 1950s to 12 oz in the 1960s and 20 oz by the late 1990s.
- Between 56 percent and 86 percent of children in school consume at least 1 soft drink daily with the highest amount ingested by adolescent males. Of this group 20 percent consume 4 or more servings daily.
- Each 12 oz sugared soft drink consumed daily has been associated with a 0.18 point increase in a child's BMI (body mass index) and a 60 percent increase in risk of obesity.[64]
- Sugar-free soft drinks constitute only 14 percent of the adolescent soft drink market.[65]

The American Academy of Pediatrics recommendations include the following:

1. Pediatricians should work to eliminate sweetened drinks in schools.
2. Pediatricians should advocate for creation of a school nutrition advisory council.
3. School districts should invite public discussion

before making any decisions to create a vended food or drink contract.

4. (Any such contract) should be tempered so that it does not promote overconsumption.

5. Consumption or advertising of sweetened soft drinks within the classroom should be eliminated.[66]

Not all researchers, however, have condemned soft drinks in schools. One study by Forshee, Storey, and Ginevan, Center for Food, Nutrition, and Agriculture Policy, University of Maryland, was published in the academic journal *Risk Analysis*. Here is the article's abstract:

Risk analysis is a widely used tool to understand problems in food safety policy, but it is seldom applied to nutrition policy. We propose that risk analysis be applied more often to inform debates on nutrition policy, and we conduct a risk assessment of the relationship of regular carbonated soft drink (RCSD) consumption in schools and body mass index (BMI) as a case study. Data for RCSD consumption in schools were drawn from three data sets: the Continuing Survey of Food Intake by individuals 1994–1996, 1998 (CSFII), the National Health and Nutrition Examination Survey 1999–2000 (NHANES), and the National Family Opinion (NFO) WorldGroup Share of Intake Panel (SIP) study. We used the largest relationship between RCSD and BMI that was published by prospective observational studies to characterize the maximum plausible relationship in our study. Consumption of RCSD in schools was low in all three data sets, ranging from 15 g/day in NFO-SIP to 60 g/day in NHANES. There was no relationship between RCSD consumption from all sources and BMI in either the CSFII or the NHANES data. The risk assessment showed no impact on BMI by removing RCSD consumption in school. These findings suggest that focusing adolescent overweight prevention programs on RCSD in schools will not have a significant impact on BMI.[67]

This study was funded by the American Beverage Association (the soft drink industry); however, the author maintains that he "followed a very rigorous scientific process" and that the Association had no input into the research process.[68] Basically, this study concludes that not enough soft drink is consumed in schools to have a meaningful impact on obesity. We offer one criticism of this conclusion. Averages can be misleading. When asked how deep the river is, the farmer responded on average three feet. The traveler promptly stepped into an eight-foot-deep pool and drowned. Not all kids drink soda at school; however, some may binge.

On April 17, 2006, Neville Isdell, the chairman and CEO of Coca-Cola, was interviewed by a *Wall Street Journal* reporter. He had this to say about the obesity and schools issue.

WSJ: How well is the company responding to the obesity issue?

Mr. Isdell: We are in what I would call the bull's eye of public opinion with regard to calorie consumption. It's something I inherited and something as an industry we have not been able to rebut effectively at this point in time. It's something we are working diligently on as an industry. . . . We really need to widen the debate. For example, Diet Coke, a zero-calorie beverage, is actually in the obesity debate because there has been a demonization of carbonated soft drinks. But if it's really about obesity, why would you not want people to drink a diet soft drink?

WSJ: Why should any regular sodas be sold in middle or high schools?

Mr. Isdell: It's high schools where the current policy we have is 50% noncarbonated drinks. In the middle schools (full-calorie sodas are sold from vending machines) only after school (according to an industry wide agreement.)

I saw this interesting piece on a guy in California who came out very strongly and said, "Why am I allowed to vote and I can own a gun, but I can't choose my own soft drink?" I think when you reach high school, you do have a level of sophistication and you can be allowed to choose what you wish. . . . There are some schools where some kids are making good money bootlegging soft drinks in and selling them to students. . . . I think that is not all bad for us. After all, every kid likes being rebellious.[69]

California and some local school districts have banned soft drink sales in public schools. New York City, for example, permits only low-fat milk, water, and 100 percent fruit juice . . . no CSD, no sports drinks such as Gatorade or energy drinks such as Red Bull.[70] The most recent move was a ban on all CSD and sports and energy drinks in public schools in Connecticut. The law also sets aside $4.7 million (10 cents per served meal) to triple the amount of money paid to school districts for nutritious lunches.[71]

Four days after the Connecticut legislature decided to ban all soft drinks, including diet sodas, the big three soft drink firms, who control 90 percent of vending machines in schools, announced an agreement with health advocates who were threatening a class action lawsuit on behalf of children. There will be no litigation, such as occurred in the cigarette industry. In return, the big three will withdraw all "sweetened drinks like Coke, Pepsi and iced teas from school cafeterias and vending machines."[72] This agreement allows diet soft drinks such as Diet Coke and Pepsi to remain.

Summary and Conclusions on the CSD Industry

The carbonated soft drink industry is the largest beverage industry in the United States. Per capita CSD consumption averaged over fifty-two gallons in 2004. Coca-Cola, PepsiCo, and Cadbury Schweppes dominate the CSD industry, accounting for 89 percent of U.S. sales in 2004. The industry is mature and the leading companies' volumes have stagnated in recent years. Coca-Cola volume grew only 4.56 percent from 1998 to 2004. Its leading regular brand, Coca-Cola Classic, lost market share while its leading diet brand, Diet Coke, gained share during the same period. PepsiCo and Cadbury Schweppes performances were similar. Consumers are shifting to diet soft drinks.

Consumers also are expanding their consumption of New Age beverages, which include sports drinks (Gatorade, Powerade), energy drinks (Red Bull), tea and coffee drinks (Snapple, Starbucks Frappuccino), and bottled water (Dasani and Aquafina). The leading carbonated soft drink firms are major players in the New Age beverage sector. They sell all of the leading brands listed here except for Red Bull.

Market power in the CSD industry is the ability to elevate price without losing all sales to substitute products offered by competitors. Firms that have market power are price setters, not price takers. Each of the three leading firms in the CSD industry possesses market power.

Introducing new brands into the CSD industry and advertising both new and old brands are competitive strategies that favor the big three firms relative to entrants. This fact underpins entry barriers in the CSD industry and the observed high level of seller concentration. Entry barriers contribute to the exercise of market power. One might conjecture that the expansion of New Age beverages would limit the market power of brands in the CSD industry. Our analysis shows otherwise for two reasons. First, the leading brands in these neighboring industries are controlled by the big three CSD firms. Second, and fundamentally more critical, is that estimated brand-level own price elasticities for the leading brands in the CSD industry clearly document that market power exists at the brand level. If new age beverages were strong substitutes for carbonated soft drinks, brand-level demand curves would be much more elastic and prices would be lower. The second result implies that New Age beverages are not in the antitrust product market for carbonated soft drinks.

The documented brand-level market power in this industry, including power levels for the two leading brands, Coca-Cola Classic and Pepsi, is predominantly unilateral market power. Coordinated market power via tacit collusion games plays a very minor role in this industry. Unilateral power comes from brand loyalty and the advertising that parent firms design to enhance brand loyalty over time.

With the advent of the 1992 U.S. Federal Merger Guidelines, unilateral market power explicitly joined coordinated effects as a possible reason to prohibit a merger. We used estimated brand-level elasticities for Coca-Cola Classic and Pepsi to illustrate how one can analyze the impact of a merger on unilateral pricing power. If Coke Classic and Pepsi were to merge, their prices would increase 16.2 percent and 17.2 percent, respectively. These price results are lower if the merger creates cost efficiencies. They may also be lower if one moves from this static analysis to consider the dynamics of market share changes and elasticity changes.

Finally, we examined the link between obesity and consumption of carbonated soft drinks. Epidemiological studies by physicians and health professionals have established this linkage. A major issue is the presence of soft drinks in schools. At least one social science study refutes the impact of that presence on obesity. After assessing the research, several states have banned sweetened soft drinks from schools. In May 2006 the big three firms voluntarily announced that they would withdraw all sweetened soft drinks from public schools. This will undoubtedly accelerate the switch to diet soda. It also eliminates threatened and potentially costly litigation on the issue.

Coca-Cola, PepsiCo, and Cadbury Schweppes are global companies. Their performance in the United States may shed light on their operations elsewhere; however, differences in consumer preferences, demand, advertising, logistics, production, and marketing laws undoubtedly require a country-by-country assessment. Therein lies an opportunity for students who would understand and contribute to the success of this industry.

Notes

Ronald W. Cotterill is the director of the Food Marketing Policy Center and Professor of Agricultural Economics and Economics, University of Connecticut; William Putsis is a professor of marketing, Kenan-Flagler Business School, University of North Carolina at Chapel Hill; Adam N. Rabinowitz, and Inga Druckute are graduate research assistants, Food Marketing Policy Center, University of Connecticut. This research was supported by USDA Special Research Grant No. 2005–34178–15694.

1. Beverage Digest, *Fact Book 2005, Statistical Yearbook of Non-Alcoholic Beverages,* 10th ed. (Bedford Hills, NY: 2005).

2. Gallons per household are not equivalent to gallons per capita. The USDA estimates that in 1999 39.8 percent of soft drinks, 55.9 percent of milk, 30.9 percent of bottled water, 82.3 percent of fruit juices, 65.4 percent of ready-to-drink coffee, and 69 percent of tea drinks were purchased in supermarkets. Oral Capps, Jr., Annette Clauson, Joanne Guthrie, Grant Pittman, and Matthew Stockton, *Contributions of Nonalcoholic Beverages to the U.S. Diet,* Economic Research Service Report No. 1 (Washington, DC: U.S. Department of Agriculture, March 2005).

3. The source for the information on milk and milk substitutes is the Information Resources, Inc., *Marketing Fact Book* (Chicago, IL: Author, 1998 and 2004). See the total U.S. all outlets tables.

4. Marian Burros and Melanie Warner, "Bottlers Agree to a School Ban on Sweet Drinks," *New York Times* (May 4, 2006), p. A–1.

5. This history of the industry was compiled from a variety of sources, including the online home pages of the Coca-Cola Company, PepsiCo, Inc., and Cadbury Schweppes. In addition, various details were obtained from Wikipedia (www.en.wikipedia.org/wiki/Pepsi) and Inventors About (http://inventors.about.com).

6. See http://inventors.about.com/od/cstartinventions/a/coca_cola.htm and "Coca-Cola: History of an American Icon" (available on DVD).

7. The beverage industry classifies bottled water, energy and sport drinks, and tea and coffee drinks as "New Age Beverages" because these brands have come into existence over the past twenty years.

8. Cott Corporation. Available at www.cott.com/.

9. www.pbg.com/pbg/servlet/index.do.

10. www.ccbanet.com/.

11. www.forbes.com/business/feeds/afx/2006/04/25/afx2693923.html.

12. William Comanor, "Vertical Mergers, Market Power, and the Antitrust Laws," *American Economic Review* 57 (May 1967), pp. 259–62.

13. Timothy J. Muris, David T. Scheffman, and Pablo

T. Spiller, "Strategy and Transaction Costs: The Organization of Distribution in the Carbonated Soft Drink Industry," *Journal of Economics & Management Strategy* 1, 1 (1992), pp. 83–128.

14. See, for example, Ronald W. Cotterill and William Putsis, "Do Models of Vertical Strategic Interaction for National and Store Brands Meet the Market Test?" *Journal of Retailing* 77 (2001), pp. 83–109; David Besanko, Jean-Pierre Dube, and Sachin Gupta, "Own-Brand and Cross-Brand Retail Pass-Through," *Marketing Science* 24, 10 (2005), pp. 123–37; Moorthy Sridhar, "A General Theory of Pass-Through in Channels with Category Management and Retail Competition," *Marketing Science* 24, 10 (2005), pp. 110–22.

15. Cotterill and Putsis, "Do Models of Vertical Strategic Interaction . . ." and Robert D. Tollinson, David Kaplan, and Richard Higgins, *Competition and Concentration: The Economics of the Carbonated Soft Drink Industry* (New York: Lexington Books, 1991).

16. Ronald W. Cotterill, Andrew W. Franklin, and Li Yu Ma, "Measuring Market Power Effects in Differentiated Product Industries: An Application to the Soft Drink Industry," *Food Marketing Policy Center Research Report*, no. 32 (Storrs: University of Connecticut, April 1996). Available online at www.fmpc.uconn.edu.

17. We do so with a caveat, noting that Sudhir has demonstrated that it is possible for one to confound horizontal interaction with vertical issues empirically. Accordingly, this issue must be dealt with carefully and any results interpreted appropriately. For more detail, the interested reader is referred to Karunakaran Sudhir, "Structural Analysis of Manufacturer Pricing in the Presence of a Strategic Retailer," *Marketing Science* 20, 3 (2001), pp. 244–64.

18. Catherine Penn, "2004 R&D Survey: New Role for CEOs and Spectacular R&D Efficiencies Create High Expectations," *Beverage Industry* 95, 1 (January 2004), pp. 35–44.

19. For some interesting reading, see Robert M. McMath and Thom Forbes, *What Were They Thinking?* (New York: Three Rivers Press, 1988).

20. Richard Schmalensee, "Entry Deterrence in the Ready-to-Eat Breakfast Cereal Industry," *Bell Journal of Economics* 9, 2 (1978), pp. 305–27; Barry L. Bayus and William P. Putsis, Jr., "Product Proliferation: An Empirical Analysis of Product Line Determinants and Market Outcomes," *Marketing Science* 18, 2 (1999), pp. 137–53.

21. William P. Putsis, Jr., "An Empirical Study of the Effect of Brand Proliferation on Private Label–National Brand Pricing Behavior," *Review of Industrial Organization* 12 (1997) pp. 355–71.

22. Bayus and Putsis, "Product Proliferation . . ."

23. Ibid.

24. William P. Putsis, Jr., and Barry L. Bayus, "An Empirical Analysis of Firms' Product Line Decisions," *Journal of Marketing Research* 38 (February 2001), pp. 110–18.

25. John Sutton, *Sunk Costs and Market Structure* (Cambridge, MA: MIT Press, 1991).

26. Bayus and Putsis, "Product Proliferation . . ."

27. See, for example, J. Miguel Villas-Boas, "Consumer Learning, Brand Loyalty, and Competition," *Marketing Science* 23, 1 (2004), pp. 134–45; Demetrios Vakratsas, Fred M. Feinberg, Frank M. Bass, and Gurumurthy Kalyanaram, "The Shape of Advertising Response Functions Revisited: A Model of Dynamic Probabilistic Thresholds," *Marketing Science* 23, 1 (2004), pp. 109–19.

28. Jan-Benedict E.M. Steenkamp, Vincent R. Nijs, Dominique M. Hanssens, and Marnik G. Dekimpe, "Competitive Reactions to Advertising and Promotion Attacks," *Marketing Science* 24, 10 (2005), pp. 35–54.

29. More complex models can relax these assumptions and be used to analyze how CSD manufacturers, integrated as independent regional bottlers, and retailers interact in the market channel to determine retail prices. Our model, however, gives a very reasonable approximation of actual CSD manufacturer conduct.

30. Cotterill, Franklin, and Ma, "Measuring Market Power Effects . . ."

31. In the empirical analysis we will not include advertising spending as an independent variable because it was only available on an annual basis, whereas the empirical analysis employs quarterly data. Ideally, we would like to examine the competitive advertising game being played as well. The interested reader should see Farid Gasmi, Jean-Jacques Laffont, and Quang Vuong, "An Econometric Analysis of Collusive Behavior in a Soft-Drink Market," *Journal of Economics and Management Strategy* 1 (1992), pp. 277–311, for such an analysis in this industry, and Steenkamp, Nijs, Hanssens, and Dekimpe, "Competitive Reactions . . . ," for a more general analysis.

32. This functional form is a linear approximation of an almost ideal demand system. It is used in empirical work because it is derived from the general utility model of microeconomic theory. It is flexible, so that empirical results are not constrained, yet one can impose the constraints that economic theory predicts, which are symmetry of cross-price effects and degree zero homogeneity. Symmetry means that the change in the quantity of Coke for a change in Pepsi price equals the change in the quantity of Pepsi for the same change in Coke price. Homogeneity means that a doubling of all prices and expenditures (income) has no effect on quantity demanded. Utility theory requires all demand systems to have these properties.

33. Technically this is a partial equilibrium demand curve. It is also called a Marshallian demand curve in honor of Alfred Marshall, an early leader in the development of microeconomic theory. Later in this chapter we will introduce a total (residual) demand curve. A total demand curve allows other firms to react to a price change, which in turn affects

the quantity sold of the price mover's product via the cross-price elasticities. A total demand curve shows how a brand's quantity changes for a change in its price, given that all other brands are allowed to react and make their best response, i.e., the adjustment that maximizes their profits given the new price for the brand that initiated the price change.

34. Cotterill, Franklin, and Ma, "Measuring Market Power Effects . . ."

35. See Liang for an illustration of the generalized BNDG model. Some economists have disavowed estimating conjectural variation models and prefer to specify alternative games such as the Stackelberg or Forcheimer dominant firm model. The reaction function approach used by Cotterill et al. and the corresponding residual demand approach used by Baker and Bresnahan, which are the basis for the analysis in this chapter, are also consistent with game theory approaches. J.N. Liang, "Price Reaction Functions and Conjectural Variations: An Application to the Breakfast Cereal Industry," *Review of Industrial Organization* 4, 2 (1989), pp. 31–58; Jonathan B. Baker and Timothy F. Bresnahan, "Estimating the Residual Demand Curve Facing a Single Firm," *International Journal of Industrial Organization* 6 (1988), pp. 283–300.

36. Cotterill, Franklin, and Ma, "Measuring Market Power Effects . . ."

37. The "average" result is due to the fact that linear regression equations always go through the average value point in a data set.

38. This is consistent with a mixed strategy in game theory as described in Hal Varian, "A Model of Sales," *American Economic Review* 70, 4 (September 1980), pp. 651–59, and many game theory textbooks.

39. See U.S. DOJ *Horizontal Merger Guidelines,* available online at http://www.usdoj.gov/atr/public/guidelines/hmg.htm.

40. For advanced analysis of unilateral market power, see Ronald W. Cotterill and Lawrence E. Haller, "An Econometric Analysis of the Demand for RTE Cereal: Product Market Definition and Unilateral Market Power Effects," *Food Marketing Policy Center Research Report*, no. 35 (Storrs: University of Connecticut, September 1997); available online at www.fmpc.uconn.edu; Aviv Nevo, "Measuring Market Power in the Ready-to-Eat Cereal Industry," *Econometrica* 69, 2 (March 2001), pp. 307–42.

41. An alternative name for the total demand curve is residual demand curve. This class of demand curves is "total" because it includes the reactions of competing firms. Alternatively, they are "residual" because they are "after" the reactions of others.

42. For *N* brands the formula is:

$$\eta_i^T = \eta_{ii} + \sum_{j \neq i}^{N} \eta_{ij} R_{ji}$$

43. Ronald W. Cotterill and Pierre O. Samson, "Estimating a Brand-Level Demand System for American Cheese Products to Evaluate Unilateral and Coordinated Market Power Strategies," *American Journal of Agricultural Economics* 84 (2002), pp. 817–23.

44. K.W. Rothschild, "The Degree of Monopoly," *Economica* 9 (February 1942), pp. 24–40.

45. Cotterill and Samson, "Estimating a Brand-Level Demand System . . ."

46. Cotterill, Franklin, and Ma, "Measuring Market Power Effects . . ."

47. Not all brands in the regular soft drink category are this powerful. Cotterill, Franklin, and Ma report the following indices for Royal Crown Cola: *RI = 0.3986; CI = 0.4368; CQ = 0.0874.* At the other extreme they find that 7 Up (the uncola) has *RI = 0.99 and CI = 1.04.* This effectively means that 7 Up is so differentiated that it is a monopoly unto itself!

48. For a more complete analysis of market power in the context of the proposed acquisition of the Dr Pepper company by Coca-Cola in 1986, see: Lawrence J. White, "Case 3-Application of the Merger Guidelines: The Proposed Merger of Coca-Cola and Dr Pepper." In John E. Kwoka, Jr., and Lawrence J. White, eds., *The Antitrust Revolution,* pp. 80–98 (New York: Harper-Collins, 1989). That deal was stopped by the U.S. Federal Trade Commission because it violated the Clayton Act.

49. Jerry Hausman, Gregory Leonard, and J. Douglas Zona, "Competitive Analysis with Differentiated Products," Annales D'Économie et de Statistique 34 (1994), pp. 159–80.

50. Actually $\theta_i^M = \dfrac{Pi - MCi}{Pi}$, so these parameters are the post-merger price–cost margins.

51. The mean market shares are: $S_{\text{Coke}} = 0.45233$, $S_{\text{Pepsi}} = 0.44622$. The elasticities are $\eta_{11} = -3.0178$, $\eta_{21} = 0.6455$, $\eta_{22} = -2.8858$, and $\eta_{12} = 0.6429$ (Cotterill, Franklin, and Ma, "Measuring Market Power Effects . . . ," p. 38).

52. Hausman, Leonard, and Zona, "Competitive Analysis."

53. Although technically possible, we know of no unilateral merger analysis that has incorporated efficiency in this fashion and demonstrated a full offset to the increase in unilateral power.

54. American Academy of Pediatrics Policy Statement, "Soft Drinks in Schools," *Pediatrics* 113, 1 (2004), pp. 152–54.

55. National Center for Health Statistics, "Prevalence of Overweight and Obesity Among Adults: United States, 1999–2002" (2005); available online at: www.cdc.gov/nchs/products/pubs/pubd/hestats/obese99/obse99.htm.

56. American Academy of Pediatrics, "Soft Drinks in Schools."

57. Matthias B. Schulze, JoAnn E. Manson, David S. Ludwig, Graham A. Colditz, Meir J. Stampfer, Walter C. Willett, and Frank B. Hu, "Sugar-Sweetened Beverages, Weight Gain, and Incidence of Type 2 Diabetes in Young and Middle-Aged Women," *Journal of the American Medical Association* 292, 8 (2004), pp. 927–34.

58. Schulze et al., "Sugar-Sweetened Beverages . . ."

59. Ibid.

60. Ibid.

61. National Center for Health Statistics, "Prevalence of Overweight and Obesity . . ."

62. American Academy of Pediatrics, "Soft Drinks in Schools."

63. Burros and Warner, "Bottlers Agree . . ."

64. The BMI is a person's weight in pounds divided by height in inches.

65. American Academy of Pediatrics, "Soft Drinks in Schools."

66. Ibid.

67. Richard A. Forshee, Maureen L. Storey, and Michael E. Ginevan, "A Risk Analysis Model of the Relationship Between Beverage Consumption from School Vending Machines and Risk of Adolescent Overweight," *Risk Analysis: An International Journal* 25, 5 (2005), pp. 1121–35.

68. Amanda Gardner, "Study Refutes Soft Drinks' Impact on Kids Obesity," *HealthCentral* (2005); available online at www.healthcentral.com/newsdetail/408/528668.html.

69. Chad Terhune, "Recharging Coca-Cola," *Wall Street Journal* (April 17, 2006), p. B–1.

70. Burros and Warner, "Bottlers Agree . . ."

71. Christopher Keating, "House Puts Lid on Soda," *Hartford Courant* (April 28, 2006), p. A-1.

72. Burros and Warner, "Bottlers Agree . . ."

Selected Readings

Baker, Jonathan B., and Timothy F. Bresnahan. "Estimating the Residual Demand Curve Facing a Single Firm," *International Journal of Industrial Organization* 6 (1988), 283–300.

Cotterill, Ronald W., Andrew W. Franklin, and Li Yu Ma. "Measuring Market Power Effects in Differentiated Product Industries: An Application to the Soft Drink Industry." *Food Marketing Policy Center Research Report,* no. 32. Storrs, CT: University of Connecticut, April 1996. Available online at www.fmpc.uconn.edu.

Cotterill, Ronald W., and Lawrence E. Haller. "An Econometric Analysis of the Demand for RTE Cereal: Product Market Definition and Unilateral Market Power Effects." *Food Marketing Policy Center Research Report,* no. 35. Storrs, CT: University of Connecticut, September 1997. Available online at www.fmpc.uconn.edu.

Cotterill, Ronald W., and Pierre O. Samson. "Estimating a Brand-Level Demand System for American Cheese Products to Evaluate Unilateral and Coordinated Market Power Strategies." *American Journal of Agricultural Economics* 84 (2002), 817–23.

Gasmi, Farid, Jean-Jacques Laffont, and Quang Vuong. "An Econometric Analysis of Collusive Behavior in a Soft-Drink Market." *Journal of Economics and Management Strategy* 1 (1992), 277–311.

Liang, J.N. "Price Reaction Functions and Conjectural Variations: An Application to the Breakfast Cereal Industry." *Review of Industrial Organization* 4, no. 2 (1989), 31–58.

Nevo, Aviv. "Measuring Market Power in the Ready-to-Eat Cereal Industry." *Econometrica* 69, no. 2 (March 2001), 307–42.

Schmalensee, Richard. "Entry Deterrence in the Ready-to-Eat Breakfast Cereal Industry." *Bell Journal of Economics* 9, no. 2 (1978), 305–27.

Steenkamp, Jan-Benedict E.M., Vincent R. Nijs, Dominique M. Hanssens, and Marnik G. Dekimpe. "Competitive Reactions to Advertising and Promotion Attacks." *Marketing Science* 24, no. 10 (2005), 35–54.

9

The Sports Industry and Antitrust

Rodney Fort

By any measure, it is an uphill fight to apply and extend the dead seriousness of the antitrust laws to the mythological kingdom of professional sports.

—Steven R. Rivkin[1]

Introduction

In 1990, NFL Commissioner Paul Tagliabue remarked:

> Free market economics is the process of driving enterprises out of business. Sports league economics is the process of keeping enterprises in business on an equal basis. There is nothing like a sports league. Nothing.[2]

And he is as right about there being nothing like sports leagues as he is wrong about the nature of competition. But, as anybody who follows the business side of pro sports knows, the claim of "keeping enterprises in business on an equal basis" also rings hollow. Leagues maximize profit by purposely keeping teams on an *unequal* basis on the field because league revenues are higher when those teams that generate the highest revenues are allowed to do so. And, as demonstrated throughout this chapter, there is no evidence at all that such a motivation even remotely enters into league actions toward any teams except those in the league.

In a famous example (and there are many others in all sports leagues), the Brooklyn Dodgers and New York Giants of Major League Baseball (MLB) left for California in 1957. Shortly thereafter, William Shea (a high-powered attorney) and Branch Rickey (among the famous baseball business people in history) decided to form a new Continental League with New York teams as a primary element of their proposed league. Teams were also announced for Minnesota and points west, including discussion of Los Angeles. However, Shea and Rickey could not get the existing American League (AL) and National League (NL) teams to agree to Continental League team locations under MLB rules for a new league to join the existing AL and NL. Shea and Rickey folded their Continental League plans in 1960.

Less than two months later, the NL expanded to Houston (the Colt .45s) and, you guessed it, New York (the Metropolitans). The AL agreed to expand to Los Angeles (the Angels) and to the just-vacated Washington, D.C., market (the second generation of the Senators. The predecessor Senators had already left for another Continental League intended location to become the Minnesota Twins).

In essence, MLB owners, acting through their league, had determined that there was no room for Continental League teams in cities where MLB almost immediately put teams upon the demise of that planned competitor. Had firms in any other industry behaved this way, they would have been open to challenge under the antitrust laws. As Stephen Ross puts it, "When restraints are anticompetitive, they are illegal unless shown to be reasonably necessary to achieve a goal that is efficient or enhances consumer appeal."[3]

At the heart of antitrust issues in sports lies the reason that sports leagues truly are different: Cooperation is required in order to produce what customers want to buy, namely, league play on the field, court, or ice. Originally, economist Simon Rottenberg developed nearly everything that went on in sports leagues incorporating the need for this cooperative behavior,[4] and Walter Neale followed up, labeling this need for cooperation among firms in the industry as the "peculiar economics" of sports.[5] The following quote from one of the earliest applications of the law to sports leagues, concerning NFL pooled radio and TV rights sales, makes it clear that the courts understand the uniqueness of sports leagues:

> Professional teams in a league, however, must not compete too well with each other in a business way. On the playing field, of course, they must compete as hard as they can all the time. But it is not necessary and indeed it is unwise for all the teams to compete as hard as they can against each other in a business way. If all the teams should compete as hard as they can in a business way, the strong teams would be likely to drive the weaker ones into financial failure. If this should happen not only would the weaker teams fail, but eventually the whole league, both the weaker and the stronger teams, would fail, because without a league no team can operate profitably.[6]

Economically, it is easy to separate those acts of cooperation among team owners that are required for play from those that are undertaken instead to clinch market power or to collect its fruits. But it has proven extremely perplexing for the courts, and, indeed, observers of court decisions in sports are divided on the issue as well. In my opinion, the

results all stem from courts deciding that cooperation is an all-or-nothing issue; if team owners need to cooperate to make play happen, then they should be allowed to cooperate even when the point is beyond making play happen into the realm of profit enhancement. But one thing is clear: Sports leagues have provided a perplexing challenge to the application of the antitrust laws. Steven Rivkin also states:

> The pattern of application of the laws has by no means been rational. Glaring inconsistencies have emerged, ranging from total exemption in one sport (baseball) to guarded intrusions where other professional sports are concerned.[7]

This chapter covers North American professional sports leagues as a potential object of U.S. antitrust laws. A league is actually comprised of the owners of the individual teams, an organization of owners that meets according to league rules in order to make all decisions about league play and the league's business model. The decision-making rules are specified in league constitutions and by-laws, and are different for each league.

Cooperative behavior among the individual producers in the same "industry" is unique to sports. If we separate these decisions into two categories, it becomes clear just what the issue is with the antitrust laws and sports leagues. One category is decisions that are required in order to make play happen. This occurs when team owners act through their league as a "single entity." The other category of decisions is made by owners acting as a league in order to enhance their profits. This type of "joint venture" activity is not required to make league play happen.

The central theme of this chapter is that the distinction between single-entity behavior and joint-venture activity has not been made clearly by courts entertaining antitrust actions against pro sports leagues. Leagues must be allowed to make single-entity decisions; without them there can be no league play, by definition. But leagues may rightfully deserve antitrust scrutiny when they enter into joint-venture activities because this type of cooperation may represent restraints of trade under the Sherman Act and/or attempts to extend market power through league mergers under the Clayton Act. For example, economist Gerald Scully estimated that 80–90 percent of the value created by MLB players was extracted by owners through one form of joint venture—restrictions on player movement between teams, a joint venture supported by the Supreme Court.[8] This chapter details the evolution of this special antitrust status in pro sports and seeks to explain why it has happened.

The chapter proceeds as follows. In the second section, the role of single-entity cooperation (making league play happen) is detailed. The third section distinguishes joint-venture activity (making profits happen) and summarizes the effects on all concerned. The evolution of the special antitrust status of pro sports leagues is covered in the fourth section. Examples, relevant court decisions, and opinions about them show the "glaring inconsistencies." The fifth section shows that congressional actions and inactions have actually facilitated the special antitrust status of pro sports leagues. The sixth section applies rational actor modeling to explain this congressional behavior and to suggest how meaningful reform can happen. Conclusions round out the chapter in the seventh section.

Pro Sports Leagues: Single-Entity Cooperation and Making Play Happen

Leagues enable owners to pursue economic goals and objectives that they cannot pursue as successfully acting alone. In its single-entity role, the league needs to act in setting a season schedule, setting the rules, and organizing championships. These are the essentials to make play happen. But before moving to each of these, it is instructive to remember an important real-world feature of leagues.

A common misperception is that leagues control owners rather than the reverse. If leagues do not make owners better off than if they were acting alone, they will simply find a league that does or create their own. This does not happen often, suggesting that leagues have typically done a good job satisfying their owners. But it does happen.

Early on, the National Basketball League faced a rival, the Basketball Association of America.[9] The Association, composed primarily of arena owners, had a lock on the largest and most valuable venues. League owners defected to the association to gain access to these valuable venues; after the 1947–1948 season, the four strongest League franchises went over to the Association, and after the next season, six more defected. The National Basketball League died because it failed to satisfy owner needs to play in the most lucrative venues. Clearly, owners form leagues for important reasons.

Setting the Schedule

Without a common schedule there is no league play. But even this most basic type of single-entity cooperation has economic impacts. National Football League (NFL) founding father George Halas, of the Chicago Bears, described the economic aspects of the original scheduling of the league to Congress:

> Naturally, each team wanted to play a team which would draw the most fans. . . . It reached the point where the Giants, Green Bay and the Bears (the most successful teams) became the most sought after teams to play. . . . We had to have official scheduling. . . . By making the season more interesting to the fans, this action benefited each member club and helped to stabilize each club.[10]

Halas recognized explicitly what economists would shortly describe as the role of competitive balance in leagues.[11] In trying to generate widespread fan interest and league growth, weaker teams were needed, too.

Another important element in setting the schedule is establishing season length. There is no magic about the length of seasons, except that it helps determine profits from the regular season and the playoffs. The season length in the AL increased from 154 games to 162 games in 1961, a 5 percent increase (the NL followed suit the next year). The NFL original season was highly variable, settling to eight games in the 1940s. But eventually the season increased from twelve to sixteen games after 1976. Similar patterns hold in the remaining leagues, the National Basketball Association (NBA) and the National Hockey League (NHL).

Setting the Rules

If teams play under different rules, they are not playing the same game. In addition, there must be officials and appeals for the sake of fairness. Once again, however, even this basic single-entity determination has economic elements to it. Gerald Scully also showed that rule changes alter the balance between offense and defense in producing winning margins.[12] In turn, this changes the pattern of winning between teams, which is what fans pay to see. Raising or lowering the pitcher's mound and adopting the designated hitter rule fine-tunes the economic balance of power in MLB between hitters and pitchers. Scully points out that measures of hitting, especially slugging average, increased significantly in the AL over the NL after the adoption of the designated hitter in the AL, and attendance increased in that league as well.

Championships

Simply determining a champion is economically valuable. However, the way championships are structured also produces economic incentives for team owners. Relative to crowning the highest winning percentage as its champion, I have shown with my co-author James Quirk how playoffs reduce the chances that the team with the highest winning percentage will become the eventual league champion, even though those chances remain higher than 50/50.[13] As a result, the expected value of talent falls so that owners have a greatly reduced incentive to hoard talent to ensure the highest winning percentage relative to the rest of the teams in the league.

Prior to 1968, there were no playoffs in MLB. Indeed, there were no divisions in either the AL or NL and the winners just met in the World Series. Championship series started after divisions were created in 1968. With the 1992 expansion, MLB added another round of playoffs after three divisions were created in each league. Once again, these rounds generate additional revenues for a few owners and impact the talent choices of all owners in the league. The modern structure of all sports leagues has multilayered championships, from divisions to the eventual league champion.

Pro Sports Leagues: Joint Ventures and Making Profit Happen

Rottenberg[14] and Neale[15] also noted that once owners act together in pro leagues to set the stage for competition on the field, they may also act together to raise profits for member owners. It is important to distinguish these from economically justifiable single-entity actions. In this chapter, cooperative actions among owners in a league not required to make play happen are called joint ventures. This careful distinction is maintained throughout the chapter in order to clear up confusion. The courts have used the terms interchangeably and, in my opinion, to the detriment of clear policy outcomes.

In the rest of the chapter, joint ventures are organized under the topics of territory protection, team location, TV negotiations, and player relations. Because joint action is not mandatory, coordination will occur only when cooperation is in each team's best interest. These topics are presented here and analyzed in subsequent sections.

Territory Protection

Territory definition and enforcement clearly has market power impacts on other teams, other leagues, and fans. Through lack of congressional and court intervention, leagues have been allowed to grant exclusive territories to their members through franchise agreements. In turn, exclusive territories are the primary determinant of the revenue structure that any owner will enjoy, and protection of that revenue structure is a fundamental league task.

The owner names the franchise, enters into season play and the playoff schedule, abides by the league operating rules, and shares in league-wide broadcasting revenues and franchise fees paid by new entrants to the league. The latter franchise fee is referred to as an expansion fee, and the amounts of this fee, as well as the points in time when the league will expand, are determined by the league. But we must never forget that the league is actually comprised of the current group of team owners. The franchise agreement also specifies the responsibilities of the league to enforce operating rules and to protect the franchise territory. Members of leagues enjoy the sale value of franchise rights, logos, and properties. The rules in every pro sports league strictly govern the ability of any member of the league to encroach on existing territories. Teams cannot simply move to a new territory without careful review and approval by their league according to its constitution.

Generally speaking, selling franchises does not necessarily restrict competition. For example, when one fast-service company grants a franchise, there is plenty of other competition from other fast-service providers. Indeed, the competitively determined customer base acceptable to potential franchise buyers often is such that quite a few McDonald's restaurants are located in the same city. But in pro sports the majority of markets support only one team, certainly at the level of a metropolitan area and sometimes even regionally; minimum and maximum efficient scale is one firm. Thus, once a team from a particular league is in place, competition from competing leagues should typically not be expected.

Economically speaking, leagues carefully manage and protect exclusive geographic territories. Once exclusive territories are created and protected, there literally is no substitute team in that sport. This managed absence of substitutes allows individual teams to maximize profits as local monopolies in their sport (although they still compete with entertainment providers in general). As expected, leagues also then enter into quantity restrictions and pricing choices that raise revenues relative to a more competitive structure.

Leagues impose two types of quantity restrictions. One that we have already discussed is season length. Absent competition, it is reasonable to expect that season length is chosen to maximize league revenues. The second and more important output restriction is the artificial limit on the number of teams. The occasional formation of rival leagues and the long line of potential hosts whenever a league announces expansion both indicate that the number of pro sports teams is kept artificially low relative to the competitive level.

Of course, the whole point of exclusive territory maintenance is to allow market power for individual team owners. And output restriction and higher price should be the result. On the latter, sports teams employ a variety of price discrimination mechanisms to increase fan expenditures.

The cost of providing on-field competition does not vary by time of day, day of the week, or the age of fans, but fans' willingness to pay does vary along each of these dimensions. The result of their protected market positions typically shows through in the rate of return on team sale prices. There have been periods when rates of return on team ownership have been incredibly high, and the growth in team sale prices typically beats the real annual opportunity cost.[16] Territorial exclusivity, controlled by leagues, maintains the market power of teams in a given location, leading to all of these enhanced outcomes for members of leagues.

Team Location

Suppose an existing league is considering expanding the number of teams. The league should approve the expansion if, on net, the current team owners in the league will be better off. But this is a profit consideration that only exists because the league will grant a monopoly right and territorial exclusivity. And it should be expected that the team will be located where the net gain to the current group of owners is highest.

If members of leagues pursue profits, and competition over franchises is brisk, "the league" will extract the value of ownership, adjusted for any other impacts on the current group of owners. Members of the current league look across all potential locations and decide the expansion fee that could be charged in each place. Current owners must estimate revenue sources (gate and gate-related, television, and venue) in the expansion city and costs (operations, player costs, and the owner's opportunity cost) in order to ascertain expected future profits just from the team itself. In addition, there will be values to any related business operations (payment for services to another of the team owner's firms that actually are revenues to the owner), "costs" that are actually profit-taking

(services provided to the owner that the owner would otherwise have to pay personally, especially loans from the team to the owner; sometimes owners draw salaries as well), cross-ownership tax advantages, pass-through tax advantages, and shares of any future league expansions.

But there are other financial impacts from expansion that owners must consider. Typically, expansion teams are not very successful at first. This means revenues that depend on the quality of opponents (gate, concessions, parking, and, in some cases, local television) will be lower when teams play expansion clubs. In addition, expansion may impact the value of the league's national TV contract, especially important in the NFL, where there is only a national contract and no local broadcasting. For example, even without any NFL team, 2002 ratings in the Los Angeles area were higher than in New York with two teams and swamped all other pro teams in the area. This partly explains why the NFL expanded to Houston, rather than Los Angeles. At the margin, Houston may actually have had a higher impact on the value of the NFL national TV contract than Los Angeles.

So, the expansion fee is the net discounted present value of this stream of returns, and it is no wonder that they can be quite large ($777.8 million in the last NFL expansion in 1999, for example). But other important considerations also shed light on antitrust issues in sports. First, relocation, as opposed to expansion, poses a more complex problem for existing owners because it may or may not enhance the value of the national contract. A given team owner would consider relocation if it is in his or her personal best economic interest. But the effect of the move could be harmful to the league as a whole. This explains in part why league constitutions specify that a super-majority vote is required to approve team relocation.

A second consideration in addition to the expansion fee is that expansion and relocation can be carefully managed to enhance the bargaining power of existing owners with their host cities. Leaving economically viable team locations empty is valuable to current members of the league in bargaining with their host cities. If the host city, county, or state fails to meet an owner's subsidy demands, the owner can simply threaten to move to the open viable location. If elected officials do not want to lose the team, the owner's upper hand can be worth millions of dollars.

Examples are many, including the move of the St. Louis Cardinals to Arizona[17] and the move of the Rams from Anaheim to St. Louis.[18] But my favorite example is the case of Tampa Bay/St. Petersburg (TBSP) during the 1990s. Despite spending nearly $200 million (inflation-adjusted) on the Suncoast Dome stadium to prove that they were worthy, owner-hopefuls in TBSP did not get an MLB expansion team in 1993. Owners in Denver and Miami received the teams for that expansion round. The MLB owner-hopefuls in TBSP let it be known that they would be willing to host or buy an existing team.

Immediately following this failed attempt, in rapid succession, owners of the Chicago White Sox, San Francisco Giants, and Seattle Mariners used TBSP as a believable threat location against their host cities. Each was (eventually, in the case of the Giants) successful in using this open, viable threat location to leverage new stadiums from their state and local host governments. Heavy bargaining leverage was ensured for three member owners by expanding to Miami and Denver rather than TBSP, and hundreds of millions of public dollars were extracted. Eventually, the value of that leverage must have declined, because an owner group in TBSP did get a team in 1998. However, I have estimated that well over $300 million (inflation-adjusted) was lost, measured by payments made to cover the costs of construction while the Suncoast Dome sat practically empty, generating no revenue.[19]

So, team owners put demands on their host cities for improved lease terms, stadium renovation, and even publicly funded new stadiums and arenas. As state and local governments are understandably reluctant to subsidize sports enterprises generating hundreds of millions of dollars in revenue, the teams threaten to leave for one of the viable locations its league may have kept open. Because owners, acting as leagues, have controlled the location of teams so well, the city is at a bargaining disadvantage. Hosts are unable to appeal to some other team to replace their current team. Invariably, then, it is an all-or-nothing proposition, and cities usually (but not always) give in.

A final consideration in addition to expansion fees is that expansion and relocation also can be used to preclude competition from existing or potential rival leagues. In leaving believable threat locations open, owners run the risk of inviting the formation of a rival league. Rival leagues typically gain initial access in one or two large-revenue markets, required to gain TV contracts, and put the rest of their teams in smaller markets, uncovered by the dominant league. If fans view the rival as competitive, demand and revenues decline for teams in the dominant league and the price of players is bid up as well. Prices fall, costs rise, and profits must fall for owners in the dominant league.

Strategic expansion and relocation can preclude rival competition; if the rival league cannot gain access to some larger-revenue market areas, it is unlikely to form in the first place. MLB always has been best at covering the top thirty population centers.[20] There is a much higher variance in other leagues. Some cities just are not basketball or hockey towns, as the NBA and NHL have the worst coverage of top thirty population centers. And the same may be true of football, because the NFL also has plenty of room to expand to cover the top thirty population centers.

In my opinion, the best example of precluding

competition is in MLB during the later 1950s. Up to that time, MLB teams were all east of the Mississippi River, leaving the rest of the country to the minor leagues. However, the Pacific Coast League (PCL) thrived with teams in Los Angeles, San Francisco, Vancouver (BC), San Diego, Hollywood, Seattle, Portland, and Sacramento. While often supplying extremely talented players to MLB (e.g., Joe DiMaggio, Ted Williams, Tony Lazerri, Rube Waddell), many players of similar caliber simply stayed in the PCL because life was good there.

During U.S. House of Representatives antitrust hearings in the early 1950s, members of the Celler Committee scolded MLB for its reluctance and, under threat of antitrust action, told MLB to design a procedure that would show how a rival league could obtain officially sanctioned MLB status (the same rules that the Continental League tried to use in the example at the beginning of this chapter). The PCL was so prosperous that its principals actually tried to gain official recognition as a third major league under these guidelines. However, the guidelines were unreasonable; attendance requirements actually were larger than the level enjoyed by all but a few of the MLB teams of the time. As a result, the PCL's campaign for major league status stalled.

In the meantime, MLB's Brooklyn Dodgers and New York Giants moved west in 1957, occupying the anchor cities for the PCL, Los Angeles and San Francisco. With this ready-made historical MLB rivalry now in their area, baseball fans shifted loyalty away from their old PCL teams and toward the MLB's new Los Angeles Dodgers and San Francisco Giants. Shortly, California was nearly emptied of PCL teams (only the Padres remained in San Diego), and the PCL occupied less lucrative markets like Phoenix, Salt Lake City, and Spokane. The PCL was relegated to AAA minor league status, and nearly all of its teams were either purchased by MLB teams or entered into close contractual relations with MLB teams. Clearly, the relocation of the Dodgers and Giants ended all chances for the PCL to obtain major league status, precluding the entry of a rival league.

The case of the PCL and MLB is just one example of how relocation protects against rival leagues. Leagues have always moved their teams around quite a bit, except for the last thirty years in MLB. No league beats the NBA in team moves, either by the number of examples or the number of times a given team has moved. Two NBA teams have been in four different cities. The Hawks moved from the "Tri-cities" (Moline and Rock Island, Illinois, and Davenport, Iowa), to Milwaukee, to St. Louis before lighting in Atlanta, and the Kings rolled from Rochester, to Cincinnati, to Kansas City before settling in Sacramento. And there are four three-city teams. Although teams typically move less in the NHL, if you count the merging of the original Minnesota North Stars with the Cleveland Barons, that team has moved five times: first to Oakland, a regional California affiliation name change, then on to Cleveland, Minnesota, and Dallas. All of this movement should be to higher-valued locations, helping to preclude the formation of rival leagues.

If there is one thing we know, it is that every pro sport has faced rival leagues, but the single dominant league outcome always prevails. Mergers and assimilations characterize nearly every rival league episode. The NFL faced seven rival leagues and rose victorious out of every episode. Mergers and assimilations typically occurred by offering the owners of the most successful teams in the rival league very inexpensive franchises in the dominant league. Those owners then just moved their entire team, lock, stock, and barrel, into the dominant league. Sometimes assimilations happened by melding some teams in the rival league with dominant league teams.

A common misperception is that this power of leagues to control the number and location of their teams derives from the U.S. Supreme Court's famous *Federal Baseball* decision.[21] Here is an excerpt of Justice Holmes's majority decision, creating the "antitrust exemption" for MLB:

> The business is giving exhibitions of baseball, which are *purely state affairs* (italics added) . . . the fact that in order to give exhibitions the Leagues must induce free persons to cross state lines. . . . is not enough to change the character of the business . . . That which in its consummation is not commerce does not become commerce among the States because the transportation that we have mentioned takes place. . . . If we are right . . . the restrictions . . . and the other conduct charged against the defendants were not an interference with commerce among the States.[22]

Clearly, the context of *Federal Baseball* is about player inputs in MLB. And that exemption in MLB has been eroded due to free agency arbitration decisions, and eventually the Curt Flood Act (1998) ended the exemption as far as labor relations are concerned (detailed below). But all leagues still continue to exercise complete control over team numbers and locations. So, that power to control team locations never really could have been blamed on *Federal Baseball,* even in MLB. As we shall see below, the source of that control actually is Congress.

TV Negotiations

Finally, for this section, joint-venture behavior also dominates league negotiation with media providers, players, and their host cities. The most striking observation about these joint-venture negotiations is the exercise of market power. Because individual owners could handle these negotiations separately (and often do), economic intuition leads us to suspect that leagues produce better results for owners than they could get on their own for at least part of

the broadcast schedule in MLB, the NBA, and the NHL and for the entire schedule for the NFL.

League negotiations with media providers are a joint venture that could be done individually by team owners. Indeed, in all leagues except the NFL, which only sells rights at the national level, individual owners negotiate their own local TV agreements. Owners act together through their leagues to confront media providers (network, cable, and satellite TV) with a league monopoly on national broadcast rights. The profits flow primarily from advertisers to the teams in sports leagues through media providers.

Player Relations

Nothing requires team owners to deal as leagues with players. For example, GM, Ford, and Chrysler bargain independently with organized labor. So, once again, we are led to conclude economically that the joint venture provides a better outcome for owners than acting individually toward players' labor unions. Indeed, as an example that they can negotiate individually, to date all individual team owners have reserved individual salary negotiations to themselves.

The Special Antitrust Status of Pro Sports Leagues

From the last section, it would seem that sports leagues are prime candidates for lawsuits under the antitrust laws. Leagues are organized to guarantee that teams enjoy market power through territorial exclusivity. Leagues also, by and large, put teams where they please, either through expansion or decisions over team relocation. Leagues also offer superior outcomes for member owners in negotiations with media providers and players. All of these exercises of market power are possible violations of the antitrust laws. While the efficiencies of single-entity cooperation determine whether there can be league play or not, the potential inefficiencies of joint ventures become the matter of concern from the policy perspective. Interestingly, this definition is apparently easier stated than implemented because it remains a matter of confusion in the legal process.

Let's see just how it is that leagues have come to enjoy special antitrust status under the law. While courts have played a role, so has Congress. As much as possible, the same categorization of topics follows from the last section under the joint-venture approaches in sports leagues: territory protection, team location, TV negotiations, and player relations.

Territory Protection

Early on, Rivkin noted there was nearly no case law on the issue of territory protection but cited some distantly related actions that might "presage considerable future litigation by would-be applicants."[23] Much later, things were pretty much the same, according to Ross and Dimitroff:[24]

> Member teams may find it economically advantageous to vote against having another team sold or relocated, especially into their territories. Potential buyers and sellers of major league baseball teams, however, have historically been left without a federal antitrust remedy for such actions, no matter how arbitrary, capricious, or mean-spirited, because, early in the century, the Supreme Court concluded that baseball was exempt from the antitrust laws.

Ross and Dimitroff found nothing to go on substantively and just discussed the setting under which a successful antitrust challenge of this type might occur. But there were two interesting cases on territory exclusivity.[25] In *Mid-South Grizzlies*[26] and *Seattle Totems,*[27] two teams from other leagues sought entry into the NFL and NHL, respectively, and sued when denied. The courts found that leagues were within their rights to deny entry because the plaintiffs were not trying to compete with the existing leagues.

Team Location

Lehn and Sykuta[28] detail the genesis of court thinking on franchise location from *San Francisco Seals,*[29] to *LA Raiders,*[30] to *San Diego Clippers.*[31] In *San Francisco Seals,* the NHL blocked the owner of the team trying to move from San Francisco to Vancouver. The court decided the NHL was a single entity and that the antitrust laws did not apply in this case because a firm cannot conspire with itself. In *LA Raiders* and *San Diego Clippers,* courts decided exactly the opposite. In the first case heard on *LA Raiders,* the California district court judge gave three arguments: granting single entity would preclude any antitrust liability on any dimension; single-entity type organizations had been found guilty of violating antitrust laws in the past; and any team could pull out and still continue to be a team because many current NFL teams had actually done that prior to joining the NFL.[32]

One of the dissenting judges in the second portion of *LA Raiders* actually hit the nail right on the head from the economic perspective:

> The purposes for which the NFL should be viewed as a single entity, impervious to Section 1 [of the Sherman Act] attack, must be functionally defined as those instances in which member clubs must coordinate intra-league policy and practice if the joint product is to result. (Parenthetical added for clarity.)[33]

The judge clearly understood the separation between cooperation required to make play happen and cooperation that simply makes for greater profits; not all joint-venture activities are single-entity activities, and reasonable care should be taken to separate the two. But clearly the courts have not adopted such a clear perspective.

And the problem is not an easy one. Lehn and Sykuta observed that, in *LA Raiders,* the court failed to recognize that territorial restrictions promote incentives for individual owners to invest in product quality and reputation of the NFL, the franchise grantor. In addition to this, Fisher et al.[34] and Carlton et al.[35] argue that league control over team location is also welfare enhancing as well as profit enhancing in dealing with externality effects on all other teams in the league.

More recently, the NFL cited *LA Raiders* as justification for not blocking the move of the Cleveland Browns to Baltimore in the late 1990s. However, the league ignored *LA Raiders* entirely when dealing with Ken Behring's proposed move of the Seahawks to the Los Angeles area. The NFL also hindered the move of the Rams from Los Angeles to St. Louis, until a mutually agreeable payment was made to the league stadium fund. For all practical purposes, the NFL simply puts teams where it wants them.

It is easy to see why the league behaved this way regarding these team moves. The NFL's behavior had nothing to do with fan happiness and everything to do with owner and league wealth maximization. The move of the Browns to Baltimore allowed one of the league's owner-icons, Art Modell, to enjoy a considerable increase in income from a new location and stadium at no cost to the league. A team was lost from one long-time NFL city, Cleveland, but gained by another long-time NFL city that had gone without a team for a few years, Baltimore. On net, Modell was better off and the league was not hurt, especially because the NFL expanded back into Cleveland shortly thereafter.

In the Seahawks case, a move from Seattle to Los Angeles would have erased a prospective large expansion fee from the future owner of the extremely valuable and vacant Los Angeles market. League members were better off with that decision, looking forward to expansion fees that are rapidly approaching the $1 billion mark. And it should not be ignored that the NFL earned $43 million or so from the Rams when they moved to St. Louis.

Another dimension of team location is the impact of these choices by the dominant league on other leagues in the same sport. Interestingly, except for the mother of all inter-league suits, *Federal Baseball,* surprisingly little activity involves one league suing another, and with surprisingly little impact. Roberts[36] points out that *AFL v. NFL,*[37] *Philadelphia World Hockey,*[38] and *USFL v. NFL,*[39] each concerning the acts of the dominant league to preclude the success of a rival league, had little impact on the usual dominant league outcome (see below). And other cases, like *NASL v. NFL*[40], did cause alterations in the behavior of leagues, but not of great impact. So dominant leagues enjoy their status but have fended off suits by a few rivals. This is further bolstered by government attitudes toward the merger of leagues, detailed in the next section.

TV Negotiations

Another antitrust issue is pro sports broadcasting. In the late 1950s, after Federal Trade Commission (FTC) investigation, the Department of Justice (DOJ) held that league negotiations on the part of all member teams for a league-wide broadcasting contract were an antitrust violation. This move could have been heralded as a solid move forward for consumers of broadcast games, but Congress basically reversed the DOJ's ruling. Under the Sports Broadcasting Act of 1961, league-wide TV contracts in all sports are exempted from antitrust.

Congress also took one further step that harms broadcast viewers and benefits leagues. If an owner does not sell out a game, he can kill a contracted broadcast in their own home viewing area. The effect of this so-called blackout is to reduce the number of people who can enjoy a given game if the game is not sold out at the gate. Acts of Congress reinforce market power in broadcasting rather than suppress it.

In the related area of league choice over which games are broadcast, we see another place where the difference between single entity and joint venture is blurred. Ross, in discussing the resurrection of the single-entity logic in *Chicago Bulls*,[41] makes the following analogy. In *Chicago Bulls,* Judge Richard Posner (familiar to economists interested in the rent-seeking literature) argued that a league was like a corporation with divisions, sometimes in competition with each other but directed by the same governing structure.[42] Earlier, Roberts had offered a similar idea: Nobody bats an eye when the GM board of directors decides factory location but cries of conspiracy erupt when a league decides to move a team and play games in one city versus another.[43] Ross points out the clear difference in a manner entirely keeping with the economic distinction:[44]

> The critical difference between General Motors and a sports league, however, is that ultimately the decision whether Saturn should refurbish a run-down Oldsmobile plant (good for Oldsmobile) or build a more expensive plant far away from the traditional culture of Detroit (good for Saturn) will be made either by senior executives or a board of directors concerned only about maximizing revenues for the entire corporation, whereas league decisions are made by the self-interested owners themselves.

Player Relations

Turning to player relations, the antitrust issue concerns how owners have used their market power over output to gain market power over inputs. Players have only one major league option, and, in the past, team owners have acted together to cre-

ate a monopsony situation in which players had to bargain over their salaries with only a single team owner. Action under the antitrust laws was one approach tried by players, but the issue always hinged on whether or not players actually had the right to take individual antitrust action against sports team owners and leagues.

The linchpin, of course, is *Federal Baseball* in which the antitrust exemption left players with no alternative protection until collective bargaining became a reality in MLB when Marvin Miller took over leadership of the players' association in 1966. There were subsequent challenges to *Federal Baseball,* but *Toolson*[45] and *Flood*[46] saw the courts simply leave the *Federal Baseball* precedent in place for MLB. Interestingly, courts did not extend the exemption from baseball to other sports. Cases tracing their lineage back to *Radovich*[47] have effectively restricted *Federal Baseball* only to baseball.

Once modern labor relations under the National Labor Relations Act (1935) swept through sports, the new arena became the relationship between labor relations law and antitrust. The issue hinges on whether the league is a single entity; you can't bring an antitrust suit against team owners if they actually are not competitors! Both the courts and Congress played a role here. The decisions are a wonderful hodgepodge of blurred distinction between single-entity and joint-venture definitions.

The list of cases is long,[48] and facilitated by looking at the most recent, *Brown.*[49] The Supreme Court essentially determined that a certified player union is precluded from bringing or sponsoring antitrust suits against its league. This clearly means that the only avenue for players to handle disagreements with owners is through collective bargaining. But the court did not base its decision on a single-entity argument, despite the fact that both the National Labor Relations Board (NLRB) and the Fifth Circuit Court had upheld in *NASL v.*

NLRB[50] that a league is a joint employer with all of its joint venture partners, so that leagues are compelled to bargain as a single unit.[51] Roberts puts bluntly what he thinks the court missed:[52]

> Given the inherently joint nature of the league's athletic competition product, it is impossible for one team to agree separately with the players union on a wide range of employment terms such as the number and location of games, length of season, playing field rules, when and how players will move from one to another, and the like. With respect to all of the other employment terms that theoretically could be negotiated for one team, a single team's entering into permanent or even interim agreements with the union that would differentiate its employment terms from those of the other league member clubs would risk altering the relative athletic prowess of the teams and thus the nature and quality of the athletic competition product that all of the teams jointly produce and own.

For Roberts, then, it seems that because individual negotiations would interfere with what it takes to make play happen, we just have to live with all of the other joint-venture outcomes that are not required to make play happen but end up simply enhancing profits.

Ross and Lucke also point out that the courts have had difficulty in entertaining all of the interests involved, especially those of the fans.[53] For example, in *Brown*, they argue that the court focused only on the relative interests of owners and players to the exclusion of fan interests. To Ross and Lucke, "Both opinions' exclusive focus on the rights of labor and management without regard to consumer interests led the majority to conclude that the only differences between professional athletes and ordinary factory workers were that the former were better paid and had greater bargaining power."[54] Their point is that in deciding the upper hand for owners, fan interests would be hurt.

Recent NLRB opinions and arbitration outcomes allow players in all pro sports leagues to sue individually if behavior prohibited under the antitrust laws leads to a breakdown in labor negotiations. MLB players were the last group of players to gain this protection, and it literally required an act of Congress. Following the MLBPA strike in 1994–1995, Congress sought a way to reduce the chances of future work stoppages. The result was the Curt Flood Act of 1998. The Flood Act puts MLB players on the same antitrust footing as other professional athletes; MLB players may sue under the antitrust laws in the special case where antitrust violations lead to a breakdown in labor negotiations. Congress made it clear that the Flood Act was limited only to labor relations and no other aspect of baseball.

Addendum: Three Other Cases Bearing on Single Entity

Courts have rendered opinions on the joint venture actions of leagues in three other cases. In *McNeil,* the famous case that broke true free agency in the NFL, the court rejected the NFL's request for summary judgment based on the claim that a single-entity requirement justified the league's actions.[55] In *Chicago Professional Sports,* a case predating *Chicago Bulls* but also concerning broadcasting limitations, the court treated the NBA as a single entity even though these restrictions are a joint venture not required to make play happen.[56] Finally, in *Sullivan,* the court again rejected the "single entity" argument of the NFL in a case that restricted sale of a team through a public offering.[57]

Congress and Sports Antitrust

An easy summary of the last section is that the courts simply have a difficult time with sports leagues; single-entity and joint-venture issues appear difficult to handle in the legal setting. One of the most crucial issues repeatedly raised by the courts as they recognized this difficulty is the fact that Congress has chosen to act in a particular way toward sports. Again, Rivkin offers the following quote from *Toolson:*

> Congress has had the ruling (in *Federal Baseball*) under consideration but has not seen fit to bring such business under these laws by legislation having prospective effect. . . . We think that if there are evils in this field which now warrant application to it of the antitrust laws it should be by legislation.[58]

Rivkin also notes that a very similar statement was made by the court in *Radovich,* challenging the applicability of *Federal Baseball* to another league, the NFL.[59]

A description of what has transpired in Congress follows.[60] Although the main outcomes involved team location choices, delving into these congressional records reveals that Congress could not help but understand each and every one of the items raised throughout this chapter. By way of a preview, Johnson offered the following observation on Congress and sports from the mid-1950s through the end of the 1970s:

> Since the mid-1960s, however, Congressional perceptions of professional sports have changed and, on occasion, Congress has enacted legislation opposed by the leagues. Nevertheless, the political power of club owners, combined with the persistence of the idyllic image of sports within Congress, makes such instances rare or dependent upon extraordinary circumstances.

Celler Hearings, 1951 and 1957

As early as 1951, Congress investigated the power of leagues over team location and movement. Congressman Emanuel Celler began the proceedings with some opening remarks:

> Organized baseball affords this subcommittee with almost a classroom example of what may happen to an industry, which is governed by rules and regulations among its members rather than by the free play of competitive forces. Without knowing at this time whether such regulation is in the best interest of baseball because of its many unique characteristics, we may at least learn something of importance about how an industry operates itself instead of being forced to comply with the antitrust laws.[62]

However, at the end of the 1951 hearings, Congress chose not to revisit the antitrust status of MLB on the output side. Congress did, however, make it clear to MLB that its reluctance to expand westward was puzzling, and encouraged the league to consider such movement and, as an incentive, to design an entry system for admitting new, competitive major leagues.

Shortly thereafter, the Dodgers and Giants moved to California, as discussed in an earlier section. This instigation on the part of Congress probably doomed the potential for a reduction in MLB's market power. Congress could certainly have facilitated competition between MLB and the PCL but chose not to. Instead, the very successful PCL was reduced to minor league status despite its attempt to join in as another major league.

Kefauver Hearings, 1958 and 1959

Similarly, after hearings in 1958 and 1959 led by Senator Estes Kefauver,[63] Congress again chose to let stand the market power of MLB. Almost immediately, in 1962, the rise and then demise of the still-born Continental League occurred. In a similar way to the PCL episode, MLB was allowed to define what it meant to be a major league and then deny major league status to the Continental League.

Noll and Zimbalist reported on congressional inquiry into antitrust after the last version of the Washington Senators left for Texas in 1971 (the Rangers began play in 1972).[64] That inquiry led to a recommendation that MLB's antitrust exemption be removed. However, Congress only recommended "further study," and there was no further action by the entire House.

Sisk Hearings, 1976 (and After)

In 1976, Congressman B.F. Sisk led congressional hearings on the issue of market power in sports in general.[65] There was clear testimony from every leading analyst on the harm done to consumers by the market power of the leagues. But, true to form, Congress again made no moves against the power of pro leagues over team location.

In the early 1990s, another wave of antitrust interest followed the possible move of the San Francisco Giants to Florida, but no action was ever taken. Perhaps the most interesting congressional twist of fate ever occurred during investigation of the movement of the NFL's Cleveland Browns to Baltimore. A plan was hatched to actually give the NFL an exemption similar to the one provided for MLB by *Federal Baseball!* The hope was that location stability would return to the NFL. Thankfully, from the antitrust perspective, no further action beyond the inquiry occurred.

Mergers and Antitrust

As if the lack of legislative interest in antitrust were not enough, Congress has been an active facilitator of pro sports league mergers.[66] In MLB, the AL was a successful rival to the NL in 1902–1903. For the 1904 season, an agreement was reached establishing MLB as a single league. Despite the fact that the antitrust laws had been in force and used in other areas for over ten years, Congress made no effort to even investigate this "agreement" that restored complete control over entering players and the mobility of players in the league.

In other cases, rather than carefully applying antitrust laws for the benefit of sports consumers, Congress actually took formal steps to sanction mergers. The most recent version of the American Football League (there have been four) was by all accounts a successful rival to the NFL in the mid-1960s. But Congress formally exempted the AFL–NFL merger from antitrust in 1966. Congress did not act to formally exempt the mergers between either the NBA and American Basketball Association or the NHL and World Hockey Association. But it did bring pressure to make those mergers happen. James Quirk and I argue that this merger activity has played a primary role in the elimination of effective economic competition in pro sports.[67]

Thus, despite repeated investigation, congressional action has either not been forthcoming or it has been directed toward enhancing market power in pro sports. Congress has failed to intervene in league practices concerning team movement and location, reversed antitrust decisions by the DOJ, passed blackout laws in broadcasting, and acted to exempt or facilitate league mergers in every sport. Indeed, Congress rejected at least fifty bills prior to 1974 that would have removed the exemption created by *Federal Baseball*.[68] No wonder Justice Blackmun was so blunt even back to *Flood:*

> We continue to be loath, even 50 years after *Federal Baseball* and almost two decades after *Toolson*, to overturn those cases judicially when Congress, by its positive inaction, has allowed those decisions to stand for so long and, far beyond mere inference and implication, has clearly evinced a desire not to disapprove them legislatively.[69]

Ross and Dimitroff document another even dozen rejected bills aimed at eliminating *Federal Baseball* from 1994 to 1996.[70] So why has Congress behaved this way? And if acts of Congress have not been forthcoming, why not some other form of regulation?

Figure 9.1 **Rational Actor Antitrust Politics Triangle**

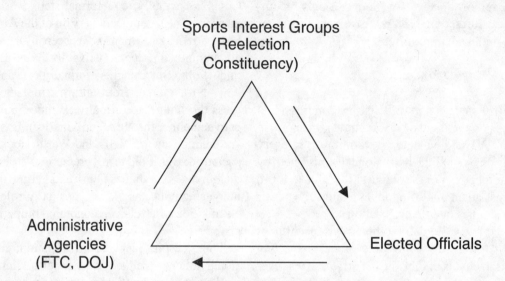

Rational Actor Politics and Antitrust

Because congressional outcomes are political ones, it is worth examining a rational actor explanation of the relationship between government and the application of U.S. antitrust laws to the business of sports. A viable explanation for this seemingly paradoxical relationship derives from a rational actor explanation of sports policy.[71] First, the actors in this process fit a simple "triangle" characterization, shown in Figure 9.1. There are the members of concentrated sports business interest groups: owners, direct beneficiaries like fans and businesses at the stadium, and indirect beneficiaries like surrounding businesses and landowners. Then there are elected officials who make policy of interest to the members of the sport business groups. At the last vertex are the administrative agencies that carry out policy toward sports, in this case antitrust policy (FTC and DOJ). Most of the recent work on administrative agencies shows that directors pursue their personal career

welfare by seeking the rewards that are in control of Congress: increases in budget and the program success that follows.

Members of Congress seek reelection ordering their activities around subcommittees covering policy provision. And the sports business interest groups form their reelection constituency on this particular policy dimension. Of course, the reelection constituency is only part of defined geographic constituencies. For a policy area like sports, it is quite common for part of the reelection constituency to be more generally defined, for example, by the national sports interests (leagues and broadcasters). I have detailed how these more nationally oriented interest groups lobby at the congressional level.[72]

Given that elected officials seek reelection, we should expect them to pursue policies that increase the amount of vote-generating resources given at the margin in the policy arenas where they work. Politicians evaluate the gains and losses among competing groups from any policy choice and provide policies that enhance their chance for reelection. Not all members of any reelection constituency will get precisely what they want, and surely many members of their general geographic constituency may be harmed in this process. But we have known since the works of Mancur Olson that this will happen in small, dispersed, hard-to-detect amounts, while the benefits to reelection constituencies will be obvious and concentrated on obvious beneficiaries.[73]

The direction of the arrows in Figure 9.1 is important for this rational actor story because they indicate that the reelection constituency dominates the outcome. Powerful reelection constituencies tell elected officials the antitrust policy they desire. Representatives do their best to provide it, subject to the competition among groups in this particular policy area. Administrative agencies carry out the congressional dictate. The policy results flow back to the reelection constituency that monitors their success.

It may appear that the outcomes are perverse if taken alone and measured from the perspective of "the general welfare," but ultimately one tracks the outcomes to the reelection interests of elected officials providing special-interest policy. This implies that the seeming lack of interest in sports antitrust, and the inconsistent treatment when it does intervene, actually serves the reelection interests of members of Congress. And here is an explanation consistent with this rational actor characterization.

Suppose you are a member of Congress with a team in your geographic jurisdiction. The team is enjoyed by some of your constituents, broadly speaking, but it also contributes to the wealth of a particularly potent part of your constituency. A vote to limit sports league market power would reduce the economic welfare of this potent group. As long as reelection drives your decisions at the margin, you will not vote against sports or encourage the FTC and DOJ to do so.

And this is precisely the setting facing members of Congress in roughly the top thirty population areas in the United States. All have at least one sports team in their jurisdiction. This means that the pro sports league support group will include many influential state and local politicians. Asking them to support antitrust intervention in pro sports leagues is asking them to act against their own re-election interest. And the same goes for members of the U.S. legislature.

Even such a simple explanation suggests that pro sports leagues continue to enjoy their favored antitrust status because that outcome is in the best interests of those people most interested in this small portion of the federal policy arena. The most potent reelection forces favor the status quo in sports antitrust. It should be expected that federal legislators see to it that these potent forces get what they want.

Examples of the quid pro quo inherent in Figure 9.1 abound. Adams and Brock detail a number of cases.[74] Adding a few they missed, plus some modern examples, generates the following list. Shortly after the Celler hearings in 1951, MLB teams moved to the Pacific coast so that Congress did get some political returns. Shortly after Dallas got an expansion NFL franchise, the Sports Broadcasting Act (1961) granted antitrust exemption in cooperative sale of broadcast rights. Partly in response to congressional interest (and partly due to the threat of the Continental League), MLB added a team in New York in 1962 and also moved west again with the Los Angeles Angels. Expansion in Atlanta and New Orleans occurred at about the same time the NFL was formally allowed to merge with the AFL in 1966. Tampa Bay and Seattle received expansion franchises at about the same time Congress failed to impose additional limitations on the league's ability to black out home games, around 1974. In the 1990s, expansion teams went to Miami and then Tampa Bay shortly after the owners voted to block the Giants' move to Tampa Bay. Interestingly, this happened after hearings instigated by Florida Senator Connie Mack and Colorado Senator Tim Wirth (remember, Colorado also received an expansion team).

As recently as 2000, hearings led by Senator Mike DeWine of Ohio (and chair of the Senate Subcommittee on the Judiciary at the time, handling antitrust issues) saw MLB promising to mend its competitive balance problems. Probably not coincidentally, DeWine's home-state Reds and Indians had been faring poorly on the field. It appears that leagues, also elements of powerful interest groups, know that Congress must receive a return every once in a while. According to Adams and Brock, "Apparently, the willingness of monopolistic club owners to expand membership in their cartel is the quid pro quo for continued congressional tolerance of structural arrangements in clear contravention of the antitrust laws."[75]

The lesson from the rational actor perspective is that the reelection imperative confronting politicians drives their decisions. Politically potent groups control reelection by providing money and votes to politicians who serve their interests. In this sense, it is difficult to blame politicians rather than the system in which they operate. Politicians who work against the powerful group risk losing in the next election. It seems unreasonable to expect politicians to commit political suicide on a regular basis.

Competition Policy and Rational Actor Politics

Standard regulatory approaches to sports problems have also been suggested, and some attempts to put them into action have occurred, but none have seen the light of day. Senator Marlow Cook introduced federal legislation creating a separate federal agency to regulate sports in 1972.

It never gained broad legislative support, but columnist Charles Rhoden tried to resurrect the idea.[76] Rivkin suggested that a national sports council was the best way to facilitate cooperation between leagues, Congress, and the public.[77] Zimbalist argued that sports are a commodity supported through public expenditure, and, he called for public-utility style regulation.[78] Others, like Joseph Bast at the Heartland Institute, have suggested fan ownership of teams.[79]

Another competition policy prescription is much more direct. A number of writers detail the usual antitrust approach to breaking up the leagues.[80] For example, suppose the NFC and AFC were turned into two separate competing pro football leagues. The idea is that competition between the leagues would remedy many of the ills currently attributable to NFL market power. Details are in the works cited, including the problems that might arise and just how bad they may actually be. And there is a "debate" in the literature on the efficacy of any antitrust intrusions in sports.[81]

But the important observation on all of the foregoing concerning regulatory intervention, either through administrative agency and public ownership, or directly by breaking up the leagues, is that it has never happened. The rational actor insight is that only under predictable circumstances will there arise any impetus for such intervention. New powerful interest groups must arise to do battle with the status quo. From the perspective in Figure 9.1, those on the outside looking in at the current triangle outcome must become insiders. Until this happens, our rational actor approach suggests that the chances for strident competition policy to be applied in sports are pretty low. Noll and Zimbalist put it this way:

> Unfortunately, the same forces that have impeded effective legislation also stand in the way of antitrust action that would lead to divestiture. Like Congress, the Antitrust Division of the Department of Justice is

susceptible to political pressure not to upset sports, and so a large, influential monopoly remains unregulated and de facto immune from antitrust prosecution by the government.[82]

It would be naïve to think that just listing the good things about interventions fostering economic competition is enough to make it happen. After all, current political margins dictate the ongoing state of affairs in pro sports in the first place. Calls for alterations in the level of economic competition in sports must first come to grips with this simple fact of life: Unless new powerful interest groups replace the current ones, politicians will not change the economic outcomes in pro sports.

However, those with an interest in reforming pro sports do have some hope. When a problem becomes important enough to voters, a new political mobilization can occur that alters the status quo (the environmental movement begun in the 1970s comes to mind). But this is an expensive and slow process. Those bent on such change must successfully accomplish an overwhelming educational mission and overcome the high costs and free-riding behavior associated with organizing a politically potent group. Then, once mobilized, the new reelection constituency contender must do battle. Given the obstacles to overcoming it, it is small wonder that market power has ruled in pro sports.

There are signs that at least fans may be mobilizing. Fan dissatisfaction, although perhaps not at a fever pitch, is quite high on the heels of lost partial seasons in both MLB and the NBA and a completely lost season in the NHL. Web pages advocating the rights of fans and alternative ownership arrangements have begun to appear. The Internet dramatically reduces the costs of forming organizations. Perhaps fan interest groups will rise to do political battle with the current pro sports supporters.

Conclusions

Commissioner Tagliabue is correct—there is nothing like a sports league—but his claims as to why are somewhat disingenuous. This chapter provides another reason that there is nothing like a sports league, namely, the special antitrust status of North American professional sports leagues. The crux of this difference lies in the distinction between single-entity cooperation required to make play happen and joint-venture activity that makes market power and profits happen.

The courts have made statements that make it clear they understand the unique characteristics of sports leagues. But then the actual court decisions appear to be quite confused on the issue of single-entity versus joint-venture behavior. In areas of territory protection, team location, TV negotiations, and player relations, courts sometimes find that joint ventures are the same thing as single-entity cooperation. This has led to a hodgepodge of difficult-to-decipher decisions. Indeed, legal scholars in the area of sports antitrust disagree on the issue as well.

Out of all this, one might hope that legislative activity in the area of sports antitrust would be less confusing. But, alas, such is not the case. In precisely the same areas (territory protection, team location, TV negotiations, and player relations), Congress has either failed to intervene at all (in the case of *Federal Baseball*) or, worse yet, its activities have actually facilitated market power in these areas. Further, the same is true in the area of mergers.

A (simple) rational actor model of the sports antitrust policy arena explains why Congress may act the way it does. Elected officials provide concentrated benefits to powerful reelection constituencies in this arena, and all of them favor the status quo of market power and weak application of antitrust. This explanation also provides insights into the lack of any other regulatory intervention in sports (federal regulatory agency, national sports council, public-utility style regulation, public ownership, breaking up the leagues). Again, the status quo reigns over these alternatives due to the power of the current reelection constituencies. So, unless other groups rise to do battle with the status quo, the most reasonable expectation is more of the same: Leagues will be free to protect the exclusive territories of member team owners, to locate their teams to their greatest financial and strategic advantage against possible rival leagues, and to exercise the upper hand in TV negotiations and dealings with players.

Notes

1. S.R. Rivkin, "Sports Leagues and the Federal Antitrust Laws." In R.G. Noll, ed., *Government and the Sports Business,* p. 408 (Washington, DC: Brookings Institution, 1974).

2. *Sports Illustrated,* September 10.

3. S.F. Ross, "Competition Law as a Constraint on Monopolistic Exploitation by Sports Leagues and Clubs," *Oxford Review of Economic Policy* 19 (2003), pp. 569–84; see p. 582.

4. S. Rottenberg, "The Baseball Players' Labor Market," *Journal of Political Economy* 64 (1956), pp. 242–58.

5. W.C. Neale, "The Peculiar Economics of Professional Sports," *Quarterly Journal of Economics* 78 (1964), pp. 1–14.

6. Rivkin, "Sports Leagues and the Federal Antitrust Laws," p. 388, referring to *United States v. National Football League,* 116 Supp. 319 at 323 (E.D.Pa. 1953).

7. Ibid., pp. 388–89.

8. G.W. Scully, "Pay and Performance in Major League Baseball," *American Economic Review* 64 (1974), pp. 915–30.

9. J. Quirk and R.D. Fort, *Pay Dirt: The Business of Professional Team Sports* (Princeton, NJ: Princeton University Press, 1992).

10. *NFL Report,* 1999, p. 2.

11. The original work on competitive balance is all in Rottenberg, "The Baseball Players' Labor Market."

12. G.W. Scully, *The Business of Major League Baseball* (Chicago, IL: University of Chicago Press, 1989).

13. R. Fort and J. Quirk, "Cross-Subsidization, Incentives, and Outcomes in Professional Team Sports Leagues," *Journal of Economic Literature* 33 (1995), pp. 1265–99.

14. Rottenberg, "The Baseball Players' Labor Market."

15. Neale, "The Peculiar Economics of Professional Sports."

16. See Quirk and Fort, *Pay Dirt: The Business of Professional Team Sports,* chapter 2, and R. Fort, "The Value of Major League Baseball Ownership," *International Journal of Sport Finance* 1 (2006), pp. 3–8.

17. W. Adams and J.W. Brock, "Monopoly, Monopsony, and Vertical Collusion: Antitrust Policy and Professional Sports," *Antitrust Bulletin* 42 (1997), pp. 721–47; see p. 739.

18. F.M. Fisher, C. Maxwell, and E.S. Schouten, "The Economics of Sports Leagues and the Relocation of Teams: The Case of the St. Louis Rams," *Marquette Sports Law Journal* 10 (2000), pp. 193–218.

19. R. Fort, *Sports Economics,* 2nd ed. (Upper Saddle River, NJ: Prentice-Hall, 2006), chapter 10.

20. J. Quirk and R.D. Fort, *Pay Dirt: The Business of Professional Team Sports,* and Fort and Quirk, "Cross-Subsidization, Incentives, and Outcomes in Professional Team Sports Leagues."

21. *Federal Baseball Club of Baltimore v. National League of Professional Baseball Clubs,* 259 U.S. 200 (1922).

22. Quirk and Fort, *Pay Dirt: The Business of Professional Team Sports,* p. 185.

23. Rivkin, "Sports Leagues and the Federal Antitrust Laws," p. 403.

24. M.E. Ross and S.D. Dimitroff, "Whose Field of Dreams: Antitrust Relief Against Restrictions on the Sale or Relocation of Major League Baseball Teams," *Antitrust Bulletin* 42 (1997), pp. 521–39; see p. 522.

25. A.N. Wise and B.S. Meyer, *International Sports Law and Business,* Vol. 1 (Boston: Kluwer Law International, 1997), pp. 42–43.

26. *Mid-South Grizzlies v. National Football League,* 720 F.2d 772 (3d Cir. 1983).

27. *Seattle Totems Hockey Club, Inc., v. National Hockey League,* 783 F.2d 1347 (9th Cir.), denied, 479 U.S. 932 (1986).

28. K. Lehn and M. Sykuta, "Antitrust and Franchise Relocation in Professional Sports: An Economic Analysis of the *Raiders* Case," *Antitrust Bulletin* 42 (1997), pp. 541–63.

29. *San Francisco Seals, Ltd., v. National Hockey League, et al.,* 379 F. Supp. 966 (Cal. Ct. App. 1974).

30. *Los Angeles Memorial Coliseum Commission v. National Football League,* 519 F. Supp. 581, 582 (C.D. Cal. 1981); *Los Angeles Memorial Coliseum Commission v. National Football League, et al.,* 726 F.2d 1381 (9th Cir. 1984).

31. *National Basketball Association, et al., v. SDC Basketball Club, Inc.,* 815 F.2d 562 (9th Cir. 1987).

32. Lehn and Sykuta, "Antitrust and Franchise Relocation in Professional Sports: An Economic Analysis of the *Raiders* Case," p. 546.

33. Ibid., p. 554.

34. Fisher, Maxwell, and Schouten, "The Economics of Sports Leagues and the Relocation of Teams: The Case of the St. Louis Rams."

35. D.W. Carlton, A.S. Frankel, and E.M. Landes, "The Control of Externalities in Sports Leagues: An Analysis of Restrictions in the National Hockey League," *Journal of Political Economy* 112 (2004), pp. S268–88.

36. G.R. Roberts, "Professional Sports and the Antitrust Laws." In P.D. Staudohar and J.M. Mangan, eds., *The Business of Professional Sports*, pp. 136–40 (Urbana, IL: University of Illinois Press, 1991).

37. *American Football League v. National Football League*, 205 F. Supp. 60 (D. Md. 1962).

38. *Philadelphia World Hockey Club v. Philadelphia Hockey Club*, 351 F. Supp. 462 (E.D. Pa. 1972).

39. *United States Football League v. National Football League*, 842 F.2d 1335 (2d Cir. 1988).

40. *North American Soccer League v. National Football League*, 670 F.2d 1249 (2d. Cir.), cert. denied, 459 U.S. 1074 (1982).

41. Ross, "Competition Law as a Constraint on Monopolistic Exploitation by Sports Leagues and Clubs."

42. *Chicago Professional Sports, Ltd., v. National Basketball Association*, 95 F.3d 593 (7th Cir. 1996).

43. Roberts, "Professional Sports and the Antitrust Laws," pp. 142–43.

44. Ross, "Competition Law as a Constraint on Monopolistic Exploitation by Sports Leagues and Clubs," p. 578.

45. *Toolson v. New York Yankees*, 346 U.S. 356 (1953).

46. *Curtis C. Flood v. Bowie K. Kuhn et al.*, 407 U.S. 258 (1972); aff'g and 443 F.2d 264 (2d Cir., 1971), 316 F. Supp. 271 (S.D.N.Y. 1970).

47. *Radovich v. National Football League*, 352 U.S. 445 (1957).

48. G.R. Roberts, "*Brown v. Pro Football, Inc.*: The Supreme Court Gets It Right for the Wrong Reasons," *Antitrust Bulletin* 42 (1997), pp. 595–639; see footnotes 86 through 89.

49. *Brown v. Pro Football, Inc.*, 116 S.Ct. 2116 (1996).

50. *North American Soccer League v. NLRB*, 613 F.2d 1379 (5th Cir.), cert. denied, 449 U.S. 899 (1980).

51. Roberts, "*Brown v. Pro Football, Inc.*: The Supreme Court Gets It Right for the Wrong Reasons," pp. 596, 631.

52. Ibid., p. 637.

53. S.F. Ross and R.B. Lucke, "Why Highly Paid Athletes Deserve More Antitrust Protection Than Ordinary Unionized Workers," *Antitrust Bulletin* 42 (1997), pp. 641–79.

54. Ibid., p. 644.

55. *McNeil v. National Football League*, 790 F. Supp. 871 (D. Minn. 1992).

56. *Chicago Professional Sports Ltd. Partnership v. National Basketball Association*, 961 F.2d 667 (7th Cir. 1992).

57. *Sullivan v. National Football League*, 34 F.3d 1091 (1st Cir. 1994).

58. Rivkin, "Sports Leagues and the Federal Antitrust Laws," p. 391.

59. Ibid., p. 391.

60. Fort, *Sports Economics,* 2nd ed., chapter 11, and A.T. Johnson, "Congress and Professional Sports: 1951–1978," *Annals AAPSS* 445 (1979), pp. 102–15.

61. Johnson, "Congress and Professional Sports: 1951–1978," p. 103.

62. *Organized Baseball,* Hearings Before the Subcommittee on the Study of Monopoly Power of the Committee on the Judiciary, House of Representatives, 82nd Congress, 1st Session, Serial No. 1, Part 6, 1951; Celler's remarks are on p. 2. Subsequent hearings under Celler are in *Organized Professional Team Sports,* Hearings Before the Antitrust Subcommittee of the Committee on the Judiciary, House of Representatives, 85th Congress, 1st Session, Serial No. 8, Parts 1 and 2, 1957.

63. *Organized Professional Team Sports,* Hearings Before the Subcommittee on Antitrust and Monopoly of the Committee on the Judiciary, United States Senate, 85th Congress, 2nd Session, July, 1958, and *Organized Professional Team Sports,* Hearings Before the Subcommittee on Antitrust and Monopoly of the Committee on the Judiciary, U.S. Senate, 86th Congress, 1st Session, July 1959.

64. R.G. Noll and A. Zimbalist, "Sports, Jobs, and Taxes: The Real Connection," in R.G. Noll and A. Zimbalist, eds., *Sports, Jobs, and Taxes: The Economic Impact of Sports Teams and Stadiums*, p. 503 (Washington, DC: Brookings Institution, 1997).

65. *Inquiry into Professional Sports,* Select Committee on Professional Sports, House of Representatives, 94th Congress, 2d Session, part 2, September, 1976.

66. Quirk and Fort, *Pay Dirt: The Business of Professional Team Sports*; J. Quirk and R. Fort, *Hard Ball: The Uses and Abuses of Market Power in Professional Sports* (Princeton, NJ: Princeton University Press, 1999); and R. Fort, "Antitrust in Pro Sports," in P.D. Staudohar, ed., *Diamond Mines: Baseball & Labor*, pp. 112–15 (Syracuse, NY: Syracuse University Press, 2000).

67. R. Fort and J. Quirk, "Introducing a Competitive Economic Environment into Professional Sports," in W.Hendricks, ed., *Advances in the Economics of Sports,* Vol. 2, pp. 13–15 (Greenwich, CT: JAI Press, 1997).

68. Rivkin, "Sports Leagues and the Federal Antitrust Laws," p. 392.

69. Ibid., p. 394.

70. Ross and Dimitroff, "Whose Field of Dreams: Antitrust Relief Against Restrictions on the Sale or Relocation of Major League Baseball Teams," p. 522.

71. Fort, "Antitrust in Pro Sports," and Fort, *Sports Economics,* chapter 12.

72. Fort, *Sports Economics,* chapter 12.

73. M. Olson, *The Logic of Collective Action: Public Goods and the Theory of Groups* (Cambridge, MA: Harvard University Press, 1965).

74. Adams and Brock, "Monopoly, Monopsony, and Vertical Collusion: Antitrust Policy and Professional Sports."

75. Ibid., p. 729.

76. *The Sporting News,* April 5, 1993.

77. Rivkin, "Sports Leagues and the Federal Antitrust Laws."

78. A. Zimbalist, *Baseball and Billions: A Probing Look Inside the Big Business of Our National Pastime* (New York: BasicBooks, 1992).

79. J.L. Bast, "Stadium Madness: Why It Started, How to Stop It," Policy Study no. 85, Heartland Institute, Chicago, IL, February 23, 1998.

80. R.G. Noll, Testimony on *Inquiry into Professional Sports,* Select Committee on Professional Sports, House of Representatives, 94th Congress, 2d Session, part 2, September, 1976, pp. 131–36; I. Horowitz, Testimony on *Inquiry into Professional Sports,* Select Committee on Professional Sports, House of Representatives, 94th Congress, 2d Session, part 2, September, 1976, pp. 131–36; S.F. Ross, "Monopoly Sports Leagues," *Minnesota Law Review* 73 (1989), pp. 643–761; S.F. Ross, "Break Up the Sports League Monopolies," in P.D. Stau-dohar and J.M. Mangan, eds., *The Business of Professional Sports,* pp. 164–68 (Urbana, IL: University of Illinois Press, 1991); Fort and Quirk, "Introducing a Competitive Economic Environment into Professional Sports"; Quirk and Fort, *Hard Ball: The Uses and Abuses of Market Power in Professional Sports*; and Fort, "Antitrust in Pro Sports."

81. Arguments against antitrust impositions of this sort are in G.R. Roberts, "Professional Sports and the Antitrust Laws"; G.R. Roberts, "The Case for Baseball's Special Antitrust Immunity," *Journal of Sports Economics* 4 (2003), pp. 302–17; W.F. Shugart, II, "Preserve Baseball's Antitrust Exemption, Or, Why the Senators Are Out of Their League"; and D.R. Marburger, ed., *Stee-rike Four! What's Wrong with the Business of Baseball?* pp. 148–56 (Westport, CT: Praeger, 1997). The opposing view is in S.F. Ross, "Antitrust, Professional Sports, and the Public Interest," *Journal of Sports Economics* 4 (2003), pp. 318–31; B.K. Johnson, "Why Baseball's Antitrust Exemption Must Go." In D.R. Marburger, ed., *Stee-rike Four! What's Wrong with the Business of Baseball?* pp. 138–41 (Westport, CT: Praeger, 1997); and B.K. Johnson, "An Overlooked Implication of Baseball's Antitrust Exemption." In P.D. Staudohar, ed., *Diamond Mines: Baseball & Labor*, pp. 104–08 (Syracuse, NY: Syracuse University Press, 2000).

82. Noll and Zimbalist, "Sports, Jobs, and Taxes: The Real Connection," p. 505.

II

Firm Studies

10

General Motors

Lost Dominance

Seth W. Norton

From iconic rock songs to the voting behavior of NASCAR fans, the automobile is a cultural focal point. It has been one since the emergence of a vibrant motor vehicle industry early in the twentieth century. Moreover, in the world of American automobiles, no entity has garnered more attention than the General Motors Corporation. For much of the twentieth century, General Motors (GM) has been a dominant firm.

A dominant firm is a special type of enterprise in economics.[1] A dominant firm is characterized by disproportionate size compared to rivals and generally considerable dominance in economic performance, resulting in greater profits and market value for its equity and often in greater returns to investors. Sometimes dominant firms, such as Alcoa, Standard Oil Company, or United States Steel Corporation, and more recently Microsoft or Wal-Mart, have been the object of antitrust or regulatory actions by the government and sometimes opposition to their existence or specific business practices.

GM has some dominant firm characteristics. For one, General Motors is a large firm. In 2004, its assets were nearly $480 billion.[2] GM employs about 325,000 workers. GM has production operations in 33 countries and sells cars in 200 countries. GM owns other motor vehicle manufacturers: Holden, HUMMER, Opel, Vauxhall, and Saab. It has joint ventures with Toyota in the United States and with other firms throughout Europe and Asia. However, by conventional economic standards, its status as a dominant firm is questionable. GM has lost market share in both an absolute and relative sense. In recent decades, GM's market share has fallen compared to native domestic producers, compared to foreign firms that export automobiles for sale in the United States, and compared to foreign firms that have domestic operations within the United States.

Dominant Firms in Theory and Practice

Dominant firms are a bit of a hybrid in the study of competition. Dominant firms, at least the dominant firm with a competitive fringe model, behave like monopolists and exercise the monopolist's price-setting behavior—by choosing the profit-maximizing price/quantity configuration.[3] However, the dominant firm does so only after considering the supply effects of the smaller or "fringe firms." The latter behave largely as small, competitive "price takers," selling all they can at the price determined by the dominant firm and presumably following something akin to the customary "price equals marginal cost" rule of economic theory.

The contrasting behavior for the dominant and

small firms stems from the fact that the types of firms differ profoundly. A dominant firm often has lower costs and, hence, can capture greater market share and to a point set the terms of exchange— price and quantity for the entire market—or the dominant firm has some feature of product superiority that in turn leads to market dominance over its smaller rivals. Thus, the presence of a dominant firm raises an important question. What gives the dominant firm its competitive advantage?[4] More precisely, why are its costs lower than its rivals' costs, or what product benefits does it provide buyers that other firms cannot just as easily provide?

The presence of a dominant firm raises another question. Why do other firms not imitate the success of the dominant firm and, thus, reduce its dominance? There is a compelling logic that dominant firms should ultimately lose their competitive advantages. In the absence of some restrictions on competition, competing firms should seek to obtain their share of the dominant firm's profits. Indeed, a strong presumption among economists is that dominant firms will inevitably decline, and there is ample evidence that dominant firms eventually do lose market share.[5]

Despite this evidence, it remains a matter of great interest whether dominant firms always eventually decline and how long their dominance endures. For example, some economists and antitrust experts argue that laws regulating competition should be directed at accelerating the decline of dominant firms and constraining dominant firms' business practices that impede competition.[6] Those observers often argue that the government should aggressively enforce antitrust laws to ensure that dominant firms do not illegally retard the natural tendencies for increased competition in markets characterized by dominant firms. Consequently, the study of particular dominant firms and the general pattern of dominant firms warrant a special place in the study of competition.

It light of these considerations, it makes sense to study GM. Understanding its behavior and performance is a subject worthy of analysis. However, that assertion understates the economic relevance of GM. In many respects, GM's rise to dominance in the mid-1920s was stunning. It was swift and entailed surpassing a formidable rival, the Ford Motor Company. At the time, Ford was itself the dominant firm in the United States automobile industry and, on many dimensions, the pioneering mass-production assembly firm in the world. GM not only replaced Ford as the leader of mass-production assembly, it also emerged as the leading prototype of industrial management. Alfred P. Sloan, its long-time president and chairman of the board of directors, was a pioneer in the development of management of the large industrial enterprise. His achievements entailed the coordination of hundreds of thousands of employees in numerous large plants across the world, development of a coherent marketing strategy with emphasis on product positioning and new-product development, governing a publicly owned corporation with thousands of shareholders, and dealing with a correspondingly powerful labor union, the United Automobile Workers, in governing the operations of its plants. Sloan also pioneered in the development of effective partnerships with a vast dealer network that at one time included as many as 17,360 independently owned dealers dispersed in communities across the United States, as well as extensive similar operations in other countries.[7]

The uniqueness of GM extends further. The firm sustained its dominance for a remarkable period. Some scholars studying competition advocate aggressive public policies to limit dominant firms' size and behavior. Such scholars often stress the slowness of dominant firms to lose their dominance.[8] General Motors is a classic case in point. The firm's market share rose dramatically in the mid-1920s to nearly 40 percent. It maintained that position until World War II, when war production replaced much of civilian industry, including automobiles. In the years after World War II, General Motors resumed its dominance and even increased it. In the years 1946–1955, its market share was 45 percent and it rose progressively, with a share of domestic production of 59 percent for the period from 1976 to 1985. In short, General Motors strongly dominated the automobile industry for sixty years.[9]

While the record indicates that GM's dominance was sustained, it was noteworthy that GM's dominance was in an extremely important industry. In simplest economic terms, it is a foundational industry. Roughly 6.6 million American jobs have been closely connected to the automobile industry —in automobile assembly, various component suppliers to the industry, or people involved in the sales and distribution of automobiles.[10] During World War II, GM's manufacturing capacity for the war effort was approximately 10 percent of the nation's aggregate metal product manufacturing capacity.[11] The motor vehicle industry is a bellwether industry—its success has long been a signal of the state of the American economy. To dominate such an industry, to such a degree, for so long, is a remarkable performance, and it merits a close examination.

An alternative approach to studying GM would be to focus on the automobile industry rather than GM. That approach would stress the interaction of General Motors with its primary domestic rivals —Ford and Chrysler—as well as some smaller rivals for a while and major European and Asian rivals in recent decades. That approach would not stress the dominant firm features but would stress the interaction of GM with its rivals—as a "tight oligopoly," in deterring price competition via GM's price-setting leadership, fixing sales levels, and perhaps retarding product development of small or high-mileage cars.[12] The analysis of the struc-ture, conduct, and performance of the automobile industry is especially relevant for examining antitrust policy, international trade, labor policies, and government regulation of fuel economy standards and safety standards for automobiles.[13] Those are certainly important issues of public policy and analysis. However, the rise and fall of General Motors is an epic story in American economic history that is especially noteworthy for understanding the economics of both firms and markets, and it is our present focus.

GM's Rise to Dominance

The 1920s witnessed conspicuous prosperity. There were several economic downturns, but they proved to be short-lived. Like parties held at Gatsby's estate in F. Scott Fitzgerald's novel of the times, *The Great Gatsby*, the economy "roared." No part of the economy seemed to roar more than the automobile industry. U.S. sales of cars and trucks were a bit less than 2.3 million in 1920, but by 1929 the comparable number was more than 5.3 million.[14] This significant growth was due in large part to the industry's dynamic nature. During the period, there were fourteen major product innovations, twenty-two major new competitors entered the market, and forty-three producing firms exited the automobile industry.[15] Rising incomes led to increased sales, and entrepreneurs in the industry devised products that satisfied customers. In particular, during this period, car production shifted to what came to be the "dominant design" for passenger cars—the all-steel, closed-body car.

In the midst of this era, General Motors replaced the Ford Motor Company, headed by its legendary founder, Henry Ford, as the leading automobile manufacturer. GM was not a new enterprise. William C. (Billy) Durant brought General Motors into existence in 1908 by the merger of five existing firms: Chevrolet, Pon-

Figure 10.1   **GM's Market Share, 1910–1940**

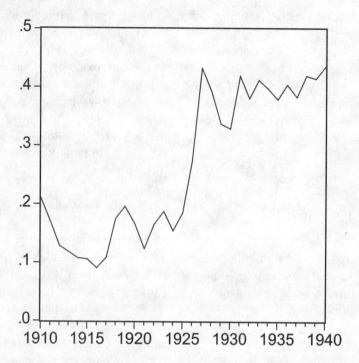

Source: General Motors Corporation, Annual Reports, various years. Sales are in $ (millions).

tiac, Overland, Buick, and Cadillac, and some suppliers. Durant acted on the assumption that there was substantial consumer demand and that potential production efficiency would result from an automobile manufacturer of large size. However, GM's performance did not measure up to Durant's aspirations and the assessment of the financial community. Durant left the firm in 1920. Alfred P. Sloan assumed leadership of GM in 1923 when he became the chief executive of the firm. Sloan brought order to a chaotic enterprise, and GM survived various competitive challenges, but Ford continued to dominate GM and the industry. However, in the middle of the 1920s, things changed: GM's performance surged in nearly every dimension.

The Data

Figure 10.1 contains data on GM's market share for the 1910–1940 period. The data show that the market share of the firm declined in the years after its formation. The numbers reflect the lack of a coherent strategy during the years when the firm was operated much like a holding company in which the divisions seemed to be competing more with each other than with other firms. Market share fluctuated considerably in the early 1920s along with the aggregate economy, and GM seemed unable to coordinate operating decisions across the divisions as well as its sales to dealers with dealers' sales to final consumers. However, in the mid-1920s, GM's market share rose dramatically.

Figure 10.2   **GM's Net Sales, 1920–1929**

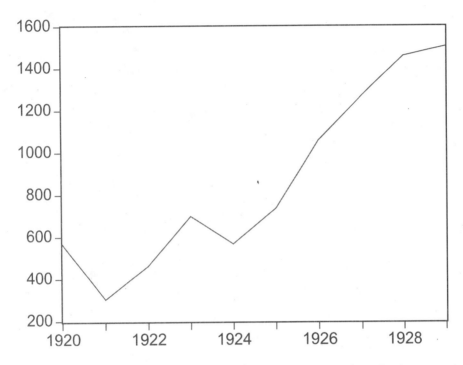

Source: General Motors Corporation, Annual Reports, various years. Sales are in $ (millions).

It fell a bit as Ford brought the Model A on line in 1928, but recovered and then stabilized around the 40 percent level.[16]

Figure 10.2 shows GM's net sales (in millions) for a shorter period. Again, fluctuations in the early 1920s are evident. However, the dominant feature is the dramatic increase starting in 1925. U.S. sales went from a bit more than $300 million in 1921 to about $1.5 billion in 1929.[17] A similar pattern holds for profits. In the period 1927 through 1937, GM earned over $2 billion while Ford lost $200 million.[18] Another piece of evidence for GM's ascendancy and its continued dominance is a comparison of its stock price and a portfolio of non-GM motor vehicle manufacturers for the 1920–1938 period. The data are shown in figure 10.3.[19]

The data show a dramatic rise for GM relative to its competitors during the mid-1920s with modest declines in 1932 and 1937. Overall, GM's stock price strongly dominated its non-GM rivals except for a few downturns and its languishing period in the early 1920s. In short, GM's stock price performance also documents its ascendancy over its competitors and its sustained dominance through the 1930s.

Consensus Explanations

Most accounts of the rise of GM stress three factors: GM's product market strategy, the adoption of the multidivisional form, "the M-form," and its vertical integration strategy. The pyramid of

Figure 10.3   **GM's Stock Price over Non-GM Auto Firms' Stock Price**

Source: Global Financial Data. Original data from the Cowles Commission.

demand refers to GM's marketing strategy that emerged early in the 1920s.[20] It was essentially a market segmentation strategy based on income. GM would produce and sell a car "for every purpose and purse." The separate operating divisions would each have a segment in the market. For example, the Cadillac division would develop and sell luxury cars, while the Chevrolet division would compete with Ford's low-priced Model T.

Sloan describes the product strategy that eventually emerged and came to dominate the industry:

> The product policy we proposed is the one for which General Motors has now long been known. We said first the corporation should produce a line of cars in each price area, from the lowest price up to one for a strictly high-grade quantity-production car, but we would not get into the fancy-price field with small

production; second, that the price steps should not be such as to leave wide gaps in the line, and yet should be great enough to keep their number within reason, so that the greatest advantage of quantity production could be secured; and third, that there should be no duplication by the corporation in the price fields or steps.[21]

One difficulty with the pyramid of demand strategy is that the firm had to coordinate the product offerings and general pricing strategies of the divisions, or the divisions might compete against each other and, in the process, reduce the total profitability of the firm. If the operating divisions had authority to make their own "product positioning" decisions, i.e., choosing the best combination of product-quality levels and price, then they could easily move toward the most profitable product areas and maximize divisional profits but not the entire firm's profits. A uniform product policy had to reflect unity among the operating divisions. Thus, it was possible that GM might give too much discretion to the component operating divisions. Indeed, some scholars argue that GM was too decentralized in its early years and that GM's performance was inhibited because it failed to coordinate product policy as well as production and investment policies across divisions. On the other hand, firms can be too centralized and limit some of the competitive advantage associated with giving decision-making authority to those closest to the problems that need to be solved. The balancing of those conflicting tensions was addressed by the second major consensus explanation for GM's rise—the multidivisional firm or M-form.

In the early years of the twentieth century, large firms tended to be organized around two competing organizational forms: the functionally organized firm (sometimes called the unitary form or "U-form") and the holding company.[22] These organizational approaches to business strategy were opposites, reflecting extreme centralization in the case of the functionally organized firm and extreme decentralization in the case of the holding company. The Ford Motor Company embodied the functional form, while GM in the early years seemed to embody the holding company format.

Firms organized by the functional form were the first modern firms. They were characterized by central offices that directed all activities in their functional or business domain. There were typically separate departments for finance, production, personnel, purchasing, logistics, sales, and marketing. The functional form gained the advantages of specialization and could be successful, but failed to achieve the necessary coordination for large, multiproduct firms with production and sales operations dispersed over large geographic areas. The flow of information to the central office was inadequate. Indeed, the larger the enterprise, the bigger the problem.

The holding company was the U-form's opposite. Holding companies emerged in the nineteenth century. Their *modus operandi* was little activity at the central office and little managerial control. The holding company amounted to a decentralized collection of nearly autonomous companies under common ownership.

The M-form emerged early in the twentieth century as a synthesis of these two forms. In the M-form, there are separate functionally organized divisions based on product or geographic units with a central office. In the typical M-form, senior management and the head office direct the firm's activities by raising financial capital, allocating capital across divisions, appointing and evaluating divisional managers, coordinating firm-wide policies, and setting the strategic direction. Divisional managers commonly direct all other activities, including design, engineering, manufacturing, marketing, personnel, procurement, research and development, and sales, although some of these functions may reside with central staff at the head office.

Alfred Sloan instituted a reorganization of GM prior to his becoming president of the corporation. GM adopted the new form organization in January 1921.[23] Sloan's reorganization reflected an attempt to reconcile the problems of coordination and control of central operations with the advantages of efficiency attributable to delegation of authority to those with the most relevant information. GM, along with DuPont, Sears, Roebuck, and Standard Oil of New Jersey, pioneered in the development of the M-form.

The development of the M-form at GM permitted divisional managers to specialize in knowledge relevant to operating their respective divisions and to link responsibility and decision-making authority. The firm could take advantage of economies of scale when purchasing common components such as spark plugs and bearings and, at the same time, reap the benefits of localized personnel and production decisions.

A crucial feature of the M-form in the rise of GM in the United States auto industry was the complementarity between GM's pyramid of demand product policy and the coordination of cross-divisional product policy to achieve a firm-wide, coherent strategy of product positioning and pricing.[24] Prior to the reorganization of the firm, there was insufficient coordination in product and pricing policy between Cadillac, Chevrolet, Oakland, and Oldsmobile. There may have been more competition among these divisions than between GM and Ford. By using the committee structure of the central staff and the entire firm, GM used the M-form to develop the coherent marketing strategy that eventually surpassed the technological mastery of Ford's production-intensive, low-priced model T, operated via an eventually outmoded, functional organizational form.

The third consensus explanation for the rise of GM was the firm's vertical integration strategy. Simply put, GM brought increasing percentages of its supply activities in-house.[25] GM pursued an active strategy of vertical integration backward into component parts nearly from the creation of the firm. Billy Durant viewed the availability of parts as complementary to large-scale production. By 1920, GM was involved in manufacturing numerous parts, including gears, axles, crankshafts, radiators, electrical equipment, roller bearings, warning signals, spark plugs, bodies, plate glass, and body hardware. After the departure of Durant as president, the short-lived presidency of Pierre DuPont (December 1920 to May 1923), and the ascension of Alfred Sloan at GM, the firm continued to integrate backward into component parts, presumably to ensure the coordination of parts supply and thus to achieve greater economies of scale and scope in production.[26]

One problem with the consensus explanations is that they do not account for the timing of the striking rise in performance during the mid-1920s. The concept and many of the details of the pyramid demand were well in place by 1920. Similarly, the M-form was in place by 1921. Vertical integration into component parts may have played a role, but that integration strategy was implemented primarily incrementally. There was a 12 percent decrease in the value of purchased component parts between 1925 and 1926. However, there was also a 10 percent decrease between 1923 and 1924.[27] The dominant pattern is a trend, not a break in the degree of vertical integration. Thus, there is not a clear basis for a discontinuity in vertical integration, and there is no basis to conclude that the explosive performance during the mid-1920s is simply the result of increased vertical integration. Perhaps the Fisher-Body acquisition may provide an explanation of a small event that had a big payoff, but there are problems with that explanation because GM had a lot of control over Fisher-Body before the mid-1920s.

Another possibility is that GM's rise was a series of actions GM took regarding its vast dealer network to synchronize its production with final consumer demand. GM moved to requiring substantial information regarding final consumer demand from the individual dealers and requiring the operating divisions to synchronize production levels to correspond closely with anticipated consumer demand and to react swiftly to changes in consumer demand.[28]

Whatever the exact causal nexus, it seems clear that something happened in 1925 that radically altered GM's performance in both an absolute and relative sense. It might simply be that the firm finally worked out the problems of coordinating a large enterprise—fitting the product strategy with the organizational strategy, resulting in large gains in performance. A certain answer at present seems elusive.

Sustained Dominance

The story of GM's rise and its replacement of Ford as the leading automobile manufacturer are noteworthy, but its continued dominance through the Great Depression and through more than three decades after World War II is at least equally noteworthy. During World War I and the Korean conflict, GM provided considerable manufacturing support for the military operations, but those activities were secondary to the market-driven, profit-making business operations of the firm.[29] However, during World War II, GM was primarily a maker of war equipment, and automobile production ceased. GM reorganized its operations to deal with military contracts, and the firm spent considerable effort addressing the unique human resource challenges facing production requirements with labor shortages and an untrained workforce. Despite the overriding concerns and necessity of wartime production, Sloan and GM's top management gave careful thought to the postwar economy and GM's strategy once hostilities ceased. The firm planned for postwar prosperity and growing automobile demand. Their forecasts were generally accurate, and the firm sustained its unusual performance and even added to it for an extended period. The common presumption among economists that dominant firms eventually decline did not hold true for a remarkably extended period.

Market Dynamics

Alfred P. Sloan's explanation for GM's rise to dominance stressed the three pillars described above, but Sloan also stressed the fact that the automobile market underwent important changes during the 1920s and in the years that followed. Sloan also emphasized that those changes benefited GM and hurt Ford. There is no doubt that GM's strategies were a better fit with the market changes

and GM adapted better to the changes in the market. There is considerable ambiguity about whether these factors were central to GM's initial rise in performance during the mid-1920s or whether they only contributed to GM's sustained success in the decades that followed. Moreover, the adaptations of the 1920s were refined and further developed in the decades to come. Thus, it is difficult to ascertain whether their primary contribution was in GM's rise or its sustained dominance. In any case, part of GM's success included the good strategic fit of GM with the changes in the marketplace.

Sloan identified four changes in the automobile market that proved on net beneficial to GM's business strategy, organizational design, and long-term superior performance. They were: the used-car trade-in, installment sales, the closed body, and the annual model.[30]

Up until sometime in the early 1920s, most car purchases were made by first-time buyers. Their purchases reflected the diffusion of the automobile as a new transportation medium and its continued acceptance by American consumers. As first-time buyers came back to the car dealers to purchase their second car, they frequently used their first car as a down payment on their second car. The transition for a majority of vehicle buyers occurred at some unknown time in the early 1920s. In the process, an active used-car market developed in the United States. While used cars were a potential competitive threat to new-car sales, the diffusion of the automobile product concept and product improvements, including improved reliability, dominated the possible adverse effects of the used-car market so that sales of new cars continued to grow.

GM recognized the market dynamics and sought to facilitate the growth of the new-car market even as total new-car sales entered into a seven-year plateau starting in 1923.[31] GM formed GMAC, its car-financing arm, in 1919.[32] In the early years of the automobile industry, banks appeared reluctant to finance automobile purchases, and to some degree to provide sufficient financing for automobile dealer financing for wholesale purchases. GM refined its financing services during the 1919–1924 period. The strategy aimed at lowering transaction costs for retail customers and easing the potential burdens and bad debt liabilities for dealers. The financing system that was implemented proved to be well conceived and well administered. Default rates were minuscule. The net result was substantially enhanced retail sales and dealer financial stability. GM thrived along with the system.

During the period 1919–1929 a major innovation was the introduction of the all-steel body. Dodge was a pioneering firm, but other firms quickly followed. The percentages of cars that were all-steel closed bodies was 10 percent in 1919 and increased in each of the following years to 17, 22, 30, 34, 43, 56, 72, and 85 percent.[33] It became the "dominant design." A dominant design is the one design that "wins allegiance in the marketplace."[34] It is the product design that meets the requirements of many classes of users and in which numerous product features are implicit. Most surviving competitors will produce a product that conforms to the dominant design. For GM, the increasing sales of closed bodies meant increased use of the Fisher Body, in which GM had acquired 60 percent of interest in 1919. In 1926, GM purchased the remaining 40 percent of Fisher Body, made it one of the GM divisions, and moved to increase the coordination of production of automobile bodies with chassis assembly. In short, the boom in closed-body sales led to a particular variant of GM's vertical integration strategy. Increased sales of closed-body Chevrolets was a core motive for the acquisition.

The fourth innovation was the annual model. GM did not set out to create annual models. The firm did recognize in the 1920s that, as buyers came

to rely on the automobile for basic transportation, they also expressed preferences for more "comfort, convenience, power and style."[35] As GM's marketing and engineering staffs observed buyer preferences, new models began to reflect product offerings that served those preferences. For example, in 1926, the Cadillac Division introduced "styling" as a separate concept and specialty within the industry.[36] Similarly, in 1925, GM's Chevrolet Division introduced the K Model. Alfred Sloan describes the model:

> The K Model had among its new features a longer body, increased leg room, a Duco finish, a one-piece windshield with automatic wipers on all closed cars, a dome light in the coach and sedan, a Klaxon horn, an improved clutch and a sound rear-axle housing in place of the old one, which had given so much trouble. It was far from being a radically new car, but it was much better than it had been and in the particulars noted above it gave the first real expression of what we had in mind to do. The K Model came on a rising market in 1925 and recovered Chevrolet's position sharply with factory sales of 481,000 cars and trucks, a 64 percent gain over 1924 and a level 6 percent above the 1923 peak.[37]

By observing potential buyer preferences and in turn pursuing engineering advances to meet customer demand, GM began significant annual model changes after 1923. The policy was not initially deliberately annual but eventually turned into introduction of annual models. In the 1930s, GM recognized that annual models had become "regularized" and began to officially designate them.

The four changes in the marketplace—used-car sales, consumer financing, closed bodies, and annual models—enhanced GM's performance and helped it secure its place as the dominant firm. One reason is that the Ford Motor Company had made substantial commitments to the low-priced, open-body Model T and was generally much less sensitive to the latent demand for advanced product features and some of the details of the retail transaction. Sloan notes that these changes helped GM pass Ford and maintain its dominance in the years prior to World War II.[38] GM's performance compared to Ford's strongly suggests that, as the environment changes, optimal business strategies also must change and managers that correctly adapt to market changes do better than those who strictly adhere to past platforms.

Additional Contributions

Other factors played a role in GM's protracted dominance. Like the case of market changes, it is difficult to account for how important these factors were in sustaining GM or even in its initial rise.

The economics of retail sales entail subtle relationships.[39] There is a potential conflict of interest between manufacturers and their dealers regarding the optimal margins for each party.[40] This basic economic problem, the "double marginalization" problem, means that, if each party sets a profit-maximizing margin independently of the joint effects of both margins on the customer, sales can be hurt for both parties. However, if one party yields to the maximizing behavior of the other party, the cooperative party will lose all profits. Thus, there is considerable need for cooperation between the manufacturer and each dealer—an essentially vertical relationship. Moreover, some dealers may compete with other dealers of the same brand if their potential customers overlap, and some dealers would be better off if they also carried the brands of competing manufacturing firms. Thus, there is a need for horizontal coordination among dealers, and the manufacturer may be in the best position to facilitate the horizontal coordination.

In the early years of the automobile dealerships, manufacturers often treated them as mere merchants and ignored the subtle coordination issues. In contrast, Alfred Sloan made extensive visits to the vast dealer network that GM created and assisted in financing and in organizing dealer-wide involvement in decision making.[41] For some time, GM enjoyed some competitive advantages in distribution.

As the automobile industry evolved, automakers favored dealers who sold only their brands and generally followed the manufacturers' preferences. Automakers often tried to "solve" the double marginalization problem by "forcing" extra cars on dealers. Manufacturers often required dealers to cut their margins to achieve sales. When dealers balked at the forcing practice, automakers used "termination threats," i.e., potential loss of the dealership, to compel dealer acceptance of extra cars and thus lower dealer margins. Eventually dealers filed lawsuits and sought legislative remedies from the practice.

In the post–World War II period, manufacturer–dealer relations changed notably. Manufacturer rules against selling competing brands were eroded by the *Standard Stations* case that restricted exclusive dealing arrangements. Other governance issues regarding dealer networks were addressed and resolved in federal and state legislation. These legal provisions, commonly known as "dealer day in court" laws, and a federal law passed in 1956, substantially altered the automobile marketing channel. Nearly simultaneously, GM made a concerted attempt to enhance relations with its dealers.[42]

The public policy approach to dealer governance had at least one important effect on GM. The scope of competition through dealer governance was restricted and, therefore, GM could rely on other sources of competitive advantage—its brand names and product policy and its organizational efficiency, both long-term strategies developed by Sloan. In short, dealer competition was standardized, and GM focused on other competitive strengths.

The National Labor Relations Act was passed in

1935 as part of Franklin Roosevelt's New Deal.[43] That act enabled large industrial unions to seek collective bargaining recognition. The considerable profitability of GM made it a prime target for the principal union, the United Automobile Workers. The UAW successfully organized the major automobile manufacturers after some stormy recognition struggles. During World War II, peaceful labor relations existed as the War Labor Board mandated a pattern wage formula. The wage formula entailed 3 percent for productivity increases plus a cost-of-living adjustment. The GM/UAW agreement of 1948 after the war was remarkably similar and became the pattern for the automobile industry as well as other manufacturing industries.[44]

That agreement was instrumental in the formation and evolution of a dominant heavy manufacturing industrial relations system that stressed pattern agreements across industries, elaborate contracts with multiple job categories, and strict job descriptions, quasi-judicial contractual administration, and an emphasis on stability of labor–management relations.

The net effect for GM was similar to the standardization of the dealer network system through court decisions and legislations. Pattern agreements across firms in the same industry tended to take the employment relationship out of competition.[45] GM, as a dominant firm, could continue to enjoy the benefits of its organization and product policy and follow less than aggressive strategies in other domains. Accordingly, labor-management conditions did little to erode GM's competitive advantages during the three decades of GM's protracted postwar dominance.

Yet another possible contribution was incentive compensation.[46] One problem with large firms like General Motors, which are owned by large numbers of investors, is that the managers may have weak incentives to pursue strategies that primarily benefit stockholders. One partial solution is to reward managers for enhancing stockholder wealth. GM pursued such a strategy early in the firm's history and offered a bonus plan as early as 1918. While the system was altered on several occasions, the essential features had great continuity. Managers at both the operating divisional level and the corporate levels were rewarded when the firm did well. The compensation was typically partly or wholly with stock ownership. Moreover, individual managers had to earn the right to be considered for a bonus.

Unambiguous evidence regarding the effects of the incentive compensation at GM does not exist. GM's sustained dominance stems from many other forces. Nevertheless, Sloan and other GM executives consistently argued that the compensation system aligned the interests of the firm's managers with the stockholders. They attribute GM's remarkable performance during the Great Depression as a partial consequence of the compensation system, including its effects in encouraging cooperation within the firm and encouraging loyalty from GM's executives.[47]

The Schumpeterian Legacy

Joseph Schumpeter was an Austrian-born economist who taught at Harvard University. Schumpeter emphasized a historical as opposed to theoretical or mathematical approach to economics and emphasized the role of entrepreneurs and innovation as part of the competitive process.[48] Generalizing on the historical process of invention and change, "creative destruction" in his terminology, Schumpeter noted the benefits of dynamic monopolies as opposed to the alleged benefits of static, competitive markets. Schumpeter also discussed the role of discontinuity in economic life and the destabilizing effects of innovation and the restructuring of economic organization that moved an economy to a new, stable equilibrium.

Schumpeter's contribution to economic understanding is imposing. However, the contemporary economic historian Nathan Rosenberg has provided detailed studies showing that competitive innovation in the commercial process involves more than just invention.[49] Commercialization of technical advances often requires considerable product improvement or process enhancement, improved reliability, and protracted inventive activity. At least part of GM's continued dominance in the U.S. auto industry can be attributed to this type of activity, which Sloan believed pervaded nearly all aspects of GM's operations and product offerings.

Sloan asserted that nearly every feature of automobile manufacturing improved after 1920. Engineers at GM pursued improved efficiency and product attributes with ceaseless commitment. Both the product and the processes of making the products improved.[50] New GM cars offered enhanced comfort, convenience, power, and style. Moreover, the products became increasingly reliable. Sloan identified four improvements that were particularly noteworthy and exceeded general improved reliability. These were ethyl gasoline and high-compression engines, automatic transmissions, balloon tires and front end suspensions, and Duco finishes.

To obtain higher levels of engine compression, "engine knock" had to be removed. Researchers at GM discovered gasoline additives that noticeably reduced engine knock. Moreover, GM set up Ethyl Gasoline Corporation—a venture with Standard Oil of New Jersey—and helped to diffuse the adoption of ethyl gasoline. Researchers at GM also directly reduced engine knock through product design. Similarly, GM Research Laboratories and various engineering staffs developed two operative automatic transmissions that could be economically produced and led to wide adoption by consumers. GM also developed balloon tires and a front-end suspension that provided a notably smoother ride. Finally, GM worked cooperatively with DuPont to develop a fast-drying, secure car finish. The innovation provided attractive colors, improved finish durability, and reduced drying time to eight hours from between two and four weeks. The last effect markedly lowered manufacturing inventory costs.

In the ensuing decades, GM continued a long line of automotive inventions.[51] These include the torque converter, bonded brake linings, high-compression V-8 engine, fiberglass body, rear engine, air-cooled engine, independent rear wheels, rear transmission, flexible drive shaft, dual brakes, simplified overhead cam engine, front-wheel drive, collapsible steering column, and side beams to resist side impact. Some observers claim that fringe firms were better noted for their inventions or that their ultimate demise led to less innovation in the industry while the larger firms long resisted aggressive product competition.[52] Whatever the merits of that contention, GM's innovative record is impressive and must account in part for the firm's sustained dominance.

Demise of General Motors

GM's competitive dominance peaked in the mid-1970s. In the following decades, GM has faced severe downturns in its business, forced restructurings, and severe retrenchment. At times, conspicuous operating losses have made some observers skeptical of the viability of the firm. Two forces converged to erode GM's competitive position: new rivals that challenged GM's production and marketing leadership, and significant changes in the automobile market.

Imports

The magnitude of GM's decline is evident on several fronts. Table 10.1 contains data on GM's

Table 10.1

GM and Import Market Shares, 1950–1980

Year	GM	Imports	GM/Imports
1950	45.48	0.26	175.92
1955	50.76	0.81	62.67
1960	43.64	7.58	5.76
1965	50.07	6.11	8.20
1969	46.79	11.24	4.16
1975	43.41	18.17	2.39
1980	46.41	28.18	1.65

Source: Automotive News, *Market Data Book*, 1981.

Table 10.2

GM's Relative Market Share

Year(s)	GM/Ford	GM/ Chrysler	GM/All others
1913	0.30	NA	0.25
1923	0.43	10.00	0.63
1933	1.95	1.64	3.15
1946–55	1.88	2.37	3.75
1956–65	1.76	3.64	8.50
1966–75	2.00	3.18	27.00
1977	2.46	4.54	14.75
1992	1.75	4.67	1.68
2003	1.23	2.00	1.23
2005	1.19	1.87	0.793

Source: Lawrence J. White, *The Automobile Industry Since 1945* (Cambridge: Harvard University Press, 1971). *Ward's Automotive Yearbook,* various years. Automotive News, *Market Data Book,* various years.

market share and the market share of all import sales, as well as the ratio of GM's market share to the import market share. Imports of foreign-made automobiles were nearly nonexistent in 1950. They were not much greater in 1955—a boom year for domestic auto sales. However, by 1960 imports had made a noticeable initial inroad into the U.S. motor vehicle market. The 1960s and 1970s saw continued growth of imports. While GM's market share in the domestic market remained stable, its competitive position relative to imports clearly was eroding. Rising oil prices resulting from the growing strength of the Organization of Petroleum Exporting Countries (OPEC) cartel and high miles-per-gallon imports were instrumental in the expanding import share of the market.

GM and the other U.S. automakers and the United Automobile Workers sought protection from foreign competition. In the early 1980s, the industry successfully lobbied for "voluntary" export restraints (VERs) to give U.S. automakers "breathing room" to reposition their products and operations.[53] The net effect of the program included increased prices on domestically produced vehicles and imports and sizable profits for American firms. Japanese firms also responded by expanding into luxury cars and opening operations in the United States. The latter operations, labeled "transplants,"

brought their innovations into the United States. The transplants were an "end-run" around explicit or tacit protectionism. Moreover, they accelerated GM's decline and provided evidence of GM's competitive weaknesses.

Domestic Decline and Transplants

Table 10.2 highlights GM's decline. The data show GM's market share compared to the domestic market share of Ford, Chrysler, and all other domestic producers. The ratio represents the concept of "relative market share," a frequent measure of a firm's performance among business strategy experts.[54]

Three patterns are evident. First, with the exception of a decline in GM's market share relative to Chrysler from 1923 to 1933, the rise and dominance of GM is seen from 1923 to the mid-1970s. Second, GM's position vis-à-vis Ford peaked in 1977 and vis-à-vis Chrysler in 1992. After those years, GM is in decline. Thus, its lost dominance includes its position with respect to its classic domestic rivals. Third, GM's relative market share

Table 10.3

Global Vehicle Production: GM and Toyota

Year	GM	Toyota	GM/Toyota
2000	8,494,000	5,888,260	1.44
2002	8,227,000	6,309,616	1.30
2004	8,745,838	7,547,177	1.15

Source: Automotive News, *Market Data Book,* 2005.

compared to all other U.S. producers is particularly instructive. The figure peaks in the 1966–1975 period when GM dominated the remaining fringe producers. In the ensuing years, GM's relative market share falls dramatically, reflecting both falling performance and the competitive advantage of foreign firms now operating in the United States as transplants. By 2005, GM's share was less than all other producers, a dramatic decline for the once dominant motor vehicle producer.

Table 10.3 provides another perspective on GM's demise. The data in the table show the worldwide production levels for recent years—2000, 2002, and 2004 for GM and Toyota—and also show GM's relative vehicle production with respect to Toyota's. The data show that the trend toward lost dominance is unabated and pervasive, including the bulk of GM's operations. By 2004, GM's production relative to Toyota's was barely above 1.0.

The Economics of Modern Manufacturing

To gain some perspective on both GM's sustained dominance and its comparative decline in the last twenty-five years, some background on the nature of manufacturing is in order.[55] Modern manufacturing is a wondrous cluster of human action and ingenuity. In the automobile industry more than 60 million vehicles are produced annually.[56] The combination of machine and human specialization and the requisite coordination toward the common end of producing the multiple vehicles is nearly unimaginable.

From Craft to Mass to Lean

Initial automobile production followed a craft production model.[57] Craft production involves skilled workers making products to a customer's specifications—catering to individuals' preferences. A craft worker must know the product design, machine operations, and tooling and must integrate these into operations. Machines are general purpose and volume is low. Supply organization is diffuse. Beyond customer preferences, product standardization is low.

Mass production in automobiles is widely associated with Henry Ford and the Model T.[58] Ford's innovative production system and its numerous reproduced operations are characterized by interchangeable parts and attachment of them to each other via the assembly line. Ford used the same gauges throughout the entire manufacturing process and on the moving assembly line. The operations relied on extreme division of labor, specialized machines, and numerous unskilled workers. Ford's product, the Model T, was limited and standardized—the opposite of craft production. The emphasis was overwhelmingly high volume.

Under Sloan's direction, GM expanded upon Ford's production model with innovations in marketing as well as organization and management—the consensus explanations for GM's rise. Notably, GM, as well as the other surviving domestic manufacturers and foreign operations, were essentially mass-production operations. Because mass production emphasizes high volume, some observers conclude that unlimited economies of scale drive competition in the auto industry or that GM's long-run dominance stemmed from scale economy differentials with its rivals. However, that conclusion is commonly criticized.[59] There are, to be sure, substantial economies of scale in automobile manufacturing and in other business practices. For example, GM's annual advertising budget has exceeded $3.4 billion, and that fact may entail some economies of scale in marketing.[60] In terms of plant scale economies, a common view is that scale economies dissipate after about the 200,000 vehicles per year range of production.[61]

A striking feature of modern manufacturing has been the emergence of a post-mass-production strategy.[62] A set of production techniques, combined with innovation in organizational design and business strategy, has coalesced and evolved to an identifiable strategy that falls under the rubric of "lean production." The manufacturing strategy is closely identified with Japanese firms and particularly Toyota and the Toyota Production System (TPS).[63]

The architects of the TPS, Eiji Toyoda and Taiichi Ohno, recognized in the early post–World War II years that the Japanese domestic motor vehicle market was too small and too fragmented to pursue the mass-production strategy.[64] Instead, they pursued an innovative strategy that rested upon the steadfast elimination of *muda,* or waste, and especially the elimination of wasteful inventories. Indeed, Toyota's economical just-in-time (JIT) inventory system, or *kanban,* is one of the widest known features of the TPS. However, elimination of inventory required reinvention of the organization of production and the employment relation, including empowering workers to respond to localized information.

The reinvention of the organization of production itself focused on two features: the assembly plant and supplier relations. In the first case, Toyota adopted a "scientific" perspective—an emphasis on experimentation with alternative organization and the measurement of performance.[65] The latter focused on two indices: yield, or the number of cars actually produced, and quality. The innovative plant organization included the use of teamwork groups

with an emphasis on *kaizen*—continuous improvement in quality. Notably, workers were instructed to stop the assembly line if necessary to prevent defective products from progressing through the plant. Workers learned to trace mistakes to their respective source. As workers gained problem-solving experience, the amount of "rework" at the end of the assembly line fell sharply—a marked contrast with mass-production practice elsewhere. By 1990, Toyota assembly plants had almost no rework space and activity, whereas mass-production practice plants commonly devoted 20 percent of the plant area and 25 percent of total hours to fixing mistakes.[66]

The reinventing of the organization of production also included the supplier functions. The mass-production supply model seemed to follow two extremes, vertical integration (in-house supply of major components from supplying divisions within the firm) and spot-market suppliers operating as arm's-length independent firms selected on the basis of low-bid competition. Toyota, in contrast, developed a hybrid structure that might be termed "relational," with an appropriate sense of partnership or alliance. Indeed, the relational supply arrangement has proved central to the *kanban* and supplier efficiency.[67]

In the Toyota supply arrangement, the parties stress cooperation—creating value rather than appropriating value. There is an emphasis on sharing the gains from cooperation. In the supplier arrangement, Toyota puts special emphasis on selecting partners and coming to implicit understandings of commitments and performance, relying on the understanding and only short, simple contracts. Toyota devotes considerable effort to helping suppliers improve their efficiency. Toyota also encourages and requires extensive information sharing with suppliers.

Evidence exists that Toyota's supplier arrangement increases value and that Toyota shares the increased value with its suppliers.[68] By sharing the increased value, Toyota has developed a favorable reputation. Firms want to be Toyota suppliers. However, Toyota also exhibits the threat of punishment to its suppliers in order to strengthen cooperation. The threat rests on Toyota's two-supplier policy. While Toyota relies on a single supplier for a component for the life of the model, Toyota commonly has another supplier of similar components for another model. If one of the suppliers behaves opportunistically rather than cooperatively, Toyota could shift to a new supplier for the next model life. Accordingly, loss of continued business serves as a powerful deterrent to supplier opportunism. Additionally, Toyota carefully monitors supplier performance and uses performance in choosing future suppliers with noteworthy effects on quality and innovation.[69]

Toyota also reinvented the employment relation.[70] Besides the team organization noted above, Toyota workers have had powerful incentives to perform well. These include lifetime employment, incentive compensation, and a steep wage progression to "bond" workers to Toyota, as well as opportunities for heavy investment in skill acquisition, comparative freedom in job design and descriptions, comparative absence of the status conflicts between "blue collar" and "white collar" categories, and relief from the monotony of factory work.

These three ingredients are conspicuous elements of the TPS. However, they do not exhaust the successful strategic factors underlying Toyota's success. On the production side, the TPS also includes rapid die changes, shorter production runs, and cross-functional product development. Toyota also developed an intrinsically cooperative marketing channel with an extensive distribution network. Similarly, its marketing strategy stressed repeat buying, brand loyalty, and attractive product mix that strongly complemented the manufacturing advances associated with lean production.

The die-changing example is particularly noteworthy. Dies are heavy metal forms that are among the most expensive tools in the industrialized world.[71] These heavy metal forms are made out of strong steel alloys and are used to stamp sheet metal into parts, such as fenders, that are used in automobile assembly. Toyota seems to be more proficient in coordinating the specification and building of dies. Also, dies are changed in cycles of production runs. The technology of rapid die changes was developed in the United States in the 1950s, but Toyota adopted rapid die changes of five to ten minutes while American manufacturers long retained methods taking eight to twelve hours.[72]

It also merits noting that Toyota and other Japanese producers have successfully operated at higher scales than other firms, which may attest to the existence of scale economies in the lean production model.[73] Toyota started operating at higher plant scales in the 1960s. By the 1980s, Toyota and other producers were operating plants in the 400,000-to-800,000 vehicles-per-year range.[74] The successful operation at larger scales seemed to be linked to plant shop organization and the use of more than single-vehicle model plants. Moreover, the presence of scale economies is also documented in sophisticated econometric analysis.[75]

Complementarity in Business Strategy and Organizational Design

Milgrom and Roberts note that one of the crucial requirements for successful firms is that managers understand the complementarity of different business activities. It is an essential foundation for successful management and organization for managers to comprehend the fit between production activities and the firm's environment. Moreover, the nexus can be subtle and the relationships can be nuanced.[76]

Nature of Complementarity

It is common to define complementarity in terms of the relationship between two inputs and prices and quantity of the inputs. However, that definition is too limited because many times inputs are thought of too narrowly. Conventional microeconomics stresses the choice of labor and capital inputs and their prices, not organizational or strategic inputs. Consequently, Roberts describes two choice variables as being complementary if "doing more of one of them increases the returns to doing more of the other."[77]

The variety of pairs of choice variables that could be considered complementary would be prices, service levels, frequency of product redesign, debt–equity ratios, intensity of performance pay, allocation of decision authority, and others. Moreover, complementarity is not just an issue of making the right choices among variables under a manager's control, but also making the right choices regarding the environment in which a firm operates. Thus, a choice variable is complementary with an element of the environment if an increase in the level of the environmental variable increases the return to introducing or increasing the choice variable. For example, use of managerial incentive compensation (a firm's choice variable) can be complementary with personal income tax rates (a variable that is the product of the political environment).[78]

Strategic and Organizational Implications

Roberts identifies two important implications regarding complementarity for GM's rise and demise.[79] First, when multiple-choice variables and complementarity among those variables exist, no small adjustment in the set of choices can increase performance unless the environment changes. Second, when choice is multidimensional, then no change, however big, in just some proper subset of the choice variables can improve performance.

Coherent Versus Incoherent Strategies

Complementarity in production, organization, and strategy raises some provocative questions regarding GM's past and future. The power of complementarity is evident in the case of the discovery of gasoline additives resulting in ethyl gasoline, octane measures, and refinements in engine design. They fit well together and surely enhanced GM's performance in the period of dominance. Similarly, the discovery of Duco finishes fit well with GM's product variety strategy and with GM's efforts to economize on inventory. No doubt the fifty years of dominance for GM includes many examples of complementarity in production, organization, and strategy. Productive links between those elements of a business constitute coherent strategies.

A contrast occurred in the midst of GM's decline and Toyota's ascendancy in the 1980s. During this period, Toyota's lean production was challenging GM's entrenched mass production. GM endeavored to change, but merely illustrated the necessity of wide-ranging and substantial changes in order to survive in a competitive environment and the insufficiency of GM's changes. Toyota developed extremely flexible factories and broad product lines. These strategic inputs fit well together. By the early 1990s, Toyota could produce more than 350 different engine/transmission/fuel system combinations in batches of one—each successive item coming off the line was different from the one before. GM invested substantial sums in making a production system that increased its flexibility. However, GM did not adequately increase the complementary strategic inputs: accelerate its product development process, adjust its product mix and production scheduling, alter and improve its human resource practices, as well as other potential practices that are complementary with increased production flexibility. In contrast to the Toyota Kamingo engine plant with its 350 varieties, GM had assembly lines that produced only a single product line.[80]

The messages of complementarity and coherence are clear. Toyota affirmed a strategy that fit well with its environment, and GM did not. No amount of change, even substantial change in production flexibility, would halt GM's loss of competitive advantage unless numerous complementary inputs also changed. Many did not.

Impediments to Coherence

The message seems straightforward. GM needs to change many dimensions of its business in order to survive. However, an analysis of GM's competitive environment shows that the requisite changes may not occur. Several factors play a role.

The first issue is complexity. The myriad of potential complementary inputs is staggering. When American executives visited Toyota and other Japanese plants, numerous activities in Japan differed from American practices. Distinguishing substantive differences from cultural artifacts is challenging. One wonders if the exercise sessions before work or singing the company song are merely benign activities or genuine complements. The list of potential complements is pretty long, e.g., the ability to stop the production line, no rework area, workers in uniforms, and teams. U.S. firms adopted quality circles, but they typically failed miserably. Evidently, a solid understanding of what does and what does not constitute a complement is essential to developing coherent strategies.

Market Dynamics

Henry Ford failed to grasp market-wide changes in the motor vehicle market in the 1920s and 1930s.

Any coherent strategy may need to be altered when the environment changes.

Government policies regarding emission standards, mileage standards, and fuel prices certainly have affected GM. Similar, and unforeseen, changes could certainly play a role in the future and may render GM less competitive than it is currently.

It is important to note that in past decades GM has actually benefited from market dynamics. GM did not pioneer the minivan or the SUV, but profits from these vehicles have contributed to GM's financial success during this period. Indeed, some accounts claim that GM made 90 percent of its profits on SUV and pickup sales.[81]

On the other hand, in 2005 GM incurred substantial losses. Rising oil prices hurt sales of these vehicles. Oil prices seem to be high because of high world demand, not just OPEC's output restrictions. Continued high oil prices or even rising oil prices could further erode GM's competitive position and, perhaps, its viability. Some industry analysts speculate about a possible bankruptcy for GM with reference to the recent bankruptcy of the Delphi Corporation, formerly a supply unit within GM. Delphi had operated as an independent automotive supply firm since 1999 but filed for Chapter 11 bankruptcy in October 2005.[82]

In the 1920s, the changes in the market for automobiles helped GM sustain its ascendancy over Ford. At the present time, the opposite effect seems operative. Beyond the problem of oil prices, demographic changes may also hurt the demand for light trucks and reduce sales. For example, the generation of drivers now reaching driving age is the largest since the post–World War II baby boom. These drivers are likely to increase demand for "family cars" with a reputation for reliability. Based on the 2000–2005 period, BMW, Toyota, Nissan, and Honda—not GM—would seem to have the best prospects.[83]

Additionally, continued high or rising fuel

prices may spur hybrid vehicle sales. Hybrids combine electrical energy with conventional fuels to economize on fuel costs. However, it is by no means evident that GM will dominate its rivals, foreign or domestic, in developing this product line. Thus, market dynamics may accelerate GM's permanent demise.[84]

Corporate Governance

GM's critics have focused on several reasons for the firm's demise. Michael Jensen argues that it is directly attributable to problems of corporate governance.[85] These problems stem in turn from overcapacity attributable to dynamic economic changes or what he calls the "modern industrial revolution." For GM, the excess capacity flows directly from the organizational and production innovations associated with modern manufacturing practices. Jensen argues that, due to institutional rigidity, including rigidity of boards of directors, exit or reduction in excess capacity is often not pursued despite its overwhelming value. In fact, poor corporate governance often results in continued investment and capacity expansion, the opposite of exit or capacity reduction.

Jensen examines some evidence regarding the effectiveness of corporate governance for a sample of 432 large firms, and looks at two decision variables that should reflect the performance of boards of directors and top managers: the productivity of research and development (R&D) and net capital expenditures. Jensen examines the market value of the sample firms based on the firms' expenditures in these two areas compared to the market value on a benchmark investment of the same amount of funds in hypothetical securities with the same risk. Jensen is thus using the basic economic concept of opportunity cost to evaluate how well the firms performed compared to a reasonable alternative use of the investments that the corporation chose

Table 10.4

Estimated Value of Productivity of R&D and Capital Expenditures (in millions)

Bottom performers		Top performers	
Firm	Value	Firm	Value
General Motors Corp.	($101,977)	General Electric Co.	$28,240
British Petroleum	($26,414)	Lowes Corp.	$29,128
Ford Motor Company	($25,048)	Bristol Myers Squibb	$30,505
Chevron Corp.	($17,314)	Wal-Mart Stores	$38,142
DuPont (E.I.) de Nemours	($14,979)	Philip Morris Cos. Inc.	$42,203

Source: Michael Jensen, "Presidential Address: The Modern Industrial Revolution, Exit, and the Failure of Internal Control Systems," *Journal of Finance* 48, no. 3 (1993), 860–61.

Note: Numbers are the mean of Jensen's estimates using three different assumptions.

not to pursue during the 1980–90 period. Jensen's procedure entails calculating the market value of the sample firms at the end of the period and subtracting the discounted value of each firm's investment expenditures in R&D and net capital during the period.

Jensen uses three different assumptions regarding the ending equity value of the firms. Thus, he provides three different estimates of his performance measure. Table 10.4 contains an average of three of Jensen's measures (in $millions) for the top five and bottom five of his sample of companies.

GM is the worst performer on the list. Its value is negative and about four times the value of British Petroleum, the next entry of the bottom performers. The contrast with Wal-Mart and Philip Morris is striking. GM's "opportunity loss" (the gap between GM's actual performance based on its strategy and the hypothetical return on an equivalent risk investment) amounts to over $100 billion. GM spent a net value of $67.2 billion on R&D and other capital projects. It could have acquired both Honda and Toyota for a mere $21.5 billion. Jensen argues that GM made bad investments during this period, and its corporate governance—the quality of the board of directors and top managers—led to this debacle.

His conclusions are difficult to refute, but looking at the implementation of those bad investment strategies, e.g., the X cars of the 1980s, GM's demise cannot solely be placed on its top management. These cars sold well in the early 1980s but eventually had serious engine and transmission problems and had bad repair records. In short, GM spent a lot money to make bad cars. Corporate governance may have been at the core of these bad investments, but the production and quality problems must have also been pervasively bad.

Organized Labor

Organized labor, particularly the United Automobile Workers, has also been an impediment to adopting a coherent strategy. The UAW and GM had strained relationships at times in the post–World War II years. However, GM's profitability and the union's pragmatic approach combined with institutionalized human resource function at GM led to extended peaceful coexistence at the national level, although shop floor tensions developed in the 1970s and later led to excessive absenteeism, grievances, and wildcat strikes in some plants.[86]

The stable industrial relations system centered on "job control unionism."[87] The arrangement entailed strict and detailed job descriptions, hierarchical job ladders, strong links of wage rates to jobs, and an obvious link to mass production of standardized goods. Proponents of lean production argue that job control unionism does not fit well with the employee relations model for world class manufacturing. The performance of the X cars and plant-by-

plant comparisons of GM versus Toyota plants do not refute that argument. More generally, it is hard to believe that developing a coherent automobile manufacturing strategy would not also require a restructuring of employee relations, including employment guarantees, intensive investment in skills, worker empowerment over a range of tasks, flexibility in assignments, and team assignments. The "New Deal," or mass-production model, seems to have left GM at a competitive disadvantage. It is hard to imagine that GM could move in this direction without the robust cooperation of the UAW or even some initiative by the UAW in moving toward employment relations closer to the Toyota model. On that score, there is a bit of a paradox regarding Toyota's employment relations, including the idea of flexibility and worker empowerment. Toyota plants are quite flexible in terms of job descriptions. However, the tasks are not. They are highly scripted. For example, there is only one acceptable sequence to install a seat. That strategy seems at odds with the GM/UAW tradition.[88]

Toward an Uncertain Future

In the early 1980s and later in the early 1990s, GM seemed to be in serious financial difficulties. The firm altered its governance strategy and moved on several fronts to improve its performance. In the early 1980s, the size of GM's competitive disadvantage was hard to comprehend. In 1981, data obtained from Isuzu by GM showed that Isuzu had about a $2,450 cost advantage over GM in producing an inexpensive, "small" (presumably subcompact) car in approximately the $5,000 price range.[89] After ten years of process improvement, the gap narrowed considerably, to perhaps about half of the cost advantage of earlier decades. Progress continues. In 1998, GM's labor hours per vehicle were 31.98 hours while the comparable 2004 figure was 23.09.[90]

Nevertheless, GM must make progress in reducing excess capacity and exiting unprofitable lines of business in adjusting to the realities of the modern industrial revolution. GM must also address the shortcomings of past decisions. The X cars are gone, but the "legacy costs" of previous decades—noncompetitive health care and pension obligations and commitments—may burden the firm much more than scrapped product investments of an earlier era. Indeed, some legacy costs seem staggering and growing. Some analysts believe GM has pension and other post-employment benefit liabilities as high as $68 billion. These items are not currently reported (and not required to be reported) on its balance sheet.[91] In contrast, Toyota and other growing rivals do not face such onerous future costs. Thus, while both GM and the UAW will be pressured to continue to modernize the firm's operations, the greatest threats to GM's survival may be burdens from the past.

Cooperative efforts by GM and the UAW may be insufficient to prevent GM from the ignominy of bankruptcy.[92] Increasingly, articles in the business press indicate that investment experts at bond-rating companies, such as Moody's or Standard and Poor's, are making grim statements about GM's continued financial viability. These firms closely monitor the debt of firms that are under financial stress. The reports emphasize problems for GM on both the cost (too high) and revenue sides (too low). On the cost side, analysts cite the burden of retirees' health-care costs, the liability burden (pensions and health care) for some employees at the bankrupt GM supplier, Delphi, who formerly worked for GM when that firm was a unit with GM, and some large programs that pay certain former workers to be part of a nonworking job bank program. On the revenue side, analysts cite the failure of good-quality GM cars to sell in the marketplace and a product mix that is excessively skewed in favor of fuel-intensive products in the face of rising fuel prices. To avoid

bankruptcy, GM and the UAW will have to work out some seemingly intractable problems. Indeed, bankruptcy may be the only orderly way for GM's managers, its creditors, and its workers to rearrange their operations in a way that preserves some form of the once-dominant enterprise.[93]

Conclusions

The story of General Motors is rich. The firm dominated a core industry in the world's largest national economy and throughout the world. The dominance was protracted and the firm's strategy and management were celebrated by experts in strategy and widely imitated throughout the world. For thirty-seven years, GM was number one on the Fortune 500 list.[94] Understanding the sources of GM's dominance enhances our understanding of successful firms and the functioning of markets.

The story is not one of eternal bliss, however. Like all dominant firms in competitive environments, rivals have challenged its dominance and successfully eroded GM's competitive advantages. For more than two decades, the once-mighty firm has struggled. GM's market share has eroded, and its financial performance within the industry and in comparison with other large firms has languished.

The firm currently faces imposing challenges. Its directors, managers, and workers face the twin requirements of adjusting their strategies and their claims on the firm's resources to compete with their rivals and developing a strategy to adjust their operations to meet uncertain market dynamics.[95]

Notes

Financial support from the Earhart Foundation is gratefully acknowledged. Thanks to Teresa Duncan and Marta Norton for editorial assistance.

1. Dennis W. Carlton and Jeffrey M. Perloff, *Industrial Organization,* 3rd ed. (Reading, MA: Addison-Wesley, 2005), pp. 107–20.

2. See General Motors, *Annual Report,* 2004, and www. gm.com.

3. Carlton and Perloff.

4. Ibid.

5. Dean Worcester, "Why Dominant Firms Decline," *Journal of Political Economy* 65 (August 1957), pp. 338–47.

6. William G. Shepherd, *The Economics of Industrial Organization,* 4th ed. (Upper Saddle River, NJ: Prentice-Hall, 1997), chapter 3 and pp. 206–07.

7. Alfred P. Sloan, *My Years with General Motors* (New York: Currency and Doubleday, 1990), p. 295. Originally published in 1963.

8. Shepherd.

9. James W. Brock, "Automobiles," in Walter Adams and James Brock, eds., *The Structure of American Industry,* 11th ed., p. 100 (Upper Saddle River, NJ: Pearson, Prentice-Hall).

10. Brock, p. 96.

11. Sloan, p. 378.

12. R. Preston McAfee, *Competitive Solutions* (Princeton, NJ: Princeton University Press, 2002), pp. 27–28. Also see Brock, p. 107.

13. John E. Kwoka, Jr., "Automobiles," in Larry L. Deutsch, ed., *Industry Studies,* 3rd ed., pp. 3–26 (Armonk, NY: M.E. Sharpe, 2002).

14. Ward's *Automotive Yearbook,* various years.

15. James M. Utterback, *Mastering the Dynamics of Innovation* (Cambridge, MA: Harvard Business School Press, 1996), p. 37. Data are for 1919–1929.

16. Seth W. Norton, "Information and Competitive Advantage: The Rise of General Motors," *Journal of Law & Economics* 40 (April 1997), pp. 245–60.

17. Sloan, p. 214. Sales fell significantly in the 1930s, especially in 1932 and 1933, but rebounded thereafter.

18. Paul Milgrom and John Roberts, *Economics, Organization and Management* (Upper Saddle River, NJ: Prentice-Hall, 1992), p. 4.

19. Data are from Global Financial Data.

20. The pyramid of demand strategy and GM's success with it may have enhanced profits for GM by limiting entry of new firms by facilitating brand proliferation by GM. For the logic and evidence of such effects in a nondurable goods case, see Richard Schmalensee, "Entry Deterrence in the Ready-to-Eat Breakfast Cereal Industry," *Bell Journal of Economics* 9 (Autumn 1978), pp. 305–27.

21. Sloan, p. 65.

22. Milgrom and Roberts, pp. 78–79 and 544–52.

23. Sloan, p. 45.

24. Milgrom and Roberts, pp. 4–5.

25. Ramon Casadesus-Masanell and Daniel Spulber, "The Fable of Fisher Body," *Journal of Law & Economics* 43 (April 2000), pp. 67–104.

26. Ibid., pp. 92–96.

27. Ibid., p. 93.

28. Norton.

29. Sloan, pp. 375–89.

30. Ibid., pp. 149–68, 238–47, and 302–12.

31. Ibid., p. 163.

32. Ibid., p. 152.

33. Ibid.

34. Utterback, pp. 23–55.

35. Sloan, p. 163.

36. Ibid., pp. 267–72.

37. Ibid., pp. 153–54.

38. Ibid., p. 149.

39. Ibid., pp. 279–301.

40. Lawrence J. White, *The U.S. Automobile Industry Since 1945* (Cambridge, MA: Harvard University Press, 1971), pp. 136–70.

41. Sloan, pp. 283–89.

42. White, pp. 151–62.

43. Thomas A. Kochan, Harry C. Katz, and Robert B. McKersie, *The Transformation of American Industrial Relations* (New York: Basic Books, 1986), pp. 21–46.

44. Sloan, pp. 390–406.

45. Harry C. Katz, *Shifting Gears* (Cambridge, MA: MIT Press, 1985), pp. 15–47.

46. Sloan, pp. 407–28.

47. Ibid., p. 416.

48. Joseph A. Schumpeter, *The Theory of Economic Development* (New York: Oxford University Press, 1961), pp. 128–56.

49. Nathan Rosenberg, *Perspectives on Technology* (Cambridge, UK: Cambridge University Press, 1976), pp. 61–107.

50. Sloan, pp. 219–37.

51. White, p. 214.

52. Brock, pp. 107–08.

53. Kwoka, pp. 11–12.

54. Arthur A. Thompson and A. J. Strickland, *Strategic Management* (Boston: Irwin McGraw-Hill, 1999), p. 250.

55. John Roberts, *The Modern Firm* (Oxford: Oxford University Press, 2004), pp. 47–51.

56. Kwoka, p. 3.

57. James P. Womack, Daniel T. Jones, and Daniel Roos, *The Machine That Changed the World* (New York: Harper-Collins, 1991), pp. 22–26.

58. Womack, Jones, and Roos, pp. 26–47.

59. Brock, pp. 103–06.

60. Ibid., p. 105.

61. Ibid., p. 103.

62. Milgrom and Roberts, pp. 109–10.

63. Roberts, pp. 64–65 and 201–07.

64. Womack, Jones, and Roos, p. 52.

65. Ibid., pp. 49–58.

66. Ibid., pp. 56–57.

67. Roberts, pp. 201–06.

68. Ibid., p. 206.

69. Ibid., p. 203.

70. Womack, Jones, and Roos, pp. 54–55.

71. Ibid., pp. 116–17.

72. Kwoka, pp. 14–15.

73. Marvin B. Lieberman and Rajeev Dhawan, "Assessing the Resource Base of Japanese and U.S. Auto Producers: A Stochastic Frontier Production Function Approach," *Management Science* 51(July 2005), pp. 1060–74.

74. Ibid., pp. 1064–65.

75. Ibid., pp. 1069–74.

76. Milgrom and Roberts, pp. 106–16.

77. Roberts, p. 34.

78. Ibid., p. 36.

79. Ibid., pp. 57–63.

80. Ibid., pp. 39–40.

81. Brock, p. 101.

82. Carol Loomis, "The Tragedy of General Motors," *Fortune* (February 20, 2006), p. 72.

83. "Built to Last," *Wall Street Journal* (February 27, 2006), p. D-3.

84. "BMW Will Join Daimler and GM in Hybrid Venture," *Wall Street Journal* (September 8, 2005), p. B-4.

85. Michael Jensen, "Presidential Address: The Modern Industrial Revolution, Exit, and the Failure of Internal Control Systems," *Journal of Finance* 48 (July 1993), pp. 831–80.

86. Katz, pp. 73–131.

87. Womack, Jones, and Roos, pp. 42–43; Katz, pp. 38–47; Kochan, Katz, and McKersie, pp. 28–29 and 239.

88. Steven Spear and H. Kent Bowen, "Decoding the DNA of the Toyota Production System," *Harvard Business Review* (September–October 1999), pp. 96–106.

89. Kwoka, p. 14.

90. Harbour Consulting, *Harbour Report*, 2005, pp. 20–21.

91. "For GM, Pension-Accounting Shift Could Dwarf Gain on GMAC Deal," *Wall Street Journal* (April 5, 2006), p. C-3.

92. Loomis, p. 60.

93. Ibid., p. 75.

94. Ibid., p. 62.

95. The market dynamics are a wild card. Loomis points out that the Internet may profoundly affect the automobile sales and the nature of competition in the automobile business (p. 67). See John E. Kwoka, "Automobiles: The Old Economy Collides with the New," *Review of Industrial Organization* 19 (2001), pp. 55–69.

Selected Readings

Milgrom, Paul, and John Roberts. *Economics, Organization and Management.* Upper Saddle River, NJ: Prentice-Hall, 1992. A comprehensive, analytical description of business organization using applications of microeconomics with rich factual details about business history.

Roberts, John. *The Modern Firm.* Oxford: Oxford University Press, 2004. A rich account of economic forces that affect production and organizational choices and the foundations of business strategy. Contains many factual accounts of successful and unsuccessful enterprises.

Sloan, Alfred P., Jr. *My Years with General Motors.* New York: Currency and Doubleday, 1990. Originally published in 1963. A corporate autobiography of GM's long-term CEO and chairman.

Utterback, James, M. *Mastering the Dynamics of Innovation.* Boston: Harvard Business School Press, 1996. An account of the role of innovation in industrial competition. Has applications to the rise of General Motors and the emergence of the American automobile industry.

White, Lawrence J. *The U. S. Automobile Industry Since 1945.* Cambridge, MA: Harvard University Pres, 1971. Details the structure, behavior, and performance of the American motor vehicle industry using a microeconomic framework, with the analysis focusing on the period from World War II to 1970.

Womack, James P., Daniel T. Jones, and Daniel Roos. *The Machine That Changed the World.* New York: HarperCollins, 1991. Provides a summary history of automobile manufacturing throughout the world and a detailed discussion of the advent of "lean production" in Japan and its diffusion to other industries and throughout the world.

11

Microsoft

Who Is Microsoft Today?

Don E. Waldman and Rochelle Ruffer

Introduction

In 1975, Bill Gates and Paul Allen founded Micro-Soft (the hyphen was later removed). The market for personal computers was in its infancy, but Gates and Allen believed personal computers would play a great role in the future. It is fascinating to read about the early years in Bill Gates's life and how he got involved with computers. There is no doubt both Gates and Allen were bright young men without whom Microsoft would probably not be the company it is today.[1] Since its inception, Microsoft has been a leading player in the operating systems market, and early on it also rose to dominance in the software market. During its thirty years in existence, there have been many key strategies that have helped Microsoft become a powerful player in the market. This chapter will focus on the strategies used by Microsoft to gain market power and the resulting antitrust court cases that came about as a result of that power.

This chapter begins with a discussion of the products and current financial situation of Microsoft. We will provide a time line of the new product introductions and legal events that helped to make Microsoft the company that it is. Once we have a sense of the current size and magnitude of Microsoft, we will briefly discuss the early history of the company. We will then introduce the economic concepts that are important for understanding its business practices over the years. Next, we provide a discussion of the four practices that were under scrutiny in the original antitrust cases. Finally, we discuss the antitrust cases surrounding Microsoft since 1993 including the Jackson ruling of the 1998 case, the Appeals Court decision, as well as the results and implications of the 2002 Consent Decree.

Who Is Microsoft Today?

Table 11.1 includes data on Microsoft from its beginning year (1975), and every five years through 2005. Microsoft started as a company with 3 employees and has grown to a company of 61,000. Of the 61,000 total employees in 2005, 39,000 are located in the United States and 22,000 are international employees. The breakdown of the 61,000 employees and their job assignments is as follows: 24,000 are involved with product research and development, 18,000 are in sales and marketing, 12,000 are in product support and consulting, 2,000 are in manufacturing and distribution, and 5,000 are in general and administration.[2]

In 1975, Microsoft generated $16,000 in revenue and focused on one product, its Disk Operating System (DOS). Microsoft generated almost $40 billion in revenue in 2005. The product line

Table 11.1

Microsoft's Total Revenue, Employment, and Spending on Research and Development (R&D)

Year	Revenue (millions)	Number of employees	R&D (millions)	R&D/Revenue (%)
1975	0.016	3	—	—
1980	8	38	—	
1985	140.42	1,001	—	
1990	1,183	5,635	177.45*	15
1995	5,937	17,800	831.18*	14
2000	22,956	40,000**	3,775	16.4
2005	39,788	61,000	6,184	15.54

Source: Michael A. Cusumano, and Richard W. Selby, *Microsoft Secrets* (New York: Free Press, 1995), p. 3; 2000 and 2005 Microsoft Annual Reports from Microsoft Web site: www.microsoft.com (March 2006).

*These numbers were estimated using figures for R&D/Revenue and Revenue from Cusumano and Selby, p. 3.

**The 2000 Annual Report says "nearly 40,000 employees."

of Microsoft has also expanded over the last thirty years. Table 11.2 shows the different product segments and the sources of that revenue.

As Table 11.2 shows, Microsoft is involved in many different aspects of the computer industry, from operating systems to software to instant messaging to video game systems. These product innovations have helped to shape Microsoft. The other major issues impacting Microsoft are the antitrust court cases. These cases and the ramifications of the outcomes are discussed later in the chapter. However, it is helpful to have an idea of the major events in Microsoft's history. Table 11.3 provides a time line of the important new product introductions and legal events in Microsoft's history. It is difficult to summarize the rich history in one table, but the information in Table 11.3 highlights the important events.

The information in the preceding three tables shows the growth in size and the diverse product base of Microsoft. The reader may next wonder about Microsoft's relative performance or size in particular product markets. Table 11.4 shows Microsoft's market share of some of its leading products as well as the market share of some of its competitors. The data range from 2003 to 2005,

but in general Microsoft is a leading competitor in most of the product markets.

The market share information for the Web browser market is somewhat contradictory. By most accounts, Microsoft's Internet Explorer (IE) has almost 90 percent of the browser market. This is the figure we have cited in Table 11.4. However, there is one source that tracks monthly browser usage statistics and estimates that Internet Explorer dominates the market with only 64.7 percent, while Firefox has approximately 24.5 percent of the browser market. They show the downward trend in Internet Explorer's dominance from approximately 85 percent of the market in 2003 to 64.7 percent now. Most other sources are still showing Internet Explorer with approximately 90 percent. It will be interesting to see if, over time, Firefox is able to break into some of Microsoft's share. This same source also provides statistics on operating system usage and shows that Microsoft Windows has approximately 88.9 percent of the operating system market, followed by only 3.4 percent for Linux.[3]

Interestingly, in November 2005, Microsoft unveiled its newest video game console system, Xbox 360. While exact figures are not yet available, the

Table 11.2

Sources of Microsoft Revenue, 2005

Product segment	Sources of revenue from product segment	2005 Revenue (millions)	Percentage of 2005 revenue	Percent growth from 2004–5
Client	Operating systems including Windows XP Professional and Home, Media Center Edition, Tablet PC Edition	$12,234	30.75	6
Server and tools	Server products including server software licenses and client access licenses (CALs) for Windows Server, Microsoft SQL Server, Exchange Server	$9,885	24.84	16
Information worker	Including licensing of MS Office System products	$11,013	27.68	3
Microsoft business solutions	Business management software including software sales (larger portion of revenue) and services sales	$803	2.02	6
MSN	Personal communications services including e-mail and instant messaging, and online information offerings	$2,274	5.72	3
Mobile and embedded devices	Including Windows Mobile software, Windows Embedded operating systems, MapPoint, and Windows Automotive.	$337	0.85	36
Home and entertainment	Video games including Microsoft Xbox video game console system, PC games, the Home Products division (HPD), and TV platform products for the interactive television industry	$3,242	8.15	13
Total	All seven segments	$39,788	100.01*	8

Source: 2005 Microsoft Annual Report.
*Numbers do not add to 100 due to rounding.

market share distribution is predicted to shift from that reported in Table 11.4 to Microsoft having 38 percent, Sony 32 percent, and Nintendo 22 percent of the video game market in North America.[4]

The Notation for the Industry

The computer and software industry is filled with acronyms. Before we begin to introduce all of the different acronyms, we thought it most helpful to provide a table of the common abbreviations that will help you to read this chapter. While most of these acronyms mean nothing to you right now, they will be introduced throughout the text. Table 11.5 serves as a helpful reference for you in remembering the meaning of all these acronyms.

Table 11.3

Microsoft's Important Product Introductions and Legal Events

Year	Product released to public or important legal event
1975	BASIC for the Altair computer
1977	FORTRAN (and later COBOL and Pascal) for microcomputers with an 8080 microprocessor
1981	DOS 1.0—the operating system for IBM's first microcomputer
August 1982	Multiplan—Microsoft's first spreadsheet software
November 1983	Microsoft Word
September 1985	Excel for the Macintosh, Microsoft's newest spreadsheet software program
November 1985	Windows 1.03, two years after it was announced
October 1987	Excel for Windows
March 1988	Apple announces it will sue Microsoft over Windows 2.03. Case dismissed in 1992.
1989	Gates discontinues relationship with IBM with his refusal to establish OS/2 as industry standard.
1989	MS Word for Windows
May 1990	Windows 3.0
1990	FTC begins investigation on four of Microsoft's practices.
1993	FTC charges Microsoft with illegally controlling the market for PC-compatible operating systems.
1994	Department of Justice and Microsoft agree to a consent decree, which is ultimately rejected in February 1995 by Judge Sporkin.
1995	Windows 95 and Internet Explorer 1.0 released.
August 1996	Internet Explorer 3.0, completely rebuilt version, is launched.
1997	Internet Explorer 4.0 designed for Windows 95, Windows 98, and Windows NT
1998	Department of Justice files complaint that Microsoft was illegally monopolizing the browser market. Judge Jackson gave ruling in June 2000.
1998	Windows 1998 and Internet Explorer 5.0
June 2001	Appeals court ruling including removal of Judge Jackson from any further participation in the case.
2001	Windows XP and Internet Explorer 6.0
November 2002	Consent decree with eight major provisions
November 2005	XBOX 360 game
February 2007	Windows VISTA

Source: www.thocp.net/companies/microsoft/microsoft_company.htm and www.thocp.net/companies/microsoft/microsoft_company_part2.htm

Microsoft's Beginnings

The picture painted above is a far cry from how Microsoft started. Microsoft started in 1975 as a small company with two employees, Bill Gates and Paul Allen. In February of 1975, after work-ing eight weeks on a BASIC program for the first "personal computer" Altair 8080 model, Paul Allen delivered the BASIC program to Micro Instrumentation and Telemetry Systems (MITS) in Albuquerque, New Mexico. The program was written without an existing keyboard or the actual

Table 11.4

Microsoft and Leading Competitor Market Share Information by Product

Market/ Product	Product name	Market share (percent)
Web browser market*		
	Internet Explorer	87
	Mozilla Firefox	8
Applications software**		
	Microsoft Office	95
	Apple Computer's iWork	2.7
	Corel WordPerfect Office	1.6
Operating systems market***		
	Microsoft Windows	55.1
	Linux	23.1
	Unix	11
	Novell Netware	9.9
Personal finance software****		
	Quicken	68
	Microsoft Money	27
Video game market in North America*****		
	Sony Playstation 2	57.5
	Microsoft XBox	24
	Nintendo Game Cube	18.5

Sources: *"Mozilla Firefox Losing Market Share?" from www.searchenginejournal.com, 8/15/2005 article.

**Ina, Fried, "Apple's iWork Emerges as Rival to Microsoft Office," CNET News.com, Jan. 23, 2006. Published on www.zdnet.com.

****Market Share Reporter* (Detroit, MI: Gale Research, 2005).

**** *Market Share Reporter* (Detroit, MI: Gale Research, 2004).

*****Market Share Reporter* (Detroit, MI: Gale Research, 2006).

computer on hand, but the 8,000 lines of programming language code worked on the Altair, and Microsoft was in business.[5] The 8080 computer chip was revolutionary for the time. By today's standards, it would be considered a "dinosaur." The 8080 chip ran with 2 MHz of clock speed and 64 KB of memory. By contrast, the Intel 386DX processor introduced in 1992 had 33 MHz of speed and 16 MB of memory. The Intel Pentium M Processor introduced in 2005 has 2.13 GHz of speed.[6]

Since BASIC was Microsoft's first (and only) product, Allen helped to market the product by working with MITS as their software director for a while. In the meantime, Gates continued to work on improving Altair BASIC before it was officially released for sale. During this time, Gates gained a reputation for providing a reliable product and always working to improve that product. Even early on, Microsoft expanded its product by developing programs in FORTRAN, COBOL, and Pascal for chips other than the 8080. Microsoft chose to write these languages for a computer operating system, CP/M-Control Program for Microcomputer, which was not initially, but later became, the industry standard.[7] Writing for CP/M was the first of many instances when Microsoft made a choice that took it down the path for success.

Additionally, Gates also had the foresight to launch into foreign markets early. In 1978, he and Kazuhkio Nishi, who founded ASCII (American Standard Code for Information Interchange), signed a one-page contract for Nishi to become the Microsoft representative for the Far East. As a result, Gates was involved in the design of the first Japanese microcomputer.[8] The Gates–Nishi relationship continued until 1986.

Microsoft's first significant industry move began with the release of the 8086 chip by Intel in April 1978. Many believed the Intel 8086 chip would never become the industry standard. Microsoft, however, saw an opportunity to position itself as an industry pioneer and agreed to write BASIC for the 8086 chip.

Table 11.5

Industry Standard Abbreviations

Acronym	Definition
AOL	America On Line: A specific Internet service provider.
API	Application Programming Interface: A set of definitions of the ways one piece of computer software communicates with another. It is a method of achieving abstraction, usually between lower-level (for example, an operating system) and higher-level (for example, an advanced application) software.
ASCII	American Standard Code for Information Interchange: This early computer standard code is used for information interchange among data processing systems, data communications systems, and associated equipment. The ASCII character set contains 128 coded characters and consists of control characters and graphic characters.
BASIC	Beginners' All-purpose Symbolic Instruction Code: A high-level programming language designed in 1964. BASIC was designed to be an "easy-to-learn" programming language and thus became a commonly used programming language for microcomputers.
CP/M	Control Program for Microcomputer: The operating system for which Microsoft chose its early languages. It became the industry standard with the early computers and was a leading competitor of DOS in the early 1980s.
DOS or MS-DOS	Disk Operating System: DOS is the first operating system that Microsoft created, based on the QDOS (Quick and Dirty DOS) bought from Seattle Computer Products. It was later referred to as MS-DOS.
DR-DOS	Digital Research DOS: A direct competitor of MS-DOS.
GUI	Graphical User Interface: method of displaying text and graphics on a computer screen using pictures and images formed by patterns of dots.
IAP	Internet Access Providers (or sometimes referred to as Internet service providers): A firm that provides access to the Internet. AOL is an Internet service provider.
ICP	Internet Content Providers: Any firm or individual that provides content on the Internet. For example, any company or individual with a Web site.
IE	Internet Explorer: Microsoft's Web browser.
IHV	Independent Hardware Vendors: Any firm other than Microsoft that produces or develops hardware.
ISV	Independent Software Vendors (or developers): Any firm, other than Microsoft, that develops software.
JVM	Java Virtual Machine: Java can be installed on any operating system and, once installed, can be used as a platform for software that is separate from Windows. All copies of Java include a JVM that translates byte code into instructions for the operating system.
OEM	Original Equipment Manufacturers
OS	Operating System
OS/2	The operating system that IBM worked on as a competitor of Windows.

Economic Theory

Later we will examine in detail many of Microsoft's business practices that eventually led to antitrust action against the company. Before doing so, however, it is necessary to understand the characteristics of Microsoft's products. Microsoft's two main product markets are operating systems (Windows) and applications software (Word and Excel). The economic concepts discussed below are all important factors in explaining Microsoft's market power; however, an understanding of the importance of these concepts in the computer industry often makes it difficult to figure out if Microsoft's conduct is anticompetitive and/or illegal, or just aggressive, but legal, business conduct.

Multi-Sided Platform Markets

Microsoft's most important product, its Windows operating system, is a multi-sided platform. The value of a multi-sided platform to one group depends on the participation of another group and vice versa. A firm providing a multi-sided platform, therefore, needs to attract two or more groups to its product.[9] A simple example of a multi-sided platform is a shopping mall. A shopping mall has significant economic value only if it attracts both a variety of stores and customers. Thus, shopping malls are multi-sided platforms and a mall developer knows that it must attract both stores and shoppers.

As Evans, Nichols, and Schmalensee note, "an operating system is more valuable to application developers the more end-users are potential buyers of programs written for it, and an operating system is more valuable to end-users the more attractive applications have been developed to work on it."[10] Pricing decisions are complex in multi-sided platform markets. For example, it may make more sense for a firm to offer its product below cost in one market because increased sales in that market result in increased sales in the other market. Consider that Microsoft and all other operating system manufacturers do not charge fees to software developers to use their application programming interfaces (APIs) even though it is costly for them to develop these APIs. Evans, Nichols, and Schmalensee summarize the economic literature: "the economic literature on two-sided markets makes it clear that there is nothing inherently inefficient or anticompetitive in this sort of pricing, even if pricing on one side of the market is below the marginal cost incurred there."[11]

The multi-sided platform nature of Microsoft's products also impacts Microsoft's product design decisions. Consider, for example, the bundling of new APIs into Windows. One of the best methods for Microsoft to tie software developers to Windows is to bundle additional APIs into the Windows operating system for no additional cost. Adding APIs attracts more software developers, which in turn attracts more Windows end-users, which in turn ties more original equipment manufacturers (OEMs) to Windows and Microsoft. From a social efficiency perspective, because the marginal cost of placing new APIs onto Windows is virtually zero after the APIs are developed, it's economically efficient to place them on the operating system at zero additional cost to the OEMs. The catch, however, is that the additional APIs help Microsoft to maintain its control in the operating system market; therefore, this efficient behavior might be viewed as being anticompetitive.

Economies of Scale

Economies of scale are often associated within this industry. This is the basic idea that long-run average costs will fall as output increases. The implication is that firms with large levels of output (or a large *installed-base*) will have lower average costs and will be able to charge lower prices. In the case of software development, the high fixed costs of developing software and the low marginal costs are the source of significant economies of scale. In addition, the high research costs of developing software are considered to be *sunk costs*. Sunk costs are fixed costs that cannot be recovered after they are spent. As a result of the large sunk costs associated with software development, application software developers want to sell as many copies as possible to take advantage of economies of scale and, therefore, want to write their applications for the operating system with the most users.[12] It follows logically that, because Windows dominates the operating system market, software developers want to write their applications for Windows.

Network Externalities/Positive Network Effect

Network externalities is another important economic concept that can be applied to Microsoft's market dominance. Network externalities exist if one consumer's utility from using a product increases as more consumers use the same product. The telecommunications market, for example, exhibits large network externalities because a consumer's utility from using a telephone increases as the number of telephone users on the network increases. There are very large network externalities in the computer operating system market because of the positive connection between the number of users of an operating system and the number of software applications available for that system.[13] The concept of network externalities will come into play when we discuss the antitrust cases surrounding Microsoft's behavior and its control over the operating systems market.

The basic concept is that consumers are better off (that is, have higher expected utility) purchas-

ing computers with an operating system that is used by many other consumers because there will be many more applications written for such operating systems. Furthermore, a large installed-base of users attracts: (1) corporate customers who want to use an operating system that new employees are familiar with; and (2) academic customers who want to use software that will allow them to share files easily with colleagues at other institutions.[14] There will also be more technical support for an operating system as more consumers use it.[15]

Network externalities are related to Windows' market dominance because independent software vendors (ISV) write more applications exclusively for Windows, which ensures a larger number of applications for Windows than for any other operating system. The much larger number of applications makes Windows a more attractive operating system for consumers and thus increases the demand for it, which provides yet another reason for software developers to continue to write applications exclusively for Windows. This self-reinforcing cycle is referred to as a *positive feedback loop*.[16]

As a result of this positive feedback loop, there is a significant first-mover advantage in markets with large network externalities, and the firm that enters the market first and establishes itself as the industry standard is likely to eventually dominate the market, at least for some extended period of time. This is referred to as a *tipped market*. Other examples of tipped markets include the VHS-formatted system over Beta-formatted videocassettes and IBM-compatible PCs over Apple computers.[17]

Microsoft's Practices

Microsoft has been accused of using a variety of practices to gain control over the operating system market. In this section, we analyze a number of these practices.

Licensing Agreements

Microsoft has been accused of using a variety of licensing agreements to attempt to monopolize the operating systems market. In his dealings with competitors, Bill Gates consistently used his knowledge of licensing agreements and his strategic abilities to write licensing agreements with the explicit objective of gaining advantages over his competitors.

After writing the Microsoft BASIC program for the 8080 computer chip, Allen and Gates signed a licensing agreement with MITS that gave MITS exclusive rights to license BASIC. The agreement, however, included a clause stating that "The Company (MITS) agrees to use its best efforts to license, promote, and commercialize the Program (BASIC). The Company's failure to use its best efforts . . . shall constitute sufficient grounds and reasons to terminate this agreement . . ."[18] Due to this wording, Gates was later able to get out of the MITS/Pertec (MITS was bought by Pertec) contract by arguing that MITS had not put forth its best efforts in promoting BASIC. This permitted Gates to move beyond his agreement with MITS and sell BASIC to MITS's competitors.

Later in Microsoft's history, Gates's knowledge of contracts and his willingness to push the envelope beyond industry norms helped Microsoft establish MS-DOS as the industry standard. Microsoft initially developed DOS for IBM.[19] Microsoft received a lump-sum payment from IBM to adapt QDOS (Quick and Dirty Operating System) to the IBM PC and an additional $500,000 instead of royalties for the rights to DOS, BASIC, and several language compilers.[20] It was standard practice at the time for the OEMs to maintain the proprietary legal rights over the source code on their computers, but Microsoft's contract with IBM prohibited IBM from licensing DOS, while placing no restrictions on Microsoft.[21] When IBM introduced its first IBM-PC on August 12, 1981, the computer ran on Microsoft's MS-DOS operating system. By December 1984, it was clear that MS-DOS was established as the dominant operating system in the market. By June 1986, income from licensing MS-DOS accounted for half of Microsoft's annual revenues of $60.9 million.[22]

Licensing agreements also helped Microsoft in its legal battle with Apple over Microsoft's introduction of Windows version 2.03. After Microsoft introduced Windows 2.03, Apple announced it was suing Microsoft because the graphical user interface (GUI) operating system on Windows 2.03 looked very similar to the GUI on a Macintosh. A GUI is a method of displaying text and graphics on a computer screen using pictures and images formed by patterns of dots. The Apple Macintosh computer has a built-in GUI. Microsoft Windows placed a GUI on top of text-based MS-DOS.[23] With a lawsuit filed on March 17, 1988, Apple hoped to obtain a court order to stop the sale and distribution of Windows and to receive all of the profits Microsoft had earned from Windows 2.03. Apple also requested that all existing copies of Windows 2.03 be destroyed. Microsoft responded to Apple's lawsuit by referring in its defense to an existing 1985 licensing agreement between Microsoft and Apple that granted Microsoft the right to use the visual displays already incorporated into six of the existing Microsoft programs at the time, including Windows version 1.0. Microsoft's main argument was that the 1985 agreement implicitly included Windows version 2.03. Apple pressed its suit and eventually expanded it to include a claim against Windows version 3.0.[24] In April 1992, however, the Apple lawsuit was dismissed. Microsoft had spent $9 million in attorneys' fees, but had won a critical court decision.

Marketing Strategy

Microsoft employed a number of marketing strategies in the early years of MS-DOS and Windows to increase the popularity of its operating systems.[25] These strategies included a strong commitment to product development. Microsoft, for example, took over three years to launch Windows, and it required a development team of more than twenty-four full-time developers, as well as testing and documentation teams. By the time Windows was released, it had seen four product managers and three development directors.[26] While Gates has been criticized for the length of time Microsoft takes to develop new products, there is no doubt that the firm devotes the resources necessary to produce a continuing stream of new products.

Microsoft also aggressively markets its products. Microsoft is famous for its no-expenses-barred philosophy of rolling out its new products. In 2005, Microsoft spent $8,677 million in sales and marketing.[27] When Microsoft introduced Windows 3.0 on May 22, 1990, it did so with approximately 6,000 people watching at the City Center Theater in New York City. Customers from nineteen other cities around North America and the world were watching via live satellite television. Microsoft spent $3 million on the opening-day marketing blitz for Windows 3.0 and planned to spend an additional $7 million promoting its new operating system. The marketing strategy included advertising, distributing 250,000 free demonstration diskettes, and organizing Windows 3.0 seminars.[28] The aggressive marketing campaign, along with continuing product improvements, helped Windows 3.0 become a product that consumers were hesitant to abandon.

Microsoft's strategic practices included the slow delivery of versions of its languages compatible with the CP/M operating system, which was the leading competitor of MS-DOS in the early 1980s. When Microsoft shipped its languages for CP/M, it priced the CP/M version 50 percent higher than the MS-DOS version. Microsoft went so far as to sell an inferior version of BASIC for use with non-MS-DOS operating systems. This inferior version of BASIC did not include graphics, which made it very difficult for software developers to write applications for non-MS-DOS operating systems.[29]

Finally, Microsoft fought a long battle with IBM to sever its relationship with the computer giant so that Microsoft could develop Microsoft Windows on its own. Up until 1989, Microsoft had been working with IBM on a GUI operating system called OS/2. In 1989, at a software developers meeting in Las Vegas, when IBM pushed Gates to commit to establishing OS/2 as the industry standard, Gates refused. As a result, the software developers left Las Vegas believing that Windows, not OS/2, would dominate the market for operating systems.[30] Microsoft is also known for spending huge sums on research and development (R&D).[31] According to Microsoft's annual reports, Microsoft spent $6.3 billion in 2002, $6.6 billion in 2003, $7.78 billion in 2004, and $6.2 billion in 2005. Typically Microsoft spends 14–16 percent of their revenue on R&D.[32] This type of sunk-cost commitment to product development and product innovation is bound to have an effect on market share.[33]

Microsoft's Battle in the Software Market

In addition to Microsoft's control of the PC operating systems market, it has developed and promoted many software applications as well.[34] Some of Microsoft's early attempts at developing applications software, like its Multiplan spreadsheet program in 1982, were not very successful. Multiplan was developed to run on computers with 64K of memory. While Multiplan initially received great reviews, it quickly lost popularity when Lotus 1-2-3 hit the market. Lotus 1-2-3 was aimed at 256K machines and had many more capabilities than Multiplan or VisiCalc (Multiplan's earlier competitor).[35] This is a great example of how first-mover advantage can sometimes help a product gain momentum. Since Lotus 1-2-3 was the first product to address the needs and wants of those consumers using 256K machines, it was difficult for Multiplan to break into that product niche already created by Lotus. In addition, Microsoft's delay in providing a rapid upgrade to Multiplan enabled Lotus 1-2-3 to gain market dominance with 80 percent of the market.[36]

In 1985, Microsoft launched its attack on Lotus 1-2-3's market control with the creation of Microsoft Excel. Excel hit the ground running with praise from all the leading magazines, including *Business Software, PC Magazine,* and *Computer Letter.*[37] On August 16, 1987, Bill Gates announced to his Microsoft executives via e-mail that Microsoft had become the number one software company, beating Lotus for the first time since 1983.[38] After passing Lotus in market share in 1987, Gates was excited about the prospects for the soon-to-be-released Excel 2.0. Excel 2.0 was meant for high-end machines, and thus it was quite impressive that it captured approximately 12 percent of the spreadsheet market by the end of 1988. Microsoft aggressively marketed Excel, including offering free trial copies and nationwide seminars to customers who switched from Lotus 1-2-3 to Excel 2.0. Overall, Microsoft invested more than $5 million to drive Excel to the top of the market.[39] Microsoft's strategy worked. Microsoft Excel's market share of spreadsheet programs increased from less than 10 percent at the beginning of 1988 to almost 90 percent in 1997. Lotus 1-2-3's market share went from almost 70 percent to less than 10 percent in that same time frame.[40]

One of Microsoft's primary reasons for success in the software market has been its persistence. Microsoft continually revises its software products with the objective of dominating each market, even if they begin behind in the race for dominance. In the case of spreadsheet programs, we have seen that Microsoft scrapped an earlier spreadsheet program, Multiplan, for an eventually more successful program, Excel. Another such example of persistence is with word-processing software. Microsoft initially launched its word-processing software, Word, to compete with WordStar. In 1986, there were two leading word-processing programs. WordPerfect held approximately 20 percent of the market and WordStar (Micropro) had approximately 10 percent of the market. Microsoft Word DOS was a direct competitor of those two programs. In the next few years, WordPerfect increased its market share to almost 50 percent by 1990. During the same time, Microsoft Word also gained popularity, taking over the second place spot in 1988.[41] In early 1989, it was estimated that in the previous year, 937,000 copies of WordPerfect had been sold compared to just 650,000 copies of Microsoft Word.[42] The key turning point was the development of Microsoft Word for Windows, which reached the market in late 1989. While WordPerfect and other word-processing programs were good programs, the bottom line is that Word won the Windows market. A change in operating systems (from DOS to Windows) caused a change in the leaders in the word-processing market.[43] Also in 1990, Word was making large inroads in the Apple world, and when the fourth version of Word was released, 100,000 Macintosh users immediately purchased it. By the end of 1990, Microsoft Word had made *MacWorld's* monthly top ten list of bestsellers sixty-nine times and was first in Macintosh word-processing programs.[44] Microsoft Word's market share rose from 10 percent in 1990 to over 90 percent in 1997.[45]

Even when developers moved to the packaged productivity software (office concept), Microsoft seems to have dominated the market. In April 2004, Corel launched its WordPerfect Office 12 suite with the specific goal of capturing the 10 percent market share that Microsoft did not claim. It is estimated that Microsoft Office has approximately 90 percent of the productivity software market, but that didn't stop Corel from trying to make a comeback.[46] The battle continues with Microsoft still on top.

Early Signs of Antitrust Troubles Ahead

As early as June 1990, Microsoft was being investigated by the Federal Trade Commission (FTC) for its marketing practices. In particular, the FTC focused on four of Microsoft's practices: preannouncement of products, exclusionary per-processor licenses for MS-DOS and Windows, unreasonably long-term licensing agreements, and restrictive nondisclosure agreements. Each of these four practices will be considered below.

Preannouncement of Products

Microsoft has historically preannounced its products well before the actual release dates. In April 1990, Novell (which purchased Digital Research in 1991) introduced DR-DOS, a direct competitor of MS-DOS. This program was introduced to critical acclaim, and experts considered DR-DOS to be a serious potential threat to MS-DOS's market share.[47] Microsoft, however, announced an expected release date for MS-DOS version 5.0 that was within one month of the launch date for DR-DOS. The MS-DOS 5.0 did not actually arrive until fourteen months later, but the early preannouncement discouraged hardware vendors and other customers from buying DR-DOS.[48] And even earlier, Microsoft announced its intention to transform MS-DOS into a GUI to compete with Apple's graphical interface. The introduction of Windows was officially announced on November 10, 1983, but Windows was not officially released until November 1985. These are two examples of Microsoft's strategic use of preannouncement of products.

Exclusionary Per-Processor Licenses for MS-DOS and Windows

As early as 1983, Microsoft chose to work individually with each OEM in setting the licensing fees for its MS-DOS operating system.[49] During these early years of MS-DOS's dominance, Microsoft negotiated these fees based on a number of factors, including the total number of *central processing units* (CPUs) shipped by an OEM, charging lower fees to OEMs that agreed to ship most of their machines with an operating system preinstalled. The rationale for this policy was to discourage computer users from pirating operating systems.[50] These types of licenses were referred to as *CPU licenses* and they accounted for as much as 50 percent of Microsoft's licenses in 1992.[51]

The CPU licenses usually required an OEM to pay for a specified minimum number of licenses. This minimum number was typically greater than the total number of computers the OEM anticipated shipping over the period covered by the licensing agreement. The OEM paid the license fee based on the total number of computers shipped, regardless of whether or not the computers were shipped with MS-DOS preinstalled. This created a huge incentive for OEMs to install MS-DOS on all the computers they shipped. Because the OEMs were paying for MS-DOS regardless of whether or not the operating system was installed on a computer, there was no incentive for the OEM to install a non-Microsoft operating system on a computer unless an end-user requested it. Furthermore, consumers had to pay an additional fee if they wanted a non-MS-DOS operating system installed on their computers.[52]

In 1988, Microsoft began its policy of offering OEMs reduced royalty fees for MS-DOS if they paid for each computer shipped, regardless of whether or not the computer was bundled with MS-DOS. At the time, Microsoft claimed that this simplified the accounting procedures associated with the licenses. In any event, Microsoft's operating systems quickly became so popular with the OEMs and end-users that the OEMs were reluctant to bundle any other operating system with their computers. In fact, the OEMs usually wanted the licensing fee discount. Microsoft also aggressively pushed its per-processor contracts on OEMs and claimed that technical problems would occur if Windows was run on a non-MS-DOS operating system. Remember that the early versions of Windows ran on top of MS-DOS, which was still the basic operating system. Microsoft continued to make this claim even though it never had software developers run beta tests* using DR-DOS with Windows, and there were few technical problems ever reported to Microsoft that stemmed from using Windows with a non-MS-DOS operating system.

Long-Term Licensing Agreements

Microsoft's CPU licenses typically ran for two years and the per-unit fee decreased as the number of computers shipped increased. Thus, to get the discounts, OEMs often ended up negotiating for a larger number of CPU licenses than they actually shipped. Microsoft allowed the OEMs to roll over any unused licenses to the following year, which increased the incentive for the OEMs to continue to install MS-DOS on their machines in future years.[53]

Restrictive Nondisclosure Agreements

As Microsoft developed and refined Windows and it became the dominant operating system in

the world, software developers needed the APIs for Windows in order to develop new software products. Microsoft followed a number of procedures to make it difficult for independent software developers to write application programs for competing operating systems or to develop applications that competed with Microsoft's applications like Word and Excel. In particular, Microsoft refused to document all of the important APIs in Windows. This gave Microsoft software developers a large advantage when writing application programs for Windows. In addition, Microsoft denied access for beta tests for DR-DOS with Windows 3.1 as well as DR-DOS with Windows for Workgroups products. Beta tests were always necessary for any new or updated operating system so that software developers have a chance to see if there are any incompatibility issues between the software and the operating system. Not only did Microsoft deny DR-DOS access, but it put a check on its beta-testing version of Windows to produce an error message if the program developers were using DR-DOS. The error message specifically stated to "contact Microsoft for a version of MS-DOS or else risk incompatibility with DR-DOS." While there were no real incompatibility problems ever reported, the intent of the error message was to create uncertainty in the minds of the software developers.[54] All of these actions made it more difficult for DRI, the creator of DR-DOS, to test for incompatibility with Microsoft products prior to the release of those products.

The Microsoft Antitrust Saga

To this point we have emphasized the history and economic reasons for Microsoft's rise to dominance of the personal computer operating system market. By historical standards Microsoft is a very young company, having been established in 1975. All of Microsoft's recent history, however, has

---

* A *beta test* is the final stage in the testing of new software before its commercial release, conducted by testers (called *beta testers*) other than its developers.

been closely tied to one or more ongoing antitrust actions filed by the U.S. Department of Justice (DOJ). Four major provisions of the U.S. antitrust law are relevant to these cases. Most important are sections 1 and 2 of the 1890 Sherman Antitrust Act, the nation's first comprehensive antitrust law. These sections read in part:

> *Section 1:* Every contract, combination in the form of a trust or otherwise, or conspiracy, in restraint of trade or commerce among the several states, or with foreign nations, is hereby declared to be illegal. . . .
>
> *Section 2:* Every person who shall monopolize, or attempt to monopolize, or combine or conspire with any other person or persons to monopolize any part of the trade or commerce among the several States, or with foreign nations, shall be deemed guilty of a misdemeanor. . . .

In 1914 the Sherman Act was amended by the Clayton Act to include two important provisions that are important for understanding the Microsoft cases. The Clayton Act aimed to prevent certain specific types of business conduct and included the following two sections:

Section 2 forbade price discrimination "where the effect of such discrimination may be to substantially lessen competition or tend to create a monopoly in any line of commerce." The section provided for three defenses—discrimination based on the quantity sold; the different costs of selling or transportation; or the need to meet a competitor's lower price. With these defenses, particularly the quantity defense, section 2 of the Clayton Act contained many large loopholes.

Section 3 forbade *tying contracts,* which forced a purchaser to buy good X in order to obtain good Y; and *exclusive dealing arrangements,* which forced a buyer to purchase its entire supply of a commodity from one seller.

One important legal distinction that is important to understand in the context of the Microsoft cases is the distinction between business conduct that is per se, or inherently, illegal, and business conduct that may or may not be illegal depending on the economic circumstances. This latter type of behavior is decided under the *rule of reason* precedent handed down in 1911 in perhaps the most famous and important of all antitrust cases, the *Standard Oil of New Jersey* case.[55] In the 1911 *Standard Oil* case, the Supreme Court ruled that only *unreasonable* attempts to monopolize violate the Sherman Act. This precedent has come to be known as the *rule of reason,* which plays an important part in many antitrust cases. As we will see, the rule-of-reason precedent played an important role in the Microsoft cases.

The DOJ filed its most significant and broad-based case against Microsoft in May 1998. This case bounced back and forth between the District Court for the District of Columbia and the Court of Appeals for the District Court for six years. The Microsoft antitrust saga, however, began five years before the filing of the 1998 case. In 1993 the FTC charged Microsoft with a variety of activities aimed at illegally controlling the market for PC-compatible operating systems. Earlier in this chapter, we analyzed these practices, which included the preannouncement of products, exclusionary per-processor licenses for MS-DOS and Windows, unreasonably long-term licensing agreements, and restrictive nondisclosure agreements. When the FTC staff presented its case before the full Federal Trade Commission, the Commission deadlocked by a 2–2 vote, and therefore did not issue a preliminary injunction against any of Microsoft's behavior.[56] Typically, this would have marked the end of the case, but in a highly unusual move, the DOJ decided to pursue the FTC's investigation, and on July 15, 1994, the DOJ proposed a consent decree.[57] When both Microsoft and the DOJ agreed to this consent decree, this, too, should have marked the end of the action; but in February

1995 Federal Judge Stanley Sporkin rejected the proposed decree. Sporkin believed the decree failed to effectively protect the public from Microsoft's power. The Court of Appeals, however, overturned Sporkin and accepted the consent decree.

Under the conditions of the 1995 consent decree Microsoft agreed to stop offering large discounts to OEMs for licenses based on the *total* number of computers shipped instead of the number of copies of MS-DOS *actually* shipped. Microsoft also agreed to end its use of long-term contracts that committed OEMs to purchasing large volumes of software in the future. Finally, Microsoft agreed to end its policy of requiring nondisclosure by software developers. This final provision ended Microsoft's practice of requiring software beta testers not to disclose details of Microsoft's operating systems for three years after the systems came to market. The nondisclosure requirement had restricted the ability of programmers to move from one company to another unless the programmer moved from another company *to* Microsoft.

By the time the consent decree was finalized in August 1995, a much larger issue was looming over Microsoft and the computer industry: the development of the Internet and Internet browsers to surf the Internet for information. In August 1995, Netscape's Navigator browser dominated the international browser market. Netscape's history was much like that of a shooting star that is super-bright one second and fading quickly the next. Founded at the University of Illinois–Urbana-Champaign in November 1994 as the successor to Mosaic Communications Corporation, Netscape shipped its Navigator version 1.0 in December 1994 and almost immediately came to dominate the market for Internet browsers. Netscape's market share of the Internet browser market peaked at over 90 percent in April 1996. Over the next two years, however, Microsoft's IE browser rapidly caught up to Netscape and by June 1998, the two

browsers essentially shared the market equally. In November 1998, America On Line (AOL) agreed to purchase Netscape for $4.2 billion worth of AOL stock. By the time the deal was completed in March 1999, however, the value of the AOL stock had increased to $9 billion, making this a very expensive acquisition for AOL.[58] In the end, it did not turn out well for AOL or Netscape. By July 2003, Microsoft's IE dominated the browser market with over a 90 percent market share. Furthermore, AOL had severely weakened its Netscape subsidiary by making IE the default browser for AOL users. AOL agreed to use IE as its default browser in exchange for Microsoft's agreement to place a *Free AOL & Unlimited Internet* icon on the Windows desktop. Microsoft presented AOL with a financial deal that AOL could not refuse, even though it cost its Netscape subsidiary dearly in the marketplace. Netscape has had some success in recent years with its introduction of its Mozilla-Firefox open-source browser, but IE continues to dominate the market with approximately a 90 percent market share.[59]

The 1995 consent decree failed to address directly the following major charge in the DOJ's 1998 complaint: Microsoft was monopolizing the Internet browser market by illegally tying its IE browser to its Windows operating system. According to the DOJ the 1995 consent decree had banned the tying of IE to Windows, and therefore the DOJ complained to the District Court that Microsoft was in contempt because it was violating the provisions of the decree. On December 11, 1997, the District Court entered a preliminary injunction banning the tying of IE to Windows.[60] Microsoft filed an appeal of this injunction, and on May 12, 1998, the Court of Appeals granted a stay of the injunction. Six days later, the DOJ and twenty state co-plaintiffs filed a formal antitrust complaint. They charged Microsoft with, among other things, violating section 2 of the Sherman Act as amended by section 3 of the Clayton Act. They were charged with attempting to monopolize the market in Internet browsers by tying IE to Windows. The complaint also charged that Microsoft had purposefully adopted a series of illegal practices in an attempt to monopolize the market for PC-compatible operating systems.

The complaint sought the following remedies against Microsoft. First, the DOJ asked for a ban on the tying of IE or any other Microsoft software product to Windows. Second, Microsoft was to be prohibited from forcing any OEM, Internet Access Providers (IAP), or Internet Content Providers (ICP) not to distribute any non-Microsoft browsers or any non-Microsoft software. Third, DOJ wanted Microsoft to be barred from placing restrictive conditions on its contracts with OEMs. For example, some of these restrictive conditions prohibited OEMs from removing any Microsoft icons, folders, or items from the start menu. Fourth, for a period of three years, Microsoft was to be required to include Netscape Navigator along with IE in all versions of Windows shipped and OEMs were to be permitted to delete the IE from their versions of Windows. Finally, the DOJ asked that Microsoft be permanently banned from shipping Windows with IE unless it made it possible for OEMs to delete the IE icon on the desktop. As we shall see, Microsoft might have been better off accepting this offer from the government and avoiding the tremendous negative publicity and the huge financial costs of fighting the case through the courts. In the end, the courts broadened the scope of the charges against Microsoft and the final consent decree handed down a much more restrictive set of behavioral guidelines for Microsoft. But in 1998 it was not in Bill Gates's nature to admit antitrust wrongdoing or to allow the threat of antitrust action to affect Microsoft's behavior.

The 1998 Antitrust Case

The 1998 case was randomly assigned to Judge Thomas Penfield Jackson of the District Court for the District of Columbia. It turned out that this random assignment had major legal and economic consequences. Because major antitrust cases tend to last for decades (for example, the AT&T monopolization case was filed in 1969 and finally ended with a consent decree in 1981) and because of the rapid technological advance in the computer industry, Judge Jackson decided to expedite the trial by putting it on a "fast track." This greatly limited the number of witnesses and the length of the trial. Witnesses were limited to twelve on each side with three rebuttal witnesses permitted. Remarkably, the entire trial was completed in seventy-six days, and Jackson handed down his decision on April 3, 2000. Bill Gates testified only by video deposition, and most of his testimony consisted of the government's attorneys questioning him about his own e-mail messages dealing with competitive relationships. Gates spent most of the time in the deposition arguing that he had no recollection of these e-mails.

Netscape was cooperating with the government and provided many pieces of evidence showing that Microsoft commonly pressured companies to use Microsoft's IE instead of Netscape's Navigator.[61] For example, in a June 13, 1996, message, a Netscape employee reported that Microsoft had offered a Dutch Internet service provider free browsing software and a $400,000 marketing fund. "This was extended on the understanding that [the service provider] would NOT purchase any s/w [software] from Netscape." In another message, an Internet service company tells a Netscape employee that "we have ceased distribution of Netscape. Your product is excellent but totally lacking in marketing support and we could never justify the $20 setup cost when Microsoft will fly a blimp with our name on it for free." A June 10, 1996, message to Netscape from Kurt Brecheisen, president of a company called Global Telecom, said: "Microsoft gave me a deal I couldn't refuse.

Free dialer, browser, developer kit, freely distribut-able, etc. . . . I know Netscape is better, but $0 vs $18K is impossible to beat."

Microsoft's most successful method of getting firms to switch from Navigator to IE was to offer free advertising on the Windows desktop. We al-ready noted that even Netscape's parent AOL used IE as its default browser in return for placement of the AOL icon on the Windows desktop. But in addition to AOL, Microsoft was able to persuade many other major browser users to switch their default browsers from Netscape to IE in return for placement of a link on the Windows desktop. Major firms that changed their default browsers from Navigator to IE included MCI in March 1996, CompuServe in June 1996, AT&T and Netcom in July 1996, Prodigy in October 1996, and Sprint in December 1996.[62]

On June 7, 2000, Judge Jackson issued his ruling.[63] It was not a good day for Microsoft. He found that Microsoft was a monopolist in the market for Intel-compatible PC operating systems, had illegally tied IE to Windows, had attempted to eliminate Netscape from the browser market, and had also violated the Sherman Act with its aggres-sive behavior toward most of its competitors and potential competitors. Jackson proposed the most radical remedy possible, one that the DOJ had not even requested, the breakup of Microsoft into two companies, an operating systems company and a software company. Microsoft, of course, immedi-ately appealed.

The Appeals Court Decision

Before examining the first Appeals Court ruling handed down on June 28, 2001, it is interesting to look at what turned out to be a very important element of the final adjudication of the case: the decision of the Appeals Court to remove Judge Jackson from any further participation in the case.[64]

Evidence indicated that Jackson had spoken with members of the press about the case long before he handed down his ruling. Furthermore, it was clear from press reports that the judge had been expressing his basic disbelief in Microsoft's de-fense, particularly the important issue of whether IE was integrated into Windows for technologi-cal reasons. In an interview with John R. Wilke of the *Wall Street Journal,* for example, Jackson commented that "it was quite clear to me that the motive of Microsoft in bundling the Internet browser was not one of consumer convenience. The evidence that this was done for the consumer was not credible. . . . The evidence was so compel-ling that there was an ulterior motive."[65] Jackson also commented in these interviews that Gates's "testimony is inherently without credibility" and "[i]f you can't believe this guy, who else can you believe?"[66] On the day he ordered the breakup of Microsoft, Jackson told Wilke, "Falsus in uno, falsus in omnibus": "Untrue in one thing, untrue in everything."[67] Jackson also told Ken Auletta of the *New Yorker* that "I thought [Microsoft] would learn."[68] In a college campus talk, the judge stated that "Bill Gates is an ingenious engineer, but I don't think he is that adept at business ethics. He has not yet come to realize things he did (when Microsoft was smaller) he should not have done when he be-came a monopoly."[69] In another interview, Jackson declared that "[i]f I were able to propose a remedy of my devising, I'd require Mr. Gates to write a book report" on Napoleon Bonaparte, "[b]ecause I think [Gates] has a Napoleonic concept of himself and his company, an arrogance that derives from power and unalloyed success[.]"[70]

According to Auletta, Jackson became "increas-ingly troubled by what he learned about Bill Gates and couldn't get out of his mind the group picture he had seen of Bill Gates and Paul Allen and their shaggy-haired first employees at Microsoft."[71] Furthermore, Jackson told Auletta that he saw in Gates "a smart-mouthed young kid who has extraordinary ability and needs a little discipline. I've often said to colleagues that Gates would be better off if he had finished Harvard," and that "they [Microsoft and its executives] don't act like grownups!" "[T]o this day they continue to deny they did anything wrong."[72]

To summarize Jackson's thinking about Microsoft, the judge told the *New York Times* the following story about a North Carolina mule trainer. "He had a trained mule who could do all kinds of wonderful tricks. One day somebody asked him: How do you do it? How do you train the mule to do all these amazing things? Well, he answered, I'll show you. He took a 2-by-4 and whopped him upside the head. The mule was reeling and fell to his knees, and the trainer said: You just have to get his attention. . . . I hope I've got Microsoft's attention."[73]

It turned out that in addition to Microsoft's attention, Jackson received the attention of the Court of Appeals. In a unanimous decision the court ruled that "the District Judge's impatience with what he viewed as intransigence on the part of the company; his refusal to allow an evidentiary hearing; his analogizing Microsoft to Japan at the end of World War II; his story about the mule—all of these out-of-court remarks and others, plus the Judge's evident efforts to please the press, would give a reasonable, informed observer cause to question his impartiality in ordering the company split in two." The court then noted that "disqualification is mandatory for conduct that calls a judge's impartiality into question." The court, however, refused Microsoft's request to vacate the entire case because of Judge Jackson's behavior. Instead, the court ruled that the law only "requires . . . disqualification from the judge's hearing any further proceedings in the case." The court then vacated the remedy of divestiture proposed by Jackson, but accepted all of his findings of fact in the case and remanded (sent back) the case back to the District

Court to consider alternative remedies. To preside over the remanded case, the Court of Appeals randomly reassigned the case to Judge Colleen Kollar-Kotelly.

The Appeals Court said much more in its decision than simply that the remedy was vacated and Judge Jackson disqualified. Based on the District Court's findings of fact, the Appeals Court overturned many of Jackson's rulings. Most importantly, the Appeals Court ruled that there was insufficient evidence to define the market for Internet browsers as a separate market, and, therefore, the court vacated Jackson's ruling that Microsoft had attempted to monopolize the market for Internet browsers. On the issue of tying, the court noted that Judge Jackson had simply "concluded that Microsoft's contractual and technological bundling of the IE web browser (the "tied" product) with its Windows operating system ("OS") (the "tying" product) resulted in a tying arrangement that was per se unlawful." The Appeals Court, however, stated that based on Supreme Court precedents, "the rule of reason, rather than per se analysis, should govern the legality of tying arrangements involving platform software products." The Appeals Court gave the DOJ the opportunity upon remand to the District Court to retry the tying issue under the rule of reason, but the DOJ chose not to do so. One of the greatest public misconceptions about this case is that Microsoft was found guilty of tying IE to Windows, when in fact that ruling was completely vacated by the Appeals Court. Furthermore, because the court ruled that the government had failed to prove that the browser market constituted a separate economic market, the court also overturned the ruling that Microsoft had attempted to eliminate Netscape and monopolize the browser market.

The Appeals Court, however, ruled that Microsoft was guilty of illegally maintaining its monopoly in the market for *Intel-compatible PC operating systems* and that Microsoft had violated the Sherman Act with its aggressive behavior toward most of its competitors and potential competitors. This ruling went to the very heart of Microsoft's power; it more seriously threatened Microsoft than a more limited finding that Microsoft had tied IE to Windows. We now turn to an analysis of the Appeals Court's major rulings against Microsoft.

Domination of the Browser Market

The Appeals Court found that domination of the browser market was an important factor in maintaining Microsoft's monopoly in operating systems. The District Court condemned a number of provisions in Microsoft's licensing agreements with OEMs because it ruled that Microsoft's imposition of those provisions served to reduce usage of Netscape's browser and, therefore, protect Microsoft's operating system monopoly. The court's reasoning concerning how Microsoft's domination of the browser market protected its market power in the operating system market is complex, and warrants additional explanation.

According to the Appeals Court, a browser must have a large market share in order to attract software developers to write applications relying upon the APIs exposed by the browser. Applications written to a particular browser's APIs, however, would run on any computer with that browser, *regardless of the underlying operating system.* This gets at the heart of the importance of network externalities in the computer industry. According to the Court, "[t]he overwhelming majority of consumers will only use a PC operating system for which there already exists a large and varied set of . . . applications, and for which it seems relatively certain that new types of applications and new versions of existing applications will continue to be marketed. . . ."[74] If Netscape Navigator captured a large share of the browser market and software

developers produced many applications written for Navigator, then users could opt to use any operating system that supported Navigator and they could opt not to use Windows. This might eventually destroy Windows' monopoly in the operating systems market.

Once the Appeals Court accepted the linkage between domination of the browser market and domination of the operating system market, it was able to conclude that "Microsoft's efforts to gain market share in one market (browsers) served to meet the threat to Microsoft's monopoly in another market (operating systems) by keeping rival browsers from gaining the critical mass of users necessary to attract developer attention away from Windows as the platform for software development."

The Appeals Court affirmed Judge Jackson's conclusions that Microsoft had used many anticompetitive methods to dominate the browser market including:

1. Writing source code for IE that was so intertwined with source code for Windows that deleting IE would cripple many Windows operations.
2. Making it impossible to use the Add/Remove function in Windows to delete IE.
3. Prohibiting OEMs from deleting IE from the desktop and start menu in Windows.
4. Prohibiting OEMs from creating an initial boot sequence that resulted in promoting any Internet service providers (e.g., AOL) that used Navigator as their default browser or promoted Navigator in any way.
5. Prohibiting OEMs from promoting any browser except IE.
6. Placing an icon on the Windows desktop for any major ISP that agreed to use IE as its default browser as long as the ISP further agreed not to promote the use of Navigator on its Web site.

7. Providing preferential treatment to software application developers who used IE as their default browsers in their applications.

8. Threatening Apple that it would stop producing a version of Microsoft Office for Macs if Apple continued to use Navigator as its default browser or if Apple continued to place a Navigator icon on the Mac desktop.

Suppression of Other Forms of Competition

The court also dealt with issues other than Microsoft's attempt to monopolize the browser market. Another potential threat to Microsoft's Windows monopoly was posed by Java, a set of technologies developed by Sun Microsystems. Java is a type of middleware* that can be installed on any operating system and, once installed, can be used as a platform for software that is separate from Windows. Programs written for Java will run on any computer operating system that includes a Java runtime environment (JRE).

Beginning in May 1995, Netscape began distributing a JRE with every copy of Navigator, so that any computer with Navigator could run programs written for Java. All copies of Java include a so-called Java Virtual Machine (JVM) that translates byte code into instructions for the operating system. The Appeals Court found that "Microsoft took steps to maximize the difficulty with which applications written in Java could be ported from Windows to other platforms, and vice versa." While

Microsoft was supposedly working with Sun to improve Java for Windows, it was covertly working to sabotage Sun's version of Java. Recall that Microsoft used the same strategy to undermine IBM's efforts to produce its OS/2 operating system by simultaneously working with IBM on developing IBM's OS/2 operating system and against IBM by developing Windows.

While working with Sun on Java, Microsoft developed its own version of a Java Virtual Machine that was fundamentally incompatible with Sun's JVM. On computers with Windows, applications ran faster on Microsoft's JVM than Sun's JVM. However, Java applications written for the Microsoft JVM did not work on Sun's JVM. The District Court found that Microsoft's development of its JVM violated the law, but the Appeals Court disagreed because of the technological superiority of Microsoft's JVM on computers with Windows. The Appeals Court ruled that "[i]n order to violate the antitrust laws, the incompatible product must have an anticompetitive effect that outweighs any procompetitive justification for the design. . . . The [Microsoft] JVM, however, does allow applications to run more swiftly and does not itself have any anticompetitive effect."

Microsoft also entered into many agreements with leading software developers to ensure that Microsoft's JVM became the developers' default JVM. According to the Appeals Court, Microsoft coerced the developers into these agreements by making technical information and support about Windows conditional on the software developers' agreements to exclusively promote Microsoft's JVM.

Microsoft's work with Sun on a JVM included a set of software development tools to assist software developers in writing applications for Microsoft's JVM. In its dealings with software developers, Microsoft deceived the developers regarding the Windows-specific nature of the software tools

---

* *Middleware* is a general term for any programming that serves to glue together or mediate between two separate and often already existing programs. Typically, middleware programs provide messaging services so that different applications can communicate. In this case, Java glued together an operating system and some application software.

provided by Microsoft. For example, the software developers were never told that Microsoft's tools could only work properly on Microsoft's JVM. As the District Court noted, and the Appeals Court accepted, even Java "developers who were opting for portability over performance . . . unwittingly [wrote] Java applications that [ran] only on Windows." In the words of the Appeals Court, "the developers who relied upon Microsoft's public commitment to cooperate with Sun and who used Microsoft's tools to develop what Microsoft led them to believe were cross-platform applications ended up producing applications that would run only on the Windows operating system."

Internal Microsoft documents presented during the trial showed that Microsoft purposefully deceived Java developers with the objective of causing ISVs unknowingly to create Windows-dependent Java applications that the developers thought would run on any version of Java written for any operating system. The court pointed out that "One Microsoft document, for example, states as a strategic goal: 'Kill cross-platform Java by grow[ing] the polluted Java market.'" The Appeals Court concluded that "Microsoft's conduct related to its Java developer tools served to protect its monopoly of the operating system in a manner not attributable either to the superiority of the operating system or to the acumen of its makers, and therefore was anticompetitive."

Intel is the world's largest producer of microprocessors for computers and a virtual monopolist in PC-compatible microprocessors. Intel's success depends critically on a close working relationship with Microsoft because Microsoft writes Windows code to work efficiently with Intel's microprocessors. Like Microsoft, in 1995 Intel was developing a Windows-compatible JVM. This made Microsoft very uneasy because if Intel developed a Windows-based JVM, it could easily develop a cross-platform JVM that could threaten

Microsoft's monopoly in the operating system market. In August 1995, Bill Gates told Intel that its "cooperation with Sun and Netscape to develop a Java runtime environment . . . was one of the issues threatening to undermine cooperation between Intel and Microsoft." Despite Gates's implied threat, by 1996 Intel had developed its own version of a JVM that worked not only with Windows but also with other operating systems. As a result, Microsoft threatened Intel that "if it did not stop aiding Sun [with Java], then Microsoft would refuse to distribute Intel technologies bundled with Windows." Microsoft carried through by threatening to support an alternative microprocessor technology rather than Intel's technology. Gates sent a message to Intel that "[i]f Intel has a real problem with us supporting this [alternative technology] then they will have to stop supporting Java Multimedia the way they are. I would gladly give up supporting this if they would back off from their work on JAVA."

According to the Appeals Court, "The District Court, however, found that Microsoft's 'advice' to Intel to stop aiding cross-platform Java was backed by the threat of retaliation, and this conclusion is supported by the evidence cited above. Therefore we affirm the conclusion that Microsoft's threats to Intel were exclusionary, in violation of section 2 of the Sherman Act."

The Consent Decree

Upon remand to the District Court, Judge Kollar-Kotelly ordered the parties to attempt to reach a settlement. The DOJ and nine of the eighteen states reached an agreement, but nine other states and the District of Columbia refused to accept the proposed settlement.[75] On November 12, 2002, the judge accepted and signed the final judgment in the case.

The consent decree is aimed at eliminating Microsoft's conduct that the Appeals Court found to be in violation of the Sherman Act. The major provisions are:

1. **Prohibition of Retaliation**—Microsoft is prohibited from retaliating against any OEM by renegotiating its relationship with that OEM. Specifically, Microsoft is prohibited from withholding any form of non-monetary consideration from an OEM because the OEM is, or is contemplating, developing, distributing, promoting, using, selling, or licensing: (1) any software that competes with Microsoft software; (2) any product or service that distributes or promotes any non-Microsoft middleware; (3) shipping a PC that includes both a Windows operating system product and a non-Microsoft operating system; or (4) shipping a computer that will boot with more than one operating system. The decree lists the following specific forms of nonmonetary consideration that Microsoft is prohibited from withholding: the provision of preferential licensing terms; technical, marketing, and sales support; enabling programs; product information; information about future plans; developer support; hardware or software certification or approval; or permission to display trademarks, icons, or logos.

2. **Requirement of Uniform Licensing Agreements**—To deal with Microsoft's rampant use of price discrimination, the decree requires Microsoft to charge a uniform royalty for Windows to all OEMs, and requires Microsoft to publish its royalty schedule on its Web site. Microsoft is allowed to charge different royalties for non-English versions of Windows, and it is permitted to offer "reasonable volume discounts," as well as some development allowances. However, Microsoft is required to make sure that all discounts are available to all OEMs on a uniform basis. Based on the reasoning that there is nothing inherently anticompetitive about volume discounts based on actual units sold, the court permitted one exception to this general

rule by permitting Microsoft to establish one uniform discount schedule for the ten largest OEMs and another uniform discount schedule for the eleventh through twentieth largest OEMs.

3. **Prohibition of Restrictive Behavior Toward OEMs**—Microsoft is prohibited from engaging in a wide variety of anticompetitive behavior in its dealings with its OEM licensees. Specifically, Microsoft is prohibited from preventing:

- Any OEM from installing and displaying icons, shortcuts, or menu entries for any non-Microsoft middleware (or any product or service that distributes, uses, promotes, or supports any non-Microsoft middleware) on the desktop or Start menu, or anywhere else in a Windows operating system where a list of icons, shortcuts, or menu entries for applications are displayed.
- The installation and display on the desktop of shortcuts of any size or shape used for the promotion and distribution of any non-Microsoft middleware, provided that such shortcuts do not impair the functionality of Windows.
- The automatic launching at the conclusion of the initial boot sequence, subsequent boot sequences, or upon connections to or disconnections from the Internet, of any non-Microsoft middleware product if a Microsoft middleware product that provides similar functionality could be automatically launched at that time in the boot-up sequence.
- Users from launching non-Microsoft operating systems, non-Microsoft boot-loaders, or similar programs from a computer's basic input/output system.

4. **Requirement of Technology Disclosures**—For a period starting at the earlier of the release of Service Pack 1 for Windows XP or twelve months after the submission of the final consent decree, Microsoft is required to disclose the APIs and doc-

umentation used by Microsoft middleware to all software developers (ISVs), independent hardware vendors (IHVs), Internet access providers (IAPs), Internet content providers (ICPs), and OEMs. Furthermore, starting nine months after the submission of the proposed final consent decree, Microsoft is required to make available for use by third parties, at reasonable and non-discriminatory terms, any communications protocol* that is implemented in a Windows operating system product.

5. **Prohibition of Retaliation Against ISVs and IHVs**—Microsoft is prohibited from retaliating against any ISV or IHV because an ISV or IHV develops, uses, distributes, promotes, or supports any software that competes with Microsoft software (or with any software that runs on any software that competes with Microsoft software). Microsoft is also prohibited from entering into any agreement relating to a Windows operating system product that conditions the grant of any consideration from Microsoft on an ISV's agreement to refrain from developing, using, distributing, or promoting any software that competes with Microsoft software (or with any software that runs on any software that competes with Microsoft software). However, Microsoft is permitted to enter into agreements with ISVs that place limitations on an ISV's development, use, distribution, or promotion of software if those limitations are reasonably necessary to and of reasonable scope and duration in relation to a bona fide contractual obligation of the ISV to use, distribute, or promote any Microsoft software or to develop software for, or in conjunction with, Microsoft. This exception

gives ISVs the right to agree to limit the development of non-Microsoft software in exchange for the right to work with Microsoft on developing Microsoft software products.

6. **Prohibition of Restrictive Behavior Toward IAPs, ICPs, ISVs, IHVs, or OMEs**—Microsoft is prohibited from granting any consideration to any IAP, ICP, ISV, IHV, or OEM in exchange for an agreement to distribute, promote, use, or support any Microsoft software. In addition, Microsoft is prohibited from providing placement on the Windows desktop or elsewhere in Windows to any IAP or ICP in exchange for an agreement to refrain from distributing, promoting, or using any software that competes with Microsoft middleware.

7. **Requirement of an Ability to Disable Windows Middleware Products**—For a period starting at the earlier of the release of Service Pack 1 for Windows XP or twelve months after the submission of the final consent decree, Microsoft is required to allow end-users (via a mechanism readily accessible from the desktop or start menu such as an Add/Remove icon) to enable or remove access to each Microsoft middleware product or non-Microsoft middleware product by displaying or removing icons, shortcuts, or menu entries on the desktop or start menu, or anywhere else in a Windows Operating system product where a list of icons, shortcuts, or menu entries for applications are displayed. Microsoft must also permit end-users, OEMs, and non-Microsoft middleware products to designate a non-Microsoft middleware product to be launched in place of a Microsoft middleware product (or vice versa) in any case where Windows would otherwise automatically launch a Microsoft middleware product. Microsoft must also ensure that a Windows operating system product does not automatically alter an OEM's configuration of icons, shortcuts, or menu entries installed or displayed by the OEM without first seeking confirmation from the end-user.

Communications protocol means the set of rules for information exchange to accomplish predefined tasks between a Windows and a server operating system product connected via a network, including, but not limited to, a local area network, a wide area network, or the Internet. These rules govern the format, semantics, timing, sequencing, and error control of messages exchanged over a network.

8. **Requirement of Licensing of Microsoft Intellectual Property**—Microsoft is required to license at reasonable and non-discriminatory royalties to ISVs, IHVs, IAPs, ICPs, and OEMs any of its intellectual property rights that are required to exercise any of the options or alternatives expressly provided to them under this consent decree.

Even a cursory examination of the consent decree shows that the final decree went well beyond the relief sought by the DOJ in its 1998 complaint. There are far more limitations placed on Microsoft's behavior, and the 2002 decree deals broadly with the entire middleware market rather than primarily the browser market. The final decree even deals with future software products and technologies. The only specific remedy suggested by the government in 1998 not included in the 2002 decree was a ban on tying Microsoft's IE browser to Windows. The reason for this omission was simply that the Appeals Court overturned Judge Jackson's ruling that Microsoft had illegally tied IE to Windows.

Comparing the 2002 decree with the remedies sought in the 1998 complaint raises an intriguing question: Would Microsoft have been better off signing the DOJ's proposed 1998 consent decree? By signing the 1998 decree Microsoft would have saved a vast amount in legal expenses, and, perhaps more importantly, Microsoft would have avoided a great deal of the negative publicity associated with the trial. Microsoft estimated that by October 2003 it had spent $3 billion on its defense and it had almost $1 billion more on reserve to fight the appeal.[76] From a publicity standpoint there were few, if any, more devastating moments in Microsoft's history than when Bill Gates in his video deposition repeatedly stated under oath that he could not remember sending one incriminating e-mail message after another even though the messages were clearly

sent by him from his personal PC. On the other hand, some economists and legal experts believe that the DOJ was so determined to litigate against Microsoft's overwhelming market power in the operating system market that signing the 1998 proposed consent decree would only have delayed the inevitable case. According to this reasoning, Microsoft was better off litigating the case to a conclusion so that it could get back to the critical business of improving its market position in a rapidly changing market, where the threats to its power come from a new set of middleware technologies such as Google's search engine.

In any event, the conclusion of the case placed Microsoft in an entirely different competitive mindset. Bill Gates and the entire Microsoft executive leadership were convinced that the company had to moderate its aggressive conduct toward competitors. Recall that Judge Jackson had stated the following: "[i]f I were able to propose a remedy of my devising, I'd require Mr. Gates to write a book report" on Napoleon Bonaparte, "[b]ecause I think [Gates] has a Napoleonic concept of himself and his company, an arrogance that derives from power and unalloyed success[.]" and "[Microsoft and its executives] don't act like grownups!"[77] The consent decree forced Microsoft to grow up quickly and behave like other firms with substantial market power. For the first time, Microsoft began to recognize that it had a legal obligation to operate under a different set of competitive rules than other firms.

Has Microsoft abided by the requirements of the 2002 decree? The evidence to date suggests it has. In fact, Microsoft began complying well before the final decree was signed. Microsoft's compliance is consistent with a theory that firms typically change their behavior during the litigation period of a case before a final settlement is reached.[78] According to this theory, the act of filing a monopolization case reduces the probability that an accused firm will behave aggressively toward competitors. Because competitors recognize this reduction in the threat of aggressive behavior, they become bolder in their attempts to compete with the accused monopolist. Furthermore, potential entrants assume that the accused monopolist is less likely to retaliate against them if they enter, and, therefore, the filing of the case can result in an increase in the rate of entry. As a first empirical example of this type of change in corporate behavior, consider IBM's conduct following the filing of the DOJ's 1969 monopolization case. IBM became so concerned about its antitrust troubles from 1969 to 1981 that it became almost passive in its dealings with competitors. In fact, IBM became almost paralyzed in terms of dealing with the threat to its power posed by Microsoft. Every IBM action was analyzed internally for its impact on the government's case. In the end, the case was finally dismissed, but by then IBM's control over the computer industry had been destroyed.

Similar responses to government antitrust enforcement have been identified during widely varying time periods, including DuPont in the cellophane industry in the late 1940s, United Shoe Machinery in the shoe machinery industry in the 1950s, and Grinnell (ADT, the home and business security company) in the market for central-station protective services in the 1960s.[79] What is unusual about Bill Gates and Microsoft is that, even after the DOJ filed its 1993 complaint and Microsoft agreed to a consent decree in 1995, Microsoft remained remarkably aggressive in its dealings with competitors. In fact, Gates and Microsoft appeared almost oblivious to the antitrust attacks. The firm's behavior undoubtedly helps explain Judge Jackson's view about Bill Gates and the senior Microsoft leadership.[80]

The 1998 case, and particularly the negative publicity surrounding the trial, dramatically changed Gates's and Microsoft's corporate attitude.

Like IBM and DuPont before them, Microsoft suddenly and dramatically modified its behavior beginning as early as 2001. In December 2001, Microsoft supplied a version of Windows that included a new "set programs and defaults" feature. This feature made it easy for Windows users to disable access to Microsoft's programs and instead set non-Microsoft products as system defaults. For example, with this version of Windows, OEMs could easily set Navigator as their default browser. A few months later, Microsoft announced that it was documenting and making available for license many communications protocols.

By July 2003, Microsoft had further modified its behavior in a wide variety of ways. First, Microsoft eliminated all of its price discrimination policies by supplying a uniform set of license agreements for Windows for all OEMs and publishing these agreements on a Web site that is accessible to OEMs. Today Microsoft updates these license agreements every spring. All available discounts are made available on a uniform basis to any OEMs. Second, Microsoft voluntarily trained its worldwide staff of lawyers and OEM sales employees to comply with the company's new nondiscriminatory pricing policy. From November 2001 to July 2003, Microsoft trained over 12,500 employees concerning the company's new marketing policies. Third, prior to Microsoft's release of Service Pack 1 for Windows XP in September 2002, Microsoft made public the documentation for approximately 290 APIs for Service Pack 1. In addition, Microsoft made available licenses for more than 100 communications protocols. These communication protocols made it easier for independent software developers to create software for tasks such as file services, print services, and media. Documentation of these communications protocols required over 5,000 pages and ten Microsoft technical writers to work full-time for nine months. Finally, in August 2002, Microsoft instituted a "DealPoint" program that required that all sales agreements coming out of the Windows Division be approved by both a lead business person and a lead lawyer to make sure that the agreements did not violate Microsoft's new policies.

Conclusion

Microsoft has been hard-hit in the last few years with court cases. To a certain extent, the outcomes of the antitrust cases have caused it to change some of its business practices. Even with the modified behavior, Microsoft is a leader in operating systems and software, as well as other products in which it has ventured. Since 1975, Microsoft has expanded into many different markets that were not even imaginable when the company was first formed. Given the rapidly advancing technology, it is difficult to predict the future of Microsoft. Perhaps one day, Google, or even Apple, will supplant Microsoft.

How might Google overtake Microsoft and become the most dominant firm in the broadly defined computer technology industry? Google could take control over the next important open-computer architecture for Web search services.[81] Google could produce its own set of proprietary APIs that work on any search engine and permit a wide variety of search functions to be performed on any computer with Google's set of APIs installed. Furthermore, Google could work closely with Linux to perfect these APIs for the Linux operating system. The Google APIs could permit users to use all types of application software from games and music to word processing and graphic design. Computer manufacturers could then offer computers loaded with Google and its APIs on a Linux, not a Windows, operating system.

As for Apple, it already is completely dominant in the market for portable music with its phenomenally successful iPods, and every one of those

iPods depends on an Apple-based bootable drive.[82] Now imagine that Apple develops a new operating system—Apple OS 10.5—for its computers and decides to load a copy of its old operating system on every iPod. Furthermore, the old OS X on the iPod can be downloaded for free on any Intel-based computer. Using this strategy, Apple might steal considerable market share away from Windows.

Are the above scenarios possible? Only time will tell.

Notes

1. For more on the early years prior to the start of Microsoft, see Rochelle Ruffer and Don E. Waldman, "Microsoft," in D. I. Rosenbaum, ed., *Market Dominance: How Firms Gain, Hold, or Lose It and the Impact on Economic Performance,* pp. 152–57 (Westport, CT: Praeger, 1998).
2. 2005 Microsoft Annual Report, www.microsoft.com (March 2006).
3. www.w3schools.com/browsers/browsers_stats.asp, March 2006 figures.
4. *Market Share Reporter* (Detroit MI: Gale Research Group, 2006).
5. Ruffer and Waldman, "Microsoft," p. 155.
6. Intel Microprocessor Quick Reference Guide from www.intel.com/technology/computing/mi06031.htm, accessed on April 18, 2006.
7. According to Daniel Ichbiah and Susan L. Knepper, in *The Making of Microsoft,* CP/M was developed in 1974 by Gary Kildall. CP/M became the industry standard for microcomputer business applications. After IBM chose MS/DOS as its operating system in the 1980s, the CP/M market declined significantly (Rocklin, CA: Prima Publishing, 1991), p. 275.
8. Ruffer and Waldman, "Microsoft," p. 155.
9. David S. Evans, Albert L. Nichols, and Richard Schmalensee, "U.S. v. Microsoft: Did Consumers Win?," *NBER Working Paper Series,* working paper 11727, October 2005, p. 37. For citations that review the economic literature on multi-sided platforms, see footnote 103.
10. Ibid., p. 38.
11. Ibid., pp. 37–38.
12. *United States v. Microsoft Corporation,* Civil Action No. 98–1232, November 5, 1999, District Court for the District of Columbia, paragraph 38, p. 18.
13. Michael L. Katz and Carl Shapiro, "Network Externalities, Competition and Compatibility," *American Economic Review* 75 (June 1985), p. 424.

14. *United States v. Microsoft Corporation, op. cit.,* paragraph 39, pp. 18–19.

15. Ruffer and Waldman, "Microsoft," p. 159.

16. *United States v. Microsoft Corporation, op. cit.,* paragraph 39, pp. 18–19.

17. Ruffer and Waldman, "Microsoft," p. 159.

18. James Wallace and Jim Erickson, *Hard Drive: Bill Gates and the Making of the Microsoft Empire* (New York: HarperCollins, 1992), p. 92.

19. For a thorough discussion of Microsoft's relationship with "Big Blue," see Wallace and Erickson, *Hard Drive,* pp. 139–206.

20. Michael A. Cusumano and Richard W. Selby, *Microsoft Secrets* (New York: Free Press, 1995), p. 158.

21. Ruffer and Waldman, "Microsoft," pp. 156–57. Also see the discussion of how luck came into play with Gates receiving the IBM contract.

22. Ichbiah and Knepper, *Making of Microsoft,* p. 74.

23. Ibid., p. 276.

24. Ibid., pp. 192–95.

25. See Ruffer and Waldman, "Microsoft," pp. 157–59, for a full discussion of the practices that helped Microsoft's rise to dominance.

26. Ichbiah and Knepper, *Making of Microsoft,* p. 192.

27. Microsoft's 2005 Annual Report.

28. Ichbiah and Knepper, *Making of Microsoft,* p. 239.

29. Cusumano and Selby, *Microsoft Secrets,* pp. 159–60.

30. Ruffer and Waldman, "Microsoft," p. 158.

31. For a discussion of early R&D expenditures, see Ruffer and Waldman, "Microsoft," pp. 161–62.

32. Microsoft Annual Reports, www.microsoft.com.

33. John Sutton, *Sunk Costs and Market Structure* (Cambridge, MA: MIT Press, 1991).

34. Stan J. Liebowitz and Stephen E. Margolis, in *Winners, Losers, & Microsoft* (Oakland, CA: Independent Institute, 2001), provide an interesting chapter on "spreadsheets and word processors" (pp. 163–200) with many visual graphs showing market share, prices, and ratings of software programs.

35. Ichbiah and Knepper, *Making of Microsoft,* pp. 109–11.

36. Cusumano and Selby, *Microsoft Secrets,* pp. 138–39.

37. Ichbiah and Knepper, *Making of Microsoft,* p. 206.

38. Ibid., p. 203.

39. Ibid., p. 209.

40. Liebowitz and Margolis, *Winners, Losers,* p. 176.

41. Ibid, pp. 180–81.

42. Ichbiah and Knepper, *Making of Microsoft,* pp. 125, 127–29, 132, 136.

43. Liebowitz and Margolis, *Winners, Losers,* pp. 180–81.

44. Ichbiah and Knepper, *Making of Microsoft,* p. 140.

45. Liebowitz and Margolis, *Winners, Losers,* pp. 180–81.

46. David Worthington, "WordPerfect Vies for a Comeback," *BetaNews,* www.betanews.com, March 5, 2004.

47. Ruffer and Waldman, "Microsoft," pp. 163–64.

48. Cusumano and Selby, *Microsoft Secrets,* p. 160.

49. Ruffer and Waldman, "Microsoft," p. 165.

50. *United States v. Microsoft Corporation, op. cit.,* paragraph 65, pp. 33–34.

51. Ruffer and Waldman, "Microsoft," p. 165.

52. Ibid., p. 166.

53. Ibid., p. 166.

54. Ibid., pp. 166–67.

55. *United States v. Standard Oil of New Jersey* 221 US 1 (1911).

56. *United States v. Microsoft Corporation* No. 94–1564 (DDC filed July 15, 1994). Amended versions filed with the court on July 27, 1994.

57. Ibid.

58. Evan Hansen, "AOL Lays Off Netscape Developers," July 15, 2003, http://msn-cnet.com/AOL+lays+off+Netscape+developers/2100–1032_3–1026078.html.

59. Robert McMillan, "Mozilla Gains on IE: Study Shows Microsoft Has Lost a Percentage of Market Share to Open Source Browser," July 9, 2004, www.pcworld.com/news/article/0,aid,116848,00.asp.

60. See *United States v. Microsoft Corporation,* No. 98–1232 (DDC filed May 18, 1998).

61. "U.S. Releases E-Mail to Back Up Testimony," *Washington Post* (October 24, 1998), p. D-4.

62. Michael A. Cusumano and David B. Yoffie, *Competing on Internet Time* (New York: Touchtone, 1998), pp. 116–17.

63. *United States v. Microsoft Corporation,* Civil Action No. 98–1232, November 5, 1999, District Court for the District of Columbia.

64. *U.S. v. Microsoft,* 253 F.3d 34 (D.C. Cir. 2001).

65. John R. Wilke, "For Antitrust Judge, Trust, or Lack of It, Really Was the Issue," *Wall Street Journal* (June 8, 2000), p. A-8.

66. Joel Brinkley and Steve Lohr, "Retracing the Missteps in Microsoft's Defense at Its Antitrust Trial," *New York Times* (June 9, 2000).

67. Wilke, "For Antitrust Judge. . . ," p. A-8.

68. Ken Auletta, *World War 3.0: Microsoft and Its Enemies* (New York: Random House, 2001), p. 14.

69. Peter Spiegel, "Microsoft Judge Defends Post-trial Comments," *Financial Times* (London), Oct. 7, 2000.

70. Auletta, *World War 3.0,* p. 397, and also Ken Auletta, "Final Offer: What Kept Microsoft from Settling Its Case," *New Yorker* (January 15, 2001), p. 41; available online at: www.kenauletta.com/finaloffer.html.

71. Auletta, *World War 3.0,* pp. 168–69, and Auletta, "Final Offer," p. 46.

72. Ibid.

73. Joel Brinkley and Steve Lohr, *U.S. v. Microsoft: The Inside Story of the Landmark Case* (New York: McGraw-Hill, 2000), p. 278.

74. *United States v. Microsoft Corporation,* Civil Action No. 98–1232, November 5, 1999, p. 30.

75. The remaining nine states continued to fight the case through the District Court, but only Massachusetts carried the case back to the Appeals Court. On June 30, 2004, the Appeals Court rejected all of Massachusetts' arguments and, therefore, affirmed the 2002 consent decree. *Commonwealth of Massachusetts, ex rel. v. Microsoft Corporation,* Appeal from the United States District Court for the District of Columbia, No. 98cv01233, decided June 30, 2004, www.usdoj.gov/atr/cases/f204400/204468.pdf.

76. Brad Smith: Microsoft Legal Settlements with the Computer & Communications Industry Association (CCIA) and Novell, November 8, 2004, www.microsoft.com/presspass/exec/bradsmith/11–08–04cciatranscript.mspx.

77. Ibid.

78. Don E. Waldman, *Antitrust Action and Market Structure* (Lexington, MA: D.C. Heath, 1978).

79. Ibid.

80. *United States v. Microsoft,* Civil Action No. 98–1232 (CKK), Joint Status Report on Microsoft's Compliance with the Final Judgments, July 2, 2003.

81. Charles H. Ferguson, "What's Next for Google?" *MIT Technology Review* (January 2005), www.technologyreview.com/InfoTech/wtr_14065,258,p2.html?PM=GO.

82. Robert X. Cringely, "Has Google Peaked? The Biggest Threat to Microsoft Might Not Be Those G-men at All, But Apple," August 25, 2005, www.pbs.org/cringely/pulpit/pulpit20050825.html.

12

Schlitz

Why the Schlitz Hit the Fan

Avi Goldfarb

Introduction

The Schlitz Brewing Company produced more beer from the 1940s through the early 1970s than any other company except Anheuser-Busch; however, by 1980 they were a minor brewer on the national scene. In 1973, Standard and Poor's wrote of Schlitz, "With further increases in market share expected over the next few years, the shares offer attractive long-term growth potential."[1] They did not have a kind word to say after 1976. Schlitz produced over 24 million barrels in 1976, yet by 1981 they produced only 14 million. Market share collapsed from 15 percent of the national beer market in 1976 to 7 percent by 1981. What caused this collapse and why did it happen so quickly?

The most common reason given for the collapse of Schlitz is a series of apparent marketing mistakes starting in 1974 when Schlitz began to downsize its marketing department. This argument, not surprisingly, is particularly strong in the marketing literature. David Aaker devotes a section of his book to explaining Schlitz's collapse as a textbook case of bad marketing.[2] Jacques Neher blames a power shift within the company from the marketing department to accounting. He blames a "growing bean counter mentality," and then the gradual elimination of the senior marketing staff over the course of the 1970s.[3]

It is undeniable that there were a number of questionable decisions made at Schlitz over the course of the decade; however, I will argue that these were not as important to the collapse of Schlitz as the rise of Miller brewing. In fact, it seems that to some degree the "mistakes" were caused by Miller's rise. Miller had been bought by Phillip Morris in 1969 and, using the parent company's marketing and distribution power, began a steady rise to the number two position in the industry. Miller's rise was slow at first, but then skyrocketed shortly after the Miller management team was replaced by a number of former Phillip Morris executives. They introduced a number of new brands, following a strategy of brand proliferation that had proven successful in the cigarette industry. With the launch of one of these new brands, Miller Lite, in 1974 (it went national in 1975), Miller sales skyrocketed. Miller was in closer competition with Anheuser-Busch than with Schlitz from the beginning of its rise. Philip Van Munching wrote, "Anheuser-Busch and Miller set their sights on each other and let fly."[4] Schlitz got caught in the cross fire. Figure 12.1 shows sales of Schlitz, Anheuser-Busch, and Miller as a fraction of their combined sales. Essentially, Miller and Schlitz switched places in the late 1970s. Total industry market shares show a similar trend.

According to the marketing literature on the sub-

Figure 12.1 **True Market Shares**

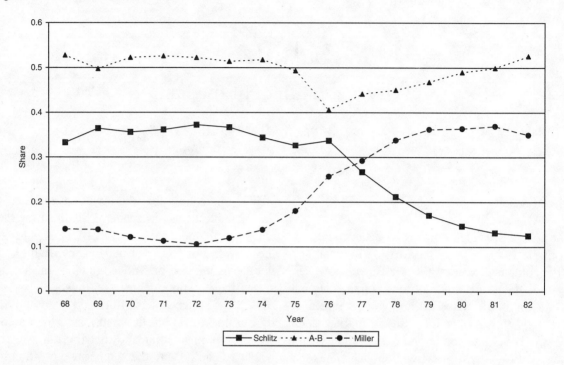

ject, the beginning of the collapse of Schlitz can be traced to the introduction of a new brewing process called accelerated batch fermentation (ABF) in the early 1970s. ABF reduced both fixed and variable costs. It allowed much larger breweries to be built at lower prices, and it reduced the length of fermentation from twelve days to four. Approximately one year later, the competition started to "spread the news: 'Schlitz is making green beer.'"[5] While none of the other major brewers had access to this technology, marketing experts such as Aaker and Neher argue that it was implemented at Schlitz and not elsewhere because cost-savings motivations took center stage at the expense of long-run concerns. Thus, the marketers argue, the weakness of Schlitz's marketing department led to the first "mistake." It is this "mistake" that I argue was a rational response to the introduction of Miller Lite and the rise of Miller as a major player in the indus-

try. I argue that Schlitz took higher short-term profits because they knew that Miller would gradually erode their market share and, hence, reduce future profits. As a former advertising manager at Schlitz said, "Schlitz sacrificed its reputation in its pursuit of bigger profits."[6] One family owned nearly 80 percent of the shares and controlled fourteen of seventeen seats on the board. The family depended on the dividends for its income. The board "wanted nothing less than an immediate return."[7] When the choice was high profits short-term or low profits indefinitely, the board had good reason to seem myopic. The simultaneous decline over the 1970s in competitor Pabst's sales (without any of these "mistakes") provides supporting evidence for the role of Miller's rise in Schlitz's collapse.

There are four subsequent mistakes made by the company that are not as easily explained. Much of the brewing industry ran into problems with the

Department of Justice (DOJ) in the mid-1970s regarding questionable sales practices involving kickbacks to distributors earlier in the decade. The other breweries settled the cases quickly, but Schlitz chose to take its case to court and suffered bad publicity as a result. In 1976, new Food and Drug Administration (FDA) regulations regarding which ingredients needed to be printed on the bottles prompted Schlitz to change the preservatives it used (it had been using silica gel). The company did not spend sufficient time testing the new process, and tiny green flakes appeared in the beer. The company claimed the problem was isolated and delayed the recall for months. This greatly damaged the beer's reputation. In order to recover their reputation, they began a new advertising campaign in 1978, which consisted of tough men yelling at the customers to drink Schlitz. The failed campaign was quickly dubbed, "Drink Schlitz or I'll kill you."[8] The final mistake made by the company was a 1978 refusal by the board of directors to accept a generous buyout offer from R.J. Reynolds. The cigarette maker's marketing and distribution power may have been able to help Schlitz as Phillip Morris had helped Miller. In 1982, a weakened Schlitz was bought by Stroh's, as much for its brewing capacity as for its brand. While these subsequent mistakes led to Schlitz's complete collapse, it was the switch to ABF that led to the sharpest decline in market share.

In this paper I show that the collapse of Schlitz is intricately related to the rise of Miller. Using a Hotelling-style spatial model with lagged demand and a lag in learning about quality changes, I show that the introduction of the ABF process was a rational response to Miller's introduction. More importantly, I show that intense competition between Miller and Anheuser-Busch pushed Schlitz into a small niche. I first explain the details of the model followed by some basic theoretical results about the two effects that are at work in Schlitz's

loss of market share: getting swept aside in the intense competition between Anheuser-Busch and Miller and changing the production process to gain short-term profits at the expense of long-term market share. I then estimate the parameters of the model and verify that Miller and Anheuser-Busch are in closer competition with each other than with Schlitz. Using these parameters, I simulate the model to derive market dynamics. The simulations show the relative importance of the two effects and how closely this model resembles reality. These simulations show that, even with perfect foresight about the detrimental effects of its actions to its future market share, Schlitz rationally implemented the ABF process.

A Model of the Brewing Industry

I model the brewing industry using a horizontal model of competition. Horizontal differentiation means that not all consumers value the attributes of the products the same. One consumer may prefer a red product while another prefers blue; one may prefer Budweiser while another prefers Miller. I use a Hotelling-style spatial model to represent the brewing industry.[9] Before 1974 and the entry of Miller as an important player, I assume there are two firms in the industry: Schlitz and Anheuser-Busch. They compete for consumers who are uniformly distributed along a line of measure one. Each consumer has unit demand for beer. The two firms are located at opposite ends of the line (see Figure 12.2a). Consumer demands are a function of price, last period's demand, and last period's "quality" or production process. This differs from the standard spatial model in two ways. First, there is a lag in demand, which appears to be true of the brewing industry and of many other branded industries. This represents brand strength. Kevin Lane Keller describes brand awareness and brand imagery as one of the key factors in brand

Figure 12.2 **Hotelling Models**

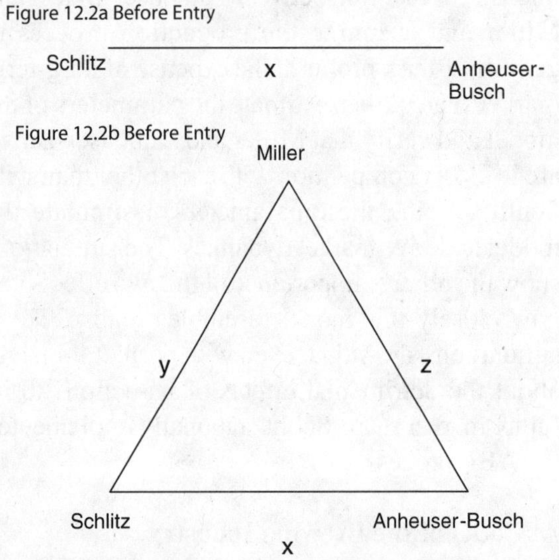

Figure 12.2a Before Entry

Schlitz ————————— x ————————— Anheuser-Busch

Figure 12.2b Before Entry

Miller

y   z

Schlitz   Anheuser-Busch

x

strength.[10] Brand awareness is assumed by all agents in the model. Last period's market share is a proxy for the overall favorability of the brand's image this period. This lagged demand captures the fact that it took time for Miller to build a strong brand image (and market share) for itself.

Second, there is the "quality" variable, adding a vertical element to the competition. Vertical differentiation means that all consumers prefer one product to another, all else being equal. A car is better if it is more fuel efficient. This is meant to capture the decision to change to ABF by Schlitz. The form used here is modeled after one used in Simon Anderson, Andre de Palma, and Jacques-François Thisse.[11] Here, however, this quality parameter shows up lagged in the demand function because it took a year for consumers to realize that Schlitz had cheapened its production process. Thus, the cost savings from a quality change occur this period, but the demand punishment is not felt until next period, making this an adapted reduced-form reputation model.

Each consumer's valuation is as follows:

$$v_t = K - c_x x_t + \delta_x x_{t-1} + F(q_{t-1}) - p_t \quad (1)$$

where v is a consumer's dollar valuation for a brand at time t, K is a fixed parameter set high enough so that the market is always covered (i.e., so that every consumer will buy beer), c_x is the travel cost per unit consumed (in perceived difference between brands), δ_x is the importance of the lag in demand, x_t is the positioning on the line of the consumer, x_{t-1} is the brand strength (measured by last period's market share), q_{t-1} is the quality variable, $F(.)$ is an increasing function in quality that determines the importance of quality changes to demand, and p_t is the price the firm charges for the good (firms cannot discriminate among customers). All symbols used in the paper are presented in Table 12.1. The adoption of ABF technology, therefore, would mean a reduction in q. Letting Schlitz be firm S and Anheuser-Busch be firm A, the indifferent consumer satisfies:

$$c_x x_t - \delta_x x_{t-1} - F(q_{S,t-1}) + p_{S,t}$$
$$= c_x (1 - x_t) \quad (2)$$
$$- \delta_x (1 - x_{t-1}) - F(q_{A,t-1}) + p_{A,t} = c_x$$

Solving for x_t and setting $F(q_{i,t-1})$ equal to $q_{i,t-1}$ for $i = S,A$, demand for Schlitz is

$$x_{S,t} = \frac{1}{2c_x}\left(p_{A,t} - p_{S,t} + c_x \right.$$
$$\left. - \delta_x (1 - 2x_{S,t-1}) - q_{A,t-1} + q_{S,t-1}\right), \quad (3)$$

noting that $x_{S,t-1} = 1 - x_{A,t-1}$, demand for Anheuser-Busch is

$$x_{A,t} = 1 - \frac{1}{2c_x}\left(p_{A,t} - p_{S,t} + c_x\right.$$
$$\left. - \delta_x (1 - 2(1 - x_{A,t-1})) - q_{A,t-1} + q_{S,t-1}\right) \quad (4)$$

Table 12.1

Variables

Variable	Definition
v_t	Dollar value of the product to a consumer
K	Fixed parameter (high enough to ensure market covered)
c_x	"Travel" cost between Anheuser-Busch and Schlitz
c_y	"Travel" cost between Miller and Schlitz
c_z	"Travel" cost between Anheuser-Busch and Miller
x_t	Consumer location between Anheuser-Busch and Schlitz
y_t	Consumer location between Miller and Schlitz
z_t	Consumer location between Anheuser-Busch and Miller
$\delta\|\mathbb{I}\|$	Importance of the lag in demand (state dependence)
$F(.)$	Increasing function in quality that determines the importance of quality to demand
q_{t-1}	Quality in the previous period
p_t	Price in the current period
Subscript A	Anheuser-Busch
Subscript S	Schlitz
Subscript M	Miller
$C(x_{i,t}, q_{i,t})$	Cost of production (based on demand and quality)
β	Discount factor
$s_{i,t}^{D}$	Market share
$s_{i,t-1}^{D}$	Market share in the previous period
D	Quantity demanded
W	Vector of demand shifters (empirical section only)
U	Vector of parameters in the simulation

Costs are a function of both demand and quality for the current period, $C(x_{i,t}, q_{i,t})$. I assume that the quality variable is a fixed cost. In reality, ABF represented both fixed and marginal cost savings. ABF plants were much larger than other plants. Schlitz could build one plant with the same capacity as two Anheuser-Busch plants for only a slightly higher cost.[12] ABF also decreased fermentation time, leading to marginal cost savings. I have included only the fixed-cost savings in order to keep the model tractable. I expect that the addition of marginal cost would not change the overall results. Therefore, I assume separable and quadratic costs:

$$C\left(x_{i,t}, q_{i,t}\right) = x^2_{i,t} + q^2_{i,t} \qquad (5)$$

Firm i maximizes discounted profits[13] as follows:

$$\max_{\{p_{i,t}\}\{q_{i,t}\}} \sum_{t=0}^{\infty} \beta^t \Big[x_{i,t}\left(p_{S,t}, p_{A,t}, q_{S,t-1}, q_{A,t-1}, x_{i,t-1}\right) p_{i,t}$$
$$- C\left(x_{i,t}, q_{i,t}\right) \Big] \qquad (6)$$

The two firms compete simultaneously and find a Nash equilibrium in prices and qualities. To get the steady states for both the two-firm and three-firm problems, I solve for the open-loop equilibrium, proving by construction that a steady state exists.[14] These results will be subgame perfect (firms are time consistent). My propositions are derived using the steady states and are, therefore, subgame perfect. In the simulations, I use a perfect foresight model to determine the dynamics between steady states. This is not subgame perfect. Because the steady states show most of the key results and the dynamics are consistent with the steady-state results, the lack of subgame perfection over the interim period does not likely change the results (see pp. 329–30 for more details on the computational algorithm).

In order to model the effects of Miller's rise as a major player in the industry, I impose the entry of a new firm into the industry. The third firm (Miller) is placed equidistant from the first two (see Figure 12.2b). This model is similar to the circular city model.[15] Without subscripts, x, y, and z represent the names of the lines, while with subscripts, x_i, $y_{i,t}$, $z_{i,t}$ represent the positions of consumers along the lines. The distance along each of the three connecting lines is one-third, thus keeping the total market size unchanged at one. The travel costs along each line may differ, thus adding asymmetry to the competition. As will be shown below, the travel costs represent the inverse of the cross-price effects on quantity. In the most realistic model, the travel costs between Schlitz and Miller (on line y) are highest,

and those between Anheuser-Busch and Miller (on line z) are lowest.[16] Also, after entry by Miller, only Schlitz is able to change its production process and, hence, its quality. In the simulations, these restrictions are relaxed in order to distinguish between different aspects of the model. The steady-state prices and qualities from the two-firm competition are used as the starting point in three-firm competition for all three firms. Schlitz is assumed to start with all of the consumers along the y line (where it competes with Miller). Similarly, Anheuser-Busch has all the consumers along the z line. Schlitz and Anheuser-Busch split the x line equally to begin. Thus, there are now six separate "demand functions," two along each line:

$$x_{S,t} = \frac{1}{2c_x}\left(p_{A,t} - p_{S,t} + \frac{1}{3}c_x - \delta_x\left(\frac{1}{3} - 2x_{S,t-1}\right) - q_{A,t-1} + q_{S,t-1}\right)$$

$$x_{A,t} = \frac{1}{3} - \frac{1}{2c_x}\left(p_{A,t} - p_{S,t} + \frac{1}{3}c_x - \delta_x\left(\frac{1}{3} - 2\left(\frac{1}{3} - x_{A,t-1}\right)\right) - q_{A,t-1} + q_{S,t-1}\right)$$

$$y_{S,t} = \frac{1}{2c_y}\left(p_{M,t} - p_{S,t} + \frac{1}{3}c_y - \delta_y\left(\frac{1}{3} - 2y_{S,t-1}\right) - q_{M,t-1} + q_{S,t-1}\right)$$

$$y_{M,t} = \frac{1}{3} - \frac{1}{2c_y}\left(p_{M,t} - p_{S,t} + \frac{1}{3}c_y - \delta_y\left(\frac{1}{3} - 2\left(\frac{1}{3} - y_{M,t-1}\right)\right) - q_{M,t-1} + q_{S,t-1}\right) \qquad (7)$$

$$z_{A,t} = \frac{1}{2c_z}\left(p_{M,t} - p_{A,t} + \frac{1}{3}c_z - \delta_z\left(\frac{1}{3} - 2z_{A,t-1}\right) - q_{M,t-1} + q_{A,t-1}\right)$$

$$z_{M,t} = \frac{1}{3} - \frac{1}{2c_z}\left(p_{M,t} - p_{A,t} + \frac{1}{3}c_z - \delta_z\left(\frac{1}{3} - 2\left(\frac{1}{3} - z_{M,t-1}\right)\right) - q_{M,t-1} + q_{A,t-1}\right)$$

Note that $\dfrac{\partial x_{S,t}}{\partial x_{S,t-1}} = \dfrac{\delta_x}{c_x}$. A similar result holds for all other "demand functions." I assume that this derivative is constant. In other words, I assume that there is a constant amount that the lag affects current demand across regions of competition. Thus, the parameter of interest is the amount that lagged demand affects current demand, δ, such that $\delta = \dfrac{\delta_x}{c_x} = \dfrac{\delta_y}{c_y} = \dfrac{\delta_z}{c_z}$. The actual demand functions facing each firm are the sums of the demands in each direction from the firm:

$$D_{S,t} = x_{S,t} = y_{S,t}$$
$$D_{A,t} = x_{A,t} = z_{A,t} \quad (8)$$
$$D_{M,t} = y_{M,t} = z_{M,t}$$

Each maximizes profits as in equation (6) using $D_{i,t}$ instead of $x_{i,t}$. Again, there is simultaneous competition in prices and qualities. The goal of this exercise is to examine what happens to market shares and qualities after the (assumed exogenous) shock of entry by Miller.

Theoretical Results

The most important aspect of this model for the dynamic interactions of the firms is the lagged nature of the effect of the quality on demand and of demand itself. This is what makes it worthwhile for Schlitz to take profits by cutting its quality while it still has market share and can demand a higher price. The idea that decisions today affect tomorrow's results is the central underlying theme of this model and of much of the marketing literature on brand development and management.[17]

There are two ways in which Schlitz's market share erodes as a result of entry by Miller. The first is not a result of dynamic interaction and is a well-known result of static Hotelling models. If there are three firms in a horizontally differentiated industry, the two firms that are placed closer to each other will compete more fiercely and will thus gain market share at the expense of the other. The second reason for Schlitz to lose market share is a result of the dynamics: It takes advantage of high market share today to take short-term profits by reducing its costs at the expense of tomorrow's demand. It knows it will lose market share over time and will have to charge a lower price. It therefore reduces its quality to have higher profits today in anticipation of lower market share tomorrow. These two ideas are formalized in Proposition 1. Lemma 1 proves the existence of a steady state, which is needed in

the proof of the proposition. A steady state means that every year firms find it optimal to maintain the same strategy.

Lemma 1 *There exists a steady state in both problems to be examined: (i) two firms where both can change quality, and (ii) three firms where all can change quality.*

Proposition 1 *Entry by Miller (firm M) with, $c_y > c_x > c_z$, $0 < \delta < 1$, and $0 < \beta < 1$ will cause Miller and Anheuser-Busch (firm A) to gain market share at the expense of Schlitz (firm S) in the long-run three-firm steady state where all can change quality. In addition, Miller and Anheuser-Busch will have higher qualities than Schlitz.*

Note that if $c_y = c_x = c_z$, and all can change qualities, then each will have a market share of one-third and each market will be split evenly in the long run. Thus, in the long run, even in a symmetric problem, Schlitz will lose some market share (dropping from one-half to one-third). When $c_y > c_x > c_z$, the model indicates that Schlitz will lose more than Anheuser-Busch and will be behind Miller as well. The proofs of Lemma 1 and Proposition 1 are in Appendix A.

Proposition 1 gives the two main reasons that Schlitz's market share collapsed after Miller's entry in 1974. First, when Miller and Anheuser-Busch compete more fiercely with each other, they take share away from Schlitz. Second, Schlitz anticipates losing share and therefore reduces quality to get higher profits today at the expense of future demand. In the simulations, I determine the relative importance of these two effects.

Empirical Evidence

Identification

I develop and estimate an empirical model to find starting values for the simulations. Demand for Anheuser-Busch beer is the sum of the demand of the different consumers, $D_{A,t} = x_{A,t} + z_{A,t}$. Similarly, demand for Schlitz beer is $D_{S,t} = x_{S,t} + y_{S,t}$ and demand for Miller is $D_{M,t} = y_{M,t} + z_{M,t}$. In order to better understand the substitutability of the three brewers' beers, four parameters need to be estimated: δ, c_x, c_y, and c_z. and. Each of these is identified by imposing the structure of the model above. There are testable restrictions that result from this model formulation. $x_{S,t}$ can be written as:

$$
\begin{aligned}
x_{S,t} = \frac{1}{2c_x}p_{A,t} - \frac{1}{2c_x}p_{S,t} + \frac{1}{6} - \frac{1}{6}\delta \\
+ \delta x_{S,t-1} + \frac{1}{2c_x}q_{S,t-1} - \frac{1}{2c_x}q_{A,t-1}
\end{aligned}
\tag{9}
$$

The other demands give similar results. Recall that $D_{S,t}$ can be written as the sum of $x_{S,t}$ and $y_{S,t}$. $D_{A,t}$ and $D_{M,t}$ can be expressed similarly. Therefore the substitutability of the different breweries' products can be derived as follows:

$$
\frac{\partial D_S}{\partial p_A} = \frac{1}{2c_x} \quad \frac{\partial D_S}{\partial p_M} = \frac{1}{2c_y} \quad \frac{\partial D_S}{\partial p_S} = -\frac{1}{2c_x} - \frac{1}{2c_y} \tag{10}
$$

$$
\frac{\partial D_A}{\partial p_S} = \frac{1}{2c_x} \quad \frac{\partial D_A}{\partial p_M} = \frac{1}{2c_z} \quad \frac{\partial D_A}{\partial p_A} = -\frac{1}{2c_x} - \frac{1}{2c_z} \tag{11}
$$

$$
\frac{\partial D_M}{\partial p_S} = \frac{1}{2c_y} \quad \frac{\partial D_M}{\partial p_A} = \frac{1}{2c_z} \quad \frac{\partial D_M}{\partial p_M} = -\frac{1}{2c_y} - \frac{1}{2c_z} \tag{12}
$$

Thus, this model imposes the restriction that the absolute value of the effect of own price on demand be equal to the sum of the cross effects. It also imposes the restriction that the cross effects of price of i on demand j be equal to the cross price effect of j on demand for i. These are strong (and testable) assumptions. Thus, c_x, c_y, and c_z can be identified from the following regression:

$$
\begin{aligned}
s_{i,t}^D = \gamma_0 + \gamma_1 p_{S,t} + \gamma_2 p_{A,t} + \\
\gamma_3 p_{M,t} + \gamma_4 s_{i,t-1}^D + \phi W_t + \varepsilon_t
\end{aligned}
\tag{13}
$$

$s_{i,t}^D$ is the market share of good i in time t, $s_{i,t-1}^D$ is market share in the previous period, and Z_t is a vector of demand shifters. If $i = S$ (Schlitz),

$$
\gamma_1 = -\frac{1}{2c_x} - \frac{1}{2c_y}, \gamma_2 = \frac{1}{2c_x}, \gamma_3 = \frac{1}{2c_y}, \text{ and } \gamma_4 = \delta.
$$

The parameter estimates are similarly derived for Anheuser-Busch and Miller. (Note that this will pose an additional restriction that the δ's are identical in each equation. There are also restrictions in the cross equations.) Because the prices are endogenous, cost-function instruments such as wages and material prices are needed. Ideally, this would be estimated as a vector autoregression using all three firms' prices and quantities; however, the sample size required is beyond that of any data set for the beer industry in the 1970s. Weekly, or at least monthly, data would be needed.

I estimate δ using a panel of twenty-two different breweries over twenty-seven years. Therefore I get δ from the following equation, using various cost shifters as instruments[18]:

$$
s_{i,t}^D = \gamma_0 + \gamma_1 p_{i,t} + \delta s_{i,t-1}^D + \phi W_{i,t} + \varepsilon_{i,t} \tag{14}
$$

Empirical Results

My data set consists of quantities sold, advertising expenditures, capacities, and prices for twenty-two different brewers annually from 1956 until 1982 (there is not data on all brewers for all years, although there is for Schlitz, Anheuser-Busch, and Miller) with a total sample size of 351. I also have annual data on brewery worker salaries, cost of raw materials, quantities of beer imported, per capita U.S. income, industry output, and industry advertising expenditures.[19] I estimate two models, first, using the complete data set to estimate δ, and, second, using only the nine years after Miller's entry in 1974 and before Schlitz was purchased by Stroh's in 1982 to get estimates of c_x, c_y, and c_z.

Because there is a lag in the panel, I first-difference the data and then use market shares from the second and third lags as instruments to account for the endogeneity of the lag (reducing the sample size to 295). This follows recommendations in William Greene.[20] As instruments for price and advertising, I use wages in the brewing industry, capacity, and a weighted index of the costs of materials (courtesy of Victor Tremblay). The lagged values of each of these are also used, for a total of eleven instruments. The vector of demand shifters includes own advertising as a fraction of total advertising, imports, and income per capita.

The regression on the panel to estimate δ yields the estimates in Table 12.2. Note that only advertising and last period's quantity are significant. The others, however, give the expected signs. I use δ = 0.6 in my simulations, though the results can be generalized to other values for δ. I conduct OLS regressions to get the other parameter estimates that I use for the simulations that follow. Regressing Schlitz quantity on prices of all of the beers (without an intercept), I find that the own-price effect is –0.0032, the cross-price effect with Anheuser Busch is 0.0142, and the cross-price effect with Miller is 0.005. This gives $c_x = \dfrac{1}{2\gamma_2}$ of approximately 35 and c_y of approximately 105. Regressing Miller quantity on prices of all other beers, I get cross effects of 0.0070 and 0.0402 for Schlitz and Anheuser-Busch, respectively. This gives $c_y \approx$ 71 and $c_z \approx$ 12.5. The results from the Anheuser-Busch regression also yielded c_x greater than c_z, although the magnitudes were different. Thus the evidence suggests that Miller and Anheuser-Busch are closer substitutes for each other than they are

Table 12.2

The Determinants of Market Share

Variable	Coefficient	Standard error
Advertising expenditures	0.0886*	0.0487
Imports ($000s)	0.00385	0.00452
Income per capita ($000s)	0.00256	0.00808
Last period share	0.669**	0.224
Constant	0.000303	0.00111
Price	0.000163	0.000608
# Observations	295	

*significant at the 90 percent confidence level.
**significant at the 95 percent confidence level.

for Schlitz, and that Schlitz is closer to Anheuser-Busch than to Miller. While the two c_y's are not exactly the same and the restriction imposed by the own-price parameters does not hold, this may be a result of the small sample size. I use the relative values of the parameters found in these regressions for my simulations, so $c_y = 3c_x = 9c_z$. I therefore use c_y = 6, c_x = 2, and c_z = 0.8. (This converges faster than, but to similar results as, c_y = 9, c_x = 3, and c_z = 1.) I keep c_x = 2 for the two-firm model as well. Using advertising instead of price also yields that Miller and Anheuser-Busch were in closer competition with each other than either was with Schlitz. The general results of the simulations hold as long as $c_y > c_x > c_z$.

It is important to be cautious in interpreting these results. The data and empirical method do not fully control for endogeneity. While the results are sufficient to derive the general calibration and simulation results in the next section, data limitations inhibit efficient and unbiased estimation.

Simulations

Algorithm

In economics, simulation methods are used to understand the consequences of actions that were not actually taken by firms, consumers, and governments. In this section, simulation methods are used to gain a better understanding of why Schlitz failed. In particular, a market is simulated in which Schlitz does not change quality. This allows for an exploration of what would have happened to Schlitz's sales without changing its brewing technology to ABF.

The algorithm used for solving this model closely resembles methods used in Kenneth Judd's chapter on perfect foresight models.[21] I first computed the steady states for the two-firm and three-firm problems using dynamic programming methods. I then use these steady states as the values for the first and the final period in a finite time maximization problem. The steady state is computed analytically in the proof of Lemma 1. The entrant's starting values for p_i and q_i were assumed to be identical to those of the symmetric incumbents. The number of periods is set so that the results for p_{it} converge to the steady-state levels long before the last period. Because of the lack of subgame perfection in the closed-loop algorithm, the closed loop q_{it} is slightly smaller (roughly 15 percent) than the open loop q_{it}. This difference is small enough that it should not affect the overall trends. The path after entry was calculated using the following algorithm:

1. Choose initial conditions for $U^0 = \left\{ p_{i,t}, q_{i,t} \right\}_{i=1 \, t=0}^{3 \quad T}$

and stopping criterion $\varepsilon = 0.0001$. For $t = 0$ use the values from the two-firm steady state for q and p. Also use market shares of 0.5 for the incumbents and of zero for the entrant. Thus, the incumbents split line x between them and each has full market share over the line in which it competes with the entrant. For $t = T + 1, \ldots, T + k$, use the three-firm steady-state values for q, p, and market share.

2. For each firm, taking the values for the opposing firms from the previous iteration (as in

the algorithm to calculate the steady state), use Broyden-Fletcher-Goldfarb-Shanno (BFGS) quasi-Newton methods to maximize

$$\sum_{t=0}^{T+k} \beta^t \left[D_{i,t} \left(p_{i,t}, p_{-i,t}, q_{i,t}, q_{-i,t}, D_{i,t-1} \right) p_{i,t} - C \left(D_{i,t}, q_{i,t} \right) \right]$$

over $\left\{ p_{i,t}, q_{i,t} \right\}_{t=1}^{T}$. Get $U^{l+1} = \left\{ p_{i,t}^*, q_{i,t}^* \right\}_{i=1 \, t=1}^{3 \quad T}$, the values that maximize the above expression. k is the number of subsequent periods of steady-state values included.[22] Here, the subscript $-i$ refers to all brands besides brand i.

3. If $\left\| U^{l+1} - U^l \right\| < \varepsilon$ stop. Otherwise go to step

2 with $U^l = U^{l+1}$.

The three-firm results were calculated in three different ways. First, it was assumed that all could change their qualities. Then it was assumed that only Schlitz could change its quality, and the others took theirs as fixed from the steady state of the two-firm competition and only competed in price. Finally, the results were calculated assuming none could change their qualities, meaning each was only maximizing over price. I also experimented with different values for δ and for c_x, c_y, and c_z. Using the algorithms, I computed the results of the following subsection. The maximization steps converge to seven decimal places, and then the final iterations up to four. Combined this gives three-decimal-point accuracy.

Results

The results of my simulations closely resemble the actual dynamics in the industry. The simulation that most closely resembles reality (from the econometric results) has $\delta = 0.6$, $c_x = 2$, $c_y = 6$, $c_z = 0.8$, and only Schlitz able to change quality (because it was the only firm with ABF technology).

Figure 12.3   **Market Share Simulation Results When Only Schlitz Changes Quality (cy > cx > cz)**

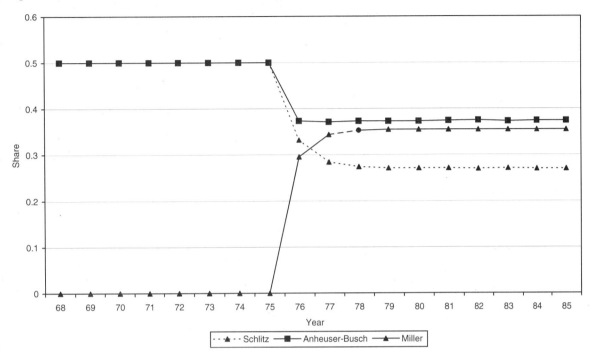

Although the data and empirical strategy suggest cautious interpretation, the simulations do closely match industry dynamics. $\beta = 0.9$ for all simulations. I will henceforth call this specification the standard specification. The market shares resulting from this specification are displayed in Figure 12.3. Anheuser-Busch takes the largest market share, with Miller a close second. Schlitz ends up well below both. Comparing this to Figure 12.1 shows that many of the dynamics of the real interaction appear to be captured in the model. One notable exception is the sharp drop and recovery of market share by Anheuser-Busch in 1976 and the corresponding rise in Schlitz sales. This was a result of a strike at Anheuser-Busch factories and therefore does not show up in the simulation. There are two other notable differences. First, it takes roughly five or six years for the real-world interactions to reach the new steady state, while it takes only three

or four in the simulation. Second, Schlitz's market share is much lower in reality than in the model. In the model, it is only eight percentage points below Miller and ten below Anheuser-Busch, while in reality it is roughly twenty-three points behind Miller and forty below Anheuser Busch. There are two possible explanations: one from changes in reality and the other from parameter misspecification. The model only reflects the first of Schlitz's "mistakes," therefore the later mistakes are not taken into account. The model reflects the effects of the 1974 changes, not of those in 1976 and 1978. Therefore the actual decline of Schlitz continued for longer than the model suggests. The other possibility is that δ and the transportation costs are misspecified. Simulations run with $\delta = 0.8$ cause convergence to occur more slowly. Larger differences in transportation costs would lead to a lower share for Schlitz. While my econometric

Figure 12.4 **Market Share Simulation Results When Only Schlitz Changes Quality (cy = cx = cz)**

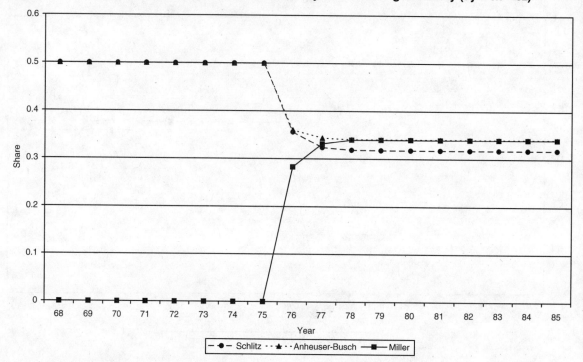

results are weak, there is no reason to believe all of these variables would change in the desired directions. Therefore, the first explanation is more likely for the differences between the model and reality. The general trends of the model, however, do resemble reality.

Raising β will speed up the rate of convergence to the steady state and decrease the incentive to change the quality. The impact, however, of $\beta = 0.95$ and $\beta = 0.97$ is negligible on the overall results, except that the magnitude of the drop in quality is smaller (though market share trends are only slightly different).

Splitting these general effects into the separate effects that cause Schlitz to lose market share in the model is informative about the relative importance of each effect. Section 3 of this paper describes these two effects as (1) Schlitz getting pushed aside by the intense competition between Miller

and Anheuser-Busch, and (2) Schlitz lowering its quality because it is the only one that can. Figure 12.4 shows what happens to market shares when each has identical transportation costs, but only Schlitz can change its quality. Because Miller and Anheuser-Busch are symmetric, they converge to the same steady-state share. Schlitz, however, is now only two percentage points below them in market share. This is only a quarter of the difference between the market shares for Schlitz and Miller.

In Figure 12.5, none of the companies can change their qualities, although allowing all to change their qualities leads to similar results. Schlitz is now roughly six percentage points below Miller and eight below Anheuser-Busch. Therefore, it appears that the effect of Schlitz's getting pushed aside by intense competition between Miller and Anheuser-Busch was more important

Figure 12.5   **Market Share Simulation Results When No Firm Changes Quality (cy>cx>cz)**

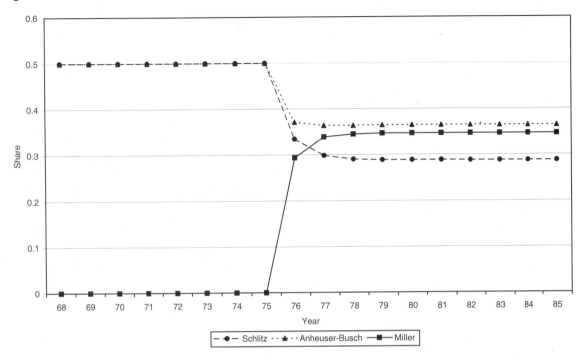

to the loss of Schlitz's market share than was the change in quality. When combined, the two effects do not seem to complement each other and further decrease Schlitz's market share. Their individual effects add up to the total effect on market share.

The results when $\delta = 0.2$ are shown in Table 12.3. With the lack of importance of the lag in demand, convergence happens almost immediately; however, the model still converges to roughly the same steady state. Similar results occur with $\delta = 0.4$ and $\delta = 0.8$. The only major difference between the different δ's is the rate of convergence to the steady state. Changing the relative sizes of the transportation costs does not change the rate of convergence, but it does change the steady-state level. For example, with $c_x = 2$, $c_y = 3$, and $c_z = 1$, Schlitz has a steady-state market share of 29 percent, while Miller has 35 percent and Anheuser-Busch has 36 percent. With, $c_x = 2$, $c_y = 12$, and $c_z = 0.4$, Schlitz's market share

drops to 22 percent (including only one-sixth of the line on which it competes with Anheuser-Busch). Miller has 37 percent and Anheuser-Busch's share rises to 41 percent.

It is interesting to note at whose expense the different firms gain share. Table 12.4 shows the results of competition along the different lines in the standard specification. Notice how quickly Anheuser-Busch takes share away from Schlitz. Schlitz actually regains some of that lost share over time. This is a result of Schlitz trying to take advantage of the fact that it will take time for Miller to gain market share. Thus, Schlitz keeps prices relatively high in the early periods in order to keep profits high in these periods. This makes it less competitive against Anheuser-Busch in 1975, 1976, and 1977 before Miller surpassed it in market share. Also of note is that Miller gains share much more quickly against Anheuser-Busch

Table 12.3

Market Shares (delta = 0.2)

	1972	73	74	75	76	77	78	79	80	81
Only Schlitz can change quality, cx = 2, cy = 6, cz = .8										
Schlitz	0.5	0.5	0.5	0.292	0.265	0.265	0.264	0.264	0.264	0.264
A-B	0.5	0.5	0.5	0.377	0.382	0.382	0.382	0.382	0.382	0.382
Miller	0	0	0	0.331	0.353	0.353	0.354	0.354	0.354	0.354
Only Schlitz can change quality, cx = cy = cz = 2										
Schlitz	0.5	0.5	0.5	0.341	0.323	0.322	0.322	0.322	0.322	0.322
A-B	0.5	0.5	0.5	0.342	0.339	0.339	0.339	0.339	0.339	0.339
Miller	0	0	0	0.317	0.338	0.339	0.339	0.339	0.339	0.339
None can change quality cx = 2, cy = 6, cz = .8										
Schlitz	0.5	0.5	0.5	0.292	0.278	0.277	0.277	0.277	0.277	0.277
A-B	0.5	0.5	0.5	0.377	0.375	0.375	0.375	0.375	0.375	0.375
Miller	0	0	0	0.331	0.348	0.348	0.349	0.349	0.349	0.349

than against Schlitz. This intense competition between Miller and Anheuser-Busch is what causes Anheuser-Busch to take so much share away from Schlitz. Remember that transportation costs shelter Schlitz more from Miller than from Anheuser-Busch, while Anheuser-Busch is more sheltered from Schlitz than from Miller. Therefore Anheuser-Busch gains more against Schlitz while Miller gains more against Anheuser-Busch.

The quality changes, shown in Table 12.5, are another interesting aspect of the story. These changes are all essentially one-time changes during the first period of entry. In the standard specification, the quality drops rapidly to one-half of the two-firm steady-state level. There are two interesting aspects of the quality change. The first is that if all the firms can change their quality, then Schlitz will change its quality the most. This may explain why Schlitz spent the resources to develop ABF technology while the other firms did not. The result in the model follows from the fact that Schlitz is relatively sheltered from the competition between Miller and Anheuser-Busch and, hence, does not need to com-

pete as heavily (recall that a higher quality, like a lower price, means more competitive behavior). The other interesting aspect of these results is that when Schlitz is the only firm that can lower its quality, it does so more than it does when all firms can change. Thus, Schlitz clearly had a large incentive to adopt the ABF process once it had been developed. The results of the simulated model are consistent with Schlitz's behavior over time.

The price competition has more interesting dynamic aspects than the quality competition. As Table 12.6 shows, Schlitz charges very high prices in the first years after entry (in all three specifications). Then, once the steady state is reached, prices are below those of the competition. Anheuser-Busch keeps prices relatively steady, and Miller starts with very low prices to gain market share rapidly and then settles on a price only slightly lower that of Anheuser-Busch. These observations reflect the reality that Schlitz prices relative to other beers were higher in 1974 and 1975 than in the late 1970s, that Anheuser-Busch prices were relatively steady, and that Miller prices rose over the decade.

Table 12.4

Market Shares Along Each Line When Only Schlitz Can Change Quality
(and cx = 2, cy = 6, cz = .8, and Delta = .6)

Firms		1972	73	74	75	76	77	78	79	80	81	82	83	84
x	Schlitz	0.5	0.5	0.167	0.103	0.094	0.101	0.108	0.113	0.116	0.117	0.119	0.119	0.119
	A-B	0.5	0.5	0.167	0.230	0.239	0.232	0.225	0.220	0.217	0.216	0.214	0.214	0.214
y	Schlitz	0	0	0.333	0.229	0.19	0.173	0.163	0.158	0.155	0.153	0.152	0.151	0.151
	Miller	0	0	0	0.105	0.143	0.161	0.170	0.175	0.178	0.180	0.181	0.182	0.182
z	A-B	0	0	0.333	0.143	0.132	0.141	0.148	0.153	0.157	0.159	0.159	0.160	0.160
	Miller	0	0	0	0.191	0.201	0.192	0.185	0.18	0.177	0.175	0.174	0.173	0.173

Table 12.5

Quality When Delta = .6

		1973	74	75	76	77	78	79	80
Only Schlitz changes, cx = 2, cy = 6, cz = .8	Schlitz	0.450	0.450	0.353	0.348	0.347	0.347	0.347	0.347
All can change quality, cx = 2 cy = 6, cz = .8	Schlitz	0.450	0.450	0.301	0.297	0.296	0.296	0.296	0.296
	A-B	0.450	0.450	0.333	0.333	0.333	0.333	0.333	0.333
	Miller	NA	0.450	0.317	0.321	0.322	0.322	0.322	0.322
Only Schlitz changes, cx = cy = cz = 2	Schlitz	0.450	0.450	0.371	0.368	0.368	0.368	0.368	0.368
All can change quality, cx = cy = cz = 2	Schlitz	0.450	0.450	0.304	0.300	0.300	0.300	0.300	0.300
	A-B	0.450	0.450	0.304	0.300	0.300	0.300	0.300	0.300
	Miller	NA	0.450	0.298	0.299	0.300	0.300	0.300	0.300

One important question remains. By how much did Schlitz profit by being able to change its quality? The total discounted profit for Schlitz when it could change its quality was 1.735. The total discounted profit when it could not change its quality was 1.577. This gain was largely a result of higher profits in the first few periods. For example, when it could change its quality, Schlitz's profit in the year of entry is 0.271, while Anheuser-Busch has a profit of only 0.162. When it cannot change its quality, Schlitz's profit in the year of entry is 0.236, a substantial drop. The long-run steady-state profits each period of Schlitz, however, are below those of Anheuser-Busch and of Miller when it can change its quality, and higher when it cannot. This may partly explain why Schlitz had high profits

Table 12.6

Prices When Delta = .6

		1973	74	75	76	77	78	79	80
	Schlitz	1.92	1.920	1.198	0.977	0.929	0.919	0.917	0.916
Only Schlitz changes,	A-B	1.92	1.920	0.943	0.937	0.943	0.945	0.945	0.945
$cx = 2$, $cy = 6$, $cz = .8$	Miller	NA	1.920	0.745	0.906	0.935	0.94	0.941	0.941
	Schlitz	1.92	1.920	1.076	0.951	0.931	0.928	0.928	0.928
Only Schlitz changes,	A-B	1.92	1.920	1.070	1.007	0.998	0.997	0.997	0.997
$cx = cy = cz = 2$	Miller	NA	1.920	0.774	0.961	0.991	0.996	0.997	0.997
	Schlitz	1.92	1.920	1.190	1.019	0.984	0.977	0.976	0.975
None change quality,	A-B	1.92	1.920	0.943	0.918	0.920	0.921	0.921	0.921
$cx = 2$ $cy = 6$, $cz = .8$	Miller	NA	1.920	0.745	0.890	0.914	0.919	0.920	0.920

from 1973 to 1976, immediately after the quality change, followed by a sharp drop-off in 1977 that continued until it was purchased by Stroh's in 1982.[23] Therefore, Schlitz's change in quality, and the resulting long-term loss of profits, was a rational response to entry by Miller. Real stock prices reflect the changes in Schlitz's prospects. In 1974, when Schlitz first changed to ABF, the stock price was relatively high and industry analysts praised Schlitz as "the lowest cost producer among the Big Three."[24] Stock prices only collapsed two years later when the model predicts that profits would start to fall.

Conclusions

The model presented in this paper reflects many aspects of the competition between Miller, Anheuser-Busch, and Schlitz in the 1970s. It shows that the collapse of Schlitz's market share was the inevitable result of entry by Miller "near" Anheuser-Busch and their subsequent intense competition. It also shows that the decision by Schlitz to adopt ABF production technology was a rational

response to this entry, and that Schlitz had a larger incentive to change its production process in order to cut costs (even if it hurt long-run demand) than either Miller or Anheuser-Busch. The changes that occurred at Schlitz in 1976 and in 1978 are not explained by the model. Thus, the "flaky beer" episode and the "Drink Schlitz or I'll kill you" advertising campaign do appear to have been a result of poor decision making by the company and appear to have exacerbated the Schlitz trend's toward lower market share and lower profits.

Further evidence for this model is provided by Pabst Brewing, the third-largest brewer for much of the 1960s and early 1970s. I did not include Pabst in my model because the algebra and the computations would have become prohibitively difficult. The Pabst story, however, does fit in with other predictions of the model. Pabst experienced a decline similar to that of Schlitz without any of the "mistakes." Pabst's share grew in the early 1970s to a peak of 10.5 percent in 1976. A rapid decline followed, and Pabst's share had fallen to 6 percent by 1982, swept aside by the competition between Miller and Anheuser-Busch. Though the 1976 peak occurred one year later than Schlitz's peak, the pattern is the same. Pabst's slower decline actually seems to fit the model better because it did not have access to ABF technology. It therefore could not obtain the same short run that Schlitz could. This kept Pabst's reputation intact, allowing it to grow for one extra year.

There is one important aspect of competition that is not addressed in this paper: advertising. In the brewing industry, competition in advertising may be as important as competition in price. Note the regression results give a significant and positive coefficient for the effect of advertising share on market share. In the mid-1970s, Anheuser-Busch and Miller both rapidly increased their advertising expenditures. Schlitz either could not or would not keep up. Preliminary econometrics show that Miller was a closer substitute to Anheuser-Busch than to Schlitz in advertising as well as in price; this is consistent with the transportation costs used in the simulations. Thus, an interesting extension would be to put advertising competition into the model.

By the late 1970s Schlitz was "no longer the most carefully pronounced name in Milwaukee."[25] Its collapse started with the rise of Miller as a major brewer in 1974 with the introduction of Miller Lite, and continued through the "mistakes" of the late 1970s. While the results from the data and empirical method used in this paper should be interpreted with caution, this paper has shown that Schlitz's adoption of ABF technology in 1974 may have been a rational response to Miller's rise. Schlitz may have sacrificed long-run profits for short-term gain.

Appendix A: Proofs

Proof of Lemma 1(i)

I first prove the existence of the steady state for the two-firm problem. I prove the existence by construction, solving the first-order conditions of the infinite dimensional maximization problem and assuming the existence of the steady state. I then solve for that steady state.

Firm S's problem:

$$\max_{\{p_{S,t}\}\{q_{S,t}\}} \sum_{t=0}^{\infty} \beta^t \left[\frac{1}{2c_x}\left(p_{A,t} - p_{S,t} + c_x - \delta_x\right. \right. $$
$$\left. \left. \left(1 - 2x_{S,t-1}\right) - q_{A,t-1} + q_{S,t-1}\right)p_{S,t} - x^2_{S,t} - q^2_{S,t} \right] \tag{15}$$

Firm A's problem:

$$\max_{\{p_{A,t}\}\{q_{A,t}\}} \sum_{t=0}^{\infty} \beta^t \left[\frac{1}{2c_x}\left(p_{S,t} - p_{A,t} + c_x - \delta_x\right. \right. $$
$$\left. \left. \left(1 - 2x_{A,t-1}\right) - q_{S,t-1} + q_{A,t-1}\right)p_{A,t} - x^2_{A,t} - q^2_{A,t} \right] \tag{16}$$

FOCs (will give a maximum because the function is concave in the $p_{i,t}$'s and $q_{i,t}$'s):

$$p_{S,t}: \quad \frac{p_{S,t}}{2c_x} + \frac{2\beta\delta_x}{2c_x}\frac{p_{S,t+1}}{2c_x} + \left(\frac{2\beta\delta_x}{2c_x}\right)^2 \frac{p_{S,t+2}}{2c_x} + \dots = $$
$$x_{S,t} + \left(\frac{2}{2c_x} + \frac{2}{2c_x}\left(\frac{2\beta\delta_x}{2c_x}\right) + \frac{2}{2c_x}\left(\frac{2\beta\delta_x}{2c_x}\right)^2 + \dots\right)x_{S,t} \tag{17}$$

$$p_{A,t}: \quad \frac{p_{A,t}}{2c_x} + \frac{2\beta\delta_x}{2c_x}\frac{p_{A,t+1}}{2c_x} + \left(\frac{2\beta\delta_x}{2c_x}\right)^2 \frac{p_{A,t+2}}{2c_x} + \dots = $$
$$x_{A,t} + \left(\frac{2}{2c_x} + \frac{2}{2c_x}\left(\frac{2\beta\delta_x}{2c_x}\right) + \frac{2}{2c_x}\left(\frac{2\beta\delta_x}{2c_x}\right)^2 + \dots\right)x_{A,t} \tag{18}$$

$$q_{S,t}: \quad \frac{\beta p_{S,t+1}}{2c_x} + \frac{\beta p_{S,t+2}}{2c_x}\left(\frac{2\beta\delta_x}{2c_x}\right) + \frac{\beta p_{S,t+3}}{2c_x}\left(\frac{2\beta\delta_x}{2c_x}\right)^2 + \dots - 2q_{S,t} = 0 \tag{19}$$

$$q_{A,t}: \quad \frac{\beta p_{A,t+1}}{2c_x} + \frac{\beta p_{A,t+2}}{2c_x}\left(\frac{2\beta\delta_x}{2c_x}\right) + \frac{\beta p_{A,t+3}}{2c_x}\left(\frac{2\beta\delta_x}{2c_x}\right)^2 + \dots - 2q_{A,t} = 0 \tag{20}$$

Noting $\dfrac{\delta_x}{c_x} = \delta$, these can be simplified to:

$$p_{i,t}: \quad \sum_{j=0}^{\infty}\left[-(\beta\delta)^j\,\frac{p_{i,t+j}}{2c_x}+\frac{x_{i,t}}{c_x}(\beta\delta)^j\right]+x_{i,t}=0 \quad (21)$$

$$q_{i,t}: \quad \sum_{j=0}^{\infty}(\beta\delta)^j\,\frac{p_{i,t+1+j}}{2c_x}=2q_{i,t} \quad (22)$$

Setting, $x_{i,t} = x_i$, $p_{i,t} = p_i$, and $q_{i,t} = q_i$, for all t because of the steady state, equations (3) and (4) can be simplified to

$$x_S = \frac{1}{2c_x(1-\delta)}\left(p_A - p_S + c_x - \delta_x + q_S - q_A\right) \quad (23)$$

$$x_A = \frac{1}{2c_x(1-\delta)}\left(p_S - p_A + c_x - \delta_x + q_A - q_S\right) \quad (24)$$

In a steady state, equations (21) and (22) become

$$\left(1+\frac{1}{c_x}\left(\frac{1}{1-\beta\delta}\right)\right)+x_i=\frac{p_i}{2c_x}\left(\frac{1}{1-\beta\delta}\right) \quad (25)$$

$$\frac{\beta p_i}{2c_x}\left(\frac{1}{1-\beta\delta}\right)=2q_i \quad (26)$$

where the x_i in equation (25) would be replaced by the appropriate expression in equation (23) or (24). There are now four equations and four unknowns (equations [25] and [26] with $i = 1,2$). Solving for the unknowns gives a unique answer.

$$p_S = c_x - c_x\beta\delta + 1 \quad (27)$$

$$p_A = c_x - c_x\beta\delta + 1 \quad (28)$$

$$q_S = \frac{\beta(-c_x + c_x\beta\delta - 1)}{4c_x(\beta\delta - 1)} \quad (29)$$

$$q_A = \frac{\beta(-c_x + c_x\beta\delta - 1)}{4c_x(\beta\delta - 1)} \quad (30)$$

Therefore the steady state exists, and it is unique.

The proofs of the existence of the unique steady state for the three-firm problem mimic the proof of the two-firm problem except that the algebra becomes much less tractable.

Proof of Lemma 1(ii)

There exists a unique steady state in the three-firm problem where all can change quality.

Firm S's maximization problem is:

$$\max_{\{p_{S,t}\}\{q_{S,t}\}}\sum_{t=0}^{\infty}\beta^t\left\{\begin{bmatrix}\frac{1}{2c_x}\left(p_{A,t}-p_{S,t}+\frac{1}{3}c_x-\delta_x\left(\frac{1}{3}-2x_{S,t-1}\right)-q_{A,t-1}+q_{S,t-1}\right)+\\\frac{1}{2c_y}\left(p_{M,t}-p_{S,t}+\frac{1}{3}c_y-\delta_y\left(\frac{1}{3}-2x_{S,t-1}\right)-q_{M,t-1}+q_{S,t-1}\right)\end{bmatrix}p_{S,t}\\-\left(x_{S,t}+y_{S,t}\right)^2-q^2{}_{S,t}\right\} \quad (31)$$

The problems for firms A and M are defined similarly. Firm S's first-order conditions are:

$$p_{S,t}: \quad \sum_{j=0}^{\infty}\left[-(\beta\delta)^j\,p_{S,t+j}\left(\frac{1}{2c_x}+\frac{1}{2c_y}\right)\right.$$
$$\left.+\left(\frac{1}{c_x}+\frac{1}{c_y}\right)(\beta\delta)^j\left(x_{S,t}+y_{S,t}\right)\right] \quad (32)$$
$$+x_{S,t}+y_{S,t}=0$$

$$q_{S,t}: \quad \sum_{j=0}^{\infty}(\beta\delta)^j\,\frac{p_{S,t+1+j}}{2}\left(\frac{1}{2c_x}+\frac{1}{2c_y}\right)=2q_{S,t} \quad (33)$$

Firms A and M have similar first-order conditions. In a steady state, these FOCs become the following reaction functions:

$$p_S = -\frac{\left(3c_y\left(q_A - p_A - q_S\right) - 2c_y c_x\left(1-\delta\right) + 3c_x\left(q_M - p_M - q_S\right)\right)\left(c_y c_x\left(\beta\delta - 1\right) - c_y - c_x\right)}{3\left(c_y + c_x\right)\left(c_y c_x\left(\delta + \beta\delta - 1\right) - c_y - c_x\right)} \tag{34}$$

$$q_S = \frac{\beta p_S\left(\dfrac{1}{c_x} + \dfrac{1}{c_y}\right)}{4\left(1 - \beta\delta\right)} \tag{35}$$

$$p_A = -\frac{\left(3c_x\left(q_M - p_M - q_A\right) - 2c_x c_z\left(1-\delta\right) + 3c_z\left(q_S - p_S - q_A\right)\right)\left(c_x c_z\left(\beta\delta - 1\right) - c_x - c_z\right)}{3\left(c_x + c_z\right)\left(c_x c_z\left(\delta + \beta\delta - 1\right) - c_x - c_z\right)} \tag{36}$$

$$q_A = \frac{\beta p_A\left(\dfrac{1}{c_x} + \dfrac{1}{c_z}\right)}{4\left(1 - \beta\delta\right)} \tag{37}$$

$$p_M = -\frac{\left(3c_z\left(q_S - p_S - q_M\right) - 2c_z c_y\left(1-\delta\right) + 3c_y\left(q_A - p_A - q_M\right)\right)\left(c_z c_y\left(\beta\delta - 1\right) - c_z - c_y\right)}{3\left(c_z + c_y\right)\left(c_z c_y\left(\delta + \beta\delta - 1\right) - c_z - c_y\right)} \tag{38}$$

$$q_M = \frac{\beta p_M\left(\dfrac{1}{c_y} + \dfrac{1}{c_z}\right)}{4\left(1 - \beta\delta\right)} \tag{39}$$

These equations can be solved to derive a unique steady state. Each of the unknowns can then be expressed in terms β, δ, c_x, c_y, and c_z.

Proof of Proposition 1

First I will show that $q_S < q_A$, q_M. Much of the work for this problem was done in Lemma 1. It remains to be shown that the derived expressions give $q_A - q_S > 0$ and $q_M - q_S > 0$. First taking p as fixed, the above is trivially true because

$$\frac{1}{c_x} + \frac{1}{c_y} < \frac{1}{c_y} + \frac{1}{c_z} < \frac{1}{c_z} + \frac{1}{c_z}$$

(recall

$$q_S = \frac{\beta p_S\left(\dfrac{1}{c_x} + \dfrac{1}{c_y}\right)}{4\left(1 - \beta\delta\right)}, \quad q_A = \frac{\beta p_A\left(\dfrac{1}{c_x} + \dfrac{1}{c_z}\right)}{4\left(1 - \beta\delta\right)}, \quad \text{and}$$

$$q_M = \frac{\beta p_M\left(\dfrac{1}{c_y} + \dfrac{1}{c_z}\right)}{4\left(1 - \beta\delta\right)} \quad .)$$

Thus showing that $p_S < p_A$, p_M will complete this part of the proof. Using the expression derived in Lemma 1, $p_A - p_S$ and $p_M - p_S$ are positive for $0 < \delta < 1$, and $0 < \beta < 1$. Therefore $p_S < p_A$, p_M, which implies $q_S < q_A$, q_M.

The next step is to show that Schlitz has less than half of both the x and y markets. Note that there are two forces working in opposite directions: $q_S < q_A$, q_M would make Schlitz lose share; however $p_S < p_A$, p_M means Schlitz will gain share. Recall firm S's steady-state demand in market x is given by

$$x_S = \frac{1}{2c_x(1-\delta)}\left(p_A - p_S + \frac{c_x}{3} - \frac{\delta_x}{3} + q_S - q_A\right) \quad (40)$$

If $p_S = p_A$ and $q_S = q_A$, then $x_S = x_A = \frac{1}{6}$. Thus, if $p_A - p_S + q_S - q_A < 0$, then firm S loses market share to firm A. Because

$$p_A - p_S + q_S - q_A = \quad (41)$$

$$p_A\left(1 - \frac{\beta\left(\frac{1}{c_x} + \frac{1}{c_z}\right)}{4(1-\beta\delta)}\right) - p_S\left(1 - \frac{\beta\left(\frac{1}{c_x} + \frac{1}{c_y}\right)}{4(1-\beta\delta)}\right)$$

Therefore, for Schlitz to lose market share in market x:

$$\frac{p_A}{p_S} < \frac{1 - \dfrac{\beta\left(\dfrac{1}{c_x} + \dfrac{1}{c_y}\right)}{4(1-\beta\delta)}}{1 - \dfrac{\beta\left(\dfrac{1}{c_x} + \dfrac{1}{c_z}\right)}{4(1-\beta\delta)}} \quad (42)$$

At first glance it is not obvious when this expression will hold; however, plugging in the expressions for p_S and p_A does give $p_A - p_S + q_S - q_A < 0$. This occurs because an increase in c_y (or a decrease in c_z) will cause the right side to increase more than the left. In other words, the derivative of the right-hand side with respect to c_y or to c_z is

higher in absolute value than the same derivative taken on the left-hand side (the derivatives are monotone over $0 < \delta < 1$ and $0 < \beta < 1$.) Because there is equality when all transport costs are equal, this implies that equation (42) is true. A similar result holds for competition in market y.

Appendix B: Data

Most of the data used in this paper were collected by Carol and Victor Tremblay. Please refer to their book for details about data collection and to obtain a copy of the data.[26] Prices for Miller were obtained from December issues of the *Chicago Tribune* from 1973 until 1982, and then rescaled to conform to the price values in the main data. Budweiser prices were used as a base in order to rescale.

Notes

Inna Galperin provided excellent research assistance. Thanks to Victor and Carol Tremblay for comments.

1. *Standard & Poor's Industry Surveys,* 1973, L34.

2. David A. Aaker, *Managing Brand Equity: Capitalizing on the Value of a Brand Name* (New York: Free Press, 1991).

3. Jacques Neher, "What Went Wrong," *Advertising Age* (April 13, 1981), pp. 61–64, and "Schlitz: Lost at Sea," *Advertising Age* (April 20, 1981), pp. 49–52.

4. Philip Van Munching, *Beer Blast: The Inside Story of the Brewing Industry's Bizarre Battles* (New York: Random House, 1997), p. 48.

5. Jacques Neher, "What Went Wrong," p. 64.

6. Jacques Neher, "Schlitz: Lost at Sea," p. 52.

7. Jacques Neher, "What Went Wrong," p. 64.

8. Jacques Neher, "Schlitz: Lost at Sea," p. 52.

9. See Luis M.B. Cabral, *Introduction to Industrial Organization* (Cambridge, MA: MIT Press, 2000) for more details on differentiation (horizontal and vertical) and on Hotelling models. Dennis W. Carlton and Jeffery M. Perloff, *Modern Industrial Organization* (Boston: Addison-Wesley, 2005), also provides rich detail on Hotelling models.

10. Kevin Lane Keller, *Strategic Brand Management: Building, Measuring, and Managing Brand Equity* (Upper Saddle River, NJ: Prentice-Hall, 1998), p. 50.

11. Simon P. Anderson, Andre de Palma, and Jacques-François Thisse, *Discrete Choice Theory of Product Differentiation* (Cambridge, MA: MIT Press, 1992), pp. 159 and 244.

12. "Gussie Busch's Bitter Brew," *Forbes* (Jan. 1, 1974), p. 22.

13. Discounting means that profits today have a higher value than profits next year. In this case, I use a modeling technique that assumes that next year's profits are β times the value of this year's profits where $0 < \beta < 1$.

14. Dennis W. Carlton and Jeffery M. Perloff, *Modern Industrial Organization,* and Jean Tirole, *The Theory of Industrial Organization* (Cambridge, MA: MIT Press, 1988), provide explanations of Nash equilibrium. Kenneth Judd, *Numerical Methods in Economics* (Cambridge, MA: MIT Press, 1998) provides details on the definition of an open-loop equilibrium.

15. See Dennis W. Carlton and Jeffery M. Perloff, *Modern Industrial Organization,* chapter 7, for example.

16. This is consistent with the alcohol content of their flagship brands, according to Carol Horton Tremblay and Victor J. Tremblay, "Advertising, Price, and Welfare: Evidence from the U.S. Brewing Industry," *Southern Economic Journal* 62 (1995), pp. 367–81. The cheaper process may also have further distanced Schlitz from Anheuser-Busch and Miller.

17. David A. Aaker, *Managing Brand Equity: Capitalizing on the Value of a Brand Name.*

18. This uses a straightforward instrumental variables technique. For details, see William H. Greene, *Econometric Analysis,* (Upper Saddle River, NJ: Prentice-Hall, 1996), Chapter 16, and Damodar N. Gujarati, *Basic Econometrics* (New York: McGraw-Hill/Irwin, 2003), chapters 19 and 20.

19. Details of the data are in Appendix B and in Carol Horton and Victor J. Tremblay, "Advertising, Price, and Welfare: Evidence from the U.S. Brewing Industry," and in Victor J. Tremblay and Carol Horton Tremblay, *The U.S. Brewing Industry: Data and Economic Analysis* (Cambridge, MA: MIT Press, 2005).

20. William H. Greene, *Econometric Analysis,* p. 641.

21. Kenneth Judd, *Numerical Methods in Economics* (Cambridge, MA: MIT Press, 1998).

22. Ibid., p. 114.

23. According to Victor J. Tremblay and Carol Horton Tremblay, in *The U.S. Brewing Industry: Data and Economic Analysis,* Schlitz's average profit-to-sales ratio from 1973 to 1976 was 5.5, compared to an industry average of 2.1. From 1977 to 1982 Schlitz's average profit-to-sales ratio fell to –0.4, compared to an industry average of 1.4.

24. *Standard & Poor's Industry Surveys,* 1974, L42.

25. Jacques Neher, "What Went Wrong," p. 61.

26. Victor J. Tremblay and Carol Horton Tremblay, *The U.S. Brewing Industry: Data and Economic Analysis.*

Selected Readings

Aaker, David A. *Managing Brand Equity: Capitalizing on the Value of a Brand Name.* New York: Free Press, 1991.

Anderson, Simon P., Andre de Palma, and Jacques-François Thisse. *Discrete Choice Theory of Product Differentiation.* Cambridge, MA: MIT Press, 1992.

Apps, Jerry. *Breweries of Wisconsin.* Madison, WI: University of Wisconsin Press, 1992.

Cabral, Luis M.B. *Introduction to Industrial Organization.* Cambridge, MA: MIT Press, 2002.

Carlton, Dennis W., and Jeffrey M. Perloff. *Modern Industrial Organization.* Boston: Addison-Wesley, 2005.

"Gussie Busch's Bitter Brew." *Forbes* (Jan. 1, 1974), 22–27.

Keller, Kevin Lane. *Strategic Brand Management: Building, Measuring, and Managing Brand Equity.* Upper Saddle River, NJ: Prentice-Hall, 1998.

Neher, Jacques. "What Went Wrong." *Advertising Age* (April 13, 1981), 61–64.

———. "Schlitz: Lost at Sea." *Advertising Age* (April 20, 1981), 49–52.

"Schlitz, R. J. Reynolds Leave Door Open for the Possibility of Merger Discussions." *Wall Street Journal* (May 19, 1978), 6.

Tirole, Jean. *The Theory of Industrial Organization.* Cambridge, MA: MIT Press, 1988.

Tremblay, Carol Horton, and Victor J. Tremblay. "Advertising, Price, and Welfare: Evidence from the U.S. Brewing Industry." *Southern Economic Journal* 62 (1995), 367–81.

Tremblay, Victor J., and Carol Horton Tremblay. *The U.S. Brewing Industry: Data and Economic Analysis.* Cambridge, MA: MIT Press, 2005.

Van Munching, Philip. *Beer Blast: The Inside Story of the Brewing Industry's Bizarre Battles.* New York: Random House, 1997.

13

TiVo

Product Versus Incumbent Advantage

Pai-Ling Yin

Introduction

When TiVo was founded in August 1997, it began a revolution in the home-entertainment industry. TiVo was a pioneer of the Digital Video Recorder (DVR) technology, allowing consumers to effortlessly record TV programs onto a hard drive. Viewers could then pause and "instantly replay" live TV and fast-forward through previously recorded programs. DVRs were an emerging consumer electronics category that changed the way that consumers experienced television. DVR technology had the potential to disrupt the balance of players and change the landscape of the home-entertainment industry.

TiVo was the initial market leader of DVR technology with arguably the best product and service on the market. The company's name was turned into a verb as consumers referred to using their DVRs to record a TV program as "TiVo-ing" the show. But after nearly ten years TiVo had not gained a dominant market position or even assured its long-term survival. With a superior product and first-mover advantage, why had TiVo not yet "won" the market?

This chapter examines one aspect of the challenge that TiVo faced as an innovator in the home-entertainment industry: competition with incumbent players in the industry. The chapter opens with a description of the TiVo product and

service, and then describes its potentially disruptive effect on the television industry structure. Not only did TiVo have to deal with the usual challenges of convincing consumers to adopt a new technology, but they also had to deal with resistance from an incumbent industry. The chapter then proceeds to describe how TiVo tried to deal with both adoption and industry partners. Ultimately, TiVo's efforts were unable to garner enough subscribers before a powerful second mover entered the DVR market: the cable operators.

TiVo's story to date is another example of superior products struggling in the marketplace due to the confluence of exploding demand from new users, high inertia among those who have already adopted the new technology, and the ability of one player in the industry to control channels of distribution.[1]

TiVo Product Advantage

At first glance, a DVR is a digital version of a VCR but with many more levels of functionality. These functions completely transform the way a consumer experiences TV in ways that were not feasible with VCRs. A DVR is essentially a large hard drive for storing information digitally. It can record hundreds of hours of programming without requiring hundreds of bulky videocassette tapes. One could even record ten straight hours of TV while not at home because there was no need to switch tapes. A DVR allows consumers to record an hour-long program, start watching that program fifteen minutes later, and then fast-forward through the commercials, catching up to the real-time broadcast by the end of the program. Consumers could also pause a TV program that they were viewing to answer the phone, for example, or replay a section that they had missed because the DVR continued to record the rest of the program, functions that VCRs could not easily provide.

TiVo's user-friendly features for recording differentiated TiVo from other DVRs and made it a quality product/service. TiVo was designed with a user interface that made DVR technology easily accessible and highly functional for consumers. TiVo was compatible with cable, satellite, and over-the-airwaves TV systems. Once the box was set up and the subscription activated, TiVo users could access two weeks of electronic program guide (EPG) information on their TV screen and record shows by simply clicking on the program.

Several "smart" services made TiVo a product superior to conventional DVRs. VCRs were notoriously difficult to program, so many consumers did not actually use them to record shows while they were away from home. The TiVo "Season Pass" feature allowed a customer to record an entire season of a show automatically simply by selecting it once; the TiVo box would even know not to record if the show was not being aired one week by consulting the EPG. Consumers could also use the "Wishlist" feature to have the TiVo record a particular show, actor, director, or style of programming, whenever and on whatever channel it might be playing. TiVo would use spare hard-drive space to record programs that the customer might enjoy based on historical viewing habits and whether he or she gave a show or genre a positive or negative rating. This feature allowed customers to try out new shows without having to sift through hundreds of cable channels to find something they might enjoy.

Consumers purchased a TiVo machine with 40 to 140 hours of recording time and then installed the machine and activated the service, which cost either $12.95 per month or a one-time, lifetime fee of $299. Installing TiVo was not always straightforward; most users needed help from the customer service desk during installation. However, once the TiVo unit had been set up and activated, it received high marks from consumers for its user-friendly interface and rich feature set. TiVo's churn rate—the rate at which customers gave up their subscriptions—was extremely low. At less than 1 percent per month and about 10 percent per year, it was lower than churn rates for other subscription services such as cell-phone service (about 33 percent per year), cable TV service (about 30 percent per year), and DirecTV (about 18 percent per year).[2] Once TiVo got a customer, it kept them. High inertia among TiVo customers could help TiVo fend off competitors, as long as TiVo got to the new customers first.

TiVo's Disruptive Potential

With TiVo's user-friendly features and subscription services, the DVR became immensely more valuable to consumers than VCRs ever had been. With DVR technology, consumers now had the power to watch shows when they wanted ("time-shifting" their viewing) and to skip over the commercials. With TiVo, the consumer could easily mix and match programs from different networks to create a personalized program lineup. This changed the established order of the home-entertainment industry. A number of players did not want to see DVR adoption, let alone TiVo adoption, proceed rapidly.

Figure 13.1 depicts the structure of the home-entertainment ecosystem with various service

Figure 13.1 **The Home-Entertainment Ecosystem**

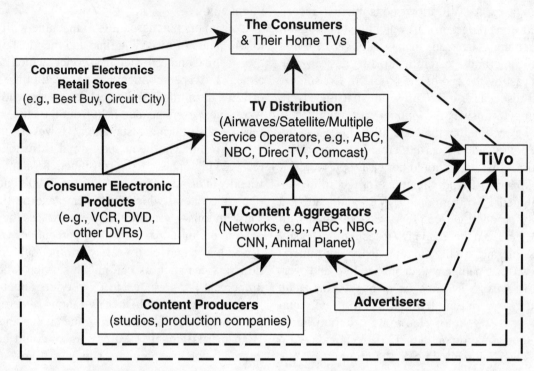

Source: Adapted from: David B. Yoffie and Pai Ling Yin, "Strategic Inflection: TiVo in 2005," Harvard Business School, revised December 20, 2005, p. 23.

providers (such as television content providers, advertisers, and consumer electronics stores) interacting with each other to get their product (be it a show, commercial, or product) to the consumers at the top. Under this current system, content (TV programs) was created by studios in anticipation of a cut of the large advertising revenue from commercials shown while the program aired. Content aggregators (networks) mediated between the content providers (some networks produced content themselves) and the advertisers, because they controlled the scheduling and choice of the content and commercials to be distributed. Distribution was achieved either through airwave broadcasting (which depended on advertising for 90 percent of its revenues) or, increasingly, through satellite

and cable subscription services.[3] Cable system operators received 65 percent to 70 percent of their revenues from subscriber fees and also generated revenues from installation charges and sales of Video-On-Demand (VOD) movies and events.[4]

The satellite and cable providers were highly concentrated, traditionally operating as monopolies or duopolies in their localities. Distribution was the "bottleneck" in the system. The only way advertisers or content could get to TV consumers was through the networks, cable, or satellite operators.

TiVo threatened to disintermediate the industry value chain, destroying the current revenue model and potentially eliminating the need for some players. TiVo offered consumers the ability to fast-forward through commercials, threatening advertisers. In 2004, an estimated 88 percent of consumers with DVRs skipped ads.[5] By 2005, roughly 2 percent of TV ads were being skipped, and more than 10 percent might be skipped by 2009.[6] This behavior threatened the revenue streams of TV networks that depended on the money they received from advertisers. Under the traditional system, advertisers were willing to pay more for commercial spots at times when there were more viewers; for example, commercials aired during "prime-time" shows paid a premium price for that time slot. TiVo allowed consumers to time-shift and watch prime-time shows at non-prime-time hours and then to fast-forward through the commercials in the program. In a TiVo world, advertisers would not have any incentive to pay for traditional ads, let alone pay premium prices for prime-time advertising slots. Finally, TiVo threatened the content aggregators by allowing consumers to much more easily search, identify, and retrieve content from any channel, making topic-specific networks related to food, sports, or children's programs potentially unnecessary.

The cable and satellite companies were initially resistant to DVRs. Just as the VCR had posed a threat to broadcast content, they felt the DVR would even more easily allow consumers to substitute recorded content for real-time broadcasts. These distributors preferred the VOD services that they had developed, and they urged the industry to stick to that technology instead of adopting DVRs. While VOD services permitted time-shifting, they also retained some control of the consumer's viewing experience in the hands of cable and satellite operators by limiting content selection and allowing the operators to attach some advertising to the content. DVR technology put more control into the consumers' hands: They could record and watch anything that aired on TV without having to deal with a cable or satellite company as an intermediary.

TiVo attempted to deal with the integrated nature of the entertainment industry by establishing its own network of industry connections. TiVo had attracted several entertainment companies as equity investors, including AOL (which owned a 14 percent stake in the company), NBC (8 percent), Sony (5 percent),[7] Cox, Philips, Advance/Newhouse, CBS, Discovery, Showtime, TV Guide, Disney, and NBC.[8] Although many of these companies faced challenges as DVR technology penetrated their markets, they wanted to be in on the wave of new technology. When Michael Ramsey, founder and CEO of TiVo, Inc., decided to retire in early 2005, TiVo brought Thomas Rogers on as president and CEO.[9] Rogers had a long history in the entertainment industry. He worked at NBC for twelve years, serving part of this time as the president of NBC Cable. By attracting these potential enemies as investors, TiVo made its competitive world friendlier, as they now had an interest in TiVo succeeding.

Adoption Challenges

Educating the Consumer

The issues that TiVo faced in its early years were the usual issues faced by entrants with a new technology. The entrant faces low demand for its product in the early stages, as only a small group of technically savvy consumers have high enough willingness-to-pay for the product. However, over time, demand begins to increase at a rapid rate. More consumers learn about the product and how to use it. Adoption begins to increase because the price of the product also starts to fall as competitors put pressure on price and find more efficient production processes. The higher demand in turn develops a real market for the new technology and its inputs, driving the costs of production down further. At the same time, the technology quality and performance are improving, further attracting

Figure 13.2   **S-shaped Adoption Curve**

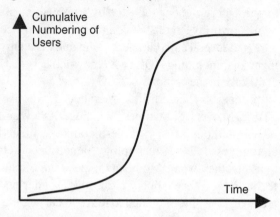

more consumers. At some point, these trends begin to taper off when the market becomes mature and saturated with the product. These dynamics create an S-shaped pattern of technology diffusion into the market as shown in Figure 13.2.[10]

Given the expected dynamics of adoption for the DVR industry, TiVo faced two major challenges. First, it was under pressure to reach the first inflection point in Figure 13.2 where the number of users would begin to explode as soon as possible. The bursting of the "dot-com bubble" on Wall Street sent TiVo's shares plummeting from $78 to $5 by the end of 2000.[11] TiVo could not continue for much longer selling low volumes of the product at already low margins.

One critical aspect to adoption is distribution. With a new technology, potential customers will not necessarily be informed enough to seek a product, so it is important to ensure that they are exposed to the product. In the early years, DVRs particularly depended on consumer electronics retail sales forces (at Best Buy or Circuit City, for example) both to help educate consumers and get the product distributed to them. However, the profit margins required by these stores to carry a product further raised the cost of adoption faced by a potential customer.

Second, TiVo wanted to make sure that the technology adopted was not just any DVR, but the TiVo DVR. The early years of the DVR market were fairly competitive. Besides TiVo, ReplayTV was founded in 1997[12] and 2Wire started up in 1998.[13] While this competition should have helped drive the price of DVRs down, the specialized design of the TiVo DVR (intended to protect user data and prevent TiVo from being easily imitated) also meant that it was more costly to make. TiVo had to both educate the market about the technology (potentially helping competitors) in addition to educating the market about why TiVo's superior quality warranted the price premium relative to competitors' products.

The importance of capturing a new user before a competitor could do so is illustrated in Figure 13.3. The solid line represents the adoption costs faced by consumers in the time-order they adopt a new technology as reflected in the S-shaped technology adoption curve from Figure 13.2. Those consumers can be thought of as ordered from technologically sophisticated to technologically unsophisticated on the horizontal axis in Figure 13.3. The adoption costs of the high-tech consumers are low (taking into account that they are not as sensitive to higher prices), which is why they are the first to adopt. The adoption costs of the low-tech consumers are higher, because they only adopt when price and quality are good enough (and when they are informed of the product's existence). However, once any of these consumers have adopted, they face switching costs (perhaps driven by simple inertia of not wanting to change products). These switching costs may be lower or higher than the adoption costs, depending on the level of inertia or other forces that would lead consumers to be locked into the particular version of the product they adopted. However, in general, the switching cost will be higher for the low-tech customers than the high-tech customers. In addi-

Figure 13.3 **One Possible Relationship Between Adoption Costs and Switching Costs**

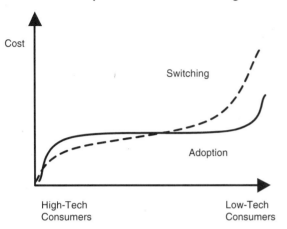

over other brands. In addition, TiVo discovered that consumers were taken aback by the fact that they had to pay a monthly service fee to use a product that they had purchased in a retail store.[15] Because of the general lack of experience with DVRs, TiVo had difficulty convincing those who had already adopted a non-TiVo DVR that TiVo was worth its premium price.

TiVo was the first to market among its competitors and did manage to become an early market leader with high brand recognition. In June 1999, TiVo had 1,000 early adopters as subscribers; by the end of the year TiVo had 18,000 subscribers. Growth was initially promising with new subscriptions increasing by 650 percent in 2000 over 1999 (see Table 13.1). However, new subscription growth in 2001 declined to only two times the previous year's additions and stagnated for 2002.

If TiVo could capture more of the new users in the DVR market more quickly, it could sustain market leadership by using switching costs to its advantage. The existing TiVo users were ardent fans. Polls revealed that up to 97 percent of TiVo users were "very satisfied" and would recommend TiVo to a friend.[16] Many stated that TiVo had changed their lives. TiVo's core consumers were not just "techies" who always had the newest technologies; TiVo had a strong following in people whose lives revolved around their passions and were comfortable enough around technology to appreciate the advanced features of the product. TiVo's challenge was educating and convincing average consumers that the TiVo product was valuable to them and superior to the competitors' product. If TiVo could do that, experience had shown that customer turnover was likely to be low.

However, TiVo knew that it would not manage a critical mass of new consumers without a stronger means of distribution. Therefore, TiVo attempted, with limited success, to partner with various entities to address this problem.

tion, to the extent there are any switching costs, the consumer will only switch if the utility from the alternative product is greater than the cost of switching. As a result, TiVo needed to capture as many of the new adopters as possible before its competitors did, or else it would face the more challenging battle of convincing DVR users to switch to TiVo rather than convincing altogether new users to adopt TiVo.

The company spent over $250 million on sales and marketing in 2000 and 2001 to build awareness of the TiVo brand and to educate consumers about TiVo's "personal TV service."[14] TiVo could not clearly list all of its box's features and benefits in just a thirty-second ad. It eventually aired ads focused on how TiVo could help consumers overcome a specific TV-related problem, such as automatically recording an entire season of a show with Season Pass so they did not have to remember to set their VCRs. Despite a spike in brand recognition following the advertising, TiVo management found that their advertising largely benefited the DVR market in general and not their product in particular. Even when consumers understood the DVR technology, they were still sometimes confused about what specifically TiVo had to offer

Table 13.1

TiVo Subscriptions, 1999–2005 (in thousands)

Quarter ended	Net new subscriptions			Cumulative subscriptions		
	Via TiVo	Via DirecTV	Total	Via TiVo	Via DirecTV	Total
30-Jun-99			1			1
30-Sep-99			1.5			2.5
30-Dec-99			15.5			18
30-Mar-00			14			32
30-Jun-00			16			48
30-Sep-00			25			73
30-Dec-00			63			136
31-Jan-01*			18			154
30-Apr-01	22	13	35	160	29	189
31-Jul-01	22	18	40	182	47	229
31-Oct-01	24	27	51	206	74	280
31-Jan-02	40	60	100	246	134	380
30-Apr-02	24	18	42	270	152	422
31-Jul-02	21	21	42	291	173	464
31-Oct-02	30	16	46	321	189	510
31-Jan-03	75	39	114	396	228	624
30-Apr-03	37	42	79	433	270	703
31-Jul-03	34	56	90	467	326	793
31-Oct-03	59	150	209	526	476	1002
31-Jan-04	130	200	330	656	676	1,332
30-Apr-04	68	196	264	724	872	1,596
31-Jul-04	63	225	288	787	1,097	1,884
31-Oct-04	103	316	419	890	1,413	2,303
31-Jan-05	251	447	698	1,141	1,860	3,001
30-Apr-05	72	247	319	1,213	2,107	3,320
31-Jul-05	40	214	254	1,253	2,321	3,574
31-Oct-05	55	379	434	1,308	2,700	4,008
31-Jan-06	183	173	356	1,491	2,873	4,364

Source: Table constructed from TiVo Quarterly and Annual Reports, 2001–2006.
*Only reports subscriptions for month of January.

Distributing the Product

Despite TiVo's somewhat adversarial position with content distributors, it was in the company's interest to pursue distribution arrangements with cable and satellite companies. The established relationship between those companies and their subscriber base offered ready access to potential customers. Establishing friendly relationships with these companies proved necessary for TiVo to penetrate the home-entertainment industry.

During the late 1990s, TiVo partnered with DirecTV, the largest U.S. satellite TV operator. The two companies worked together to launch a set-top box (the box that sat on top of a TV and allowed cable and/or DVR access) that integrated the DirecTV satellite box with TiVo's DVR technology and began offering it to DirecTV's 13 million customers. TiVo designed the boxes and had rights to share data and advertising revenues, but DirecTV took responsibility for manufacturing, marketing, installing, and servicing TiVo DVR accounts. TiVo subscribers were activated through DirecTV starting in April 2001. DirecTV customers received a basic DVR subscription rate of just $4.95 per month, and the service was included free in DirecTV's premium package.[17] DirecTV paid a low monthly fee per household to TiVo. In mid-2003 the average monthly fee paid to TiVo was $3.00 but was expected to drop to close to $1.00 in 2005.[18]

TiVo partnered with DirecTV as a way to gain access to the established base of potential customers. By 2005 DirecTV had generated 66 percent of TiVo's cumulative new subscriptions (see Table 13.1). However, DirecTV began offering its own DVR as a TiVo competitor in October 2005.

Incumbent Advantage

DVR Competition from Distributors

Although the cable industry had initially resisted DVR technology, by 2002 it had accepted that DVRs were in the market to stay. Rather than lose out to TiVo, the cable industry decided that it was better to introduce its own lower-quality version of the product and preempt further expansion by TiVo into the home. This became a particularly urgent activity when household adoption of satellite began to slow growth in cable's share of households. Satellite company Echo Star's Dish Network was estimated to be the second-largest provider of DVR devices after TiVo (including the DirecTV partnership). That company offered DVR capability based on technology from a company called OpenTV. Similar to the DVR boxes that the cable companies would come to offer, the Dish Network DVRs had limited functionality, but Dish had become an aggressive distributor, occasionally giving its products away for free with no monthly charge.

There were two major DVR providers to the cable industry: Motorola provided the DVRs for Comcast and RCN, while Time Warner, Cox, and other cable

operations offered Scientific Atlanta's Explorer 8000 (which had been the first integrated set-top box for the cable industry). Some cable operators used both technologies. While both the Motorola and Scientific Atlanta's boxes lacked TiVo's advanced features, some versions had multiple tuners and could record in high definition. The cable companies were racing to get their DVRs in their customers' homes before TiVo could. Most were willing to give away the hardware for free and charged only $8–$10 for the monthly subscription.[19] Any losses the cable industry would incur from this penetration-pricing campaign would have been outweighed by the long-run subscription and revenues from customers who chose cable over satellite and benefits from retaining more control over their consumer base than if those consumers used TiVo's DVR.

Despite the fact that TiVo had a head start in capturing new adopters in the DVR market, and was able to get some distribution help through its partnership with DirecTV, the cable industry had several advantages that could allow it to catch up. First, the cable companies already had 66 percent of the TV-owning households since 1999.[20] The cable companies could easily push a product to their own installed base of consumers, whereas TiVo and DirecTV had to pull customers to retail stores or satellite subscriptions as newer entrants to the home-entertainment industry. Although this was not a costless endeavor, exchanging the old set-top box for a DVR-capable box could be combined with upgrading half of their current cable customers from analog to digital services. Second, demand for DVRs was still growing, so the industry was still on the steeper part of the adoption curve in Figure 13.2. As a result, the cable companies could still compete with TiVo for the increasing number of new adopters. Finally, the challenges that TiVo faced as a premium product were an advantage to the cable and satellite companies, who chose to offer a low-end product. The lack of

Figure 13.4   **Cable Versus TiVo Share of DVRs in U.S. Households**

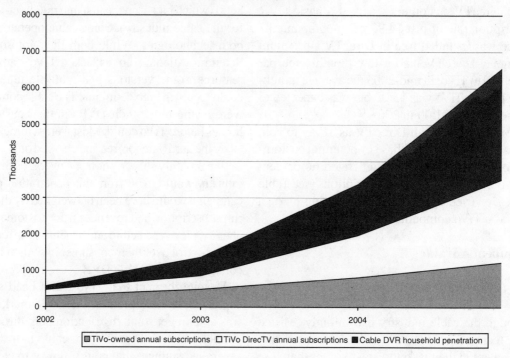

knowledge about product choices and attributes in this new market made it easier for the cable and satellite distributors to compete with TiVo on price with low-end products for new customers. The high inertia among consumers (while churn rates were 30 percent, this also implied that 70 percent of customers remained with their existing subscriptions) meant that with 66 percent of TV-owning households, the odds were in favor of the cable industry being able to retain its subscription customers as DVR customers once they offered that option to their customer base.

The results of cable's entry on the market share of the DVR adopters are shown in Figure 13.4. Non-DirecTV TiVo penetration grew much more slowly between 2002 and 2005. DirecTV TiVo penetration grew more rapidly, but neither source of TiVo customers grew as quickly as the penetration of cable DVRs. Indeed, if it were not for TiVo's relationship with DirecTV, TiVo's share of the DVR market would have been swamped by both cable and satellite distributors. If TiVo had captured much more of the market before the cable companies entered, or if the cable companies had entered at a later point on the S-curve of adoption, when the market had already been saturated, or if the cable industry had not had the incumbent distributional advantage of a large installed base of subscribers, the cable companies may not have been able to capture as much of the market despite their late entry into DVRs. However, in this case, various factors coincided such that the incumbent advantage proved to be a formidable challenge to product advantage.

DirecTV to Comcast

DirecTV announced it would sell its 4 percent share of TiVo in January 2004 after News Corp., which owned TiVo competitor NDR, acquired a controlling interest in DirecTV's parent, Hughes Electronics. DirecTV's new parent company, News Corp., had decided to exclusively offer a DVR made by subsidiary company NDR by the end of 2005. TiVo still had an advertising services agreement signed with DirecTV that lasted through 2007, allowing both companies to sell and distribute TiVo's advanced advertising capabilities. But News Corp. had made it clear that the relationship would likely end there.[21] Clearly, the loss of the DirecTV relationship was cause for great concern at TiVo.

TiVo had to look for a new distribution partner. In March 2005 TiVo signed a nonexclusive licensing and marketing deal with Comcast Corp. that would run for seven years from first deployment, with the option to extend year by year for a further eight years.[22] While TiVo had sold an integrated satellite-DVR box, roughly at cost, to DirecTV, Comcast wanted TiVo to adapt its software to run on its existing hardware, mainly Motorola-made boxes, so that it would not have to introduce a new box to customers. TiVo was obliged to deliver a technical solution given these parameters, and Comcast would handle the marketing and distribution. Similar to the DirecTV deal, Comcast would pay TiVo an upfront nonrecurring engineering fee to allow TiVo adapt its software, then only about one dollar per subscriber, per month, as time went on. The two companies also agreed to an advertising deal that would span all DVRs deployed with the TiVo system.

Although TiVo's deal with Comcast would potentially give it access to over 20 million subscribers, the nonexclusivity of the arrangement meant that TiVo still had to compete for those customers. Comcast was already deploying its own set-top box with DVR functionality. Additionally, in March 2006, Comcast threw its support behind a Cablevision plan to offer a remote storage digital video recording (RS-DVR) service. The service would allow subscribers to record programs onto Cablevision's network servers, eliminating the need for set-top boxes like TiVo's. Both Comcast and Time Warner Cable senior officers expressed interest in the system and declared that their companies would follow suit if Cablevision's attempt proved successful.[23]

Comcast has also been a long-time supporter of VOD. These types of services had been slow to get started due to the technical problems of setting up a system that could quickly transmit digital programs to individual cable boxes when they were demanded. As broadband access and service improved, VOD services would become a more serious competing technology.[24]

The Future for TiVo

Despite consistent rave reviews for the TiVo product, the company had not achieved a significant penetration into the TV market. Fierce competition in the DVR market had developed very quickly, and TiVo had not been able to capture enough of the market before the content distributors were able to leverage their installed bases to create a distribution advantage and capture the large growth in new DVR adopters.

New Competition

In 2005, a new class of content distributor was entering the equation: telecommunications companies. It was believed that the future existence of the telephone companies depended on their ability to enter the video market, bundling video with phone and Internet access. SBC, Verizon, and others hoped to bring brand recognition and very deep pockets to the battle for video distribution. Several telecommunications companies were aggressively laying fiber-optic networks able to offer superior bandwidth and to deliver a wide array of digital services to their customers. Similar to the content distributors, these entrants also had the advantage of a large installed base of consumers to whom they could distribute their products.

Strategic Options

Given TiVo's customer satisfaction and loyalty it was possible that TiVo could still carve out a niche for itself in the DVR market, just as Apple had in the computer market. Alternatively, TiVo could instead focus on pursuing more partnerships, like the Comcast deal, that would open up high-volume distribution channels. These partnerships did not yield nearly the revenue per customer that TiVo's stand-alone business did, but they made broader distribution possible. If TiVo could achieve significant subscriber volumes (into the tens of millions), then its advertising and data-gathering services could take off. TiVo could develop a large alternative revenue stream by placing ads in programming, targeting ads, and providing fine-grained feedback to advertisers and TV networks about consumer viewing behavior.

TiVo had considered entering the content-distribution business for years. The company had already taken a first step by partnering with Netflix, Inc., in the fall of 2004 to develop a system that would allow TiVo owners to download films provided by Netflix. In the summer of 2005, TiVo entered into the realm of content distribution by striking a trial deal with the Independent Film Channel to broadcast several of the cable channel's shows over broadband. Delivering content over the Internet was considered to be the new frontier for many in the entertainment industry. Mike Ramsay was particularly interested in using TiVo technology to make the thousands of programs that were rarely broadcast over mass media but could be delivered on demand over the Internet, available to consumers with specialized interests.

By distributing material using their customers' broadband Internet connections, TiVo could bypass the existing methods of cable or satellite content distribution.[25]

Finally, TiVo could try to replay the fast adoption–capture game outside the United States. There were many who believed that DVRs could penetrate the TV market worldwide and that TiVo should be a first mover in this potential market. TiVo was already partnered with venture capitalists and other industry players in a project in Asia called TiVo Greater China (TGC, Inc.) that was exploring the market for DVR services in China, Hong Kong, Taiwan, and Singapore.[26] The company was also considering activity in Japan, where the DVR market was already strong. It was believed that TiVo's user-friendly interface would appeal to consumers, allowing TiVo to penetrate the already developed market. The international market could potentially offer big rewards if TiVo were able to capture a large portion of it as a first mover. However, this strategy bore a significant threat to stretch TiVo's resources too thin and TiVo did not have a successful track record as a first mover.

Conclusion

With a large potential market of over 100 million U.S. households with TVs, TiVo knew when it pioneered the DVR market that it would soon face competition as other companies picked up on the exciting new technology. As the innovator, TiVo faced the challenge of educating the market to ensure adoption of the new technology while also trying to differentiate itself as a premium product. TiVo needed to capture the new users before large companies with established customer relationships, like cable and satellite companies, could switch their installed-customer base over to a competing technology. Despite having a technology superior to that of many of its competitors and high customer satisfaction, TiVo has had difficulty capturing the new DVR adopters once cable and satellite companies offered DVR technology.

TiVo turned to distribution partnerships with companies such as DirecTV and Comcast to try to overcome some of these challenges. However, these partnerships bring their own problems as they leave TiVo in a dependent and vulnerable position, as evidenced by DirecTV's pullout. TiVo will face challenges as the home-entertainment landscape continues to shift. Competition from other technologies, such as RS-DVR and VOD, will continue to challenge the TiVo technology.

TiVo has not enjoyed the market success that is often expected for the best product in the market. It faced strong competition very quickly, and then was swamped by industry incumbents attracting a large share of growing numbers of new users. The incumbents had the advantage of larger installed bases of customers that created an immediate distribution channels. TiVo has maintained its product as largely superior in the DVR market, but this had not guaranteed success. Characteristic of new technology markets, lack of information can allow inferior products to beat premium products, based solely on lower price, especially among the new adopters. As the company considers its future strategic options, it needs to remember the lessons about the power of product advantage versus industry structure and incumbent advantage.

Notes

The author gratefully acknowledges the research and writing assistance of Abby Tinker.

1. Another example is the browser war between Microsoft Internet Explorer and Netscape, documented in Timothy F. Breshahan and Pai-Ling Yin, "Economic and Technical Drivers of Technology Choice: Browsers," *Annales d'économie et de statistique* (forthcoming), and Timothy F. Breshahan and Pai-Ling Yin, "Standard Setting in Markets: The Browser War," in Shane Greenstein and Victor Stango, eds., *Standards and Public Policy* (Cambridge, UK: Cambridge University Press, in press).

2. David Farina, Mary O'Toole, and Ralph Schackart, "TiVo, Inc.," William Blair & Company, March 17, 2003, p. 25; and Bob Parks, "Where the Customer Service Rep Is King," Business 2.0, June 2003, Business 2.0 Web site, www.business2.com/articles/mag/print/0,1643,49462,00.html, accessed July 1, 2003.

3. Some local advertising would negotiate directly with distribution operators.

4. Farina, O'Toole, and Schackart, "TiVo Inc.," p. 12.

5. Paul Bond, "Households Double Pp on Digital Video Recorders," July 22, 2005. http://labs.news.yahoo.com/news?tmpl=story&u=/nm/20050722/media_nm/television_survey_dc, accessed August 8, 2005.

6. Jessica Hodgson, "TiVo Technology Could Leave 10%of TV Ads Unwatched," *Wall Street Journal* (June 23, 2005).

7. Ibid.

8. TiVo, "Partners," www.tivo.com/5.4.asp, accessed March 25, 2006.

9. Ibid.

10. This pattern was documented early on in the diffusion of hybrid corn usage by Zvi Griliches, "Hybrid Corn: An Exploration in the Economics of Technological Change," *Econometrica* (October 1957), and further studied by subsequent authors (see Edwin Mansfield, *The Economics of Technological Change* [New York: W. W. Norton, 1968]; Bronwyn Hall, "Innovation and Diffusion," in J. Fagerberg, D. Mowery, and R.R. Nelson [eds.], *Handbook of Innovation* [Cambridge, UK: Oxford University Press, 2004]; and chapter 5 of R. Preston McAfees' *Competitive Solutions: A Strategist's Toolkit* [Princeton, NJ: Princeton University Press, 2002]). Some of the diffusion concepts were popularized in Richard Foster, *Innovation: The Attacker's Advantage* (New York: Summit Books, 1986).

11. David B. Wilkerson, "TiVo's Fast Forward: Is the Video Pioneer Moving Too Hastily to Save Its Future?" *Market Watch* (Nov. 25, 2005).

12. http://www.digitalnetworksna.com/about/replaytv/.

13. David B. Yoffie and Pai-Ling Yin, "Strategic Inflection: TiVo in 2005," December 20, 2005, p. 9.

14. Farina, O'Toole, and Schackart, "TiVo Inc.," p. 10.

15. "Research Notes 3Q 2002," Leichtman Research Group, Inc., p. 1.

16. Yoffie and Yin, "Strategic Inflection," p. 6.

17. Richard Shim, "DirecTV Cuts Fee for TiVo Service," CNET News.com Web site, September 3, 2002, http://news.com.com/ 2100–1040–956384.html, accessed July 2, 2003.

18. Yoffie and Yin, "Strategic Inflection," p. 3.

19. Ibid., p. 8.

20. Federal Communications Commission, *12th Annual Report to Congress on the Status of Competition in the Market for the Delivery of Video Programming*, March 3, 1996.

21. Wilkerson, "TiVo's Fast Forward."

22. Yoffie and Yin, "Strategic Inflection," p. 10.

23. "Comcast, Time Warner Back Cablevision DVR Service," *Reuters*, March 30, 2006.

24. Daniel Gross, "The Buddy System," *New York Metro* (October 18, 2004).

25. Yoffie and Yin, "Strategic Inflection," p. 12.

26. Ibid., p. 14.

Selected Readings

Breshahan, Timothy F., and Pai-Ling Yin. "Economic and Technical Drivers of Technology Choice: Browsers." *Annales d'économie et de statistique* (forthcoming).

———. "Standard Setting in Markets: The Browser War." In Shane Greenstein and Victor Stango, eds., *Standards and Public Policy.* Cambridge, UK: Cambridge University Press. In press.

Farrell, Joseph, and Paul Klemperer. "Coordination and Lock-In: Competition with Switching Costs and Network Effects." *Handbook of Industrial Organization* 3 (2004).

———, and Garth Saloner. "Installed Base and Compatibility: Innovation, Product Preannouncements, and Predation." *American Economic Review* 76, no. 5 (December 1986), 940–55.

Foster, Richard. *Innovation: The Attacker's Advantage.* New York: Summit Books, 1986.

Forman, Chris, Avi Goldfarb, and Shane Greenstein. "Geographic Location and the Diffusion of Internet Technology." *Electronic Commerce Research and Applications* 4, 1(Spring 2005), 1–10.

Goldfarb, Avi. "The (Teaching) Role of Universities in the Diffusion of the Internet." *International Journal of Industrial Organization* 24, no. 2 (2006), 203–25.

Goolsbee, Austan, and Peter J. Klenow. "Evidence on Learning and Network Externalities in the Diffusion of Home Computers." *Journal of Law and Economics* 45 (October 2002), 317–43.

Griliches, Zvi. "Hybrid Corn: An Exploration in the Economics of Technological Change." *Econometrica* (October 1957).

Hall, Bronwyn. "Innovation and Diffusion." In J. Fagerberg, D. Mowery, and R.R. Nelson, eds., *Handbook of Innovation.* Cambridge, UK: Oxford University Press, 2004.

Mansfield, Edwin. *The Economics of Technological Change.* New York: W. W. Norton. 1968.

McAfee, R. Preston. *Competitive Solutions: A Strategist's Toolkit.* Princeton, NJ: Princeton University Press, 2002.

Yoffie, David B., and Pai Ling Yin. "Strategic Inflection: TiVo in 2005." Harvard Business School Case 704425, revised December 20, 2005.

About the Editors and Contributors

Robert M. Adams is an economist in the Division of Research and Statistics of the Federal Reserve Board. His policy responsibilities include the analysis of the competitive effects of proposed bank mergers and acquisitions. His research centers on issues involving industrial organization, antitrust, banking, and bank productivity. Prior to joining the Federal Reserve Board, Dr. Adams worked as a staff economist at the Department of Justice, Antitrust Division. He received his Ph.D. in economics from Rice University.

Frank J. Chaloupka is a professor of economics and the director of the Health Policy Center at the University of Illinois at Chicago. Professor Chaloupka is the associate editor of *Nicotine & Tobacco Research* and *Tobacco Control: An International Journal.* He has published widely on health issues as they relate to tobacco, alcohol, and illicit drugs in journals such as the *American Economic Review, Journal of Political Economy, Journal of Health Economics, Economic Inquiry,* and *British Medical Journal.* Professor Chaloupka received his Ph.D. in economics from City University of New York.

Ronald W. Cotterill is a professor of agricultural economics and economics, and director of the Food Marketing Policy Center at the University of Con-

necticut. He received a joint Ph.D. in economics and agricultural economics from the University of Wisconsin. Professor Cotterill is an internationally known expert on the organization and performance of industries. He is editor of *Agribusiness,* a leading research journal on food industries, has testified before Congress on economic issues, and has served as expert economist on antitrust matters for private firms and agencies, including the Federal Trade Commission and several state attorneys general. His research on industrial organization and antitrust policy addresses issues of market power, price transmission, differentiated product pricing, cooperatives, mergers, price fixing, and monopolization.

Inga Druckute is a Ph.D. student at the Department of Agricultural and Resource Economics and Graduate Research Assistant at the Food Marketing Policy Center, University of Connecticut. Her major field of interest is industrial organization. Ms. Druckute received her B.A. in economics from Vilnius University, Lithuania, and her M.S. in agricultural and resource economics from the University of Connecticut.

Rodney Fort is a professor of economics at Washington State University. His fields of interest include industrial organization and the economics of sports. Professor Fort serves on the editorial boards of *Journal of Sports Economics, Eastern Economic Journal,* and *International Journal of Sports Finance.* He has published several books, including *Pay Dirt: The Business of Professional Team Sports, Hardball: The Abuse of Power in Pro Team Sports,* and *Sports Economics.* He has also published numerous articles in academic journals, such as *American Economic Review, Journal of Political Economy, Journal of Economic Literature, Economic Inquiry,* and *Journal of Sports Economics.* Professor Fort received his B.S. in environmental studies from Utah State University and his Ph.D. in economics from the California Institute of Technology.

H.E. Frech III is a professor of economics at the University of California, Santa Barbara and adjunct professor at Sciences Po in Paris. He has been a visiting professor at Harvard and the University of Chicago. His research includes health care, industrial organization, and regulation and antitrust policy. Professor Frech has published numerous books and articles in journals such as *American Economic Review, Journal of Political Economy, Quarterly Journal of Economics, Journal of Law and Economics,* and *Antitrust Law Journal.* One recent book is *Competition and Monopoly in Medical Care.* He received his Ph.D. in economics from the University of California, Los Angeles.

Avi Goldfarb is an assistant professor of marketing at the Rotman School of Management, University of Toronto. His research interests include branding, the economic impact of information technology, and online behavior. He has published numerous articles in academic journals, including work that has appeared or is forthcoming in *Journal of International Economics, Journal of Economics and Management Strategy, International Journal of Industrial Organization,* and *Journal of Urban*

Economics. Professor Goldfarb received his B.A. in economics from Queen's University, Canada, and his Ph.D. from Northwestern University.

Lee R. Mobley is a senior economist and research fellow at RTI International. She left her associate professorship at Oakland University, Rochester Michigan, in 2000 to devote more time to health market research. Dr. Mobley is an expert in health economics, spatial analysis, spatial statistics, and geographic information systems. She has applied these tools to the study of hospital market behavior, access to health care, managed care penetration, spatial clustering in disease risk factors, and how the physical environment impacts risky behaviors and screening for cancer. She has published articles in *Health Economics, Economic Inquiry, Applied Economics, Review of Industrial Organization,* and *Antitrust Bulletin.* Dr. Mobley earned both a master's in fine art–sculpture, and a Ph.D. in economics from the University of California, Santa Barbara.

Steven A. Morrison is a professor and chair in the Department of Economics at Northeastern University. He is also the managing editor of *Journal of Transport Economics and Policy.* In 2003 the Transportation and Public Utilities Group of the American Economic Association (TPUG) presented him with its "Distinguished Member" award, which is given to members "who have made significant contributions to the field and to the Transportation and Public Utilities Group during their careers." Professor Morrison is the author of numerous articles relating to transportation economics and the airline industry, and he is coauthor (with Cliff Winston) of *The Economic Effects of Airline Deregulation* and *The Evolution of the Airline Industry.* He received a B.A. in economics from the University of Florida and a Ph.D. in economics from the University of California–Berkeley.

Jon P. Nelson is a professor emeritus of economics at Pennsylvania State University. He has served as a consultant to the U.S. Department of Labor, U.S. Department of Transportation, National Science Foundation, and other government agencies and private organizations. His fields of interest include industrial organization, technological change, advertising economics, and environmental economics. Professor Nelson is the editor of *Advances in Applied Economics: Advertising and Differentiated Products* and has numerous articles in academic journals, such as *Review of Economics and Statistics, Journal of Law and Economics, Antitrust Bulletin, Journal of Regulatory Economics, Journal of Economic Behavior and Organization,* and *Review of Industrial Organization.* Professor Nelson received his B.S. and Ph.D. in economics from the University of Wisconsin–Madison.

Seth W. Norton is Norris Aldeen Professor of Business at Wheaton College. He has also taught at the University of Michigan and Washington University, St. Louis, and has received the Burlington-Northern Foundation Award for outstanding teaching at Washington University. Professor Norton has also been the recipient of fellowships from the John M. Olin Foundation and the Earhart Foundation. He was the Julian Simon Fellow at PERC—the Center for Free Market Environmentalism, Bozeman, Montana. His interests include industrial organization, finance, marketing, and strategic management. Professor Norton has published in a variety of subject areas, and his work has appeared in *Cato Journal, Constitutional Political Economy, Economic Development and Cultural Change, Journal of Business, Journal of Corporate Finance, Journal of Economics & Management Strategy, Journal of Institutional and Theoretical Economics, Journal of Law & Economics, Marketing Science,* and *Strategic Management Journal.* Professor Norton received

his B.A. in history and his Ph.D. in economics from Northwestern University.

Stanley I. Ornstein is a vice president at Analysis Group, Inc., an economic and financial consulting firm. He specializes in applied microeconomics and industrial organization and their application in the areas of antitrust and competitive issues more broadly. Previously, he was a research economist and the associate director of the Research Program in Competition and Business Policy, Anderson Graduate School of Management, University of California, Los Angeles. He has been a consultant to corporations and law firms on antitrust and other business litigation matters for over thirty years. He has published over twenty-five articles, books, and chapters in books. Dr. Ornstein received a Ph.D in economics from the University of California, Los Angeles and a M.S. in business administration from San Diego State University.

William Putsis is currently professor and marketing area chair at the Kenan-Flagler Business School at the University of North Carolina at Chapel Hill. Prior to this time, he was professor of marketing and department chair at the London Business School, associate professor at the Yale School of Management, Yale University, and assistant professor at Cornell University. His research and academic pursuits focus on the empirical application of game theoretic models of competition, competitive strategy, the marketing of private label products, new product diffusion and product line strategy, international marketing, advertising and communications research, and sports marketing. He has numerous scholarly articles published in journals such as *Journal of Marketing Research, Marketing Science, Journal of Business, Journal of Business Research, Managerial and Decision Economics, Marketing Letters, Applied Economics, Journal of Forecasting,* and *Review of Industrial*

Organization. He serves on the editorial board of *Marketing Science, Journal of Marketing, International Journal of Research in Marketing, Review of Marketing Science,* and *International Journal of Marketing Education.*

Adam N. Rabinowitz is a Ph.D. student the Department of Agricultural and Resource Economics and graduate research assistant at the Food Marketing Policy Center, University of Connecticut. His major field of interest is industrial organization. Mr. Rabinowitz received his B.A. and M.A. in economics from the University of Nevada, Las Vegas.

Rochelle Ruffer is an associate professor of economics at Youngstown State University. She received her Ph.D. in economics from the University of Wisconsin–Madison. She is trained as an industrial organization economist and has published previously on Microsoft. Her research interests include the scholarship of teaching and learning. In 2001–2002, she was one of three economists to participate in the Carnegie Foundation for the Advancement of Teaching's CASTL (Carnegie Academy for the Scholarship of Teaching and Learning) program.

Carol Horton Tremblay is an associate professor of economics at Oregon State University. Her research interests include applied econometrics, labor economics, health economics, and industrial organization. She has published numerous articles in journals such as *Health Economics, Journal of Human Resources, Journal of Industrial Economics, Review of Economics and Statistics,* and *Review of Industrial Organization.* She has also published a book with Victor Tremblay, *The U.S. Brewing Industry: Data and Economic Analysis.* Professor Tremblay received her B.A. in economics from University of California, Irvine, and her Ph.D. in economics from Washington State University.

Victor J. Tremblay is a professor of economics at Oregon State University. He has been a visiting professor at the University of Wisconsin–Madison and at Aomori Public College, Japan. His field interests include industrial organization and applied game theory, and his research has focused on the economics of advertising, especially as it applies to the brewing and cigarette industries. Professor Tremblay is special editor of industry issues for *Review of Industrial Organization.* He has published numerous articles in academic journals, such as *Journal of Industrial Economics, International Journal of Industrial Organization, Review of Industrial Organization, Antitrust Bulletin,* and *Journal of Business.* He has also published a book with Carol Tremblay, *The U.S. Brewing Industry: Data and Economic Analysis.* Professor Tremblay received his B.A. in economics from the University of California–Los Angeles, and his Ph.D. in economics from Washington State University.

Don E. Waldman is the Richard M. Kessler Professor of Economic Studies at Colgate University. He is the author of six books, including *Industrial Organization: Theory and Practice,* 3rd edition (with Elizabeth J. Jensen), *Microeconomics, the Economics of Antitrust: Cases and Analysis,* and *Antitrust Action and Market Structure.* He has also published numbers articles in academic journals, such as *American Economic Review, Antitrust Bulletin,* and *Review of Industrial Organization.* He has received excellence-in-teaching awards from Cornell University, the University of Maryland–Baltimore County, and Colgate University. Throughout his career, he has served as a consultant and expert witness for both the government and private firms. Professor Waldman received his Ph.D. in economics from Cornell University.

Pai-Ling Yin is an assistant professor of strategy at the Harvard Business School. Her research interests include technology and strategy, online auctions, and market tipping. She has published several cases on high-tech companies used in the HBS curriculum, and her academic work has appeared or is forthcoming in books and journals, including *Annales d'économie et de statistique* and *Communications of the ACM*. Professor Yin received her B.A. and B.S. in economics, French, and math from Indiana University–Bloomington, an MSc in regulation from the London School of Economics and Political Science, and her Ph.D. in economics from Stanford University.

Index